PUBLIC PROGRAM
ANALYSIS

PUBLIC PROGRAM ANALYSIS

APPLIED RESEARCH METHODS

Theodore H. Poister
Institute of Public Administration
The Pennsylvania State University

AN ASPEN PUBLICATION®
Aspen Publishers, Inc.

1978

Rockville, Maryland
Royal Tunbridge Wells

Aspen Publishers, Inc.
1600 Research Boulevard
Rockville, Maryland 20850

Library of Congress Cataloging in Publication Data

Poister, Theodore H.
    Public program analysis.
    Bibliography: p.
    Includes index.
1. Evaluation research (Social action programs)
2. Social sciences—Statistical methods.
3. Social science research. I. Title
H62.P575   300'.1'8   77-27308
ISBN 0-8391-1190-8

CONTENTS

PREFACE

This book is designed to provide instruction in research methods as applied to the analysis of public programs. Its general purpose is to provide an overview of the relevance of information developed by program analysis, the range of criteria and research approaches employed in evaluating program performance, and the principal kinds of considerations to be taken into account in the design of program analyses. Its major objective is to teach the kinds of skills needed to do program analysis, as opposed to books that discuss the conduct of program analysis or its political implications without showing how to do it. This book is aimed at preparing students seeking public sector employment or related careers for either 1) actually doing this kind of work themselves, or 2) if they are working in nonanalytical positions, being able to assess the merit of analytical work that comes across their desks.

A critical feature of the book is the integration of quantitative analysis with the more qualitative aspects of problem definition, general research design, development of measures, and data collection procedures. Students in the policy sciences often learn social science statistical methods in a vacuum and are not taught the use of these techniques within a general framework of applied policy/program analysis. First, this book illustrates applications of quantitative techniques to investigate needs and demands for public programs, the internal operations of public programs, and their impact on their environments. It employs hypothetical illustrations and examples drawn from existing studies relating to programs in a wide variety of substantive areas and conducted at different levels of government.

Second, the book places a strong emphasis on the relationships that such issues as problem specification, development of operationalized measures, and research design bear to appropriate applications of statistical techniques. Rather than taking the data as "given," as often seems to be the case in statistics courses, this book attempts to link consideration of the question "How do we analyze the data?" with the prior issue of "What data should we collect in the first place?" With respect to the statistical techniques themselves, attention is given to both mechanics and applications, stressing limitations as well as advantages.

In writing this book the author is drawing on continuing experience in teaching a two-term course in program analysis at the graduate level and a new one-term introductory course in the subject at the graduate/upper division undergraduate level. Typically, such courses use a basic social science statistics text, an introductory book or reader on program evaluation, a text on survey research, and various books and journal articles on such subjects as measurement, research design, cost/benefit analysis, systems analysis, and possibly operations research, as well as examples of completed studies. It is left for the instructor to pull these sources together in a way that is meaningful to students and to provide some degree of continuity for the course.

The organization of the book moves back and forth between qualitative and quantitative concerns. The chapters in the first section provide an indication of what program analysis is all about and a discussion of problems of formulating research questions and developing valid measures. Of particular importance is chapter 2 on the use of the systems approach in the development of a conceptual framework for structuring program analysis. The chapters in the second section then introduce the topics of statistical analysis and sampling. An important aspect of this sequence is the emphasis placed on the *descriptive* examination of bivariate associations, the process of elaboration, and in general the development and interpretation of statistical tables contained in chapter 5.

Given an understanding of the purposes and the "language" of analysis provided in these first two sections, the third section discusses various general approaches to applied program analysis including benefit-cost and cost-effectiveness analysis, experimental and quasi-experimental models, cross-sectional analysis, and survey research. Survey research is, however, presented as a mode of data collection that may be applicable for any type of design as well as a general approach in its own right. Chapters in the fourth section discuss more advanced statistical techniques. Although the initial chapters on statistics establish the theoretical basis underlying inferential statistics, the latter chapters on statistics present the underlying assumptions on which a technique is based, the computations involved, and an indication of appropriate applications, without attempting to explain its mathematical foundations.

This text can be used in different ways depending on course content and students' backgrounds. Use of all four sections is intended for a full length (possibly two-term) course in which no statistics prerequisites are imposed, as many students coming into the field of public administration have avoided statistics and methodology in general during their undergraduate careers. For a one-term introductory course with no prerequisites, the chapters in section four should probably be omitted. If, on the other hand, basic skills in statistics are required or can be assumed, the chapters in section two might be reviewed very briefly (or assigned to students on their own without devoting class time to these topics) with adequate time for the rest of the book to be covered.

ACKNOWLEDGMENTS

Developing any type of methods text obviously requires help in many ways. The author owes a great debt of gratitude to Robert J. Mowitz, Director of the Institute of Public Administration of The Pennsylvania State University, first, for recognizing the need for this kind of book and encouraging the author to undertake the effort, and second, for providing the generous institutional support which made it possible to complete the project in "real" time. Without this kind of backing, undertaking such a project would be unrealistic. Other faculty members at the Institute, most notably Thomas C. Webster and Robert D. Lee, Jr., were helpful both in terms of providing moral support and reading draft chapters.

If the author has had an alter ego in the last few months of putting the book together, it has been James C. McDavid, a good friend and colleague at the Institute who has given much of his own time to critique the manuscript and presented the author with many important ideas regarding emphasis and clarity of presentation. In its attempt to teach material that often seems difficult for students to cope with, this text has benefited substantially from his insightful feedback.

Other colleagues at Penn State have also been very helpful with various parts of this text, in terms of both substance and mode of presentation. These include William J. Sauer of the Department of Sociology, Jack Barnette, Associate Director of the Center for Education Research and Evaluation, Kant Rao of the Department of Business Logistics and the Pennsylvania Transportation Institute, and Rex H. Warland of the Department of Rural Sociology, all of whom have been helpful in critiquing various chapters relating to their particular interest. In addition, Jesse V. Burkhead, Professor of Economics and the author's former teacher at the Maxwell School of Syracuse University, was extremely helpful in reviewing draft material and making suggestions that were critical for finalizing the chapter on economic analysis.

The author has also been highly fortunate with respect to the high quality work put in on the project by graduate assistants at the Institute of Public Administration, including Dennis J. Demuth, Alan Klein, David J. Sallack, and Susan K. Miller. In addition, the work of Anne H. Magoun, research assistant, in helping to finalize the manuscript and going beyond the call of duty in editing page proofs was indispensable, and her efforts are particularly appreciated. The typing and manuscript preparation work was expertly supervised by Gail M. Dillon, ably assisted by Deborah Strunk, Marie L. March, and Takako Pike. Finally, the author appreciates the extra effort made by Maria Coughlin, production editor at University Park Press, in pulling the book through the production process in coherent fashion. Completing this book has indeed been a joint enterprise involving many people; I thank you one and all.

To

Arthur William Poister

who has always been a model
of excellence and humanity

APPLIED PROGRAM ANALYSIS

CONCEPTS AND PRINCIPLES OF PROGRAM ANALYSIS

—The U.S. Department of Agriculture's school lunch program is based in part on the idea that providing nutritiously balanced meals to children from low income families will lead to improved health.

Is there any evidence that the program is actually producing these results?

Are children other than the intended recipients receiving these meals?

Are the children even eating the food or are they turning up their noses at the "more nutritious" foods included?

—The Urban Mass Transportation Administration provides both capital grants and operating assistance to local transit authorities in an effort to revitalize the nation's urban transit systems.

To what degree has service actually been improved?

Has this led to increased ridership, increased mobility in general, and increased access to jobs in particular?

Is it likely to have any impact on the problems of traffic congestion or excessive fuel consumption?

What about the distribution of intended benefits—are the primary target groups actually benefiting the most?

—The costs of Pennsylvania's special education programs have been rapidly escalating in recent years.

What benefits are being produced by these programs?

What are reasonable expectations for what they should be able to accomplish?

Which treatment modes—such as mainstreaming, separate home rooms, or itinerant teaching—seem to be best suited for children with different types of problems?

Can we produce the same services at less cost?

—Routine patrol activities have traditionally been the backbone of most city police departments. Does routine patrol, in fact, act as a deterrent to crime and reassure the public against the fear of crime?

How do various patrol and deployment strategies—such as team policing, foot patrol, increased fleet utilization, and "directed" patrol as opposed to routine patrol—compare in terms of meeting these objectives?

Can women officers be assigned to sector patrol and be expected to perform as well as men?

These questions illustrate the kinds of issues that applied public program analysis is intended to address. In general, how does a certain public program operate and how well is it performing? Given such substantive concerns, then, how do we analyze the program to identify its critical features and analyze its performance?

This text is concerned with research methodologies for designing and carrying out such program analyses. **Program analysis** as discussed in this book refers to the use of applied research methods to study problems in the functioning of public programs. Its primary and most legitimate purpose is to provide information on an objective basis for improved decisions regarding the original design, implementation, continuation, or modification of a program. Rather than assuming that a given program is producing the intended results, or, if the results have not been forthcoming, assuming that this is simply a matter of insufficient resources allocated to the program, we need to measure whether results are in fact being produced, determine why certain programs are not producing results, and compare alternative programs and strategies in terms of demonstrated ability to produce results (Mowitz, 1970, p. 42). Program analysis refers to the use of scientific methods to provide this input to decision making as opposed to conclusions based solely on intuition, impressions, casual observation, or conventional wisdom.

Interest and activity in program analysis have increased dramatically in recent years, particularly in the federal government (Abert and Kamrass, 1974). Its products are intended to serve program managers, higher level policy makers in substantive policy areas, central executives, budget officers, and more recently, legislators (Wholey et al., 1970; Beckman, 1977; Lee and Johnson, 1977). This trend is part of a broader effort to inject rationality into public policy-making (Rossi and Wright, 1977, p. 6). As such, increased interest in program analysis has been reinforced by other trends in public administration toward increased planning, management information systems, and developments in financial management such as performance budgeting, program budgeting, and zero-based budgeting. However, it should be clear at the outset that the product of program analysis is only one of many inputs into decision making; objective analysis is by no means a substitute for the political process. Rather, the role of program analysis is to make recommendations, not decisions, based on structuring alternatives and comparing them in terms of some specified objective criteria.

This chapter is intended to introduce various concepts associated with program analysis and to give the reader an idea of the many kinds of program analysis undertaken by, or conducted to serve the needs of, public administrators. Furthermore, consideration is given in a normative sense to principles or standards to be applied to program analysis with an eye to the kinds of requirements they impose on program analysis in terms of research design and methodology.

CONCEPTS OF PROGRAM ANALYSIS

The term **policy analysis** generally refers to the analysis of the determinants, characteristics, and implications of public policies and programs, particularly of the relationship between the content of policies and programs and the substantive consequences and outcomes they produce. Public **policies** are guidelines for public action, prescribing in general terms the means for moving toward a desired course of events or outcome. **Programs** are sets of organized activities conducted by governmental institutions in pursuit of established policy objectives; they can be thought of as vehicles for carrying out policy. Thus, program analysis is a subset of the general field of policy analysis.

As broadly defined in this book, program analysis includes any serious research effort relating to the design and functioning of a public program. In terms of research objectives, it may be **descriptive** in nature (basic fact finding studies), aimed at the **explanatory** level of analysis concerned with programmatic cause and effect relationships, or concerned primarily with **projecting** or **forecasting** program-related variables into the future (Johnson, 1975, pp. 79–80). Furthermore, in terms of substantive content, whereas much of the interest in program analysis in recent years has been tied to programming in the human services—primarily health, education, and welfare—program analysis and the methodologies covered in this text are used in all program areas, from criminal justice through housing and transportation programs, to environmental and economic development programs, and even military programs (Abert and Kamrass, 1974).

Focuses of Program Analysis

Although there are many ways to classify different kinds of program analyses, one useful way of differentiating among them is by whether they focus primarily on the program itself, the environment, or relationships between the two. Thus we can think of three classes of program analyses, each implicitly addressing a somewhat different set of topics:

1. studies of the needs and demands for a program generated by the environment;
2. analyses of the internal operation of the program itself; and
3. studies of the impact of the program on the environment.

Although truly comprehensive analyses are rare, a given piece of program analysis may contain all three of these elements.

Needs and Demands Studies   One kind of program analysis is aimed at identifying the needs or demands for a particular service or program. These needs and demands studies may be done as part of the initial program planning process for new programs or as a continuing planning or evaluation function leading to the modification of ongoing programs. Most public programs focus on some identifiable subject or problem area, such as a particular target population, group, or clientele; a geographic area or areas; or some social, economic, or physical condition that generates needs or demands for the program in the first place.

In economic terms, a **demand** for a public service exists when taxpayers desire the service to be performed and are willing to pay its costs through taxes, or when users are willing to pay for a service through fees or service charges. **Needs** reflect the claims of clientele groups or potential recipients that they require certain services, or a general recognition that a certain service is necessary for the public welfare even though there is no effective economic demand for it. Many studies are aimed at identifying the existence, characteristics, and magnitude of these needs and demands for current or possible future programs.

The information obtained in needs assessments may be useful in determining the required dimensions of the relevant program; providing insight as to how it might be organized; and estimating the worth of implementing, continuing, or changing a program through analysis of projected costs and benefits. Needs and demands studies are more than descriptive; often they attempt to determine cause/effect relationships leading to problems or suggesting solutions. This kind of analysis may provide indications of controlling factors that must be taken as "givens" and points in the causal chain where intervention may be expected to produce change, or it may identify trends that can be used to project changes in needs and demands over time.

Program Operation Studies   Many program analyses focus on the internal operation of the program by the organizational unit or units conducting it. These program operation studies, or **process studies,** are not concerned directly with the needs for the program or the program's ability to meet those needs but rather with the process of how the program is carried out. Process studies examine the mix of resources utilized by the program, the quality of these resources, and the way in which they are transformed into the units of service that are produced by the program.

Unlike needs and demands studies and impact studies, process studies focus on factors that for the most part are within the control of the program management. These studies may also consider administrative aspects of conducting the program such as the performance of program personnel or communications systems, organizational aspects such as the optimal degree of centralization or decentralization of service delivery, or the technological and substantive considerations in providing the service. Although not directly measuring final effects, they may be geared to contribute to an overall assessment of program effectiveness. However, the primary concern in most process-oriented studies lies with the mechanics of program operation, improving the productive function, viewed as an internal management problem.

Program Impact Studies   The third class of program analyses includes those studies aimed at analyzing the substantive results of an ongoing or completed program. As they attempt to measure the effects of public programs on the problems they are designed to alleviate, **impact studies** may well represent the most important contribution that social scientists can make to social practice (Riecken, 1972, pp. 86–87).

Impact studies address the question of what behavioral patterns or physical conditions in the environment have been altered as a result of the program's operation. Although they are often primarily concerned with measuring the degree to which the program is accomplishing its intended objectives, the scope of the more comprehensive impact studies is broadened to cover the full range of possible consequences. Among the three classes of program analysis, impact studies pose the most critical problems of study design and methodology and have proven the most difficult to carry out; yet they produce the most important information for decision makers when carried out successfully.

Evaluation Research

Although the term program evaluation as used in much of the literature connotes the study of program impacts or effects (Weiss, 1972b; Hatry et al., 1973), most program analyses come under the heading of **evaluation research,** broadly defined as the use of research methods to measure the worth or performance of a program in terms of certain stipulated criteria. As discussed by one proponent of program evaluation (Weiss, 1972b, pp. 16–17), evaluation research is intended to address the following kinds of decisions:

1. to continue or discontinue the program;
2. to improve its practices and procedures;
3. to add or drop specific program strategies and techniques;
4. to institute similar programs elsewhere;
5. to allocate resources among competing programs;
6. to accept or reject a program approach or theory.

Certainly the most direct kinds of program evaluation are impact studies that identify and measure the effects of a program on its environment, and this is the surest basis for assessing the value of a program to the society. However, other aspects of program performance can be evaluated through process studies, especially when the efficacy of program strategies is unchallenged. The suitability of basing program evaluations on process studies is largely a matter of the varying criteria that are applied as discussed below. Moreover, there is a growing and encouraging tendency to link studies of process and impacts together in program evaluations in order to explain why impacts do or do not occur in terms of program operation (Bernstein and Freeman, 1975, p. 20).

Although needs and demands studies are not usually considered evaluations, they are also often used as benchmarks in program evaluation as illustrated by a comparative evaluation of police services relative to needs in two dissimilar police districts in Washington, D.C. (Bloch, 1974). Furthermore, needs assessments often attempt to evaluate the probable worth of alternative programs designed to alleviate the problems under study. Although not strictly equivalent, then, as broadly defined in this book, the terms *program evaluation* and *evaluation research* are used interchangeably with program analysis.

Furthermore, no sharp distinction is made in this text between program evaluation and *program-related* policy analysis, as policy analysis is viewed as a broader extension of program analysis. Whereas program analyses are usually set-piece studies of the functioning of discrete activities, projects or programs carried out at a relatively fine grade of detail, the focus is more squarely on policy itself when whole systems of programs come under consideration, and a detailed understanding of the effects of any one program is of less interest than comparisons among the programs and assessments of their interactions and combined effects. Similarly, while program analysis is primarily concerned with current programs, policy analysis is more forward-looking, addressing the issues of 1) what will happen if existing policies continue into the future, and 2) what is likely to happen if new programs are adopted. Our ability to answer these questions depends for the most part on the capability of available forecasting tools and information about strategy/outcome relationships produced by conventional program evaluation. In general, evaluation research concerns the development of information on specific issues regarding program operation, while policy analysis involves the synthesis and analysis of this information in light of desired ends in order to structure policy-making situations (Williams, 1972, pp. 4–5).

Performance Evaluation Criteria

The worth of public policies and programs should be evaluated in terms of the contributions they make to the welfare of the society. Does the policy or program result in changes that produce desirable, observable benefits to the society or sectors of the society? The desirable benefits that are anticipated to result from the implementation of policies and programs are defined as policy goals and objectives through the political process, and examination of the appropriateness of these goals and objectives is one function of policy analysis. The attainment of appropriate goals and objectives should be the principal standard against which operating programs and other policy strategies are evaluated.

Three central challenges facing evaluators are to determine 1) the program's goals and objectives, 2) the indicators of its success or failure, and 3) the causal relationships between program operation and apparent results (Gardiner, 1975). These challenges arise primarily from the fact that goals and objectives are often vague and inconsistent, with identified linkages between program design and intended objectives that are tenuous at best.

The criteria employed to evaluate policies and programs all relate to goals and objectives, either focusing on the objectives themselves or on the means/ends relationships between strategies and objectives. As presented below, they represent concepts that must be operationalized as specific standards defined in terms of the particular objectives and values involved in a given program area. Chapters 2 and 3 deal at some length with identifying objectives and operationalizing performance indicators tied to these criteria.

Effectiveness   As used in this book, **effectiveness** refers to a program's performance in light of specified objectives. Measuring effectiveness looks at the question of whether the program is producing the desired kinds of results, comparing actual accomplishments with standards of what is expected of the program. The effectiveness criterion refers to the real-world consequences of the program and involves the identification and measurement of physical or behavioral changes in the environment that are attributable to the program in relation to the program's intended objectives. The primary concern of effectiveness analysis is not whether the program is being operated as planned, but whether its operation is producing the intended effects in the environment.

Although effectiveness is often interpreted strictly in terms of goal achievement, some evaluations go beyond goal-oriented effects to consider all consequences that can be traced to the program; goal-oriented effects are a subset of the full range of impacts that might be produced by the program. A thorough effectiveness analysis of a program's impact on the environment would take into account secondary, unintended, external, and counterproductive impacts, as well as the intended, goal-oriented effects (Weiner and Deak, 1972, pp. 57–60). Effectiveness is the central criterion in evaluation research, and measuring the effectiveness of public programs is the single dominating concern of this book.

Efficiency   The concept of **efficiency** refers to the relationship between a program's products and the costs incurred by operating the program, based on the desire to maximize the value of product per unit of cost or to minimize the cost per unit of product. The efficiency criterion, employed in the interests of eliminating waste and making more productive use of scarce resources, is primarily concerned with better ways of operating the program rather than more effective program approaches for accomplishing objectives. Of course, the two are not necessarily unrelated, as an alternative program approach may prove to be more efficient as well as more effective.

In the analysis of public programs and policies there are really two kinds of efficiency that may be of interest. **Technological efficiency,** or engineering economy, refers to the objective function of producing some specified product or carrying on some specified activity at a minimum effort or cost, or maximizing the amount of product or activity per unit of effort or cost. This kind of analysis might be concerned primarily with internal operating efficiency—such as comparing alternative strategies for deploying garbage trucks and crews in order to minimize the total hours required to collect refuse in a neighborhood—or it might be concerned with maximizing a program's intended effects, given a specified limit on costs. For example, a **cost-effectiveness** approach might be used to compare two strategies for housing rehabilitation loan and grant programs to determine which one will result in the greatest number of completed rehabilitations, given the same amount of initial funding. Recently, the term **productivity** has come back in vogue with a more specialized meaning, referring to improvements in the efficiency of personnel, equipment, operating procedures, or program strategies, which lead to the provision of more effective or higher quality services (Committee for Economic Development, 1976).

On a more global plane, **economic efficiency** refers to the relationship between the total costs and total benefits of a public program or project, and to the criterion of allocating resources so as to maximize citizens' satisfaction derived from the use of those resources. A full-fledged **benefit-cost analysis** attempts to measure in dollar terms all the costs incurred by and benefits derived from the program, including indirect costs and the full range of impacts. The question being addressed by this type of analysis is whether a program should be undertaken by government or to what extent it should be funded. Although efficiency measures are discussed throughout this book, cost-effectiveness and benefit-cost analysis are treated at length in chapter 11.

Adequacy   Although program objectives are sometimes established in terms of the total elimination of a problem, constraints often force the scope of objectives to be reduced to a partial or incomplete solution. The objective may be to reduce the dimensions of a problem by a certain percentage or to treat high priority cases only. The criterion of **adequacy** refers to the degree to which attainment of a program's objectives would eliminate the problem (Deniston et al., 1972, p. 142). In part, adequacy is a matter of effort; a particular program strategy might be highly effective, for example, but the level of funding might be totally inadequate in relation to the magnitude of demonstrated need for the program. Even where objectives have been set realistically in terms of incremental progress toward total solutions, adequacy is a measure of the amount of effect or impact relative to these stated objectives (Suchman, 1967, pp. 63-64).

Consideration of the adequacy of public policy often leads to concern with systems of programs or the lack thereof, posing the question of whether attainment of individual program objectives will also result in accomplishing some larger objective. For example, a program to eliminate the problem of acid mine drainage in Appalachia may be effective in terms of eliminating one source of water pollution, and yet be inadequate relative to the greater objective of protecting water quality in the region because of the lack of a policy to control the problems of municipal and industrial wastes.

Appropriateness   On a higher level of policy analysis, the concept of **appropriateness** refers to the worth of a program's objectives themselves rather than to the means or strategies employed to achieve them (Poland, 1974, p. 336). Logically prior to the question of whether a program is operating efficiently and effectively in attaining its objectives is the issue of whether these objectives are the proper ones for the society or community to be seeking. Analysis of the appropriateness of a program centers on the question of whether its objectives reflect the values of society.

Two other concepts that are useful in the analysis of programs and policies, but which relate most directly to appropriateness considerations, are equity and responsiveness. In considering **equity,** the analyst examines the distribution of the benefits derived from and the costs imposed by the program or policy. The concept refers to a "fair" distribution of costs and benefits as defined by public policy for a particular context; a fair distribution of benefits in a given program area, for example, might be determined in terms of some measure of need for the service, the charging of equal fees for equal services, or on the basis of geographic coverage.

In the area of social programming, a redistribution of income, opportunities, or other benefits may be a primary objective, in which case equity effects would be considered within the framework of overall program effectiveness. In other cases in which equity objectives are not explicit, it may be appropriate to apply a general standard of equity as a higher order objective. For example, an analysis of a public works program might investigate whether facilities that are built impose uncompensated costs on adjacent land parcels, or more generally, whether projects are concentrated in some areas at the expense of other areas.

The concept of **responsiveness** is used in this book to refer to the degree to which a program meets the needs and desires of its users and clients. It relates to both the design and conduct of a program as well as its objectives. For example, there may be a strong desire on the part of residents in a black, low income neighborhood for more effective police patrol as a deterrent to crime; yet, the actual behavior of patrol-men may be considered offensive by the area's residents, thus making the program unresponsive in the eyes of the intended recipients of the program's benefits. In general, the responsiveness criterion is most useful in analyzing programs aimed at particular target populations. Although a program's objectives might be highly appropriate with respect to society as a whole, responsiveness is concerned with whether the program is sensitive to the needs and preferences of its target groups.

Thus, in considering the appropriateness of a given policy or program, the analyst is asking whether 1) it is desirable from a social policy standpoint, 2) it is equitable, and 3) it is responsive to the perceived needs of the intended clientele. Program analytic methods can be employed to provide insight as to the general desirability of policy objectives and the relative priority to be placed on attaining these objectives as seen by a cross-section of citizens. Sometimes the process works the other way around. Given the confusion surrounding the purposes of many programs, evaluation research may enlighten the issue by identifying the de facto objectives that are being served; it would then be up to policy makers to determine whether the objectives are appropriate. At a more operational level, evaluation research can also be used to determine how program costs and benefits are distributed and to examine the match between clients' perceived needs and actual service delivery.

There is clearly some degree of hierarchy among these criteria, although the ability to treat them separately as discrete criteria is not always clear-cut. For example, the issues of internal operating efficiency and an adequate level of program operation are relevant only if the program strategy has proven to be effective. In turn, the criterion of effectiveness in meeting program objectives is subordinate to the higher order criteria of appropriateness, economic efficiency, equity, and responsiveness. Thus, moving from higher level to lower level performance criteria, program analysis can be designed to answer the following questions.

—Are the program's objectives and the type of program in general desirable from a social policy standpoint? (appropriateness—may also relate to equity and responsiveness)
—Are the intended results of the program worth the costs? (economic efficiency)
—Is the program achieving its specified objectives? (effectiveness)

—Is the internal operation of the program efficient in terms of the utilization of resources? (technological efficiency)
—Is the scope or magnitude of program effects commensurate with the need for the program? (adequacy)

Although program evaluations most often operationalize the criteria of effectiveness, technological efficiency, and adequacy, there is a presumption in such cases that the higher order criteria of appropriateness, economic efficiency, equity, and responsiveness are being satisfied.

Other Criteria

The criteria described above are performance criteria in that they are geared to assessing the product, or payoff, of a public program. This payoff, as measured in terms of effectiveness, efficiency, or adequacy can be evaluated against previously determined standards—a **pure payoff approach**—or can be compared to the payoff produced by alternative or competing programs. By contrast, some less analytical evaluations are concerned not with payoff but rather with input (Scriven, 1972). Such **intrinsic evaluations** are concerned with the quantity and quality of program staff, facilities and equipment, materials and operating procedures; they relate to program *design* specifications rather than the *performance* specifications to which most evaluation research is geared.

Program-Related Administrative Studies Administrative studies that examine the administrative feasibility, management practices, or legal compliance of ongoing programs may be considered to be on the periphery of program analysis, but they are not directly concerned with the usefulness of a program or its components in a substantive sense. They look at programs from a management perspective rather than a programming perspective intended to suggest ways of improving programs in terms of achieving policy objectives. For example, many demonstration programs are assessed in terms of administrative feasibility, whether the program can indeed be conducted in the prescribed manner in a given environmental setting, rather than whether it can produce the desired results (Williams, 1972, p. 4).

Monitoring refers to tracking the progress of program implementation and operation, usually by funding agencies or central offices not actually involved in implementation (Waller et al., 1976). Monitoring usually entails the development of an information system that is updated periodically to meet reporting requirements of certain activities, the expenditure of funds, and numbers and characteristics of program participants. As such, monitoring is primarily concerned with the quality of inputs to the program rather than with measuring performance. As defined above, monitoring involves progress reporting more than analysis, and it is, therefore, an administrative control function as much as a programming function.

Another type of program review that relates to the control function is the fiduciary **audit,** intended to determine whether the program is being operated in accordance with legislative intent and following legally required management practices. Traditional audits are tied to the criterion of **managerial accountability** rather than the performance criteria discussed above, but more recently at the federal level the scope of audits conducted by the General Accounting Office has been broadened to include assessments in terms of effectiveness and efficiency (Comptroller General of the United States, 1972).

PROGRAMMING AND EVALUATION

Program analysis should be considered as an integral part of a continuing planning/programming function whose purpose is the development of new program strategies and improvement of program performance. As indicated in Figure 1.1, evaluation is an activity that often comes at the end of this process, but it may also occur at every stage and provide feedback to every stage of the programming process.

Evaluations of program performance sometimes reveal problems or suggest program alternatives that lead back into basic research and initial program development. Program plans are often evaluated before they are set in motion, particularly in terms of economic analysis as discussed in chapter 11, and performance evaluations at later stages frequently provide feedback for plan revision or updating activities.

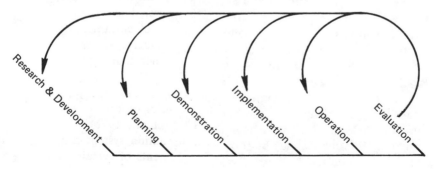

Figure 1.1   Planning/programming process.

Evaluation of demonstration programs is critical for comparing alternative strategies under consideration and determining whether promising strategies can be made to work out in the field (Suchman, 1967, pp. 137–140). The results of these evaluations provide crucial input to further research and development and planning activities. Similarly, the implementation stage as a discrete step in the programming process should be evaluated closely, as poor implementation has been found to be an important source of program failure (Pressman and Wildavsky, 1973; Williams, 1975). Finally, the performance of ongoing programs is evaluated to measure actual impact and to provide surveillance of the continuing operation and the need for adjustments to changing environmental conditions over time. In general, evaluations at these different stages will require different research approaches (Suchman, 1972, pp. 56–64).

One important distinction to be made along these lines is that between formative and summative evaluation (Scriven, 1972). If the developmental work on a program is considered to have been completed and the decision pending is one of continue/discontinue or adopt/not adopt the program as constituted, a summative evaluation might well be in order. **Summative evaluations** are intended to provide a final assessment of a program's value to aid the administrator in deciding whether or not to use the program, but not in deciding how to try to improve it. They have less need to explain the why's and wherefore's of a program's performance, because they are intended primarily to indicate how well or how poorly the program performs.

Formative evaluations, on the other hand, are designed to provide feedback to program developers to aid in improving the usefulness of the program. In addition to measuring program performance, they break down its functioning in an attempt to discern which program elements are successful and which are not, and those aspects that function as intended along with those that should be modified or scrapped in favor of new approaches. Formative evaluations are much more challenging to design and conduct as they require understanding of the internal operation of the program; the desire for good formative evaluations has provided the main impetus for the linking of impact and process studies, as mentioned above. Whereas summative evaluations serve a definite purpose, in a very basic sense all analysis is formative inasmuch as our accumulated knowledge from all sources on program performance may be brought to bear in program design sometime in the future.

Levels of Objectives

The design of program analyses is often complicated by the fact that many programs are characterized by multiple objectives. Although some of them consist of semi-independent, mutually supporting or conflicting objectives, many fit into hierarchies of objectives in which anticipated program accomplishments increase in importance as one moves from lower level, specific objectives to higher level, more general objectives. These levels of objectives, which also differ in terms of time horizons, can be grouped into immediate objectives, intermediate objectives, and long range or ultimate objectives (Suchman, 1967, pp. 51–56).

An example would be a program designed to increase the ability of coal miners in Appalachia to work with newly developed deep mine technologies. Although the ultimate objective of the program is to increase the amount of coal mined underground in the region economically and within certain environmental constraints, intermediate objectives would be the mastery of the requisite skills by miners and a subsequent improvement in on-site labor productivity. Immediate objectives would be to establish and operate relevant training programs and to enroll miners in these programs. Such a program could be analyzed and evaluated at each level in the hierarchy of objectives.

The various levels of objectives are tied together by assumptions about how the attainment of lower level objectives is expected to lead to the attainment of higher level objectives. This represents the theory that underlies the program. If this theory is not valid, that is, if the causal hypotheses in the theory are not corroborated by experience, the program cannot be expected to be successful in accomplishing its objectives. The validity of the theory underlying the program is only as strong as the weakest assumption connecting levels of objectives, as ultimate objectives can only be attained (by the program under consideration) through the accomplishment of lower level objectives.

In the example, although the assumption that increased labor productivity will lead to increased volumes of coal being mined may be true, the training program will not accomplish this objective unless the training sessions do in fact result in the mastery of the new skills by the coal miners. On the other hand, if mastery of these skills does not contribute to labor productivity, or if increased labor productivity does not lead to increased total production, then the ultimate objective will not be reached through the program even if it does produce miners who are skilled in the new technology.

In the first instance, the problem facing program analysts would be to discover why the skills are not being learned or used by the miners and to find ways of improving the program to overcome these deficiencies. In the second instance, however, a finding that the assumptions connecting intermediate objectives with ultimate objectives are false would suggest that a program for training miners, however successful in attaining immediate and intermediate objectives, is not adequate for achieving increased production. In the first instance, the techniques used by the program are not effective; in the second instance, the overall program approach is not adequate to meet the problem at hand.

The assumptions that make up the underlying theory of a program must either be tested by research or simply accepted on the basis of faith or conventional wisdom, and the heart of program analysis concerns the empirical testing of these assumptions. Whereas a comprehensive analysis would address the assumptions underlying each level of objectives, in practice, partial analyses are often conducted concentrating on a particular level. One might logically begin with the lower level objectives on the grounds that if they are not being met the program cannot be working in terms of higher level objectives; or conversely, an analysis may focus on ultimate objectives to look at overall effects, particularly if monitoring activities provide some indication that the program is working at the lower levels. Program analysis aimed at lower levels often consists primarily of process studies, especially as they may be concerned more with activities rather than objectives to be attained, while those dealing with ultimate objectives are much more likely to focus on impacts.

Scale of Programming

Program analysis should be geared to the problems and decisions facing administrators and other decision makers, and these tend to vary with the scale of programming with which the analysis is concerned. As the subject of analysis moves from individual, very specific projects to larger programs that include different kinds of projects, to whole packages of complementary programs in a given substantive problem area, the set of concerns that may be addressed expands considerably. This is particularly true of large programs at the federal and state levels that are administered through the intergovernmental system.

With respect to the varying characteristics of evaluations according to level of policy concern and general purpose, one typology of evaluations conducted by federal agencies has been developed as follows:

1. **Program impact evaluations** are assessments of the overall effectiveness of national programs in meeting their objectives, or of the relative effectiveness of two or more programs in meeting common objectives.
2. **Program strategy evaluations** are assessments of the relative effectiveness of different strategies or techniques used in a national program.
3. **Project evaluations** are assessments of the effectiveness of individual projects in achieving their stated objectives; usually required by the federal program but often carried out by the projects themselves.
4. **Project ratings** are comparative assessments of local projects in achieving similar objectives, most appropriate when the projects are operating in similar local environments (Wholey et al., 1970).

These types of evaluation should be keyed to the needs of different users; program impact evaluations tend to be aimed at policy decisions regarding funding levels or the general direction of a program, while program strategy evaluations feed into programming decisions based on relative strengths and weaknesses of alternative techniques. Project evaluations, on the other hand, tend to be tailored to specific characteristics of individual projects to assist both program managers and project directors in assessing the impacts of a project, while project rankings employ uniform standards to provide program managers with information on the comparative effectiveness of projects within a given program.

PRINCIPLES OF PROGRAM ANALYSIS

As defined above, program analysis is the use of scientific research methods to develop objective, factually based information to aid decision makers in the planning, development, and operation of public programs. The two fundamental principles inherent in this definition are 1) that program analysis requires a sound research effort as opposed to conventional wisdom or studies of the "quick and dirty" variety and 2) that program analysis should be applied to real, substantive issues and aimed at providing information that has practical utility to program managers and policy makers. Thus, an evaluation of any piece of program analysis should be concerned with both the quality of the research—its **research validity**—and the extent to which it produces results that are used in the policy-making process, its **policy validity**.

Utilization

Although the increased emphasis on program analysis is part of a growing trend at all levels of government, the usefulness of this kind of undertaking has by no means gained universal acceptance on the part of administrators and public officials. Although program/policy analysis is much more commonplace now than 10 years ago, there is still distrust in and resistance to this kind of effort in many quarters. More importantly, even though the quantity of program analysis has increased dramatically in the past few years, there are still "few cases of actual effective utilization of evaluation research for expected purposes" (Bernstein and Freeman, 1975, p. 5).

Citing the relative lack of comprehensive program evaluations in state and local government, one reference (Hatry et al., 1973) provides the following explanations.

—Evaluations can be expensive and time consuming.
—Many managers believe that "the value of my program cannot be measured."
—Explicit and systematic program evaluations can be controversial.
—State and local governments often have lacked personnel skilled in quantitative techniques and analysis.
—The track record of the quality and timeliness of evaluations (including federally sponsored evaluations) seems poor.

These reasons hint at the two main obstacles that have impeded the widespread use of the results of public program analysis, namely 1) bureaucratic inertia and the urge for survival, and 2) the mediocre and even poor quality of much of the analysis that is performed.

Institutional Framework   One scholar has neatly summarized the institutional pressures that form the organizational context within which program analysis must function as follows.

> Even rudimentary knowledge of organizational behavior indicates the salience of the drive for organizational perpetuation, personnel's needs for status and esteem and their attachment to the practice skills in which they have invested a professional lifetime, conservatism and inertia and fear of the unknown consequences of change, sensitivity to the reactions of various publics, costs, prevailing ideological doctrines, political feasibility, and the host of other considerations that affect the maintenance of the organization. (Weiss, 1972a, p. 319)

In this environment, which fosters the instinct to preserve the status quo and to resist change and uncertainty, program evaluations—especially when conducted by outsiders—are often considered as threats. Thus, efforts are made to avoid evaluations based on the following kinds of rationalizations. 1) The effects of the program are long range; thus, the consequences cannot be measured in the immediate future. 2) The effects are general rather than specific; thus, no single criterion can be used to evaluate the program, and indeed, even using many measures would not really get at complex general consequences intended. 3) The results are small, but significant; thus, they cannot be measured effectively because instruments are not sufficiently sensitive. 4) The effects are subtle, and circumstances may not be ordered appropriately to get at the qualities that are being changed. The measurement would disturb the processes involved. 5) Experimental manipulation cannot be carried out because to withhold treatment from some persons would not be fair (Borgatta, 1966, p. 186).

When evaluations are undertaken and produce negative results, the conclusions and their implications may be resisted further on the following grounds. 1) The effectiveness of the program cannot really be judged because those who could use the services most did not participate. 2) Some of the persons who received the services improved greatly. Clearly, some of the persons who recovered could not have done so if they had not received attention. 3) Some of the persons who most needed the program were actually in the control group. 4) The fact that no difference was found between the persons receiving services and those not receiving services clearly indicates that the program was not sufficiently intensive. More of the services are obviously required. 5) Persons in the control group received other kinds of attention (Borgatta, 1966, p. 187). An important point to note here is that although these postures are often adopted as a bureaucratic smokescreen, in other cases they constitute valid points that do indeed pose difficult methodological challenges to program analysts.

On the other hand, although a cardinal principle of program analysis is that it should be undertaken with the general purpose of program involvement, agencies sometimes "abuse" evaluation by using it for less legitimate reasons. One list of such "pseudo-evaluations" (Suchman, 1967, p. 143) is as follows.

> Eye-wash—an attempt to justify a weak or bad program by deliberately selecting only those aspects that "look good." The objective of the evaluation is limited to those parts of the program that appear successful.

> White-wash—an attempt to cover up program failure or errors by avoiding

any objective appraisal. A favorite device here is to solicit "testimonials" which divert attention from the failure.

Submarine—an attempt to "torpedo" or destroy a program regardless of its worth in order to get rid of it. This often occurs in administrative clashes over power or prestige when opponents are "sunk" along with their programs.

Posture—an attempt to use evaluation as a "gesture" of objectivity and to assume the pose of "scientific" research. This "looks good" to the public and is a sign of "professional" status.

Postponement—an attempt to delay needed action by pretending to seek the "facts." Evaluative research takes time and, hopefully, the storm will blow over by the time the study is completed.

Substitution—an attempt to "cloud over" or disguise failure in an essential part of the program by shifting attention to some less relevant, but defensible, aspect of the program.

Added to this list is the fact that many evaluations are undertaken solely because it is required by a federal policy, usually as part of a grants program, rather than because of a real desire to develop and use feedback on program performance.

The Action Setting   On an operational level, actual program evaluations are carried out within agency contexts in which the dominant program concern is service delivery, not analysis. In this "action setting" (Weiss, 1972b) there may be many seeming incompatibilities between program imperatives and research requirements, issues that surface in subsequent chapters of this book. Although the evaluator might prefer that the program operation remain static during the course of the evaluation, for example, it might be continually shifting in response to numerous internal and external factors, forcing a more flexible research approach.

In general, the evaluation effort may be viewed primarily as interference by program managers. In addition to the status rivalry that sometimes develops between outside evaluators and program personnel, friction may also be created by the extra requirements on agency staff for data collection, possible changes in record-keeping, criteria imposed on the selection of program participants, and possibly the use of control groups who will not receive program benefits. Strategies that have been suggested for easing such tensions include developing support at the outset from higher administrators, involving practitioners in the evaluation, minimizing the disruptive effects of the evaluation on program operation, emphasizing that the purpose is to test program theories and techniques as opposed to evaluating agency management, and feeding back useful information to program personnel whenever possible (Weiss, 1972b, pp. 104–107).

Responsive Program Analysis

The institutional barriers to effective program analysis are being overcome, particularly as the track record improves over time. As indicated above, however, this is only half of the problem; both to prove functional and to gain credibility, evaluations must be responsive to the needs of decision makers as well as be based on sound research methods.

One scholar-practitioner in the field (Coleman, 1975) has developed a set of principles for successful policy analysis—that which is geared toward utilization by being responsive to policy requirements. In general, they are based on the recognition that we are concerned with **decision-oriented** or **action-oriented** research as opposed to the **conclusion-oriented** traditional academic research, and that this generates a different set of requirements.

The foremost characteristic of evaluation research, as opposed to traditional research, is that the problems to be analyzed and the effects to be studied are dictated by the nature of the program intervention and the operating context. To be successful, evaluation research must be structured in these terms and focus on the salient issues arising from them. Within this framework, however, a study can still take different directions and serve different purposes; to increase the likelihood of utilization, a study should be keyed to pending decisions or the needs of the most likely potential users.

Other principles for designing and conducting responsive program analysis, adapted from the same source (Coleman, 1975), include the following.

> **Timeliness**—partial information made available at the time a decision or action must be taken is worth more than complete information after that time.
>
> **Accuracy**—results that are approximately correct with a high degree of certainty are worth more than those which are derived more elegantly, but with a greater probability of being grossly incorrect.
>
> **Representation**—when competing interests have a stake in the outcomes, it may be desirable to have replications conducted by different study groups under the auspices of the different interested parties.

Dissemination of Results Additional principles for encouraging the use of program analytic results relate to their transmission from evaluators to decision makers (Adams, 1975). The first involves linking evaluation with program planning and development. If planning and development personnel conduct the evaluation, or if they can be included in the process, or at least be kept informed along the way, the evaluation is more likely to become input in the planning process. In general, agency planning and development units can serve as middlemen to interpret evaluation results to decision makers.

Second, the format of reporting and disseminating results is important in its own right. Higher level administrators and public officials do not have time to read long-winded reports written in academic or technical language, especially when they stress method and analysis while downplaying results. If separate "action reports" are not developed to overview technical reports, executive summaries should be made available. These should be brief and well organized, emphasizing results, recommendations, and implications for program decisions.

Research Principles

Individuals constantly make thumbnail analyses or quick evaluations based on judgment or intuition combined with accumulated experience. Evaluation as a process refers to judging something or choosing among alternatives in light of given criteria. Although the criteria *should* be clearly defined, people often have only a vague notion of the objectives to which a decision should be geared; and in any case the criteria can be and often are applied on the basis of very incomplete or superficial information. In effect, many evaluations are made on the basis of assumptions of fact whose validity is untested.

Administrators commonly rely on such "back-of-the-envelope" analyses, either because they feel that the matter does not warrant fuller attention or because time constraints do not permit it. The worth of this approach, however, should not be totally rejected; sometimes it provides accurate assessments, and often is the only expedient course to take. The problem, obviously, is that such efforts often lead to faulty conclusions (Bernstein and Freeman, 1975, p. 16).

Program analysis, on the other hand, should be based on research to develop more complete information and test such assumptions. It refers to a process that attempts to be objective, systematic, and comprehensive rather than subjective, sporadic, and partial. These are scientific criteria that distinguish program analysis and evaluation from judgmental assessments.

It should be apparent that it will often be impossible to fully satisfy standards of scientific rigor within the "action setting" of program analysis. Yet as one authority points out, there has been a reluctance to recognize that scientific adequacy is a matter of degree and that there may well be a number of research approaches appropriate for a given problem (Suchman, 1967, p. 82). **Validity,** the degree to which a study's conclusions do in fact represent the real world condition they support to represent, is a *continuum* rather than an absolute. The evaluator should strive to design and conduct research so as to enhance the validity of his findings, but given the institutional constraints and requirements of responsiveness to the policy process discussed above he will often be forced to make trade-offs between scientific rigor and the demands of the operating context.

Program Analysis as Applied Research   Although **basic research** in the social services is concerned with theory building and identifying the causal laws that govern relationships among systems of variables in their natural state, the function of evaluation research is to measure the effects of planned, purposeful intervention on these relationships. As such, it is primarily a form of **applied research** (Suchman, 1967, p. 75), whose main function is to test the application of knowledge as embodied in the design of a program; this form of applied research may also lead to the discovery of new knowledge. The term is descriptive of the principle characteristics of public program analysis in that it involves the use of legitimate *research,* as *applied* to operating programs.

Basic research is often too general to have direct relevance for program management. It is often criticized as being too academic or theoretical to apply to the operating level. Basic research attempts a much higher level of generality, so that its findings can be considered to hold true across a wide range of circumstances; these results contribute to the development of new program approaches, which must then be tested under operating conditions, the function of program analysis.

Evaluation research is characterized by more **contingencies,** factors outside the control of the researchers or their ability to identify them explicitly, which nevertheless may influence the relationships under study (Suchman, 1967, p. 76). Contingent factors may facilitate or hinder a program's achieving its intended results; and if their role cannot be determined, the findings of the study cannot validly be transferred to other settings where the same contingencies may not obtain. Program analyses are conducted in specific time and space settings and for the most part are best suited for providing prescriptions for these particular operational circumstances.

The point is that because the transferability of the findings of program analysis is limited by the variation in contexts, there is a great need for continued replications of studies on the effects of program treatments in alternative settings. Repetitive studies of similar program applications should be conducted to corroborate or disconfirm the theoretical basis of a program approach, to distinguish between the real effects of the program and freak or extraneous effects of nonprogram forces. If similar findings emerge from a number of replications, our faith in the general applicability of the program approach is substantiated, whereas dissimilar or contradictory findings should generate hypotheses regarding the effects of salient nonprogram variables.

Value Framework Although the term objectivity implies impartiality in terms of policy preferences and openness toward research questions rather than preconceptions as to what the results should indicate, evaluators cannot be neutral or totally independent of the framework of values that govern the general direction of the study. This is so because, as discussed above, program evaluation hinges on the criteria employed. **Objectivity** really refers to a process of gathering relevant data and examining the evidence in terms of specified criteria and standards. Establishing the criteria and standards in the first place is a **subjective** process in which value systems are applied to policy areas and program contexts. Thus, the question of "who puts the value in evaluation" is of the uppermost importance in that it determines the basis on which a program is judged (Whitaker, 1974).

The evaluator will usually have a role in determining the relative emphasis to be placed on effectiveness, efficiency, adequacy, and equity criteria in a given evaluation, and moreover, in the absence of a clear consensus on what the program's objectives are he may have great influence over the specification of the objectives to which these criteria are keyed. Beyond this the evaluator will have more subtle influence over the basis on which the program is evaluated, in terms of operationalizing performance indicators and establishing the basis of analysis.

In the absence of clear policy guidance as to what the mix of objectives and criteria should be in a given study, one approach the evaluator might consider would be to try to develop a balanced set of indicators reflecting the perspective of various interested parties, rather than tilting the study toward any single perspective. For example, a needs assessment conducted in a large suburban school system tried to achieve such a balance by incorporating feedback on program performance from several different perspectives, including those of teachers, students, administrators, other staff, community leaders and lay citizens, including parents (Taylor, 1977). Whatever perspectives and operationalized criteria are adopted, however, the important principle is that to be objective, the evaluator should make the criteria and standards explicit—clearly identified in all reports—and then proceed to measure performance against these criteria and standards based on empirical evidence.

METHODOLOGICAL OVERVIEW OF PROGRAM ANALYSIS

This book is designed to provide instruction on research methods frequently employed in the analysis of public programs. The prospective evaluator should be warned, however, that a firm command of methods alone is not sufficient for the design and conduct of high quality evaluation research. Rather, carrying out program analyses that are strong in terms of both research and policy validity also requires a close familiarity with the operation and general context of the program under review as well as an understanding of the substantive issues of concern to decision makers. An evaluator coming from the outside without substantial experience in the program area should make every effort to educate himself in these matters before tackling an evaluation.

The methods themselves involve a mix of quantitative and nonquantitative skills. The bulk of the analysis uses the general set of social science research methods and statistical techniques covered in this book. A complementary approach is to employ methods of economic analysis. There are also other bodies of more specialized techniques, collectively referred to as operations research methods, which are sometimes used in program analysis but are not covered in this book. For the most part these techniques involve the development of mathematical models, often based on the use of probabilities to represent alternative choice situations or simulate operating systems in order to reach an optimal solution given specified objectives and constraints (Morse and Bacon, 1967; Gupta and Cozzolino, 1974; Adams, 1975, chapters 13 and 14). In addition, some methods used primarily in urban and regional planning, relating to population, land use, and economic development patterns, are sometimes useful in program analysis (Krueckeburg and Silvers, 1974).

Regardless of the particular analytic techniques used, the design and conduct of a piece of program analysis moves through the steps of the general research process as follows.

1. **Problem Specification**—This involves development of the **substantive framework** of the research including identification of the key

issues to be addressed, specification of the alternatives to be considered, and formulation of specific hypotheses or research questions to be examined.

2. **Design of Research Strategy**—Given substantive issues and specific research questions, the next step is the development of an **analytical framework** to examine them. The approaches taken range from primarily descriptive case studies to highly sophisticated experiments. This research design process focuses on determining what evidence should be collected and what comparisons should be made, and how conclusions are to be reached, but inseparable from this are the development of operationalized measures and the identification of data sources.

3. **Data Gathering and Processing**—Collecting the necessary data is often the most time consuming and costly part of the study. Data processing usually involves preparing the data to be entered into a computer system for analysis.

4. **Data Analysis**—Analysis means breaking down cases into groups, making comparisons, looking for relationships among the variables of interest. The mode of statistical analysis and the particular techniques used will depend on the research design and the types of measures employed.

5. **Conclusions, Recommendations and Report Writing**—Applied program analysis should produce conclusions about the issues and research questions concerned, and these in turn often lead to the development of recommendations. These are the product of the research effort, and if they are not communicated clearly, as discussed earlier, the work will be of little relevance.

The validity of a study can be weakened or lost in any one of the steps outlined above, and the analyst must be concerned with the proper application of method throughout. However, the competent use of techniques will not always guarantee success. The problem of evaluation research has been characterized as "vague goals, strong promises, and weak effects," which pose a great challenge to researchers in terms of identifying and measuring program impact as well as distinguishing real program effects from pseudo-effects (Rossi, 1972, pp. 16–23). The methods available are not always equal to the task of measuring program performance, often producing inconclusive results; the evaluator must take pains to avoid overinterpreting results and stating conclusions that are not fully justified by the analysis. The state of the art is advancing, however, and will continue to do so with both *innovative* and *careful* applications of the research methods and analytical techniques presented in this book.

REFERENCES

Abert, J. G., and M. Kamrass (eds.). 1974. Social Experiments and Social Program Evaluation. Cambridge, Mass.: Ballinger Publishing Co.

Adams, S. 1975. Evaluative Research in Corrections. Washington: National Institute of Law Enforcement and Criminal Justice, LEAA.

Beckman, N. (ed.). 1977. Symposium on Policy Analysis in Government: Alternatives to 'Muddling Through.' Public Administration Review 37 (May/June): 221–263.

Bernstein, I. N., and H. E. Freeman. 1975. Academic and Entrepreneurial Research. New York: Russell Sage Foundation.

Bloch, P. B. 1974. Equality of Distribution of Police Services: A Case Study of Washington, D.C. Washington: Urban Institute.

Borgatta, E. F. 1966. Research Problems in Evaluation of Health Service Demonstrations. Milbank Memorial Fund Quarterly 44(2):182–199.

Caro, F. G. (ed.). 1971. Readings in Evaluation Research. New York: Russell Sage Foundation.

Coleman, J. S. 1975. Problems of Conceptualization and Measurement in Studying Policy Impacts. In: K. M. Dolbeare (ed.), Public Policy Evaluation. Beverly Hills, Cal.: Sage Publications, Inc., pp. 19–40.

Committee for Economic Development, 1976. Improving Productivity in the State and Local Government. New York: CED.

Comptroller General of the United States. 1972. Standards for Audit of Governmental Organization Programs, Activities and Functions. Washington: General Accounting Office.

Deniston, O. L., I. M. Rosenstock, W. Welch, and V. A. Getting. 1972. Evaluation of Program Effectiveness and Program Efficiency. In: F. J. Lyden and E. G. Miller (eds.), Planning-Programming-Budgeting. 2nd ed. Chicago: Markham, pp. 141–170.

Dolbeare, K. M. (ed.). 1975. Public Policy Evaluation. Beverly Hills, Cal.: Sage Publications, Inc.

Gardiner, J. A. 1975. Problems in the Use of Evaluation in Law Enforcement and Criminal Justice. In: K. M. Dolbeare (ed.), Public Policy Evaluation. Beverly Hills, Cal.: Sage Publications, Inc. pp. 177–183.

Gupta, S. K., and J. M. Cozzolino. 1974. Fundamentals of Operations Research for Management. San Francisco: Holden-Day, Inc.

Hatry, H. P., R. E. Winnie, and D. M. Fisk. 1973. Practical Program Evaluation for State and Local Government Officials. Washington: Urban Institute.

Johnson, R. W. 1975. Research Objectives for Policy Analysis. In: K. M. Dolbeare (ed.), Public Policy Evaluation. Beverly Hills, Cal.: Sage Publications, Inc. pp. 75–92.

Kraemer, K. L. 1973. Policy Analysis in Local Government. Washington: International City Management Association.

Krueckeberg, D. A., and A. L. Silvers. 1974. Urban Planning Analysis: Methods and Models. New York: John Wiley and Sons, Inc.

Lee, R. D., Jr., and R. W. Johnson. 1977. Public Budgeting Systems. 2nd ed. Baltimore: University Park Press.

Lyden, F. J., and E. G. Miller (eds.). 1972. Planning-Programming-Budgeting. 2nd ed. Chicago: Markham.

Morse, P. M., and L. W. Bacon (eds.). 1967. Operations Research for Public Systems. Cambridge: M.I.T. Press.

Mowitz, R. J. 1970. The Design and Implementation of Pennsylvania's Planning, Programming, Budgeting System. Harrisburg: Commonwealth of Pennsylvania.

Poland, O. F. 1974. Program Evaluation and Administrative Theory. Public Administration Review 34(July/August):333–338.

Pressman, J. L., and A. Wildavsky. 1973. Implementation: How Great Expectations are Dashed in Oakland, or Why It's Amazing that Federal Programs Work At All. Berkeley: University of California Press.

Riecken, H. W. 1972. Memorandum on Program Evaluation. In: C. H. Weiss (ed.), Evaluating Action Programs: Readings in Social Action and Education. Boston: Allyn and Bacon, Inc., pp. 85–104.

Rivlin, A. M. 1971. Systematic Thinking for Social Action. Washington: Brookings Institution.

Rossi, P. H. 1972. Testing for Success and Failure in Social Action. In: P. H. Rossi, and W. Williams (eds.), Evaluating Social Programs: Theory, Practice and Politics. New York: Seminar Press, pp. 11–49.

Rossi, P. H., and W. Williams (eds.). 1972. Evaluating Social Programs: Theory, Practice and Politics. New York: Seminar Press.

Rossi, P. H., and S. R. Wright. 1977. Evaluation Research: An Assessment of Theory, Practice, and Politics. Evaluation Quarterly 1(February):5–52.

Scriven, M. 1972. The Methodology of Evaluation. In: C. H. Weiss (ed.), Evaluating Action Programs: Readings in Social Action and Education. Boston: Allyn and Bacon, Inc., pp. 123–136.

Struening, E. L., and M. Guttentag (eds.). 1975. Handbook of Evaluation Research. Vol. I and II. Beverly Hills, Cai.: Sage Publications, Inc.

Suchman, E. A. 1967. Evaluative Research: Principles and Practice in Public Service and Social Action Programs. New York: Russell Sage Foundation.

Suchman, E. A. 1972. Action for What? A Critique of Evaluative Research. In: C. H. Weiss (ed.), Evaluating Action Programs: Readings in Social Action and Education. Boston: Allyn and Bacon, Inc., pp. 52–84.

Taylor, R. G., Jr. 1977. Assessing the Need for Change: A School District Experiments with Multiple-Survey Techniques. Phoenixville, Pa.: Phoenixville Area School District.

Waller, J. D., D. M. Kemp, J. W. Scanlon, F. Tolson, and J. S. Wholey. 1976. Monitoring for Government Agencies. Washington: Urban Institute.

Weiner, P., and E. Deak. 1972. Environmental Factors in Transportation Planning. Lexington, Mass.: D. C. Heath & Co.

Weiss, C. H. (ed.). 1972a. Evaluating Action Programs: Readings in Social Action and Education. Boston: Allyn and Bacon, Inc.

Weiss, C. H. 1972b. Evaluation Research. Englewood Cliffs, N.J.: Prentice-Hall, Inc.

Whitaker, G. P. 1974. Who Puts the Value in Evaluation? Social Science Quarterly 00(April):759–761.

Wholey, J. S., J. W. Scanlon, H. G. Duffy, J. S. Fukumoto, and L. M. Vogt. 1970. Federal Evaluation Policy. Washington: Urban Institute.

Williams, W. 1972. The Organization of the Volume and Some Key Definitions. In: P. H. Rossi and W. Williams (eds.), Evaluating Social Programs: Theory, Practice, and Politics. New York: Seminar Press, pp. 3–8.

Williams, W. (1975.) Implementation Analysis and Assessment. Policy Analysis 1 (Summer):531–566.

2

THE SYSTEMS APPROACH

The first step in the design of a program analysis, and one that is of singular importance in determining whether its results provide worthwhile and usable information, is to lay out the research questions to be addressed in terms of the program's actual and intended operation. This entails identifying the critical and secondary variables that describe the program's operation and context as well as the relationships, known or presumed, among them. Developing this framework of program logic requires the evaluator to become thoroughly familiar with all substantive aspects of the program's design and operation: what goes into the program, how these things are used separately and in combination, what changes they are expected to produce in the environment and how these changes are expected to occur, and what forces outside the program might influence its operation. This kind of understanding of a particular program can then be used to formulate specific research questions about the program's performance, such as what is the rate at which resources are transformed into intermediate products or what is the degree to which specified program activities are succeeding or failing to produce changes in the environment?

This chapter describes systems analysis as a way of laying out a public program as an operating system to facilitate performance evaluation and the analysis of alternatives. Over the past two decades widespread interest has developed in both government and private industry in the use of systems analysis as a management approach and as a general approach to problem solving (Beer, 1966, 1972; Smithies, 1969; Churchman, 1968). As an approach to program analysis, systems analysis is not an analytical methodology, but rather a way of conceptualizing the problems (and alternative solutions) to be addressed. Thus the concepts of systems and program analysis are closely bound together in a two-directional relationship: While analysis is critical to the systems concept of program management, the systems approach is a useful way of formulating a substantive framework for problem specification and resolution in a program analysis.

The systems analysis approach is controversial, in part because it is often identified with a body of quantitative techniques keyed toward considerations of economic and technological efficiency, at the expense of behavioral approaches which place a greater emphasis on the importance of human factors. There is a bias in the systems approach—and in program analysis in general—toward efficiency and other more tangible considerations because they are easier to quantify and measure, but it should be noted that systems analysis is a general approach that can incorporate the softer, human dimensions of a problem.

Systems analysis is a critical part of the approach to program analysis advanced in this book because of the need to base performance evaluation on specified objectives and the importance of linking studies of process to assessments of program impact. A large scale review of evaluation efforts in federal agencies led to the conclusion that the worth of many evaluations has been limited, primarily because of the following three reasons:

Lack of Definition—The problem addressed, the program intervention being made, the expected direct outcome of that intervention, or the expected impact on the overall society or on the problem addressed are not sufficiently well defined to be measurable.

Lack of Clear Logic—The logic of assumptions linking expenditure of resources, the implementation of a program intervention, the immediate outcome to be caused by that intervention, and the resulting impact are not specified or understood clearly enough to permit testing them.

Lack of Management—Those in charge of the program lack the motivation, understanding, ability, or authority to act on evaluation measurements and comparisons of *actual* intervention activity, *actual* outcomes, and *actual* impact (Horst et al., 1974).

While the lack of management follow-through relates to the institutional factors discussed in chapter 1, the first two problems are directly concerned with problem specification. Because program objectives and intended effects are often not clearly defined, and because the underlying assumptions about *how* program strategies are expected to produce these effects are often not clearly understood, evaluations are often *not* keyed to the central issues of a program's performance. The systems approach as presented here is primarily a tool for structuring analyses in terms of these central concerns.

SYSTEMS THEORY AND SYSTEMS ANALYSIS

Systems are sets of interacting elements, or structures of subsystems (Black, 1968). Systems theory focuses on the explanation of the organization and behavior of phenomena in terms of dynamic interactions among interdependent elements within a contextual environment. It has been characterized as a supradiscipline that draws on concepts from various disciplines and is aimed at developing principles and models that are applicable to systems across a wide range of phenomena (Sutherland, 1973). Systems analysis, which is derived in part from systems theory, is operational rather than theoretical. It refers to the application of analytical methods as an aid to the management of manmade systems in which key factors can be manipulated to improve performance.

General Systems Theory

Two pioneers in the field, Ludwig von Bertalanffy (1951; 1968) and W. Ross Ashby (1964; 1965; 1968), are primarily responsible for developing the foundations of general systems theory as a way of explaining common patterns in the structure and functioning of phenomena in a number of different fields. A noted contributor to the theory from the vantage point of the social sciences is the economist, Kenneth E. Boulding (1956; 1964). The basic tenet of general systems theory is that structure and function of both natural and social/cultural phenomena can be best understood through investigation of aggregations of interacting elements rather than by concentrating on the elements themselves. Thus, for example, focusing on whole organisms as being constituted of several subsystems, each with a different structure and function, will lead to a greater understanding of biological organization. Of basic importance to the theory is the recognition that adding up the elements will not equal the whole system in terms of understanding its total significance; given the dynamics of interactions among its essential variables, a system is greater than the sum of its parts.

General systems theory holds that many different kinds of phenomena, including both entities and processes, exhibit an organizational pattern of systems containing subsystems, which themselves might be made up of smaller subsystems. Boulding (1956) has characterized the theory as the "skeleton of science" aimed in part at pointing out similarities in theoretical constructions of different disciplines. In addition to interdependencies among subsystems and their organization in hierarchies of systems and suprasystems, the major themes of systems theory relate to exchange across system boundaries, the dependence of systems on their environments, adaptation to the environment, and the ability of a system to achieve a "steady state" in its relationship with the environment (Emery, 1969). Systems theory has been applied to many areas of interest to social scientists, ranging from political systems (Easton,

1953; Deutsch, 1966) to urban growth and decay (Forrester, 1969) to the structure and function of complex organizations (Katz and Kahn, 1966).

Most systems we are concerned with in public administration are open, goal-seeking systems. **Open systems** are systems in exchange with their environment, as opposed to closed systems that are isolated from their environments. Open systems export to the environment and depend on the import of material and energy input from it. They are subject to **disturbances** from the environment (beneficial or harmful events that affect the system) and may be able to cause disturbances in the environment. Therefore, only partial control over an open system is possible from within because some of the controlling factors lie in the environment.

While with nongoal-seeking systems subsystems react to stimuli from other subsystems or the environment with no overriding purpose, **goal-seeking systems** function with control mechanisms characterized by feedback loops. This is the concern of cybernetics, the study of communication and control. In a goal-seeking system, the **feedback loops** channel both positive and negative information on system performance (feedback) to a decision center, which adjusts the system's functioning accordingly. This continuous monitoring and reevaluation serves to assure that the system remains on course toward its objective function. An oft-used example in the engineering realm is a thermostatically controlled heating system. The objective—the maintenance of a specified temperature—is pursued by the continuous monitoring of the temperature and the consequent activation and deactivation of the furnace as needed to maintain that temperature.

Systems Analysis

Systems analysis involves both the development of a conceptual framework for investigating a given problem and the application of analytical techniques to operating systems. One proponent of the use of systems analysis (Lee, 1970) has identified three kinds of applications of the systems approach: solving a single problem, devising a means of systematically solving a recurrent problem, and designing a means of providing information to be used as the basis of decision making. Systems analysis entails the use of scientific methods to identify, analyze, and compare alternative solutions to a problem.

Systems analysis is not concerned directly with the development of theoretical models to explain the organization of independent or natural phenomena, but rather with the analysis of man-controlled systems as an input to improved system operation. It is frequently employed as a design tool, as well as to evaluate the performance of existing systems. In addition, it can sometimes be used to compare the operation of an existing system with suggested alternatives, providing information feedback used in the planning, modification, or operation of systems. In a full-fledged plan development or program design process, for example, a systems analysis approach would include the following steps: 1) definition of objectives, 2) identification of limiting constraints, 3) generation of alternatives, 4) analysis and selection of an alternative, 5) development and pilot implementation, and 6) evaluation and modification (ICMA, 1972). One of the most useful forms of program analysis, whether at the planning stage or in the evaluation of ongoing programs, involves the comparison of two or more alternative delivery systems operating in similar environments and evaluated on the basis of the same set of performance criteria.

The two hallmarks of applied systems analysis are 1) a comprehensiveness in treating elements as they function in larger systems rather than in isolation, and 2) a concern with the design and performance of systems in terms of specified objective functions. In part the systems approach represents an attempt to raise problems to a higher plane to make certain that all relevant considerations are taken into account. This placing of the problem in its broader context is aimed at counteracting the tendency to **suboptimize**, which refers to "optimizing" in terms of subsystem performance regardless of overall system effects. Its purpose is to focus attention on the higher order effects produced by subsystem alterations.

Systems analysis can be conducted at both macro and micro levels, depending on purpose (Martin, 1969). At the macro level interest is focused on subsystem interactions and the performance of the system as a whole in terms of aggregate measures of goal achievement, costs, and secondary impacts. With regard to public programs, macro level analysis would be especially concerned with comparing levels of system outputs with needs and demands. At the micro level attention would shift to detailed analysis of elementary subsystem functions to identify strengths and weaknesses in the system's internal operation and suggest adjustments to improve performance.

Some program analysis treats the program as a whole and concentrates on "input" and "output" without regard to its internal workings. Such "blackboxing" of the system is appropriate when the desire is solely to discover whether or not intended effects are indeed occurring, a pure payoff approach to program evaluation. However, as discussed in the preceding chapter, there is a growing tendency to attempt to analyze how programs function in order to explain why successes and failures are encountered and where in the system the breakdowns are located. Decomposing the system into subsystems and analyzing them in terms of separate and joint effects greatly facilitates this kind of formative evaluation.

System Characteristics

Systems can be described in terms of five attributes that help structure program logic: objectives, environment, resources, components, and management (Churchman, 1968).

Objectives A program's objectives should be developed in light of its general goals and missions. **Goals** are idealized outcome states that are often somewhat vague and timeless, in the sense that they are never expected to be fully achieved. **Objectives**, on the other hand, represent concrete outcomes that are expected to be achieved within specified time horizons. They should be set realistically, in terms of capabilities and feasibility, as attainable stepping-stones on the way to idealized goals. As an example, the goal of decent housing for all the residents of a city does not provide an operational definition of exactly what a program is intended to do. However, the objective of upgrading 600 dwelling units from substandard to standard condition (as defined by the city's housing code) in two years specifies a clear-cut milestone to be achieved in moving toward the goal of providing decent housing for everyone.

A program's objectives are the things it is seeking to accomplish; observable physical, socioeconomic, behavioral or psychological changes it is designed to produce in the environment. Although it might seem that a program's objectives should be readily apparent, often they prove difficult to define in a form that is sufficient to serve as the basis of program analysis. To be operational, objectives must be stated in a manner that is clear, specific, and measurable. Statements of objectives should describe them in a number of dimensions so that criteria can be set for determining whether or not they are being met. Objectives first of all should specify a **target**, some group, condition, or problem at which the program is aimed, and the nature of changes that are desired to take place regarding that target. Furthermore, objective statements should indicate the *magnitude* of change the program is expected to produce and the *time frame* in which the changes are expected to occur.

The fact that most programs have multiple objectives sometimes leads to problems in setting the criteria for evaluation. Although a program may be geared to a series of different levels of objectives linked together in a logical sequence, long range objectives may differ from short range objectives, and a program may even be characterized by conflicting objectives. Here it is also important to differentiate between procedural objectives and outcome objectives (Cook and Scioli, 1975, p. 97). **Procedural objectives** are targets regarding the direct products of program activities, objectives for internal administration in implementing a program and providing for service delivery. Examples would be to conduct 100 cellar-to-roof housing inspections per week or to respond to all calls for service for part 1 property crimes within 10 minutes. **Outcomes objectives**, on the other hand, are targets external to program operation. They relate to the positive changes in the environment the program is expected to produce, the real outcomes that justify the program's existence in the first place. Corresponding examples of outcomes objectives might be to force the upgrading of 70 percent of all substandard dwelling units to meet the requirements set by a city's housing code, or to solve 25 percent of all part 1 property crimes. Procedural objectives should be identified in the specification of program design, but they should be subordinated to the attainment of outcomes objectives in a performance evaluation.

Environment A program should be designed to pursue its objectives within the confines of its environment, the set of factors that lies outside the program but have direct relevance to its operation. The **environment** consists largely of **givens**, factors that are beyond the control of program management, so that the criterion for determining whether a factor is part of the system or its environment is whether or not it can be manipulated by those conducting the program. The environment, then, provides the substantive and administrative context within which the program operates.

Much of the environment is made up of constraints and opportunities, which in a way are two sides of the same coin. **Constraints** are limitations on the program's operation, whereas **opportunities** are potentials available to it; institutional factors, for instance, could both impede and facilitate a program's effectiveness. Consider, for example, a school district's vocational education program intended to provide students with carpentry, masonry, and other construction skills to enhance their ability to earn a livelihood. Tight union restrictions on entry into apprenticeships in the building trades could hinder the ability of graduates to realize the benefits of their training, whereas on the other hand a Comprehensive Employment and Training Act (CETA) program in the area might provide opportunities for short time employment and further on-the-job training.

Other types of constraints and opportunities include socio-economic, legal, financial, psychological, and technological factors or contingencies that relate to the nature of the problem to which the program is addressed, or to the means for carrying out the program. All of these environmental factors should be taken into account in attempting to analyze why a program is or is not working. The environment generates the needs and demands to which public programs are responding. While needs and demands in some circumstances may be modified by program efforts, in the main they are givens; the program should be designed to meet needs or demands within the framework of environmental constraints.

It should also be pointed out that environmental constraints vary as to the degree to which they are beyond the influence of the program. Although by definition environmental factors cannot be manipulated by program management, some problems arising from environmental factors may be mitigated by program strategies, while others must be accepted as bedrock, immutable constraints. For example, a regional library commission that serves in part as a clearinghouse for its members might fail to meet 30 percent of all requests it receives to locate books and other materials. In analyzing the causes of this problem, it might find that 20 percent of all initial request forms received from users are not completed sufficiently to identify the materials desired, while 10 percent of all requests are for materials that are simply not available in the system. The first problem is a short term constraint whose effects can be reduced by remedying the intake process in the libraries; the second problem stems from a deeper constraint beyond the control of the program.

Resources   **Resources** are the things within the system that are available to program management for pursuing objectives. In contrast to environmental factors, within appropriate budgetary and other constraints, program personnel do have control over the mix of resources employed and the way they are used. Resources are typically measured in terms of manpower, money, materials, equipment, and facilities. For the most part, resources represent the direct costs of operating the program and can be measured in dollar terms.

Components   The **components** of a system are its subsystems, the interacting parts of a program designed to achieve its objectives. The components are the activities that use the available resources and constitute the program's operation; they describe how the program functions in converting the resources to products. Taken together, the components or subsystems really constitute the program. They are geared to supporting objectives that should be subordinated to system objectives and, in general, as subsystem performance improves, overall system performance should improve. If this is not the case, either the system design is faulty or the system is not being managed and supported as planned.

Program components may consist of complementary or alternative approaches designed to jointly produce the desired effects. For example, a state's program to hold traffic accidents on its highways to an acceptable level may consist of four principal components, each of which can be further broken down into subsystems: driver training and licensing, vehicle licensing and inspection, highway maintenance, and traffic patrol. Each of these components uses a different set of resources in different activities toward the achievement of intermediate objectives that support the program's overall objectives.

Alternatively, one program component may serve as a support function for another. Consider a community volunteer agency whose objective is to meet the needs of individuals requiring or desiring certain services. One component, the production component, would consist of the actual provision of services to individuals by volunteers; its elements might relate to transportation, domestic household work, recreation, and so forth. The other component, the support component, would entail recruiting volunteers, contacting individuals in need of services, and matching volunteers to needed services. A good formative evaluation would examine both subsystems in order to pinpoint the sources of weakness in service delivery and to examine ways of improving overall performance.

Management   The **management** attribute of the system is the control center that plans and directs the system's operation. It considers all the other attributes of the system in setting system and component objectives, in designing the subsystem structure, in determining the use of resources and their allocation among components, and in controlling system performance. This control function is carried out through feedback loops through which management monitors program performance in light of its objectives and makes adjustments in resource allocations and component operations accordingly. Information systems, designed according to the principles of cybernetics, monitor operations and provide relevant information to decision makers. Program management is a continuous process of planning and modifying the system not only in terms of strategies and component operations, but also, on a macro level, in terms of modifying objectives, depending upon their appropriateness and adequacy.

THE SYSTEMS APPROACH TO PROGRAM ANALYSIS

The systems approach is a good way of building a conceptual framework for structuring the analysis of program performance. Whether or not the systems approach is employed, it is essential to begin a program evaluation with a complete and accurate understanding of how the program is designed to operate, including a description of the goals and objectives it is aimed at achieving, the mix of resources employed and how they are used, the underlying theory that explains how the program's operation is expected to accomplish its objectives, outside factors that influence the program's design and influence its functioning, and the way in which the program is intended to interact with other programs in pursuing higher order objectives. Systems analysis is simply a direct and comprehensive method of developing this detailed understanding of program design.

Developing or reconstructing a program design is often a much more challenging task than might be supposed, because of the complex milieu of substantive factors and institutional arrangements in which programs function, the often complicated and sometimes contradictory nature of program design itself, and organizational or bureaucratic pressures that may be grafted onto or even supersede substantive program considerations. Although general program directions and strategies are initiated by legislated public policy, which is often vaguely defined in the first place, they are pieced together with increasing amounts of detail through administrative decision making at successively lower layers of governmental organization, which concludes at the operating level. As it evolves, a program may well be shaped by a variety of clientele demands and the maintenance expectations of individuals and groups operating the program, as well as by competing views of the relative importance of objectives and the most promising ways of pursuing them. In the course of this process, program objectives and means may be altered or displaced so that the questions "What is the program supposed to do?" and "How is it supposed to do this?" are not easily answered.

Systems Thinking

The systems approach as advocated in this text is basically an organizing tool, a way of thinking about a problem and structuring an analysis in terms of the major issues, the critical variables, and the linkages among variables and among subsystems.

Subsystem Interactions   The focus on subsystem interactions and interdependencies as they affect overall system performance is particularly relevant from the perspectives of higher policy levels. Poor overall performance is often the result of a lack of coordinated management from a systemwide perspective, with subsystems aimed at maximizing objective functions that may not be at all well tuned to overall system requirements. Obviously, this problem is especially critical when management responsibilities for major subsystems are fragmented among various agencies; in the systems approach to policy analysis there is not necessarily a strong correlation between program-system structure and organizational structure.

For example, a study of Virginia's drug abuse control programs focused on five interrelated subsystems: education, law enforcement, the courts, corrections, and treatment programs (Joint Legislative Audit and Review Commission, 1975). Among the study's major findings were the following.

—Rather than having reduced drug usage, the educational programs in the high schools have apparently led to increased experimentation with drugs.
—Although state law directs that law enforcement efforts be concentrated on persons engaged in drug trafficking and more harmful (hard) drugs, roughly 75 percent of all drug-related arrests involved possession of marijuana, mostly for small amounts. Yet, best estimates of the total magnitude of the problem indicate that most users are not arrested.
—Roughly two-thirds of drug-related court cases concern marijuana, whereas only 10 percent relate to distribution offenses of any kind. Over 50 percent of all cases resulted in no conviction, whereas of those persons found guilty and sentenced, 61 percent of the sentences were entirely suspended.

Thus, the educational component may well be counterproductive, leading to increased usage of drugs—a boomerang effect—which has become the object of the de facto priorities of the law enforcement agencies involved. In turn, the law enforcement effort, although not reaching the great majority of drug users, is consuming substantial amounts of resources to arrest persons on possession charges, which has the practical effect of overloading the courts system with cases with which it is inclined to deal leniently. Clearly, the major subsystems are operating in a highly dysfunctional manner rather than as critical components of an integrated goal-seeking system, and the set of programs taken together constitutes a costly, relatively ineffective approach to control over drug problems.

Program Logic The systems approach as an organizing tool basically involves a reasoning process (based on previous research and familiarity with the program area) aimed at identifying the essential variables in the program and the environment and indicating the presumed relationships among them. The resulting systems model should represent the underlying logic of the program, including the program-induced causal patterns that are expected to produce desired results and the environmental variables that are thought to influence program effectiveness. The cause-effect relationships so identified represent assumptions that should be formulated as working hypotheses to be tested in evaluation research.

Figure 2.1 shows a system of variables developed for an evaluation of a set of drug abuse treatment programs. The variables inside the dashed line represent the program-system, and those on the outside are environmental variables. Because the primary objective in this case is the reduction of crimes committed by persons with drug abuse problems, the dependent variable is expressed as the arrest rate of individuals having participated in these programs. As indicated by the figure, there are a number of program factors that are thought to influence arrest rate; the single most important hypothesis, however, would be that participation in these programs will lead to reduced arrest rates. Looking at the program operation variables, those within the system, we see that the operating characteristics thought to influence posttreatment arrest rates directly are the type of treatment and the retention rate; the model further suggests that two other program operation variables, staff teamwork and morale and staff/patient ratio, directly influence retention rate. These also constitute hypotheses to be tested.

The environmental variables shown in Figure 2.1 indicate that there are factors, such as age, education, family background, and employment experiences, that are assumed to influence arrest rates but that are clearly beyond the control of the programs. This suggests the need to measure the influence of these variables and, more importantly, to compare clients in terms of these variables in order to determine which environmental conditions, if any, seem to facilitate the success of specific types of treatment in reducing arrest rates. The hypothesized influence of the variable, age, is particularly interesting in that it is assumed to influence posttreatment arrest rates directly *and* indirectly through its influence on the type of program clients enter. (To see how to operation-

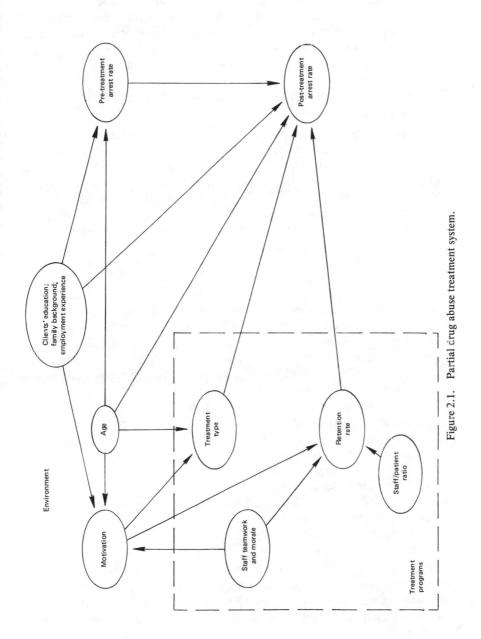

Figure 2.1.   Partial drug abuse treatment system.

alize this one part of the analysis, the reader can look ahead to Tables 5.2 through 5.4 in chapter 5.) One more interesting point concerning the environmental variables is that the factor termed motivation has a two-directional relationship with the program. For the most part it is an externally determined constraint that influences whether patients remain in their program or drop out early; however, over time patients' motivation may be tempered by their contact with program staff.

Program Measures

Conceptualizing a program as an objective-seeking system that operates within environmental constraints, the analyst can classify the key variables that measure program operation and effects as they relate to the underlying theory of how resources are used to achieve objectives. Figure 2.2 shows the three major categories of program variables—process measures, linking variables, and effectiveness measures—and the assumed relationships among them that serve to outline the program logic. The process measures represent the ongoing operation of the program and the attainment of *procedural* objectives, while the effectiveness measures are indicators of the extent to which *substantive* objectives are being accomplished. Quite often the underlying logic will include a number of linkages between program process and the production of intended impacts that must be specified if the reasons for program success or failure are to be examined. For the most part these linking variables represent the attainment of intermediate objectives which are held to be necessary in order for real impacts to occur. The theory underlying a program is based on the assumption of a chain of events triggered by the production of outputs and leading through intermediate results to final impacts. If all the links in this causal sequence can be identified, the underlying theory can be stated as a series of "if-then" assumptions that should be examined in a formative evaluation. Depending on the number and complexity of the causal sequences involved, the systems model of program logic might be stretched out in more steps than shown in Figure 2.2 (representing numerous linking variables and impacts), and it might be expanded vertically to represent parallel streams of causal sequences relating to different subsystems or components.

Impact Indicators   Variables that serve to indicate whether impacts are actually being produced by the program are the most important, and often the most difficult, to identify in a program evaluation. A full-fledged evaluation would attempt to identify and measure unanticipated impacts as well as the desired goal-oriented impacts, which stem directly from program objectives. Frequently, however, a major problem is to obtain a clear definition of the program's objectives in the first place; effectiveness measures are operational definitions of criteria that indicate

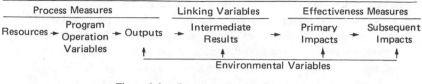

Figure 2.2.   Program-related variables.

success or failure in achieving objectives. In Figure 2.2 the term **primary impacts** refers to the major, direct effects intended to be produced by the program, while **subsequent impacts** are longer range, and usually more general and less direct, effects that might be expected to evolve over time. For example, the primary impact of a neighborhood health center might be specified as improved health status of the resident population as measured by the reduced incidence of certain types of illnesses and limiting health conditions, while a subsequent impact intended as a spinoff over time might be improved social functioning as reflected by improvement in such indicators as employment levels, maintenance of families as household units, and crime rates.

In the absence of clear-cut objectives around which there is a strong consensus, a number of strategies are available to the analyst. First, he can attempt to force them from program personnel, and this might well be a healthy exercise for them, *if* it can be made to work. Second, he can define the objectives himself based on observation and familiarity with the program, previous studies done on similar programs, written guidelines and regulations that may apply, and points of view solicited from any interested parties. In order to avoid too narrow a focus based on the analyst's own values, the safest approach here is to try to maintain a balance by including all the objectives that surface in the review, regardless of incompatibilities. Third, the evaluator can start with an open-ended approach, beginning with a number of broad goal statements and working with program personnel in successive rounds of attempts to refine them into a set of specific objectives. This last approach may be the wisest (Weiss, 1972, p. 28), particularly in developing program areas where in general there is little consensus as to what constitutes success.

Unanticipated impacts are even more difficult to identify because they may not be hinted at by the program logic. In some cases, programs have almost the opposite effects from those that are intended and exacerbate the problems they are aimed at alleviating. In a housing program, for example, a rigid codes enforcement component might have the adverse effect of encouraging the abandonment of marginal properties, leading to a decrease in the available housing stock and further neighborhood deterioration. Other unanticipated impacts may result from programs that generate important side effects while working toward their objectives. A notable example is the aid for dependent children program, which has been found to contribute to the breakdown of family structure while attempting to assure financial support for children.

Weiss (1972, p. 33) makes the point that unanticipated efforts can be negative, neutral, or even good, as in a readings skill educational program that leads to better citizenship in addition to improved reading ability. The identification of unanticipated impacts is one of the most challenging aspects of program analysis and planning and one of the reasons why analysts and evaluators need to be familiar with the substantive aspects of a program as well as with research tools. Weiss recommends that evaluators brainstorm about all the possible unanticipated effects of a program in advance of structuring projects, while remaining flexible enough to incorporate those that emerge later in their analysis (1972, p. 33).

Impact indicators tend to create the greatest difficulties in data collection and require the most ingenuity in developing reliable and valid operational measures. In part this is because, although some program measures are generated directly by the program's operation and are therefore readily available, impact data are often "out there in the field," less accessible and requiring more time and money for collection. Reliability may be a problem in terms of the use of multiple observers or reliance on soft measures, or due to a level of precision and sensitivity that is inadequate to identify incremental differences in impacts. In addition, program impacts may be difficult to sort out from other phenomena, leading to a problem of validity that presents challenges to the development of measures as well as overall research design and analytic approach. Such problems can be especially critical in relation to the mix of impact indicators employed to represent multiple objectives, as they can lead to a distortion of criteria in the direction of those impacts that are more easily measured and for which data are more accessible (Rivlin, 1971, p. 142).

Linking Variables As discussed above, formative evaluations depend on an understanding of how various aspects of program process are linked with the production of intended impacts. While the process measures as shown in Figure 2.2 represent program operation and actual service delivery, the linking variables represent the intermediate results that are necessary in order to complete the causal sequence of program logic. These intermediate results occur in the environment, but they are not the real impacts upon which the program is focused. Rather, they are bridging variables, or channels through which the provision of service is expected to generate impacts. Depending on the nature and complexity of the program, the specification of linking variables might not be necessary, or, on the other hand, it may be appropriate to examine a whole sequence of linking variables.

The intermediate objectives that are represented by linking variables often refer to gaining access to clients in need of the program, the initial response to a new program, and participation rates in programs. In general the theory underlying many programs is that high quality services must first be provided, and then utilized, for the program to be a success. The utilization factor is not a significant impact in its own right, but rather an intermediate step that must occur if the program is to have any real impact. As mentioned above, for example, a new neighborhood health center might be established to provide a number of in-house and outreach services with the basic objective of improving the health status of the target area population. For this to be successful, three types of intermediate objectives should be of concern and incorporated in a formative evaluation as linking variables: 1) initial target area penetration, people beginning to make use of the services; 2) user satisfaction, which is necessary to increase target area penetration and sustain usage; and then 3) continuous and comprehensive utilization, individuals and households making use of a variety of complementary services on a regular basis. This sequence of intermediate results must occur if the center is to have any impact on overall health status; each of these three linking variables can be operationalized with multiple indicators to permit the evaluator to examine the agency's progress in moving toward the effective utilization of its services.

Process Variables   The process side of a program to be specified in a comprehensive evaluation includes resources, program operation variables, and outputs. The resources used by a program are usually easier to identify and measure than other types of variables. They are usually stated as quantities of manpower, money, materials, and equipment, but they can also be measured as direct costs in dollar terms, as discussed in chapter 11. Resources are themselves one of the major concerns of monitoring efforts, but more importantly they are taken into consideration in analyses attempting to identify associations between alternative resource mixes and types with levels of outputs and impacts.

If the analysis is to go inside the "black box" in order to examine how the system operates, it will need to consider **program operation variables**, those that describe the components of the program and the conversion process by which resources are transformed into products.

Program operation variables represent the general program approaches embodied in a program design or the specific strategies, techniques, and types of treatment that constitute service delivery. The use of program operation variables will depend on the scope and complexity of the program as well as the level and analytical framework of the evaluation. The program being examined may itself utilize varying strategies and alternative approaches, which can be compared in terms of performance, or essentially there may be a single program approach that is basically constant rather than variable. In the latter case, the major program operation variable might be specified as a simple program/no program dichotomy. At higher levels of analysis in which many programs are being compared, numerous indicators may be required to capture the variation in different aspects of program operation. In forward-looking benefit-cost or cost-effectiveness analysis, the alternatives to be compared in terms of efficiency are represented by program operation variables. (See chapter 11.)

Outputs are the direct products of the program/system; they have no inherent value, but rather are important because they are intended to lead to the production of desired impacts. Outputs do not represent the physical, socio-economic, or behavioral changes that are the real objectives of the program, but rather volumes of activities or physical entities that are the immediate products of the program. They are usually measured in terms of workload, numbers of cases treated, or units of service provided. Outputs can be thought of as being at or near the boundary between program and environment; to a great extent managers can manipulate output levels, given available resources, but in some cases outputs are measured in terms of the volume of frequent actions taken for which a standby capacity is maintained but which are triggered by variable environmental stimuli, such as the number of fire alarms responded to in the past 6 months. It should also be kept in mind that it is often desirable to include measures of the quality as well as the quantity of outputs produced, looking at *how quickly* alarms are responded to, for example, in addition to counting *how many* alarms were answered.

A common shortcoming of many evaluations is the reliance on output measures rather than true impact measures. Outputs alone cannot justify a program's existence because they do not constitute benefits in their own right; rather, programs are designed to produce outputs that in turn are expected to generate real impacts. In a juvenile deliquency prevention program, for example, outputs might be measured by such variables as the number of hours spent in counseling individuals, the number of job training programs conducted, and the number of school contacts made. Impacts, however, would be measured by the number of first offenses and the recidivism rate among juveniles. Outputs are a critical link in the program logic that should be analyzed in formative evaluations in relationship to both resources and impacts. Output targets are often set by managers as *procedural* objectives; whether these targets are met and whether the mix of outputs being produced is optimal are often important issues in explaining observed program performance and suggesting ways of improving it.

In many program evaluations, the most relevant outputs are those that measure the units of service produced or made available, while linking variables might represent units of service consumed or utilized. Real impacts, then, would be the changes in the target population or target area that occur because services were provided and utilized. For example, in an evaluation of specialized transportation services for elderly and handicapped persons, outputs might be specified by such measures as vehicle miles and vehicle hours operated, or even seat-miles operated, while linking variables representing utilization might be measured in terms of the number of passenger trips made or the number of passenger miles traveled on the system. The primary impact or direct effects would be measured by the extent to which the perceived need or desire for trips on the part of elderly and handicapped persons has been reduced by making increased service available. The intended subsequent impact, a more normalized lifestyle, might be represented by the number and kinds of activities that users participate in at present that were difficult or impossible previously due to the lack of transportation.

Environmental Factors Environmental variables are critical in developing explanations for why a program succeeds or fails in various respects because they represent conditions that facilitate or impede achieving objectives. When possible they should be identified as short term or long term constraints, such as a temporary downturn in a local economy because of national trends as opposed to the general lack of prosperity in an area because of the permanent loss of basic industries. In addition, it is desirable to identify constraints as being either completely beyond programmatic influence or subject to possible amelioration over time, as discussed earlier.

Furthermore, in structuring a problem or developing a program specification, rather than simply listing the relevant environmental factors, it is important to identify presumed relationships among environmental variables and other measures, as illustrated in Figure 2.1. As an oversimplified example, consider the specialized transportation services for elderly and handicapped persons discussed above. Given a ceiling on expenditures, outputs such as vehicle miles and seat miles operated will be dependent in large part on the technological constraints of vehicle operation and costs, while the vehicle miles operated per hour will be further influenced by such "area" constraints as street pattern and traffic volumes. Attainment of the intermediate objective of utilization of the new service by handicapped persons can be expected to be heavily influenced by such client characteristics as the nature of the disability, perceptions of the convenience or inconvenience afforded by the new service, and willingness to try something new. More importantly, utilization of the service and the degree of impact this might have in permitting a more normalized lifestyle will be greatly dependent on other environmental variables such as the existence of architectural barriers that might still prohibit participation in a full range of activities despite the availability of transportation.

Two problems arise in incorporating environmental factors in a program analysis. First, what the constraints are may not be apparent. Again, ferreting out those factors that might be relevant is largely a matter of experience and familiarity with the substance of the program. In the initial process of variable identification at least, the analyst should think expansively and include variables that would seem to be on the periphery of the program's environment. Pilot work or exploratory analysis may then indicate whether such variables should actually be included in the analysis.

The second problem is that the important environmental factors may not *vary*; with respect to a single program the major constraints may be constant, thereby not permitting comparisons aimed at determining their effects. When this is the case, the best way to analyze the influence of environmental factors on program performance may be through replications, comparing similar programs in varied settings.

Program Specification

The scope and complexity of the causal sequences that form the basis of program logic vary with the type and scale of program being examined. Program specification may or not involve multiple causal sequences and the feedback of results from some subsystems into the operation of others. Figure 2.3 shows the specification of a housing improvement program including two components, regulatory and rehabilitation.These in turn consist of multiple subsystems of elements, each of which is thought to contribute directly to the goal of improved housing conditions.

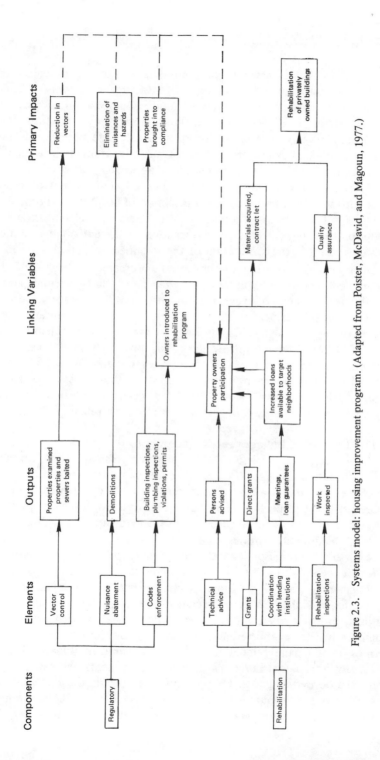

Figure 2.3. Systems model: housing improvement program. (Adapted from Poister, McDavid, and Magoun, 1977.)

The model indicates how the components are expected to achieve the objectives of increased code compliance, reduction of vectors (rodents), elimination of nuisances and hazards, and rehabilitation of privately owned dwellings. Each arrow in the diagram represents a cause-effect assumption that is a link in the program logic. The first set of such assumptions relates to the production of outputs. Implicit in each element is an implementation plan or tactical approach that is intended to meet output targets. Although outputs can be controlled with much greater certainty than impacts, the production of outputs as specified is not always automatic. The linkage between element and output is the assumption that implementation or operation of the activity as planned will in fact result in the production of the specified outputs.

An assumption relating to the codes enforcement element of the regulatory component in Figure 2.3, for example, is that focusing a codes inspection effort on the target neighborhoods will produce a certain number of inspections per month and citations for codes violations for a given percentage of all dwelling units that are not in compliance with codes. Whether these output targets will be attained is uncertain. Although the targets and schedule may be reasonable, resources may be expended without achieving the specified output levels if 1) the inspectors are unnecessarily slow, or fast but not thorough in their work, or 2) homeowners or occupants resist the effort by refusing permission for their properties to be inspected.

The next set of linkages relates outputs to intermediate results, in general based on the assumption that producing the specified mix and levels of outputs will trigger the causal sequence underlying the program logic. Some of these may be critical links that are basically open to question: will the inspection of major repair and improvement projects ensure the quality of materials used and workmanship, and will contacts with local lending institutions and offers of loan guarantees actually lead to revised redlining policies and make more loan money available in the target neighborhoods? At this point an important subsystem interdependency should be noted; one critical assumption in the program logic is that codes enforcement—through inspections, citing violations, and providing information—will induce property owners to participate in the rehabilitation program. In addition, participation is shown as being partially dependent on the increased funding available.

Finally, the model indicates how the components are expected to achieve the desired impacts. Of particular interest is the fact that the codes enforcement outputs are expected to serve both to induce owners to bring properties into compliance themselves and/or to enter the rehabilitation program. Of further interest is the positive effect that increased codes compliance, vector reduction, and nuisance elimination are anticipated to have on housing rehabilitation activity, indicated by dashed lines.

Thus, accomplishing the set of interrelated objectives of this program is dependent upon a number of program elements whose outputs are intended to trigger parallel and interdependent causal sequences. Operationalizing the variables in these sequences (measures as discussed in chapter 3) and stating each causal linkage in the model as an assumption to be tested provides a strong substantive framework for evaluating this program's performance. Does codes enforcement lead to increased compliance and interest in the rehabilitation program? Do increased compliance, rodent control, and nuisance elimination lead to greater participation in the rehabilitation program? Does the provision of grants and loans in fact lead to the rehabilitation of substantial numbers of dwellings? Examining these issues would be the heart of a worthwhile evaluation.

The issue of identifying the critical factors and cause-effect assumptions to examine necessarily leads into a consideration of research design, discussed in chapter 9. The primary concern is that analyzing cause-effect relationships between programs and impacts requires comparisons across varying program designs or between a program and "no program" situation. However, an evaluation focusing on a single program is likely to encounter a lack of variation in the program operation variables, i.e., the program is actually a constant structure of relatively static subsystems, as implied in Figure 2.3. Analysis of this one program alone will amount to a descriptive case study with little analytical content and an inability to test causal hypotheses about the production of impacts. A full discussion of this issue is deferred until chapter 9, but the following brief comments are in order at this point:

—The single program can be examined intact in comparison with a situation characterized by a similar environment but a complete lack of the program; in the case of the housing program this could be a set of comparison neighborhoods or the same target neighborhoods *before* the program is implemented. This might provide an assessment of overall impact but would not facilitate a highly analytical examination of the interworkings of subsystems.
—Alternatively, if the housing program in question is to be implemented in various neighborhoods across a metropolitan area, the detailed specifications might be varied in terms of levels of

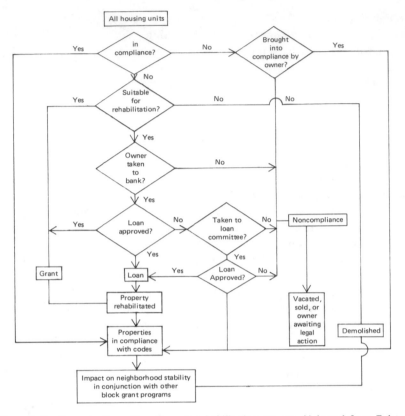

Figure 2.4. Property disposition through rehabilitation process. (Adapted from Poister, McDavid, and Magoun, 1977, p. 48.)

output to permit useful comparisons. Beyond that, the inclusion of components might be varied to examine questions about major subsystem interaction; for example, including the codes enforcement element in some areas but not in others in order to analyze its impact on rehabilitation.

—Finally, questions about subsystem interactions, the relative mix of components and elements, and alternative levels of output could be assessed through comparing a series of project evaluations in different cities. This might work if the projects were similar in terms of objectives and major program approach but sufficiently varied in terms of actual design features; furthermore, valid results would depend on incorporating the salient environmental variables

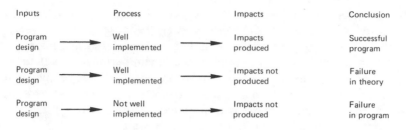

Figure 2.5.   Types of program failure.

into the analysis in an attempt to sort out program effects from nonprogram effects.

—Even given a single program with little or no internal variation in structure or output levels, some explanation of apparent results, and particularly the lack of results, can be obtained through the process study approach. Figure 2.4, for example, is basically a flow chart representing the entrance of properties with code violations into the system, their progress through various steps in the process, and their final disposition as either rehabilitated, demolished or vacated, sold, or awaiting legal action. If, at the end of a two-year period, the rate of properties being brought into compliance is disappointingly low, tracking cases through the process as illustrated in Figure 2.4 would help locate bottlenecks and pinpoint problems.

Explaining Program Failure

The logic of a sequence of events, or causal process, leading from outputs to impacts points up the issue of explaining the failure of programs to achieve their objectives, which is often a critical aspect in formative evaluations. These explanations boil down to two categories of reasons: 1) the program may not be producing the outputs designed to trigger the causal process, a **failure in program**, or 2) the program may be producing the intended outputs but these may *not* in fact lead through the hypothesized causal process to the desired impacts, a **failure in theory**. These two types of failure are modeled in Figure 2.5. It should be noted that this examination of program failure is based on the classification of variables shown in Figure 2.2

If a failure in program is encountered, the theory has not been tested fairly. No conclusions can be drawn about the validity of the underlying theory if the program has not been implemented as planned.

In fact, this is sometimes a major problem in experimenting with new program stategies (Gramlich and Koshel, 1975, p. 520). In general, when failure in program implementation is encountered, the importance of linking of process study to impact assessment becomes paramount.

On the other hand, if a program is found to have been implemented correctly, but the intended impacts are not being produced as anticipated, the underlying theory is invalidated, at least as it applies to the context in which it is being tested. It may be that the program logic is basically incorrect, or it may be that the fit of program design to the operating context has not been specified thoroughly enough. The need to learn why the theory does not seem to work further emphasizes the importance of including environmental variables in the analysis and replicating studies in similar, and different, contexts.

A Note on Boundary Problems   At times difficulties arise concerning the most appropriate scope for a program analysis. This depends on the purpose of the project and the questions to be addressed, and, as we have seen, these range from macro level issues to small scale operating concerns. Most program analyses are partial analyses in that they address only certain aspects of a program's operation or selected criteria of program performance. The analyst must be sure to take into account all those factors that truly impinge on the problem at hand but he does not want to be encumbered by the time and money costs of extra baggage. One strategy in the conceptualization of formative studies that is intended to remedy operating problems is a step by step contraction of the system's boundaries to reduce it to manageable proportions. This is accomplished by excluding apparently unnecessary elements followed, if necessary, by a gradual expansion of boundaries in order to take into account additional factors to improve understanding of the problem (Lee, 1970, p. 34).

Of course, the decision to focus on a certain level in a program hierarchy is arbitrary in the sense of there being no true, inviolate boundaries, as any program can be thought of as constituting a subsystem of some larger system. This kind of decision is usually based on knowledge or assumptions that the problem at hand can be corrected at a given level or that in any case, the decision makers have little control over the higher order system.

The system should be defined so as to meet the needs of the analyst studying a problem, rather than as an elaborate structure illustrating all the presumptions of systems theory. As has been seen, there is often no real need to break a program or activity down into subsystems. In some situations, analysis will concern only a partial system or only certain system attributes, as in traditional needs and demand studies. If the problem facing him does not neatly conform to a systems model, the analyst should *not* bend it to fit such a model. Systems analysis is by no means a rigid requirement of every program analysis project, but rather an organizing tool that is frequently helpful in conceptualizing problems and formulating a framework for analysis.

REFERENCES

Ashby, W. R. 1964. An Introduction to Cybernetics. London: Chapman & Hall and University Paperbacks.

Ashby, W. R. 1965. Design for a Brain. London: Chapman & Hall and Science Paperbacks.

Ashby, W. R. 1968. Principles of the Self-organizing System. In: W. Buckley (ed.), Modern Systems Research for the Behavioral Scientist. Chicago: Aldine Publishing Co.

Beer, S. 1966. Decision and Control: The Meaning of Operational Research and Management Cybernetics. London: John Wiley and Sons, Inc.

Beer, S. 1972. Brain of the Firm: A Development in Management Cybernetics. New York: Herder and Herder.

Bertalanffy, L. von. 1951. General Systems Theory: A New Approach to the Unity of Science. Human Biology 23:303–361.

Bertalanffy, L. von. 1968. General Systems Theory. New York: George Braziller.

Black, G. 1968. The Application of Systems Analysis to Government Operations. New York: Praeger.

Boulding, K. E. 1956. General Systems Theory—The Skeleton of Science. Management Science. 2(3):197–208.

Boulding, K. E. 1964. General Systems Theory as a Point of View. In: M. D. Mesarovic (ed.), On General Systems Theory. New York: John Wiley and Sons, Inc., pp. 25–38.

Churchman, C. W. 1968. The Systems Approach. New York: Delta Books.

Cleland, D. I., and W. R. King (eds.). 1969. Systems, Organizations, Analysis, Management: A Book of Readings. New York: McGraw-Hill Book Co.

Cook, T. J., and F. P. Scioli, Jr. 1975. Impact Analysis in Public Policy Research. In: K. M. Dolbeare (ed.), Public Policy Evaluation. Beverly Hills, Cal.: Sage Publications, Inc., pp. 95–117.

Deutsch, K. W. 1966. The Nerves of Government: Models of Political Communication and Control. New York: Free Press.

Dolbeare, K. M. (ed.). 1975. Public Policy Evaluation. Beverly Hills, Cal.: Sage Publications, Inc.

Easton, D. 1953. The Political System: An Inquiry into the State of Political Science. New York: Alfred A. Knopf.

Emery, F. E. (ed.). 1969. Systems Thinking. Baltimore: Penguin Books.

Forrester, J. 1969. Urban Dynamics. Boston: M.I.T. Press.

Gramlich, E. M., and P. P. Koshel. 1975. Is Real-World Experimentation Possible? The Case of Educational Performance Contracting. Policy Analysis (Summer):511–530.

Horst, P., J. N. Nay, J. W. Scanlon, and J. S. Wholey. 1974. Program Management and the Federal Evaluator. Public Administration Review (July/August):300–308.

International City Management Association. 1972. Applying Systems Analysis in Urban Government: Three Case Studies. Washington: International City Management Association.

Joint Legislative Audit and Review Commission. 1975. Program Evaluation—Virginia Drug Abuse Control Programs. Richmond: Virginia General Assembly.

Katz, D., and R. L. Kahn. 1966. The Social Psychology of Organizations. New York: John Wiley and Sons, Inc.

Lee, A. M. 1970. Systems Analysis Frameworks. New York: John Wiley and Sons, Inc.

Martin, E. W., Jr. 1969. The Systems Concept. In: D. I. Cleland and W. R. King (eds.), Systems, Organizations, Analysis, Management: A Book of Readings. New York: McGraw-Hill Book Co.

Mosher, F. C. 1969. Limitations and Problems of PPBS in the States. Public Administration Review (March/April):160–167.

Mowitz, R. J. 1970. The Design and Implementation of Pennsylvania's Planning, Programming, Budgeting System. Harrisburg: Commonwealth of Pennsylvania.

Poister, T. H., J. C. McDavid, and A. H. Magoun. 1977. Applied Program Evaluation for Small and Medium-Size Cities. University Park: Institute of Public Administration, The Pennsylvania State University.

Rivlin, A. M. 1971. Systematic Thinking for Social Action. Washington, D.C.: The Brookings Institution.

Smithies, A. 1969. A Conceptual Framework for Program Budget. In: D. I. Cleland and W. R. King (eds.), Systems, Organizations, Analysis, Management: A Book of Readings. New York: McGraw-Hill Book Co., pp. 163–183.

Sutherland, J. W. 1973. A General Systems Philosophy for the Social and Behavioral Sciences. New York: George Braziller.

Weiss, C. H. 1972. Evaluation Research. Englewood Cliffs, N.J.: Prentice-Hall, Inc.

Wright, C., and M. D. Tate. 1973. Economics and Systems Analysis: Introduction for Public Managers. Reading, Mass.: Addison Wesley Publishing Co.

MEASUREMENT AND DATA SOURCES

3

One of the most demanding aspects of social science research is the development of adequate measures. In program analysis this may be somewhat less problematical inasmuch as we are less concerned with theories and more directly interested in concrete, observable phenomena than those engaged in basic research. Nevertheless, in evaluating public programs the definition of variables that are appropriate for the purposes at hand and the collection of reliable data are critical. To a great extent, the difficulties that face a program analyst regarding the development of an adequate data base constitute problems of measurement.

Measurement involves the classification and description of cases in terms of a particular attribute. Essentially it is a process of comparing a given attribute of individual cases to a uniform standard, thus permitting comparisons among cases as to whether they are equivalent and the extent to which they possess the attribute in question. The objectivity of a measure depends on the clarity with which categories or gradations of the standard are defined and the degree to which the proper fit of cases to the standard can be ascertained.

OPERATIONALIZED MEASURES

Most of the information items used in program analysis are measures of needs and demands, resources, environmental factors, and program outputs and impacts. Usually we do not measure these variables directly, but rather observe indicators of them. Whereas research questions and hypotheses may be formulated in terms of general concepts, to proceed with data collection and analysis requires that the variables be defined in terms of operationalized measures that are concrete, precise, and specific. For example, to address the question of whether auto availability decreases the demand for mass transit, we might employ the operationalized hypothesis that members of households owning more automobiles make fewer trips on city buses.

Notice that although now our hypothesis is operational, it is somewhat more limited than the original research question, and in some ways may be misleading. The concept of auto availability might be translated into a number of operationalized definitions, and possibly the evidence collected would produce differing conclusions depending on which measure is actually used. Relying on the number of automobiles owned by a household as the indicator may underestimate actual auto availability, which might also depend on vehicles that household members drive regularly but do not own (such as company cars) and cars owned by friends made available to household members. Conversely, autos that might be owned by household members but not licensed or maintained in operating condition would inflate our operational measure of auto availability.

Concepts and Indicators

An **operationalized indicator** is one that is defined in terms of the procedure used in taking the measurement. This leaves no doubt as to what the measure *is*, but there may well be varying interpretations of what it is an appropriate measure *of.* To be more specific, our operationalized measure of auto availability might be the number of licensed automobiles that household members say they own in responding to a survey question, or alternatively, the indicator might be the number of automobiles registered in the names of household members by the Motor Vehicle Bureau. If our data are collected reliably we know exactly what the measure is, but we are less certain that it is a valid measure of auto availability and even less certain that it is a good indicator of some more generalized concept, such as affluence.

Theoretical concepts are not defined in these concrete terms. They are not operational because they are defined in terms of other concepts that are assumed to be already understood. Take, for example, the concept of adequate housing. To most of us this would connote housing conditions that are clean and sanitary, afford protection from natural elements, enhance physical and mental health, provide enough space for a minimum of privacy, and perhaps afford some comfort and aesthetic value. However, these descriptors are as unoperational as the original concept of adequate housing.

A principal problem regarding the development of good measures is the definition of operationalized measures that are valid indicators of the concepts or more general measures they are intended to represent. Because many concepts tend to be multidimensional, the use of multiple operationalized measures is often appropriate. The classification of housing units as standard versus substandard (or as compared to a standard of "decent, safe, and sanitary" housing) applied by many governmental units serves as an example. In such classification schemes housing units are rated in terms of structural soundness, the existence and functioning of sanitary facilities, and the ratio of rooms or floor space to occupants. Yet these operationalized measures are only indicators of some of the more tangible aspects of housing conditions and may not represent other dimensions of the concept—adequate housing—such as aesthetic appeal.

Such problems, however, may often be less worrisome in the conduct of applied program analysis than in basic social science research, in which interest tends to center around core concepts. As public programs are aimed at producing tangible and specific impacts, operationalized measures are more often directly representative of the phenomena of interest. The concept of transit demand, for example, may refer to more than the actual number of trips taken because there may be a latent demand for the service that is not manifested in trip-making. Yet what is of interest to planners may be the volume of actual ridership, given a specified level of service.

The issue of general concepts versus operationalized measures is an open question with respect to program analysis and depends largely on the purposes of the individual study. For example, consider a program in an urban area that is intended to improve housing conditions by assisting homeowners in weatherproofing their homes and improving their heating systems. Appropriate measures of this program's effectiveness might include the increase in the number of winter days when a temperature of 68° is maintained (controlling for fluctuations in the weather) and the amount of home heating fuel saved by such efforts. As the program has very specific immediate objectives, these operationalized measures provide a very direct measure of its effectiveness. On the other hand, if one is really interested in the more far-reaching goal of assuring adequate housing, such measures would tap only one dimension of this desired quality. A study of the adequacy of the program would require measures that encompass many more aspects of the concept of adequate housing.

Regardless of whether one is interested in operationalized measures or more generalized concepts for which they serve as indicators, data analysis and the conclusions drawn from it are assured of validity only with respect to the operationalized measures employed. Transferring conclusions from the operational to the conceptual level is something of an act of faith because one can only be certain of results with respect to the actual measures used. The more one believes that his operational measures are valid indicators of the general concepts he is interested in, the more confidence he can have in drawing conclusions about these concepts. Concluding that one method of teaching reading is superior to a second on the basis of certain test scores is valid only to the extent that the tests employed provide a good measure of reading ability.

Validity and Reliability

In many respects the difficulties inherent in the development of good measures are the same as those that are of primary concern in the design and conduct of quality research in general. Indeed, the purpose of most program analysis is measurement in a more general sense, as in the measurement of needs or demands for a particular service or the measurement of the effects of an ongoing program. The principal criteria of a good measure, validity and reliability, are also the primary concerns in drawing conclusions based on the collection and analysis of data. In a sense the development of a sound research approach and application of appropriate statistical methods in a program evaluation are aimed at obtaining valid and reliable measurements of program performance.

Validity refers to the degree to which a measure provides a true indication of whatever it is intended to represent; **reliability** refers to the stability or dependability of the measures, the consistency with which a measure is taken over repeated applications. Reliability is a necessary, but not sufficient, condition for validity, because if it is not reliable, a measure will reflect inconsistencies in the measurement process as well as the relevant characteristics of the individual cases. A measure can be reliable, however, and still not be valid because validity depends on the nature of a measure as well as its reliability. To be valid, a measure also must be appropriate; it must be an indicator that truly represents the attribute or characteristic of interest.

Types of Reliability A traditional distinction between reliability and validity is that unreliability is caused by **unsystematic** or **random error** in the measuring instrument, while any **systematic error** that creates a **bias** in the measure constitutes a source of invalidity (Suchman, 1967, pp. 116–118). Unsystematic error or chance variation may be present in any measuring instrument; the problem is to contain unreliability at an acceptable level.

Four types of reliability have been identified that can also be considered as tests for reliability: 1) congruency of several indicators, 2) consistency of an instrument used repeatedly by a single observer, 3) consistency of an instrument used by many observers, and 4) constancy of an instrument over time (Zetterberg, 1965, p. 124). Regarding the first, if a number of indicators produce the same pattern of measurements over a number of observations, this is a sign that they are reliable. For example, a highway department may use two methods of measuring the quality of the roads it is responsible for: 1) road condition observation forms filled out by on-site inspectors, and 2) a mechanized street-roughness indicator. If the two produce consistently similar results over a sample of highway stretches, this is evidence that they are *reliable* measuring instruments. However, whether they provide *valid* indicators of road quality may still be debatable.

If repeated applications of an instrument by a single observer to the same subject produce the same, or nearly the same, measurement, the instrument yields a high degree of precision. If the repeated applications produce random fluctuations around a supposedly true value, the measure is less precise; **precision** concerns the tolerance or expected range of error produced by a measure.

The reliability of a measure is enhanced if multiple observers obtain the same results. This is an indication of the **objectivity** of an instrument, the extent to which it is based on the application of a uniform standard as opposed to the subjective interpretations of those taking the measurements. Also, a measure lacks reliability if it produces differing results over time. For example, reported crime statistics are often unreliable for analyzing trends over time because classification schemes or reporting procedures have changed over the years. Sometimes the object of a measure will, in fact, vary over time, such as the blood pressure of an individual under varying conditions; a reliable measure should provide an indication of the range of variability (Suchman, 1967, p. 118).

This latter type of reliability can present thorny problems for evaluators, who are often concerned with identifying and measuring changes produced by public programs. If an apparent change over time is noted, is it a matter of unreliable measures or a reliable measure of an actual changing condition? This question can be addressed in part by statistical techniques and in terms of the magnitude of change observed, but the primary basis for such a decision depends on whether changes or fluctuations over time follow some logical pattern or can be explained or predicted by meaningful factors, in which case actual changes are assumed to have occurred.

Types of Validity   With respect to the development of good measures, validity concerns the worth of an instrument in providing measures that are appropriate indicators of the criteria or attributes of interest. It deals with the substantive meaning or interpretation of a measure. The overall validity of a study's conclusions is limited by the weakest aspect of that study. With respect to measurement, the primary threat is the use of measures that are not truly relevant; indicators that are unrelated or only tangentially related to the subject of interest. Furthermore, even when the intent of a measure is relevant, the way in which it is taken may introduce a systematic bias in the values recorded, thereby invalidating the measure.

Suchman has identified four types of validity or bases for asserting the validity of a measure (Suchman, 1967, pp. 120–121). **Face validity** refers to the obvious relevance of a measure as determined by the evaluator himself. These measures are probably the easiest to develop and can involve direct counting of objects, or some relatively objective type of measurement. For example, if one is interested in the intensity of use of a recreational facility, one measure would be merely to count the number of people using the facility. Less directly, if one is concerned with the health care of infants and children in a given area, one may investigate the incidence of diseases that are normally considered to be preventable, e.g., poliomyelitis, diphtheria, measles. This measure indicates the extent to which infants and children in this area are not receiving the appropriate immunization.

Consensual validity, on the other hand, is that conferred upon a measure by experts on the basis of their special familiarity with the subject. An example of a consensual measure might be found in a special education program in which one objective is to raise the level of achievement of the participants. Because special education is one of those nebulous fields in which there is no widespread agreement on what constitutes achievement or how achievement is measured, an evaluator might consult a group of professionals in this field to collectively develop performance measures that they agree should serve as indicators of whether or not reasonable expectations are being achieved.

Correlational validity refers to a finding that a measure co-varies over a cross-section of cases with other measures that are already considered to be valid indicators of the same attribute. In the case of a burglary prevention program, two valid measures of an area's relative safety from burglaries may be the number of burglaries committed and the mean income of the residents of the area. If a survey taken on a sample of city precincts found that the number of burglaries also varied with the number of street lights per block, this measure could also be considered a measure of susceptability to burglary.

Finally, **predictive validity** is the substantiation of a measure that can be used to predict other measures that are considered valid—a correlation between present and future measures (Nunnally and Durham, 1975, pp. 290–93). For example, take the selection process used in deciding which Peace Corps volunteers will actually be given field placement. The process involves multiple psychological tests, continuous observation by previously trained personnel, and personal interviews, all of which are conducted in the training period before placement. On the basis of these multiple and varying types of measures a selection is made. In other words, a prediction is made that those selected can and will perform the work of Peace Corps volunteers in an acceptable manner.

To determine whether or not these instruments do measure what they are assumed to measure on the basis of predictive validity, one would have to examine whether or not the measures taken during training are in fact strongly associated with indicators of actual performance in the field later on.

Problems in Reliability and Validity Suchman has also identified five potential sources of unreliability and invalidity that should be considered during the design or selection of measuring instruments, their use in collecting data, and subsequent data processing (Suchman, 1967, pp. 118–119). First, when measures are taken on individuals, these subjects may be affected by mood, motivation, fatigue, and so on in such a way as to momentarily alter their attitudes or behavior, thereby distorting the measures being taken. Occurring on an unsystematic, random basis, this lessens the reliability of the measures. By the same token and because of any number of possible reasons, perceived or real, these people may intentionally or subconsciously alter their behavior or provide misleading responses to survey questions systematically in a given direction, for example, to conceal certain attitudes or habits or to create a desired kind of impression. This is more serious because it invalidates the measure as an indicator of whatever is intended to be measured.

Second, observer reliability and validity can be affected by the same factors. An individual taking traffic counts, for example, can become lackadaisical and easily overcount or undercount passing vehicles. If in this process there is no systematic tendency either to undercount or overcount vehicles, but simply a lack of precision, this represents a problem of reliability. If, however, there is an inherent tendency simply to miss vehicles and thereby undercount them, it becomes a problem of validity.

Third, situational reliability may be suspect if the conditions under which the measure is taken vary randomly from case to case. For example, reliability would be suspect if some participants in a group training program happen to be observed by a psychiatrist during periods of intense instruction whereas others are observed during more relaxed periods in their schedules.

Fourth, apart from these other factors, the measuring instrument itself may be unreliable and lack objectivity; for example, a survey questionnaire may include ambiguous or unclear items that generate random responses or "noise." Alternatively, a survey instrument may contain many leading questions, and by the range of alternative responses provided it may further bias the data so obtained, perhaps in the direction most likely to confirm the researcher's expectations. Whether this occurs intentionally or by accident, it drastically weakens the validity of the data.

Finally, errors may be made in coding or processing the data; for example, errors in transferring data to computer cards will reduce the reliability of the measures actually used in data analysis. If this happens on a systematic basis, with all 10's punched as 100's, for example, these data become invalid.

If the analyst is aware of these potential sources of unreliability, he can attempt to control them in the design of his measures and data acquisition procedures. Unsystematic error is likely to occur in any study; the challenge is to keep it within reasonable limits given the purposes and requirements of the study. It is often contended that a lack of reliability may not be important in developing aggregrated measures and estimates inasmuch as random errors will tend to cancel each other out. However, individual cases will be affected, and thus disaggregations and comparisons are highly vulnerable to unreliable measures. In general, however, assuring that the measures used are valid poses the more difficult challenge, at least conceptually, to the evaluator.

SELECTING MEASURES

Clearly, the validation of a measure is relative rather than absolute, and in the final analysis it is a question of whether a measure seems to be doing what we need done. The term **sensitivity** is often used to refer to the adequacy of a measure in terms of its ability to differentiate among cases in a way that is meaningful for the purposes of the research. In part, sensitivity relates to the level of refinement of a measure, the closeness of gradations on a scale and the precision with which cases can be placed on a finely gradated scale. Beyond this, a measure must be sensitive to the relevant varying characteristics of interest. For example, aggregate measures of total income for a number of less developed countries could be highly precise—sensitive to production increases, for instance—but still not useful for a particular research purpose because they are not sensitive to shifts in the distribution of income within countries.

The development of program measures can be viewed as a two-part process in which an appropriate construct or criterion is established, and then an empirical indicator of that construct is operationalized. With respect to program impacts, then, the first task is to identify appropriate criteria for evaluating impacts, and the second is to define valid indicators of these criteria. For example, one of the principal criteria for evaluating the effectiveness of the performance of a police department might be a specified percentage reduction in the number of crimes committed.

The question then becomes one of defining an operationalized measure of crime rate. The number of crimes reported to the police would certainly be one indicator, but it is likely that not all crimes are reported. The measure may be biased in that some types of crimes are less likely to be reported than others. Furthermore, if a lack of effective police performance, as perceived by residents, decreases their propensity to report crimes, this operationalized measure could have an inverse relationship with the impact it is intended to represent. An alternative might be to use the number of crimes estimated on the basis of a victimization survey, but this operationalized measure may also have its weak points.[1] Validity is a matter of degree, and thus the use of complementary measures might well be the best solution.

Moving from a concept or criterion to an operationalized indicator depends on the purpose of the criterion in the first place; it all depends on how you count. As one indicator of efficiency, for example, how does one best determine the ratio of students to faculty members at a large university? Does it include part time and nondegree students as well as full time matriculated students, and should faculty members engaged primarily in research be included along with those with full time teaching responsibilities? Again, the appropriate procedure for calculating the ratio depends on its intended use. The ratio of full time students to total faculty can be calculated reliably if complete informa-

---

[1] See articles by Skogan (1976) and Ennis (1967) for a discussion of the need for victimization surveys, and Schneider (1975) for a discussion concerning the use of both official data and victimization surveys.

tion is available; it may or may not be valid for a number of uses depending upon the nature of the questions being addressed.

An operationalized measure will usually be a valid indicator of something, but often not what it is intended or interpreted to be. Some IQ tests lack reliability when interpreted as being accurate to the specific score, because when applied repeatedly to a single subject they usually produce a range of scores varying by 12 points or so (Huff, 1954, pp. 53–57). These measures may be considered to be reliable when interpreted in terms of such ranges, but the question of validity still remains. As a measure of native intelligence an IQ test may be suspect in that it is oriented to one dimension of intelligence (ability to reason and learn as opposed to the ability to be creative or lead people, for example) and may depend on what has been learned rather than the potential to learn (Huff, 1954, pp. 53–57). Furthermore, the content of many IQ tests is centered around white middle class values and customs; therefore, such tests would be better indicators of acculturation than basic intelligence. They may be suitable for some purposes for which they are designed, but not others.

Measures of effectiveness are often the most difficult to develop because the objectives to which they relate are not clearly fixed or because the necessary information is costly or difficult to acquire. Looking at the federal government's swine flu program, for example, one appropriate measure of impact would be the number of swine flu cases that were prevented by the inoculations. However, developing this measure would require an estimate of the number of people who would have contracted the disease without the program, a difficult estimate to make.

Types of Measures

Many different types of indicators are used as operationalized measures in program analysis. Each has advantages and drawbacks, and the decision to use some types and not others in a given study will reflect a consideration of trade-offs regarding the quality of measurement as well as the relative ease or feasibility in obtaining different kinds of measures. The following discussion is not geared to a rigorous classification of operationalized measures, but rather is intended to introduce alternative approaches to the development of useful measures in an applied setting.

Hard and Soft Measures   Measures vary widely in the extent to which they are based on procedures that involve precise, well defined observations that can be relied upon to produce consistent results for different subjects (or cases) and recorders. We often refer to **hard measures** as those that leave little doubt about the criteria and standards employed in taking the measure. **Soft measures** are less clear-cut in terms of the basis on which the measurement is taken, and therefore, less explicit about the real meaning of scores or values recorded for individual cases.

Although we often speak about hard versus soft measures, the reader should recognize that measures fall somewhere along a continuum in this regard rather than in one category or the other; some measures are "harder" or "softer" than others. Hard measures are usually based on physical observations or precisely defined counting procedures. They tend to be more objective, more quantifiable, and more specific in terms of the scales employed than soft measures. Soft measures are more subjective, more qualitative, and less specific in terms of what they mean.

For example, one could measure the volume of traffic on a street by counting the number of vehicles passing a given point in specified time periods, a relatively hard measure, or for each time period he could characterize traffic as light, average, or heavy by watching the street but not counting vehicles (a much softer measure). If we have a number of observers at different points on the street network taking these measures, we would have much less confidence in comparing traffic flows based on the second measure because we have no assurance that light, average, and heavy traffic mean the same thing to all the observers.

Hard measures are usually preferred by analysts because of their greater reliability. Because one has a much more exact idea of what hard measures are, he can have much greater confidence in interpreting their values or scores and in making comparisons across cases or situations. However, hard measures are limited in the sense that they usually apply to the more tangible aspects of a situation and tend to relate to single dimensions of the subject of interest. Hard measures are often very difficult to devise for less tangible aspects of a program, such as the extent to which people feel a need for a given service or the degree of satisfaction felt by its clientele. Frequently then, some mix of hard and soft measures is appropriate for measuring certain aspects of public programs. Although the softer measures may have less reliability, this may be outweighed by the fact that they complement hard measures in providing a more valid overall indication of whatever is being measured.

Proximate and Surrogate Measures When a desired measure proves difficult or impossible to obtain, it may be replaced by another measure that can be thought of as representing it indirectly. A **proximate measure** is one that is thought to be directly related to, and used to represent indirectly, the measure that is really of interest. For example, a good measure of the effectiveness of a concerted effort to improve the quality of a city's refuse collection operation might be the increase in the percentage of respondents who say that they are satisfied with that service in surveys taken before and after the improvements are implemented. Rather than go to the expense of such surveys, however, an analyst might rely on the reduction of complaints registered with city hall about refuse collection as an indicator of increased citizen satisfaction; this would constitute a proximate measure.

Often, measures of immediate effects or even outputs are used as proximate measures of a program's ultimate effects, especially when the desired impacts lie in the distant future. For example, in an evaluation of the new management incentive program whose long term objective is improved management performance, the change in management turnover rates might be used as a proximate measure. Similarly, the effectiveness of a smokers' clinic will normally be evaluated using the percentage of participants who actually stop smoking as a proxy variable, although the long range objective is improved health.

Proximate measures are usually used as a convenience or because they are the only available measures. The important consideration regarding their worth, of course, is validity. If they do relate directly to the true measures they are substituting for, then proxies are valid indicators. However, the links relating them to the true measures are often tenuous or at least untested. In fact, the use of immediate effects as proxies for ultimate effects, or of outputs as proxies for impacts, begs the question of the logic of the assumptions underlying the program if they have not been previously validated. For example, with respect to a tree-planting program, the number of new trees planted along city streets in a given neighborhood, an output indicator, might be used as a proxy to measure increased satisfaction on the part of residents, the real impact.

Surrogate measures are also used to represent other measures. Rather than indicators that are substituted for other single measures, however, **surrogates** are single measures that are used to represent clusters of variables simultaneously. For example, a race variable might be used as a surrogate for the "welfare sector" on the basis that minorities have a much greater incidence of lack of education or occupational training, poverty, and dependence upon social services. Clearly, there is much slippage in using race to represent these conditions, but its use as a surrogate may be warranted by convenience. A surrogate is a measure that is intended to capsulize, however imperfectly, the information contained by a group of interlinked variables.

Unobtrusive Measures   Inherent in many types of measures is the possibility that the pieces of information that are noted and recorded may be influenced in part by the measurement procedure or situation itself. The problem of reactive measurement is of concern especially with respect to personal interviews and direct observation procedures in which people are aware that their behavior is being watched. To a degree, people's behavior, or statements about their behavior, attitudes, and opinions in direct observation or interview situations are responses to the stimulus of being observed or interviewed. Their actual behavior may be influenced in any number of ways by such a stimulus, and as is discussed in chapter 10, measures obtained in personal interviews may be reactive effects induced by the subject's motivation or perception of self, the interviewer's behavior, or the survey instrument.

As is seen below, there are many sources of data, and some pose much less threat of reactive measurement than others. Webb et al. have coined the term **unobtrusive measures** to refer to those kinds of measures that are nonreactive in that they "do not require the cooperation of a respondent and . . . .do not themselves contaminate the response" (Webb et al., 1966, p. 2). The classes of unobtrusive measures include physical evidence, public and private archives, simple unobtrusive observation of behavior, and contrived or concealed observation. Although these often entail straightforward counting operations, sometimes they involve more innovative approaches developed on an ad hoc basis to fit a particular context and avoid the problem of reactivity. For example, rather than surveying elderly people participating in a congregate feeding program about their preferences for different types of food—because of difficulties in eliciting information from older people in general as well as problems of biased responses—noting what foods are most often left uneaten would serve as an alternative indicator.

Although unobtrusive measures have the advantage of not contaminating data through the measurement procedure, questions concerning the validity of individual measures can be critical in that they are often indirect indicators and, in the case of archives, results of data collection processes over which present users have no control (Webb et al., 1966). Furthermore, ethical questions regarding the right to privacy may arise with certain kinds of unobtrusive measures.

Social Indicators   In some analyses the use of very generalized measures reflecting some aspect of the quality of life may be appropriate to determine whether impacts have occurred (Taylor and Hudson, 1972; Wilcox et al., 1972; Andrews and Withey, 1976). **Social indicators**, gross measures intended to represent society's well being, are generalized quality of life indicators. For example, the measure of Gross National

Product (GNP) was developed as an indicator of the national economic health. Other commonly used indicators of economic well being are median family income and the national unemployment rate.

Social indicators are very highly aggregated measures intended to convey a single impression of a general condition for large populations. Thus, they often do not afford the kind of breakdown to permit comparisons that are desirable in many analyses. They do, however, lend themselves to analyses of trends in general conditions over time. Second, as single measures they often fail to tap the multidimensionality of the concepts to which they are attached and may, therefore, invite criticisms of validity. In this regard social indicators often act as surrogate variables for a number of more specific measures with which they presumably co-vary.

In many instances, the generality and level of aggregation of social indicators detracts from their usefulness in evaluating the effects of a particular program. The indicators are composite measures and it is difficult to link them directly with particular program strategies that may well relate to only one aspect of what the measure represents and involve only a fraction of the population covered by the measure. They are more useful for analyzing the net effect of a number of forces (including public programs) over time. However, in some instances they do lend themselves to discrete program analyses. For example, the impact of county boards of health might be analyzed by comparing overall morbidity and mortality rates for counties with and without boards of health.

The concept of social indicators has attracted increased interest in recent years because of their wide coverage, availability, and summative nature. In particular, interest has grown in developing indicators that can be used to make comparisons among urban areas or to mark changes in individual areas over time. The following are a few selected indicators that might be considered to represent aspects of the quality of urban life (Flax, 1972).

Quality	Indicator
Housing	Cost of housing a moderate income family of four.
Health	Infant deaths per 1,000 live births.
Mental health	Reported suicides per 100,000 population.
Public order	Reported robberies per 100,000 population.
Poverty	Percentage of households with income less than $3,000 per year.
Racial equality	Ratio between nonwhite and white unemployment rates.
Community concern	Per capita contributions to United Fund appeals.

Indexes Indicators of various aspects or dimensions of the attribute to be measured are often combined to form a single measure or **index**, such as the air quality index or the familiar consumer price index. For example, the Shevky-Bell urbanization index incorporates three measures: 1) the ratio of children under 5 to women of childbearing age, 2) the proportion of women with jobs outside the home, and 3) the percentage of single family detached homes (Shevsky and Bell, 1954, pp. 17-18). Although many indexes used in program analysis consist of hard indicators, they may also represent softer measures such as the attitude indexes discussed in chapter 10.

Many of the indexes used are *additive* in nature. The value of the index taken on by a case is the sum of its value on each of the component measures. For example, the Uniform Crime Index is intended to measure the extent of serious crime in an area relative to population size. It is the sum of the number of crimes committed per 100,000 population in each category of part 1 crimes; i.e., murder, manslaughter, rape, robbery, aggravated assault, larceny, burglary, and auto theft.

The formula to be used in computing an index will depend on the relationships the component measures bear to the thing the index is intended to represent. For example, in trying to measure the level of service (LOS) provided by an urban transit system to individual households, an index might be developed based on accessibility to routes, frequency of service on those routes, and average schedule speed on the routes. Because distance from the household to the nearest stop on the route is inversely associated with LOS—the closer the stop, the greater the LOS—it should be put in the denominator. Furthermore, because LOS to an individual household is improved by each additional bus route that passes, say, within a half mile, the index should be additive to represent the service provided by multiple routes where appropriate. Thus, such an index might look like:

$$\text{LOS} = \frac{F_1 \times S_1}{D_1} + \frac{F_2 \times S_2}{D_2} + \cdots + \frac{F_N \times S_N}{D_N}$$

where F = frequency, the number of buses passing by the stop per hour during peak periods; S = average speed of buses on the route during peak periods; D = distance between household and nearest stop in tenths of miles. The subscripts in the formula indicate that this index is to be computed for, and summed across, any routes within a half mile of the household. Indexes clearly are not economical in the sense of reducing data collection costs because all the individual measures incorporated by an index must be obtained for each case. They are used because they afford a single measure that can be interpreted as representing multiple dimensions or combined effects that may be more convenient for statistical analysis than the use of a number of separate measures. Their chief disadvantage is that they mask conflicting trends among the individual members; they can be interpreted only as single, comprehensive, and hopefully well balanced, indicators of the concept to which they are linked. In order for an index to be truly representative, its component measures should not be redundant (representing the same aspects) and should be weighted according to their relative importance or relevance to the concept.

Weighting these measures is almost as critical as selecting them in the first place. The basis for the weights should be founded on some kind of evidence of relative importance, but this is often very difficult to determine, and weighting schemes may be highly subjective. On the other hand, the relative importance of the various factors to be incorporated in an index might be established by more objective means. The component measures of the transit level of service index might be weighted according to their relative importance as established by a survey of riders. A fire hazard index might be constructed by weighting factors such as structure type, number of stories, and population density by the relative degrees to which they are found, through statistical analysis, to be associated with the outbreak of fires.

Use of Existing Measures

The reader should not be misled into thinking that program analysts are always left to their own devices and required to develop original measures for each new project. As program analysis, especially ex post facto program evaluation, becomes more widespread, a pool of operationalized measures is being developed in various program areas, which may well include adequate indicators for the analyst's purposes.[2] In preparing for a study an analyst should not only become familiar with the program to be studied but also with similar studies conducted in the same area, elsewhere, or at other times. He can learn from both their strong points and weaknesses, and replications of studies, with or without adjustments, are important contributors to the total body of

---

[2] The Urban Institute has published a number of reports that discuss different types of measures commonly used to assess performance in a variety of city service areas from solid waste collection to crime control, libraries, recreation, and transportation. See the Urban Institute, 1974 and subsequent Urban Institute publications relating to effectiveness measurement in individual program areas.

knowledge about a program area. Repeated use of common indicators permits comparisons of the effectiveness of alternative program strategies or the conditions under which a given approach seems to work.

While some of the most difficult measures relate to psychological outlook, attitude scales (see chapter 10), and abnormal or retarded behavioral patterns, a number of these instruments have been developed, tried, and tested and are documented for easy access to future users, often accompanied by response distributions and interpretations from previous applications (Weiss, 1972, p. 35). For example, in one effort to develop an approach for monitoring mental health treatment programs, it was decided to rely on a core set of four types of outcome measures: 1) client distress, 2) social functioning, 3) client satisfaction, and 4) family burden. Standardized measuring instruments are available that are generally appropriate for measuring these outcomes; the decision often reduces to choosing one from among a number of a certain type of existing techniques or trying to develop a new instrument that will be better suited to the particular information needs (Schainblatt, 1977; National Institute of Mental Health, 1976, chapter 7).

Measures relating to numerous program areas and purposes have been developed, and these can be consulted for possible use.[3] Many such measures that have been used often have been "validated" through a general consensus or through correlation or predicting ability. Yet the potential user must be his own judge of whether they are valid indicators of the things he wants to measure. In evaluating the performance of public programs, researchers should avoid falling into the trap of using certain measures simply because they are available or examining certain aspects of performance mainly because they are "measurable."

In some cases it might be a good idea to identify the desired characteristics of key measures and then search for measuring tools that satisfy these requirements. For example, in developing a system for measuring the performance of programs for the mentally retarded across the state, the Michigan Department of Mental Health determined that the measures should 1) permit *uniform* assessments of various programs, 2) provide *client-oriented* performance indicators, 3) provide multidimensional indicators in terms of self-help capabilities and other characteristics, 4) consist of *objective* rather than subjective measures, and 5) provide measures that are *relevant* to the purposes of the

---

[3] In the area of education, for example, see the sources listed by Isaac and Michael (1976, p. 108), Ferriss (1969), and United Nations Department of Social Affairs (1967). In the area of health care, see Kogan (1974) and Moriyama (1968). For measures relating to police services see Hatry (1975) and American Justice Institute (1977).

assessment. One prominent method of assessing adaptive behavior, the Progress Assessment Chart, was then piloted in one region of the state and tested in terms of both reliability and validity, cost of implementation, and feasibility (Milan and Hallgren, 1976, p. 7).

Use of Multiple Measures   Because operationalized indicators, including indexes, often constitute only partial measures that tap selected facets of the quality or characteristic of interest, reliance upon single measures or even classes of measures may produce misleading results, or results that can only be interpreted within a very limited frame of reference. An alternative is to employ a set of measures that, taken together, round out a picture of the phenomenon being measured. This may be particularly advantageous in terms of measuring such concepts as efficiency and effectiveness. The intent in using multiple measures, and especially different types of measures—complementary hard and soft indicators or survey data used in conjunction with less reactive measures, for example—is to increase confidence in overall validity by obtaining a more complete indication of how cases compare on a spectrum of measures. For example, the adequacy of street lighting in city neighborhoods might be measured by 1) using a light meter to measure illumination, and 2) conducting surveys to obtain indicators of residents' perceptions and evaluations of street lighting. The survey data might be made more objective and more meaningful by using display devices such as a street lighting simulator or a street lighting display board as a standardized basis for eliciting survey responses (Workshop in Political Theory and Policy Analysis, 1975).

As a second illustration, consider the LOS index discussed above. Although it includes some indicators of the *availability* of service, it does not measure the *quality* of the service provided. Door-to-door travel time is often used as a surrogate measure for LOS in this regard, but it fails to take into account many aspects of service such as personal safety, comfort, and schedule reliability that might be important to potential users. As can be seen, there will be variation in reliability among these measures, and each may pose problems in operationalization. Each operational measure may in turn contain some irrelevant connotations, but the effect of such irrelevancies will be reduced by the use of multiple measures.

If a set of multiple operationalized measures produces consistent results—if individual cases measure or rank similarly on the various scales—there is less uncertainty regarding interpretation, as "the possibility of slippage between conceptual definition and operational specification is diminished greatly" (Webb et al., 1966, p. 5). This constitutes a confirmation of the validity of the individual measures through their high intercorrelation. If, however, multiple measures yield differing results, it does not necessarily signify a lack of validity; rather, they may be indicators of different things. In basic research involved with propositions of a conceptual nature this poses a dilemma; the researcher can either recognize that he is testing a number of separate, noncomprehensive hypotheses or he can redefine his basic concepts to a point of clarification that will not lead to conflicting empirical measures (Blalock, 1972, pp. 13-19).

This is often less problematic in applied program analysis where interest lies with individual attributes rather than generalized concepts. For example, if we are looking at the effects of a comprehensive effort to provide adequate housing, we may use a number of measures relating to structural soundness, cleanliness and sanitary facilities, floor space, heating systems and utilities, and comfort and aesthetic values. If these measures provide mixed results, they will be providing useful information about those areas in which the program is working well and those in which it is not. A low degree of correlation among a set of operationalized performance indicators, for example, may well mean that they are useful in providing relevant measures of different aspects of a program's operation (Parks, 1975, p. 187). The use of multiple measures is especially appropriate for providing a balanced view of program effectiveness, as single indicators can often provide distorted measures of performance (Rivlin, 1971, p. 142).

Data Sources

A program analyst may collect data from any number of sources including agency records, documents, published data sets, interviews, structured observation or testing, and other types of surveys. They will all vary in terms of availability and ease of access, quality, and time and money costs, and because data collection usually represents a major, if not *the* major, cost of a research project, consideration must be given to trade-offs among data sources in terms of usefulness versus cost in the development of operationalized measures. In some situations the nature of the problem will dictate that one particular kind of data be used; conversely, in other instances the analyst may have a choice among alternative data sources or use data from two or more sources in a single study.

Primary data refers to original data collected by the researcher himself (or under his direction) for his own purposes, while **secondary data** is data that are already in existence and collected intact by the researcher or compiled by him for use in his own analysis. This includes not only published data sets, but any data that have been developed through institutional recordkeeping, routine program operation and monitoring, or other research processes.

Secondary data have the obvious advantage of requiring less effort to collect. Although they may have to be transformed in some way, compiled from or broken down into smaller sets before being processed for the user's needs, this usually involves much less effort than going to primary sources. The chief limitation is that the current researcher has no control over how secondary data are developed. Thus, if there is any doubt about the original measuring procedures, the researcher should make every effort to determine how the data were generated, so that he can evaluate their reliability.

A potential secondary data source may be very attractive if it is readily accessible, but one must beware of using it if it does not really provide valid indicators of the factors to be measured. The temptation of available data should not outweigh the need for valid measures. For example, an index of current neighborhood property values maintained by an association of realtors might be considered to measure the impact of a housing program aimed at stabilizing or increasing property values, but it would not necessarily afford a good indication of housing conditions. If it were to be used for either purpose (it might serve as a proximate measure of housing conditions) the researcher would first want to find out how it was developed. Is it based on a windshield survey, recorded property transactions, or a sample survey of properties, for example?

An additional problem frequently arising with secondary data is that even when they have an appropriate information content, they may not exist in the form required by the research design; they may be too highly aggregated to permit the kind of analysis or comparisons the researcher has in mind. On the other hand, if no alternatives are available, the research approach may have to be adjusted to accommodate the data. Although not a desirable state of affairs, it is sometimes a necessary one given time and money constraints.

Although secondary data may be perfectly suited for some tasks, others will require the gathering of primary data to provide reliable and valid program information. As stated above, this usually requires much greater effort, but within the constraints of feasibility, primary data can be tailored to the purposes at hand. **Interview surveys**, discussed more fully in chapter 10, can be used to obtain information of a factual, behavioral, or attitudinal nature from target groups, the larger population, or those involved in service delivery regarding needs and demands, program operation, or impacts.

There are other kinds of surveys, noninterview surveys, that involve surveying conditions or behavior with physical measuring instruments or through human observation. Examples of this type of **observational survey** would include a survey of traffic conditions in a downtown area with the use of mechanical counters, the use of a boarding and alighting survey to count the numbers of passengers using various stops on a rapid rail transit line, the rating of street and alley cleanliness by visual inspection using a series of gradated photographs as benchmarks, and "windshield surveys" of exterior property maintenance in selected neighborhoods. Closely related to this would be testing procedures used in educational programs.

Surveys, whether they involve interviews or observation only, connote a direct approach and a relatively widespread reconnaissance. **Elite interviews**, another form of primary data gathering, are equally direct but highly selective (Dexter, 1970). Program managers or other individuals located in strategic positions relating to a program's development, implementation, or operation might be interviewed to gain insight regarding performance.

In other situations, it might be useful to examine internal memoranda or working documents for the same purpose. Finally, another type of primary data might be obtained through participant observation such as the analyst attending meetings with program personnel or participating in regular activities to see firsthand how the program works. In some situations, rather than participant observation, some form of concealed observation might be appropriate to ensure nonreactive measurement.

Frequently, program analyses use data from a wide variety of sources to obtain complementary measures and indicators of different aspects of program performance. For example, an urban transit system evaluation and plant update recently conducted by the author employed the following types of data:

—on board interviews of passengers
—counts of passengers boarding and alighting at various stops
—a telephone survey of a sample of area residents
—unobtrusive riding checks to assess driver performance
—unstructured interviews with supervisors and a sampling of employees

—maintenance records and parts inventories
—monthly operating data on vehicle miles, hours, passengers, and
revenues broken down by route
—financial records of revenue and expense items over the past 3 years.

MEASUREMENT AND ANALYSIS

In selecting measures the researcher should be thinking ahead to the
analysis of the data once they have been collected and processed. Two
important considerations that relate to the types of measures used as
well as the analytical approach and types of statistical methods that will
be appropriate are the unit of analysis and the levels of measurement
employed.

Units of Analysis

Although there is often little question as to what the unit of analysis
should be in a study, frequently there are valid alternatives and the
researcher must decide which one best serves his purpose. A complete
study may well incorporate separate analytical components, each with a
different unit of observation, but a single piece of statistical analysis
will be based on only one type of unit. The choice of that unit will
depend on both how well it lends itself to the analysis of research
questions and the feasibility of obtaining data on that basis.

Consider a study on the effectiveness of preventive police patrol in
a city. Possible units of observation might include patrol sectors or
subsectors or temporal units such as month, date, or shift. It might
also consist of a combination such as the shift in a sector (each shift in
each sector would constitute one case). Units of analysis that are
appropriate in other kinds of police-related studies, such as the officer
or team of patrolmen, or the incident, might not be as useful in this
instance because they fail to provide a spectrum wide enough to measure the incidence of crime. These would be more likely to be useful as
variables measured across the range of spatial or temporal units of
observation.

The unit of analysis relates directly to the subject under study and
will depend to a great extent on the specific purpose of the research. If
the intent is, for example, to determine the likelihood that different
types of households are victimized by different kinds of crimes, the
household would be an appropriate unit of analysis. If, however, the
desire is to analyze the nature of victimizations and the way in which
the police deal with different kinds of incidents, the incident might be a
more useful unit of analysis.

A prime consideration in the selection of an appropriate unit of analysis is the level of aggregation it implies. A low level of aggregation permits more detailed comparisons to be made but may result in an overwhelming amount of costly and relatively uninteresting data. Higher levels of aggregation, on the other hand, can often provide greater coverage at reduced cost, but too highly aggregated data will obscure crucial variation.

The level of aggregation must be scaled to the immediate purposes at hand. In considering applications for instituting new commercial airline routes, for example, it might be appropriate to look at travel volumes on a weekly, monthly, or even annual basis. However, the scheduling of specific flights will require estimates of travel volume on an hourly basis; monthly estimates will not provide an indication of the critical variation, that occurring between peak and off-peak periods of the day. Similarly, an evaluation of a demonstration health care project might focus on the individual recipients, whereas a study of a nation-wide effort in the same area might use each local program (or project) as one observation.

Levels of Measurement

Although we often think of measures as indications of dimensions and quantities—or the amount of something that characterizes an observation—not all measures provide this much information. Measures can be divided into four levels according to the type and precision of information they convey, and in developing operationalized measures researchers should always be aware of the level of measurement involved in the indicators being considered. Concepts and phenomena to be measured very often are limited, or lend themselves naturally, to one specific level of measurement, and when feasible alternatives are available there are often trade-offs between reliability and validity versus usefulness and cost that should be taken into account.

Nominal Scales   Each successive level of measurement includes the properties of lower levels in addition to further characteristics that increase its information content. The first level consists of **nominal scales**, measures that classify observations according to a set of exhaustive and mutually exclusive categories. Observations must fit the definition of one and only one category in the scale and thus can be compared as being equivalent or nonequivalent. Examples would be a race variable whose values are defined as white, black, or other (this last category to meet the requirement of an exhaustive classification scheme) and the variable marital status made up of single, married, widowed, separated, and divorced categories. The definition of the categories or values must be sufficient to provide for an unambiguous classification of individuals; in the above example, the first category might be "single-never married" to distinguish between it and the last three categories.

Nominal scales are classifications of cases according to the existence or lack of some characteristic or attribute; they indicate nothing about the degree to which an attribute is present. Although they provide only the minimum of information necessary for measurement, nominal scales are frequently used either because simple classification is sufficient for the purpose or due to difficulties in securing additional reliable information. How fine a breakdown of categories is needed again depends on the purpose; too few categories will fail to differentiate adequately among cases whereas the use of too many will obscure common characteristics that are of interest and make statistical analysis meaningless. If a researcher is unsure as to how fine a classification is appropriate, he may begin by developing a large number of detailed classes and then, depending on the distribution of cases and the workability of the initial classification scheme, collapse the classification into fewer categories that are easier to work with.

Ordinal Scales Measures that classify cases into categories that are not only exhaustive and mutually exclusive, but also are ranked according to the degree to which they represent a given characteristic, are called **ordinal scales**. For example, urban neighborhoods may be classified on an ordinal scale of economic viability or stability with the categories of healthy, endangered, blighted, and deteriorated; each category representing a lesser degree of economic viability than the last.

In some cases, a given set of categories may be considered to constitute either a nominal or ordinal scale, depending on the interpretation given to the criteria used in defining the categories. Students in a special education program, for example, might be classified in the following manner: physically disabled, socially-emotionally disturbed, mentally retarded-educable, profoundly retarded. When viewed as an indication of the source of learning disability or the general instructional stream the students are following, these categories would make up a nominal scale; if they are considered as indicators of the degree of difficulty in learning or the amount of progress that can reasonably be expected, they may be thought of and used as an ordinal scale.

Interval and Ratio Scales **Interval and ratio scales** measure the degree to which a characteristic is represented in or by a case with the use of numbered scales with equal intervals between the numbers. Thus we can know not only that one case is greater than another on a given attribute, but how much greater. These scales are most analogous to a yardstick: they are measuring devices with equal interval gradations designed to measure degrees of attributes in terms of numbers of specified standard units. A given number of units represents the same amount anywhere along the scale, so that the difference between 5 and 10 inspections, for example, is exactly the same as that between 20 and 25 inspections.

Interval scales measure quantities in terms of equal units but do not have a natural 0 point which would represent a complete absence of the quality or characteristic being measured. Thus, units can be added and subtracted, but cannot be multiplied and divided. The Fahrenheit temperature scale is a good illustration. Because 0° does not represent a true absence of heat, we can know that 20° is 10° more than 10°, but have no basis for asserting that 20° is twice as hot as 10°. A ratio scale is an interval scale with a natural, rather than arbitrary, 0 point. Thus if Officer A hands out 20 parking tickets on a day and officer B hands out 10, we can say that the difference is 10 tickets, and that Officer A did hand out twice as many tickets as Officer B.

Ratio scales are the most informative level of measurement and are, therefore, the kind that should be used when the opportunity presents itself. In practice, in applied program analysis, interval measures that are not also ratio scales are relatively rare, and the term **interval** is commonly used to refer to both interval and ratio scales. When true interval measures do arise, however, as is the case with certain attitude scaling techniques, care must be taken not to treat them as having all the properties of ratio scales. The most important point to remember regarding levels of measurement is that computational and statistical techniques are dependent upon the assumptions inherent in the various levels of measurement. A particular technique is often appropriate for one kind of scale and not others and, therefore, researchers must concern themselves with levels of measurement to be assured of making appropriate applications of techniques.

One last point along these lines is that because the higher levels incorporate all the assumptions of lower levels of measurement, one can always back down to lower levels in making interpretations or applying quantitative techniques. An interval scale, for example, can always be treated as a nominal scale with each number, or grouping of values, representing a category. Although this is sometimes done to facilitate certain types of analysis or to increase a measure's validity if suspect, there is clearly a loss of information.

REFERENCES

American Justice Institute. 1977. Measuring Police Department Effectiveness and Productivity. Sacramento: AJI.

Andrews, F. M., and S. B. Withey. 1976. Social Indicators of Well Being: The Development and Measurement of Perceptual Indicators. New York: Plenum Press.

Blalock, H. M., Jr. 1972. Social Statistics. 2nd Ed. New York: McGraw-Hill Book Co.

Dexter, L. A. 1970. Elite and Specialized Interviewing. Evanston, Ill.: Northwestern University Press.

Ennis, P. H. 1967. Field Surveys II: Criminal Victimization in the United States: A Report of A National Survey. Washington: U.S. Government Printing Office.

Ferriss, A. L. 1969. Indicators of Trends in American Education. New York: Russell Sage Foundation.

Flax, M. J. 1972. A Study in Comparative Urban Indicators. Washington: Urban Institute.

Hatry, H. P. 1975. Wrestling with Police Crime Control Productivity Measurement. In: J. L. Wolfle and J. F. Heaphy (eds.), Readings on Productivity in Policing. Washington: Police Foundation, pp. 86–128.

Huff, D. 1954. How to Lie with Statistics. New York: W. W. Norton.

Isaac, S., and W. B. Michael. 1976. Handbook in Research and Evaluation. San Diego, Calif.: EDITS Publishers.

Kogan, L. S. 1974. Indicators of Child Health and Welfare: Development of the DIPOV Index. New York: Center for Social Research, Graduate Center, City University of New York; distributed by Columbia University Press.

Milan, M., and S. Hallgren. 1976. The Uniform Client Assessment of the Mentally Retarded: A Pilot Study. Lansing: Michigan Department of Mental Health.

Moriyama, I. M. 1968. Problems in the Measurement of Health Status. In: E. B. Sheldon and W. Moore (eds.), Indicators of Social Change: Concepts and Measurements. New York: Russell Sage Foundation, pp. 573–599.

National Institute of Mental Health. 1976. A Working Manual of Simple Program Evaluation Techniques for Community Mental Health Centers. Rockville, Md.: National Institute of Mental Health.

Nunnally, J. C., and R. L. Durham. 1975. Validity, Reliability and Special Problems of Measurement in Evaluation Research. In: E. Struening and M. Guttentag (eds.), Handbook of Evaluation Research. Beverly Hills: Sage Publications, Inc., pp. 289–354.

Nunnally, J. C., and W. H. Wilson. 1975. Method and Theory for Developing Measures in Evaluation Research. In: E. Struening and M. Guttentag (eds.), Handbook of Evaluation Research. Beverly Hills: Sage Publications, Inc., pp. 227–288.

Parks, R. B. 1975. Complementary Measures of Police Performance. In: K. M. Dolbeare (ed.), Public Policy Evaluation. Beverly Hills: Sage Publications, Inc.

Rivlin, A. M. 1971. Systematic Thinking for Social Action. Washington: The Brookings Institution.

Schainblatt, A. H. 1977. Monitoring the Outcomes of State Mental Health Treatment Programs: Some Initial Suggestions. Washington: Urban Institute.

Schneider, A. 1975. Measuring Change in the Crime Rate: Problems in the Use of Official Data and Victimization Survey Data. Eugene: Oregon Research Institute.

Shevsky, E., and W. Bell. 1954. Social Area Analyses. Stanford: Stanford University Press.

Skogan, W. G. 1976. Victimization Surveys and Criminal Justice Planning. University of Cincinnati Law Review 45(2):167–206.

Struening, E. C., and M. Guttentag (eds.). 1975. Handbook of Evaluation Research. Beverly Hills: Sage Publications, Inc.

Suchman, E. A. 1967. Evaluative Research. New York: Russell Sage Foundation.

Taylor, C. L., and M. C. Hudson. 1972. World Handbook of Political and Social Indicators. New Haven: Yale University Press.

The Urban Institute. 1974. Measuring the Effectiveness of Basic Municipal Services: Initial Report. Washington: Urban Institute and the International City Management Association.

United Nations Department of Social Affairs. 1967. Statistics Needed for Educational Planning. Conference of European Statisticians. Statistical Standards and Studies No. 11. ST/CES/II, Vol. 2. New York: United Nations.

Webb, E. J., D. C. Campbell, R. D. Schwartz, and L. Sechrest. 1966. Unobtrusive Measures. Chicago: Rand McNally and Co.

Weiss, C. H. (ed.). 1972. Evaluating Action Programs: Readings in Social Action and Education. Boston: Allyn and Bacon, Inc.

Wilcox, L. D., R. M. Brooks, G. M. Beal, and G. E. Klonglan. 1972. Social Indicators and Societal Monitoring; An Annotated Bibliography. San Francisco: Jossey Bass Inc., Publishers.

Workshop in Political Theory and Policy Analysis at Indiana University. 1975. Measuring Urban Services: A Multi-Mode Approach. Bloomington: Department of Political Science, Indiana University.

Zetterberg, H. L. 1965. On Theory and Verification in Sociology. Totowa, N.J.: Bedminster Press.

INTRODUCTION TO STATISTICS

INTRODUCTION TO STATISTICS

4

The subject of statistics often creates anxiety for students of public administration, even when they may not have a very clear idea of what it entails. In its more common usage, the word **statistics** refers to the collection of quantitative data, or to pieces of quantitative data themselves. Statistics are often considered as bits of information expressed numerically. Thus we have vital statistics on births, deaths, marriages, divorces, and communicable diseases; economic statistics on employment, production, prices, and sales volumes; and governmental statistics on expenditure levels, employees, and outputs such as the numbers of conferences convened, clients served, or demonstration projects conducted. As should be apparent from earlier chapters, the analysis of public programs often involves the heavy use of such quantitative data.

A second, more specialized meaning of statistics refers to the body of techniques, or methodologies that have been developed for the collection, presentation, and especially the analysis of quantitative data. These statistical techniques have two very broad functions, description and induction. **Descriptive statistics** are used to summarize quantitative information so as to make it more manageable and useful, while **inferential statistics** serve the purpose of making generalizations or inferences on the basis of limited observation. Descriptive statistics provide information pertaining to the cases at hand; inferential statistics are used to draw conclusions about a larger number of cases. Many of the chapters of this text are concerned with the structure of applied research projects in terms of what indicators to measure, what comparisons to make, what data to collect, and how to collect the data. Statistics are tools for analyzing data within the framework of this overall design, aimed at facilitating and making manageable the task of drawing valid and meaningful interpretations from masses of quantified information.

The field of statistics includes a growing "tool kit" of techniques that is useful for making these descriptions and inferences. This text presents a variety of statistical techniques, as applied to problems in the analysis of public programs. The presentation is generally non-mathematical, requiring only a knowledge of simple arithmetic operations and a little college algebra. Most of the computations involved are not very complicated; the main point is to understand the logic underlying these techniques and the assumptions on which they are based. The primary objective of this text is to lead the student to a knowledge of when and how to apply individual techniques, rather than a knowledge of their underlying mathematical support.

This chapter provides an introduction to statistical analysis, intended in part to acquaint the uninitiated student with some of the "language" of statistics that will be used in many subsequent chapters. The first section discusses the arrangement of data in frequency distributions, and the second section presents a number of simple descriptive statistics. The third section introduces the concept of the normal distribution and its unique characteristics.

PATTERNS OF VARIATION

Most aspects of public programs, from needs and demands through efficiency and effectiveness levels, are characterized by variation, and this variation is the source of the information we obtain about a program. Managers are concerned with variation in staff abilities, workloads, and productivity levels, etc., and they are interested in the varied outcomes produced by alternative strategies. Understanding the patterns of variation of the relevant factors, as well as the interconnections among these variables, is what the statistical analysis of program related data is all about. A data set drawn up on a number of drug abuse projects, for example, which contained no variation in terms of client characteristics and needs, general program approaches, specific treatments, staffing patterns, unit costs, and impact measures would not be highly informative. It might enable us to make a summative assessment of this program as a whole, but by itself it would not facilitate the kinds of comparisons that might lead to suggestions for improving overall performance or more effective matching of specific treatments to different kinds of clients.

Variables are measures that can take on a number of values, indicators that vary from one case to another. **Values** are the categories, or degrees on the measurement scale being employed, used to classify and describe individual cases of a given variable. The difference between variables and values in this sense is analogous to the distinction made in biology between characteristics and traits: human eye color is a characteristic or variable whereas blue eyes is a trait or value of that variable.

As discussed in the previous chapter, variables can be measured with four different types of scales: nominal, ordinal, interval, and ratio. While nominal and ordinal scales take on qualitative, rather than numerical values, such measures obtained for a large number of cases provide data that can be analyzed quantitatively because we are usually interested in the numbers of cases that take on particular values. **Cases** are the **units of analysis**, the objects that are observed and measured; a case will take on one value of a given operationalized variable. In an analysis of an educational program, for example, the unit of analysis might be the individual student, with each student or case taking on a particular value of the variable, standardized test score. Alternatively, the school might be the unit of analysis, with each school in the data set taking on one value of the more highly aggregated measure, "average" standardized test score. Cases are also referred to as **observations.**

A **data set** is an organized package of individual pieces of information; we usually think of it as consisting of the values of a number of variables taken on by a number of cases. The **population**, or **universe**, to which the data pertain is the total number of projects or cases that are of interest. If the data pertain to a **finite population**, one with a fixed number of cases, the data set may contain information for the entire population or any subset of it, termed a sample. Sometimes we are interested in generalizing to **infinite populations**, those with indefinitely large numbers of cases, for example the population consisting of the reporting forms to be processed by an agency in the foreseeable future. Infinite populations may be hypothesized, but never completely observed. **Empirical data,** on the other hand, those actually collected and analyzed, are obtained by observing or measuring a finite number of cases.

Frequency Distributions

It is usually convenient to obtain an overall impression of the pattern of variation characterizing any measure of interest by organizing the data into frequency distributions. A **frequency distribution** is a classification of cases by their values on a scale (whatever the level of measurement) that shows the number of cases (the frequency) that take on the different values. For example, recidivists (repeat offenders) in a juvenile corrections center might be classified by the type of current offense, as shown in Table 4.1.

Suppose we are interested in the number of felony arrests made by individual police officers over a 6-month period. Figure 4.1 shows this number for each of 60 officers, first as unorganized raw data and second, as an array, an ordering of the 60 values from lowest to highest.

Table 4.1.   Recidivisms by offense type

Offense type	Recidivisms
Assault	387
Theft	2,099
Antisocial behavior	773
Drugs	278
Juvenile offenses	574
Total	4,111

Data drawn from Pennsylvania, 1976.

With an array of this size or larger it is difficult to obtain much information by visual inspection beyond the general range of the cases; in this example we can see at a glance that most of the officers made fewer than 10 felony arrests. A much clearer picture of these same 60 cases is presented by the frequency distribution in Table 4.2, which shows the number (frequency) of officers making each number (level) of arrests. The absolute frequency is usually denoted by a lower case f.

Grouped Data   From Table 4.2 we can see that although five officers made no arrests, only two made one arrest each. The number of

A. Raw Data

1	0	5	3	8	10	5	7	9	6
8	11	4	5	12	6	4	5	6	4
6	2	0	1	0	7	8	3	10	5
4	0	7	0	2	6	3	4	5	9
7	4	9	5	11	3	8	5	6	3
3	6	5	2	7	4	14	2	10	4

B. Data Array

0	0	0	0	0	1	1	2	2	2
2	3	3	3	3	3	3	4	4	4
4	4	4	4	4	5	5	5	5	5
5	5	5	5	6	6	6	6	6	6
6	7	7	7	7	7	8	8	8	8
9	9	9	10	10	10	11	11	12	14

Figure 4.1.   Felony arrests by officers (6 months).

Table 4.2. Frequency distribution: felony arrests by officers (6 months)

Number of arrests	f	Number of arrests	f
0	5	8	4
1	2	9	3
2	4	10	3
3	6	11	2
4	8	12	1
5	9	13	0
6	7	14	1
7	5		60

officers then increases to the point that nine officers made five arrests each, and thereafter the number of officers decreases gradually as the number of arrests increases. Our visual impression of the number of arrests made by the officers could be made more compact by combining numbers of arrests into categories or intervals, which would then have greater frequencies of officers. We might say, for example, that 11 officers made zero to two arrests, 23 officers made three to five arrests, 16 officers made six to eight arrests, and so on. In doing so, however, we would lose some information and have less exact knowledge about the number of arrests per officer.

Grouping the data is advantageous for visual inspection when the variable takes on many different values. If, for example, we were looking at the number of moving traffic citations per officer instead of felony arrests, the observations might range from zero to more than 100, and a frequency distribution of the data in ungrouped form would be much more difficult to evaluate by visual inspection. It would likely consist of a list of 100 or more values, each with a corresponding frequency of zero, one, or two. Grouping the number of citations into intervals of 10 or 20 would produce a much more meaningful frequency distribution, even though some detail would be sacrificed.

In other situations, the data are automatically grouped to a degree in that the variables of interest are continuous variables whose values by necessity are rounded off to some point for computational purposes. The variables we have been looking at so far are **discrete variables**, ones with a limited number of possible values. In dealing with an incident, for example, an officer either makes an arrest or does not, so the number of arrests he makes in a 6-month period must be zero or some whole number. Given a value in a discrete interval scale, you automatically know what the next highest value is. **Continuous variables**, on the other hand, can theoretically take on an infinite number of values. The percentage of arrests resulting in convictions, for instance, can be 43.6982...percent. Although the concept of continuous data is useful in connection with more advanced statistics, empirical data always seem to be in discrete form because of measurement crudity and the need for rounding. Such data may represent grouped data in which each specified point actually represents a small spread of possible values around it. Furthermore, discrete variables often come in grouped form and must be treated as such.

Setting limits to the intervals used to group continuous variables is somewhat more problematic because of the importance of establishing intervals that neither overlap nor have gaps between them. Consider a study of the average annual income of 218 small groups of participants in an alcoholism rehabilitation program. Although we have not covered the concept of averages, suffice it to say that if precisely computed, the average income of a group could turn out to be something between $9,999 and 10,000 or even between $9,999.49 and 9,999.50. Thus, if we establish intervals of $0 to 4,999, $5,000 to 9,999, etc. the average income of a group could fall between two intervals. One useful convention for avoiding this type of problem is that used in Table 4.3. The lowest category includes every group whose income is less than $5,000. A group with an average income of exactly $5,000 would fall in the second interval, which would contain incomes up to but not including $10,000. This is the most practical way of assuring that each case will fit into one and only one interval. Note that with discrete variables this is not necessary because cases cannot fall between two adjacent values on the scale.

The size of intervals used should be mentioned here. In general, fewer and larger intervals summarize the data more but provide less detail. If the variable is to be analyzed in conjunction with other variables, the

Table 4.3.   Frequency distribution, grouped data: average annual income

Income	f	F_u	F_d
0 and under $ 5,000	30	30	218
$ 5,000 and under $10,000	45	75	188
$10,000 and under $15,000	80	155	143
$15,000 and under $20,000	40	195	63
$20,000 and under $25,000	15	210	23
$25,000 and under $40,000	8	218	8

intervals should be large enough so that each has a sufficient number of cases. On the other hand, they must be small enough to provide a useful differentiation among cases; i.e., possible differences among cases within an interval should not be very important because they will be ignored by the classification scheme. It should also be noted that the highest interval in Table 4.3 is three times as large as the others. This has been done because there are relatively few cases in this income range, but it can be misleading if not interpreted carefully. It is a good idea to use equal intervals except where small numbers of cases make this undesirable, in effect where the size interval being used elsewhere in the distribution would not result in the actual grouping of many cases.

Finally, Table 4.3 also shows **cumulative frequency distributions**, conventionally denoted by an upper case F. The upward cumulative frequencies (F_u) indicate the number of cases falling below the upper limit of each interval, so that as we move to higher cutoff points we find increasing accumulations of cases. Cumulative frequencies can also be calculated moving downwards through the intervals to show the number of cases with incomes above various levels, as shown in the column headed F_d.

Graphical Presentations

Univariate frequency distributions can be conveniently displayed in graphic form, which sometimes is more striking and more easily and quickly interpreted by some people. Although ungrouped data can be presented in graphs, and often are when the distributions of two variables are being observed simultaneously over the same set of cases, graphs showing single variable distributions are more often constructed using grouped data.

One common type of graph places the intervals along the horizontal axis with the magnitudes of frequencies on the vertical axis, and represents the frequency of cases in each interval with vertical bars. Figure 4.2 *A* illustrates this kind of graph, called a **histogram**, for the grouped income data used above. The relative heights of the bars represent the relative magnitudes of the corresponding frequencies. If all the intervals are of equal width, the areas of the bars will also be proportional to the frequencies. However, because the highest interval in the grouping of this income data is three times as wide as the other intervals, such is not the case in this example. An interpretation of the relative areas here would be misleading, and Figure 4.2 should be interpreted in terms of the height of the bars only. Bar graphs such as this are also used to display frequency distributions of nominal and ordinal data.

A. Histogram

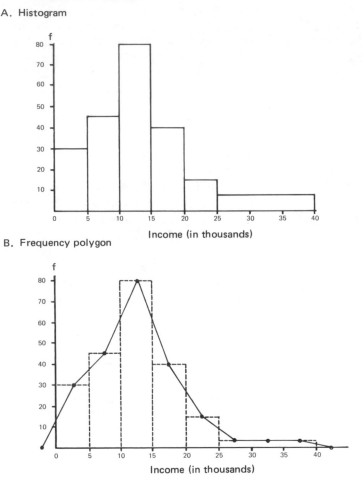

B. Frequency polygon

Figure 4.2.   Histogram and frequency polygon.

Another way of presenting this same information graphically is to connect the midpoints of these bars with straight lines. This kind of line graph, termed a **frequency polygon**, is illustrated in Figure 4.2*B*. It has been superimposed over the histogram (with minor modification) to show the correspondence between the area covered by the frequency polygon and that included within the bars of the histogram. The endpoints of the frequency polygon have been placed at the midpoints of the imaginary intervals in the distribution so that the corners of the outside bars of the histogram that are cut off by the frequency polygon are equal to the two new areas incorporated into the frequency polygon. For every other portion of the histogram that is cut off there is a corresponding ing additional area, so that the areas covered by the two graphs are equivalent. It should be pointed out that the histogram on which the frequency polygon is based has been altered in one respect. The height of the bar over the widest area has been reduced by two-thirds so that the area rather than the height of the bar is proportional to the frequency of the cases in that interval.

In practice, frequency polygons are often terminated at the endpoints of the outside intervals rather than the midpoints of the adjacent intervals to represent the boundaries of the distribution more realistically. In such cases, areas under the curve are not precisely proportional to the numbers of cases they represent.

We can think of the total area of the frequency polygon as unity with the area under any part of this curve representing the proportion of cases falling between the two points on the variable scale that mark off the area. In reading off numbers of cases from the graph, however, we can make specific interpretations only with respect to the midpoints: for example, 80 households reported incomes of $12,500, or between $10,000 and $15,000. This is comparable to rounding off household income to the nearest $5,000 or assuming that all the incomes in the interval average out to the midpoint. The graph does not indicate, for example, that 37 households reported incomes of $5,000 each.

Cumulative distributions are presented graphically by **ogives**. These graphs are constructed by connecting with straight lines those points that represent the number of cases falling below the upper limit (or above the lower limit) of each interval. The ogives for both upward and downward cumulative distributions of household income in the example are shown in Figure 4.3.

Line Graphs Histograms, frequency polygons, and ogives are the three basic ways of graphing univariate frequency distributions, but there are many other ways of graphically displaying statistical data. A few of these are presented below, and other graphical methods are discussed in chapter 5.

Graphical presentations are often advantageous because they convey an impression more clearly or more dramatically than a statistical table or narrative description. Because they are powerful mediums of displaying data, care must be taken to make them accurate and easily interpretable. A book entitled *How to Lie with Statistics* (Huff, 1954), written some 20 years ago, provides an illuminating discussion of the misuses of statistics. The book is based on the premise that although correct statistics (facts) do not tell lies in and of themselves, they can

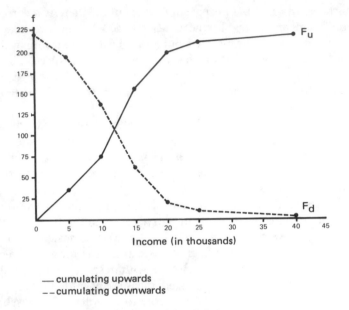

— cumulating upwards
-- cumulating downwards

Figure 4.3.   Ogives.

easily be interpreted incorrectly and presented in ways calculated to produce misleading impressions. The user of a text such as this should take pains to present his data fairly and learn to check the basis of presentation of data in analyses and reports he may read and act on. One of the classic ways of lying with statistics is through the use of biased charts, as is seen below.

One frequently used type of graph is a line graph showing the variation in some measure over time. Figure 4.4A shows such a graph depicting the number of stillbirths in a county for every fifth year over a period of 35 years. It is a straightforward presentation showing that beyond relatively minor year to year fluctuations there has been a gradual downward trend in the number of stillbirths over this period.

Figure 4.4B and C illustrates two ways of graphing identical data, which relate to the number of people participating in a given program in two consecutive years. The first impression to be gained from a quick look at Figure 4.4B is that there was a dramatic increase in the number of participants from 1975 to 1976. In fact, however, the recorded gain from 4,000 to 4,010 participants is not likely to have any practical significance for the management of the program at all. The dramatic effect of the graph is achieved by truncating the scale below 4,000 and stretch-

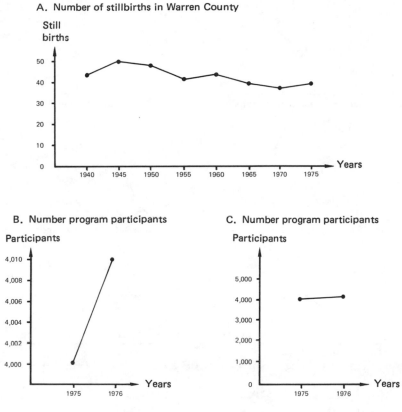

Figure 4.4.   Time trend graphs.

ing out the interval containing the next 10 units along the vertical axis. Figure 4.4*C* provides a much more reasonable display of the same data, conveying the immediate impression that there has been almost no change at all.

DESCRIPTIVE STATISTICS

There is no reason to expect that variables in an empirical data set will usually form the same type of distribution; empirical data can come in any distribution imaginable. The graphs in Figure 4.5 illustrate some of the different types of distributions that can be manifested by interval variables; think of them, for the present, as frequency polygons drawn over numerous, small intervals. Interval variables may have symmetrical

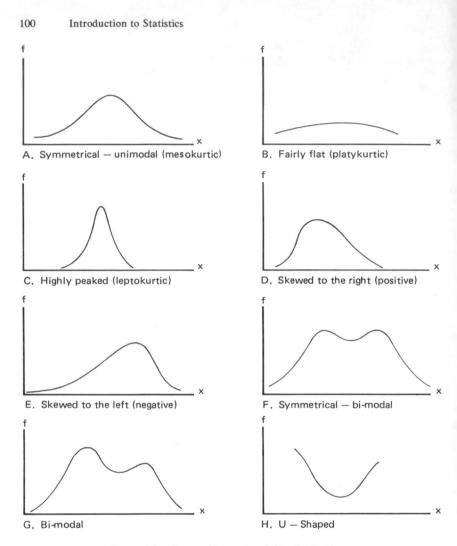

Figure 4.5.   Types of interval variable distribution.

distributions or be skewed in one direction or the other; they may be unimodal, bimodal, or trimodal; they may be highly peaked or very flat; and they may exhibit a concentration of cases near the center of the distribution or none at all. Different variables in the observable world tend to be distributed differently. The general form of a frequency distribution is one way of describing the pattern of variation a measure exhibits.

Measures used to summarize certain characteristics of frequency distributions are termed **descriptive statistics**. They are single measures that in some way represent the complete distribution, thus making its interpretation a more manageable job. In actuality, the basis of most quantitative analysis is the comparison of descriptive statistics between two or more groups of observations differentiated according to other variables of interest. Most of the more advanced statistics discussed in later chapters are not descriptive statistics, but rather inferential statistics used in drawing conclusions about whole populations based on sample data. Used by themselves, descriptive statistics are limited in the sense that they refer directly to only those cases that have been observed and included in the data set, even if these are a small fraction of all the cases of interest; no scientific inference is being made to extend conclusions based on descriptive statistics to a larger population.

In summarizing the distribution of a variable with descriptive statistics, information is invariably lost. What is really of interest is the fact that not all the cases are identical, that indeed there is variation from case to case that might be useful in addressing research questions. The amount of variation in part determines the potential richness of the data, and this richness may be reduced when summarizing measures are used. Thus it is usually wise to look at a number of descriptive statistics in combination. The first step in data analysis should be to examine the frequency distributions and descriptive statistics for all the variables of concern to the researcher.

There are two principal classes of descriptive statistics; measures of central tendency and measures of dispersion. The former are measures of location or typicality that report "average" values taken on by the variable. They are usually used as the single best representation of the overall distribution. Measures of dispersion provide an indication of the amount and nature of variation around the central points or "average" values of the distribution. In one sense they provide a measure of the extent to which measures of central tendency are in fact typical of the distribution. In addition, a number of relational measures are discussed in the following sections.

Measures of Central Tendency

Summarizing the distribution of nominal variables is less complicated than that of interval variables. The cases taking on each value (or in each category) of a nominal variable are tabulated and the total numbers of cases in the categories are noted and compared, often on some standardized basis. The category with the greatest number of cases is sometimes called the **modal category**, and this is the one measure of central tendency appropriate for nominal scales. The modal category, or **mode,**

$$\overline{X} = \text{mean average}$$

$$\Sigma = \text{summation}$$

$$X_i = \text{individual cases}$$

$$N = \text{number of cases}$$

$$\overline{X} = \frac{\Sigma X_i}{N}$$

$$\overline{X} = \frac{1 + 0 + 5 + \ldots + 2 + 10 + 4}{60}$$

$$\overline{X} = \frac{319}{60}$$

$$\overline{X} = 5.32$$

Figure 4.6.   Computation of mean from ungrouped data: felony arrests per officer.

is the most typical category of the distribution. There are a number of measures of central tendency used with interval data and each provides somewhat different information about the distribution. For example, from the frequency distribution in Table 4.2 we can see that the mode is 5, but this tells us nothing about the values taken on by other cases.

Mean Average   The measure most commonly used with interval data is the arithmetic mean or **mean average**, usually denoted by $\overline{X}$. This is defined as the sum of the values of all the cases divided by the number of cases. It is an arithmetic measure because it is based on a computation of the values in the distribution. It should be recognized that when used with discrete data, the mean average may well be some quantity that cannot be taken on by an individual observation. Figure 4.6 illustrates a computation of the mean average from the data on felony arrests presented earlier in Table 4.2, using ungrouped data.

The mean can be thought of as the balancing point of the values of all the cases in the distribution. It may not be that value that occurs most frequently, but in terms of the interval units on the measuring scale, it is the most representative value. Two special properties of the mean should be noted. First, in absolute terms, the sum of the differences between the mean and the values of the cases below it equals that between the mean and the values of the cases above it. The negative differences equal the positive differences and thus the sum of all the differences from the mean equals 0. This property can be stated as:

$$\Sigma(X_i - \overline{X}) = 0$$

A second property of the mean is that the sum of the squared deviations of each value from the mean will be less than the sum of squared deviations from any other number. This "least squares" property serves as the basis of some more sophisticated techniques discussed in later chapters. In notational form this property can be represented as:

$$\Sigma(X_i - \overline{X})^2 = \text{minimum}$$

Median Average In contrast to the mean, the median average does not take into account all the values in the distribution. Rather, the median is the value taken on by the middle case, regardless of the values of other observations. It is a *positional* rather than arithmetic measure, with the property of having the same number of cases with smaller values as there are with larger values. If the number of cases is odd, therefore, the median is the value of the middle case, while with an even number of cases it is the mean average of the two middle cases. To find the median case or cases, divide one more than the total number of cases by two; the median average is the corresponding value. Continuing the same example, with 60 observations $(N + 1)/2$ is 30.5. Thus the median average is one-half the combined values of the 30th and 31st cases, ordered from highest to lowest. From the frequency distribution in Table 4.2 we can see that these two cases both have five arrests, so the median average itself is 5.

In this example the median turned out to be slightly less than the mean of 5.32; the two are quite close because the distribution has a heavy concentration in its middle range. The mean average takes fuller advantage of the interval level of measurement in that it is an arithmetic measure involving all the values in a distribution. We would also find that in drawing repeated samples from the same population, the mean will vary less than the median from sample to sample. Thus it is usually considered to be a more reliable measure and is in fact used more often. However, as an arithmetic measure the mean is more sensitive to extreme values than the median.

In a highly skewed distribution, one that is characterized by extreme values on either the low or high end but not both, the mean will be pulled in the direction of the extreme values, away from the cases in the middle of the distribution. The median is not particularly sensitive to the extremes, because each is just one more case, and is therefore more representative of the "typical" cases in the distribution. Income distributions, for example, are usually skewed to the right (or high side) and are therefore often reported in terms of median income. Figure 4.7 illustrates the difference between the mean and median (denoted Md) in a skewed distribution.

Weighted Average One reason why mean averages are attractive is that they provide flexibility in computation. In some situations analysts may have need to compute **weighted averages**, in effect, the mean average of a set of mean averages, each weighted by the number of cases it is based on. A weighted average is the sum of the products of each mean multiplied by the number of cases it is based on, divided by the

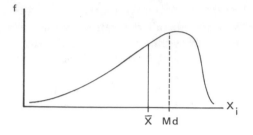

Figure 4.7.   Mean and median in a skewed distribution.

total number of cases. Symbolically,

$$\bar{X} = \frac{\Sigma f_i \bar{X}_i}{N}$$

Figure 4.8 illustrates the computation of the weighted average of the number of participants in 159 programs operated by a federal agency around the country. The analyst knows the number of programs being operated in each of six regions and the mean number of participants in the programs for each region. Each regional mean is weighted by the number of programs in the region and the sum of these products is then computed and divided by the total number of programs. The resulting weighted average is exactly the same as the mean calculated using the original data on each of the 159 programs. This procedure depends on the characteristic of the mean average, which reflects the value taken on by each individual case, and it therefore cannot be applied to median averages with the same results.

Region	f_i Number of Programs	$\bar{X}_i$ Average number of participants	$f_i \bar{X}_i$
Region I	22	205	4,510
Region II	31	184	5,704
Region III	18	177	3,186
Region IV	36	260	9,360
Region V	12	221	2,652
Region VI	40	162	6,480
	N = 159		= 31,892

$$\bar{X} = \frac{\Sigma f_i \bar{X}_i}{N}$$

$$= \frac{31,892}{159}$$

$$\bar{X} = 200.6$$

Figure 4.8.   Computation of weighted average.

Moving Averages Another variation of the mean average is the **moving average**, used to smooth out trend lines of interval data over time. Moving averages are appropriate when the analyst is more interested in the long term trend of the data than the fluctuations from one interval to the next along the time scale. Although short term fluctuations are sometimes of primary interest, in other situations they are viewed as "noise" that is not important and may be disruptive of the longer perspective.

To reduce this noise level and the effect of extreme cases that may occur from time to time, averages may be computed for the observations centering on one point in time and substituted for the single observation at that point. If this is done for all points on the time scale, we have a series of moving averages that accentuates the trend over time by reducing the influence of short term fluctuations.

Figure 4.9 illustrates the use of moving averages to show the trend in the amount of property loss by fire in a city from 1963 to 1975. The original annual data show substantial year to year fluctuations attributable primarily to extremely damaging large scale fires in 1964, 1968, and 1973. This obscures the longer range trend across this period. The analyst wishes to dampen the effect of these extreme fires and does so by computing 3-year averages. The first is the mean average of the fire loss for the first 3 years, centering on 1964. For 1965, the 1963 figure is dropped from the computation and the 1966 figure added, so that the moving average for 1965 is based on two of the same years as were used in the 1964 computation. This deleting and adding of cases to form moving clusters of 3 years is repeated until the final 3 are averaged to find the moving average for the next-to-the-last year. As can be seen in Figure 4.9, the moving averages illustrate a clearer trend of increasing fire loss over time than the series of single observations shows.

Other Positional Measures Other positional measures, comparable to the median, include quartiles, deciles, and percentiles. These are not really measures of central tendency, but are useful in sizing up a distribution or in making comparisons between cases or different distributions. Quartiles divide the total number of cases, ranked from highest to lowest, so that the first quartile is the value of that case that has one-quarter of all the cases below it and the third quartile is the value of that case with three-quarters of the cases below it. Deciles work in the same way with tenths of the total number of cases. Percentiles are used more often and should not be confused with percentages. For example, in educational testing a student in the 90th percentile earned

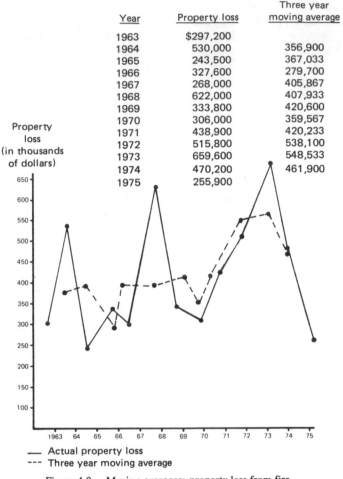

Year	Property loss	Three year moving average
1963	$297,200	
1964	530,000	356,900
1965	243,500	367,033
1966	327,600	279,700
1967	268,000	405,867
1968	622,000	407,933
1969	333,800	420,600
1970	306,000	359,567
1971	438,900	420,233
1972	515,800	538,100
1973	659,600	548,533
1974	470,200	461,900
1975	255,900	

—— Actual property loss
--- Three year moving average

Figure 4.9.   Moving averages: property loss from fire.

a score higher than that of 90 percent of the students taking the test. This, however, indicates little about the score itself, which may or may not represent correct answers to 90 percent of the questions. Like the median, these other positional measures are stated in terms of scores or values but are determined by numbers of cases. By definition, the median is equivalent to the second quartile, the fifth decile, and the fiftieth percentile.

Positional measures other than the median are computed by multiplying the number of cases by the fraction that represents the position of the case being sought, rounding that case identifier to the nearest whole number, and noting the corresponding value. To find the 31st percentile of the felony arrests distribution, for example, we would have

$$31 \text{ percentile} = (31/100)(60)$$
$$= 18.6 \cong 19$$

or the 19th case. Thus, counting up cases in either Figure 4.1 or Table 4.2, we would find that the value of the 31st percentile is 4.

Relational Measures

Proportions, percentages, ratios, and rates are all descriptive statistics that in some way relate the magnitudes of two or more quantities. These relational measures are used in two ways. First, they are used in summary fashion to express the frequency of cases in a given category as this quantity relates to some other quantity. Second, a given relational measure may be computed for each case in a data set; essentially this is using the relational measure to define a new variable rather than as a summary descriptive statistic.

Proportions   The frequencies of the categories of a nominal level variable are compared most easily by expressing the number of cases in each category as the share they constitute of the total number of cases. One such measure, the **proportion**, is computed by dividing the number of cases in a category by the total number of cases in the distribution. Unless all the cases fall in one category, the proportion will always be less than unity. Essentially, proportions show how a sum total breaks down into a number of subgroups, and therefore the proportions of cases in all the categories sum to unity.

Table 4.4 shows the number of graduates of the occupation-related programs of a state's community college system according to their present employment status, along with the corresponding proportions.

Table 4.4.   Number and proportion of community college graduates by present employment status

Present job status	Students (f)	Proportion (p)
Employed—curriculum related	2,858	0.5277
Employed—unrelated	1,113	0.2055
Unemployed	1,445	0.2668
Total	5,416	1.0000

Of the total 5,416 graduates, for example, the proportion presently employed in a field related to their curriculum is 0.5277, slightly over one-half of the graduates. In some tables like this, the proportions shown do not add up to exactly 1.000, because of rounding errors. When it is desired to make adjustments in such cases so that they do sum to unity, the convention is to adjust the proportions of the largest categories, thereby creating the least distortion. The column of proportions in Table 4.4 is referred to as the **relative frequency distribution** of the present job status variable.

Percentages   More common is the use of **percentages**, which are simply proportions multiplied by 100. As proportions sum to unity, the percentages of cases in the categories sum to 100. Percentages can also be thought of in terms of rates, indicating how many cases fall in a given category per 100 cases in the whole sample or population.

Proportions and percentages are most useful in comparing relative frequencies of cases in categories across two or more groups of observations. Table 4.5 shows the present employment status of the same 5,416 community college graduates, categorized by their field of study. This information can be used to compare the extent to which graduates from the three program areas directly use what they studied in the community college system.

As the numbers are large and as there are three categories in each of these two nominal variables, it is somewhat difficult to interpret this information. The problem is simplified by transforming the numbers into percentages, also shown in Table 4.5. Now it can be seen easily that fewer of those graduates who studied business are employed in work relating to their field of study than those graduates who were enrolled in "other" curricula. On the other hand, a smaller percentage of the engineering graduates are currently unemployed than those from business or "other" programs.

Table 4.5.   Number of community college graduates by field of study and present job status

Present job status	Business		Engineering		Other		Total	
	N	%	N	%	N	%	N	%
Employed-related	1,368	49.7	989	53.8	501	60.7	2,858	52.7
Employed— unrelated	559	20.3	444	24.2	110	13.3	1,113	20.6
Unemployed	826	30.0	404	22.0	215	26.0	1,445	26.7
Total	2,753	100.0	1,837	100.0	826	100.0	5,416	100.0

It should be noticed that these percentages are intended to address certain questions and not others. They have been calculated vertically to show breakdowns of the variable in the rows of the table, employment status. The question of what share of all the unemployed graduates came from business or engineering curricula would require horizontal percentages for which the row totals would each be 100 percent. In a table with two or more nominal variables, the choice of the direction in which to compute percentages depends on the question to be addressed, and this is usually made explicit in the overall research design. If we are interested in learning about the efficacy of various curricula in preparing students for careers, then the set-up in Table 4.5 is appropriate. By convention, percentages are usually calculated vertically. It is therefore common practice to place in rows the variable whose categories are to be expressed as relative shares, with the variable used to divide the cases into groups placed in the columns.

In interpreting percentage data, care should be taken to ascertain the base, or total number of cases, on which the percentages are computed. The numbers in Table 4.5, for example, do not indicate the percentage of all those graduates who are employed who are working in jobs unrelated to their field of study. This is because the base for the percentages in the figure is the total number of graduates, including those who are not employed at all. Thus, it is a good idea to report the base on which percentages are calculated along with the percentages themselves, or to make sure that all numbers are reported as well as percentages. In addition, when the total number of cases is much less than 50, it is preferable to report findings in terms of the actual numbers rather than percentages, or to report both.

Ratios The relative magnitudes of two groups of items or individuals or two categories of a nominal scale can also be compared by direct ratios. **Ratios** measure the magnitude of the first group or category in units of the second and are computed by dividing the first by the second. The second quantity, the base of the ratio, is the denominator. Ratios may be expressed in terms of the initial raw numbers, or by dividing the numerator by the denominator. Thus the ratio of business graduates to engineering graduates in Table 4.5 is 2,753 to 1,837, or 1.5; this means that there are 1.5 business graduates per one engineering graduate.

Proportions are a special class of ratios in which the denominator is the total number of cases observed. A proportion is the ratio of a subset of these cases to the whole set of cases. Other ratios involve two mutually exclusive quantities and may be less than or greater than unity. For example, a student/faculty ratio might be 25 to 1 whereas the corresponding faculty/student ratio would be 0.04 to 1.

Ratios have many uses in public program analysis, particularly as indicators of efficiency. Thus, we might be interested in the ratio of passenger miles travelled to seat miles provided by an urban transit system, or the ratio of the dollar value of the benefits generated by a job training program to the dollar cost of running that program. Ratios are often computed to express one measure in terms of units of another variable in order to make it more meaningful or operational. For example, cost analysis usually proceeds on the basis of unit costs such as the cost per vehicle mile of providing transit service or the cost per patient treated in a clinic.

Rates Ratios can be computed on any base that is convenient, the base being the magnitude of the denominator. In cases where the use of a quantity expressed in units of 1 in the denominator is likely to yield ratios of small decimal values, ratios are often based on denominators multiplied by large round numbers. This class of ratios is referred to as **rates**. For example, birth rates are conventionally reported in terms of the number of births per 1,000 females of childbearing age, accident rates by the number of accidents per 10,000 miles driven, and crime rates by the number of specific types of crimes committed per 100,000 population.

It is often useful to define variables as relational measures in terms of rates, ratios, proportions, or percentages rather than as single quantities. Such measures provide standarized variables that permit meaningful comparisons to be made on a uniform basis. For example, in comparing the incidence of outbreaks of influenza across the counties in a state, it would be helpful to define the variable as an incidence rate, the number of reported cases of influenza in a year per 100,000 population, rather than simply to compare raw numbers of cases. The use of absolute numbers, where percentages, ratios, or rates seem to be more appropriate may be a simple mistake, or, if intentional, an example of "how to lie with statistics."

Table 4.6 illustrates the utility of rates in the presentation of data. Rates enable more meaningful interpretation of the data. Table 4.6 breaks down data obtained from Table 4.1 by whether recidivists were placed in private institutions or on probation for their first offense. Because the great majority came from probation, this might suggest that this more lenient action is less effective in preventing repeat offenses. Quite a different picture emerges if we look at recidivism **rates**, however, because there were far fewer first offenders in private institutions. The

Table 4.6.   Recidivisms and recidivism rates by correctional system component

Correctional component	Total recidivisms (N)	First offenders (NFO)	Proportion (p)	Recidivism rate (N/100NFO)
Private institutions	229	524	0.437	43.7
Probation	3,882	9,234	0.420	42.0
Total	4,111	9,758	0.421	42.1

proportion of first offenders who became second offenders, or the rate of recidivisms per 100 first offenders, is almost identical for both components of the corrections system.

Comparisons in the amount of change in a variable over time are often expressed by the use of **rates of change**, the amount of change between time 1 and time 2 as a percentage of the quantity in the base period, time 1. The formula for such a rate of change is

$$\frac{X_{T2} - X_{T1}}{X_{T1}} (100)$$

If, for example, a legal aid service handled 214 cases in 1973 and 396 cases in 1976, the rate of change in its caseload would be $182 \div 214 = 0.850$, or $+85$ percent.

Measures of Dispersion

Measures of dispersion reflect the homogeneity of the distribution, a measure of the extent of the variation among the cases in the distribution. Used in conjunction with measures of central tendency, they provide an indication of the locus of the distribution and the degree to which cases are spread out or concentrated around its central points. A brief example illustrates the usefulness of both kinds of descriptive statistics. A study designed to aid in scheduling nurses to the in-patient wards of hospital might estimate the average number of patients in these wards daily, but the use of this estimate may not result in an appropriate nurse to patient ratio a majority of the time. Additional information about the degree of variation in the number of patients from day to day should help in determining whether scheduling to meet the average patient load is adequate or whether some alternative strategy should be employed.

Variation Ratio   The measure of dispersion used in conjunction with nominal scales is termed the variation ratio. It measures the degree to which the modal category dominates the distribution or the extent to which the cases are concentrated in that one category. The **variation ratio** is defined as 1 minus the proportion of cases in the modal category.

$$1 - \frac{fm}{N}$$

The higher this ratio, the greater the variation among the observations. In the community college example used above, the modal category in the employment status variable is employment related to curriculum for all three groups of graduates, but this classification is most typical of those graduates from "other" fields of study. The variation ratio for these graduates is only 0.393 (1 − 0.607) as compared with 0.462 and 0.503 for engineering and business graduates, respectively. Therefore, we can say that the variation within the category of "other" fields is less than the variation in the business or engineering categories.

Range and Quartile Deviation   Two measures of dispersion based on the spread of values between designated cases are the range and the quartile deviation. The **range**, which is used much more frequently, is the difference between the values of the highest and lowest cases. In the felony arrests example this would be the difference between 14 and 0, or 14. With grouped data it is the difference between the midpoints of the extreme categories. The range has the advantage of indicating the limits of the complete distribution but can also be somewhat misleading when extreme values are present.

The quartile deviation is one-half the range from the first to the third quartile. Also known as the **semi-interquartile range**, this measure is used for the most part in the fields of psychology and education. Symbolically,

$$Q = \frac{Q_3 - Q_1}{2}$$

This is one-half the range of the middle range of cases, and as the first and third quartiles vary less from sample to sample than the extreme values, this measure is more stable than the range. It provides an idea of the compactness of the central portion, but does not indicate anything about the other one-half of the cases, which can usually be expected to exhibit greater variation.

Standard Deviation   Whereas the two measures of dispersion discussed above provide an indication of the spread of the cases in the overall distribution or the central portion of it, other measures reflect the extent to which all of the cases taken together typically deviate from the mean. The one used most often by far is the **standard deviation**, and again it can be thought of as an arithmetic measure in contrast to the range and quartile deviation, which are essentially positional measures. To describe the standard deviation, it is instructive to look first at another measure called the **mean deviation**, or **average absolute deviation**, which is the sum of the absolute values (ignoring plus or minus signs) of the difference between each case and the mean, divided by the number of cases. Symbolically,

$$\text{Mean deviation} = \frac{\Sigma |X_i - \overline{X}|}{N}$$

The differences are taken as absolute values because we are interested in the amount of *deviation* of each case from the mean, not the *direction*. Otherwise, this sum would equal zero, as stated earlier. Thus, the mean deviation represents the mean average deviation of the cases from the mean.

Although the mean deviation has a very direct interpretation, the standard deviation is considered to be much more useful, primarily because of its importance in the theoretical foundation of more advanced statistics. It is the square root of the sum of the squared deviations from the mean divided by the number of cases. Symbolically, it can be represented as:

$$s = \sqrt{\frac{\Sigma (X_i - \overline{X})^2}{N}}$$

This shows that we take the difference of each case from the mean, square each difference, sum the squared differences, divide the sum by the number of cases, and take the square root, in that order. Figure 4.10 illustrates the computation of the standard deviation of the number of felony arrests from the example discussed above (shown in Table 4.2).

For the moment, the exact meaning of the standard deviation of 3.18 in the example is somewhat unclear, but later it is shown how the standard deviation is used to obtain probabilities associated with a normal distribution. At present we can think of it as an abstract number that indicates the magnitude of the typical variation of cases around the mean. If all the cases take on the same value, there will be no variation and *s* will be 0. As the spread of the cases around the mean is enlarged, *s* increases. The standard deviation of a distribution will usually be greater than the mean deviation and thus overestimate the mean average deviation of cases from the mean. This is because al-

	X_i	$(X_i - \overline{X})$	$(X_i - \overline{X})^2$
$\overline{X} = 5.32$	1	−4.32	18.66
	0	−5.32	28.30
N = 60	5	− .32	.10
	.	.	.
	.	.	.
	.	.	.
	2	−3.32	11.02
	10	4.68	21.90
	4	−1.32	1.74
	319	0.00	$\Sigma = 606.84$

$$s = \sqrt{\frac{\Sigma(X_i - \overline{X})^2}{N}} = \sqrt{\frac{606.84}{60}} = 3.18$$

Figure 4.10.   Computation of standard deviation. Data taken from Table 4.2.

though the square root is taken later, the squaring of each deviation places more weight on the extreme cases. With distributions having several extreme cases, then, the quartile deviation may be more appropriate as a purely descriptive measure of dispersion.

Variance   Taking the square root in computing the standard deviation in a sense scales the measure back down to the units observed. Summing the squared deviations from the mean and dividing this total by the number of cases produces another measure termed the variance:

$$\text{Variance} = s^2 = \frac{\Sigma(X_i - \overline{X})^2}{N}$$

The **variance** is by definition the square of the standard deviation (or the standard deviation is the square root of the variance). It is a measure of dispersion that is not used often as a descriptive statistic but is of importance to more advanced statistical techniques.

The standard deviation and variance are arithmetic measures of the dispersion of observations around the mean. To a great extent the value of either is meaningless by itself, but comparing standard deviations or variances across two or more distributions can be useful in determining their relative homogeneity if the distributions have similar means. Both measures, especially the standard deviation, are most meaningful when considered in conjunction with the mean. A standard deviation of 10, for example, would indicate wide variation regarding a distribution with a mean of 12, but with a mean of 180, relatively little variation would be indicated. It is good practice, therefore, to report the two together. A useful measure for comparing the degree of homogeneity between or among distributions is the **coefficient of variation**, the ratio of the standard deviation to the mean:

$$CV = s/\overline{X}$$

As the coefficient of variation indicates the size of the standard deviation relative to the magnitude of the mean, it can be used to compare the degree to which the cases deviate from the mean among two or more distributions with differing means.

Skewness and Kurtosis Two measures that provide information about the overall shape or form of a distribution, and are used particularly in econometrics, are skewness and kurtosis. **Skewness** provides an indication of the symmetry of the distribution, whether there is a tendency for extreme cases to be above or below the mean whereas **kurtosis** is a measure of the flatness or peakedness of the distribution. Both of these measures are products of the **moment** system in which the sum of the deviations from the mean are taken to different powers and divided by the number of cases. For example, the first moment is

$$m_1 = \frac{\Sigma(X_i - \overline{X})}{N}$$

which by definition is 0. The second moment is

$$m_2 = \frac{\Sigma(X_i - \overline{X})^2}{N}$$

which we have seen is the measure of dispersion termed the variance. The third moment (sum of the deviations taken to the third power, over N) and the fourth moment (sum of the deviations taken to the fourth power, over N) provide measures of skewness and kurtosis, respectively. However, these moments are not relative measures and therefore do not facilitate comparisons of the relative skewness or kurtosis across two or more distributions using different measurement units. For this purpose, standardized measures, which are based on ratios of moments taken to different powers, are sometimes used.

Beta-one is a standardized measure of skewness defined as the ratio of the third moment squared to the second moment taken to the third power. Symbolically:

$$\text{Beta-one} = \frac{m_3^2}{m_2^3}$$

Beta-one is a measure of skewness; if the distribution is symmetrical,

Beta-one is 0. A positive Beta-one indicates a skew to the right, whereas a negative Beta-one indicates a skew to the lower side of the distribution. Beta-one can be compared across distributions to indicate their relative degrees of skewness. Because squaring the third moment will always cause the result to be a positive number, the sign is obtained before the process of squaring this number and is subsequently added to the end result of the calculation of Beta-one.

Beta-two is a standardized measure of kurtosis defined as follows:

$$\text{Beta-two} = \frac{m_4}{m_2^2}$$

A normal (mesokurtic) distribution has a Beta-two value of 3, whatever the original unit of measurement. A Beta-two of less than 3 indicates a flatter (platykurtic) distribution than a normal distribution, and a Beta-two of greater than 3 represents a more highly peaked (leptokurtic) distribution.

Computations from Grouped Data

The descriptive statistics discussed above can all be calculated from grouped data, in some cases more easily than in others. These operations provide added convenience over ungrouped data when computations involving a large number of observations are carried out by hand. With the widespread availability of computer programs, however, they are performed much less frequently, and these computations are not included in this text.

NORMAL DISTRIBUTION

As illustrated in Figure 4.5, there are many general types of frequency distributions. One such type is the normal distribution, a theoretical distribution that can be approximated, but not perfectly matched, by empirical data. This is because the normal distribution is an infinite, continuous distribution, whereas empirical distributions are finite and to some extent always discrete. Figure 4.11 illustrates comparisons between discrete distributions, represented by histograms and frequency polygons, and continuous distributions represented by smooth curves.

Assuming a unimodal, symmetrical distribution, with cases grouped in a few large intervals, we might well have a distribution with widely differing frequencies in adjacent intervals, as shown in Figure 4.11*A*. If, however, we reduce the width of the intervals and at the same time add more cases to the distribution, we would expect the differences in frequencies in adjacent intervals to decrease, as shown in Figure 4.11*B*.

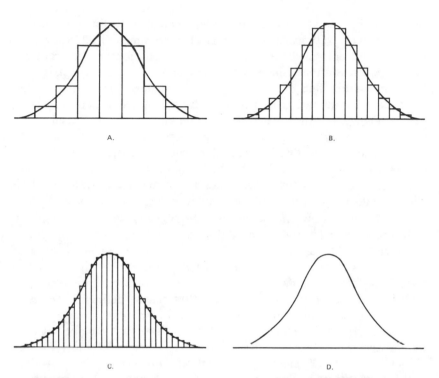

Figure 4.11.   Comparison of continuous curve with histograms and frequency polygons.

Thus, the frequency polygon would begin to smooth out. If we keep on reducing the width of the intervals and adding still more cases to the distribution, eventually we would expect a distribution in which only very gradual increases and decreases are observed between adjacent intervals and for which the frequency polygon approaches a curve rather than a series of straight lines, as illustrated in Figure 4.11C. Such a distribution, with very many small intervals, would approach a contin-uous distribution in which every conceivable value within the range of the distribution, however precisely defined, is taken on by some proportion of the cases, as represented by Figure 4.11D.

Properties of the Normal Distribution

The normal distribution is a unimodal, symmetrical distribution, as shown in Figure 4.11D. As stated above, it is a theoretical distribution in that it is a continuous distribution with an infinite number of cases; although empirical data cannot fit it exactly, they can resemble it closely. As is the case with all unimodal, symmetrical distributions, the mean, median, and mode of a normal distribution are all equivalent. Actually, the normal distribution is not one distribution but rather a family of distributions; there is one and only one normal distribution for each combination of mean and standard deviation. On the other hand, not all unimodal, symmetrical distributions are normal. Referring back to Figure 4.5, the normal distribution is shown in A (mesokurtic). Given a mean and standard deviation, there can be many other unimodal, symmetrical distributions that will be more highly peaked (leptokurtic) or less peaked (platykurtic) than the normal distribution. Depending on the relative magnitudes of the mean and standard deviation, the normal distribution will be more or less "bell-shaped."

The great utility of the normal distribution stems from known relationships between the standard deviation and areas under the curve. Specifically, that the proportion of the total area included in an area bounded by the mean on one side and some number of standard deviations on the other is known, and is the same for all normal distributions. That is, given an area under the curve that can be defined in terms of units of standard deviations from the mean, one can know precisely what proportion of the total area under the curve that area constitutes. More importantly, because the areas under portions of the curve are proportional to the number of cases that fall into corresponding portions of the distribution, by knowing the number of standard deviations from the mean that represents an area under the curve, we can determine what proportion of the cases fall in that part of the distribution. This property of the normal distribution provides the real meaning to the interpretation of the standard deviation.

Figure 4.12 illustrates these relationships. It is known, for example, that the proportion of the area under a normal distribution between the mean and 1 standard deviation is 0.3413. Therefore we know that in a normal distribution 34.13 percent of all the cases will fall between the mean and 1 standard deviation in either direction (because the distribution is symmetrical) or that 68.26 percent of all the cases will fall between the mean and plus or minus ($\pm$) 1 standard deviation. Similarly, we know that 47.73 percent of the cases will fall in that portion of the distribution between the mean and 2 standard deviations and that 49.86 percent will fall between the mean and 3 standard deviations of a normal distribution. This means that 95.46 percent of all the cases fall within ± 2 standard deviations and 99.72 percent within ± 3 standard deviations of the mean. The normal distribution is also infinite and continuous in the sense of not being terminated by discrete lower and upper

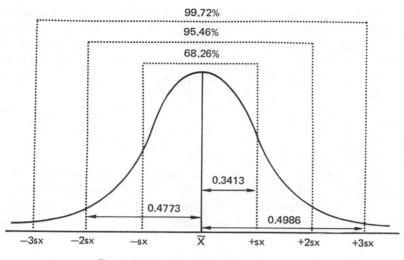

Figure 4.12.   Areas under the normal curve.

boundaries. Rather, the relative frequency of cases in the tails approaches, but never reaches, 0. As the distribution trails off in unbounded extreme values, we cannot measure its range in discrete values. However, from Figure 4.12 we can see that the effective range of a normal distribution (that which incorporates the vast majority of the cases) is somewhere around the mean ±3 standard deviations.

Standard Z Scores

The relationships between the proportion of area or cases and the number of standard deviations in a normal distribution are known not only for 1, 2, and 3 standard deviations, but for any number of units of standard deviation. The number of standard deviation units that marks the portion of the distribution between the mean and any other value taken on by the distribution is conventionally expressed in terms of *Z scores*, otherwise referred to as normal deviates or standard scores. Table A-3 in the appendix shows the proportion of the area under the curve corresponding to these individual *Z* scores. To obtain that proportion of the area under the portion of the curve between the mean and any other value of *X*, then, the procedure is to convert that *X* to a *Z* score and then to refer to Table A-3. The formula for converting to *Z* score is:

$$Z = \frac{X_i - \overline{X}}{s}$$

The Z score for a particular value of X is that X_i minus the mean, divided by the standard deviation. What this amounts to is expressing the difference between X and the mean in terms of units of standard deviation. If all the values in a normal distribution are converted to Z scores, the result would be a Z scale, **normal deviate scale**, or normal scale in standard form, a normal distribution with a mean of 0 and a standard deviation of 1. Interval data are often transformed into standard Z scores in order to express different variables in common units, i.e., units of standard deviations, regardless of whether their frequency distribution approaches a normal distribution.

When an empirical distribution is known or can be assumed to approximate a normal distribution, the properties of the normal distribution can be used to provide information on relative frequencies of various portions of the empirical distribution. Figure 4.13 illustrates a num-

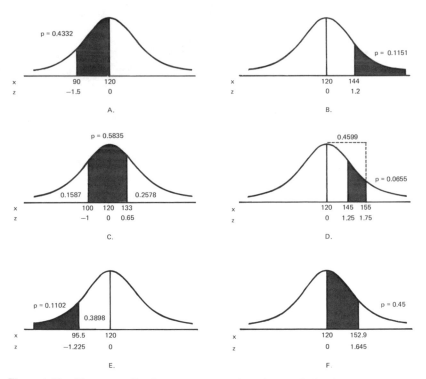

Figure 4.13. Z score applications. $p =$ proportion of cases falling in the shaded area under the curve.

ber of questions that might be addressed with the Z score technique. In all but Figure 4.13F, the problem is to determine what proportion of the cases lies within the portion of the distribution that has been shaded in. In A, for example, the problem is to find the proportion of cases taking on values between 90 and 120 in a normal distribution with a mean of 120 and a standard deviation of 20. Putting these numbers into the formula:

$$Z = \frac{X - \overline{X}}{s} \qquad Z = \frac{90 - 120}{20} \qquad Z = -1.5$$

we get a Z of -1.5. The fact that Z is a negative number simply indicates that the portion of the curve in question lies below the mean; because the distribution is symmetrical, the relationships of areas to standard deviation is constant, regardless of direction. Table A-3 shows that proportion of the area between the mean and a point represented by a Z score of 1.5 is 0.4332. Therefore, the portion of the distribution between 90 and 120 will account for 43.32 percent of all the cases in the distribution.

In B the problem is to determine the proportion of cases taking on values of greater than 144 in the same distribution. Using the same computation, we find a corresponding Z score of 1.2, and from Table A-3 we see that the proportion of cases falling between the mean and this point is 0.3849. Because the mean equals the median in a normal distribution, we know that the proportion of cases lying above the mean is 0.5; hence the proportion of cases in the upper tail greater than 144 will be $0.5 - 0.3849$, or 0.1151. Notice in this example we found the proportion of cases by subtracting the unshaded portion from the upper half of the curve (0.5 of the total area) to find the residual shaded area. In C, the proportion of cases in an area extending from below to above the mean is the sum of those proportions corresponding to the two subareas bounded by the mean. In D, a residual method is employed by subtracting the proportion of the curve bounded by the mean and the lower limit of the shaded area from the other proportion of the curve bounded by the mean and the upper limit of the shaded area.

Interpolation Figure 4.13E presents a situation in which the calculated Z score does not appear in Table A-3, but rather falls between two of the Z scores in the table. To obtain the exact proportion of the area under the curve between the mean and a point represented by a Z score of -1.225, it is necessary to interpolate between the proportions corresponding to the nearest Z scores in the table, in this case 1.22 and 1.23. The proportions corresponding to these Z scores are 0.3888 and

0.3907, respectively. The difference between the Z score in question—call it the critical Z—and the next lower Z is 0.005, whereas that between the next lower and next higher Z scores is 0.010. Therefore we have to interpolate a proportion of 0.005/0.010, or 5/10, into the interval between 0.3907 and 0.3888. Thus, the proportion corresponding to the critical Z score equals:

$$0.3888 + 5/10 \, (0.3907 - 0.3888)$$

or 0.3898. Using the residual method, then, the proportion of cases falling below 95.5 on the original X scale is 0.1102.

Figure 4.13F illustrates a different situation, but one that also requires interpolation. Given the same distribution, the problem here is to obtain that value of X that bounds the upper tail of the distribution such that exactly 5 percent of the cases lie within the tail. The first step is to determine the Z score corresponding to the value of X in question by referring to Table A-3. Because we know that the proportion of cases lying between the mean and this value of X is 0.4500, we search for this proportion in the interior part of the table and find that the nearest proportions that appear there are 0.4495 and 0.4505, corresponding to Z scores of 1.64 and 1.65, respectively. Interpolating, we find that the required Z score is 1.645. To find the corresponding value of X in the original scale, we must rearrange the Z score formula to isolate X. Thus,

$$Z = (X - \overline{X})/s \qquad X = Z(s) + \overline{X} \qquad X = 1.645 \, (20) + 120 \qquad X = 152.9$$

Therefore, we determine that exactly 5 percent of all the cases in the distribution are greater than 152.9 and that 95 percent are less than 152.9.

Other Z Score Applications   Although standard Z scores are used most often when a normal distribution is assumed, as illustrated above, they can also be used to provide less precise information about the proportion of cases under parts of the curve of distributions that are decidedly not normal. **Chebyshev's inequality**, for example, states that for any form of distribution, the proportion of cases falling within Z standard deviations of the mean is *at least* 1 minus the reciprocal of Z^2.

$$\min[p \, (\overline{X} \pm Z)] = 1 - (1/Z^2)$$

Thus we can compute the minimum (min) of the proportion of cases falling within a given number of standard deviations above and below the mean, whatever the form of the distribution we are working with. If we cannot assume that a distribution is normal but do know that it is unimodal and symmetrical, the minimum proportion of cases within a specified number of standard deviations from the mean is greater. With unimodal symmetrical distributions,

$$\min[p\,(\overline{X} \pm Z)] = 1 - (4/9)\,(1/Z^2)$$

Knowledge of this relationship can often be used to help size up the dispersion of cases around the mean average point of central tendency.

REFERENCES

Blalock, H. M., Jr. 1972. Social Statistics. 2nd Ed. New York: McGraw-Hill Book Company.

Freeman, L. C. 1965. Elementary Applied Statistics. New York: John Wiley & Sons, Inc.

Hoel, P. G., and R. J. Jessen. 1971. Basic Statistics for Business and Economics. New York: John Wiley & Sons, Inc.

Huff, D. 1954. How to Lie With Statistics. New York: W. W. Norton & Company Inc.

Loether, H. J., and D. G. McTavish. 1976. Descriptive and Inferential Statistics: An Introduction. Boston: Allyn & Bacon, Inc.

Neter, J., and W. Wasserman. 1966. Fundamental Statistics for Business and Economics. Boston: Allyn & Bacon, Inc.

Pennsylvania, Commonwealth of. 1976. Juvenile Corrections Recidivism Evaluation, Harrisburg: Division of Program Planning and Evaluation, Office of the Budget.

Tanur, J. M., F. Mosteller, W. H. Kruskal, R. F. Link, R. S. Pieters, and G. R. Rising. (eds.). 1972. Statistics: A Guide to the Unknown. San Francisco: Holden-Day, Inc.

PRACTICE PROBLEMS FOR CHAPTER 4

1. The following are data from a sample of 34 households. The variable is: number of persons per household.

1	2	10	6	2	4	5
1	2	4	5	1	1	4
3	5	9	3	1	7	6
4	6	10	3	6	8	4
2	7	7	2	3	6	

    a. Group these data, using five categories of equal width.
    b. Draw a frequency polygon with these grouped data.
    c. Calculate the mean from the ungrouped data.
    d. Calculate the standard deviation from the ungrouped data.

e. Calculate the median from the ungrouped data.
f. Calculate the skewness of the distribution, treating the data in an ungrouped fashion.

2. The following array shows the distribution of the weekly pay of the employees of a government agency.

| $195 | $210 | $185 | $195 | $175 | $220 |
| $225 | $195 | $210 | $185 | $210 | $195 |

Treating the data in ungrouped form, calculate the mode, median, mean, range, and standard deviation.

3. In a study of the times taken for a bus to travel between two points the following distribution was observed.

Time (in minutes)	f
0.0– 9.0	2
10.0–19.0	15
20.0–29.0	20
30.0–39.0	3

For the data displayed above perform the following operations.
a. Give the true class limits for each class.
b. Create a cumulative frequency distribution (cumulating up) of the number of buses taking less time than indicated by the upper limit of each class.
c. Give the cumulative frequencies (cumulating down) of the number of buses taking more time than indicated by the lower limit of each class.
d. Draw an ogive to represent this cumulative distribution.
e. Indicate the percentage of bus trips taking less time than indicated by the upper limits of the second interval.

4. In a study of the patients in two hospitals the following kinds and number of patients were found.

Types of patients	Hospital A	Hospital B
Males under 30 years	80	40
Females under 30 years	60	50
Males 30 years and over	40	90
Females 30 years and over	20	70

a. What percentage of the patients in hospital A are females 30 years and over?
b. What is the relative frequency distribution of the patients in hospital B?
c. Of all the males in hospital B, what is the proportion under 30?
d. What is the ratio of females in hospital A to females in hospital B?

5. Calculate the overall mean annual family income for the 310 cases given below.

	Mean family income	Sample size
Sample 1	8,500	120
Sample 2	9,500	100
Sample 3	11,000	90

6. Assume that the traffic counts taken at various points around a city approximate a normal distribution with a mean of 460 vehicles and a standard deviation of 32.00000.
a. What proportion of the observations would be expected to have traffic counts of greater than 508?
b. What proportion of the observations would be expected to have traffic counts in the range of 420 to 500?
c. What proportion of the observations would be expected to fall below a traffic count of 416? (Interpolate.)
d. What value of the traffic count variable would be equivalent to the ninety-seventh and one-half percentile (97.5 percentile)?

STATISTICAL ASSOCIATIONS AND RELATIONSHIPS

5

Although we are sometimes interested in measuring or providing estimates of individual parameters relating to public programs using only univariate statistical techniques, interest centers more often on analyzing associations between two or more variables. Two variables are **statistically associated** when there exists some systematic connection between their patterns of variation such that the distribution of one variable changes across subgroups of cases as divided by levels or values of the other measure. When this situation exists, one variable is said to **co-vary** with the other.

We work with statistical associations because we are interested in finding the extent to which we can explain or predict the values taken on by certain variables through their associations with other variables. As discussed in chapter 2 on the systems approach, in applied program analysis we are concerned with cause/effect relationships among needs and demands, environmental constraints, available resources, program characteristics, outputs, and impacts, because they are the keys to understanding, and therefore improving, program performance. Collecting data and examining statistical associations among operationalized indicators of these measures, then, is our primary way of analyzing how well a program works, why it works or does not work, and the conditions that facilitate or impede its success.

The newcomer to statistical analysis should be warned immediately, however, that statistical associations do *not* always represent real world causal relationships. As seen in this chapter, statistical associations may be very misleading with respect to underlying causal relationships. The identification and testing of hypotheses about causal relationships depend heavily on the adequacy of the data base and the comparisons that are structured in the first place, as well as the examination of statistical associations. Nevertheless, we move toward conclusions about causal relationships through the analysis of statistical associations, and working with these associations is the real "guts" of most statistical analysis. This chapter first looks at ways of displaying associations in graphs and tables, then discusses various attributes of statistical associations, and finally looks at the process of elaborating bivariate associations by introducing new variables.

DISPLAYING ASSOCIATIONS

Statistical associations are displayed in various types of graphs and tables, and in large part the particular format used is determined by the number of variables and the levels of measurement involved. Associations between two variables, or **bivariate** associations, are the simplest kind to work with, and their presentation is relatively straightforward. When additional variables are introduced to further specify associations or examine joint effects, the graphs and tables become a little more complicated.

Construction of the graph or table will also depend on the levels of measurement represented in the dependent and independent variables. Usually when we are working with associations we have one variable in mind, the **dependent** variable, as being influenced by the other variable, the **independent** variable. If we are hypothesizing about cause/effect relationships and examining associations to see whether the hypotheses are validated, the "cause" factor would be viewed as the independent variable and the "effect" would be the dependent variable. In the absence of previously specified hypotheses, the direction of implied causality is still often clear by virtue of chronology or logic. For example, if an association between previous work experience and participation in a job training program is based on a causal relationship, the previous work experience would have to be the independent variable, while if an association between race and income reflects a causal system, income would have to be the dependent variable.

In general, the variable of paramount interest, the one whose pattern of variation we are most concerned about understanding or explaining, should be considered as the dependent variable in a bivariate association. In program analysis measures of effectiveness and efficiency, as well as needs and demands indicators, are often used as dependent variables, whereas variables indicating environmental factors, resources consumed, and program operation characteristics often constitute independent variables. There are no hard-and-fast rules about this, however, and frequently a given variable will be used as an independent variable in one instance and a dependent variable in another. For example, in looking at associations between a number of program operation variables and one specific output measure, the output measure would be the dependent variable, whereas in subsequent analysis of associations between output levels and impact indicators, that same output measure would be used as an independent variable.

Because each level of measurement—nominal, ordinal, and interval—is possible in both the dependent and independent variable, there are a total of nine possible "types" of bivariate associations involving each permutation of two levels of measurement. Different statistical techniques for analyzing associations are appropriate for these different combinations, as is seen in later chapters. In terms of data displays, however, we are concerned primarily with the distinction between category or class type variables as opposed to continuous interval measures. Some of the more common types of graphs and tables are illustrated below and are briefly discussed in terms of how to construct and interpret them.

Graphical Presentations

Figure 5.1 shows one way to compare the distribution of one nominal variable, in this case type of crime, by another, in this case a dichotomized race variable. The numbers of cases in this example have been converted to percentages and are represented by the relative proportions of the respective bars in the graph, shaded in according to the legend, for white and black households. This particular graph shows by visual inspection that the white households in the sample on which the data are based had a greater tendency to be victims of part 1 person crimes and a slightly greater tendency to be victims of part 1 property crimes, while the black households had a greater tendency to be victims of part 2 crimes. Notice that this type of bar graph works as a cumulative relative frequency chart, showing for example that among the white households 85 percent of the victimizations were part 1 crimes involving either persons or property.

This graph is notable for what it omits as well as what it shows. First, it should not be inferred that the *number* of white households victimized in part 1 person crimes was greater than the number of black households so victimized, because the graph does not report absolute frequencies. The same type of graph could be produced in terms of numbers, however, and then this kind of comparison could be made. Second, although the heights of bars are the same in the graphs shown in Figure 5.1, it should not be interpreted as signifying that black and white households had the same propensity to be victimized

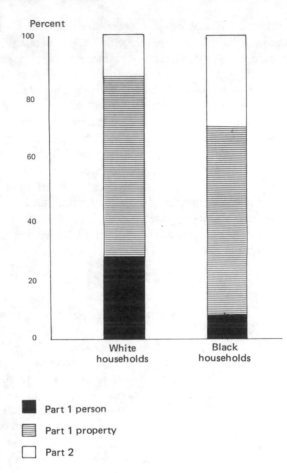

Figure 5.1. Type of crime by race.

by any type of crime. It simply shows the relative frequencies of different types of crimes.

Figure 5.2 shows a similar kind of graph, but one in which the bars have been truncated because the dependent variables are dichotomies. The height of each bar represents the proportion of survey respondents indicating that they agreed or disagreed with certain statements about police services in their neighborhoods. The figure actually presents three separate bivariate associations at once. There are three dependent variables, responses to three different but related items on a survey questionnaire, and they are all compared on the same district

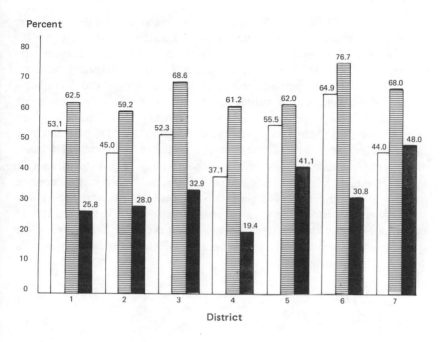

Figure 5.2. Evaluation of neighborhood police services, police treatment of citizens, and ability to solve crimes, by district. (From Poister, McDavid, and Miller, 1976, p. 82.)

basis. All three of these dependent variables are associated with district, i.e., the percentage of individuals responding favorably to any one statement varies considerably from district to district, but the graph also shows that the association with the district variable follows a somewhat different pattern for each of the dependent variables. For example, district 6 respondents had the greatest tendency to respond favorably to the first two statements on police performance, but district 7 respondents had the greatest tendency to respond favorably to the third statement. In general, this graph also shows that there is much more variation in responses to the third statement than to the second statement, which exhibits very little difference from district to district.

Figure 5.3 illustrates the use of a graphical technique to display the joint distribution of two interval level measures. It differs from the types of graphs discussed so far, primarily in that each individual case is represented in the Figure 5.3 graph, called a **scattergram**, whereas the preceding graphs provide information on summary measures such as means and proportions rather than individual cases. By convention the scale of the dependent variable is usually indicated along the vertical axis; that of the independent variable is drawn along the horizontal axis. Each dot, then, represents the values of both variables taken on by a single case. The scattergram shown in Figure 5.3 was drawn up to determine whether there was an association between the average number of passengers served daily by a transit system and the vehicle miles of service provided; the cases or observations are individual transit operations across the United States. It shows that there are more systems in the sample providing fewer than 3500 vehicle miles of service

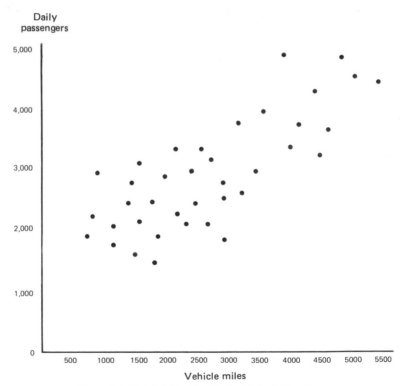

Figure 5.3. Total daily ridership by total vehicle miles.

per day than there are providing more than 3500 miles, and that there seems to be a definite tendency for the daily passengers variable to increase as the vehicle miles variable increases, or that there is a positive association between the two variables.

Figure 5.4 also shows the association between two interval level measures but is different from Figure 5.3 in two respects. First, the independent variable, age of persons served by two medical centers, has been grouped into several categories, thus treating age as an ordinal variable. Second, instead of showing the cost of services for each individual utilizing these centers, mean average costs have been computed for the subgroups of these individuals falling into the different age categories. Thus, each discrete point on the line graph indicates the average cost of medical services consumed by people in a particular age group. Although information is lost by grouping the data and using mean averages, this line graph provides a clearer indication of the overall trend of the association between age and cost of medical services, namely that costs tend to increase with age up to age 65 and tend to decrease a little beyond age 65. Notice that it should not be inferred from this graph that kinds of medical services received by older people cost more than those received by younger people; the association seen in

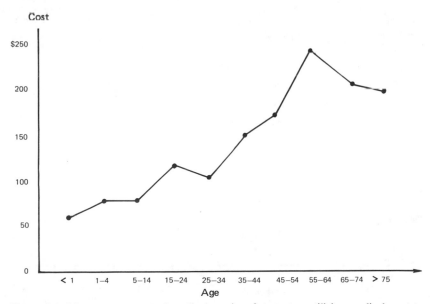

Figure 5.4. Mean average cost of medical services for persons utilizing medical centers, by age. (Adapted from Pennsylvania, 1975.)

Figure 5.4 might simply be a result of the greater frequency of visits to the medical centers by older individuals. If this were the case, the graph presented in Figure 5.4 could easily lead to misleading interpretations or illustrate a classic example of "how to lie with statistics." The problem is not with the graphical technique itself, but rather with the information (or lack of it) that is presented. If the desire of the analyst is, on the other hand, to compare the costs of services dispensed by the medical centers and consumed by individuals in different age groups, in total and regardless of number of visits, then the graph shown in Figure 5.4 would be highly appropriate.

Figure 5.5 shows a similar type of graph with a new feature added in. It is designed to show the variation in mortality rates resulting from kidney transplant operations performed in various hospitals, as associated with the number of such operations performed annually in these hospitals. As such it is really a scattergram with no replications on the independent variable (no two hospitals performed the same number of kidney transplants). The dots represent individual hospitals and indi-

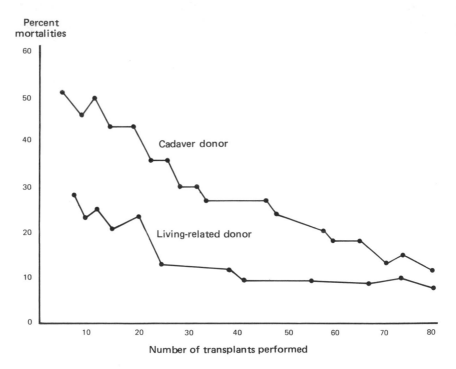

Figure 5.5. Mortality rate by number of kidney transplants and type of donor.

cate both their number of transplants and mortality rate and are connected by a line to show the general trend of mortality rate with number of transplants. The new feature is that on the same graph the association between mortality rate and number of transplants is shown separately for two sets of hospital operations, those using organs from a living, related donor, and those using organs from cadavers. Taken as a whole, then, the graph shown in Figure 5.5 incorporates three variables: mortality rate (the dependent variable), number of kidney transplants (an independent variable), and donor type (a second independent variable, sometimes referred to as a control variable). The graph shows that there is a negative association between number of transplants performed and the mortality rate incurred (mortality rate tends to go down as the number of transplants performed goes up), that this association pertains to operations using organs from living related donors as well as from cadavers, and finally, that regardless of the number of transplants performed by the hospital, mortality rates resulting from these transplants are higher with cadaveric donors than with living, related donors.

Statistical Tables

Most statistical tables fall into one of two categories, crosstabulations and comparison of means tables. Crosstabulations are appropiate when all the variables involved are nominal, or class type measures; ordinal measures are often used in crosstabulations (or crosstabs), and interval measures are often grouped and displayed in crosstabs to facilitate visual interpretations. Crosstabs are really joint frequency distributions, showing the distribution of two or more class type variables across the same set of cases.

Table 5.1 shows the crosstabulation of a college enrollment variable with the length of time spent in the Upward Bound program for a large sample of participants in that program, a bivariate frequency distribution. By convention the dependent variable is placed in the rows, with the values (in this example, yes and no) labeled in the extreme left column, or stub, of the table. The independent variable, then, is placed in the columns with its values labeled in the column headings. The title of the table should reflect its construction and purpose, with the dependent variable named first followed by the independent variable or variables with which it is crosstabulated.

Both row and column totals should be included in all crosstabulations. The row totals, shown in the extreme right-hand column, show the frequency distribution of the dependent variable in the aggregate,

Table 5.1.   College enrollment by months in program

Enrolled in college	Months in program			
	1–10	11–20	21 or more	Total
Yes	198 (26.3%)	849 (54.4%)	745 (64.0%)	1,792 (51.5%)
No	555 (73.7%)	713 (45.6%)	419 (36.0%)	1,687 (48.5%)
Total	753 (100%)	1,562 (100%)	1,164 (100%)	3,479 (100%)

From United States General Accounting Office, 1974.

in this case indicating that of the 3,479 program participants in the sample, 1,792 subsequently enrolled in college but 1,687 did not. The column totals, taken together, constitute the aggregate frequency distribution of the independent variable.

Any given row or column in the crosstabulation constitutes, by itself, a **conditional frequency distribution,** showing the distribution of one variable within a single category or "condition" of the other variable. Thus the first row in Table 5.1 shows the distribution of the months in program variable for that subsample of cases that were subsequently enrolled in college, and the middle column shows the distribution of the college enrollment variable for that subsample of cases participating in the program for 11 to 20 months.

Placing the dependent variable in the rows facilitates comparison of its conditional distributions within the various categories of the independent variable. Unless the total number of cases is very small or the association between the two variables is quite obvious, crosstabulations are usually best interpreted by converting the distribution of the dependent variable, both in the aggregate and within categories of the independent variable, into relative frequency distributions with the use of proportions or percentages. As a general rule, percentages are computed in the direction of the independent variable; with the dependent variable in the rows this yields vertical percentages that can be used to examine whether the dependent variable co-varies with the independent variable.

If there is no association between the two variables, the relative frequencies (or conditional probabilities) of the dependent variable would be identical across all categories of the independent variable and therefore equal to the relative frequencies in the aggregate (or marginal probabilities). If these relative frequencies differ from category to category, the two variables are associated. This is the case in Table 5.1; there is a systematic connection between the variation in the college enrollment variable and the months in program variable such that only 26.3 percent of those participating in the program for 1 to 10 months subsequently enrolled in college, whereas among those who were in the program for 11 to 20 months, 54.4 percent enrolled in college and among those in the program for more than 20 months, 64 percent enrolled in college.

Comparison of Means Tables Comparisons of means tables are appropriate for viewing associations between an interval dependent variable and a class-type independent variable or variables. Looking at bivariate associations, this involves listing the categories of the independent variable and the corresponding mean averages of the dependent variables taken on by the cases in each category. For example, in comparing the posttreatment arrest rates of participants in a number of drug abuse programs for different age groups we might find the following:

Age	Arrest rate	N
22 or less	0.37	(153)
23–26	0.37	(145)
27 or over	0.67	(149)
Total	0.47	(447)

This indicates that there is an association between age and posttreatment arrest rate on the average, but only between those groups of age 26 years or less and 27 years or over. Notice that this does not show a bivariate frequency distribution as does the crosstabulation discussed above. The number of cases shown represent the univariate frequency distribution of the age variable, while the dependent variable, arrest rate, is represented only by a summary descriptive statistic, mean average.

Comparison of means tables are set up more often using two or more independent variables, as illustrated in Table 5.2. This employs a cross-classification of all the cases by two class type variables, as does a crosstabulation. But in a comparison of means table, the numbers in the cells of the table are mean averages of the dependent variable, rather than number of cases. Table 5.2 shows the mean average posttreatment arrest rate for the same total number of participants in drug abuse programs as broken down by both age and type of treatment. As

Table 5.2.   Posttreatment arrest rate[a] by treatment type and age

| Age | Treatment | | Total |
	Methadone	Drug-free	
22 or less	0.61	0.34	0.37
23–26	0.34	0.44	0.37
27 or over	0.68	0.61	0.67
Total	0.51	0.40	0.47

[a] Arrest rates = mean number of arrests per year.
Reconstructed from Montclair State College and the New Jersey Division of Narcotic and Drug Abuse Control, 1973.

set out in Table 5.2, the number of cases in each subcategory of the total sample is not shown. Notice that whereas the crosstab shown in Table 5.1 incorporates two variables, the comparison of means table in Table 5.2 uses the same type of cross-classification but provides information on three variables.

In Table 5.2 the numbers in the row and column totals are mean averages for subsamples as broken down by only one of the independent variables. Thus, the column totals show the mean posttreatment arrest rates for those participating in methadone maintenance programs and those participating in programs using drug-free treatments, regardless of age. These are sometimes called **main effects**, whereas the figures in the interior cells show joint effects of the two independent variables on the dependent variable. Thus, the figures in the first column show the mean arrest rates for all those in methadone programs as broken down by age group, and these can be compared to the mean arrest rates for drug-free program participants as broken down by the same age categories. In this particular instance Table 5.2 shows that mean arrest rates do vary with age for both methadone and drug-free patients and that for every age group there is also an association between arrest rate and type of treatment.

Often, when comparison of means tables such as that shown in Table 5.2 are being analyzed, the question arises as to whether the two independent variables are associated. Because the age variable has been grouped into three intervals, the possible association between age and treatment type is best facilitated by the crosstabulation shown in Table 5.3A. It indicates that the frequency distribution of the age variable is quite different for the methadone patients than for the drug-free pa-

Table 5.3.   Association between age and treatment type

A	Age by treatment type		
Age	Methadone	Drug-free	Total
22 or less	30 (12%)	123 (62%)	153 (34%)
23–26	100 (40%)	45 (23%)	145 (32%)
27 or over	119 (48%)	30 (15%)	149 (33%)
Total	249 (100%)	198 (100%)	447 (99%)

B	Treatment type by age			
		Age		
Treatment type	22 or less	23–26	27 or over	Total
Methadone	30 (20%)	100 (69%)	119 (80%)	249 (56%)
Drug-free	123 (80%)	45 (31%)	30 (20%)	198 (44%)
Total	153 (100%)	145 (100%)	149 (100%)	447 (100%)

Reconstructed from Montclair State College and the New Jersey Division of Narcotic and Drug Abuse Control, 1973.

tients, with the former tending to have more people in the higher age groups and the latter having a sizable majority in the lowest age group.

Although Table 5.3A is set up to reflect the cross-classification set-up of the comparison of means table shown in Table 5.2, it is not really the most appropriate structure for a table designed to examine the association between age and treatment type. If these two variables are associated, and if that association reflects a direct causal relationship (for example, that individuals in certain age groups tend more to self-select into a particular type of treatment), then treatment type would be specified as the dependent variable with age as the independent variable. Thus Table 5.3B, which places treatment type in rows, might be a better way to display this bivariate frequency distribution. It shows that 80 percent of the individuals in the youngest age group were in drug-free programs while great majorities of the other two age groups were receiving methadone treatments.

Comparison of Percents Tables   Another frequently used type of statistical table is the comparison of percents table, which is a variant of the comparison of means table. It is often useful when the dependent variable of interest is a dichotomy and there are two or more independent variables. The cases or observations are cross-classified in the same manner as with the comparison of means table, but instead of mean averages, the numbers in the cells of the table indicate the proportion or percentage of all the cases falling into a given cell that take on a certain one of the values of the dichotomy.

Table 5.4 shows an example that relates to the same posttreatment arrest/treatment type/age problem examined above. Here, the dependent variable has been specified not as the rate of arrests per individual, but rather as the percentage of individuals who have been arrested at least once after beginning treatment.

This kind of table should not be confused with two other types in which percentages also appear in the cells of the table. First, crosstabulations are often converted into percentages, as discussed above, and may be displayed with only the percentages shown in the cells. In such crosstabs, however, the percentages should sum to 100 percent, whereas in comparison of percents tables as shown in Table 5.4, the percentages do not represent relative frequency distributions and do not sum to any particular number. In other situations, comparison of means tables are encountered in which the dependent variable happens to be a percent. For example, an analysis using census tracts as observations and focusing on the association of unemployment rate with region and racial composition might specify the dependent variable as the percentage of members of the labor force currently (at the time the census was taken) unemployed. If the racial variable is specified as percentage of the population that is nonwhite, and then grouped into several intervals, a comparison of means table could be constructed with regions in the

Table 5.4.   Percent arrested after beginning treatment by treatment type and age

Age	Treatment		Total
	Methadone	Drug-free	
22 or less	38%	25%	28%
23–26	27%	31%	28%
27 or over	34%	35%	35%
Total	33%	28%	30%

Reconstructed from Montclair State College and the New Jersey Division of Narcotic and Drug Abuse Control, 1973.

columns, percent nonwhite intervals in the rows, and mean averages of the variable, percent unemployed, in all the cells. Here the dependent variable would be a percent to start with, an interval level measure ranging from 0 to 100, and the summary statistic used would be the mean average. In the comparison of percents table shown in Table 5.4, the dependent variable would be a (nominal level) dichotomy as summarized by the descriptive statistic, proportion, or percentage.

Interaction   With comparison of means tables having two or more independent variables, we are often interested in learning whether there is any peculiar interaction in their joint effects on the dependent variable beyond a straightforward combining of their separate main effects. If there is no interaction, the magnitude of the differences in means across categories of one independent variable will be the same for all categories of the other independent variable or variables. If, on the other hand, the differential effect of one independent variable on the dependent variable changes from category to category of another independent variable, then in addition to their separate main effects, the two independent variables are said to have an **interaction** effect.

Table 5.5 shows some hypothetical data on the average savings in the operating costs of home heating using solar energy systems as opposed to different competing fuels. The data would be obtained from an experiment using alternative heating systems in pairs of identical housing units at various locations around the country, and general climate would be a variable of primary interest. Table 5.5*A* shows that mean average cost savings varies by both competing fuel and climate in the aggregate, that an association with competing fuel is apparent for all three types of climate, and that an association with climate is apparent for all three competing fuels. Table 5.5*A* also shows that there is no peculiar effect of interaction between competing fuel and climate on cost savings. For those experimental units in warm climates, the differential effect of cost savings between natural gas and fuel oil is $40 ($140 to $180), and the same holds true for the experimental units in moderate and cold climates. Furthermore, the differential effect between fuel oil and electricity for the warm climate units is $85 ($180 to $265), and this also holds for the moderate and cold climate units. If we work the table the other way, we will get the same findings, e.g., that the difference of $90 between warm and moderate units where natural gas is the competing fuel is the same as that for those units where fuel oil or electricity is the competing fuel.

Table 5.5*B*, on the other hand, shows interaction between the two independent variables. For warm climate units we see differences of $65

Table 5.5. Average savings in home heating costs using solar assisted systems, by general climate and competing fuel (operating costs only)

A	No interaction			
	Climate			
Competing fuel	Warm	Moderate	Cold	Total
Natural gas	$140	$ 50	−$ 10	$ 60
Fuel oil	$180	$ 90	$ 30	$ 95
Electricity	$265	$175	$115	$170
Total	$190	$ 90	$ 32	$105

B	Interaction			
	Climate			
Competing fuel	Warm	Moderate	Cold	Total
Natural gas	$115	$ 55	$ 0	$ 50
Fuel oil	$180	$ 90	$30	$ 95
Electricity	$270	$160	$75	$145
Total	$190	$ 90	$25	$ 98

and $90 as we move from natural gas to fuel oil and then from fuel oil to electricity, respectively, but for moderate climate units those differences are $35 and $70 and for cold climate units the differences are $30 and $45, respectively. Thus, we observe a pattern of interaction in which the differential effect of competing fuel is greatest for warm climate units and least for cold climate units. If we make the same kind of comparison working horizontally across the table, we see that the differential effect of climate is greatest for those experimental units with electricity as the competing fuel and least for those whose competing fuel is natural gas.

Patterns of interaction are not always as consistent as in the above example, but should always be examined in terms of practical implications. For example, an analyst might find that in the aggregate neither of two independent variables, one a program operation variable and the other an environmental factor, is strongly associated with the dependent indicator of a program's effectiveness, but that their interaction shows a quantum jump in the mean average effectiveness level for one particular combination of environmental factor and program strategy.

Some patterns of interaction are even more pronounced by virtue of actual reversals in the direction of a bivariate association within different categories of a second independent variable. Returning to Table 5.2, for example, the comparison of means indicates that for the youngest age group and the eldest age group the average arrest rate was lower for the participants in drug-free programs, while for those participants in the middle age group, the arrest rate was lower for the methadone treatment.

EXAMINING STATISTICAL ASSOCIATIONS

Up to this point we have been concerned primarily with the displaying of data to facilitate making comparisons to determine whether two variables in a data set are associated. With crosstabulations the interpretation is best made in terms of relative frequencies; if the conditional frequency distributions of the dependent variable are identical to its distribution in the aggregate, no association exists and the two variables are statistically independent. If there is variation among the conditional frequency distributions, however, the two variables are associated. With comparison of means tables, if an interval level dependent variable is not associated with some class type independent variable, its mean average will not vary from category to category of this independent variable. When mean averages do vary across categories of the independent variable, the two are associated.

When variables are statistically associated, we usually become concerned with various attributes of these associations, such as the extent to which they are associated and the nature of the association. If the associations we are working with are based on a probability sample drawn from a larger population, we may also be interested in their statistical significance. In this chapter we only consider the issue of statistical significance in passing, because it is discussed in depth in other chapters. This section is primarily concerned with interpreting the strength and nature of associations.

Strength of Association

The **strength of a statistical association** refers to the extent to which the variation in the dependent variable can be statistically explained or predicted by virtue of knowing values of the independent variable. In general, the greater the differences in the proportion of cases taking on values of the dependent variable across categories of the independent variable in a crosstab, the stronger the association; the greater the differences in mean averages in a comparison of means table, the stronger the association between the dependent and independent variables.

Returning to Table 5.1, for example, the association between months in the program and whether or not the individual enrolled in college would be termed a moderately strong association, because although in the aggregate a bare majority of the participants enrolled in college, only about one-quarter of those in the 1 to 10 month group did so, whereas almost two-thirds of those in the 21 month or more group did so. There is no rule of thumb for knowing how great a difference in these percentages, termed **epsilon**, is required for an association to be considered moderate or strong. Rather, the interpretation is judgmental and depends upon the practical significance of the differences observed. In this case, for example, we would probably conclude that the differences between 26.3 percent college enrollment, 54.4 percent enrollment, and 64.0 percent enrollment are of some consequence in assessing the effectiveness of the Upward Bound program.

By contrast, the association shown in Table 5.6 between months in the program and the current status of those who did enroll in college (minus 90 missing cases for which the information was not available) is very slight. Although an association does exist between the two variables, in that the conditional relative frequencies are not identical, the differences in the proportion who are still enrolled or have already graduated, as opposed to those who have dropped out, are minimal. Almost certainly, it would make no difference to program planners or decision makers that 48.9 percent of those who were in the Upward

Table 5.6.   Current status in college by months in program

Enrolled or graduated	Months in program			
	1–10	11–20	21 or more	Total
Yes	91 (48.9%)	414 (51.8%)	366 (51.1%)	871 (51.2%)
No	95 (51.1%)	386 (48.2%)	350 (48.9%)	831 (48.8%)
Total	186 (100%)	800 (100%)	716 (100%)	1,702 (100%)

From United States General Accounting Office, 1974.

Bound program for 1 to 10 months and then went on to college are either still enrolled or have graduated. The same is true of 51.8 percent of those who were in the program for 11 to 20 months and then enrolled in college and for 51.1 percent of those who were in the program for 21 months or more and then enrolled in college. If we were to assume that the statistical associations shown in these two tables reflected underlying causal relationships, we would conclude that the time spent in the program has an important effect on whether participants go on to enroll in college, but that for those who do enroll in college, the length of time spent in the program is of no consequence in terms of whether the individual will drop out before he graduates.

Assessment of the strength of associations exhibited in comparison of means tables is not quite so clear-cut, given only the information shown in the table. In general, if the magnitudes of differences between mean averages in a table were considered to be of some practical significance, they would indicate moderate or strong associations. However, in some cases it is difficult to judge the importance of differences between means without an idea of the extent of variation around those means.

Perfect Associations   Most of the associations we work with in the analysis of public program performance, as in social science research in general, are probability relationships rather than absolute relationships. In interpreting the associations revealed in statistical tables, we usually make tendency statements about the values of the dependent variable taken on by subsets of cases as grouped by independent variables. This is in contrast to the more mechanistic relationships encountered in many of the physical sciences in which a dependent variable may be completely a function of single or multiple independent variables; for example, H_2O at temperatures above 32° is liquid, but at temperatures below 32° it is solid.

In some areas of program analysis we do work with such mechanical or functional relationships. In analyzing or forecasting a state's revenues from a liquid fuels tax, given a uniform tax rate, the amount of revenue generated in a month is totally a function of the level of fuel consumption, as indicated in Figure 5.6. Most of the time, however, we cannot be nearly as precise in describing relationships, and this lack of precision stems from two sources:

1.   Given the complexity of the web of causal relationships that underlie the measures and effects we observe, along with our limited knowledge about all these relationships, we are often not able to specify very precisely the particular combination of constraints,

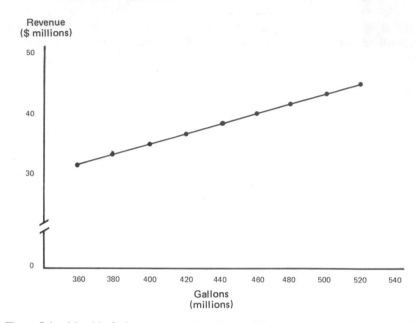

Figure 5.6.   Monthly fuel tax revenue by gallons of fuel sold (tax rate = 9¢/gallon).

contingencies, and interactions that will lead to a given set of effects, and

2. apart from this problem, there is a greater degree of randomness in many of our observations and findings because of the presence of the human variable, whether recognized explicitly in the research context or not.

In much of our work we are concerned with the strength of observed associations precisely because the association is neither non-existent nor total, but rather somewhere in between these two extremes. For example, Table 5.7A shows the distribution of survey respondents according to income and their responses to an item on recreation programs. Without converting to percentages we can easily see that the response variable is quite strongly associated with income. Interpreting this table, we would say something like "low income respondents have a greater tendency to rate the programs as poor, intermediate income respondents have a tendency to rate them as fair, and high income respondents tend to rate the programs as good."

Although this interpretation might suffice for most purposes, we sometimes need a clearer indication of the strength of a particular

Table 5.7. Rating of recreation programs by income

A	Imperfect association			
	Income			
Response	Low	Intermediate	High	Total
Good	10	30	35	75
Fair	20	50	20	90
Poor	60	20	5	85
Total	90	100	60	250

B	Perfect association			
	Income			
Response	Low	Intermediate	High	Total
Good	0	0	60	60
Fair	0	100	0	100
Poor	90	0	0	90
Total	90	100	60	250

association relative to other associations or of what the strength of that association might be. A number of normed measures of association have been developed and are discussed in later chapters in conjunction with contingency analysis and analysis of variance. Most of them provide indications of relative strength of association on scales ranging from a complete lack of association to a perfect association.

The term **perfect association** usually refers to one in which the error in predicting the dependent variable for any given case is reduced to zero by virtue of knowing the value of the independent variable for that case. In other words, all the variation in the dependent variable is connected with, or can be explained by, the variation in the independent variable. A less restrictive interpretation of perfect associations is sometimes used (Loether and McTavish, 1976, pp. 199–201). The functional relationship between fuel sold and revenues generated, shown in Figure 5.6, is an example of a perfect association between two interval level measures. An example of a perfect association between two class type variables as displayed in a crosstabulation is shown in Table 5.7B. Although there is considerable variation in the survey responses in the aggregate, within each income group there is none. All low income respondents rated the recreation programs as poor, all intermediate income respondents rated them as fair, and all upper income respondents rated them as good. Thus the systematic connection in the variation of these two variables accounts for all the variation in the response variable, and an individual's response to the survey item can be predicted with 100 percent certainty, given his income level.

Nature of Associations

A separate attribute of a statistical association is its substantive nature, how the dependent variable tends to vary with respect to the independent variable. The nature of associations is often described in terms of both direction and consistency. If the variables involved are ordinal or interval measures, the association is either **positive**, with the dependent variable tending to increase as the independent variable increases, or **negative**, with the dependent variable tending to decrease as the independent variable increases. With more than two categories of the class type variables involved, the consistency of such a positive or negative trend can also be noted.

Returning to Table 5.2, for example, we see that in the aggregate, the mean posttreatment arrest rate for those participants 27 years old and over is greater than that for the participants 26 years old or younger. Thus, the arrest rate is positively associated with age. Notice that the "positive" nature of this association has a mathematical rather than a value laden reference, i.e., this does not signify that the arrest rate "gets better" as age increases. Within the two treatment categories shown in Table 5.2, the nature of the association between age and arrest rate differs. For the drug-free participants only, the mean arrest rate increases from the youngest age group to the middle age group and again from the middle age group to the oldest age group. Thus the association between arrest rate and age for this group is **linear** in nature; a consistently positive association. On the other hand, for the methadone patients, the arrest rate drops from the youngest group to the middle group and then increases from the middle group to the oldest group, reflecting a **curvilinear** association.

Similar interpretations can be derived from crosstabulations. Table 5.8, for example, shows an indicator of satisfaction with police performance in victimization situations, crosstabulated with crime classification. Considering the type of crime to be an ordinal measure reflecting the seriousness of the crime, we would say that the association is curvilinear, with the percent responding that they were satisfied decreasing substantially from part 1 person to part 1 property crimes and

Table 5.8.   Satisfaction with police by type of crime

| Satisfaction | Type of crime | | | |
	Part 1 person	Part 1 property	Part 2	Total
Satisfied	14 (70%)	27 (39%)	10 (45%)	51 (46%)
Dissatisfied or uncertain	6 (30%)	42 (61%)	12 (55%)	60 (54%)
Total	20 (100%)	69 (100%)	22 (100%)	111 (100%)

From Poister, McDavid, and Miller, 1976, p. 117.

then increasing somewhat from part 1 property crimes to part 2 crimes. We might conclude that in general the trend of this association is negative, but that it is not consistently so.

Table 5.9 shows the association between the same dependent variable and the estimated response time taken by the police to answer the call for service. Here the direction of the association is definitely negative, with the percent satisfied decreasing as the estimated response time increases; and it is linear, with some decrease in the percent satisfied for each successively higher response time category. Notice that the magnitude of the increase or decrease in the dependent variable does not have to be even in order for the association to be termed linear, but rather the direction of difference from category to category must be consistent.

Statistical Significance

The description and interpretation of statistical associations as discussed above pertains to the data at hand, whether the data set constitutes the total population of interest, some type of probability sample, or a chunk or judgment sample. When the observed associations are based on sample data, the intent is usually to make inferences about the larger population, and with probability samples, tests of statistical significance are often appropriate.

Many of the particular tests available are discussed in subsequent chapters in this text, but it might be helpful to point out their usefulness at this point. In discussing the nature and strength of statistical associations in this chapter, we have been commenting on their **practical significance**, their substantive content and possible implications for evaluating programs and suggesting improvements. Their **statistical significance**, on the other hand, is concerned with whether sample

Table 5.9. Satisfaction with police by estimated response time

| Satisfaction | Estimated response time | | | | Total |
	10 minutes or less	11-20 minutes	21-45 minutes	more than 50 minutes	
Satisfied	21 (72%)	11 (35%)	6 (32%)	4 (25%)	42 (44%)
Dissatisfied or uncertain	8 (28%)	20 (65%)	13 (68%)	12 (75%)	53 (56%)
Total	29 (100%)	31 (100%)	19 (100%)	16 (100%)	95 (100%)

From Poister, McDavid, and Miller, 1976, p. 117.

associations are likely to represent similar associations in the larger population as opposed to having a reasonable likelihood of occurring by chance in a random selection process, even if in the larger population there is a complete lack of association between the variables in question. In the latter situation, the hypothesis to be tested is a statement to the effect that in the larger population the two variables are not associated; rejecting the hypothesis, then, leads to the conclusion that the two variables are in fact associated in the larger population. The reader should note that even when associations are found to be statistically significant, they may or may not have practical significance.

Statistical Associations and Causal Relationships

Throughout this chapter it has been emphasized that in describing associations among variables and even in testing for statistical significance, we are working with statistical relationships that may or may not reflect underlying real world cause/effect relationships. In some situations we may not even be concerned with the specific causal sequences involved. For some purposes **predictive** models are sufficient, those that can be used to predict values of certain variables based upon their demonstrated associations with other variables, without regard to the underlying patterns of causality. For example, a racial composition variable might be used as an operational predictor of the expected case load for a number of social service agencies even though we know that the web of causal influence, which generates the need for their services, is much more intricate.

More often, however, we are interested in developing **explanatory** models, which explain the variation in effect type variables as the direct result of causal factors. That is, ultimately we are interested in identifying causal relationships and therefore examine statistical associations in order to gain insight into these causal relationships. Without a proper data base in the first place, however, the utility of statistical analysis in moving toward conclusions about causal relationships may be severely limited.

To begin to claim that an observed statistical association in a particular data set represents an underlying causal relationship requires that we have 1) an explanatory theory that would lead us to expect the observed association, and 2) an ability to rule out rival hypotheses. It is preferable to start with hypotheses regarding cause/effect relationships, which might well arise from tracing the logic on which a particular design is based, and then develop test implications that would be expected to materialize if the hypotheses are true. The **test implication** concerns an observable association between two or more operationalized indicators that should occur if the causal hypothesis is true. Data are collected to test this working hypothesis, either descriptively or inferentially. If the anticipated association is observed and the working hypothesis therefore accepted, we say that the data tend to substantiate the causal hypothesis or that at least the data are consistent with that hypothesis.

However, there may well be other explanations for the occurrence of the observed association. Our causal hypothesis may in fact be false although the test implication materializes because the association is the result of some other causal influence. The greater the extent to which we can rule out such competing explanations, the more confident we become in concluding that the hypothesized causal relationship is valid. One way we sometimes take rival hypotheses into account, if our data set includes variables that could serve as indicators of these other possible influences, is to incorporate them into our statistical analysis. If we do so, and the association of interest still holds, we have moved a step closer to claiming a causal hypothesis. We have clearly not proven that the hypothesized causal relationship is valid but we have failed to eliminate it, and we have eliminated a rival explanation.

At this point, we might say that we have substantiated the causal hypothesis within the confines of our data base. But is this data base adequate for testing this particular hypothesis? The adequacy of the data base itself is a concern of the overall research design and will not be treated here in any detail. Suffice it to say that the use of experimental controls is the preferred approach for narrowing the range of possible explanations for observed associations and ruling out rival hypotheses. This might involve, for example, the use of matched pairs of individuals in test groups and their counterpart control groups to eliminate their previous experience as an explanation of observed differences in some effects type variable between the two groups.

With less structured data sets, much more reliance is placed on statistical analysis in moving toward conclusions about causal relationships. With cross-sectional data analysis, which typically involves a data set consisting of a single sample taken at one point in time, statistical controls are used as a poor man's substitute for experimental controls. Statistical associations are analyzed in depth to determine whether causal hypotheses are substantiated by the data and whether some rival hypotheses can be eliminated, but within the confines of such a data base, cause/effect type relationships can never really be demonstrated.

In thinking about whether statistical associations reflect underlying causal relationships, we are raising the question of whether or not certain observed associations are spurious. In general terms, a **spurious** association is one that does not directly represent a causal relationship, but rather is an indirect product of some other causal relationships. Operationally, a spurious association is a statistical association that disappears when additional variables are taken into account. As an example, consider the very strong positive statistical association that emerged between foot size and reading ability among a sample of students in grades one through four in a certain school district. Does this represent a direct causal relationship? Certainly not. If we take an age variable into account, the association will disappear. It is a spurious association based on the fact that both foot size and reading ability are functions of age. The point is that the interpretation of statistical associations in terms of causal relationships is a difficult process, particularly with less structured data sets. The following section discusses how to proceed in elaborating bivariate associations by incorporating additional variables into the analysis.

ELABORATING STATISTICAL ASSOCIATIONS

The process of expanding upon the analysis of bivariate statistical associations by taking additional variables into account is sometimes referred to as **elaboration**. It is a fundamental aspect of statistical analysis because it permits us to check the consistency of bivariate associations and observe the "behavior" of selected variables when looked at in different combinations. By examining what happens to bivariate associations when different third and fourth variables are taken into account as well as looking at the bivariate associations involving these variables directly, we gain a more complete and (it is hoped) more accurate description of the nature and strength of the statistical relationships among a number of measures. With less structured data bases in particular, the process of elaboration is our primary means of examining alternative explanations of observed differences in effects, thereby helping us to move from strictly statistical interpretations of observed associations toward tentative conclusions about underlying cause/effect relationships.

Third Variable Effects

Elaboration typically begins with the examination of a bivariate association of particular interest and then proceeds with the introduction of a third variable in order to determine what happens to the original association when this new measure is taken into account. The analyst is interested in knowing whether the new variable is associated with the two original variables and whether it affects the original bivariate association, i.e., whether it remains the same for the most part, is altered substantially, or disappears when the new variable is brought into the analysis.

This analysis is conducted by disaggregating the cases into sub-samples according to the categories or levels of the new variable, and examining the association between the original two variables within each of these subsamples. The new variable is often termed a **control** variable, and is used in this manner to identify the way in which a dependent variable co-varies with a particular independent variable, after this third variable has been taken into consideration. Although the results of such analysis are often described in terms of the association between two variables "controlling for" a third variable or when the third variable is "held constant," the distinction between experimentally controlling for some factor or holding it constant in any physical sense as opposed to statistically controlling for it after the data has been collected is basic. With less structured research designs that lack built-in experimental controls, we rely on statistical controls that "fix for the effects of" control variables through the process of elaboration.

Replication   Control variables are often introduced to examine a competing explanation for an observed bivariate association that would be based on the premise that the two original variables are in part functions of a third variable, the control variable, and that the original association observed is not based on a direct causal relationship, but rather is a result of these associations with the control variable. If this competing explanation is valid, the original association is a spurious one, which will wash out when the control variable is brought into the analysis. If, on the other hand, the original bivariate association does reflect a direct line of causality, it should hold up in some or all of the categories of the control variable.

Table 5.10*A* presents some data on 340 housing rehabilitation programs in communities across the country, pertaining to the type of financial incentive they provide and the percentage of eligible properties that have been entered into the programs. It shows that the participation rate does vary with the type of incentive, with those programs using combinations of loans and grants tending to have higher participation rates than those offering loans only.

One explanation for this association is that the combined incentives are simply more attractive to more property owners and therefore

Table 5.10.   Participation of eligible dwelling units in rehabilitation programs, by type of incentive

A	All Programs		
Participation rate	Loans only	Loans and grants	Total
20–40%	46 (32.9%)	38 (19%)	84 (24.7%)
40–60%	70 (50%)	106 (53%)	176 (51.8%)
60–80%	24 (17.1%)	56 (28%)	80 (23.5%)
Total	140 (100%)	200 (100%)	340 (100%)

B	Rental units eligible		
Participation rate	Loans only	Loans and grants	Total
20–40%	30 (33.3%)	25 (17.9%)	55 (23.9%)
40–60%	45 (50%)	75 (53.6%)	120 (52.2%)
60–80%	15 (16.7%)	40 (28.5%)	55 (23.9%)
Total	90 (100%)	140 (100%)	230 (100%)

C	Rental units not eligible		
Participation rate	Loans only	Loans and grants	Total
20–40%	16 (32%)	13 (21.7%)	29 (26.4%)
40–60%	25 (50%)	31 (51.7%)	56 (50.9%)
60–80%	9 (18%)	16 (26.6%)	25 (22.7%)
Total	50 (100%)	60 (100%)	110 (100%)

provide a stronger inducement to participate in the program. A competing hypothesis might be that the type of incentive is itself bound up with the eligibility requirements, and that whether or not rental units are eligible for the program funds is the real determinant of participation in the program. Wishing to examine this competing hypothesis, we break the total number of cases down into two groups, those programs in which rental units are eligible and those in which they are not. Table 5.10, B and C show these two corresponding subgroups. With the frequencies converted into percentages, it is apparent that the association observed in the aggregate holds true for both groups, with only slight deviation. Although the association is just a little more evident for those programs in which rental units are eligible and just a little weaker for the other group, for all practical purposes these associations are almost identical. Thus we find that the original association has been **replicated** in the categories of the control variable, thereby ruling out the competing hypothesis. This finding does not prove that there is a causal relationship between type of incentive and participation rate, but it does lend additional credibility to the hypothesis.

Specification   The purpose of introducing third variables is often to obtain more precise descriptions of the interrelationships among variables. In trying to learn about how a program operated and gauge its performance under different conditions, analysts are often interested in determining whether certain associations generally hold true across the board or whether they can be further specified as changing across categories of control variables.

Table 5.11 shows the present job status of former participants in a job training program by whether they were enrolled in 4-month cycles or 6-month cycles of the program. In the aggregate, the two variables are seen to be associated such that a higher percentage of those in the 6-month cycles presently have jobs. Does this indicate that as a general rule the 6-month cycles are preferable? Thinking that the type of program, whether focused on general skills or specialized skills, might also be an important factor here, we bring this into the analysis as a control variable, as shown in Table 5.11*B*. Here we see that for the specialized skills programs, the association between cycle duration and present job status is stronger than in the aggregate, whereas among those participants in general skills programs there is no association between duration and present job status. Thus the association has been further specified; it holds for special skills programs, but for general skills programs the additional 2 months does not seem to be a factor directly associated with whether or not the individual participant obtains a job after completing the program.

Distorter Variables   In some circumstances associations not only disappear when a control variable is introduced but, given the presence of the control variable, an association emerges between the original two variables that is contradictory to their association in the aggregate. For example, in the aggregate, two variables might have a positive association, but fixing for the effects of the control variable yields a negative association. The misleading positive association in the aggregate is a result of the effects of the control variable on the two other variables, which is thus shown to be a **distorter** variable.

Table 5.11. Job status of training program participants by program type and duration

A

Job status	All participants		
	Duration		
	4 Months	6 Months	Total
Obtained job	49 (0.54)	171 (0.81)	220 (0.73)
No job	41 (0.46)	39 (0.19)	80 (0.27)
Total	90 (1.0)	210 (1.0)	300 (1.0)

B Broken down by program type

Job status	General skills			Special skills		
	4 Months	6 Months	Total	4 Months	6 Months	Total
Obtained job	24 (0.6)	36 (0.6)	60 (0.6)	25 (0.5)	135 (0.9)	160 (0.8)
No job	16 (0.4)	24 (0.4)	40 (0.4)	25 (0.5)	15 (0.1)	40 (0.2)
Total	40 (1.0) (0.4)	60 (1.0) (0.6)	100 (1.0)	50 (1.0) (0.25)	150 (1.0) (0.75)	200 (1.0)

For example, Table 5.12*A* shows the bivariate association between survey responses to an item on affirmative action and the respondents' socioeconomic status. In the aggregate there is a modest association between the two, suggesting that working class respondents tend to favor the idea of affirmative action more than do middle class respondents. When race is brought into the picture, however, in Table 5.12*B*, the direction of the association changes. Among both blacks and whites, middle class respondents have a greater tendency to favor affirmative action than do working class respondents. The distorted view of the association between socioeconomic status and position on affirmative action in the aggregate results from the fact that blacks have an overwhelming tendency to be in the working class whereas whites in the sample fall primarily in the middle class, combined with the fact that blacks in the sample tend to have a more favorable view of affirmative action than do whites. Thus, the race variable distorts the association between socioeconomic status and position on affirmative action.

Suppressor Variables   Although elaboration usually begins with pairs of variables that are statistically associated in the aggregate and attempts to determine whether they can be "explained away" with other variables in the data set, sometimes the process works in the reverse. At times the apparent lack of association between two variables in the aggregate may conceal important associations between them within subsamples of the observations. Most commonly, two variables may be associated within subsamples but in different directions, with the net effect of cancelling each other out and showing no association in the aggregate. This possibility indicates the importance of elaborating associations beyond the bivariate stage even when anticipated associations do not materialize initially.

Table 5.13 illustrates the effect of a **suppressor** variable, again using hypothetical survey data. In the aggregate (*A*) no association is found between the response to an item on a tax increase and a housing tenure variable; 45 percent of all homeowners and 45 percent of all renters in the sample responded that they were in favor of a tax increase. Yet, when income of the respondent is taken into account (*B*) definite associations emerge between these two variables. For those in the lower income category, renters are seen to have a greater tendency to favor a tax increase while for those respondents in the upper income category, homeowners favored the idea more than renters. Thus, housing tenure is associated with position on a tax increase, but the association is specified in one direction for lower income respondents

Table 5.12. Position on affirmative action by socioeconomic status and race

A

By socioeconomic status

Position on affirmative action	Socioeconomic status		
	Working class	Middle class	Total
For	80 (73%)	60 (67%)	140 (70%)
Against	30 (27%)	30 (33%)	60 (30%)
Total	110 (100%)	90 (100%)	200 (100%)

B

By race and socioeconomic status

Position on affirmative action	Blacks			Whites		
	Working class	Middle class	Total	Working class	Middle class	Total
For	70 (78%)	10 (100%)	80 (80%)	10 (50%)	50 (63%)	60 (60%)
Against	20 (22%)	0 (0%)	20 (20%)	10 (50%)	30 (37%)	40 (40%)
Total	90 (100%)	10 (100%)	100 (100%)	20 (100%)	80 (100%)	100 (100%)

Table 5.13. Respondents favoring tax increase by housing tenure and income

A

All respondents

Position on tax increase	Housing tenure		
	Renters	Owners	Total
For	106 (45%)	74 (45%)	180 (45%)
Against	130 (55%)	90 (55%)	220 (55%)
Total	236 (100%)	164 (100%)	400 (100%)

B

Broken down by income

Position on tax increase	Low income			High income		
	Renters	Owners	Total	Renters	Owners	Total
For	96 (47%)	24 (25%)	120 (40%)	10 (31%)	50 (74%)	60 (60%)
Against	108 (53%)	72 (75%)	180 (60%)	22 (69%)	18 (26%)	40 (40%)
Total	204 (100%)	96 (100%)	300 (100%)	32 (100%)	68 (100%)	100 (100%)

and in the other direction for upper income respondents. In the aggregate, these associations are totally suppressed because of their conflicting directions.

Patterns of Elaboration

When control variables are introduced to further examine a bivariate association, the effect may be to find it replicated in the various subsamples created by the control variable, specified differently from subsample to subsample, washed out completely and nonexistent in the various subsamples, or having changed its basic nature when the control variable has been taken into account. Similarly, an association that was nonexistent in the aggregate may emerge within categories of the control variable. When we find that observed associations are altered when control variables are considered, we usually examine the way in which the control variable is associated with the original variables in order to complete the analysis and describe the overall pattern of relationships.

Independent Causation A study employing cross-sectional data analysis to examine the performance of fire departments across the country might be interested in determining whether one-way street patterns facilitate shorter response times to fire alarms. Suppose that data were collected on 175 fire departments in a sample of communities, 105 with predominantly one-way street patterns and 70 with predominantly two-way street patterns, and that the mean response time for the former was 4.6 minutes, but was 7.6 minutes for those with predominantly two-way patterns. In the aggregate the two variables are associated in a way that would tend to support the hypothesis that street pattern does make a difference in terms of response time to fires.

Now consider the competing explanation: the abovementioned association is a function of population density; higher density areas might tend to have more one-way street patterns, but they also tend to have fire stations located closer together, and this is the real reason why areas with one-way street patterns also have shorter response times. To examine this hypothesis we would cross-classify the observations by both density and predominant street pattern, and compare their mean average response times, as shown in Table 5.14A. Although density does make a difference with respect to response time, the 3-minute differential between one-way and two-way street patterns is evident for each level of density. Thus the competing hypothesis is ruled out, although density does seem to have a separate effect on response time.

To complete this particular aspect of the analysis, we would look at the crosstabulation of predominant street pattern and population

Table 5.14. Associations among mean response time to fires, predominant street pattern, and population density

A

Mean response time to fires
by predominant street pattern and population density
(no interaction)

	Street pattern		
Density	One-way	Two-way	Total
Low	3.5 (30)	6.5 (20)	4.7 (50)
Medium	4.5 (60)	7.5 (40)	5.7 (100)
High	7.0 (15)	10.0 (10)	8.2 (25)
Total	4.6 (105)	7.6 (70)	5.8 (175)

B

Predominant street pattern
by population density

	Density			
Street Pattern	Low	Medium	High	Total
One-way	30 (60%)	60 (60%)	15 ((60%)	105 (60%)
Two-way	20 (40%)	40 (40%)	10 (40%)	70 (40%)
Total	50 (100%)	100 (100%)	25 (100%)	175 (100%)

C

Mean response time to fires
by predominant street pattern and population density
(interaction)

	Street pattern		
Density	One-way	Two-way	Total
Low	4.0 (30)	5.5 (20)	4.6 (50)
Medium	5.0 (60)	7.5 (40)	6.0 (100)
High	6.0 (15)	11.0 (10)	8.0 (25)
Total	4.9 (105)	7.4 (70)	5.9 (175)

density, as shown in Table 5.14*B*. With an identical 60 percent of the communities in each density class having predominantly one-way street patterns, the two variables are seen not to be associated with each other. This explains how the density variable can be associated with average response time and yet not have any effect on the bivariate association between street pattern and response time. The pattern of associations that emerges from this analysis is termed **independent causation** and might be diagrammed as such:

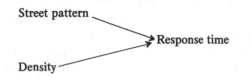

Two independent variables have separate effects on the dependent variable, and each of these two bivariate associations is replicated across the categories of the other independent variable. Because the two independent variables are themselves unassociated, neither bivariate association is washed out, suppressed, or distorted by virtue of the other variable.

In the example shown in Table 5.14*A*, it happens that there is no interaction between the two independent variables as they affect the dependent variable. The differential effect of street pattern is the same for all density levels, and vice versa. This is not necessarily the case in all patterns of independent causation, however. In Table 5.14*C*, the results have been altered slightly so that there is an interaction effect of street pattern and density on response time. Here the effect of street pattern is quite marginal for low density areas, where traffic is not congested in any event, but much more pronounced for high density areas. Nevertheless, as indicated by the subsample sizes in parentheses, the two independent variables are not associated and the pattern of independent causation still applies.

Causal Sequence   It sometimes works out that a third variable brought into the analysis will not exert a separate effect on the dependent variable, but will be associated with the two original variables in a causal sequence, describing a pattern of association in which one variable is seen to influence another, which in turn seems to influence the third, usually the dependent variable of primary interest.

Consider an analysis of the absentee rate of a sample of 600 employees in a department, 400 males and 200 females. On the average the males were found to have been absent 2 days over the past 3 months while the women were absent on the average of 4 days during the same period. Although this association might reflect some basic differences attributable to sex itself, it might also be a function of some other factor that is related to both sex and absenteeism. Suppose that income is suggested as such an explanatory factor and that in an attempt to control for income, the data shown in Table 5.15A are developed. The table shows that the mean absentee rate varies directly with income level and that within individual income categories, there is no difference in average days absent between men and women. Thus, the association between sex and absenteeism was found to be a spurious one that evaporated when income was taken in account.

Table 5.15B shows the crosstabs between sex and income. It shows clearly that the male employees have a much greater tendency to be in the highest income category whereas women have a much greater tendency to be in the lowest income group; 25 percent of both the men and women are in the middle income category. If this association reflects a causal relationship (based on education, career orientation, discrimination, etc.) between the two, it would be that sex affects income, not the other way around. Therefore we have identified (as far as we can go without experimental controls) a causal sequence in which sex influences income which in turn influences absenteeism. We would diagram this as follows:

$$Sex \rightarrow Income \nrightarrow Absenteeism$$

The slashed arrow from "Income" to "Absenteeism" indicates a negative association. Our interpretation of this would be that sex does influence days absent, but only as it works through differentials in

Table 5.15. Associations among absenteeism, sex, and income

A	Absenteeism[a] by sex and income		
Income	Male	Female	Total
$ 6,000–10,000	5.0	5.0	5.0
$10,000–15,000	3.0	3.0	3.0
$15,000 and above	1.0	1.0	1.0
Total	2.0	4.0	2.7

B	Income by sex		
Income	Male	Female	Total
$ 6,000–10,000	50 (0.125)	125 (0.625)	175 (0.29)
$10,000–15,000	100 (0.250)	50 (0.250)	150 (0.25)
$15,000 and above	250 (0.625)	25 (0.125)	275 (0.46)
Total	400 (1.00)	200 (1.00)	600 (1.00)

[a] Days absent in past 3 months

income, not because of any inherent differences between male and female employees. If in this example sex did have an effect on days absent apart from its relationship with income, then this would have been reflected in the comparison of means table in 5.15A. If, for example, within each income category, the mean average days absent for women were higher than that for men, we would conclude that there is an association between sex and absenteeism beyond the effects of income.

Antecedent Variables   The role played by the newly introduced variable will depend in part on which variables happen to be examined first. In the above example, the original bivariate association was that between sex and absenteeism. When income was brought into the analysis, it was found to be partly a function of sex, and the effect of sex on absenteeism washed out when income was controlled for. In that process, income was established as a **linking** variable, one that turned out to be useful in interpreting the association between sex and absenteeism.

If, on the other hand, we had started with the association between income and absenteeism, we would have found that the original association was replicated for both sexes. Sex, the new variable, would have been found to constitute an **antecedent** variable rather than one that linked income and absenteeism.

When we test for the spuriousness of an association on the basis that it is a function of some third variable that influences both of the original variables, we are testing to determine whether some antecedent variable can explain away the observed association. If so, the original association will disappear, or at least weaken, when we control for the antecedent variable.

Table 5.16A presents the association between the type of job training program participated in and the current job status of 150 former program participants. It shows that those who were in special skills programs have a much greater tendency to have obtained a job than those in general skills programs. The analyst finds that these data tend to support his hypothesis that the special skills programs are more suitable to the current labor market, but he also has the suspicion that this observed association could be a function of age rather than a real difference in program impacts. He therefore examines the same association controlling for age, as shown in Table 5.16B. The results show that the association between program type and present job status holds, indeed is stronger, when controlling for age, eliminating the age variable as the rival explanation.

Table 5.16. Job status of training program participants by program type and age

A

By program type

Job status	General	Specific	Total
Obtained job	29 (32%)	40 (67%)	69 (46%)
No job	61 (68%)	20 (33%)	81 (54%)
Total	90 (100%)	60 (100%)	150 (100%)
	(60%)	(40%)	

B

By program type and age

	Young			Medium			Older		
Job status	General	Specific	Total	General	Specific	Total	General	Specific	Total
Obtained job	16 (40%)	8 (80%)	24 (48%)	9 (30%)	14 (70%)	23 (46%)	4 (20%)	18 (60%)	22 (44%)
No job	24 (60%)	2 (20%)	26 (52%)	21 (70%)	6 (30%)	27 (54%)	16 (80%)	12 (40%)	28 (56%)
Total	40 (100%)	10 (100%)	50 (100%)	30 (100%)	20 (100%)	50 (100%)	20 (100%)	30 (100%)	50 (100%)
	(80%)	(20%)		(60%)	(40%)		(40%)	(60%)	

C

Percent securing jobs by program type and age

Age	Program type		
	General	Specific	Total
Young	40%	80%	48%
Medium	30%	70%	46%
Older	20%	60%	44%
Total	32%	67%	46%

Nevertheless, age is also found to be associated with program type (by comparing the percentages in parentheses below the column totals), but in a direction contrary to what was anticipated by the analyst's rival hypothesis. There is a definite tendency for younger participants to have participated in general programs and for older participants to have participated in special skills programs, negating the possibility that the reason for the better showing of specialized programs was attributable to the younger, more marketable, clientele.

Although the results in Table 5.16B show that program type is associated with present job status, controlling for age, they also indicate that age has an association with present job status, even when program type is controlled for. Among those in general skills programs, for example, 40 percent of the younger participants obtained jobs, 30 percent of the middle age group participants obtained jobs, and only 20 percent of the older participants did so. The same trend holds for all of those participating in specialized skills programs. Thus, both variables are seen to be associated with present job status, each controlling for the other.

This is perhaps best summarized in the comparison of percents table shown in Table 5.16C, which is facilitated by the fact that the dependent variable, present job status, is a dichotomy. It shows the percentages of program participants who presently have jobs, as grouped by both age and program type. For each program type, the percentage having jobs decreases as age increases, whereas for each age group, the percentage with jobs at present is greater for those in specialized programs than in general programs. (Inspection of this table will indicate that there is no peculiar interaction between the two independent variables, but this is not critical for the present argument.) It should also be noticed that the magnitude of differences in percents is much greater between the two program types (32 percent and 67 percent) than that among the three age groups (48 percent, 46 percent, and 44 percent).

Thus, interpreting the overall pattern of associations among these three variables, we find first that the original association between program type and present job status was not spurious; it held and was even strengthened when age was taken into account. Second, we find that age is associated with program type, with the younger individuals tending to participate more in the general programs. Here then we have a causal sequence in which age seems to influence program type, which in turn seems to influence present job status. Thus, the antecedent variable, age, did not explain away the association between program type and job status, but it is a part of the causal sequence.

In this problem, however, we have a variant of the causal sequence pattern, rather than the strictly linear pattern found in the previous problem dealing with sex, income, and absenteeism. In that problem, the first variable in the sequence, sex, was not found to be associated with the dependent variable when the linking variable, income, was accounted for. Here, however, we did find that when controlling for program type, age was still associated with present job status, although this association was weaker than that between program type and job status. Thus we have a variant of the causal sequence pattern in which the primary sequence (age to program type to job status) is supplemented by the additional influence of age on job status. This variant would be diagrammed as follows:

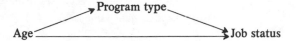

As a second example of the effect an antecedent variable might have, consider the analysis of highway patrol effects on accident rates on state highways, in which the underlying program logic indicates that there should be a negative association between the two; that as patrol levels go up, accident rates go down. To test this hypothesis, information is collected from a sample of 178 stretches of highway in the state, including data on patrol level and the number of recorded accidents per million vehicle miles. Collapsing the various levels of police patrol into two levels, designated high and low, and comparing the mean accident rates between the subsamples of roadways in these two groups indicates that there is a positive association between the two. The mean average number of accidents per million vehicle miles for the low patrol highways is 3.00, while that for the high patrol highways is 3.48. This could reflect an underlying causal relationship in direct contrast to the program logic, indicating that the program is dysfunctional, or the observed bivariate association might be a function of variation in traffic flow. It might be hypothesized that the observed positive association between patrol level and accident rates is a spurious one that results from the fact that most accidents occur on high traffic volume roads and that the higher levels of patrol are also assigned to these same roads.

Table 5.17A shows a comparison of mean accident rates on subsamples of roadways as grouped by both patrol level and traffic volume. It shows that accident rates have a linear positive association with traffic volume for both low patrol and high patrol level highways, thus establishing that traffic volume is definitely a relevant factor. However,

Table 5.17.   Associations among accidents, patrol level, and traffic flow

A	Accidents per 100 million vehicle miles by patrol level and traffic flow		
	Patrol level		
Traffic flow	Low	High	Total
Light	2.70	2.40	2.65
Intermediate	3.40	3.00	3.22
Heavy	4.20	3.90	3.93
Total	3.00	3.48	3.23

B	Traffic flow by patrol level		
	Patrol level		
Traffic flow	Low	High	Total
Light	60 (63%)	8 (10%)	68 (38%)
Intermediate	30 (32%)	25 (30%)	55 (31%)
Heavy	5 (5%)	50 (60%)	55 (31%)
Total	95 (100%)	83 (100%)	178 (100%)

the table also shows that patrol level is associated with accident rates, but in the opposite direction of their association in the aggregate. At each level of traffic volume, the mean accident rate for the high patrol level roads is less than that for the corresponding low patrol level roads, thus indicating that the data are consistent with the underlying program logic, once traffic volume is taken into account. Here, the antecedent variable, traffic volume, is acting as a distorter variable, whereas accident rates are negatively associated with patrol level within categories of traffic volume; in the aggregate this association is positive.

Traffic volume is distorting the effect of patrol level on accidents through its association with both patrol level and accidents. The association between traffic volume and accidents is seen in Table 5.17A, but examination of that between traffic volume and patrol level requires a crosstabulation between traffic flow and patrol level, as shown in Table 5.17B. This indicates a strong association between traffic flow and patrol level in the direction that was anticipated; the high patrol level roads also tend to be heavy traffic volume roads, while the low patrol level roads tend to be those with light traffic volumes.

The overall pattern of association exhibited in this problem would be a variation of the causal sequence that appeared in the previous problem. Traffic volume, the antecedent variable, is associated with both patrol level and accidents, its association with accident rates remaining valid when patrol level is controlled for. On the other hand, patrol level is associated with accident rate, when traffic volume is controlled for. Thus, this pattern of association would be diagrammed as follows (the slashed arrow from patrol to accidents indicates a negative association).

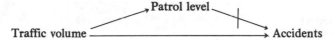

Traffic volume ——————————————————→ Accidents

SUMMARY

Examining statistical relationships among variables is the real guts of most statistical analysis. We are interested in looking at statistical associations as they may represent cause/effect relationships among program related variables, but we are limited in this regard by the confines of our data base. The validity of extending conclusions about statistical associations to real world causal relationships depends on the extent to which the data at hand provide fair comparisons that are not distorted by factors we are unable to take into account.

Bivariate associations are often misleading with strong statistical associations materializing spuriously as the result of the effect of some additional variable or, more dangerously, because of biases in the data base. Conversely, bivariate associations that are weak or nonexistent may be suppressed by failure to take other variables into account. The process of elaboration is an approach to test rival explanations and specify statistical relationships more precisely by bringing additional variables into the analysis. With this process, some associations may be explained away as a function of other variables, previously suppressed associations may emerge, distorted relationships may be straightened out, and apparent causal sequences may be identified; elaboration pushes the usefulness of statistical analysis to the limits of the available data. Yet, the worth of such statistical analysis in terms of shedding light on real world cause/effect patterns depends ultimately on the adequacy of the data base in the first place. Providing for this adequate and proper data base is the function of research design, as discussed in chapter 9.

REFERENCES

Loether, H. J., and D. G. McTavish. 1976. Descriptive and Inferential Statistics: An Introduction, pp. 119–202. Boston: Allyn & Bacon, Inc.

PRACTICE PROBLEMS FOR CHAPTER 5

1. The table below shows the mean average per capita amounts of state aid given to local governments in metropolitan and nonmetropolitan areas, by region.

Region	Metropolitan areas	Nonmetropolitan areas	Total
South	$26.69	$38.62	$32.29
North Central	36.00	48.03	40.89
Northeast	38.80	51.27	41.02
West	64.30	74.42	66.01
Total	$39.90	$46.92	$42.42

   a. Ignoring the breakdown by region, is there an association between state aid and metropolitan versus nonmetropolitan areas? Discuss.
   b. Does region seem to influence the amount of state aid and the difference in aid received by metropolitan and nonmetropolitan areas? Discuss.

2. The data in panels A and B of the table opposite show the present job status of former prisoners under three alternative types of release: direct release (no treatment), parole, and a halfway house program. Answer the following questions regarding the data in these tables. The purpose of the analysis is to examine the effects of the new halfway house program as compared with the traditional direct release and parole.

   a. Using the data in panel A, does the type of postrelease treatment program seem to have any effect on an ex-convict's employment possibilities? If such a relationship exists, describe the association.
   b. Examine the contingency table breaking the data down by type of crime in panel B. Is the type of crime committed by the ex-convicts associated with the type of postrelease treatment they received? (i.e., are the two independent variables associated?) If so, how?

A

Job status by type of postrelease treatment

Job status	Direct release	Parole	Halfway house program	Total
Obtained employment	30 (30%)	70 (35%)	25 (56%)	125 (36%)
Unemployed	70 (70%)	130 (65%)	20 (44%)	220 (64%)
Total	100 (100%) (0.29)	200 (100%) (0.58)	45 (100%) (0.13)	345 (100%) (1.0)

B

Job status by type of postrelease treatment and type of crime

Job status	Rape				Robbery				Auto theft			
	Direct release	Parole	Halfway house program	Total	Direct release	Parole	Halfway house program	Total	Direct release	Parole	Halfway house program	Total
Obtained employment	3 (9%)	5 (7%)	2 (17%)	10 (8%)	8 (23%)	14 (26%)	10 (59%)	32 (30%)	19 (59%)	51 (72%)	13 (81%)	83 (70%)
Unemployed	30 (91%)	70 (93%)	10 (83%)	110 (92%)	27 (77%)	40 (74%)	7 (41%)	74 (70%)	13 (41%)	20 (28%)	3 (19%)	36 (30%)
Total	33 (0.28)	75 (0.62)	12 (0.10)	120 (1.0)	35 (0.33)	54 (0.51)	17 (0.16)	106 (1.0)	32 (0.27)	71 (0.60)	16 (0.13)	119 (1.0)

c. Using the data in panel *B*, when controlling for the type of postrelease program received, does the offense for which the individuals were incarcerated seem to influence whether or not they can obtain employment? If such an association exists, describe its nature.

d. For the data in panel *B*, does the type of postrelease treatment received by the ex-convict seem to influence the possibility of employment, controlling for the type of crime for which he was convicted? Describe any associations you might find. Does this elaboration influence your conclusions about the worth of the halfway house program?

3. The table below shows the crosstabulation of a transit usage variable with an employment indicator as obtained through a telephone survey of 959 households in a community.

	Number of persons working 20 hours per week or more		
Transit usage	0	1 or more	Total
User households	102	184	286
Nonuser households	170	503	673
Total	272	687	959

a. Does transit usage by households seem to be contingent on whether or not there are people working 20 hours per week or more, and if so, how?

b. The tables below show these 959 households broken down further by whether or not they own automobiles. How do you interpret the association between transit usage and the employment variable, controlling for automobile ownership?

	No automobiles			Own automobiles		
	Employed workers			Employed workers		
Transit usage	0	1 or more	Total	0	1 or more	Total
User households	52	16	68	50	168	218
Nonuser house-holds	39	12	51	131	491	622
Total	91	28	119	181	659	840

   c. Controlling for the number of employed workers, does transit
       usage seem to be contingent on automobile ownership?
   d. Is there an association between automobile ownership and the
       number of employed workers? Assuming that the dominant
       direction of causality in such an association would run from
       employment to auto ownership, how would you summarize the
       overall pattern of associations among these three variables?
4. In an experiment designed to determine whether women could per-
    form sector patrol police duties as well as males, officers of both
    sexes were rated on a behaviorally anchored scale (from 10 = very
    poor to 80 = outstanding) by trained evaluators who observed their
    performance in various types of incidents. Panel A of the table on
    the next page shows the average ratings on 1,277 incidents for male
    and female officers, further broken down by the sex of the evaluator,
    for three types of incidents.

   a. Describe the main effects of the three independent variables:
       sex of officer, sex of evaluator, and type of incident.
   b. Looking in the aggregate at all three types of incidents taken to-
       gether, is there an interaction effect of sex of officer and sex of
       evaluator on performance ratings? Discuss.
   c. Controlling for the type of incident, do your findings in parts
       a and b above hold up or are they modified?
   d. Panel B shows the number of rateable incidents for male and
       female officers by sex of evaluator and type of incident. Are
       there any associations among these three variables? Within
       each type of incident, would you say that there was a fairly
       even assignment of male and female evaluators to male and fe-
       male officers?

Mean average performance rating by sex of officer, sex of evaluator, and type of incident

A

	Car stops			Family disturbance			Man with a gun			Total		
	Evaluator			Evaluator			Evaluator			Evaluator		
Sex of officer	Male	Female	Total	Male	Female	Total	Male	Female	Total	Male	Female	Total
Male	60	62	61.0	58	42	49.4	60	50	55.1	59.5	54.4	56.9
Female	66	80	71.9	54	65	59.3	64	70	67.1	62.0	73.3	67.1
Total	62.4	67.9	65.0	56.2	51.2	53.6	61.2	56.6	58.9	60.5	61.1	60.8

B

Sex of officer by sex of evaluator and type of incident

	Car stops			Family disturbance			Man with a gun			Total		
	Evaluator			Evaluator			Evaluator			Evaluator		
Sex of officer	Male	Female	Total	Male	Female	Total	Male	Female	Total	Male	Female	Total
Male	230	223	453	98	113	211	68	65	133	396	401	797
Female	150	110	260	82	76	158	30	32	62	262	218	480
Total	380	333	713	180	189	369	98	97	195	658	619	1,277

PROBABILITY FUNDAMENTALS

6

One of the fundamental concepts underlying much quantitative analysis, and one that needlessly mystifies many students upon first encounter, is probability. For our purposes, **probability** can be defined as an informed estimate of the likelihood of some specified occurrence in a structured trial or experiment, or as the theoretical relative frequency of occurrence of a certain kind of event in the long run. Probability concepts are basic to an understanding of inferential statistical techniques and also serve as an important aid to structuring decision situations.

In common parlance the word probability is used in a number of ways, as in statements such as "I'll probably go to the basketball game tomorrow night" or "Who murdered Jones? It was probably his wife," but in statistics we are not interested in such circumstances involving single events or past occurrences about which we lack complete information. Statistical probabilities are indications of likelihoods over a large number of cases or a total population, often a hypothetical population, and are based on observations or theories of long run patterns. For example, if we observe that of all the initial contacts made by a social service agency the proportion that results in a follow-up visit to the agency within 1 week is 0.35, and if nothing changes with respect to the contact strategy or the targeted groups contacted, we can say that the probability that the next initial contact will produce a follow-up visit within 1 week is 0.35. This assumes that we have no evidence that would lead us to believe otherwise, in effect that the rate of follow-ups generated by future initial contacts will continue to follow the pattern set by past initial contacts. If, on the other hand, we have reason to believe that the initial contacts are now being made in areas where those contacted are less receptive to the agency and its services, we would revise our probability downward. In this case, the probability would be different because the proportion of follow-up visits would be changing. The important thing to remember about probabilities is that they are directly governed by proportions: probabilities are proportions in the long run.

PROBABILITY CONCEPTS

Statistical probabilities are usually thought of in terms of the likelihood of some occurrence in a fair trial or random experiment. A **random experiment** or fair trial in this sense can be defined as a controlled inquiry in which pure chance permits more than one possible outcome. It might consist of flipping a coin, an observation of some naturally occurring phenomenon in the world, or the selection of an individual or group of individuals from a larger group. The common characteristic of all these types of experiments is that in each repetition of the experiment, one of the possible outcomes will occur as a result of chance effect.

The set of all possible outcomes of an experiment is termed the **sample space**. Identification of the sample space is important because probabilities are indicators of relative likelihood only with reference to a given experiment and sample space. In problems or applications involving probabilities, interest centers on an event or a number of events. An **event** is a specified single outcome or combination of outcomes that can result from a given experiment. If in one trial the designated outcome or event occurs, it is a **success**; if not the event is a **failure**. Over a large number of repeated trials, which must be independent of each other but perfectly identical in terms of the procedures used to conduct the experiment, the proportion of successes, however defined, can be calculated. This proportion, then, is the probability of the occurrence of the specified event in any single trial. In the example cited above involving initial contacts and follow-up visits to the agency, the outcomes might be defined as 1) follow-up visit within 1 week, 2) follow-up visit in the 2nd week, and 3) no follow-up in the first 2 weeks. The event of interest was specified as 1) a follow-up visit within 1 week, and the experiment in this case was making an initial contact and observing the outcome in the next 2 weeks.

Although probabilities are often illustrated in introductory texts with examples of shooting dice or choosing cards, they can be understood just as easily in terms of sampling experiments involving the random selection of individual cases from a larger population. This will also lead us into the discussion of sampling principles in chapter 8. A **random selection** is one in which each individual case in the population has an even chance (or probability) of being chosen, as would be the case, for example, if each individual is assigned a number and then one number is selected from a table of random numbers such as that contained in appendix Table A-2. It constitutes a random experiment as defined in this chapter because the outcome of such a random selection is a result of pure chance.

Consider an English as a Second Language (ESL) program run by a school system in which 200 adults are enrolled. If one person is to be selected at random, the probability that any given individual will be selected is 0.005, obtained from the proportion (1/200) that individual constitutes of the total enrollment. Now suppose that of this population of 200 adults, 120 or 60 percent are native Spanish speakers and that the remaining 80 adults or 40 percent are non-Spanish, non-English native speakers. If an individual is chosen from this group at random, then, the probability of choosing a Spanish speaker is 0.6. Notice that we will actually obtain either a Spanish speaker or a non-Spanish speaker, not someone we would classify as a 60 percent Spanish speaker. The probability of 0.6 means that there are 6 chances out of 10 that the person we choose will be a native Spanish speaker, and that if we repeat this experiment many times we would expect that of all the individuals selected the proportion of Spanish speakers would approximate 60 percent. Note that in this example the possible outcomes are 1) Spanish speaker and 2) other native language; the event is the selection of a Spanish speaker, and the experiment is the random selection of an individual from the program's enrollment.

To understand why the probability of randomly selecting a Spanish speaker in this example is 0.6, it is useful to picture what might happen if we made a number of successive random selections from the same population and looked at the proportion of Spanish speakers in the sample that accumulates, as illustrated in Figure 6.1. We are talking here about sampling with replacement, with the individual who is chosen in one selection being put back into the population before the next selection, so that the circumstances of each trial are identical, the random selection of one individual from the same population of 200 program participants. With only a few trials, the proportion of Spanish speakers in the accumulating sample may deviate substantially from 0.6 and will fluctuate considerably with additional selections, moving above and below 0.6. With more trials the magnitude of these fluctuations decreases markedly as each additional selection has less relative impact on the overall proportion, and the trend in the variation of the proportion of Spanish speakers is concentrated more narrowly on 0.6.

With additional trials the trend smooths out even more and hones in precisely at 0.6; this is the **limit**, the point at which the fluctuating proportion of successful events will finally settle, given a sufficiently large number of trials. The limit, in turn, defines the probability of an

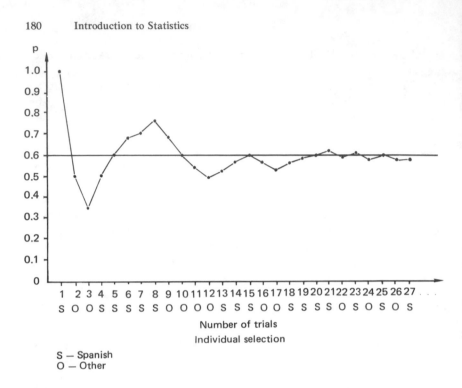

Figure 6.1.   Accumulating proportions of Spanish speakers chosen in random selections.

event occurring in a single trial. Note that in this example using sampling with replacement, an infinite number of trials can be conducted since the population of 200 adults will never be exhausted. The proportion of events may not approach the limit of 0.6 until hundreds of trials have been completed. When 200 trials have been conducted, it may well be that not all individuals have been selected in a trial; some may have been selected more than once and some not at all, and the proportion of Spanish speakers may not equal 0.6. It is even conceivable that at the end of 200 trials, 200 non-Spanish speakers and no Spanish speakers will have been selected, but with more trials the proportion of Spanish speakers will eventually approximate 0.6.

We do not really have any a priori logic to explain the tendency of a proportion of events to approach the limit with a large number of trials; it is not a logical necessity. Rather, it has been observed to happen this way consistently, it seems "natural" that this would be the case, and we have no reason to question the assumption that it will always pertain. This tendency follows the **law of large numbers**, which states that in the long run over a large number of trials or selections the proportion of various outcomes will "even out" according to their relative frequencies in the set of cases or items serving as the basis of the experiment.

It should be clearly understood that each successive trial in a series such as that described in the example above is independent of the trials that come before and after it. The probability of a specified event occurring does not change from trial to trial. The law of large numbers, sometimes referred to as the law of averages, cannot be interpreted in the short run; as shown in Figure 6.1, many short series of trials will not approximate the limit. Over the long run, however, the proportion of events does gravitate toward the limit, which in turn governs the probability of obtaining an event in a single trial. Thus, probabilities are proportions in the long run.

Probability Interpretations

Probability theory is a very abstract subject, and there is no single all-encompassing interpretation of what probability means; the word itself can only be defined in terms of primitive concepts such as "chance effect." However, it is a convenience that probabilities can be applied to practical problems and manipulated in ways that produce useful information, even in the absence of a clear definition. Mathematical probabilities are simply numbers assigned to outcomes in a sample space, but given their utility on an operational level, the question of how probabilities in a given problem are assigned in the first place is paramount.

One basis for assigning probabilities is past observation of the relative frequencies with which the outcomes in question have occurred. Such **experiential probabilities** or **objective probabilities** are very attractive in terms of providing realistic assessments of relative likelihoods, if the experience from which the relative frequencies are drawn conforms to the present circumstances to which probabilities are being assigned. The question is always whether or not the relative frequencies are appropriate for the situation at hand. In evaluating alternative arrangements for dealing with applications for entry visas to the U.S., for example, a consular officer may wish to know the probability that in any given week at least one applicant will require special considerations beyond the usual procedure for processing visas. He may look at the number of such special cases over the past month as a proportion of the total number of applicants, and on the basis of this relative frequency compute the desired probability. However, the question remains whether the experience over the past month is typical of the population of visa applicants in general; if not, the probabilities so derived may not be valid indicators of the relative likelihood of the event of interest. Perhaps basing the probabilities on the relative frequencies occurring over a year would give us greater confidence, but even so, we face the problem that the proportion of special cases may be increasing or decreasing over time.

A somewhat different notion of probability is based on the idea that some probabilities can be determined on the basis of self-evident reasoning, without requiring any previous experience to indicate relative frequencies. Such **a priori probabilities** can be easily derived whenever it is assumed that all the outcomes in the sample space are equally likely to occur. When all possible outcomes have an equal likelihood, the probability of a single outcome is one divided by the total number of outcomes. This was really the basis for the determination that the probability of selecting a given individual at random from a population of 200 was 0.005, because, by definition, a random selection is one in which each individual has an equal likelihood of being chosen.

The difficulty in using the a priori approach is that it is not always easy to be sure which outcomes are equally probable. For example, a manager of a transit system may be interested to know the probability that the next engine breakdown will occur in bus #112. If all the buses in his fleet are the same model, have been in service for the same amount of time, and all have roughly the same mileage, he may assume that the probability that the next breakdown will involve bus #112 is one divided by the number of buses in the fleet. However, if experience shows that some buses have had very few breakdowns whereas others are really "lemons," this a priori probability would not be appropriate.

A third basis for assigning probabilities to possible outcomes is judgment or intuition. In the face of a lack of experience with relative frequencies or a sound basis for developing a priori probabilities, an analyst might assign probabilities on the basis of his general familiarity with the subject or a hunch in order to get a dimension on a problem and its resulting implications. In fact, people employ such **subjective probabilities**, involving a degree of personal belief, at least implicitly in approaching their everyday problems. It is questionable whether these judgmental probabilities are statistical probabilities or not. They might be viewed as one-time occurrences that are not subject to statistical analysis, or alternatively as complex problems about which so little is known that there is simply no basis at present for assigning relative frequency or a priori probabilities. Nevertheless, although subjective probabilities may not always have a clear correspondence to proportions in the long run, they can still be manipulated and interpreted the same as other probabilities at an operational level. For example, in considering whether or not to devise a contingency plan for implementing a new program strategy, a manager will have to take into account all financial constraints. Suppose that in part these constraints are dependent on the continuing expenditure patterns of a related program and the perceived success of that program. To help structure his own decision, the manager may try to investigate present and future trends in that related program from a wide variety of sources, and on the basis of that intelligence, formulate an estimate of the probability that expenditures in the program will level off as opposed to continuing to increase. Using this probability, the manager can develop a much clearer scenario for the implications in terms of his own program, but his analysis can only be as valid as the assumed probabilities underlying it.

PROBABILITY THEOREMS

There are a number of properties of mathematical probabilities that are useful in interpreting and manipulating them. As might already be apparent at this point, for example, probabilities range from 0 to 1, with 0 representing the complete absence of likelihood of an event occurring, and 1 indicating the complete likelihood of its occurring. If an event is defined as including all possible outcomes, its probability is 1, while an event defined as excluding all possible outcomes would have a 0 probability of occurring. If an event is specified as consisting of any subset of all possible outcomes, it will have a probability of greater than 0 and less than 1. Because a probability of 1 represents the condition that the occurrence of an event is a certainty and because an event specified to include all possible outcomes has a probability of 1, it follows that the sum of the probabilities of all possible outcomes equals 1:

$$P_1 + P_2 + P_3 + \cdots P_K = 1$$

This property of probabilities is illustrated by Table 6.1, which shows the 200 adults enrolled in the ESL program mentioned above as broken down by native language and whether or not they have had any previous training or experience in English. In parentheses are shown the proportions of each subgroup, which can also be interpreted as the probabilities that an individual selected at random from among the

Table 6.1.   Participants in an English as a Second Language program by native language and background in English

English background	Native language					
	Spanish		Other		Total	
	N	p	N	p	N	p
No English	90	(0.45)	48	(0.24)	138	(0.69)
Some English	30	(0.15)	32	(0.16)	62	(0.31)
Total	120	(0.60)	80	(0.40)	200	(1.00)

total 200 enrollees would fall into the respective subgroups. The probabilities of the four subcells of the table sum to 1.

Addition Rules

It is sometimes useful to perform arithmetic operations on probabilities, and two such procedures are presented here. First, the **addition rule** states that the probability of one event *or* another event is the sum of their individual probabilities, assuming that the two events are mutually exclusive:

$$P(A \text{ or } B) = P(A) + P(B)$$

If event A is specified as the random selection of an individual who has no English background and speaks Spanish, and B is defined as the random selection of someone with no English background whose native language is other than Spanish, the probability of either A or B occurring in a random selection is the sum of their separate probabilities, or 0.69, the probability of selecting any individual with no English background.

$$P(A \text{ or } B) = P(A) + P(B)$$
$$= 0.45 + 0.24$$
$$= 0.69$$

If the events postulated are overlapping rather than mutually exclusive, the addition rule is somewhat different. If events A and B are two subsets of outcomes that partially overlap, the probability of obtaining A or B (either A or B or both) is the sum of the probability of A and the probability of B minus the probability of A and B (both A and

B). For example, specify A as the drawing of a Spanish speaker and B as the selection of an individual with no background in English. The probability of randomly selecting an individual who fits into one or both of these categories is computed as:

$$P(A \text{ or } B) = P(A) + P(B) - P(A \text{ and } B)$$
$$= 0.60 + 0.69 - 0.45$$
$$= 0.84$$

The validity of this computation can be checked by looking at the probability of *not* obtaining A or B, in this case selecting an individual whose native language is other than Spanish and who has some previous experience with English. From Table 6.1 we can see that this probability of neither A nor B is 0.16, the complement of 0.84.

Multiplication Rules

The probability of simultaneously obtaining two events that are not mutually exclusive also depends on their separate probabilities. The **general multiplication rule** states that the probability of A and B (read both A and B or the **joint probability** of A and B) is the probability of A times the probability of B given A, written as:

$$P(A \text{ and } B) = P(A) \cdot P(B/A)$$

The probability of B given A refers to the probability of selecting an individual fitting into the category B, given the subset of all individuals in category A to choose from.

Specify A as the selection of a Spanish speaker and event B as the drawing of someone who has no English background. What is the probability of obtaining an individual who fits into both categories? First we need to know the probability of selecting someone with no English background, given that we will select a Spanish speaker. Of the 120 Spanish speakers shown in Table 6.1, 90 have no background in English; therefore, the probability of B/A is 90 divided by 120, or 0.75. Thus,

$$P(A \text{ and } B) = P(A) \cdot P(B/A)$$
$$= 0.60 \cdot 0.75$$
$$= 0.45$$

In this example, the probability of selecting a person with no English background can be said to be **contingent** on native language, because it varies between the native language categories. As we have seen, the probability of selecting a person with no English background from among the Spanish speakers is 0.75. Given a non-Spanish language speaker, the probability of having no English background is (48 ÷ 80) or 0.60, whereas for the total 200 enrollees the probability of selecting a person with no English background is 0.69. Thus, the probability of drawing a Spanish speaker is not **independent** of the probability of drawing a person with no background in English.

When the probabilities of two events are *not* independent, **conditional probabilities,** such as the probability of *B* given *A*, are not equal to their corresponding marginal probabilities, in this case the probability of *B* with or without *A*. In such instances, interest sometimes focuses on computing conditional probabilities, based on a knowledge of joint and marginal probabilities. The **conditional probability rule** states that the probability of *B* given *A* equals the joint probability of *A* and *B* divided by the probability of *A* itself, or

$$P(B/A) = \frac{P(A \text{ and } B)}{P(A)}$$

When two probabilities are independent, the probability of one given the other is, by definition, equal to the probability of the first regardless of the other. In such cases the **special multiplication rule** can be used to compute joint probabilities. It states that if *A* and *B* are independent events, the probability of *A* and *B* equals the probability of *A* times that of *B*:

$$P(A \text{ and } B) = P(A) \cdot P(B)$$

The special multiplication rule is often useful in considering the joint probability of two events arising from separate sources or experiments. Let us return to the bus breakdown problem for an illustration. Suppose that the manager of a large transit system is very concerned about the probability that a bus in service will break down and be stranded, because of the lack of a relief driver to take a back-up bus to the site of the breakdown. Suppose that on the basis of past experience he knows that the probability of a breakdown during off-peak hours is 0.4, and that from the drivers' schedule he knows that a relief driver is available 75 percent of the time during those hours. The probability that a relief driver will not be available is thus 0.25. Assuming that these two events are independent, then, he can compute the joint probability of a bus breakdown occurring when no relief driver is available as the product of their two separate probabilities as follows:

$$P(A \text{ and } B) = P(A) \cdot P(B)$$
$$= 0.4 \cdot 0.25$$
$$= 0.1$$

Thus, the probability of a bus being stranded sometime during the off-peak hours of a day is 0.1. On this basis the manager would have to de-

cide whether to accept this probability or to alter schedules or maintenance policies in order to reduce it.

Combinatorial Rules

In working with probabilities it is sometimes useful to determine the
number of sequences or groupings that can be arranged from a given
set of items. Whereas knowledge of the number of such sequences or
groupings may be useful for a number of purposes, in regard to probabilities, they are used to determine the number of all possible outcomes
of a given experiment. The two rules briefly presented in this section do
not involve manipulations of probabilities themselves, but rather of elements or items that may define outcomes.

First, we may be concerned with ordered arrangements, the number of ways in which a given number of elements can be arranged in a
sequence. Such **permutations** might involve the order in which individuals are observed, the order in which program treatments are exposed
to individuals, or the rank order of individuals on some measure. The
number of possible sequences of a number of individuals is that number **factorial**, the number times itself minus 1, times itself minus 2, etc.
Thus, three individuals can be arranged in six possible sequences
$(6 = 3 \cdot 2 \cdot 1)$ as follows: *ABC, ACB, BCA, BAC, CAB, CBA.*

If we are interested in the number of permutations of a number of
items to be selected from a larger pool of items, for example, the ordered arrangements of n elements taken r at a time, we use the **permutation rule**, which states:

$$P(n, r) = \frac{n!}{(n - r)!}$$

Thus, the number of permutations of 10 elements taken 4 at a time
(10!/6!) equals 5,040.

In other situations the number of possible **combinations**, selections
of groups of items regardless of order, is needed. For example, we
might be interested to know the number of samples of size 12 that can
be selected from a population of size 20. Using the formula for combinations,

$$\binom{n}{r} = \frac{n!}{(n - r)! \, r!}$$

we would have

$$\frac{20!}{8! \, 12!}$$

By cancelling, this reduces to

$$\frac{20 \cdot 19 \cdot 18 \cdot 17 \cdot 16 \cdot 15 \cdot 14 \cdot 13}{8 \cdot 7 \cdot 6 \cdot 5 \cdot 4 \cdot 3 \cdot 2 \cdot 1}$$

or

$$\frac{5,079,110,400}{40,320} = 125,970$$

Thus, the experiment of selecting a sample of size 12 from a population of 20 individual items would have 125,970 possible outcomes.

PROBABILITY DISTRIBUTIONS

As stated above, the set of all possible outcomes in a probability oriented experiment is referred to as the sample space. If probabilities are assigned to each of the outcomes in a sample space, the result is termed a **probability distribution.** A probability distribution is not an empirical distribution of the numbers of cases taking on different values; rather, it is an indication of the likelihood that a selected case will fall into each different category (outcome) in the distribution. Another way of defining it is that a probability distribution is the relative frequency distribution of the results of an indefinitely large number of repetitions of a specified experiment or trial.

The normal distribution discussed in chapter 4 is best thought of as a probability distribution. Although some empirical data may approximate a normal distribution and thus facilitate the computation of the proportion (or probability) of cases falling in different portions of the distribution, this is not its primary application. As is seen in chapter 7, this use of the normal probability distribution provides the basis for some inferential statistical techniques. Other inferential techniques are based on other known probability distributions in drawing conclusions about a population based on sample data.

Still other probability distributions are useful, not as the basis of formal inferential techniques, but rather because they represent the relative frequencies of the values taken on in some continuing process. The Poisson and exponential distributions are usually used in this way. Their utility stems from the fact that they describe the distribution of values in a sample taken from some continuing operation of that process. The Poisson and exponential distributions often describe variables that are indicators of workloads or demands for a service, and thus they are useful in analyzing the consequences of alternative strategies for meeting these workloads or demands.

Poisson Distribution

The Poisson distribution is a unimodal distribution that is highly skewed to the right, as illustrated in Figure 6.2. It often characterizes the number of arrivals in a waiting line or the number of cases to be processed that are initiated in specified time periods. It is a discrete

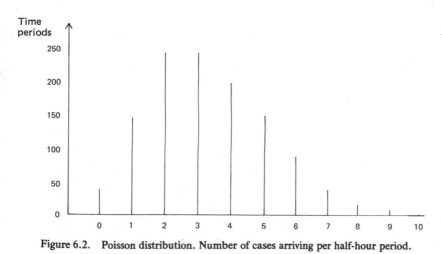

Figure 6.2.   Poisson distribution. Number of cases arriving per half-hour period.

distribution in which the values taken on can be 0 or any whole number; the unit of analysis or case is usually some time period. For example, the distribution shown in Figure 6.2 represents the number of clients arriving at an employment security office per half-hour for each of 1,000 half-hour periods.

The standard deviation of the Poisson distribution equals the square root of the mean. Knowing the mean of a Poisson distribution, then, will enable one to determine the relative frequency or probability that a given number of occurrences will happen in a time period. Table A-4 in the appendix shows such relative frequencies or probabilities for a number of Poisson distributions. Notice that although the values in the distribution include only 0 and whole numbers, the mean average is not limited to these numbers. Poisson distributions are used primarily in operations research techniques to study queuing type problems, which address such questions as the probability of a new arrival not having to wait for service, the average number of cases waiting to be serviced, or the average waiting time before being serviced.

Exponential Distribution

The exponential distribution is a continuous distribution that can take on any value from 0 to plus infinity and is very highly skewed to the right. It is illustrated in Figure 6.3. The exponential decay distribution is characterized by fewer cases taking on larger values, and is often approximated by empirical data on the length of the life of some manufactured part or the time required to serve a client or process a case. Because of the high degree of skewness, only about 37 percent of the cases

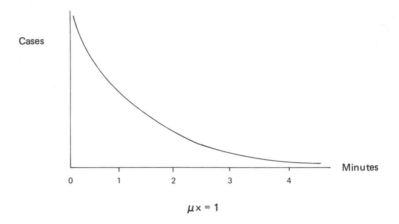

$$\mu x = 1$$

Figure 6.3.   Exponential distribution.

in an exponential distribution take on a value greater than the mean, while the majority are less than the mean. If the time required to dispose of a certain type of case follows an exponential distribution, for example, there would be some cases whose required time greatly exceeds the mean average required time, but the relative frequency, or probability, of such cases would be small. The standard deviation of an exponential distribution is equal to the mean.

Knowing the mean average of an exponential distribution (μx), one can determine the proportion of cases or the probability that a case will take on any value greater than a single specified value by dividing the value of X_i by the mean ($X_i/\mu x$) and taking the quotient into Table A-5 in the appendix. For example, if the mean average time required to dispose of a case is 10 minutes and the distribution of the required time is exponential, the probability that a case will require 5 minutes or more is 0.607, the probability of a case taking 15 minutes or more is 0.223, and the probability that a case will take 20 minutes or longer is 0.135.

Use of the properties of the exponential distribution is often made in conjunction with the Poisson distribution in waiting line problems. The latter might describe the pattern of arrivals whereas the former might characterize the time required to deal with them. For a brief introduction to this methodology, consider the operation of a complaints desk in an employment security agency on check-validation days. Assume that the number of individuals arriving at the desk per hour has a mean of 3 ($\mu n = 3$) and follows a Poisson distribution, and that the length of time it takes to deal with each complaint follows an exponential distribution with a mean of 12 minutes ($\mu s = 12$ minutes or 0.2 hours). If these two probability distributions are independent, it can be shown that on the average the complaints desk will be busy 0.6 hours ($3 \cdot 0.2$) or 36 minutes per hour. This figure, 0.6, is called the **utilization factor**; if it is greater than 1 the waiting line will continue to build up because complaints could not be handled as quickly as they arrive.

The utilization factor also represents the probability that an individual will face some waiting time between his arrival and the time the complaints' officer can talk with him. Thus, the probability of no wait can be computed as:

$$P \text{ (no wait)} = 1 - (\mu n)(\mu s)$$
$$= 1 - (3)(0.2)$$
$$= 0.4$$

Furthermore, the average length of the waiting line and the average waiting time can be easily determined. In our example, the **mean average length** of the waiting line would be given by:

$$\frac{1}{1 - \mu n \mu s} = \frac{1}{0.4} = 2.5$$

Thus, the average length of the waiting line, which will change from time to time, is 2.5 individuals. The **average waiting time** of arrivals who must wait is:

$$\frac{\mu s}{1 - \mu n \mu s} = \frac{0.2}{0.4} = 0.5 \text{ hours}$$

or 30 minutes. On the basis of this type of analysis, management might consider the merits of improving service at the complaints desk, for example by assigning two officers to the desk on check-validation days or by shifting a second employee to the desk whenever there are two or more people in the line.

EXPECTED VALUES

One concept that is closely linked to probability and reappears in subsequent chapters is that of expected values. An **expected value** is the average value of a statistic resulting from repeated trials, given a set of probabilities. Put another way, the expected value of X, written $E(x)$, is the mean of the probability distribution of X. That is, the expected value of a statistic is the sum of the products of the value of that statistic for each possible outcome times the probability of that outcome. If X equals the value of the statistic:

$$E(x) = \Sigma XP(X)$$

For example, if 60 percent of a given population are males, the expected value of the proportion of males in a random sample taken from that population is 0.60. This is shown for a population of five (three males and two females) and a random sample of two in Table 6.2. Of the 10 possible samples (outcomes) three would produce a proportion of males of 1.0, six of 0.5, and one proportion of zero. If these frequencies are transformed into relative frequencies or probabilities and multiplied by their respective proportions of males, the resulting expected value of this statistic, proportion of males in a random sample, is 0.60.

A less obvious, and more useful, example of expected value would be a comparison of the cost of correcting errors in processed data on a program's newly registered participants. The first method involves preverification of the data for each case and making any necessary corrections before the data are fed into a computer. The second method is to put the data into the computer without verifying beforehand, verifying the data from a computer printout, and then making any necessary corrections. The costs of both methods for cases that do and do not require corrections are shown in Table 6.3. Preverification is more costly for cases that do not require corrections but much less costly for those that do require corrections.

Given this reversal in cost advantage, the preferable method will depend on the probabilities of cases with and without errors. In the

Table 6.2.   Expected value of the proportion of males in a random sample of two[a]

Sample	N	p (males)	P
MM	3	1	0.3
MF	6	0.5	0.6
FF	1	0	0.1

$$\begin{aligned} E(p) &= \Sigma pP(p) \\ &= 0.3(1) + 0.6(.5) + 0.1(0) \\ &= 0.3 + 0.3 + 0 \\ &= 0.6 \end{aligned}$$

[a] Population: M M M F F $P(M) = 0.60$
Samples: MM, MM, MF, MF, MM, MF, MF, MF, MF, FF

Table 6.3. Expected values of costs of making corrections, with two methods

| Method | Error status of data cards | | E (cost) |
	No errors ($P = 0.9$)	Errors ($P = 0.1$)	
A. Preverification	$0.40	$0.50	$0.41
B. Computer verification	$0.05	$3.00	$0.345

$$\text{Method A: } E \text{ (cost)} = 0.9(0.40) + 0.1(0.50)$$
$$= 0.36 + 0.05$$
$$= 0.41$$
$$\text{Method B: } E \text{ (cost)} = 0.9(0.05) + 0.1(3.00)$$
$$= 0.045 + 0.30$$
$$= 0.345$$

example, it is assumed that the probability that the case will be error-free is 0.9 and the probability that the case will have errors requiring corrections is 0.1. Thus, for the preverification method the expected value of the cost of making corrections is $0.41 while that for the second method is $0.345. Everything else being equal, then, the expected values would indicate that the computer verification is the low cost method. If the probability of no errors were 0.8 instead of 0.9, however, the conclusion would have been the opposite; the expected value of the cost of preverification would be $0.42 while that for computer verification would be $0.64 (calculations not shown).

The expected value is our best prediction of the average value of the statistic in question over a number of trials, given a probability distribution; it may or may not be obtained over a few actual trials because probabilities are not necessarily adhered to in the short run. With a sufficiently large number of trials, however, actual values should approach expected values. Notice that the results of any one trial may not possibly match the expected value. In the above example, the expected value for the cost of preverification was $0.41, whereas an actual case would cost either $0.40 or $0.50 depending on whether it required corrections. Expected values are not predictions of the value for the next single case, but rather an estimate of the average value over a number of cases.

SUMMARY

As discussed in this chapter, probabilities are indicators of relative likelihood that have a number of uses. To the extent that the probabilities assigned to various outcomes are valid, whether determined on a relative frequency, a priori, or judgmental basis, they can be manipulated mathematically and interpreted so as to have useful applications for a number of practical problems. This chapter has provided some insight into how probabilities are used in operations research and statistical decision-making techniques; for a fuller introduction to these kinds of methods the reader should consult some of the texts listed under References. Apart from these kinds of applications, probability is also the underlying basis of inferential statistics, which are introduced in chapter 7.

REFERENCES

Hoel, P. G., and R. J. Jessen. 1971. Basic Statistics for Business and Economics. New York: John Wiley & Sons, Inc.

Loether, H. J., and D. G. McTavish. 1976. Descriptive and Inferential Statistics: An Introduction. Boston: Allyn & Bacon, Inc.

Neter, J., and W. Wasserman. 1966. Fundamental Statistics for Business and Economics. Boston: Allyn & Bacon, Inc.

PRACTICE PROBLEMS FOR CHAPTER 6

1. The number of overnight visitors per night in a state park follows a normal distribution with a mean of 600 and a standard deviation of 150, and eight attendants are scheduled to be on duty each night during the park's open season. The park supervisor has found that the proportion of nights when an attendant is absent without replacement is 0.30 and he is concerned about violating the departmental regulation that there be at least one attendant on duty for each 100 overnight visitors. Assuming that the number of visitors and the number of attendants absent are independent events, what is the probability that on any given night there will be more than 700 overnight visitors and only 7 attendants?

2. An economic analysis of a school system's proposed technical-vocational program is based partly on assumptions about the number of students who would choose this curriculum rather than the regular academic program. The analysts have projected ratios of the program's dollar benefits to operating costs (benefit/cost ratios) for three assumed levels of enrollment as follows.

Enrollment	Benefit/cost ratio	P
3,000	0.70	0.6
3,800	1.10	0.3
4,600	1.30	0.1

The third column in the above table shows the probabilities that have been assigned to each of these three outcome states based on experience in other school districts. Given this set of probabilities, what is the expected value of the technical-vocational program's benefit/cost ratio?

INTRODUCTION TO INFERENTIAL STATISTICS

7

The descriptive statistics discussed in chapter 4 provide summary measures of the cases for which information is included in a data set, but the bulk of statistical techniques involve the use of inductive procedures to extend conclusions beyond the cases immediately at hand. **Inferential statistics** use probabilities to draw conclusions about a population on the basis of evidence from a sample. They are inferential and inductive in the sense of leading to generalizations about a total population from a limited number of cases.

Almost invariably, our research interests concern a whole population, the total number of cases fitting a given classification such as the total number of participants in a given program, the total number of incidents of a given type occurring in connection with a program's operation, or the total number of projects administered by a program. Ideally, we might prefer to obtain the appropriate measures for all the cases in the population of interest and proceed with analysis on the basis of this complete information. We would still be faced by problems of valid measurement and research design, but at least we would be certain of frequency distribution and descriptive measures for the complete population. However, data collection is frequently the most costly portion of a research project, and with large populations time and effort constraints often limit actual observation and data gathering to a small fraction of cases, or **sample**, from the total population.

Given the need to rely on a sample, the most useful type would be a **representative** sample, one whose makeup represents a good cross-section of the population with respect to the variables of critical interest. We could then conclude that because the sample is truly representative, what we find to be true of the sample is also true of the population. With a sample size of a few cases or more drawn from a larger population, there are many possible samples, each unique in its individual makeup. Some of these will be highly representative of the population, some less representative, and some very unrepresentative. It should also be noted that a sample can be representative in terms of some variables and not others. Although a representative sample obviously provides the most accurate information about the population, we are rarely, if ever, in a position to determine whether the sample we are working with is representative in terms of the variables we are concerned with.

Thus, we have two options in extending conclusions from a sample to the population: 1) assume that the sample is representative and make inferences on blind faith, or 2) use probabilities to draw inferences based on the likelihood of obtaining a sample by chance if certain stated assumptions hold true. The advantage of a random sampling process is that it enables us to follow the second approach, thereby making informed inferences to the population.

The population characteristics in which we are interested are commonly referred to as **parameters**, and the corresponding characteristics of the sample are called **statistics**. Parameters include such population measures as means, medians, proportions, standard deviations, and variances. They are fixed values but usually unknowns, whereas their corresponding statistics can be computed for a given sample but vary from sample to sample. We often calculate sample statistics as our best single point estimates of population parameters.

The chapters in the first section of this book were concerned in general terms with the development and testing of program-related hypotheses. Research often begins with the formulation of **general hypotheses** expressed in terms of concepts, which are refined into **working hypotheses** expressed more specifically in terms of operationalized measures. General and working hypotheses are natural language statements that may concern one variable or, more frequently, relationships among variables. To permit testing with statistical analysis, they must be further translated into **statistical hypotheses**, statements about values of population parameters. Inferential statistics involves accepting or rejecting specific hypotheses about population parameters on the basis of sample information, or constructing interval estimates of parameters around sample statistics.

For example, consider a job training program implemented in 1975 whose intended impact is the subsequent increase in participants' earnings. The measure to be used might be the change in income between 1974 and 1976 as adjusted for inflation—termed a **gain score** (see chapter 9). The general hypothesis might be stated as "the real income (adjusted for inflation) of program participants will increase from 1974 to 1976" while the working hypothesis might read as "the average incomes reported by program participants on 1976 state income tax returns, adjusted to 1974 dollars, will be greater than the average income they reported on 1974 state income tax returns." At this level the way in which change in income is to be measured has been specified. For each case (each program participant) the income change variable will be computed by subtracting 1974 reported income from 1976 reported income expressed in constant dollars. The statistical hypothesis representing the program logic, then, would concern the parameter, mean average income change, and would be stated: "The mean average income change of program participants exceeds zero."

By convention, Greek letters are usually used to represent population parameters and Roman letters are used for the corresponding statistics, as shown in the first two rows of Figure 7.1. In keeping with this division, in this text n will be used for the population size and N will be used to denote the size of the sample. The individual cases, denoted by X_i, that make up the sample are part of the larger number making up the population. Although the descriptive or summary measures discussed in chapter 4 may be appropriately computed for either a population or sample, their formulas are usually written with Roman letters.

This chapter begins by explaining the basic logic that underlies all inferential statistical techniques, along with the kinds of assumptions they are based on. Then it moves on to consider a number of **univariate** inferential procedures, those involving hypotheses or estimates concerning a *single variable*. The final section discusses the application of statistical inferences to questions about differences in means or proportions between two groups or populations.

THE LOGIC OF HYPOTHESIS TESTING

In concluding whether to accept or reject a hypothesis using inferential techniques, we can never be certain whether or not we are correct, because we are working with incomplete information. Rather, we as-

	Mean	Variance	Standard Deviation	Size	Individual Items
Population	μ	σ^2	σ	n	X_i
Sample	$\bar{X}$	s^2	s	N	X_i
Sampling Distribution $\bar{X}$	μ	$\dfrac{\sigma^2}{N}$	$\dfrac{\sigma}{\sqrt{N}}$	$\dfrac{n!}{N!\,(n-N)!}$	$\bar{X}$

Figure 7.1.   Population, sample, and sampling distribution of X.

sume that the population parameter equals the value given by the as yet untested hypothesis. We can then compare this hypothesized parameter with the corresponding statistic to obtain an idea of how representative the sample is, assuming that the hypothesis is correct. If the statistic closely approximates the hypothesized parameter, the hypothesis may well be correct. As we shall see, however, a sample statistic that deviates widely from the presumed value of the parameter is much less likely to occur, given a random sampling process. It may be that the hypothesis is true and that we just happened to draw an improbable sample, or it may be that the hypothesis is false. At some predetermined, arbitrary point we will conclude the latter and reject the hypothesis with the knowledge that there is a certain small probability we are making a mistake.

All inferential statistical methods are based on this kind of reasoning. The probability of selecting the one sample at hand from among all the possible samples is determined, and the hypothesis is accepted or rejected accordingly. It should be understood that we are not evaluating the probability of the hypothesis being correct, because its accuracy or inaccuracy is not variable; it is absolute and not probable. Rather, we determine the probability of drawing the sample obtained, assuming that the hypothesis is true, and draw a conclusion on that basis. All inferential techniques, then, hinge on the ability to determine the probability of a given sample being selected.

Sampling Distributions

The number of all possible samples of size N that can be drawn from a population of size n is given by the formula for combinations,

$$\frac{n!}{N! \, (n - N)!}$$

as discussed in the preceding chapter. This formula for the number of combinations indicates the number of possible samples drawn in a process of **sampling without replacement.** That is, an individual member of the population cannot be included in the same sample more than once. (See chapter 8.)

With even small and moderate size samples, there is usually a very large number of possible samples. Sample size is usually of lower order of magnitude than population size, and thus the number of possible samples increases as either N or n or both get larger. If we are drawing a sample from an infinite population the number of possible samples will also be infinity.

In practice we usually draw only one sample and compute statistics on that basis. However, we can conceive of drawing all possible samples, one at a time, and calculating some statistic—the mean average of some interval measure, for instance—separately for each. If we were to do this and then plot all the values computed for that statistic in a frequency polygon, the result would be a **sampling distribution** (SD). Note that although each sample will be unique in terms of the individual cases it contains, the calculated value of the statistic will not necessarily be different for every sample; a number of different samples may all yield the same mean, standard deviation, or proportion, etc. The sampling distribution of a statistic is the frequency distribution of the values taken on by that statistic in all possible samples of size N from a given population. Although we will begin working with the sampling distribution of the mean, the reader should recognize that a sampling distribution exists for any sample statistic that might be calculated.

Sampling Distribution of $\overline{X}$ Hypotheses concerning interval level variables usually involve mean averages. As stated by a mathematical theorem, it is known that if the population has a normal distribution, the sampling distribution of the mean will also be normal with a mean equal to the population mean and a variance equal to the population variance divided by the sample size. Knowledge of these properties would provide us with enough information about the sampling distribution to make inferential tests, given a normally distributed population. Although we usually do not know whether the population is normally distributed, another theorem, the **central limit theorem**, permits us to relax the normality assumption with large sample sizes: With samples of *large N*'s drawn from *any population* (of whatever distribution) the sampling distribution of the mean will approach normality with a mean equal to the population mean and a variance equal to the population variance divided by the sample size.

Figure 7.1 indicates the relationships among populations, samples, and sampling distributions of $\overline{X}$. Whereas the individual items making up the population and sample distributions are X_i's, those making up the sampling distribution of $\overline{X}$ are individual sample means. The mean of this sampling distribution is the population mean, μ; its variance is σ^2/N. The standard deviation of this sampling distribution, referred to as the **standard error** (s.e.), is $\sigma/\sqrt{N}$, the population standard deviation (σ) divided by the square root of the sample size.

Figure 7.2 illustrates the empirical derivation of the sampling distribution of the mean ($\overline{X}$) calculated for the 70 possible samples of size 4

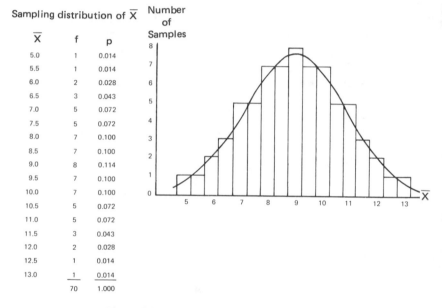

Population distribution			All possible samples — Size 4		
X_i	P		Seq. no.	X_i's	$\overline{X}$
2	0.125		1	2,4,6,8	5.0
4	0.125		2	2,4,6,10	5.5
6	0.125		3	2,4,6,12	6.0
8	0.125		.	.	.
10	0.125		.	.	.
12	0.125		68	8,10,14,16	12.0
14	0.125		69	8,12,14,16	12.5
16	0.125		70	10,12,14,16	13.0

Sampling distribution of $\overline{X}$

$\overline{X}$	f	p
5.0	1	0.014
5.5	1	0.014
6.0	2	0.028
6.5	3	0.043
7.0	5	0.072
7.5	5	0.072
8.0	7	0.100
8.5	7	0.100
9.0	8	0.114
9.5	7	0.100
10.0	7	0.100
10.5	5	0.072
11.0	5	0.072
11.5	3	0.043
12.0	2	0.028
12.5	1	0.014
13.0	1	0.014
	70	1.000

Figure 7.2   Derivation of a sampling distribution.

taken from a population of 8. The population distribution is completely flat with each member taking on a different value of the interval level variable, which might represent age, dollars, or whatever. However, the sampling distribution is more compact; even with a small N the sampling distribution of the mean approaches a normal distribution! Its range is smaller than that of the population, and there is a strong tendency for sample means to fall into the middle categories of the distribution. Also, it can be observed that although sample means vary from sample to sample, the arithmetic average of the sample means (or the mean of the sampling distribution) is equal to the population mean, as predicted by the central limit theorem. Also as illustrated in Figure 7.2, the proportion of samples yielding a given value of a statistic decreases with the extent to which they deviate from the population, e.g., in the example there are fewer samples with means of 6 or 12 than samples with means that are equal to or nearly equal to 9, the true population mean, and still fewer samples with means of 5 or 13.

You may be wondering how large N must be before we can relax the normality assumption and apply the central limit theorem. In the illustration above, the theorem was shown to apply for the most part for a given uniformly distributed population and a sample size of only 4. Yet, it will not apply so neatly with other kinds of population distributions, and you should usually have a much larger sample before using it. Statistical techniques that are based on assumptions of interval measurement and normally distributed populations are referred to as **parametric techniques**. With samples of $N \leq 30$ these techniques should not be applied unless the population distribution is known to closely approximate a normal distribution. With such small samples, it is preferable to use other, nonparametric techniques, to be discussed later in this text. However, as a rule of thumb, with $N \geq 100$ the normality assumption can almost always be relaxed and the parametric techniques employed. This can also be done when N is in the range of 50 to 100 and there is evidence to indicate that the deviation from a normal distribution is not serious (Blalock, 1972, p. 185).

Random Sampling A known sampling distribution can also be conceived as a probability distribution, one that indicates the likelihood of drawing a sample that will produce a statistic in a specified range of values in a random selection from among all possible samples. As illustrated in Figure 7.2, these probabilities are given by the proportions of samples that yield different values of a sample statistic. For example, of all possible samples of size 4 from the population shown in Figure 7.2, which has a mean equal to 9, the proportion having a mean of 5 is 0.014.

As will be seen, we usually are interested in the extremes of sampling distributions and in ranges of values rather than discrete points in the distribution. Thus we might note that of all these possible samples, the proportion that yields a mean equaling 11.5 or greater is 0.099. Because probabilities are proportions in the long run, we know that if we make a random selection of one sample from among all possible samples, the probability of obtaining a sample with a mean of 11.5 or greater is 0.099, while that of obtaining a sample with a mean of 12.5 or greater is 0.028.

In practice we draw one sample and, based on knowledge of the sampling distribution, assuming that the hypothesis is true, determine the probability of selecting that one sample from among all possible samples of that given size. To do this requires that the sample be drawn by a random sampling process, i.e., one that assures each possible sample an even chance of being the one that is actually selected. Two conditions must be met, at least in theory, as is discussed further in chapter 8. First, each individual member of the population must be given an even chance of being selected, and second, each selection of an individual to be included in the sample must be independent of every other selection. If the sample is drawn in this way, all possible samples of a given size have an equal probability of being chosen. Note that this by no means signifies that every possible *value* of the sample statistic of interest has an equal probability of resulting from a random sample selection process. Because some values of the statistic recur in many samples but others do not, random sampling will signify differing probabilities associated with different sample statistic values, as illustrated in Figure 7.2.

All inferential statistical techniques involve 1) drawing a random sample from the population, 2) computing some statistic for the sample, and 3) comparing the sample statistic with the known sampling distribution of that statistic, assuming that the hypothesis is correct, in order to 4) determine the probability of drawing that one sample if the hypothesis is in fact true. The decision to accept or reject the hypothesis is based on this probability. Because this probability is given by a corresponding proportion of all possible samples, it is crucial that the sample be drawn in a random selection process. Otherwise, we have no assurance that the sampling distribution represents the probabilities associated with differing values of the sample statistic.

Test for Population Mean, σ Known

Our first example of single sample hypothesis testing consists of a simplified problem in which more information is available than is usually the case, in order to see most directly how the underlying logic functions. In a study of labor productivity in a city government, we are interested, among other things, in the number of housing sanitation inspections made by health code officials per week. Assume that 14 inspections per inspector per week has been established as a standard but that we have reason to believe that the average number actually conducted is less. We decide to test this hypothesis using records of inspectors' activities for a random sample of inspector/weeks (the unit of analysis) over the past year. The hypothesis to be tested directly, termed the null hypothesis (H_0) as discussed below, is that the population mean equals 14. The alternate hypothesis (H_1) would be that the mean number of inspections per inspector/week is actually less than 14. The test assumes interval measurement and random sampling, and the population standard deviation is somehow known to be 6.4. Given these assumptions we draw a random sample of 108 inspector/weeks and compute a mean of 12.8 inspections per week for this sample.

Given the sample size of 108 we can apply the central limit theorem and relax the normality assumption. Therefore, we know that the sampling distribution of $\overline{X}$ will be normal with a standard error of 6.4 divided by $\sqrt{108}$ and, assuming that H_0 is true, with a mean of 14. The problem now is to determine the probability of selecting a random sample yielding a mean of 12.8 or less if the value of the population mean is in fact 14. The sampling distribution is known to be normal, so this can be done by converting the sample mean to a standard Z score, as shown in Figure 7.3. Notice that because we are working with the sampling distribution of $\overline{X}$, the value of the population mean hypothesized by H_0 is taken as the mean of this normal distribution, whereas the sample mean is the one item in this distribution whose deviation from the hypothesized mean we are trying to interpret. The standard deviation of this normal (sampling) distribution is the standard error, $\sigma/\sqrt{N}$. Thus, the formula for computing Z in this instance becomes

$$Z = \frac{\overline{X} - \mu}{\sigma/\sqrt{N}}$$

As shown in the figure, the Z is computed to be -1.9486. From Table A-3 in the appendix we find that this corresponds to a proportion of 0.4744. Thus, the probability of a sample of size 108 with a mean of between 12.8 and 14 is 0.4744, and by the residual method $(0.5 - 0.4744)$ the probability of a sample mean of 12.8 or less, if the true mean is 14, is 0.0256. This means that if the null hypothesis is true and the true population mean is 14, the probability of drawing the observed sample in a random sampling process would be only 0.0256. At this point the decision to accept or reject the null hypothesis is judgmental; we can either accept H_0 and assume that we simply drew a relatively improbable sample by chance, or we can reject H_0 on the basis that the true mean is probably closer to 12.8. In this case we might have decided to take a risk of up to 0.05 of incorrectly rejecting H_0. Thus, we would reject H_0 and accept H_1, recognizing that the probability that we are making an error is 0.0256.

H_0: $\mu_x = 14$

H_1: $\mu_x < 14$

N = 108

$\overline{X} = 12.8$

$\sigma = 6.4$

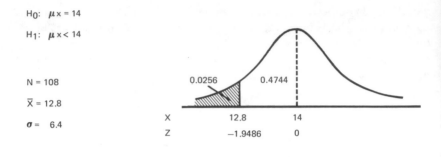

$$Z = \frac{\overline{X} - \mu}{\sigma / \sqrt{N}}$$

$$Z = \frac{12.8 - 14}{6.4 / \sqrt{108}}$$

$$= \frac{-1.2}{6.4 / 10.392}$$

$$= \frac{-1.2}{0.6158}$$

$$Z = -1.9486$$

Significance level: 0.05

Conclusion: Reject H_0, with a probability of error of 0.0256.

Figure 7.3.   Number of health code inspections made per week.

Steps in Hypothesis Testing

As illustrated in the above example, hypothesis testing is essentially a process of examining a sampling distribution to determine the probability of obtaining a given random sample by chance if the hypothesis is true. If this probability is high, the hypothesis may well be true (although this is by no means necessarily so) and we accept it. If it is low, we are faced with a dilemma posed by two possible explanations: 1) The hypothesis may be true, and we happen to have an improbable, unrepresentative sample, or 2) The hypothesis is actually false, and the sample is not so improbable or unrepresentative. When the probability is sufficiently low, we conclude that the second explanation is more likely and thus reject the hypothesis. When we reject the hypothesis on this basis, as in the example above, we are making an informed judgment and acknowledge that there is some small probability or risk that we are making an error; that the hypothesis is actually true and that we are mistakenly rejecting it on the basis of improbable, but nevertheless possible, sample evidence.

All inductive statistical tests are based on this logic. Although each individual technique is unique in terms of specifics, all proceed in a series of five steps. These are 1) identifying the assumptions on which the test is based, 2) determining the sampling distribution to be used, 3) specifying the **critical region**, that part of the sampling distribution that indicates that the hypothesis is to be rejected, 4) computing a test statistic for the sample, and 5) based on the test statistic, concluding to accept or reject the hypothesis.

Assumptions Every hypothesis testing procedure is based on a number of assumptions that must be met in order for the application of the technique to be valid. These assumptions concern both the population about which inferences will be drawn and the sampling procedure employed. Together, they determine what the correct sampling distribution should look like. An inductive statistical technique can be thought of as employing a model of what the probability distribution of the test statistic looks like, based on certain underlying assumptions. If one or more of these assumptions is incorrect, the model is not a valid representation of that probability distribution. One assumption underlying a model will be the level of measurement involved. When the level is interval, another assumption to be made concerns the distribution of cases in the population; usually with interval data there is an assumption of a normal distribution. In addition, an assumption underlying the use of every inductive technique is that the sample is drawn with a random selection procedure.

One further kind of assumption that has to be made in order to generate an expected probability distribution of the relevant sample statistic regards the value of the corresponding population parameter. This value is given by the hypothesis that is to be tested. Up to this point nothing has been said about the nature of the hypothesis being tested. Research hypotheses can be either of two forms, null hypotheses or alternate hypotheses. In general, **null hypotheses** state equalities, whereas **alternate hypotheses** postulate differences. With respect to the statistical tests discussed in this chapter, null hypotheses state that a population parameter equals a specific value, whereas alternate hypotheses state that the parameter is not equal to, greater than, or less than some specified value.

Usually, the hypotheses motivating the research are in alternate form, stating that a parameter is actually different from its presumed value. However, formal statistical tests are always made in terms of *null* hypotheses. Alternate form hypotheses are tested indirectly by testing the corresponding null hypothesis and drawing conclusions about the alternate hypothesis accordingly. If the null is rejected, the alternate is accepted, while accepting the null leads to rejecting the alternate. Statistical tests can only be made directly in terms of null hypotheses because the generation of a sampling distribution to make the test is predicated on the assumption of a single, discrete value of the population parameter.

Thus, the null hypothesis is always one of several assumptions on which a statistical test is based. In order to make a fair test of the null hypothesis, one must be certain that the other assumptions are all valid. In effect, the test is based on what the probability distribution of a sample statistic would look like, given that all the underlying assumptions are true. If the test indicates that the sample has low probability of occurring given these assumptions, we reject the null hypothesis on the basis of it being the only assumption in doubt. We conclude that the model has not yielded the correct probability distribution and attribute this to the null hypothesis being incorrect. To permit this, it is essential that all the other assumptions be well established.

Sampling Distribution   Given the underlying assumptions, the second step in inductive statistical tests is to develop the sampling distribution on which the test is to be based. Obviously, this is not done empirically by computing the statistic for every possible sample, as illustrated in Figure 7.2, as this would require complete information about the population. Rather, we have a priori knowledge of what the sampling distribution looks like either by way of mathematical theorem or empirical development for a generalized case. This will become clearer as we move through samples of varying techniques. The sampling distributions used in conjunction with the statistical methods discussed in this text are obtained from tables in the appendix.

Critical Region   As seen above, a statistical test consists of evaluating the likelihood of randomly selecting the sample at hand, assuming that the null hypothesis is true. This is accomplished by fitting a test statistic computed for the sample to the sampling distribution of that statistic to determine the probability of selecting that particular sample if the null hypothesis is in fact true. Determining this probability, given the validity of the underlying assumptions, is an objective process. However, concluding to accept or reject the hypothesis on the basis of this probability is judgmental. The decision as to how low a probability is sufficiently low to reject the hypothesis is arbitrary and depends solely on the degree of risk or error the researcher is willing to take.

Because setting the cutoff point between accepting and rejecting the null hypothesis is subjective, the researcher should guard against letting it be influenced by his desire to confirm or reject a hypothesis. To insure against this tendency, it is preferable to determine which outcomes of the test will lead to accepting and rejecting the null before the test is made. It is good practice to partition the sampling distribution into two areas in advance of the actual test. The critical region is that portion of the total sampling distribution that, if the test statistic falls within it, will lead to rejecting the hypothesis. If the test statistic falls outside the critical region, the probability of the sample occurring by chance is greater, and the hypothesis will be accepted. Establishing the critical region ahead of time by no means reduces the subjectivity of the test, but it does add to the rigor of the testing procedure.

One and Two-Tailed Tests   In the inferential tests discussed in this chapter, the sampling distributions employed are unimodal and symmetrical. Values of the test statistic that are at either extreme of the distribution have a low probability of occurring, and a decision must be made as to whether the critical region should be split between the extremes or concentrated in one tail. This depends on the form of the alternate hypothesis.

If the alternate hypothesis specifies a direction of difference, for example, that the population proportion is *greater* than some value, a **one-tailed test** should be used, in this case the *upper* tail. A sample statistic falling in the extreme lower tail would indicate a low probability of the sample occurring randomly if the null hypothesis is true, but this probability would be even lower if the alternate hypothesis is true. Thus, it would not constitute grounds for rejecting the null in favor of the alternate hypothesis. On the other hand, if the alternate hypothesis does not specify a direction of difference, stating for example that the true proportion does not equal some value, we would want to reject the null if it seems likely that the true proportion is *either greater* or *less than* the value specified by the null. Thus, a two-tailed test would be appropriate.

Type I and Type II Errors   The sensitive issue in determining the critical region concerns the **significance level**, the probability of rejecting the null hypothesis when it is actually true. When the null is rejected, it is on the basis of the sample having a low probability of being selected at random if the null is true. Yet, it may be that the null is true and that the sample consists of an improbable, but nevertheless possible, random selection of cases. Rejecting the null in this case would lead to a type I error, rejecting a true hypothesis.

Whenever the null is rejected, there is some possibility of committing a type I error. We control for this kind of error by stipulating a significance level, the maximum acceptable risk of a type I error. Establishing a significance level of 0.05, for example, means that the null is not to be rejected unless the probability of the sample, assuming the null is true, is 0.05 or less. Thus, if the null is rejected, the probability of a type I error is 0.05 or less. Setting the significance level is a purely arbitrary matter and depends solely upon the importance attached to guarding against type I error. By convention, significance levels are most frequently set at 0.05 and 0.01, but more or less stringent levels can certainly be used. In applied research this judgment may rest in large part on the nature of the problem and its context, as well as the anticipated use to which the results will be put.

While type I errors are due to chance variation of sample error, a second type of possible error represents an error in logic. A type II error, accepting a false hypothesis, is an error in inductive logic often referred to as the **fallacy of affirming the consequent** (Hempel, 1966, p. 6). Briefly, this refers to accepting an hypothesis not because the evidence proves it, but because the evidence does not dispute it. With respect to inferential statistics, when the sample is shown to have a high probability of occurring if the null hypothesis is true, we accept the null. Yet, it must be recognized that the null may be false and that the same sample may also have a high probability of occurring if the population parameter of interest is actually not equal to the value specified by the null. In effect, when we accept the null hypothesis, we are continuing to assume that it is true because our sample evidence did not indicate that it should be rejected. We are rarely in a position to determine the probability of committing a type II error, but, as will be shown below, that probability increases as we control more strictly against making a type I error.

It should be noted that in a single test only one type of error or the other is possible, a type I error if the null is actually true and a type II error if it is actually false. The problem, of course, is that we do not know which situation has actually occurred. The four possible outcomes of a test are illustrated in Figure 7.4.

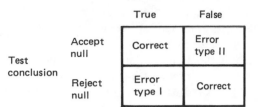

Figure 7.4.   Hypothesis test outcomes.

In practice, we control for a type I error on an arbitrary basis and recognize that we may well be making a type II error if we accept the null. Although the inability to control for type II errors is clearly a weakness, it is important to understand the implications with respect to conclusions about the alternate hypothesis. Rejecting the null means accepting the alternate. Thus, by extension, controlling for a type I error with respect to the null leads to controlling for a type II error concerning the alternate; we will only accept the alternate when we are almost certain that the null is false and that the alternate is correct. As we are usually interested primarily in the alternate hypothesis and want to guard against accepting it when it is false, this is a fortunate situation. We would rather not accept the alternate unless we are almost certain that it is true, taking a greater risk of assuming that the null is true even when it may not be.

Test Statistic and Conclusion   Upon determining the critical region of the sampling distribution, the last step is to calculate the test statistic for the sample and conclude to accept or reject the null hypothesis. It should be made clear that the conclusions drawn from single tests of hypotheses using inferential statistics are not all that certain or absolute. When the null hypothesis is rejected, there is a specified level of risk that the conclusion is incorrect, an artifact of sample error. When it is accepted, on the other hand, it may be that the null is actually false and that the test simply was not sufficiently discriminating to indicate this. For this reason, it is prudent to think of this conclusion in terms of "failing to reject" the null rather than a full fledged acceptance of it. As we are working with incomplete (sample) information, we cannot be certain of our conclusions. Thus, it is critical to make sure that the assumptions on which the test is founded are valid and to be conservative in establishing the possible test outcomes that lead to the acceptance of the hypothesis of primary interest.

STUDENT'S t DISTRIBUTION

Although the Z score application illustrated above is easy to understand intuitively, it is impractical because it requires prior knowledge
of the population standard deviation, which is rarely available. One
alternative is to use the sample standard deviation, s, as an estimate
of σ, but this is not altogether satisfactory in that s is not an unbiased
estimate. An **unbiased estimate** is one whose sampling distribution has
a mean that is equal to the population parameter being estimated.
Thus the sample mean is a statistic that provides an unbiased estimate
of the corresponding parameter; a single sample mean may overestimate or underestimate the population mean, but it does not have a
greater tendency toward error in one direction than the other. The
sample standard deviation, however, is a biased estimate tending to underestimate σ.

Whereas s itself is a biased estimate of σ, the expression $s\sqrt{N-1}$
provides an unbiased estimate of $\sigma/\sqrt{N}$, which is the standard error.
This can be used in computing a different test statistic, Student's t, as
follows.

$$t = \frac{\overline{X} - \mu}{s/\sqrt{N-1}}$$

With small sample sizes, s is highly variable from sample to sample, as opposed to σ, which is constant. This means that the t statistics will take on a greater range of values than Z and, therefore, the
t distribution will be flatter than the normal distribution. With larger
N's, the variability of s decreases, and the t distribution approximates
the normal distribution. Thus there is a different t distribution for each
sample size, moving from a flatter distribution toward a normal distribution as N increases. This means that it will be necessary to go out
to larger values of $\pm t$ to incorporate 95 percent of all samples with a
small N than to do so with a larger N.

Selected points on the t distribution are shown for various sample
sizes in Table A-6 in the appendix. The sample sizes are given in terms
of **degrees of freedom**, which in this type of problem equal $N-1$.
(Generally, the number of degrees of freedom is equal to the number
of unknowns minus the number of independent equations linking
them. Here we have N unknowns linked by one equation—that for the
mean average. See Blalock, 1972, pp. 203–204.) The numbers in the
interior columns of Table A-6 are values of t that represent selected
points along the distribution beyond which a random sample has a
certain probability of falling, as given by the significance levels stated

in the column headings. For example, with an N of 6, or with 5 degrees of freedom, 5 percent of all samples will yield a t value of greater than $+2.015$, and 5 percent will yield a t of less than -2.015. Thus the **critical** t for either a one-tailed test at the 0.05 level or a two-tailed test at the 0.10 level is 2.015.

One-Tailed t Test

Consider the problem concerning the number of visitors processed per day by an agency providing information and referral services, illustrated in Figure 7.5. The agency staffing plan was developed 4 years ago in anticipation of having to accommodate a maximum of 210 visitors per day, but personnel contend that, as the agency has become more widely known in the community, the number of visitors per day has consistently been greater than 210. To test this hypothesis the number

H_0: $\mu = 210$

H_1: $\mu \rangle$ 210

N = 95

$\overline{X}$ = 226

s = 65

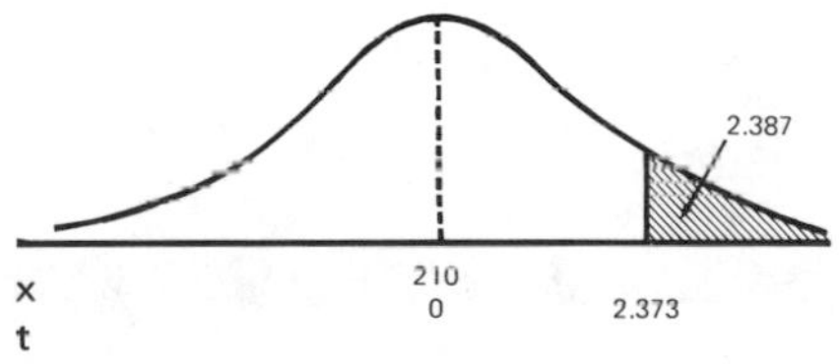

2.387

210
0

2.373

x
t

one tailed, df = 94
significance level = 0.01
critical t = 2.373

$$t = \frac{\overline{X} - \mu}{s/\sqrt{N-1}}$$

$$= \frac{226 - 210}{65/\sqrt{95-1}}$$

$$= \frac{16}{65/9.6953}$$

$$= \frac{16}{6.704}$$

$$t = \quad 2.387$$

conclusion: Reject H_0

Figure 7.5. Number of visitors processed per day.

of visitors is tabulated for a random sample of 95 days out of the past year and a half.

The null hypothesis is that the mean number of visitors is 210, and the alternate is that the mean is greater than 210. Given the assumptions of interval measurement, random sampling, and a normally distributed population, (to be discussed further below), the sampling distribution of the t statistic will be that given in Table A-6 for 94 degrees of freedom. Because H_1 specifies a direction of difference, a one-tailed test is appropriate; H_0 is to be rejected only if the sample mean is significantly greater than the hypothesized population mean. In this case it is decided to test at the 0.01 level because we want to guard against concluding that the mean is greater than 210 unless there is a very low probability that this is not the case. Because the Table does not show t values for 94 degrees of freedom, it is necessary to interpolate between the values given for 60 and 120 degrees of freedom; this process yields a critical t of 2.373.

With a sample mean of 226 and standard deviation of 65, the computation shown in Figure 7.5 yields a calculated t of 2.387, which falls in the critical region. Thus we conclude that H_0 is false on the basis of our sample having a probability of less than 1/100 of occurring if H_0 is true.

Two-Tailed t Test

Figure 7.6 illustrates a situation in which a two-tailed test is appropriate because the alternate hypothesis does not indicate whether the true mean is greater or less than the value specified by H_0. The variable of interest is the occupancy rate of public housing projects, the proportion of the housing units owned by local housing authorities that are occupied at a given point in time. The null hypothesis holds that this rate is 0.95, a conventional management rule of thumb, and we wish to determine whether the actual rate is higher or lower than 0.95. Thus we will reject H_0 if the sample mean is significantly greater or less than 0.95.

To make the test we select a random sample of 60 local housing authorities and compute the occupancy rate for each. Given the same assumptions as in the previous example, we know that the sampling distribution t will be that given in Table A-6 for 59 degrees of freedom; for a two-tailed test at the 0.05 level the critical t equals 2.001. In other words, the lowest 2½ percentage points of all possible samples of size 60 would yield a t value of –2.0 or lower and the highest 2½ percentage points of this distribution will yield t values of +2.0 or

$H_0: \mu = 0.95$

$H_1: \mu \neq 0.95$

$N = 60$

$\overline{X} = 0.92$

$s = 0.16$

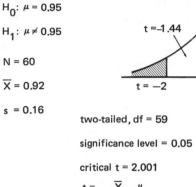

t = –1.44

t = –2   0.95   t = 2

two-tailed, df = 59

significance level = 0.05

critical t = 2.001

$$t = \frac{\overline{X} - \mu}{s/\sqrt{N-1}}$$

$$t = \frac{0.92 - 0.95}{0.16/\sqrt{59}}$$

$$= \frac{-0.03}{0.16/7.681}$$

$$= \frac{-0.03}{0.0208}$$

$$t = -1.44$$

Conclusion: Accept H_0

Figure 7.6.   Public housing occupancy rates.

greater if H_0 is true. H_0 is to be rejected if the computed t falls into either portion of this split critical region. In this example, the computed t value equals -1.44 and falls outside the critical region. Therefore, we accept H_0, that the mean average occupancy is 0.95.

Z Versus t Distribution

As has been mentioned, the t distribution approaches the normal deviate distribution as sample size increases, and with large N's (greater than 120) the two procedures produce almost identical results. For smaller samples, t values are more accurate than Z scores and provide a more conservative test, but they are only valid for populations that are normally distributed. The practical value of t is for small samples when the population distribution is known to be normal.

There is no completely satisfactory method for dealing with smaller samples drawn from populations with unknown distribution. Parametric techniques should not be employed with N's of less than 30 unless the approximation to a normal distribution is known to be good, and for sample sizes of between 30 and 120 the t distribution is probably preferable to Z when it can be assumed that the deviation from a normal distribution is not serious. These are simply rules of thumb, however, and should be applied with caution. The one overriding principle here is that when little is known about the population distribution, the researcher is much safer working with larger samples.

Probability of Type II Errors

It is worthwhile at this point to proceed with a more detailed discussion of the probability of type II errors, and their relationship to type I error probabilities. When an inferential test fails to reject the null hypothesis, the null is accepted on the basis that the sample evidence is not inconsistent with the null. However, this evidence is also consistent with many other possible hypotheses that would postulate different values for the parameter in question. By controlling for a type I error we are guarding against accepting a false alternate hypothesis at the risk of accepting a false null hypothesis. As discussed previously, research tends to be motivated by an interest in determining whether an alternate hypothesis is correct, and we would therefore rather retain a null that might not be true than accept an alternate hypothesis that might not be true.

As we control more stringently for a type I error, the probability of a type II error increases, everything else equal. This is illustrated in Figure 7.7, A and B. The probability of a type II error is given by the proportion of the true sampling distribution that is associated with accepting the false null hypothesis, i.e., those samples yielding a mean that falls outside the critical region under the usual assumption that H_0 is true. These probabilities usually cannot be determined because, obviously, the true mean is unknown. As can be seen from these first two panels, moving from the 0.05 to the 0.01 significance level in testing the same null hypothesis increases the probability of drawing a random sample that will lead to accepting the false null.

In controlling for type I errors, then, we often accept null hypotheses with no idea of the probability that they are false. This situation is ameliorated in part because the probability of a type II error decreases as the amount by which the null hypothesis deviates from the true value of the parameter increases. This is illustrated in Figure 7.7,

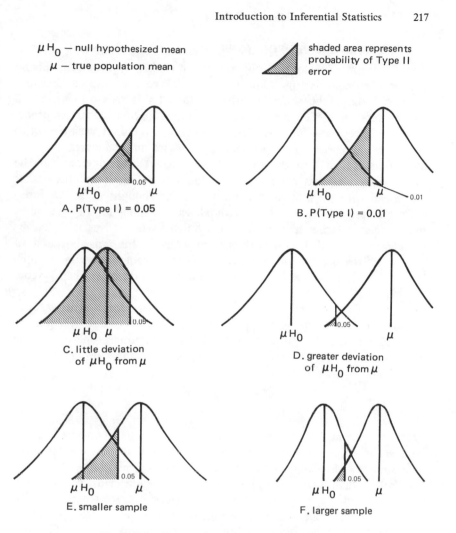

Figure 7.7.   Type I and type II error probabilities.

C and *D*. When the null hypothesis is false, but not too far off, the probability of a type II error is high, but when the null is way off (*D*), the probability of a type II error is greatly reduced because the hypothesized and actual sampling distributions overlap much less. Finally, Figure 7.7, *E* and *F* illustrate the effect of increased sample size. The null hypothesis is incorrect by the same amount in both cases, but in *F* the sample size is greater and the sampling distributions more compact; therefore, a much smaller proportion of all samples will lead to accepting the false null hypothesis.

TESTS INVOLVING PROPORTIONS

The Z score methodology can be applied to testing hypotheses involving proportions, considering them as a special case of means, because when N is large the sampling distribution of this measure is normal and centers on the corresponding population parameter. This procedure is appropriate for use with dichotomies; nominal variables with only two categories. The proportion of cases in one category of a dichotomy is equal to the mean average as calculated when all the cases falling into that category are coded with a 1 and the other cases are coded with a 0. Such a variable can be thought of as an interval scale ranging from 0 to 1 with all cases falling at the extremes, that is, certainly not a normally distributed variable. Nevertheless, by the central limit theorem, with sample sizes in the neighborhood of 100 to 120 or greater the sampling distribution of $\overline{X}$ (or the sample proportion) fulfills the normality assumption underlying the Z score technique.

It has been found that the population standard deviation of a proportion considered as a special case of mean average is equal to the square root of the proportion times its complement (one minus the proportion). Using the symbol q_u to represent this complement, we have the following formulas.

$$\sigma = \sqrt{p_u (1 - p_u)}$$

$$\sigma = \sqrt{p_u\, q_u}$$

The reader should be aware that in one sense tests involving proportions are more precise than those involving means, in that with proportions we know the value of the standard deviation, assuming that H_0 is true, rather than having to use an estimate. Working with proportions, then, we avoid the major problem in using the Z score technique with means—that is, not really knowing what the population standard deviation is—and we know the value of the standard error of the sampling distribution:

$$\text{s.e.} = \sqrt{p_u\, q_u}\ /\sqrt{N}$$

Single Sample Tests Involving Proportions

Figure 7.8 illustrates the use of the Z score technique to make a one-tailed test of a hypothesis concerning the percentage of commuters in a city whose primary mode of travel to work is the public transportation system. The data base used consists of survey responses concerning travel mode drawn from a random sample of 350 of the city's commuters.

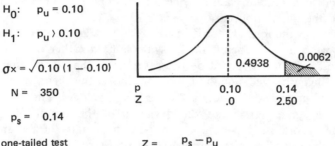

H_0: $p_u = 0.10$

H_1: $p_u \rangle 0.10$

$\sigma x = \sqrt{0.10 \, (1 - 0.10)}$

N =   350

p_s =   0.14

one-tailed test

significance level = 0.01

$$Z = \frac{p_s - p_u}{\sqrt{Pu \; qu} / \sqrt{N}}$$

$$= \frac{0.14 - 0.10}{\sqrt{0.1(0.9)} / \sqrt{350}}$$

$$= \frac{0.04}{\sqrt{0.09} / \sqrt{350}}$$

$$= \frac{0.04}{0.3 / 18.70}$$

$$= \frac{0.04}{0.016}$$

$$Z = 2.50$$

Conclusion: Reject H_0

Figure 7.8.   Public transit modal split.

Note the difference in the dependent variable between this problem and that shown in the previous example. In that case, the unit of analysis was the apartment building and the variable of interest was the percentage of occupied units in each building. That measure is a percentage that varies from case to case, and the most appropriate summary measure of central tendency is the mean average of these percentages. In the present example however, the unit of analysis is the individual commuter, and each is characterized as either using public transit for his work trip or not. If we are interested in the extent of use of public transit for work trips, then the most appropriate measure is the proportion of commuters who use the system.

In this problem the null hypothesis states that the proportion of commuters using transit is 0.10, based on past estimates, whereas the alternate hypothesis holds that this proportion is actually greater than 0.10. The sample proportion of 0.14 is consistent with the alternate hypothesis, and the purpose of the inferential test is to determine the likelihood of a random sample yielding a proportion of 0.14 if H_0 is true and the population parameter is 0.10.

Although the formula for Z in Figure 7.8 looks different from that used above, the difference is in the symbols used rather than the logic of the test. The test is based on the assumption that H_0 is true; therefore, the hypothesized population proportion is the mean of the sampling distribution and the standard error is $\sqrt{p_u q_u}/\sqrt{N}$. The formula for Z, then, is an expression of the deviation of the sample proportion from the hypothesized population proportion in units of the standard error of the sampling distribution. Given the large sample size and a random sample, we know that the sampling distribution will be normal and we can therefore make use of the probabilities associated with areas under the curve as measured in units of standard error.

Plugging the numbers into the formula, we obtain a Z of 2.5; our sample proportion is 2.5 standard errors above the mean and thus would have a low probability of occurring by chance if H_0 is true. From Table A-3 we find that if H_0 is true, the probability of drawing a random sample yielding a proportion between 0.10 and 0.14 is 0.4938, whereas that of drawing a sample yielding a proportion of 0.14 or greater is 0.0062. Testing at the 0.01 level, then, we reject H_0 and conclude that the true proportion of the city's workers who use transit is greater than 0.10.

CONFIDENCE INTERVALS AND SAMPLE SIZE

In some cases we are more interested in estimating the values of population parameters rather than testing a particular hypothesis. Sample statistics can be used to provide point estimates of their respective parameters, and some of these are better estimates than others. For example, with a normal population the mean and median are equal, but the mean provides a more efficient estimate because it fluctuates less from sample to sample.

As we have seen, an estimate is unbiased if the mean of its sampling distribution equals the value of the corresponding parameter in the population. The sample mean, for example, is an unbiased estimate because its sampling distribution centers on the population mean, whereas we have seen that the sample standard deviation provides a biased estimate tending to underestimate the population standard deviation. The sample mean, then, is a good estimating statistic because it is unbiased and relatively efficient, but this obviously does not imply that it will provide a totally accurate estimate of the population mean. The mean average computed for a random sample will not have a greater tendency either to underestimate or overestimate the population mean, but we do not know how close a given sample mean will be to the population mean; it may be a very accurate, or very inaccurate, point estimate.

Confidence Intervals

It may be preferable to establish an interval estimate of a population parameter along with the probability that it will contain the actual value of the parameter. Although an interval estimate is less precise than a single point estimate, we have an indication of how accurate it is. As is seen in later chapters, such interval estimates can be developed for numerous parameters, but the following section concerns only estimates of population means and proportions.

Confidence Intervals for Means   Confidence intervals are based on the proportion of sample means that can be expected to fall within a specified range of the population mean. We can use the Z or t distribution to determine the probability of $\overline{X}$ falling within any specified number of estimated standard errors of the population mean. For example, we know that approximately 68 percent of all sample means will fall within 1 standard error of the population mean; thus an interval ranging from 1 standard error below the sample mean to 1 standard error above $\overline{X}$ will have a probability of containing the true mean of approximately 0.68.

The logic of confidence intervals is illustrated in Figure 7.9 for a situation in which one desires to construct a 95 percent confidence interval. From the normal deviate table it can be seen that if the sampling distribution of $\overline{X}$ can be assumed to normal, 95 percent of all sample means will fall within ±1.96 standard errors from the population mean whereas 5 percent will fall outside these limits. Thus, with 95 percent of all samples, an interval that extends 1.96 standard errors above and below the sample mean will contain the true mean. It remains simply to convert a Z of 1.96 into units of the original scale and add and subtract this amount from the sample mean. An interval so constructed will contain the true mean for the 95 percent of all samples that yield a mean within 1.96 standard errors of the true mean. For the other 5 percent this interval will not contain the true mean.

Figure 7.10 shows the development of a 95 percent confidence interval estimate of the average daily travel (ADT) on a particular stretch of highway. A sample of 40 days was observed and yielded a mean of 6,000 vehicles per day and a standard deviation of 800. The t distribution is used because the population standard deviation is not known.

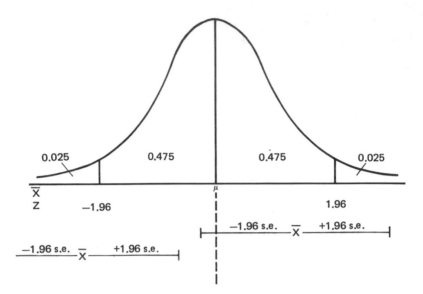

0.025   0.475   0.475   0.025

$\overline{X}$
Z   −1.96   1.96

                              −1.96 s.e. $\overline{X}$ +1.96 s.e.

−1.96 s.e. $\overline{X}$ +1.96 s.e.

Figure 7.9. Logic of confidence intervals.

The *t* value for the central 95 percentage points of the distribution for 39 degrees of freedom is multiplied by the estimated standard error to produce the amount of expected deviation from the true mean in units of ADT. This amount is then added to and subtracted from $\overline{X}$ to estab-

$\overline{X} =$ 6,000 ADT   P (Type I error) = 0.05

$s =$ 800   t (0.05,39 df) = 2.023

$N \doteq$ 40

$\overline{X} \pm t \quad \cdot \quad s/\sqrt{N-1}$

6,000 $\pm$ 2.023 · 800/$\sqrt{39}$

6,000 $\pm$ 2.023 · 128.10

6,000 $\pm$ 259.15

P (5,741 < μ < 6,259) = 0.95

Figure 7.10. Ninety-five percent confidence interval. ADT = average daily travel.

$\overline{X} = 6,000$ P (Type I error) = 0.01

s = 800   t (0.01,39 df) = 2.709

N = 40

$\overline{X} \pm t \cdot s/\sqrt{N-1}$

$6,000 \pm 2.709 \cdot 800/\sqrt{39}$

$6,000 \pm 2.709 \cdot 128.10$

$6,000 \pm 347.02$

$P (5,653 < \mu < 6,347) = 0.99$

Figure 7.11. Ninety-nine percent confidence interval.

lish the confidence interval. Our interpretation is that the probability is
0.95 that the interval 5,741 to 6,259 contains the true mean average
ADT.

Figure 7.11 illustrates the same procedure carried out to construct
a 99 percent confidence interval. Because we desire an interval that will
contain the true mean for all but 1 percent of all sample means, the
value of t is greater and the interval is therefore larger. This illustrates
the trade-off between accuracy and precision for a given sample size
and variability. This second interval provides less precision, but we have
greater confidence that it contains the true mean.

Given a desired confidence level, the precision of the interval estimate will also vary with the size of the sample on which the estimate is
based. Larger samples provide more precise estimates because they have
smaller standard errors. Table 7.1 shows the upper and lower limits of

Table 7.1. Ninety-nine percent confidence intervals with varying sample size[a]

N	t	estimated standard error	lower limit[b]	upper limit[b]	interval range[b]
20	2.861	183.53	5,475	6,525	1,050
40	2.709	128.10	5,653	6,347	694
60	2.662	104.15	5,723	6,277	554
80	2.646	90.01	5,762	6,238	476
120	2.618	73.34	5,808	6,192	384

[a] $\overline{X} = 6,000$ ADT; P (type I error) = 0.01; $s = 800$.
[b] estimates rounded to nearest integer.

99 percent confidence interval estimates of ADT based on varying sample sizes. The width of the interval decreases as N increases, but at a diminishing rate; at some point the precision gained will be outweighed by the cost of obtaining the additional sample cases.

Confidence Intervals for Proportions   The confidence interval estimate of a population proportion would be constructed around the sample proportion with the following formula:

$$p_s \pm Z \sqrt{\frac{p_u q_u}{N}}$$

Because no value of the parameter, p_u, is being hypothesized, however, it is necessary to impute some value into the equation. Because the sampling distribution of sample proportions is normal only for large N's and because large samples usually provide a fair estimate of p_u, one procedure is to use p_s as our best estimate of p_u. This is done in the example shown in Figure 7.12 developing a 95 percent confidence interval to estimate the proportion of commuters using public transit as discussed in a previous problem. An alternative procedure is to use the value 0.5 for p_u; this produces the most conservative (widest) interval estimate because the product $p_u q_u$, the estimated standard error, is maximized when p_u equals 0.5.

Finally, with respect to confidence intervals, it should be noted that the development of a confidence interval implies a whole range of two-tailed tests. As can be seen from Figure 7.9, the upper and lower limits of a confidence interval represent the cutoff points between accepting and rejecting H_0 at the corresponding significance level. Specifically, given a 95 percent confidence interval around a sample mean, we know

$p_s = 0.14$ (percent commuters using transit)

$N = 350$

$$p_s \pm Z \sqrt{\frac{p_u \, q_u}{N}}$$

$$0.14 \pm 1.96 \sqrt{\frac{0.14 \cdot 0.86}{350}}$$

$$\pm 1.96 \cdot 0.0185$$

$$0.14 \pm 0.036$$

$$P \, (0.104 \langle \, p_u \, \langle \, 0.176) = 0.95$$

Figure 7.12.   Ninety-five percent confidence interval for a proportion.

that a two-tailed test at the 0.05 level would lead to accepting any H_0 that states that the population mean is somewhere within the interval, and rejecting any H_0 that maintains that the true mean is outside the interval.

Determining Sample Size

As we have seen, the precision of a confidence interval and the ability to reject false null hypotheses improve with increased sample size. Often, in planning a research project we desire to know approximately how large a sample is required to attain a given degree of precision. For example, in a study of an employment service we might wish to develop a 95 percent confidence interval estimate of the mean number of cases closed per day with a width of six cases, a sample mean plus or minus three cases. Using the formula for confidence intervals, we can represent this as:

$$\overline{X} \pm 3 \text{ cases} = \overline{X} \pm Z(\sigma/\sqrt{N})$$

therefore

$$3 = 1.96 \, \sigma/\sqrt{N}$$

and

$$N = \left(\frac{1.96 \cdot \sigma}{3}\right)^2$$

Our remaining problem, then, is to find some reasonable value for σ, the population standard deviation. We might get an idea of σ from previous research on the same subject or using similar observations and measures, a pilot study or survey field test, or some secondary data source. If these are not available, one very rough way to estimate σ is to estimate the range of values taken on by X and divide by 6, because most of the cases will be contained in ± 3 standard deviations.

In our example, assume that a very small pilot sample provides an estimate that σ equals 12. Putting this into the equation, we have:

$$N = \left(\frac{1.96 \cdot 12}{3}\right)^2$$

$$N = 61.5$$

Thus we would conclude that we need a sample of approximately 60 days in order to develop the desired confidence interval. If we had specified a 99 percent confidence interval with the same precision (± 3 cases), the required N would have been 106. Obviously, these are order of magnitude estimates of sample size, because they are based on a rough estimate of σ, but they usually will provide a better guide in project planning than will intuitive judgment.

TWO-SAMPLE TESTS

All the single sample tests involving means and proportions that are covered in this chapter can be extended to test hypotheses concerning differences in these parameters between two populations or two subpopulations of one larger population. Basically, this involves observing differences in some mean or proportion between two samples and determining the probability that it would occur by chance if the samples are independent random samples of their respective populations. Although not illustrated in this text, these two-sample procedures can also be used to develop confidence interval estimates of the difference in means or proportions between two populations or to develop estimates of required sample size.

Two-Sample t Tests

The **difference in means test**, or **two-sample t test**, is one of the most common inferential statistical techniques in use. It may appropriate whenever the analyst is concerned with any two groups of cases in his data set and interested in finding out whether the mean averages of some variable differ significantly between these groups. For example, he may want to compare the mean average income between the male and female samples in his data set.

Although the two-sample t test is usually presented in terms of comparing samples as the name implies, it is important to point out that it really involves the application of inferential statistics to a *bivariate association*. Whatever characteristic is used to differentiate between the two samples is actually *a variable* with two categories. Thus, the technique may be appropriate whenever interest centers on the association between a (nominal level) dichotomous *independent* variable and an interval level *dependent* variable. In the example cited above, then, we would be looking at the question of whether income (interval, dependent) varies with sex (nominal, independent).

The inferential test is aimed at concluding whether an observed difference in means between the samples is likely to be a product of chance effect in a random sampling process or whether it is unlikely that the means of the two corresponding populations are in fact equal as stated by the null hypothesis. Instead of asking what is the probability of getting a particular sample if the null hypothesis is true, we are now asking what is the probability of getting these two sample means if the populations from which the samples were drawn have equal means. Stated in another way, what is the probability of drawing these two samples if they are in fact independent random samples from the same population?

This test is based on the sampling distribution of the difference between means rather than the sampling distribution of the mean itself. We are able to do this by using a theorem stating that given two independent random samples from a normally distributed population, the sampling distribution of the *difference* between the means, $SD(\overline{X}_1 - \overline{X}_2)$, will be normal with a mean equal to the difference of population means and a variance equal to the sum of the population variances divided by their respective sample sizes. The normality assumption may be relaxed with large N's but the samples must be *random* and *independent* (one not contingent upon the other in any way) in order to apply the test. Because the population variance is unknown and, as we have seen before, s^2 tends to underestimate the variance, the comparison of means test uses the t distribution rather than the normal distribution.

Based on this theorem the formula for the two-sample t statistic appears below:

$$ t = \frac{(\overline{X}_1 - \overline{X}_2) - (\mu_1 - \mu_2)}{\sqrt{\dfrac{s_1{}^2}{N_1 - 1} + \dfrac{s_2{}^2}{N_2 - 1}}} $$

The notation for the two-sample test is the same as for the single sample test, with the subscripts pertaining to the particular sample from which the individual term comes. In practice, the null hypothesis for the two-sample t test tends to be that the two means are equal. When this is the case the $\mu_1 - \mu_2$ term drops out and the formula is the one seen in Figure 7.13.

Figure 7.13 illustrates the use of this test for two random samples of students taught by two different methods. The test scores are compared to see if the teaching method actually produced a difference in the average score for the two samples of students. The null hypothesis is that the method made no difference, whereas the alternative hypothesis states that the new method should produce higher scores than the old method. Because the test statistic exceeds the one-tailed critical value of t we conclude that the new teaching method did indeed produce a significantly greater mean score (with a 0.01 probability of being incorrect).

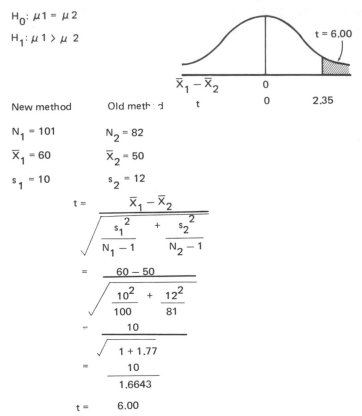

$H_0: \mu 1 = \mu 2$

$H_1: \mu 1 > \mu 2$

t = 6.00

0

0   2.35

New method	Old method
$N_1 = 101$	$N_2 = 82$
$\overline{X}_1 = 60$	$\overline{X}_2 = 50$
$s_1 = 10$	$s_2 = 12$

$$t = \frac{\overline{X}_1 - \overline{X}_2}{\sqrt{\dfrac{s_1^2}{N_1 - 1} + \dfrac{s_2^2}{N_2 - 1}}}$$

$$= \frac{60 - 50}{\sqrt{\dfrac{10^2}{100} + \dfrac{12^2}{81}}}$$

$$= \frac{10}{\sqrt{1 + 1.77}}$$

$$= \frac{10}{1.6643}$$

$$t = 6.00$$

Critical region: One-tailed test at 0.01 level, 181 degrees of freedom is 2.35.

Decision: Since 6.00 > 2.35, reject H_0 and conclude the new method yields higher test scores.

Figure 7.13.   Difference of means test.

t **Test Variations**   Although the *t* test is most often used when the null hypothesis specifies no difference, this test can also be used when an amount of difference is specified. For example, in the previous example we might have wanted to test whether the average score with the new teaching method was more than 6 points better than the mean without the new method. By using the original formula for two-sample *t* tests we can put in the numbers and come up with the following test statistic:

$$t = \frac{10 - 6}{\sqrt{\dfrac{10^2}{100} + \dfrac{12^2}{81}}}$$

$$t = 4/1.6643$$

$$t = 2.40$$

Because the value for the test statistic surpasses the critical t value (2.35) we can conclude that the new method produces a mean test score more than 6 points greater than that of the old method, with only a 0.01 probability of being incorrect.

It is also possible to apply the difference in means test as a two-tailed test if warranted by the research context, but the great majority of applications in analyzing program performance employs the one-tailed version illustrated above. Most often the substantive framework and the nature of the particular comparisons being made lead to alternate hypotheses, which specify that one mean is greater than the other, and thus a one-tailed test is appropriate. If a two-tailed test is required, the only change in conducting the test is in identifying the correct critical t value; computation of the t statistic is the same as for the one-tailed test.

It should also be noted that the computation of the t statistic shown above is based on the assumption that the variances of the two populations in question may be dissimilar; when it can be assumed that these variances are equal (even though their means may be different) the standard error of the difference in means can be based on a pooled estimate, which is more efficient in terms of developing confidence intervals or rejecting null hypotheses at a given significance level. However, by convention the method illustrated above is almost always used in practice, and the pooled estimate will not be explained in this text (Blalock, 1972, pp. 223–226). Furthermore, if the total sample size is quite small or the 2 N's are highly disparate, a correction factor should also be applied to the degrees of freedom (Blalock, 1972, p. 227).

Difference in Proportions

The difference of proportions test can best be pictured as a comparison of two sample proportions considered as special types of means. As is seen below, the major difference is that with proportions we have an unbiased estimate of the standard deviation of the population. This test, like the two-sample t test, assumes two independent random samples. However, we also require a large sample size in order to use the central limit theorem to posit a normal sampling distribution of the difference between the proportions.

Because we are assuming a normal sampling distribution, the test will use Z scores, with the difference in proportions between the samples minus the hypothesized difference in the numerator and the standard error in the denominator. In the case of the null hypothesis being that the two population proportions are equal ($p_{u1} = p_{u2}$) the formula for estimating the standard error of the sampling distribution of $p_{s1} - p_{s2}$ is:

$$\text{s.e.} = \sigma \sqrt{\frac{N_1 + N_2}{N_1 N_2}}$$

In order to get the estimate of σ, we use the formula derived previously in single sample tests involving proportions, as shown below.

$$\hat{\sigma} = \sqrt{p_u q_u} \quad \text{where} \quad q_u = 1 - p_u.$$

However, because we now have two separate estimates of p_u—namely p_{s1} and p_{s2}—the best estimate of p_u is a weighted average of the two sample proportions as illustrated below:

$$\hat{p}_u = \frac{N_1 p_{s1} + N_2 p_{s2}}{N_1 + N_2}$$

By using this weighted estimate of the population proportion, p_u, as the basis for estimating the population standard deviation, $\hat{\sigma}$, we can develop our estimate of the standard error of the sampling distribution of the difference in proportion as follows:

$$\text{estimated s.e.} = \sqrt{\hat{p}_u \hat{q}_u} \sqrt{\frac{N_1 + N_2}{N_1 N_2}}$$

where $\hat{q}_u$ equals $1 - \hat{p}_u$. Thus, the formula for Z becomes:

$$Z = \frac{(p_{s1} - p_{s2}) - (p_{u1} - p_{u2})}{\sqrt{\hat{p}_u \hat{q}_u} \sqrt{\frac{N_1 + N_2}{N_1 N_2}}}$$

The example shown in Figure 7.14 pertains to the percentage of drug addicts arrested within a 5-month period after receiving either treatment through the use of methadone or a drug-free treatment. Our purpose is to see if either program produces a significantly different arrest percentage. The difference in proportions procedure is appropriate here because we have a dichotomous dependent variable (arrest ver-

Percent arrested within a 5-month period:

$$H_0: P_{u_1} = P_{u_2}$$

$$H_1: P_{u_1} \neq P_{u_2}$$

	Type of treatment	
	Methadone	Drug free
P_s	39%	48%
N	100	100

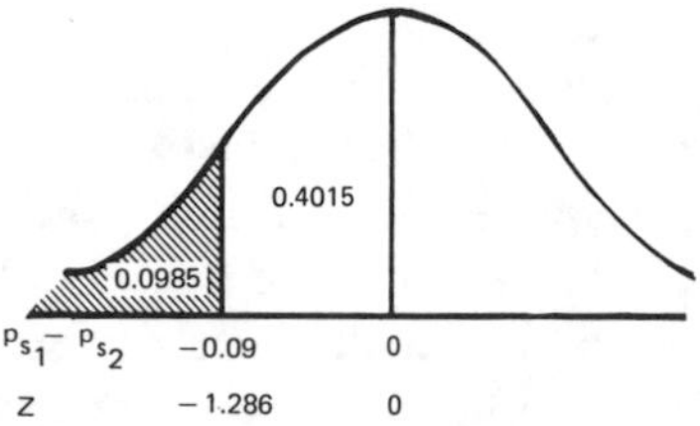

$$P_u = \frac{N_1 P_{s_1} + N_2 P_{s_2}}{N_1 + N_2}$$

$$= \frac{100\,(0.39) + 100\,(0.48)}{200}$$

$$= 0.435$$

$$Z = \frac{(P_{s_1} - P_{s_2}) - (P_{u_1} - P_{u_2})}{\sqrt{\hat{P}_u \hat{q}_u}\,\sqrt{\dfrac{N_1 + N_2}{N_1\ N_2}}}$$

$$= \frac{(0.39 - 0.48) - (0)}{\sqrt{(0.435)(0.565)}\,\sqrt{\dfrac{(100 + 100)}{10{,}000}}}$$

$$= \frac{-0.09}{(0.4957)(0.1414)}$$

$$= -1.286$$

Significance level: 0.05

Decision: There is 0.0985 probability of getting these two samples if H_0 is true; thus conclude H_0.

Figure 7.14. Difference of proportions.

sus no arrest) and a dichotomous independent variable (methadone versus drug-free).

In the example, we first compute the estimated population proportion by using weighted averages of the two sample proportions. We can then compute the standard error and the Z score of the difference in proportions. It should be noted that because the null hypothesis states equal proportions, the term $p_{u1} - p_{u2}$ drops out of the equation. By looking at Table A-3 we see that there is a 0.0985 probability of drawing these samples if the null hypothesis is correct and therefore we conclude it is true.

Extensions of Tests with Proportions   It is also possible to apply tests involving the difference of proportions. For example, we might sample black and white households in two different cities to find the proportion who feel police services are at least adequate. We might then be interested in finding out if the difference in the proportions between black and white households in each city is different between the two cities. We could then perform a test to see if the difference between the difference of proportions of black and white households who feel police services are adequate is significantly different between the two cities. The formula for Z in this case would be:

$$Z = \frac{(p_{s1} - p_{s2}) - (p_{s3} - p_{s4})}{\sqrt{\dfrac{p_{s1} q_{s1}}{N_1} + \dfrac{p_{s2} q_{s2}}{N_2} + \dfrac{p_{s3} q_{s3}}{N_3} + \dfrac{p_{s4} q_{s4}}{N_4}}}$$

In this formula, each sample proportion is actually being used as an estimate of the population proportion; as these estimates may differ, the procedure works best with four separate samples of approximately the same size (Blalock, 1972, pp. 230–232).

REFERENCES

Blalock, H. M., Jr. 1972. Social Statistics. 2nd Ed. New York: McGraw-Hill Book Company.

Hempel, C. G. 1966. Philosophy of Natural Science. Englewood Cliffs, N.J.: Prentice-Hall, Inc.

Hoel, P. G., and R. J. Jessen. 1971. Basic Statistics for Business and Economics. New York: John Wiley & Sons, Inc.

Neter, J., and W. Wasserman. 1966. Fundamental Statistics for Business and Economics. Boston: Allyn & Bacon, Inc.

PRACTICE PROBLEMS FOR CHAPTER 7

1. In 1970 the average number of traffic accidents per 10 miles of state highway was 42, and it is hypothesized that because of increased highway patrolling this rate decreased in 1972. A sample of accident rates on 144 stretches of roadway yields a mean of 38 accidents per 10 miles with a standard deviation of 24. Is the difference between the 1970 and 1972 accident rates statistically significant at the 0.05 level?

2. It is hypothesized that the mean number of square feet per occupant of dwelling units in a certain neighborhood meets the standard of 90 square feet. In a random sample of 17 households the mean is calculated to be 80 square feet per person with a standard deviation of 36. Test the null hypothesis that $\mu x = 90$ at the 0.01 level, and indicate your conclusion. (Assume that the population is normally distributed.)

3. The mean average income of a sample of 400 participants completing a mid-career training program is $9,000 annually, with a standard deviation of $2,000. Construct a 95% confidence interval to estimate the mean average income of all those who have completed the program.

4. You are planning a survey that will in part be used to estimate the mean average number of phone calls received by a community referral service per day. You want to set up a 95% confidence interval to estimate the mean number of calls, and you want the interval to have a width of 8 calls. Similar research shows that the standard deviation of the daily number of calls is likely to be about 20. How large a sample will you require to obtain this precision in an estimate?

5. Officials of a public employees union contend that over 60% of the employees of a very large organization favor the implementation of a collective bargaining system, but the organization's top management disagrees. To test the union officials' hypothesis a random sample of 576 employees are surveyed, and 65% say that they do favor collective bargaining. Calculate the Z score corresponding to the sample proportion of 0.65, assuming a true population proportion of 0.60. At the 0.01 significance level, what do you conclude?

6. In light of the growing problem of rapid obsolescence of factory workers' skills, a job retraining program is initiated in a metropolitan area. One performance measure used in evaluating this pro-

gram is the weekly earnings of factory production workers, and it is hypothesized that the mean earnings of those workers retrained in the program will be greater than those of other production workers. Samples are drawn independently from each group and the following statistics are calculated:

	Retrained workers	Other workers
Sample size	$N_1 = 101$	$N_2 = 82$
Mean	$\overline{X}_1 = \$240$	$\overline{X}_2 = \$210$
Standard deviation	$s_1 = \$40$	$s_2 = \$27$

Use the appropriate inferential technique to determine if the job retraining program has had a significant impact on the earnings of factory production workers. Test at the 0.01 level.

7. The director of an Area Office on Aging hypothesizes that the average number of visits made by program participants to senior centers is greater than 12 per month. Data collected on a random sample of 41 participants shows a mean of 15 visits per month with a standard deviation of 10. (The distribution would appear to approximate a normal distribution.)

   a. State the null and alternate hypotheses.
   b. Test the null hypothesis at the 0.05 level and indicate your conclusion.

8. Employees of the Bureau of Labor Statistics are engaged in conducting surveys of the prices of consumer goods on an ongoing basis. In part, their productivity is judged in terms of how many survey "schedules" they complete per week. As part of an evaluation of a new incentive program, a comparison is to be made regarding the mean average schedules completed between two groups: (1) participants in the incentive program, and (2) nonparticipants. Independent random samples are drawn from the two groups, and the following statistics computed:

	Participants	Nonparticipants
	$\overline{X}_1 = 24$	$\overline{X}_2 = 20$
	$s_1 = 6$	$s_2 = 5$
	$N_1 = 63$	$N_2 = 59$

   a. State the null and alternate hypotheses.
   b. Test the null hypothesis at the 0.01 level and indicate your conclusion.

SAMPLING STRATEGIES

8

As pointed out in chapter 7 much of the quantitative analysis in the area of public programs, as well as in business administration and social science research in general, is based on sample data. We are really interested in developing information relating to the complete **population** or **universe** of interest, but because of time and money limitations we often select a sample of cases from the population and proceed with our analysis on that basis. Now the validity of our findings depends on the quality of the sample and the procedures used in obtaining it as well as the issues of measurement, overall research design, and the application of statistical techniques.

Because a **sample** is a subset of cases in the population, the use of a sample necessarily involves working with less than complete information. This may or may not present a serious problem, depending on what type of sample we have and how the sample data are interpreted. As seen in chapter 7, everything else equal, the larger the sample the greater the precision in making estimates of population parameters and in testing statistical hypotheses. Thus, designing a sampling strategy very often includes consideration of trade-offs between costs and precision in terms of sample size.

Sample size, however, is by no means the only important consideration. In general, we are often interested in obtaining a **representative sample**, one that includes a healthy cross-section of cases from the population, and although we rarely, if ever, can be certain about the degree to which a sample is representative, we can sometimes take steps to increase the likelihood of obtaining a representative sample, at least according to some population characteristics. Furthermore, different types of samples are more or less appropriate depending on the researcher's purposes and the nature of the population being examined, and the applicability of various statistical methods with different kinds of samples must also be taken into account in choosing a sampling plan.

All samples fit into one of three categories: 1) probability samples, 2) judgment samples, and 3) chunks. The various types of probability samples are most often recommended because they facilitate probabilistic inferences being made to the general population, but **nonprobability samples**, judgment samples and chunks, have appropriate uses in certain contexts. This chapter discusses different types of probability and nonprobability samples and then concludes with some additional comments on considerations to be taken into account in devising a sampling plan.

PROBABILITY SAMPLES

Probability sampling procedures are those in which the selection of cases from the population is made according to known probabilities, using some random mechanism such as a table of random numbers. This random selection according to known probabilities is the distinguishing feature of probability samples because it provides a control against systematic biases in estimation and permits the calculation of the range of sampling error, and this is the basis of inferential statistics as discussed in chapter 7 and subsequent chapters.

Simple Random Sample

The simplest type of probability sample in terms of structure, and the one on which most of the inferential statistics discussed in chapter 7 are predicated, is a simple random sample. This type of sample is constructed by developing a list of all the cases in the population and selecting individual sample cases from a list on a random basis, such as numbering all the entries in the list in consecutive order and then selecting a sample of the desired size with a table of random numbers. In a simple random sampling process each individual case in the population has an equal probability of being included in the sample, and that probability is given by the **sampling fraction**, the ratio of sample size to the population size.

Given the condition that all individuals in the population have an even chance of being selected in the sample, the probability of selecting a case fitting into a specified subgroup of the population in any given individual selection is given by the proportion that the cases in that subgroup constitute of the total population. As was seen in chapter 6, then, the expected value of the proportion of cases in a specified subgroup to be included in a simple random sample is equal to its proportion in the larger population. Thus, if the sample size is large enough, the proportions of various subgroups in the sample should approximate those in the population.

Obviously, a simple random sample is no guarantee of a representative sample, because a highly distorted sample has some probability of occurring by chance in a random sampling process. In fact, the probability of a type I error is an indicator of this likelihood. However, with a simple random sample there is no systematic tendency to underrepresent or overrepresent given categories of cases, and with larger samples we do have increasing confidence that sample proportions are approximating their corresponding population parameters.

In strict terms, there are two general requirements for a simple random sample. Not only must each individual in the population have an equal probability of being selected, but each possible sample of the specified sample size must also have an equal probability of being chosen. This second requirement would necessitate the use of **sampling with replacement**, as mentioned in chapter 6, such that an individual case would be selected at random, recorded, and then put back into the population before the next selection. This procedure allows for individual cases being included more than once in the actual sample, and is hardly ever used in practice for obvious reasons.

Usually, we sample without replacement, and this has the technical effect of reducing the probability of certain redundant samples occurring to zero. Although this means that the sampling distributions used as the basis for inferential statistics will not be precisely correct, this rarely creates serious problems. First, if the sample size is a small fraction of the total population size, this effect will be negligible. With sampling fractions of 0.2 or greater there may be more substantial errors in sample estimates, but in some cases correction factors are available for coping with these problems. However, even these correction factors are not often used because as it happens the estimated standard error is an overestimate with uncorrected estimates based on sampling without replacement. Therefore, in proceeding with these uncorrected estimates, we are being conservative in applying inferential tests of significance. In other words, the actual probability of a type I error will be slightly less than that indicated by the standard tables of significance levels (see Blalock, 1972, pp. 513–514).

Very often the greatest problem in drawing a simple random sample is compiling a complete list of all the cases in the population in the first place. The master list from which the sample cases are selected constitutes the population being sampled to which inferences can validly be extended, whether or not it is identical to the population being sampled. With large populations the physical work of developing the master list, numbering the entries, and then pulling out the sample may be a cumbersome task. More importantly, there does not seem to be any clear-cut method for identifying exactly who or what all the bona fide cases are in many instances.

Where possible, existing compilations of cases that seem to represent the population of interest are often used. Although this is sometimes the only feasible way of choosing a sample, care should be taken to analyze the limitations of the available listing before actually using it. First, if possible the **elementary sampling units**, the cases actually being sampled, should be the same as the intended unit of analysis. For example, community surveys often employ samples of *households* when the unit of analysis of interest may be the *individual respondent* rather than the household itself. This is not the same thing as surveying a random sample of individuals in the community—individuals from larger households have a lesser probability of being included in the sample, for instance—and it may introduce some distortion depending on the content and purpose of the survey.

Second, the existing source that lists cases may actually constitute only a partial listing of the complete population, and the analyst must be concerned whether there is any systematic bias, in terms of which cases are listed and which are not, that might prevent him from obtaining a truly representative sample. For example, a sample pulled from a telephone directory, although it might include a fairly broad cross-section of residents, would not include households without telephones, thereby underrepresenting low income households in the community. By the same token, a sample drawn from a listing of occupied residences would tend to underrepresent transient households. In such a situation, the analyst must determine the seriousness of potential biases as weighed against the difficulty of obtaining a better sample through a different approach.

Systematic Sample

Even with a complete listing of cases in the population, the mechanics of numbering all the cases and selecting the sample with random numbers can be a very tedious process. As a matter of convenience, therefore, researchers often resort to the use of a **systematic sample**, one consisting of every Kth individual taken from the listing based on a random start. The procedure is to determine an appropriate skip factor, the number of cases to be skipped over before choosing the next case for the sample, select the first case on a random basis and then cycle through the listing pulling each case you land on with the skip factor.

Although considered by some not to meet the requirements of a probability sample (Loether and McTavish, 1976, chapter 11), systematic samples nevertheless are often used interchangeably with simple random samples on the assumption that there is nothing inherent in the procedure that would produce a biased sample. Systematic samples are obviously much easier to obtain than simple random samples or other types of probability samples, and the results can be expected to be as good as simple random samples in terms of representativeness if the original listing can be considered to be randomized in terms of the variables of interest. Note that the systematic sampling procedure precludes the possibility of selecting many combinations of cases in the sample once the order of cases on the listing has been established, and thus a systematic sample is clearly not the equivalent of a simple random sample. Yet, if there is no systematic pattern in the order in which cases are listed that relates to the variables of interest, treating a systematic sample in statistical analysis as if it were a simple random sample is often not seen as a serious problem.

Potential problems to be considered with the use of systematic samples relate to the possibility of definite patterns in the listing of cases. If, for example, there happens to be a coincidence between the skip factor and some characteristics of the cases that are relevant to the research issues, systematic sampling can lead to a heavily biased sample. For instance, a systematic sample of households in a residential development in which each tenth parcel is a corner lot, which also utilizes a skip factor of 10, will either include all corner lots or no corner lots. If location on a corner lot is related to size of lot, exposure to street noise, income, or any other characteristic that might be relevant to the research questions, the sample is bound to be unrepresentative.

A second potential problem is that the cases might have been listed in some kind of rank order such that there is a trend running through the listing. Here the question is whether or not such a trend might relate to characteristics that are of interest to the researchers. An alphabetical listing of individuals does exhibit a definite trend, for example, but it will be totally irrelevant for most purposes; in fact, it might enhance the representativeness of the sample in terms of ethnic groups (Blalock, 1972, pp. 514–516).

If such a trend is relevant to the variables under consideration, systematic sampling may still be adaptable. If the case histories of program participants to be sampled about their opinions, for example, have been filed according to length of time in the program, and this longevity is likely to be linked with opinions, then a start near the beginning of the listing might yield systematically different results than would a start further down the list. One way to counteract this trend would be to use a calculated "middle start" instead of a random start, beginning with the case that falls one-half of the skip factor from the top of the list.

A second approach would be to use a skip factor that is larger than necessary to purposefully cycle through the complete listing more than once. This method might be very cumbersome if the "listing" is actually a physical order such as houses in a neighborhood, but it is highly feasible with the more common use of systematic sampling with secondary data files. For example, if the population listed contains 2,000 entries from which a sample of 200 is to be selected, the minimum skip factor for cycling through the listing once would be (2,000/ 200) or 10. Using a skip factor of 20 or 30 will require cycling through the listing two or three times instead of once, but it will also help to guard against any anomalies in the order of the listing. In general, systematic sampling is often an expedient way of drawing a sample, and its validity in terms of applying inferential statistics can usually be assumed *if* such potential problems relating to the way in which cases are listed are taken into account.

Stratified Random Sample

Although simple random sampling is free from systematic bias in terms of representing subgroups of the population or the levels of individual variables, it does not guarantee representative samples, as noted above. It is also the case that a simple random sample might not provide the most efficient estimates (although unbiased) of population parameters nor an optimal basis for making certain comparisons. Therefore researchers often move to the use of stratified sampling as an improvement over simple random sampling to suit their particular purposes.

A **stratified random sample** is obtained by dividing the population into subpopulations or **strata** and then drawing probability samples independently from each stratum. The sampling fraction used with each stratum may be the same, in which case the result is a **proportional stratified random sample**, or different sampling fractions may be applied to different strata, yielding a **disproportional stratified random sample**. Most commonly, the component samples from the separate strata are drawn with simple random sampling or systematic sampling, used judiciously as discussed above. If a population is stratified and the strata are sampled with nonprobability methods, the overall sample is of course not a probability sample. Here the term "stratified sample" will be used to connote a probability sample.

Proportional stratified samples are often used to provide added assurance of having a representative sample. Particularly when there are one or more subpopulations of interest that are quite small, there is a fear of underrepresenting or overrepresenting them in a simple random sample. In such instances, a proportional stratified sample may be desired to assure that each subpopulation is fairly represented in the sample. Given the nature of variation and the fact that a sample may be representative in terms of one variable and highly unrepresentative in terms of another, the critical consideration here is to stratify by some relevant variable. The underlying principle here is that the stratification is useful if it results in a relative homogeneity of cases within each stratum, in terms of the characteristics under investigation, with greater diversity among the strata in terms of these characteristics.

Usually we stratify by some primary independent variable that we have reason to believe is linked with the dependent variable or variables of interest. For example, if interest centers on analyzing the use of certain kinds of medical facilities by the general population, we might stratify our sample by age in order to rule out distortions that might result from the inclusion of too many or too few elderly persons in the sample. Note that stratified sampling is often based on two or more stratifying variables, such as age and income in the above example. This would entail breaking the population down into categories of these two variables and then taking independent samples from each of the cells in the resulting crosstabulation.

Disproportional stratified sampling is often used when there is interest in improving the efficiency of inferential statistical techniques or in facilitating certain comparisons. When primary interest lies in individual subpopulations or in comparisons among them, our major concern in sampling design is to include enough cases from each subpopulation to facilitate this kind of analysis. This might involve having sufficient cases to make inferential tests about subpopulation means and proportions, or it might relate to the need for large subsample sizes in order to permit extended elaboration using the stratifying variable as an independent or control variable. In either case some subpopulations might have to be sampled more heavily than others.

When primary interest lies in making inferential tests or estimates for the population aggregate as a whole, we are interested in maximizing efficiency given a total sample size. As we have seen, efficiency in this statistical sense refers to the extent to which a sampling distribution is concentrated around the true value of the corresponding parameter; a more efficient sampling distribution (or reduced sample error) results in narrower confidence intervals or decreased probabilities of type I errors, everything else equal. Note that a proportional stratified sample itself frequently achieves a gain in efficiency by precluding the possibility of unrepresentative samples with many extreme values and a resulting large standard deviation.

If sample standard deviations vary substantially across the strata, the overall efficiency may be further strengthened by sampling disproportionally because the standard error is a function of both standard deviation and sample size. If there is very little variation in the variable of interest within certain strata, they need not be sampled heavily in order to permit a reasonably small standard error, while strata in which there is much more variation would have to be sampled more heavily in order to achieve the same standard error. Because the efficiency of the overall sample depends primarily on the least efficient stratum, it would make sense to sample more heavily in those strata with the greatest variation. In fact, where data collection costs are the same for all strata, the most efficient sampling plan is one in which the strata are sampled in proportion to their *standard deviations* rather than numbers of cases.

If there are also differences in the costs of obtaining the data from stratum to stratum, because of geographic patterns or the work involved in searching through the files of different agencies for instance, the optimal allocation of sample cases to strata is directly proportional to the standard deviation of each stratum and inversely proportional to the square root of the cost of collecting the data for each case within the stratum. Precise knowledge about relative standard deviations and data collection costs among strata is usually not available, but very rough estimates of these differences have been found to yield sample designs that closely approximate optimal allocations, if there are substantial differentials in one of these factors. If the researcher does not have reason to believe that there are substantial differentials among the strata, there is no advantage in using disproportional stratification for efficiency purposes, although he still might want to sample disproportionally to facilitate comparisons across subpopulations.

Cluster Sampling

In situations where it is unfeasible to actually list all the cases in a population, or too costly to obtain the data on the widely dispersed cases that might be selected in a simple random sample, sampling may be carried out at a higher level of aggregation. With **cluster sampling** the individual cases or elementary units are grouped into clusters or sampling units, and a random sample of these clusters is taken rather than a random sample of the individual cases. Often the clusters reflect some kind of natural grouping that lends itself to this sampling technique. In its simplest form, a **single stage cluster sample**, all the cases belonging to the clusters that have been selected are included in the sample.

Cluster sampling is sometimes used with secondary data files in order to reduce the records search. For example, in drawing a sample from a very large number of agency clients built up over the past 10 years, the clients may be "clustered" by the first letter of their last name. If the agency's client files are organized this way and if there is no reason to believe that there is any linkage between this characteristic and the variables of real interest, it may be expedient to randomly select a few letters and then process the data for all the clients in those clusters.

The most frequent application of cluster sampling, however, is in **area samples**, which are made up of cases located in certain geographic zones that have been randomly selected. Area samples are used most often in conjunction with primary data gathering, which requires interviewers or observers to be "on site" for every case. If, for instance, a sample of participants in a statewide program for the elderly is to be surveyed, a number of the local agencies carrying out the program might be selected randomly and their clients included in the sample. The obvious advantage of this kind of sampling is that it is very economical to have concentrated data collection efforts in a few selected smaller areas as opposed to a geographically dispersed data gathering effort over a much larger area.

On the surface, cluster sampling would seem to have something in common with stratified sampling, in that the clusters of cases can be thought of as strata, but the similarity ends there. With cluster sampling it is desirable to use clusters that are characterized by a substantial internal diversity of cases and less variation among the clusters themselves so that a few clusters taken together might be expected to constitute a microcosm of the general population. This is the opposite of stratified sampling, which is based on the use of strata that differ substantially from each other in terms of the key variables of interest but that have a higher degree of internal homogeneity. If a cluster sample is developed on the basis of clusters that do not meet these requirements, the resulting data may be of little use. If a survey on housing conditions in a large metropolitan area were based on a few neighborhood clusters, for example, some types of housing conditions might be heavily overrepresented in the sample and other types excluded altogether, because different types of housing conditions tend to be concentrated in different types of neighborhoods.

Area samples are often developed by a **multi-stage sampling** process in which clusters that are randomly selected in the first stage are themselves subdivided into smaller clusters that are then sampled at the second stage, and so on, until random samples of cases are drawn from those clusters that have been selected in the initial stages. For example, a survey of rural transportation needs in a state might employ a four-stage area sampling process as follows: 1) First, a few rural counties would be randomly selected, and 2) in each of these few counties a few townships would be randomly selected. 3) The townships selected in these various counties would be subdivided by a grid system and a few grids would be randomly chosen. 4) Finally, a simple random sample of households would be developed in each of the grids included in the sample, and these households (the elementary units) would actually be surveyed in terms of their transportation needs.

By definition, a cluster sample qualifies as a probability sample only if the probabilities of selecting individual cases are known. It is not necessary that all cases have an equal probability of being included in the sample, but if the probabilities differ this must be recognized and taken into account in statistical analysis. Because the number of cases or elementary units may differ substantially from cluster to cluster, an unweighted simple random sample of clusters will result in unequal probabilities for different cases in a multi-stage sampling process. For example, if 100 households are to be selected from each township cluster included in the sample, a household in a large township has a lower probability of ultimately being included in the sample than does a household in a small township *if* each township cluster has an equal probability of being selected in the first place. If the researcher desires to equalize the probability of each household's being included in the final sample, he could weight the probability of each township's being selected at the first stage by the relative number of households in each township. Thus, if one township has twice as many households as a second township, the first should be given twice the probability of being selected at the first stage. If this sampling with **probability proportionate to size** is carried out at each stage, each case or elementary unit has an equal probability of being included in the final sample.

Area sampling is frequently used when the population to be sampled is large and geographically dispersed. It should be noted, however, that area samples and any other kind of cluster samples are likely to be far less efficient in the statistical sense than simple random samples or stratified samples. Given the differences among clusters that are bound to exist, cluster sampling usually involves a much greater sampling error. The researcher can of course begin to counteract this problem by including many more clusters in his sample, but this defeats the primary purpose of the cluster strategy, namely that it is more economical to collect data only within a few clusters. A cluster sample of a given size will often result in a sample error equal to that of a much smaller simple random sample, but the average cost per case of data collection may be substantially reduced. Cluster sampling, then, may be deemed more efficient overall if the need for a larger sample in order to maintain a certain limit on sample error is outweighed by the cost savings in data collection.

Work Sampling

In efficiency oriented process studies of program operation, interest frequently centers on the amount of time spent by employees in various activities or the time in which facilities and equipment are used for different purposes. This might relate, for example, to the proportion of time spent by maintenance workers in a nonproductive state, that spent by supervisors engaged in tasks that should be performed by subordinates, the time spent by program staff in interviewing prospective clients, or the amount of time that a central information retrieval system is "down," unused or being used by personnel from various city departments. In all of these problems the relevant breakdown of time periods could be determined by continuous observation, but this is costly even over a limited time span and, in the case of employees who are aware that they are being monitored constantly might produce a Hawthorne effect (see chapter 9) in which their behavior would deviate temporarily from normal patterns.

Work sampling is a method of obtaining data for such studies through the use of separate observations taken on the same subjects over time. The procedure is to divide the total time span of the study into very momentary time slots such as 1-minute intervals with a time clock orientation, and to take a simple random sample of these time slots. At each designated time, which has been randomly selected—9:52 a.m., 10:16 a.m., 10:31 a.m., and so on, for example—the subject is observed and its momentary state noted. Of course it is of the utmost importance that the activity or usage variable of interest and the criteria for determining which category a given observation fits into be clearly defined and understood before the data collection begins in order to contain measurement error. In addition, if the subject is an individual, it is preferable that he be unaware that he is being observed in this manner.

Work sampling is really just another version of simple random sampling. It is unique in terms of the specification of the unit of analysis, namely that each time slot constitutes a case in the population to be sampled. If a sufficient number of observations are taken (see chapter 7 for the discussion of required sample sizes), the proportion of time slots that are recorded in a certain activity or use category will provide a good estimate of the proportion of the total time that is occupied that way. Given random sampling, such estimates will be unbiased in terms of the overall pattern of usage of time, whether, for example, the time spent by an employee in unproductive states happens to occur frequently or infrequently, regularly or irregularly, or for long or short periods at a time.

The use of work sampling originated with time and delay studies in industrial plants and spread to studies of office routines, but it clearly has many applications in public administration, particularly given the growing interest in productivity improvement. Advocates of this approach claim many advantages over the continuous observation of a given operation, including the following:

1. It costs much less.
2. It does not require observers with special skill and training.
3. It leads to fewer complaints from operators under study.
4. It does not distort the operator's normal work routine as much.
5. Observations may be taken over a longer period of time.
6. It can be used to analyze the operations of an entire department.
7. It can be used when time study is not feasible (Neter and Wasserman, 1966, pp. 355-356).

NONPROBABILITY SAMPLES

Although this book emphasizes the use of probability samples because they provide a basis for making unbiased inferences to larger populations with some indication of precision and the probability of error, nonprobability samples are also appropriate for certain purposes. In general, they may prove useful to gain insight into a problem or facilitate exploratory examination of some relationships when a high degree of precision and the ability to generalize conclusions are not felt to be of great importance.

Judgment Samples

While random sampling processes in which cases are selected by pure chance may yield highly distorted samples or fail to contain sufficient variation in the key variables of interest, an alternative approach is to very purposefully construct a sample on a case-by-case basis that the researcher feels does provide the kind of variation or patterns of co-variation he needs. Such **judgment samples** are put together in this way based on the researcher's judgment, impressions, or preliminary examination rather than any kind of randomized mechanism.

An example might be an analysis of the impacts of a recently established federal block grant program on the activities of various types of local government jurisdictions in a state, in which the basic methodological approach requires fairly detailed case studies of all the jurisdictions to be observed. Because time and manpower constraints may severely limit the number of jurisdictions to be included in the study and the primary research question concerns the differential impacts on jurisdictions that vary in terms of population size and characteristics as well as past programming efforts, expenditure patterns, etc., the researcher may not want to rely on a random sample, which could fail to provide the necessary mix of jurisdiction types.

Instead, based on previous familiarity with a number of jurisdictions or the use of available secondary data on these characteristics, he may build a small sample that contains the requisite variation. Although the researcher cannot make a valid use of inferential statistics to make estimates or test hypotheses relating to the general population of local jurisdictions in the state, he may conclude that the general trend of his findings can be generalized beyond the sample if, in his judgment, the jurisdictions in his sample do constitute a representative cross-section of the total number of jurisdictions. Whether this kind of judgmental inference is the same as, or superior to, generalizing to the larger population "on blind faith" and how it compares with the use of random samples and inferential statistics begs the question of the quality of his judgment in the first place and, in general, may be a debatable issue in certain research contexts.

It should be pointed out that the data obtained through interviews in sample surveys may constitute a judgment sample in technical terms because of the problem of nonresponse, even though the original set of households or individuals to be surveyed might have been developed with random sampling. Such survey data are usually, and should probably continue to be, analyzed using inferential statistics; but if there is a substantial lack of response for whatever reason, the validity of generalizing the findings to the total population of interest depends in effect on the *judgment* that the cases for which the data have been obtained do constitute a representative cross-section of that population. This is also a problem when a brief community survey is initially planned as a virtual census, with a questionnaire mailed to every household in the city. Although the absolute number of returns may be impressive, it may constitute only a small fraction of those that were mailed out, and to assume that the households who responded constitute a cross-section of that population may be totally misleading.

Chunks

In some instances samples are used that are the product of neither random sampling nor selective judgment, but rather a collection of cases whose only advantage is that they are readily available. Such samples that are used because the data have already been collected or because the cases are conveniently at hand are commonly referred to as **chunks**. Although chunks are clearly inappropriate for generalizing conclusions with any degree of confidence beyond the sample itself, they may serve as interesting case studies or purely exploratory analysis aimed at identifying likely research issues rather than actually testing hypotheses.

For example, if a researcher is interested in identifying the kinds of problems that participants in drug abuse programs have in coping with work or school-related problems, he may base his analysis on a number of participants in one particular program because he has ready access to them through a connection with the program director. This may provide some insight as to what those problems are, but its most valuable product would be the development of worthwhile hypotheses and a systematic plan for addressing them on a more generalizable basis.

As a second example, consider a project aimed at developing aggregate effectiveness and efficiency measures of urban mass transit systems and relating these to certain operating characteristics. Given the initial decision to use aggregate data analysis, yearly reports submitted voluntarily by a few transit systems to a state's department of community affairs might be very attractive as an available data source. If the results do have some practical significance, however, they can be generalized beyond those systems in the study only to the vaguely defined population of "all similar transit systems" with any degree of confidence.

So-called **voluntary samples** in which the general purpose of the study or survey is made known to individuals or groups who may then volunteer to participate may also be considered essentially to be chunks. In these situations cases are clearly not chosen randomly and the researcher is not carefully constructing a judgment sample. If organized groups are targeted for the possible inclusion of their members in a sample because the characteristics of the various groups are thought to relate to the topic being analyzed in some way, the sample may seem to be a judgment sample at the first stage, but if the individual members are then included in the sample on a voluntary basis, these component samples are really chunks.

One other type of sampling technique that is encountered fairly frequently in certain types of surveys is the **quota sample**, in which the desired numbers of cases in various categories of respondents are predetermined with people then being interviewed or observed on a "first come-first served" basis until all the quotas are filled. For example, in a local public opinion survey quotas might first be set for so many black males between 20 and 40 years old, black females between 20 and 40 years old, white males above 40 years old, etc., with interviewers on selected street corners interviewing passers-by who fit into the various categories until each quota is met. Although quota samples do have an element of judgment built in to assure the desired distribution of respondents in terms of certain characteristics, they are probably classified more accurately as "stratified chunks" given the uncontrolled nature of who might be exposed to the interview and the hit or miss pattern of who actually responds.

ALTERNATIVE SAMPLING PLANS

The basic considerations in developing a sampling strategy, relating to both type of sample and sample size, include 1) the nature of the population of interest, 2) the primary purposes of the analysis, 3) the types of statistical techniques that might be used, 4) the relative ease or difficulty in the mechanics of listing cases and drawing the sample, and 5) the costs of and resources available for collecting the data. In general, we are often interested in two criteria of the worth of a sample, **sample reliability** or the extent to which the sample is representative of the larger population (also used to refer to sampling procedure used in terms of unbiased selection of cases) and **sampling error** or the degree of precision in making estimates of population parameters. As discussed above, the general criterion of efficiency refers to usefulness of the sample data relative to data collection costs.

These kinds of considerations come into play in many ways. As discussed in chapter 7, for example, greater variation of the key variables in the population will require a larger sample to obtain the same degree of precision in making inferences than would be the case if the variances were smaller. On the other hand, the cost of collecting data on more cases might be offset by the lower per unit costs achieved by the use of systematic rather than simple random sampling of secondary data files.

When primary interest centers on drawing conclusions about a defined population based on sample data, and particularly when a high degree of precision is desired, some type of probability sample is usually in order. If a generally representative cross-section of the population is desired as a sample, a fairly large simple random sample will usually be suitable, and this provides the greatest flexibility in terms of statistical applications. On the other hand, if it is felt to be important to have a sample that is representative in terms of certain key variables that may be quite unevenly distributed in the population, a proportional stratified sample may well be preferable. If the primary purpose is to make comparisons among certain subgroups, some of which are not likely to be adequately represented in any kind of proportional sample, the researcher may turn to a disproportional stratified sample in order to facilitate this kind of analysis. As has been seen, stratified samples can also be used to gain a tighter control over sampling error.

On the other hand, when the primary purpose is to gain some insight regarding possible relationships among certain variables, particularly at exploratory stages, hand-built judgment samples developed to assure the desired kinds of variation may be optimal, regardless of the fact that they may be highly unrepresentative of the larger population. Even when a representative sample is desired, and especially when cost constraints limit the sample size to less than what would be considered adequate with simple random or even stratified sampling, a judgment sample might be appropriate if the researcher is confident that he can key in on the right variables.

Although chunks are the least desirable kinds of samples in terms of reliability and sampling error, they may still be useful for exploratory kinds of research purposes. Where accessing cases preselected on a random basis would be difficult, and particularly when time and cost constraints make random sampling impractical, the use of voluntary samples or other kinds of chunks may be the only feasible option. Sometimes the use of quota samples can provide some degree of structure to facilitate comparisons or assure a wide range of variation, but any kind of generalization of results beyond the sample itself is based on blind faith.

Although judgment samples and chunks are often employed because of time and resource considerations, these same factors lead to the use of cluster samples. With large populations that may be grouped in some kind of natural units, and especially in the case of populations geographically dispersed over large areas, cluster sampling may provide an attractive alternative to either more evenly distributed random samples or judgment samples and chunks. Although reliability and precision may be greatly decreased with cluster samples in comparison with simple random or stratified samples, cluster sampling does provide a compromise between the desire for a probability sample and cost considerations with certain kinds of populations.

Finally, it should be noted that in program evaluations that involve overt experimentation, in which certain variables are carefully manipulated while others are held constant as in a laboratory setting, the kind of samples most commonly encountered are chunks and judgment samples. (See chapter 9 for a discussion of various types of experimental models.) It may seem incongruous at first that the most elegant type of research design is often used in conjunction with the least sophisticated kind of sampling procedure, but the rigid requirements of treatment interventions and control over other factors inherent in experimental designs often effectively limit the alternatives to voluntary samples or other kinds of chunks. Thus, the findings generated by true experiments may be valid only for the observed cases, and the ability to generalize conclusions beyond the sample depends on replications and the reinforcement or modification of results.

Sampling and Statistical Analysis

The appropriateness of various statistical techniques with data from different kinds of samples needs to be mentioned here, because it is an important topic that is frequently overlooked. The formulas given in this book for inferential statistics are based on the assumption of simple random sampling; they may or may not be applicable or adaptable to other types of probability samples. Quite often analyses of data drawn from different types of samples employ the techniques presented in this book on the assumption that the samples are "random" without adequate consideration of whether or not the assumptions upon which the techniques are based really apply. The discussion that follows is intended to provide only a brief overview of some of the relationships between sample design and statistical analysis.

First, the one level of statistical analysis that is always appropriate for any kind of population or sample is descriptive statistics. This applies to the descriptive examination and measurement of associations among variables as well as the use of univariate summary statistics. With judgment samples and chunks, particularly when the general purpose is exploratory analysis, the data should be mined with descriptive statistics to uncover patterns of variation and co-variation, but usually the use of inferential statistics to extend conclusions to the more general population is not appropriate. In some instances, however, inferential techniques might be used as applied to the data *as a population* as discussed in chapter 7. Furthermore, in analyses based on experimental designs, even though the samples may well be judgment samples or chunks, inferential techniques are commonly used, but in the context of controlling for the chance effect of the random assignment of cases to treatments rather than that of generalizing conclusions to larger populations. (See chapter 9.)

The inferential statistics covered in this book are based on the assumption of simple random sampling and although systematic sampling does not meet all of these assumptions, the use of these techniques with systematic samples is usually considered valid if the samples are developed with caution, as discussed above. Similarly, although proportional stratified samples do not meet all these assumptions, they do facilitate the use of the inferential techniques and in fact will err on the conservative side, tending to overstate the probability of type I errors or understate the confidence level associated with an interval estimate.

Disproportional stratified samples and cluster samples, however, present much more challenging problems. Usually the disproportional stratification is based on key independent variables, and thus adjustments can be made in analyzing dependent variables in a more representative way. For example, in developing a point estimate of the population mean from a disproportionally stratified sample, the cases must be weighted in terms of their relative frequencies in the population; essentially this involves computing a weighted average in which the relative frequencies are the weights.

Table 8.1 illustrates this, showing the computation of the mean average outstanding taxes for a sample of 600 tax delinquent properties in a city that had been stratified by local versus absentee ownership. The sample was stratified disproportionally in the first place because the absentee owned properties constituted a relatively small percentage of all tax delinquent properties (12.8 percent) while one purpose of the analysis was to make comparisons between these two groups. (Note that

Table 8.1. Computation of weighted mean average from disproportionally stratified sample

			Outstanding tax on tax delinquent properties		
Ownership	Number	%	Sample size	Sampling fraction	$\bar{X}_i$
Locally owned	12,436	87.2	400	0.032	$682
Absentee owned	1,822	12.8	200	0.109	$971
Total	14,258	100.0	600	0.042	

$$\begin{aligned} \bar{X} &= \Sigma W_i \bar{X}_i \\ &= 0.872(682) + 0.128(971) \\ &= 594.7 + 124.3 \\ &= \$719 \end{aligned}$$

the formula for weighted average used here differs on the surface from that presented in chapter 4. This is because the weights used here, proportions, sum to unity; thus there is no need to divide by a denominator of 1. The interested student could also compute this weighted average according to the formula shown in chapter 4 using the actual frequencies of these properties in the population as weights and putting the total number of properties, 14,258, in the denominator. This procedure would yield the same result.)

Modified formulas are also available for computing other descriptive statistics and for making estimates of individual parameters based on data from disproportionally stratified samples. More complex inferential statistics such as chi square, tests of hypotheses relating to ordinal data, and all the least squares techniques covered in later chapters in this book, however, cannot be used with disproportionally stratified samples without substantial modification (see Kish, 1965). One type of inferential technique whose use is often facilitated with disproportionally stratified samples is the two-sample t test discussed in chapter 7. If the sample was stratified by the independent variable, this technique may be employed for comparing the means between two subsamples that represent differing proportions of their respective populations because use of the technique is not based on any assumption of equal sample sizes or sampling fractions. Disproportionally stratified sampling may well increase the usefulness of the two-sample t test by reducing the standard error of the difference in sample means.

With cluster sampling these problems are even more critical. With single stage cluster samples and with multi-stage cluster samples, primarily area samples that are based on the use of differing probabilities proportional to size, samples may not be very representative but point estimates of population parameters will be unbiased. However, in addition to the fact that precision is generally lower with cluster samples than with other types of probability samples, the use of the formulas for inferential statistics as presented in this book may be extremely misleading and should not be used. The errors will usually *not* be on the conservative side, and their order of magnitude is much greater than with other samples. Thus, if the application of the standard two-sample *t* test with a cluster sample were to indicate that the probability of a type I error in rejecting the null hypothesis is 0.05, the true risk of error might be as great as 0.5 (Kish, 1965).

Other sampling strategies that have not been discussed so far in this chapter also merit brief mention in this context. Specifically, **matched samples** in which a simple random sample might be selected and then a second sample constructed case by case by matching individual cases to those in the first sample on a one-to-one basis are often used for comparative purposes. With respect to statistical analysis, the important point here is that this kind of data set really consists of a single sample of matched pairs rather than two independent samples. Therefore, single sample tests rather than two-sample tests are appropriate, as will be discussed in chapter 9. If the first sample is, in fact, a probability sample that lends itself to the use of inferential statistical techniques, then the single sample of matched pairs can be analyzed on that basis.

A more confusing situation arises with the not infrequent use of data sets that contain repeated observations on a limited number of cases. In a study of highway safety in a given state, for example, data might be collected on a random sample of highway segments for each year of a 10-year period. In effect, the basic unit of analysis here is the highway segment/year. Although the analyst might be tempted to think of his sample size as the number of highway segments *times* the 10 years and proceed to analyze the data as if it were one large random sample, this is not a valid application. Essentially this would represent the artificial expansion of N by a factor of 10. The alternative, and correct, procedure in this case would be 1) to combine the highway segments and treat the data as a single time series, 2) to keep the individual highways separate or combine them in groups according to some meaningful characteristics and treat the data as a number of parallel time series, or 3) to compute one or more rate of change type variables and treat the data as a single sample for the overall 10-year period.

SUMMARY

It should be kept in mind that the primary reasons for using sample data to analyze public programs relate to time constraints, available resources and sheer practicality, as data collection is often the most costly and time consuming phase of the whole project. The objective in designing a sampling plan, then, is to maximize the usefulness and validity of the data with respect to the particular research objectives at hand, within these time and resource constraints. This chapter has presented a number of varied sampling strategies, some more suited for certain purposes than others, and the development of a sampling strategy for a particular project, regarding both type of sample and sample size, will often involve trade-offs in terms of the considerations discussed above.

A decision on a sampling strategy is in effect a commitment of resources that should be used effectively and efficiently in pursuit of research objectives, and, therefore, a careful consideration of the alternatives in light of these objectives is warranted before such a decision is made. Sometimes important considerations that should be taken into account in the determination of what kind of sample to use are overlooked, particularly those relating to the use of various statistical techniques in conjunction with different kinds of samples. It should be remembered that the validity of statistical analysis of the data depends on the sample as well as the techniques applied, and that a poor sampling plan may well be the weakest link in the overall research design. On the other hand, carefully thinking through the pros and cons of alternative sampling plans may well suggest ways of improving the data base that greatly enhance the quality of the analysis.

REFERENCES

Blalock, H. M., Jr. 1972. Social Statistics. 2nd Ed. New York: McGraw-Hill Book Company.

Kish, L. 1965. Survey Sampling. New York: John Wiley & Sons, Inc.

Loether, H. J., and D. G. McTavish. 1976. Descriptive and Inferential Statistics: An Introduction. Boston: Allyn & Bacon, Inc.

Neter, J., and W. Wasserman. 1966. Fundamental Statistics for Business and Economics. Boston: Allyn & Bacon, Inc.

Stephen, F. F., and P. J. McCarthy. 1958. Sampling Opinions. New York: John Wiley & Sons, Inc.

Sudman, S. 1976. Applied Sampling. New York: Academic Press.

GENERAL RESEARCH MODELS

9
PRINCIPLES
OF RESEARCH DESIGN

Research design constitutes the methodological approach to a research problem. In general, it serves as the "blueprint" for the overall research effort, the methodological plan for addressing a given set of research questions from the definition of measures through data collection and analysis to the drawing of conclusions. More specifically, the term refers to the basis established for testing given hypotheses, including the specification of the observations and comparisons to be made as well as the outcomes of this analysis, which will lead to accepting or rejecting the hypotheses. Although a piece of research can rarely, if ever, produce a final verdict on a program's worth, a legal analogy is not wholly inappropriate. Setting a research design is in many ways comparable to establishing what constitutes admissible evidence and fair trial procedure in a particular case and specifying those findings that should lead to the conclusion that a defendant is innocent or guilty.

While the systems approach to problem specification is used to develop a conceptual framework for analyzing a program, the research design provides an analytical framework for measuring program performance. It is aimed at assuring a fair, unbiased evaluation and as such is concerned more with obtaining adequate and proper data than with the statistical analysis of those data. Very often this implies a need for manipulating a program's implementation or operation to some extent in order to generate the adequate and proper data, rather than relying solely on data that can be readily collected from the field.

This chapter focuses on the selection and development of appropriate research designs and the application of statistical techniques with certain designs. The first section describes the underlying concerns of program evaluations including experimental error and threats to validity. The following three sections present outlines of various types of nonexperimental, experimental, and quasi-experimental research designs, respectively. Then, the use of statistical analysis with different types of designs is considered. The last section discusses various factors relating to the feasibility of alternative types of designs and their appropriateness for different kinds of program evaluations.

RESEARCH DESIGN OBJECTIVES

The primary concern of research design is the validity of the research, assurance that the findings and conclusions of a program analysis represent real world occurrences or relationships, unbiased by the way in which the analysis was structured or carried out. The quest for validity usually entails attempts to isolate cause and effect patterns and safeguard against the contaminating effects of extraneous factors. With respect to research design, then, the concept of validity developed in chapter 3 can be expanded to relate to the strength and veracity of overall conclusions as well as the appropriateness of individual operationalized measures.

The issue of appropriate research design is especially critical with respect to program impact evaluations, and the discussion in this chapter will center on analyses attempting to draw conclusions about cause/effect relationships between program stimuli or treatments and their impacts on the environment. As will be seen, designs range from highly structured, controlled experiments to much less structured, less sophisticated case studies and cross-sectional data analysis. The classic approach, in theory if not in practice, is the **true experiment**, which isolates as much as possible the effects of program stimuli from those of other factors, which might confound the results. However, less structured designs are frequently employed, and the results must be interpreted in light of their inherent weaknesses.

As discussed in chapter 5, determining that a causal relationship exists requires observing empirical associations that would be expected in light of the postulated relationship and being able to rule out all rival explanations. It is incumbent upon a research design to meet both these requirements. If the anticipated results do in fact materialize, the design must be capable of ruling out competing hypotheses, and if not, the design must have provided a fair test, free from factors that might have suppressed the anticipated effects. Even with strong designs that satisfy these requirements, it should be kept in mind that with respect to making generalizations about causal relationships, the results are best considered to represent tentative conclusions subject to further testing rather than absolute confirmation or rejection of hypotheses.

Experimental Error

The purpose of a program evaluation is to obtain a clear indication of the varying effects of alternative program treatments or the difference between operating a program and no program at all. If we conceive momentarily of every type of program evaluation as at least a very loose "experiment" in which a program is implemented and monitored, we can define **experimental error** as the imprecision and variability of the results of such evaluations; variation in the dependent variables across all the cases included in the analysis, which may be attributable to a myriad of causal factors other than program treatments. In general, the more experimental error present in the analysis, the more difficult it is to interpret the results in terms of the effects of program treatments.

Experimental error may originate from two sources, random variation and systematic bias, and the distinction between these two components may be likened to that between reliability and validity of operationalized measures. The **random error** component is due to both a lack of precision of the measures used and an inability to take into account all the factors in the complex webs of interrelationships characterizing many social program areas that might influence the dependent variables. Random error is almost always present in program evaluations, but it is less problematic if it arises from the effects of numerous, singly unimportant causal factors or unbiased measurement error; the key point is that random error is independent of program treatment variable influences.

The presence of any **systematic bias** component of experimental error represents a defect in the research design. Any factor that might influence comparisons among program treatments other than the nature of the treatments themselves represents a systematic bias. To illustrate the difference between random variation and a systematic bias, consider an experiment in which two alternative teaching methods are being compared in terms of the test scores of students in two classes. If the two methods are tried out on two classes that are equivalent in their proportions of slow, intermediate, and fast learners in the subject area and with teachers of comparable teaching skills, this may be basically a fair comparison. Because each class consists of a mixture of students with differing abilities, we would expect to find a considerable amount of variation in test scores within each class, but differences in mean average test scores between the two classes could probably be attributed to the difference in teaching methods. The variation within each class would constitute random experimental error because of factors independent of the program treatments.

On the other hand, if it happened for some reason that the better students tended to be in one class, with the poorer students in the other, there would be a systematic bias in the research design. Not only would differences in the abilities of the students produce variation *within* each class, but it might also account for a difference in mean scores *between* the two classes; thus it would not be possible to determine whether the difference in test scores is because of variation in teaching methods or variation in the composition of the classes.

Any systematic bias in a research design can produce rival explanations for observed effects, thus preventing the evaluator from determining that it is the program or treatment itself that leads to these effects rather than some other causal factor. The primary objective in building a sound research design, then, is to avoid such biases, termed **threats to validity.** Beyond the issue of systematic error, the principles of research design can also be used to strengthen an already sound design by reducing the random component of experimental error. This can be done through both the structure of the design and the sample sizes employed, and inferential statistical techniques can be used to take into account the remaining random variation.

With the more highly structured research designs, there is much less reliance in general on statistical methods. With true experiments they are used primarily to deal with the probability of chance effects due to random variation. Sometimes they are used secondarily to specify the effects of program treatments more clearly by examining differences among cases as classified by client characteristics or other environmental variables, independently of program treatment variables. With weaker research designs the evaluator is often forced to resort to methods that "statistically control" for possible influences other than program treatments that the research design fails to control. This involves examining the association between two variables while fixing for the effects of additional variables, as discussed in chapter 5, but such analysis is limited to findings of statistical associations, not verifiable relationships. Using statistical analysis to take systematic biases into account is no substitute for a strong research design that avoids them in the first place.

Other Considerations

In addition to guarding against systematic biases, research designs can also be evaluated in terms of the amount of useful information they provide. In part this is a question of reducing random error, but other factors impinge as well. Beyond the conclusion that one strategy produces better results than a second strategy, the evaluator may want to estimate the magnitude of the differences in effects; his ability to do this will depend both on random experimental error and the sampling plan employed. Some designs can lead to valid conclusions about differences in the effects of various strategies, and others are intended primarily to provide an indication of the degree of improvement in the impact criterion from before to after the program's implementation. Furthermore, designs differ widely as to the extent to which they permit the evaluator to specify the circumstances external to the program treatments themselves under which favorable results are achieved.

Finally, an extremely important practical consideration is that, with respect to a given program evaluation, there may be several candidate research designs that vary significantly in terms of the cost and feasibility of implementation. A major theme throughout this chapter relates to the degree of control over program implementation or operation required by alternative research designs; often the most attractive designs in terms of the validity and usefulness of the data generated are the most difficult to use in practice because they would require the manipulation of program variables in ways that are unacceptable to program managers and agency personnel. Similar trade-offs often exist between the quality of a research design and the time and money costs of carrying it out.

Threats to Validity

Because the overall validity of results is really the acid test of a program evaluation, some discussion of the systematic biases that threaten validity is warranted to provide a framework within which individual research designs can be examined. A classic discussion of the appropriateness of alternative research designs, with respect in particular to assessments of public program interventions, is contained in the treatise by Campbell and Stanley (1963) in which the authors itemize a list of threats to validity under two categories, threats to internal and external validity. **Internal validity** refers to the validity of results as they pertain directly to the individual program, demonstration, or set of cases under study, while **external validity** refers to the generalizability of these results to the larger set of programs, treatments, or clients that is of interest. Containing threats to internal validity is the first requirement of a sound research design, because without internally valid results the question of generalizability is a moot point.

Threats to Internal Validity   The internal validity of an evaluation is jeopardized whenever a design is vulnerable to the possibility that some factor other than program treatments actually is responsible for the effects that have been observed and attributed to program variables. There may be other substantive factors not taken into account or controlled for by the design or features of the design itself, which bias the results. If such threats are present, the conclusions drawn may be artifacts of the way in which the evaluation is conducted rather than valid representations of program impacts on the environment. Brief definitions and examples of eight classes of internal threats (Huston, 1972; Campbell and Stanley, 1963) are as follows:

History includes any set of events other than program activities or treatments that are concurrent with the program and may be influencing outcomes independently of program effects. For example, the effectiveness of a program to encourage community involvement with schools would be obscured if local teachers went on strike during the program. In general, the longer the time period under consideration, the greater the danger of historical factors rivaling the program as plausible causes of change.

Maturation denotes natural changes in people over time which can be mistaken for program effects or the lack of intended effects. A simple before and after comparison would be inappropriate for evaluating a long term health care program for instance, because as people grow older their health tends to decline; thus, there would be a systematic bias towards underestimating the program's effectiveness.

Testing refers to the effect of having taken a pretest on posttest scores. The familiarity with a particular testing format gained during a pretest may well produce an improvement on a second test, and even when different testing instruments are used the added experience of being tested in a pretest may have the same effect, which might be interpreted erroneously as a real improvement produced by the program.

Instrumentation or instrument decay refers to changes in the ways in which measures are actually taken, which by themselves can result in differences in the observed values of outcomes variables. The evaluation of a program intended to improve social adjustment, for example, might employ periodic interviews with the participants. If the psychologists conducting these interviews change their standards of judgment or interpretation in any way across the series of interviews, this could create pseudo changes in the outcomes measures.

Statistical regression may also be a problem when measures are repeated as in a before and after comparison. It refers to the likelihood that on any given observation, some cases take on extreme values which deviate considerably from their normal range. These cases will tend to "regress" to their normal values on subsequent observations. This threat is especially salient when the participants in a program have been selected on the basis of extreme scores in the first place, because there will be a systematic tendency for their scores to move in a given direction on the next test, producing pseudo program effects. Thus, the effects of a remedial reading program will be overestimated if students were placed in the program on the basis of extremely low scores on a single reading test.

Selection is a potential threat whenever an evaluation is based on the comparison of outcomes among groups of cases whose makeup has not been determined by random assignment. While the comparison groups differ in terms of the program treatments they receive, they may also differ systematically on any other variables which might influence results, and it will not be possible to sort out the program effects from these "group effects" with certainty. Although such comparison groups may be well matched on a number of important variables, the evaluator cannot be certain that non-randomly assigned groups were in fact equivalent in terms of all the factors that might have influenced final outcomes.

Experimental mortality refers to the attrition of cases during the program duration or evaluation period. If, for example, there is a systematic tendency for the less able participants to drop out of a program or to refuse to submit to measurement, the average score of the remaining cases will automatically go up even if the program has no other effect. If the evaluation is based on a comparison of groups exposed to different program treatments, differential rates of experimental mortality can compound the problem. It should be understood, however, that this is only a real problem if the analysis is limited to comparing outcomes in the aggregate or care is not taken to include in the analysis of program effects only those cases which remain in the program and are measured at all observation points. (Of course, separate analysis of attrition rates and comparisons of the dropouts with those completing the program can provide valuable insight as to whom the program is best suited for and the expected response to similar program initiatives in the future.)

Selection-maturation interaction refers to different rates or patterns of maturation among comparison groups, such that differences in observed outcomes among the groups may be produced by systematic differences in their maturation processes but be mistaken for bona fide program effects. This threat is of particular concern whenever an evaluation is based on long term comparisons among non-randomly assigned comparison groups.

Instability basically reflects a lack of reliability in the operationalized measures used in an evaluation (imprecision or unsystematic inconsistency in taking the measures), random variation in sampling persons or program components, or random fluctuations in outcome indicators across time. This is the only threat which can be contained with the use of inferential statistics.

Threats to External Validity External validity is the degree to which analytical results about the effectiveness of an individual program or set of programs under study can be extended to other similar programs. It may be especially pertinent, for instance, with respect to whether the results obtained from the evaluation of a demonstration project represent a valid indication of performance if the program is implemented on a more widespread basis. Although the results of a given program evaluation may be internally valid for the projects actually studied, they may not apply to other applications of the same program treatments if the observed programs are unique in any way, varied in the way they are actually conducted, or different in terms of the setting or client characteristics. Furthermore, the conduct of the evaluation may generate effects that can be mistaken for valid impacts, in which case the conclusions are artifacts of the evaluation rather than products of the program.

As will be seen throughout this chapter, the requirements of a research design depend on the purpose of the evaluation as well as the nature of the program and its setting. If the evaluator is basically interested in testing the effectiveness of an individual program, for example, external validity may be of less concern, but if he is interested in theory testing or examining the assumptions underlying program logic, external validity is crucial. Five general classes of threats to external validity (Bracht and Glass, 1968; Bernstein, 1976; Campbell and Stanley, 1963) include the following:

Interaction between testing and treatment includes any responses to the stimulus of being tested or observed that might interact with the treatment or be mistaken for effects of a program treatment. Pretesting might well sensitize clients or program participants in a way that would cause them to behave differently than would clients or participants in similar programs who were not tested. For example, initial interviews intended to measure homeowners' interest in burglary prevention techniques might themselves heighten that interest and make them more receptive to the program. Similarly, posttests might prompt latent reactions that would not materialize in similar situations where evaluations were not being conducted.

Selection can threaten external validity as well as internal validity if the people observed in the evaluation are not representative of the larger population of clients or prospective clients, even though these participants might have been randomly assigned to groups. If participants in a demonstration project, for example, are selected on the basis of expediency or their high potential for success, they may receive the program treatment differently from other potential recipients. If social programs intended to serve disadvantaged subpopulations are tested with relatively more advantaged subjects, the results may appear to be much more favorable than would be the case with the intended target group. Furthermore, there can be interactions between selection and measuring devices that produce misleading results. A measuring instrument that is "culture bound" with a white, middle class orientation, for instance, may fail to pick up significant effects of a program on lower income Spanish-speaking clients.

Reactive effects of experimental arrangements are produced by the patent artificiality of many evaluation settings. These may be guinea pig effects in which behavior is altered simply due to the fact that people know they are being observed, they may be more calculated adjustments in behavior geared to the self-interest of respondents and their perceptions of the likely consequences of alternative outcomes of the evaluation. In general, such reactive effects are likely to produce more positive or beneficial indicators, more program success, than would be obtained in more normal settings. They are often termed "Hawthorne effects" after the findings of the Hawthorne Western Electric experiments that in some instances productivity continued to increase when such conditions as illumination and rest periods were made worse as well as when they were improved. The interpretation of these findings was that the effects were due to the existence of an experiment and the additional attention paid to the workers rather than the experimental treatments, i.e., the changes in working conditions (Roethlisberger and Dickson, 1939).

Confounded treatment effects are impacts observed in a given program evaluation that may not apply to other similar programs because they are produced by a specific mix of treatments that might not pertain to the other situations. In a sense, any program implementation is unique in its specifics. There may exist a lack of uniformity or standardization of treatments among many similar type programs which would negate the transferability of conclusions from one to another, a problem that may be particularly salient in the assessment of a nationwide program that may take on somewhat differing characteristics in each local project. The sample of projects actually observed might not be representative of the total number of such projects. Secondly, there may be a problem of multiple treatments in which the participants in the observed projects are exposed to any number of other planned and unplanned stimuli that jointly produce the observed effects. If this mixture of treatments does not parallel those impacting on the participants of other similar programs, the results of the evaluation may not apply to these other programs.

Situational effects are closely related to confounded treatment effects in that they differentiate the programs under observation from those to which it might be desirable to transfer the results. Included in this class are threats to "ecological validity" in terms of staff characteristics, the program setting, geographic coverage, or the point in time at which the evaluation is conducted which would render the results as site or time specific. Another type of possible situation threat is the "novelty effect," the newness of a program in an evaluation setting that might generate a much more noticeable response than would occur later under more ordinary operating conditions.

NONEXPERIMENTAL DESIGNS

The nonexperimental designs are by far the least structured, but most frequently employed, evaluation research designs. The notion of experimentation connotes some degree of manipulation of the variables of interest, some control over what is to be observed as well as over the observation itself. By contrast, **nonexperimental designs** consist solely of the observation of "naturally occurring" phenomena without any attempt to manipulate them so as to permit clearer comparisons to be made. Such designs are not only attractive to the practitioner or funding agency because they absorb the least time and money costs, but they are also, in many ways, the most manageable designs in that they do not require any interference on the part of the evaluator in the operation of an ongoing program, other than data-gathering procedures. The evaluator simply monitors the program's operation, collects whatever data might be available, and assesses the program's performance on that basis.

The findings generated with such an approach are basically descriptive in nature, and the data rarely permit the kinds of comparisons to be made that facilitate the confirmation of cause/effect type hypotheses with any degree of confidence. Conclusions that the program, or certain components of it, produced specific impacts are often vulnerable to rival hypotheses, and thus the internal validity of the results is questionable. The following discussion concentrates on threats to internal validity because the weaknesses of nonexperimental designs on this score make the issue of external validity an academic one.

One-Shot Case Study

The simplest research design is the one-shot case study, in which a program is initiated and data are collected on the impact variable or variables after treatments have been administered or after the program has been in existence for a long enough period to have achieved its presumed effects. This approach can be diagrammed as:

$$X \quad O$$

in which the X represents the program treatment and the O represents the observation, moving through time from left to right. This is clearly the weakest type of design because its results are not based on any real comparisons; data may be collected for numerous individuals participating in the program and subjected to elaborate statistical analysis based on a large sample size, but there are no comparisons with individuals who were not part of the program or who received different treatments. Taking the set of postprogram observations as representing the level of impacts achieved and evaluating this in light of specified objectives involves the implicit comparison of these findings with conditions that it is presumed would continue or develop if the program had not been implemented. The case study, then, can only be as strong as the validity of these untested presumptions, the very state of affairs that objective program analysis is intended to avoid! If the findings illuminated by the postprogram observations are favorable, the case study design is generally incapable of taking into account any rival explanation that might be suggested.

One-Group Pretest-Posttest Design

The following two nonexperimental designs are generally stronger than the one-shot case study, mainly because they are more informative because of the possibility of making direct comparisons. The one-group pretest-posttest design can be likened to the case study design augmented with an explicit observation or set of observations before the program is put into effect or a group of participants enters into it. It can be diagrammed as:

$$O \quad X \quad O$$

The advantage of this design is that it provides a measure of the change in the criterion or impact variables from before the program's initiation to after its completion, assuming that instrumentation is not a problem and that any observed change represents a real change rather than a difference in measuring instruments.

The danger inherent in this approach, of course, is the tendency to assume automatically that any observed change in the direction of the desired results is attributable to the program as opposed to any other possible causal influence. The design provides no controls for potential rival interpretations based on some concurrent change in the environment (history) or natural changes in the individuals being observed (maturation), which might reasonably be expected to produce similar changes. In some applications, the threat of statistical regression might present a problem, particularly if the individuals participating in the program were chosen or selected themselves into the program on the basis of some extreme measure. Furthermore, the design is vulnerable to the threat of pretesting, rather than the program itself, leading to some change in attitude or behavior. This last possibility will be reduced or eliminated if unobtrusive measures are employed. (The reader should not be misled by the names of some of the research designs discussed in this chapter into thinking that all the measures to be analyzed are in the form of test scores. In this instance, "pretest" refers to any type of measure taken before a program is initiated or any treatment is given to a new group of participants.)

Static Group Comparison

A third type of nonexperimental design, the static group comparison, can be likened to a one-shot case study whose observations are compared with those for a second group of subjects who were not exposed to the group. Again, although disaggregated statistical analysis may well be appropriate with this design in a particular evaluation, basically it involves a comparison between two situations: treatment versus no treatment, or program exposure versus no exposure. This can be represented as:

$$X \quad O$$

$$O$$

The static group comparison is sometimes referred to as an ad hoc comparison, which alludes to its major drawback. The comparison being made is not between two groups compiled by sorting or assigning individuals before the program treatment began, but rather on the basis of an attempt to find a comparison group that matches the naturally selected treatment group as closely as possible in terms of key characteristics. To a great extent the validity of the conclusions to be drawn from such a comparison hinges on a similarity between the two groups on all the relevant variables except program exposure. To the extent to which he feels the two groups are equivalent, the evaluator is wont to attribute differences in postprogram findings to the effect of the program, but there is always the possibility that there is some difference between the two groups being compared, a selection bias, that is the real cause of the difference in observed effects.

Often the composition of the group of individuals receiving the program precludes the likelihood of finding a "duplicate" comparison group. Problems ranging from logistics to the desire for privacy may prevent the evaluator from obtaining a truly comparable group, and usual practice in such low level efforts is to resort to the use of a comparison group primarily on the basis of readily available data and a lack of marked differences. Even when the groups are similar in terms of certain outward measures, the evaluator can never be sure that they are matched on the essential characteristics; in some situations the difference between participating and not participating in the program may itself reflect some dissimilarities in attitude or perceived prospects that might be crucial to the outcome.

The static group comparison design is in a way complementary to the one-group pretest-posttest design in terms of threats to internal validity. The static group comparison is open to problems of selection and mortality, the possible loss of cases from the program as it proceeds, which could account for differences between the treated group and the untreated group, two threats that are not really problems with the one-group discussed above. On the other hand, to the extent that the ad hoc comparison provides a fair comparison, it controls for other threats to internal validity. The effect of history is not salient, because presumably it would affect the comparison group as well, whereas the threats of pretesting, instrumentation, and statistical regression are not really of concern here either because the design does not include a pretest.

Correlational Studies

Much statistical analysis is performed on cross-sectional data consisting of measures pertaining to a complete set of observations or a sample of cases thought to constitute a representative cross-section of the population of interest. Such **cross-sectional** designs, or **correlational studies** as they are often called, are characterized by a complete lack of structure in the sense of collecting data on a group of individuals who have been exposed to the same program or comparing such a group with another discrete group that has not had the program treatment. Rather than employing a longitudinal design in which observations are taken at more than one point in time in an attempt to measure change over time, the idea behind cross-sectional analysis is to capture a wide variation in the measures of interest through observation of a number of diverse cases at one point in time. The strength and salience of associations between programmatic variables and impact measures, or any other associations that might be germane, can then be identified with statistical methods.

Program evaluations based on strictly cross-sectional designs often use fairly highly aggregated units of analysis so that at least most of the cases or data points have some useful information content. For example, a correlational study of the effectiveness of fire inspections conducted on a limited request or probable cause basis in reducing the outbreak of fires might use data for census block groups, clusters of city blocks, for a 5-year period. A high percentage of the block groups would be expected to have had fire inspections, providing sufficient variation in the independent variable for searching for associations with the dependent variable, outbreaks of fires. If, instead of compiling the data for all the block groups in a city, a random sample of households were selected, the data set would be swamped with "no inspection" households, possibly obscuring an important association. With disaggregated units of analysis, cross-sectional designs are often highly inefficient.

They are often useful in exploratory research, however, and are often appropriate for needs and demands studies or attempts to measure public attitudes toward a particular program through a community survey. Cross-sectional data analysis is mentioned at this point because it shares many of the same weaknesses that plague other non-experimental designs, in particular a vulnerability to the threat of selection. In a program impact evaluation based on cross-sectional data, for example, statistical analysis would focus on comparisons of those cases that happened to have participated in the program with the rest of the cases in the sample. Even with elaboration of these comparisons in terms of using background or attitudinal indicators as control variables, however, differences in outcome measures observed in the data may have been produced by any number of factors that cannot be accounted for with the existing data. Experimental isolation, which would preclude rival explanations of observed results, is completely lacking from cross-sectional designs.

Case studies focusing on the individual participants are sometimes treated as cross-sectional designs in which variations among the participants are analyzed to determine which characteristics or types of background facilitate the "success" of the program. This approach can be useful in identifying the effects of client characteristics, but it cannot provide a firm basis for testing the program's effectiveness. The point is that without comparison of participants and nonparticipants it is often very difficult, if not impossible, to determine whether the program is having any success in the first place. Because of the complete lack of structured comparisons among preselected groups that are known to be alike in some respects and different in others, cross-sectional studies do not permit the separating out of cause and effect patterns underlying observed associations. Statistically significant associations can be interpreted with possible cause and effect explanations, but it is not possible to rule out competing explanations and confirm that a program is producing its desired impacts.

EXPERIMENTAL DESIGNS

The strongest type of research design, and some would say the only true way of isolating and measuring the effects produced by a program treatment, is experimental design. True experiments are the only designs that can satisfy the three requisite conditions of evaluative research: 1) sampling equivalent experimental and control groups, 2) isolation and control of the stimulus, and 3) definition and measurement of the criteria of effect (Suchman, 1967). The use of valid performance criteria has been stressed throughout this text as a necessary condition of any worthwhile program evaluation; it is the first two of the requirements listed above that distinguish experimental designs from less structured, and generally weaker, research designs.

The basic principle underlying any true experimental design is the comparison of two groups or sets of cases that have no systematic dissimilarities except for program treatment. To the extent that this condition is met, any differences in observed effects can be attributed to the program treatment, or lack of treatment. In true experiments the effect of the program treatment, or stimulus, is isolated because there are no systematic connections between the variation in program treatment and any other factor that might have some bearing on the outcome. Because the two groups are not different with respect to any other characteristic or circumstance that might account for observed differences in measures of effects, such differences must be the product of the program variation.

Using experimental design to isolate cause/effect relationships can be thought of as a process of elimination; the experiment is structured so as to rule out rival explanations and thus any differential effects between test group and control group can be attributed to the program stimulus. Alternatively, experimental design can be viewed as an effort to *demonstrate* the causal logic underlying a program's intended operation. Rather than observe associations between program variables and apparent effects of an ongoing program in its natural setting, in which it is uncertain whether the effects are actually attributable to the program as opposed to some other factor operating concurrently, the experimenter tries to structure a fair test of the program's effectiveness that is uncontaminated by other possible causal factors. If, under otherwise unchanging conditions, the experimenter can consistently produce the desired effects by applying the program, and they are absent when the program is not applied, he can conclude that there is probably a causal relationship between program and effects. These interpretations are really two sides of the same coin; the point is that true experiments are the most rigorous method of assessing a program's effects because they employ fair comparisons in which only the program stimulus is allowed to vary, in isolation from any other factor that might also influence the effects.

Experimental designs are by far the most demanding to implement because they require that the evaluator have control over the exposure of individuals or cases to program treatments as well as the scheduling of data collection. Thus, the evaluator must be able to manipulate the "who" and "when" of both treatment and observation. The isolation of a program's effects by true experimentation therefore requires some degree of control over the program's implementation or operation. As is discussed below, the degree of control that is required is one of the main obstacles to the use of true experimental design in the evaluation of public programs.

Principles of Experimental Design

The major components of any experiment are the treatments and experimental units. At a minimum there must be two treatments including 1) the bona fide program strategy or application whose effects are to be examined and 2) a **control** treatment in which the program strategy under consideration is withheld. The control may be a "no program" alternative but does not necessarily signify the total lack of treatment. Obviously, in an experiment involving a nutrition program the control would not be enforced starvation, but rather a continuation of the normal dietary habits of the participants before the introduction of the experiment. In general, the control should represent the prevailing status quo, the benchmark against which the experimental treatment is to be tested. Many experiments incorporate multiple treatments, comparing three alternative versions of a newly developed program strategy with a "present program" control and a second control consisting of no program at all.

Often the program is simply withheld from the control group, but in some instances a placebo is given to the controls to further isolate the root causes of differences in effects. A **placebo** provides the aura or atmosphere of the program, but not its content, and is intended to distinguish between effects of the nature of the treatment and those that result as a reaction to being given the treatment. In a **blind** test, both experimental units and controls are given what seems on the surface to be the same treatment; the participants need not be aware that there are in fact two groups, one receiving only a watered down version of the program. Thus, any reactive effects to the experiment would be expected to materialize in both groups, whereas effects brought on by the substance of the real program should occur only in the experimental group. To further guard against experimental or observer bias, **double blind** tests are sometimes used in which neither the recipient nor the evaluator is aware of who receives the treatment and who receives the placebo.

The feasibility and even the desirability of a placebo is questionable in evaluations of many public programs. In medical research in which it is desired to distinguish between the pharmacological effects of a new drug as opposed to the psychological impact on the recipient of having been administered a drug, a placebo in the form of a "sugar pill" is very helpful. Similarly, in mental health programs or alcohol abuse programs the trappings of a functioning program without real treatment might serve at least to equalize Hawthorne effects. However, in many public service programs, it is really not possible to duplicate the appearance of a program without actually mounting the real thing. Furthermore a change in attitude or increase in confidence brought about by the awareness of a public program may be an intentional part of the program strategy. Even in the field of public health, the communication of a concern and commitment or the appearance of authoritative action may be the crux of a program decision (Suchman, 1967, pp. 96-100). If the purpose of an evaluation is to measure the impact generated by a program as applied in its entirety including its more superficial aspects, then a placebo is out of place.

The **experimental units** are the cases assigned to treatments and observed during the course of the experiment, the actual units of analysis. In human resource-oriented programs the experimental units are people, but in other types of programs they may be precincts, dwelling units, hospitals; whatever the program is intended to impact upon. In general, the level of aggregation should be dictated by the level at which the impacts are expected to materialize. Everything else equal, a larger number of small units is usually preferable to a few large units, in part because this facilitates greater statistical control over the chance variation inherent in the random assignment of cases to treatments.

For example, in an evaluation designed to compare alternative methods for teaching fourth graders to read, it would be preferable to randomly assign individual students to the treatment and control groups, rather than assign existing classes or homerooms to these treatments. However, this low level of aggregation is not always feasible, as in the case of teaching methods in which school officials might not permit the evaluators to tamper with existing classroom assignments. In other experimental contexts the type of anticipated effects may dictate the use of larger experimental units. Employee motivation programs, for example, might be aimed at producing group effects while many community development programs are intended to produce general neighborhood effects; in these instances the cases to be assigned to treatments might be work units and neighborhoods, respectively. In some experiments involving demonstrations, experimental units are selected on the basis of being highly susceptible to the program treatment, in order to establish whether the program *can* work, although these cases obviously will not be representative.

Experimental Design Process An idealized experimental design process for measuring the effects produced by a given program is represented in Figure 9.1. The first steps consist of the identification of the target population for which the program is intended, and the drawing of some kind of probability sample from it to provide individual cases to be used in the experiment. Such probability samples taken from the complete population of intended program recipients, however, are rarely used in practice. Depending on the specific purpose of the evaluation, this lack of probability sampling may limit the external validity with which the results of the experiment can be generalized.

Given a set of cases to be used in the experiment, whether randomly selected or not, the third step is to divide them into two groups, an experimental or "test" group and a control group. The lack of systematic bias between the two groups is the objective of the *random* assignment of cases to treatments, and this is at the heart of experimental design. The random assignment of individual cases to experimental and control groups guards against the threat to internal validity of selection bias; although there may be considerable natural variation among the cases, their random assignment to the two groups minimizes the likelihood that in the aggregate there will be differences in characteristics between the two groups. Thus, with random assignment, there should be no systematic connection between case or client characteristics and program variables.

The random assignment of cases is the primary strategy for separating out effects of the program from those of any other source. To assure the isolation of program effects from other possible influences once the groups have been established, then, they are treated in exactly the same manner as much as possible in every respect except implementation of the program. The experimental group receives the program whereas the control group does not. If nothing else is permitted to vary between the two groups, any differences noted can be attributed to the program treatment.

Given the random assignment of individual cases to the two groups and the controlled introduction of the program treatment, with or without a placebo, the effects of the treatment can be assessed by comparing impact measures between the two groups after the experi-

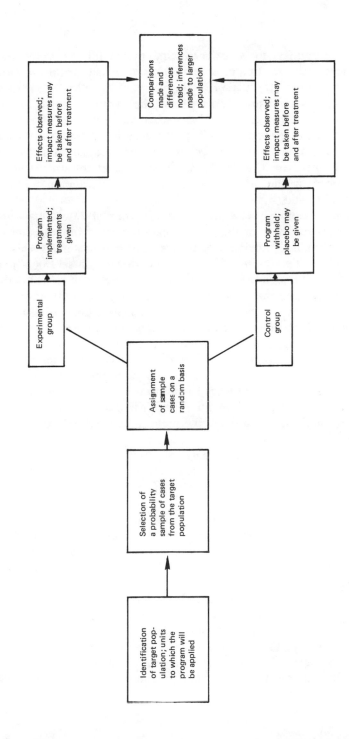

Figure 9.1. Idealized experimental design process.

ment has been in effect for a sufficient time period for the anticipated results to have occurred. Often, observations are taken on both groups before and after the introduction of the program in order to measure the magnitudes of change occurring, but the critical comparison in terms of isolating causal relationships is that between the "after" observations of the two groups. If, indeed, the experiment was based on a probability sample of the total target population, inferential statistical techniques can be used to estimate the magnitude of the difference in effects generated by the program as opposed to no program for that target population as a whole.

Additional Features   The random assignment of cases to groups and the similar treatment of the groups, except for the introduction of the program stimulus, provide a control against any systematic biases which might threaten internal validity. The threats of selection and regression are controlled for by the random assignment, while the effects of history, pretesting, maturation, and experimental mortality are accounted for by the random assignment in conjunction with the equal treatment of the groups for the duration of the experiment. Changing instrumentation is not a problem because the primary comparison is that between groups observed at the same time with the same instrument, although any differences in the way the measures are applied can invalidate the comparisons. Further randomization of other elements of the experiment may be used to guard against biases that might be linked to environmental conditions, the program delivery system, or the measurement process. For example, in the evaluation of a counseling program, randomizing the time or place of treatment or the assignment of interviewers to cases might shift some error from the systematic to the random component of experimental error (Riecken and Boruch, 1974, p. 54).

To the extent that these experimental conditions can be implemented and maintained, then, the evaluation will be internally valid; a second issue relates to the degree of precision that is attained. The results of a true experiment will still be subject to random variation among the cases, which can obscure real differences in effects between test and control groups. If the random variation is substantial, real but relatively small differential effects may be produced by the program and go unnoticed because they could occur by chance with a high probability. Although the practical consequence of such a problem is relative, i.e., a more substantial difference in effects would turn out to be statistically significant with a low probability of occurring as a function of the random variation, it is often desired to reduce the random component of experimental error as well as avoid systematic error in order to discern differences in effects more precisely.

One strategy aimed at a further reduction of experimental error is the use of **matching** in the assignment of cases to groups. The idea behind matching is to assure greater similarity between the two groups by dividing matched pairs of cases between them. The cases are matched in pairs according to values of relevant independent variables, those that are thought to influence the impact variable in addition to the effects of the program treatment, and then randomly split between the test and control groups. In general, the more variables used to determine matched pairs, the greater the confidence that a selection bias has been ruled out, *if* the right variables, those that have a bearing on the outcome, are included.

It should be understood that the cases are not necessarily individual persons. The unit of analysis might be the household, census tract, precinct, bus route, class, or any other unit. For example, an experiment designed by the Defense Department to assess the performance of solar heating systems in military base housing may use the building or structure as the unit of analysis. Groups of such structures on bases all around the country might be selected to include pairs of identical structures. If from each pair one building is assigned to the test group and the other is allocated to the control group, the two groups will be as similar as possible with respect to all the characteristics that might influence the impact measures, temperatures maintained and the percentage of home heating supplied by the solar unit. The only differnece will be that the test group structures will be retrofitted with solar heating systems but the control buildings will continue to be heated with their conventional systems.

It should be noted that if matching is to be used, cases should be matched in pairs and then assigned randomly to groups *in that order.* If an experimental group is somehow selected by itself with a later attempt to construct a control group by searching for cases that closely match cases in the experimental group, the result is not a true experimental design. The two groups might well be equivalent in terms of the variables on which the cases were matched, but if the cases are not randomly assigned to the two groups, there may be other systematic differences between them that could produce differential results.

Experimental error can also be reduced by incorporating concomitant variables into the analysis of results. For example, in the solar heating experiment there would be substantial variation in climatic conditions affecting the performance of solar systems within both the test and control groups. A **concomitant variable**, which varies among the cases but is not associated with the difference in treatments, that would be salient in this situation would be heating degree days. If statistical analysis can be used to remove the amount of variation in heating performance associated with the variation in heating degree days, the amount of random variation that remains will have been reduced, and differences between the two groups in terms of performance will be easier to interpret. As will be seen, random error can also be dealt with by additional features of an experimental design, in terms of the assignment of cases and treatments to groups.

Pretest-Posttest Control Group Design

The classic experimental design involves observations both before and after the program implementation taken on both the experimental and control groups. Using R to denote the random assignment of cases to groups, the pretest-posttest control group design can be diagrammed as follows:

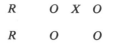

$$R \quad O \quad X \quad O$$

$$R \quad O \qquad O$$

In its simplest application the design involves only one experimental group and one control group, but it can easily be expanded to incorporate multiple test groups with alternative treatments. In the New Jersey Negative Income Tax Experiment, for example, some 1,200 families headed by able bodied males were randomly assigned to one of eight experimental groups or a control group. The eight groups received eight different incentive plans, consisting of combinations of some level of guaranteed income along with a tax rate on other income. Both test and control families were interviewed before the experiment began and periodically during its conduct in an attempt to determine whether the incentive plans produced any noticeable changes in employment behavior (Pechman and Timpane, 1975). This example represents somewhat of an elaboration of the basic pretest-posttest design in that it involves a continuing treatment and continuing set of observations.

A second example of this design would be an evaluation of alternative health insurance plans. Families in the target income range could be randomly assigned to one of four groups, test groups for three different plans and a control group, and monitored periodically for such factors as number of visits to physicians, quality of medical care received, satisfaction with the health insurance plans, and actual health status. If carried out according to plan, this research design is internally valid, but like many true experiments it may be vulnerable to threats to external validity. Although any experimental design may have limited generalizability because of either a selection problem or reactive arrangements, the pretest-posttest control group design is particularly vulnerable to the threat of interaction between program treatment and testing, producing effects that do not develop within the control group. If observed effects are only partially due to the program treatment they may not materialize when the treatment is applied but no pretest administered. In the health insurance example, an increase in the tendency to seek medical care on the part of the test groups might be because of the availability of health insurance, but in part it might have been prompted by the initial interviews that caused the respondents to think more about the advisability of seeing a physician when the need arises.

Posttest-Only Control Group Design

The advantage of the design discussed above is that although the risk exists of the beforehand observations influencing the results, it supplies data that can be used to measure the amount of change occurring before and after the experiment. In some situations, however, this might not be warranted either because of the desire to guard against the possibility of a reaction to the pretesting or because the particular nature of the subject under study does not require a before and after comparison. In such instances, the posttest-only control group design may be appropriate. This design can be illustrated:

$$R \quad X \quad O$$

$$R \quad\quad O$$

In an evaluation of a nationwide television campaign intended to encourage the reporting of health code violations, for example, a sample of cities might be randomly assigned to the experimental group in which the TV spots are aired and a control group in which they are not. After the campaign had been underway for a sufficient time a sample of households within each of these cities would be selected and interviewed about the occurrence and reporting of health code violations. If these sample households had been interviewed before the campaign was initiated, they might have been sensitized to the need for reporting such violations. Internal validity would not be hampered because such sensitizing would be expected to occur equally within both treatment and control groups, but the possible interaction of the pretesting with the TV campaign could jeopardize the external validity of the experiment. In this situation, the posttest-only design might well be preferable because it avoids this sensitizing effect. Although it does not provide a direct measure of the increase of the rate of reporting violations before and after the campaign, this increase can be inferred from the comparison of the two groups on the set of postcampaign observations.

In some cases the posttest-only design is appropriate because a before/after comparison is not occasioned by the nature of the program being evaluated. The case of an evaluation of a supportive employment program for former drug addicts is a case in point, because the primary purpose of the evaluation is not to measure improvement of individuals' behavior over some previous point in time. The program is designed to subsidize employment in service oriented jobs for ex-addicts to ease their transition from prison, and the purpose of the evaluation is to measure the impact of the program beyond the normal postprison support. Although candidates might be screened before acceptance into the program and then randomly assigned to experimental and control groups, the impact measures of work performance, drug abstinence, criminal activity, and personal relations would be taken solely on a post-treatment basis (Vera Institute, 1973).

Solomon Four-Group Design

The Solomon four-group design is a combination of the two experimental designs discussed above. The cases are randomly assigned to four groups, two pairs of experimental and control groups. The four-group design is intended to provide information on before/after changes while at the same time controlling for the possible influence of pretest observations on subsequent behavior. All four groups are observed with the same posttests at the same time, but only one experimental and one control group are pretested. If the pretest interacts with the treatment to influence effects, this can be noted by comparing the posttest observations between the two experimental groups and between the two control groups. The four-group design is diagrammed as follows:

$$R \quad O \quad X \quad O$$

$$R \quad O \quad\quad O$$

$$R \quad\quad X \quad O$$

$$R \quad\quad\quad O$$

The Kansas City Preventive Patrol experiment made use of the four-group design in part in its attempt to determine the influence of alternative levels of routine police patrol on crimes rates, citizen perception of crime, police response time, traffic accidents, and citizen satisfaction with the police (Kelling, 1974). This study is a good example of the use of more than one design in a given evaluation. The basic design employed was a pretest-posttest control group design in which 15 police beats were matched in groups of 3 on the basis of crime rates, calls for service, and socioeconomic variables and then assigned to one of three patrol levels: 1) the normal patrol level, which was the control, 2) a proactive level, with two or three times the normal amount of patrol, and 3) reactive patrol, no routine patrol. Some of the data were taken from departmental records to make before and after comparisons on crime rates and case dispositions, while encounter surveys and participant observation were also used to monitor awareness levels, police activities, and police-citizen interactions during the experiment. However, the study also made substantial use of data collected in citizen surveys conducted both before and after the experiment was put into effect. In this portion the four-group design (actually using six groups in this case) was put into use by conducting one-half of the post observations as follow-up interviews with individuals who had been interviewed in the pretest, and the other half with individuals who had not been surveyed as part of the pretest. With this design it was possible to account for the possible effect of the pretest interviews in sensitizing people to the issues involved with police patrol and leading to changes in awareness levels or perceptions of crime and the police.

Randomized Block Design

Experimental error can often be further reduced by moving beyond a simple random assignment in the establishment of experimental and control groups. If considerable random variation is expected to result from differences in client characteristics and the key characteristics can be discerned ahead of time, it may be useful to sort the participants in an experiment into blocks on the basis of these characteristics and then to randomly assign cases to experimental and control groups within each block. In essence, this amounts to replicating the same experiment with a number of different groups of cases as classified by characteristics that are thought to have some influence on the outcome separate from the effects of the program treatment. Beyond the reduction of experimental error, through an accounting of externally influenced variation, moreover, this approach is beneficial in that it permits a much more precise specification of the results. It lends itself to comparisons of the efficacy of the program strategy for different groups of cases, aimed at determining whether it is more appropriate for some kinds of subjects and less appropriate for others. This design, called the randomized block design, can be illustrated as follows:

Block 1	R	O	X	O
	R	O		O
Block 2	R	O	X	O
	R	O		O
Block 3	R	O	X	O
	R	O		O

The above diagram represents the use of the pretest-posttest control group design with randomized blocks, but the posttest-only control group design or the four-group design could also be applied to randomized blocks, if called for. An example in which a randomized block design might be appropriate is an evaluation of effectiveness of a newly introduced, individualized teaching technique aimed at increasing the percentage of remedial students in a special education program who attain a verbal achievement that is comparable to the fifth grade level or higher. Because it is anticipated that students' performance in the experiment might be influenced by the type of delivery system to which they have been exposed previously, a randomized block design based on this factor should permit much greater precision in the analysis of results. Students in the program could be classified by delivery system (organized resource room in schools as opposed to itinerant visits to homes, for example) and the experiment conducted on samples from each subgroup randomly assigned to treatment and control groups. In this case a pretest-posttest design would probably be used in order to measure the improvement in verbal abilities gained by each experimental group.

Factorial Designs

The experimental designs presented up to this point, and the examples used to illustrate them, have involved the evaluation of one program strategy or comparisons of alternative approaches to one program component. Frequently, however, program managers and planners are concerned about interactions between various program components and require information on the effectiveness of alternative combinations of various levels or types of multiple components. Such alternatives, combinations of alternative work schedules with varying levels of supervision in proposed incentive plans for example, can easily be built into the designs discussed above, using any preferred combination as a treatment. If, however, the experimenter wishes to be more comprehensive and examine the effects of all or at least many of the possible combinations, he might use a factorial design in which varying combinations of the components' alternatives are established as treatments, with cases randomly assigned to them.

An example in which this approach might be useful is an experiment designed to determine the effectiveness of various alternative approaches to promoting increased usage of contraceptives in a program aimed at controlling population growth. If there are two sets of treatments or "factors" to be experimented with in the program, birth control method (intrauterine devices, oral contraceptives, and condoms) and promotional strategy (pamphlets, group meetings, and household visits), a complete factorial design would include a test group for exposure to each combination of the two. In this example there would be a total of nine test groups, with the possible addition of a true control group that would not intentionally be exposed to the alternatives of either factor. Analysis of the results of such a design would facilitate the comparison of the effectiveness of the alternative birth control methods, apart from the question of promotional strategy, and vice versa, as well as permitting the evaluator to identify any particular combination of the two factors that was found to be particularly effective. Of course, if some of the alternative combinations would be infeasible to implement, or if the experimenters have already identified the most promising approaches from among all the possibilities, it will be more efficient to employ a "fractional" factorial design comprehending only those combinations that are really of interest.

Use of Experimental Design

Although true experiments are the strongest type of research design and the only kind of design that can control for all the threats to internal validity with greater certainty, in the past they have been used relatively little in public program evaluation. On one count experimental designs have been criticized as being too highly structured to meet the needs of decision makers relating to the management of ongoing programs (Guba and Stufflebeam, 1968). One contention is that the rigor of experimental design requires holding the program constant over the life of the experiment rather than permitting or facilitating its continual development toward improved performance. Related to this is the claim that true experiments are appropriate for summative evaluations of end results, but not for formative assessments geared to improving the program as the evaluation goes along.

Both these criticisms have some validity, and experimental design is by no means recommended as the most suitable approach for every kind of program evaluation. Yet they imply more severe constraints on experimental design than necessary, and the reader should not be misled by the cut-and-dried diagrams and initial descriptions presented above into thinking that experiments cannot be tailored in some respects to the needs of a given evaluation. In the first place, differing strategies can be built into experiments with the factorial design, precipitating in some cases the need to change single strategies. Second, if a change in program approach is desired in the midst of an experiment, it may be possible to randomly subdivide the test group or groups, with one being put on the new track while the other continues with the original treatment. This would not only allow the program to be changed, but would also provide a comparison between the original and "improved" versions.

Furthermore, observations are not limited to pretests and then posttests administered at the end of an experiment, but rather observations can be made periodically throughout its duration. Treatments can be varied from periodic interval to interval, in which case the evaluation might be considered as a whole series of experiments, if lingering effects are not thought to be a problem. In some instances, the experimental time period might be shortened so as to provide "real time" feedback that might suggest program modifications, which could then be evaluated in the next time interval. Finally, if the program can be administered in cycles, experiments run in early cycles can be used to suggest changes in later cycles that themselves can be run as experiments.

The Issue of Program Control   In general, true experiments are often difficult to implement in real world settings because of the great amount of control the experimenter is required to exert over the operating program. In part this difficulty is symptomatic of a general opposition, on the part of administrators, to evaluators "interfering" with a program's operation during the course of the evaluation. This sometimes antagonistic turfmanship on the part of program managers, however, may be heightened in the case of true experiments because they do require a closer regulation of the program operation than other types of evaluations.

The primary difficulty in implementing experiments arises from the requirement for the random assignment of cases to experimental and control groups (Stanley, 1972). Very often the feasibility of using an experimental design breaks down over disagreements about the use and composition of the control groups, and these are often based on ideological disputes. The problem is usually where to find adequate controls. In many social and human service programs, participants self-select into programs on the basis of perceived needs and potential benefits. Individuals with comparable needs who do not elect to participate in the program may not be good controls because the attitudinal differences that underlie their decision may mark attributes that would lead to different outcomes if they were to be exposed to the program. Similarly, participants are often selected into programs and assigned to particular treatments by program staff based on professional judgment; to select other people into the experiment or to assign individuals to different treatments is often seen as contradicting the rationale underlying the whole program approach.

Frequently, the problem of obtaining suitable control groups boils down to the issue of whether it is ethical to withhold a service from people who need it and for whom it is intended. This is a classic example of a conflict between the demands of scientific rigor and the imperative of providing service, and a general reluctance to deny a service that program advocates argue is necessary and useful will often preclude a true experiment. Understandable as this point of view may be, however, the opposing argument in effect contends that if the efficacy of a program is as yet unproven, the "critical need" to provide the service may be based on invalid assumptions (Borgatta, 1955).

In many instances the problem of withholding service from a randomly selected control group is not critical, for example, in situations where resources are scarce in comparison with demands or in the evaluation of pilot programs that are to be implemented on a modest scale, leaving many potential clients unserved. For example, in the Salk polio vaccine tests some children were given the vaccine while others were given an inert placebo injection in a double blind test. Because many more of these controls would die than if they had been given the vaccine, withholding it would have been "morally, psychologically, and socially impossible had there been enough for all" (Campbell, 1969, p. 419). However, because most children had to go without the vaccine that year anyway, the creation of experimental and control groups was a "highly moral allocation of that scarcity so as to learn the true efficacy of the supposed good" (Campbell 1969; Meier, 1972).

In addition, when new program approaches whose effectiveness is largely unknown are in question, the withholding of service is not apt to be considered to be so critical. Finally, true control groups can sometimes be built into experiments without the ultimate withholding of service, as with the following design:

$$R \quad O \quad X \quad O$$

$$R \qquad\qquad O \quad X \quad O$$

$$R \qquad\qquad\qquad\qquad O \quad X \quad O$$

With this design the program is staged such that randomly selected groups of prospective participants serve as controls for the first treatment group and then receive treatment themselves. This design, which might be appropriate for the evaluation of programs in which the immediacy of clients' needs is less than urgent, also facilitates a formative approach that enables the program to be changed from stage to stage, thereby gaining comparisons of alternative ways of program delivery as well as program/no program comparisons.

Maintaining Experimental Conditions   Once an experiment is put into effect, it may prove very difficult to enforce and maintain experimental conditions across its timespan. Even though the random assignment of cases to groups is intended to guarantee the independence of treatments and selection effects, in the evaluation of actual programs in real world settings it is usually not possible to maintain complete control over the course of the experiment and all other factors that might influence results. In laboratory experiments that are more characteristic of basic research, the experimenters manipulate all the influences to which the subjects are exposed, but in applied experiments involving public programs this is not possible.

The behavior and activities of clients at times when they are not actually engaged in program activities is usually not controlled, and they may be influenced concurrently by many other kinds of factors. Although the experimenter can control how the particular program is administered or not administered, any number of other factors beyond the scope of the program may impinge upon the results. A saving grace, however, is that such influences may well pertain to both test cases and controls alike, thus introducing further random variation, but not bias, into the evaluation.

Besides such contamination from random factors in the environment, the experiment may also be plagued by the **interpenetration of treatment effects**. In real world settings it is often difficult, if not impossible, to isolate the various test groups and control groups from each other, so that a group receiving one particular treatment may also inadvertently be exposed to another. This threat is especially salient in communications research, for example in an effort to compare the effectiveness of alternative modes of communication in some kind of promotional campaign, where targets of a newspaper strategy might also hear radio spots with the same message.

Furthermore, it is often difficult to control the conduct of the treatments themselves over a prolonged period of time, particularly if the people responsible for carrying them out are either overzealous or not sympathetic to the program approach. For example, in the afore-mentioned Kansas City Preventive Patrol experiment, it was found that police officers assigned to the reactive (no patrol) beats were overreacting to calls for service and other problems that occurred in those areas, presumably in part because they believed that the lack of patrol might be detrimental to the well-being of those areas (Kelling et al., 1974). Working with the human variable always makes it difficult to carry out neat, precise experiments.

Problems of External Validity   One main drawback in the design of experiments is that they are often vulnerable to threats to external validity. If the experimental arrangements are artificial or conspicuous, the results may well be vulnerable to Hawthorne effects, which would limit their transferability to other instances of the same program ap-proach. Similarly, the sensitizing effects of pretesting, which would be absent in the normal implementation of the program, and the con-founding effects of the possible contamination of test cases and inter-penetration of treatments discussed above can render the results valid for only that one experiment. Peculiarities or uniqueness in any of the situational factors—staffing, setting, time, etc.—can have the same effect. Furthermore, the fact that most experiments in the field of public program evaluation are *not* based on probability samples of the complete target population brings up the question of possible selection bias, some systematic difference between the test and control cases in the experiment as opposed to other cases to which the program might be applied.

The lack of ability to control for these threats to external validity in many experiments underscores the need to replicate such experi-ments many times over. As is discussed in the section on statistical treatment of experimental data, the foremost concern is with the inter-nal validity of the project, rather than with making inferences to the larger population. A well designed and executed experimental evaluation will provide internally valid conclusions relating to the cases or projects examined, but generalizing these conclusions to the wider range of potential applications requires repeated replications of similar experiments in a variety of settings. Only if such replications repeatedly produce the same results can we begin to have confidence in the generalizations drawn from them.

QUASI-EXPERIMENTAL DESIGNS

On an intermediate level between experimental and nonexperimental designs, in terms of controls for threats to internal validity, are a number of approaches to the evaluation of program and policy effects that improve upon nonexperimental designs by incorporating or attempting to replicate some of the principles of experimental design. Collectively termed **quasi-experimental designs**, these methods have been refined and promoted in recent years and have been accorded added legitimacy as respectable designs, if applied judiciously in certain circumstances (Campbell and Stanley, 1963; Caporaso and Ross, 1973; Riecken and Boruch, 1974). In general they represent attempts to obtain some of the strengths of experimental designs without the full control over the situation required by experiments.

Quasi-experimental designs are intended for situations in which true experimentation is not feasible or desirable, conditions in which there may be no possibility of manipulating the experimental variables and in which the randomization of cases across treatments is not possible. However, experimental stimuli often occur naturally, without the active intervention of the researcher, as the policies and programs of an experimenting society, and the quasi-experimental approaches are designed to study the impact of such "reforms as experiments" (Campbell, 1969). As such, many quasi-experimental evaluations are thought of as unplanned, natural, or post hoc experiments. Other quasi-experimental applications are sometimes thought of as "field experiments," as distinct from natural experiments, although the boundary between the two is very indistinct. As defined by some writers, **field experiments** are those in which the evaluator institutes or can manipulate the treatments as opposed to unplanned experiments in which he is reduced to observing the "experiment" and making comparisons with units beyond its scope (Caporaso and Ross, 1973, pp. 14–16). Field experiments lack the randomization of true experiments but may generate more reactive effects than natural experiments do.

If the causal impacts at work in natural experiments can be validly determined, evaluations of them may avoid problems that often beset more artificial, planned experiments, namely low external validity and an inability to produce effects of the magnitude at which they would be generated in a natural, real world environment (Caporaso, 1973, p. 12). The problem, of course, is how to obtain internally valid results in the absence of experimental controls. Quasi-experimental designs represent attempts to approximate or simulate the manipulation of treatment variables and guard against confounding variables and rival explanations based on fair comparisons extended beyond the scope of the reform whose impact is being investigated. Quasi-experiments can be distinguished from true experiments by the lack of randomized assignment of cases to treatments, but the difference between quasi-experimental and nonexperimental design is not so clear; in general, quasi-experiments have some additional features that narrow the range of possible explanations of differential effects, thereby reducing the likelihood of erroneously attributing observed impacts to program stimuli.

Quasi-experimental designs achieve some of the characteristics of true experiments through the scheduling of treatments and measurements and the use of certain modes of data analysis to provide fair comparisons. They capitalize on the fact that with naturally occurring reforms or program changes the evaluator may have some degree of control over the "whom and when" of observation, if not of treatment. One or another of the various quasi-experimental designs may be applicable in a particular evaluation, depending on the availability of data and the most salient threats to validity. Each has strengths and weaknesses and should be used selectively to fit the purposes and constraints of the evaluation. It should be clearly understood that without full experimental control the conclusions drawn from an evaluation about cause and effect patterns cannot be airtight; quasi-experiments cannot really provide the "demonstration effect," however limited its transferability, produced by true experiments. Nevertheless, in terms of practical significance, such complete control is not always necessary. As Campbell has pointed out: "The mere possibility of some alternative explanation is not enough—it is only the *plausible* rival hypotheses that are invalidating" (Campbell, 1969, p. 411). Although in the abstract no quasi-experimental design controls against all the possible threats to validity vis-à-vis a particular research problem, one of the quasi-experimental approaches may permit the evaluator to sort out the effects of program treatments from those of other likely influences.

Time Series Designs

One of the quasi-experimental approaches that has been receiving increasing attention and refinement in recent years is the extended time series design and its variations. Sometimes referred to as interrupted time series as opposed to the economists' continuous time series, the basic design consists of a number of observations at periodic intervals preceding the program or policy stimulus and a number of repeated observations after it has been put into effect. It can be illustrated as:

$$O \quad O \quad O \quad O \quad O \quad O \quad X \quad O \quad O \quad O \quad O \quad O \quad O$$

This design can be thought of in some respects as an extended one-group pretest-posttest design intended to take the longer term trend into account in assessing whether or not the program change produced any effects in the outcome variable. A change in the level of the outcome variable that is simply a part of its normal fluctuation across time, for example, but that might be mistaken as an impact of the program with the simple pretest-posttest design, would be seen not to deviate seriously from the normal pattern using time series analysis.

The particular design represented above concerns a temporary intervention, with the stimulus applied once and then withheld. Other time series involve a continuous intervention, however, in which a change is put into effect initially and then retained over subsequent observations. For example, a reduced off-peak bus fare might be introduced for a month as a temporary "experiment" in hopes of attracting new riders to the system, or such a reduction might be instituted on a permanent basis, a continuous intervention that can be diagrammed as:

$$O \quad O \quad O \quad O \quad O \quad XO \quad XO \quad XO \quad XO \quad XO \quad XO$$

The importance of distinguishing between the two lies in the fact that given a particular substantive problem, the two approaches might be expected to produced differing results. With the temporary reduced fare, for example, we might expect a short term increase in ridership followed by a return to the previous level, whereas a permanent fare reduction might induce a ridership increase that stabilizes at a higher level. With any variation of time series analysis, it is important to postulate what the expected results will be before analyzing the data in order to avoid the temptation of interpreting any change in trend as a significant impact.

Although time series designs have many applications, they are often the most appropriate designs for assessing the effects of large scale policy change with across-the-board applications, such as the nationwide effect of equal employment legislation on the employment opportunities of minorities. Time series designs often make use of highly aggregated data that do not facilitate comparisons among multiple units; often this involves using archival data compiled by routine record keeping, as opposed to primary data gathering. This approach may be particularly appropriate if a program is already underway and the evaluator must rely on existing data sources. The use of archival records, of course, incurs the risk of instrumentation problems if there have been any changes in the way the data have been collected and recorded over time.

When there is little cross-sectional variation because the intervention being examined has been applied to the total system being observed, often the most promising approach is a longitudinal approach comparing the status of that system at various points in time. The pre-intervention series can be examined to summarize a trend over time that can be used to project what subsequent levels would be if the intervention had not been introduced. On this basis it is determined whether observed values of the dependent variable after the intervention are likely to have occurred as a continuation of previous trends, or whether they are likely to reflect a change brought about by the intervention. Although some analyses use abbreviated time series designs, with only one postintervention observation point in an attempt to obtain an early reading on a recent change, it is much preferable to have extended series both before and after the intervention to compare longer term trends. It is also important to note that time series provide the clearest results when the policy change in question is made abruptly, because a gradually introduced program may produce effects that cannot be distinguished from secular trends influenced by a number of varied forces.

Figure 9.2 shows some possible outcome patterns in time series analysis; in general the validity of inferring a planned intervention effect is strongest in A and totally unjustified in F, G, and H (Campbell and Stanley, 1963, p. 38). Pattern B might be expected to result from a temporary intervention or with the use of an "operant" design in which an attempt is made to purposefully alter the trend of the series and then return it to its previous pattern as a stronger demonstration of causal influence (Glass et al., 1975). Pattern C seems to reflect some degree of intervention effect, but also shows that a tendency to increase over time was part of the series' maturation process; this might dampen somewhat the conclusion that the intervention itself produced a dramatic effect. Pattern D could represent a delayed response to an

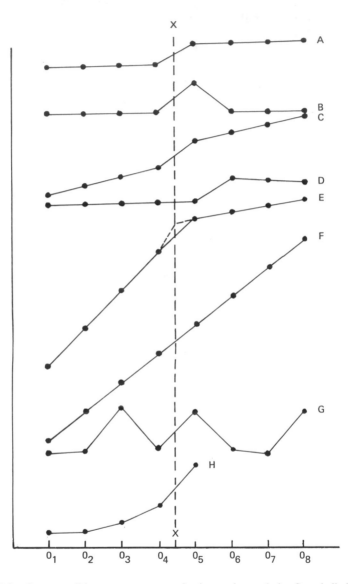

Figure 9.2. Some possible outcome patterns in time series analysis. Campbell, Donald T. and Julian C. Stanley, *Experimental and Quasi-experimental Designs for Research* (Chicago: Rand McNally & Company, 1963), Figure 3 from p. 38 ("Some Possible Outcome Patterns from the Introduction of an Experimental Variable at Point *X* into a Time Series of Measurements"). Copyright 1963, American Educational Research Association, Washington, D.C.

intervention, or this could be the effect of some entirely different stimulus. If this change is indeed a program impact, it shows a small attenuation of the effect over time after the initial impact is felt. Pattern D highlights the need to postulate what kind of intervention effects are anticipated; in this case the question of when the effect should take place and its expected duration are crucial. Pattern E might indicate an intervention effect, again possibly delayed, and would invite closer examination, if possible, of the change occurring between the two observations bracketing the intervention. Pattern F portrays a change in the level of the dependent variable across the intervention that would have occurred anyway as part of a consistent long term trend, whereas pattern G represents a change in the intervention period, probably attributable to the general instability of the series. Although pattern H shows an upsweep of the series at the intervention point, the preintervention trend shows a movement toward higher levels in any case.

Although time series data permit the analyst to take into account the prior trend and general instability of a series across time, the time series design may be particularly vulnerable to the effects of history. If any other change in the environment that might plausibly be expected to produce the results coincides with the intervention, the analyst is incapable of sorting out the effects of these competing explanations. For example, examination of data on ridership in mass transit systems in all Pennsylvania cities reveals an increase from 1971 to 1974, reversing a previous downward trend. This change may well be caused by a concerted effort by the state's Department of Transportation to promote service improvements in hopes of attracting more users, but it could represent a shift in modal choice in reaction to the energy crisis of that period and continuing high gasoline prices, which would have occurred with or without the state's program (Poister and Larson, 1976).

Multiple Time Series   Given the possible effects of history as the primary threat to the validity of time series analysis, the design is strengthened substantially if the series with the intervention can be compared with another, similar series that did not experience the intervention. Such multiple time series can be represented as:

$$O \quad O \quad O \quad O \quad X \quad O \quad O \quad O \quad O$$

$$O \quad O \quad O \quad O \qquad O \quad O \quad O \quad O$$

A good example is provided by the study of the Connecticut crackdown on speeding in an attempt to reduce the traffic fatalities; in this case the reform was a continuous intervention (Ross and Campbell,

1968). Figure 9.3*A* shows traffic fatalities before and after the crack-down; it indicates that fatalities decreased dramatically immediately after the intervention. With this simple one-group pretest-posttest de-

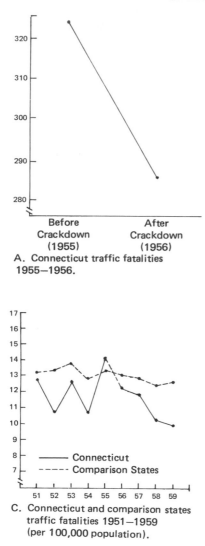

A. Connecticut traffic fatalities 1955–1956.

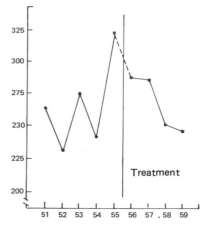
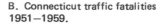

B. Connecticut traffic fatalities 1951–1959.

C. Connecticut and comparison states traffic fatalities 1951–1959 (per 100,000 population).

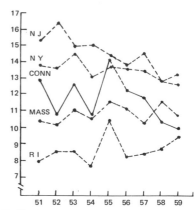

D. Traffic fatalities for Connecticut, New York, New Jersey, Rhode Island and Massachusetts (per 100,000 population).

Figure 9.3. Multiple time series. Traffic fatalities in Connecticut and comparison states. Source: Campbell, D.T., and H. L. Ross, 1968. *The Connecticut crackdown on speeding: time series in quasi-experimental analysis,* Law and Society Review, Vol. 3, pp. 38, 42, 44, 45. (Figures 1-4). Official publication of the Law and Society Association, which is copyright holder of the abovementioned article.

sign an evaluator might be tempted to conclude that the intervention did indeed produce a dramatic effect. The extended time series design, shown in Figure 9.3*B*, incorporates the measure in *A* and reveals considerable instability in the number of fatalities over time. It suggests that the reduction of fatalities across the intervention period may have been in large part a regression from an extremely high level of fatalities toward the mean average. Figure 9.3*C*, representing a multiple time series design, shows fatality rates (per 100,000 population) for Connecticut and the average of comparison states: New York, New Jersey, Massachusetts, and Rhode Island. The comparison states were chosen for their geographic and cultural similarity to Connecticut. From this design it seems that Connecticut's fatality rate dropped, in absolute terms and in relation to the comparison states, after the crackdown. The widening gap cannot be explained by a regression from the extreme high of 1955. Figure 9.3*D* further supports the argument that the crackdown had an impact on fatalities in Connecticut. Although the patterns for Connecticut and Rhode Island both show increases just before the crackdown and subsequent sharp declines, only Connecticut's rate continues to drop.

It should be noted that the comparisons in multiple time series need not always be drawn from separate groups, persons, units, or systems, but that they may consist of separate samples of times or stimulus materials (Campbell and Stanley, 1963, pp. 46–47). For example, in an analysis of the impact of the British Breathalyzer crackdown, whose primary effect would be expected to occur on weekend nights when the pubs are open, the comparison series consisted of data for commuting hours, when pubs had been closed (Ross and Glass, 1970). Regardless of the nature of the comparison series the interpretation of differential effects between the two series is based on the assumption of their equivalence in terms of all change agents except for the intervention whose impact is being evaluated. Although it will never be possible to obtain units that are identical in every other respect, interpretation of intervention effects is based on the absence of counter explanations that are plausible, based on other differences noted between the groups or units being compared.

Nonequivalent Control Group Design

One frequently used quasi-experimental approach, which attempts to replicate the pretest-posttest control group design in the absence of a true experiment, employs a separate group from the treatment group for before and after comparisons. This nonequivalent control group design, perhaps better termed a comparison group design, is diagrammed as follows:

$$O \quad X \quad O$$

$$O \qquad O$$

What this usually amounts to in practice is the before and after monitoring of a program in its normal operating setting and a search for a comparable group of cases that do not receive the program treatment but can be observed in the same way at the same points in time. This comparison group design represents an improvement over the ad hoc comparison discussed under "Nonexperimental Designs" in that it usually connotes a more closely structured comparison; the comparison cases are selected on the basis of some objective criteria of similarity *before* the program treatment is initiated, and the results provide measures of change in both groups over the same time period.

As with the ad hoc comparison and the use of comparison groups in multiple time series designs, the major threat to the validity of nonequivalent control group designs is selection; without the random assignment of an initial pool of cases to experimental and control groups, the evaluator can never be sure that program effects are not confounded with differential effects stemming from differences in underlying characteristics between the test and comparison groups. In the main, the effects of history, maturation, pretesting, instrumentation, and mortality are accounted for by this design, but if there are systematic differences between the two groups, then interactions between selection and these other threats are pertinent factors that may jeopardize internal validity.

Obtaining Valid Comparison Groups   The objective in using this design is to obtain a comparison group that is as similar as possible to the treatment group in terms of all the various factors that might affect the outcome measures. In evaluations in which the unit of analysis is the individual participant in a program, this has led in some cases to the strategy of constructing a comparison group of members who are matched closely with individuals in the test group. Such matching, if it is used, should definitely not be done on the basis of pretest scores, a common mistake made in an attempt to obtain comparable groups that "start out at the same level." Matching on pretest scores, particularly if program participants have been chosen on the basis of extreme performance (for example in a special educational program aimed at gifted students), is highly vulnerable to pseudo-effects produced by statistical regression. It is preferable to live with pretest differences between comparison groups selected on other criteria than to risk such regression artifacts (Riecken and Boruch, 1974, p. 109).

The real problem in building comparison groups is that often the characteristics on which the groups should be similar are not known, i.e., those characteristics of potential participants that most facilitate or inhibit program success. Often, the search for fair comparisons has led to the use of "unawares" or "geographic ineligibles," but as Weiss points out, the lack of awareness itself may mark some underlying differences in experience or attitude while the geographic ineligibles may be subject to differing community influences (Weiss, 1972). As always with quasi-experimental designs, the evaluator should look for possible alternative explanations before interpreting differential effects as program impacts.

Use of the nonequivalent control group design is by no means limited to situations in which the cases are individual persons. For example, in analyzing the impact of a community development program on its target neighborhoods, changes in those neighborhoods might be compared with the conditions observed at the same point in time for other comparison neighborhoods. Similarly, an evaluation of a burglary prevention program centering on a few police precincts in a city might be based on comparison with similar precincts that are not exposed to the program. Such comparison neighborhoods and precincts should be selected in terms of similar demographic, socioeconomic, and land use characteristics—all factors that might influence change in general neighborhood viability and crime rates—as well as past trends, if possible. If, for example, with the burglary prevention program comparable precincts cannot be found and looser comparisons are still desired, it might be wise to choose as comparisons a few precincts in which decreases in burglary rates are thought least likely to occur without the initiation of the program. Such deliberate stacking of the deck against evidence of the program's success is most conservative in guarding against threats of selection biases; on the other hand, such a strategy may conceal bona fide program impacts.

The burglary prevention example can be used to make two additional points regarding quasi-experimental designs. First, these designs are flexible and can be used in various combinations. The nonequivalent control group design can be viewed as a subset of the multiple times series design and often lends itself to use in conjunction with multiple time series analysis. Hence, the shortened comparison group design might be the basis for comparing the extent to which residents take precautions against burglaries in their home before and after home security evaluations and a promotional campaign, whereas multiple time series might be used to assess any changes in long term trends in burglary rates.

Second, the comparison group design is much stronger when more than two natural groups are involved. For example, the evaluation could be based on observations in one treatment and one comparison precinct, using households as the unit of analysis, but treatment effects might well be confounded with precinct effects. If three treatment precincts and three comparison precincts are built into the design, however, in effect replicating the "experiment" with two additional repetitions, the likelihood of systematic selection biases between treatment and comparison groups is greatly reduced.

Regression-Discontinuity Design

In some evaluations the randomization of cases into program participants and controls is not very practical because eligibility for the program is based on some objective criteria. For example, academic scholarships might be awarded on the basis of overall grade point average, and participation in a health insurance plan might be based in part on age. If samples of the eligibles for such programs can be randomly assigned to treatment and control groups, a full scale experiment might be possible, but this is often not the case. The use of individuals or households that are eligible but for some reason do not participate might invite a selection bias, while this certainly would result from lumping a number of ineligibles together as a control group to be compared in the aggregate with a group of participating eligibles. However, using ineligibles as "controls" while taking into account the scores of these controls as well as those of the participants on the eligibility criterion may yield a valid comparison. This is the approach taken with the regression-discontinuity design.

The logic of this approach can best be understood through a brief consideration of another design, the tie-breaking experiment. As an example, suppose that eligibility for a Neighborhood Youth Corps job training program is based on family income, and that a cutoff is set to include all those individuals in the area with family incomes of $22 per person per week or less and half of those with families with incomes of $23 per person per week (Riecken and Boruch, 1974, pp. 90–93). Because only one-half of those incomes of $23 are eligible, it might be possible to run an experiment within this narrow category, randomly assigning half to the experimental and half to the control group. If the program is successful in raising the participants' income 3 years later, the results to be expected from the experiment would be those shown in Figure 9.4A.

If we were to expand our data base and make postprogram observations on ranges of participants with family incomes going well below $23 and ineligibles with incomes going well above $23, and the program did produce its impact, we might expect findings as illustrated in Figure 9.4B. In general, income 3 years after the training project would be strongly related to income before the project, but there would be a noticeable break in this pattern in the previous income categories surrounding the cutoff category, and within the cutoff category the participants would have higher postprogram incomes than the controls.

The expected findings shown in B suggest that we should be able to infer the results of a hypothetical tie-breaking experiment from those of nonrandomly assigned treatments across the whole range of prior incomes, even if the middle category is not split between participation and nonparticipation. Figure 9.4C shows the results that might be expected if the program did produce the intended impact; with these results one could conclude quite safely that a tie-breaking experiment would have produced the results shown in A. If the results of this evaluation turned out as illustrated in Figure 9.4D, however, we would have no evidence that the desired impact was being produced.

Both the tie-breaking experiment and the regression-discontinuity design used to approximate it are weak in that if the results do in fact turn out as shown in Figure 9.4C, the effectiveness of the program stimulus can be inferred only to a narrow range of participants, i.e., only those near the cutting score. Thus, in the example described above, we might be able to conclude that the job training program does benefit participants coming from families with incomes at or near $23 per week, but this conclusion cannot be automatically extended to participants from lower income households. In specific applications, the design may also be vulnerable to problems of instrumentation and experimental mortality, depending on the types of measures used and the difficulty of conducting follow-ups on nonparticipants. However, given these limitations the regression-discontinuity approach certainly provides a more exacting analysis in this type of situation than do the nonexperimental models.

Other Quasi-Experimental Designs

Evaluations in which the assignment of cases to groups is not possible, but in which the scheduling of treatments to groups is possible, might use a rotational or **counterbalanced design** to compare the efficacy of alternative treatments. This design might be diagrammed as follows.

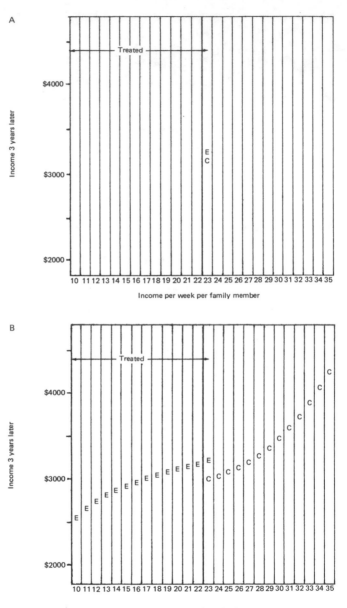

Figure 9.4. Regression-discontinuity design. *A*, Illustrative outcome for a hypothetical tie-breaking experiment in which some applicants with a per capita weekly family income of $23 are assigned at random to the Neighborhood Youth Corps and others are randomly assigned to control group status. All those with incomes of $22 and below get the training. Means for each group in average earnings subject to witholding 3 years later are indicated by the location of the *E* for Experimental Group and *C* for Control Group. *B*, Hypothetical tie-breaking experiment of *A* plus values for those in other family income classes, all of whom either got Neighborhood Youth Corps training if at $22 or below, or

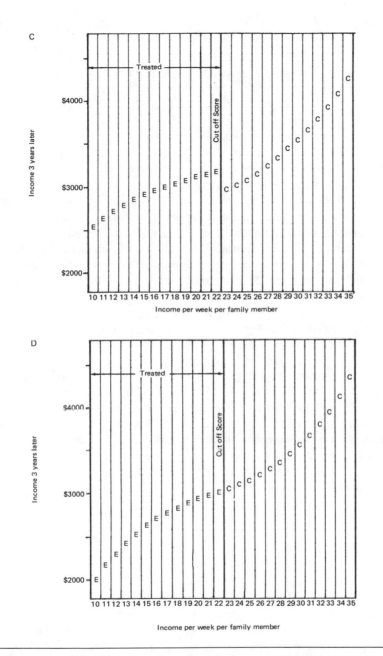

did not if at $24 and above. *C*, Hypothetical outcome for a regression-discontinuity design showing a degree of effect from Neighborhood Youth Corps similar to that illustrated in *A* and *B*. This figure is essentially the same as *B* except that there is no randomized category and no tie-breaking randomization. Instead, all at income level $22 and below have been admitted to the program. *D*, Hypothetical outcome for a regression-discontinuity design setting of *B* and *C*, but in which the treatment has had no effect. (From Riecken et al., 1974, pp. 90–93; reprinted by permission.)

$$X_1O \quad X_2O \quad X_3O \quad X_4O$$
$$X_2O \quad X_4O \quad X_1O \quad X_3O$$
$$X_3O \quad X_1O \quad X_4O \quad X_2O$$
$$X_4O \quad X_3O \quad X_2O \quad X_1O$$

It attempts to approximate experimental control or enhance precision by exposing all cases to all treatments. Each natural group is exposed to the treatments in a unique sequence; in any one time period no two groups are receiving the same treatment. Because all the groups receive all the treatments, selection is not a problem in its own right, but because they are exposed to the treatments at different times in differing sequences, the interaction of selection and maturation can produce pseudo-effects. The main limitation on the applicability of this design, however, is the threat of lingering effects that carry over from one period to another, thus clouding interpretations as to which treatment actually caused which effect. Similarly, the design ranks low in terms of external validity in that widespread application of any one of the treatments would probably not be given in conjunction with the others, making the evaluation unrepresentative of the more normal operation situation, particularly in terms of multiple treatment effects.

Separate-sample pretest-posttest designs take advantage of the possibility of the evaluator's ability to make random assignments for purposes of observation even when he can exert no influence over the assignment of cases to treatments. In its simplest form this strategy involves the random division of one natural group receiving one treatment into two subgroups, one to be pretested and the other to be posttested. This design can be diagrammed as follows, using R_0 to represent the random assignment for observation purposes only.

$$R_o \quad O \quad (X)$$

$$R_o \qquad X \quad O$$

The comparison to be made with this design is between the post-treatment observation on the second subgroup and the pretreatment observation on the first subgroup; an (X) indicates that the pretested subgroup also receives the identical treatment at the same time, but that this treatment is incidental to the analysis. This design represents an improvement over the one-group pretest-posttest design in two respects that might be pertinent depending on the plausible rival explanations in a given evaluation. First, if the possible effect of pretesting on posttest performance is considered to present a problem, this design avoids it by obtaining posttest measures only for those individuals who were not pretested. Secondly, the threat of statistical regression which is salient with the one-group pretest-posttest design is less likely with the use of a randomly split sample because, assuming no program impact, the second subsample would be expected to have as many artificially extreme scores when it is tested as would the first subsample. The major drawback to this design is the weakness it shares with the one-group pretest-posttest nonexperimental design, namely that it is vulnerable to historical effects because it does not involve any comparison between cases that receive the program and others that do not.

The separate-sample design can be improved considerably by adding a nontreated comparison group, removing the threats to internal validity of history, maturation, and mortality. This would be diagrammed as:

$$R_o \quad O \quad (X)$$

$$R_o \qquad\quad X \quad O$$

$$R_o \quad O$$

$$R_o \qquad\qquad O$$

There are two levels of comparability in this design, that between the two subsamples of the treatment group, and that between those of the comparison group and the treatment group. This design can also be thought of as a further subdivision of the nonequivalent control group design in that both the natural treatment group and the comparison group are now randomly divided into pretested and unpretested subsamples. This strengthens the design in terms of external validity, particularly in situations, such as the burglary prevention evaluation mentioned above, in which a pretest (in this case, home interviews) might interact with the treatment (home security evaluations and promotional campaign) to produce results that might differ from the more general application of the treatments without the pretest. This separate-sample pretest-posttest nonequivalent control group design is still vulnerable to the threat of selection in interaction with maturation and other threats to internal validity, a limitation that can be improved upon if the evaluation can be replicated over additional treatment and comparison units.

Mention should be made here of the notion of **patched up designs,** based on the idea of taking advantage of inherent flexibility or natural characteristics of ongoing programs that enable the analyst to build certain features into a specific evaluation design that either enhance its information content or provide added controls against threats to validity. An example might be an **institutional cycle design** that combines cross-sectional and longitudinal approaches by using participants in the second cycle, first as controls for those observed in the first cycle and then as a treatment group to be observed at the end of the second cycle, and so on as follows:

Cycle 1: X O_1

Cycle 2: R_o O_2 X O_3

                          R_o X O_4

Cycle 3: O_5 X

Comparisons O_6

                                      O_7

Consider, for example, a recently initiated program designed to help ease the transition into a nonworking lifestyle for elderly persons in their first six months of retirement; effectiveness would be measured by both attitudinal change and modified behavioral patterns. Participants in the first cycle are treated as a one-shot case study while the second cycle group is randomly divided into two groups. The third group of participants are observed before they receive the treatment.

Looking at the observations at O_1 and O_2, we would expect O_1 to compare favorably with O_2 because O_1 has received the program and O_2 has not. This comparison could be affected by history, experimental mortality, and pretesting, but it is not vulnerable to maturation or selection problems. When the second cycle is complete, O_3 can be compared with O_2 in order to measure real change over time. Pretesting is still a problem here, but selection biases and experimental mortality are not. At that same point in time the analyst can compare O_4 and O_2; the program logic would indicate that O_4 should compare favorably with O_2. This attempts to approximate actual change over time without being open to the effects of pretesting.

If these three comparisons all provide the same results, they reinforce the conclusion that the program is working. However, it should be noted that each post-program observation is based on a comparison with O_2; if O_2 is unreliable or unique in any way, this set of comparisons would still be weak. Thus, the comparison of O_4 to O_5, using third cycle personnel as the "controls," would be desirable.

One last point is that maturation could still be a problem, in that there is likely to be some natural or emotional change occurring in the first few months after retirement that might well be responsible for the apparent positive results of the program. In order to control for these, two separate samples would be drawn, one from among people who can be surveyed soon after retirement, O_6, and the second, O_7, from among persons who have been in retirement for about six months. These two samples would be compared on the same attitudinal and behavioral measures mentioned above. If the difference between O_6 and O_7 is substantially less than the difference between O_4 and O_5, then maturation can be ruled out as a rival explanation of the results discussed above, and the analyst can feel confident in concluding that the program really is working.

CONSIDERATIONS OF STATISTICAL ANALYSIS

Although particular statistical techniques are discussed in several different chapters in this book, a few general observations on analytical approaches within the framework of differing research designs is in order here. The following comments are geared toward helping the student avoid the pitfalls of certain frequent misapplications, as well as pointing out some of the more useful approaches in analyzing data generated through the use of structured research designs.

Comparisons of before and after observations on the same groups are often helpful in support of the measurement of the magnitude of impact, and detailed statistical analysis of variables representing process steps and environmental factors is also very useful in elaborating and explaining observed program effects or the lack of effects; yet with the tighter research designs the basic conclusion as to whether or not the treatment produced some differential effect depends on comparisons of the same sets of measures across groups that are treated differently.

For example, with the posttest-only control group design, and even the static group comparison, the crucial test is whether there is substantial or statistically significant difference between outcome measures for the treated and untreated groups. If the impact measure is an interval level variable, a test of statistical significance of an observed difference would probably take the form of a two-sample t test of difference in means. If the outcome measure is a dichotomized nominal measure, the analyst might test for a significant difference in proportions, while with a multiple category nominal measure the data might be organized into a crosstabulation between type of group and outcome state. Statistical analysis might then proceed along the lines of chi square and other techniques discussed in chapter 12.

The primary comparisons to be made become a little less obvious if we consider those designs that provide measurements taken before the treatment is administered, as well as after. With the Solomon four-group design, for example, the most basic comparisons are not those between pretest and posttest values for the two groups that are pretested, but rather comparisons among the posttest scores of all four groups. With interval data, this analysis would take the form illustrated in Figure 9.5. This facilitates sorting out the differences due to treatment variation from those that might be caused by the effect of pretesting on posttest performance. Assuming equal numbers of cases in all four groups, the "average" effect of the treatment with or without a pretest can be determined by comparing the aggregate mean scores of columns I and II, and that attributable to the administration of a pretest with or without the program treatment can be measured by comparing the aggregate means of rows I and II. This design also facilitates measuring the effects of the treatment, fixing for the effects of a pretest by comparing the means of cells A and B for the pretested groups and C and D for the unpretested groups. Furthermore, if we find, for example, that the difference between cells A and B is much greater than that between cells C and D, this would indicate a substantial interaction between pretesting and the treatment—that the greatest impact was produced by the combination of a pretest with the treatment—thus providing a check on the external validity of the experiment.

Although these comparisons may be performed by a descriptive interpretation of the comparison of means table illustrated in Figure 9.5, more precise estimates of the effects of the treatment, pretesting, and their interaction, as well as tests of statistical significance, can be obtained with a technique called analysis of variance, discussed in chapter 13.

As a complement to the analysis outlined above, comparisons can be made between the two groups pretested in order to obtain a closer interpretation of the amount of improvement produced by applying the treatment to a group of cases. This portion of the analysis should utilize gain scores, as discussed below.

Test status	Group		Total
	I Experimental	II Control	
I Pretested	A	B	$\overline{X}_{A\ \&\ B}$
II Unpretested	C	D	$\overline{X}_{C\ \&\ D}$
Total	$\overline{X}_{A\ \&\ C}$	$\overline{X}_{B\ \&\ D}$	$\overline{X}$

Figure 9.5.   Posttest scores from Solomon four-group design.

While t tests of difference in means or proportions are often appropriate for comparisons between two groups at one point in time, and, as is seen below, for determining whether a significant change has occurred in one group between two points in time, the t test technique is not applicable for analyzing data from time series or regression-discontinuity designs. Use of the t test of a significant difference between the last preintervention observation and the first postintervention is inappropriate because it fails to take into account the longer term time trends represented in the complete data set, the very heart of the time series design. With such an application, a statistically significant result may register that is only a part of an overall, unbroken time trend as shown in pattern F of Figure 9.2. Furthermore, although the leveling off at the intervention point of a series which steadily increases or decreases before the intervention would certainly indicate a change in trend, in that instance a t test by itself would lead to the conclusion of no significant difference.

The same kinds of problems apply to the regression-discontinuity design. Although the performance measures on a group of gifted students participating in a special education program may be significantly higher than those registered by a comparison group of less gifted nonparticipants, with both groups near the cutting edge of eligibility for the program, such a comparison cannot be used to distinguish whether this difference is what would be expected as part of a continuous relationship between where individuals fall on the criterion variable for determining eligibility and their scores on later performance measures. Rather than two-sample t tests, data from these designs are better analyzed using a technique referred to as piecewise regression analysis, discussed in chapter 15.

Use of Gain Scores

One commonly encountered statistical application is the use of significance tests to examine the difference between pretest and posttest
scores for one group, considering the sets of pretest scores and posttest
scores as two separate samples. Use of the two-sample t test in such
applications is invalid because it violates the underlying assumption of
two random, statistically independent samples. What we really have in
such situations is two sets of measures, two variables, observed for the
same sample. Thus, the proper way to examine the difference between
pretest and posttest scores for a group is to modify the data, creating a
new variable, called a **gain score**, which indicates for each individual or
case the change from pretest to posttest. The analysis then centers on
the mean average gain score. With the nonexperimental one-group
pretest-posttest design, for example, we have a pretest score, here
denoted as Y, and posttest score, denoted as Z. The gain score, X, then
is computed as $X = Z - Y$. The alternative form hypothesis that there
is in fact some improvement in scores from pretest to posttest would be
that for the larger population this gain score would be some positive
number, while the corresponding null hypothesis would contend that
the population gain score is equal to 0. The appropriate statistical
approach, then, would be a single sample t test of this null hypothesis,
using $\overline{X}$ as the estimating statistic of the parameter μ.

With two groups to be compared on a before and after basis, as
with the case of the experimental pretest-posttest control group design
or its quasi-experimental version, the nonequivalent control group design, this approach is extended to a two-sample test. Given the design

$$O \quad X \quad O$$

$$O \qquad O$$

we have two sets of variables on each of two samples. The procedure is
to create gain scores for each of the groups and then to test for a
difference in the mean average gain scores of the two groups. For
illustrative purposes, let:

$Y_1 =$ pretest scores, treatment group
$Y_2 =$ pretest scores, comparison group
$Z_1 =$ posttest scores, treatment group
$Z_2 =$ posttest scores, comparison group

Then we can compute gain scores as follows:

$X_1 = Z_1 - Y_1$, gain scores, treatment group
$X_2 = Z_2 - Y_2$, gain scores, comparison group

The mean average gain scores for the treatment and comparison group, respectively, are thus computed as:

$$\overline{X}_1 = \frac{\Sigma (Z_1 - Y_1)}{N_1} \qquad \overline{X}_2 = \frac{\Sigma (Z_2 - Y_2)}{N_2}$$

The two-sample test will then employ the test statistic

$$t = \frac{(\overline{X}_1 - \overline{X}_2) - 0}{\sqrt{\dfrac{s_1{}^2}{N_1 - 1} + \dfrac{s_2{}^2}{N_2 - 1}}}$$

to test the null hypothesis that $\mu_1 = \mu_2$. With this approach we are in fact comparing mean averages of the dependent, or impact variable, and the amount of improvement in score from pretest to posttest, across two different samples.

Matched Samples

In a previous section the possibility of matching cases in a comparison group with cases in a treatment group was presented as a means of achieving greater confidence in the equivalence of the two groups and reducing the possible influence of extraneous variables on the outcome of the evaluation. In true experiments, cases may be matched in pairs (or possibly sets of three or four or more) that are then randomly divided into treatment and control cases, whereas in less rigid designs a comparison group may be put together by finding cases that match closely individual cases already in the treatment group. When such matching procedures are employed, this must be taken into account in the statistical analysis of the data. With matched groups, in effect we have two samples, one of which is dependent upon the other; therefore we cannot use two-sample techniques, which are based on the assumption of independent samples. Although this results in a halving of the degrees of freedom in the statistical analysis, this is often outweighed by the reduction of overall variability achieved by the matching in the first place (Blalock, 1972, pp, 233–238).

Consider again the static group comparison design in which X_1 is the outcome variable for the treatment group and X_2 that for the comparison group. If these two groups are matched samples, then each value of X_1 in the first sample is linked with a particular value of X_2 in the second sample. Each pair of matched cases across the two groups in effect represents one data point, such that the value of $X_1 - X_2$ for a given pair constitutes one measure of the differential effect of the treatment. The mean average of this differential effect then is given by:

$$\overline{X} = \frac{\Sigma (X_1 - X_2)}{N}$$

where N, the number of cases over which the mean average is computed, is the number of pairs of treatment and comparison cases. A single sample t test can be used to test the hypothesis that μ (of which $\overline{X}$ is an estimate) $= 0$.

This procedure can be easily extended to the pretest-posttest type design when it is desired to use the amount of change from pretests to posttests as the impact indicator. Referring back to the pretest-posttest above example we can compute X_1 as the gain score for each case in the treatment group and X_2 as that for each comparison group case and then further compute $\overline{X}$ as the difference in gain scores between each treatment group case and its matched comparison group case. Formally, the test to be made is of the null hypothesis that the mean average difference in gain scores for each pair of treatment and comparison cases equals 0. This amounts to the same kind of single sample t test described in the previous example, which in this case can be expressed as:

$$X = (Z_1 - Y_1) - (Z_2 - Y'_2)$$

$$\overline{X} = \frac{\Sigma[(Z_1 - Y_1) - (Z_2 - Y_2)]}{N} \text{ , or}$$

$$\overline{X} = \frac{\Sigma[X_1 - X_2]}{N}$$

$$H_0 : \mu = 0 \qquad\qquad t = \frac{\overline{X} - 0}{\sqrt{s^2/N - 1}}$$
$$H_1 : \mu > 0$$

Statistical Inference

Applications of t tests and other inferential statistics alluded to in the above discussion are made in order to assess the probability that observed differences in posttest measures or gain scores might occur by chance. However, it should be pointed out that the assumptions on which these tests are based are often not met in a strict sense in experimental and quasi-experimental designs. The general assumption is that the cases being observed constitute a random sample or samples from a larger population, and the attempt is to make inferences from the sample to the larger population; the question underlying the statistical test is: If there is (or would be) no difference between treated and untreated groups in the larger population, what is the probability that a random sampling process would yield the results actually observed in the experiment?

The idealized experimental design process illustrated in Figure 9.1 provides for random (or some other probability) sampling of cases from the total target population and then for the random assignment of these cases to treatment and control groups. The random assignment of cases to groups is the sine qua non of the true experiment—however, random sampling of cases in the first place is often forgone in the interests of expediency; it simply is not feasible to take a random sample of potential participants in a drug abuse program from all across the United States and ask them to cooperate in an experiment of a newly proposed group therapy treatment that will convene two nights a week for the next 6 months.

In the absence of such a sample, experimenters select a group of test cases that they think may represent the kinds of cases for which the program is applicable. In effect, these are judgment samples as discussed in chapter 8. In some situations evaluators may purposefully choose cases that they feel provide a greater than average likelihood of success. The critical factor is then to randomly assign these cases to treatment and control groups. This random assignment serves as a guarantee of internal validity in a tightly designed experiment, even though its external validity may be open to question, in part because of the unknown degree of representativeness of the sample. The question of whether the experimenter should be concerned with basing the whole experiment on a random sample from the total target population depends on purpose. If the purpose is to determine whether a treatment can have some noticeable effect, which is usually the primary issue, then an internally valid experiment is the major criterion; the question of generalizability is really less important. Most experiments are more concerned with making fair comparisons in a specific setting rather than estimating the magnitude of effect on the total population of potential program participants; the random assignment of cases to groups is of the utmost importance whereas the random sampling of the general population is not (Riecken and Boruch, 1974, pp. 52–53). The generalizability of the results of experimentation depends on many replications in numerous settings, not on a single experiment based on a representative sample.

Given a lack of probability sampling of the set of test cases, the application of inferential statistical techniques is not valid in a very strict sense. Yet, inferential tests of significance are commonly made and inferential techniques are frequently used to develop confidence interval estimates of the magnitude of observed effects, and such applications in general can be considered to provide helpful, rather than misleading, information. Although statistical models other than those based on the assumption of random sampling might be even more appropriate in some cases, such as the urn model (Campbell and Stanley, 1963, p. 24), the random assignment of cases to groups provides an approximation to the random sampling assumption, if we think of the inference as extending only to cases that are similar to those being observed in the experiment.

USE OF ALTERNATIVE DESIGNS

In thinking about the use of alternative research designs it is well to bear in mind that many of the problems and issues addressed by program analysis can be approached in a number of different ways. A case in point is the attention paid in recent years to the question of whether increased highway patrol does lead to a reduction of accidents on state highways. The analysis of the Connecticut crackdown, discussed above, illustrates the use of the quasi-experimental multiple time series design to address this question, facilitated by an abrupt policy change that was intended to produce an immediate and substantial impact. Other studies of the same issue have used different approaches. In California, for example, a basic one group pretest-posttest design was employed to assess the results of "experimenting" with varying patrol levels on one 36-mile stretch of highway, while in Wisconsin a true experimental design was employed by assigning differing patrol strategies to a number of different test and control routes (Michaels, 1960; California, 1972). More recently, the issue has been addressed by a study in Pennsylvania that utilizes a cross-sectional design to examine associations between patrol levels and accident rates on a large number of roadway stretches across the state (Pennsylvania, 1976). All of these studies reached somewhat similar conclusions, namely that increased traffic patrol does have some effect on reducing accidents, although the strength and statistical significance of the relationship vary from one to another. This is how a body of evidence about the efficacy of some kind of program is built up; where such studies produce conflicting results, they should be examined closely to search for indications of whether the differences are an artifact of methodology or represent further specification in the effectiveness of differing program strategies in different environments or settings.

Choice of Research Design

In considering the choice of a particular research design for a given evaluation, it should also be kept in mind that validity is a continuum rather than a dichotomy, and that although an evaluation may be stronger or weaker depending on the methodology, the results of one evaluation or experiment will not be definitive for any case. In practice, the specific design that is settled on for a given project usually represents a compromise between scientific considerations of overall measurement validity and the more operational considerations of time and money constraints and the way in which the conduct of the evaluation is to mesh with ongoing service delivery. Furthermore, these practical considerations notwithstanding, there is no such thing as a single "correct" design (Suchman, 1954). Although the true experiment may seem to be the ideal design in the abstract, it may not always represent the most appropriate approach, given the particular purpose of the evaluation.

This point can be illustrated by consideration of the differing evaluation needs of different types of demonstration projects (Suchman, 1972). **Pilot projects** represent the loosest kind of demonstration whose purpose is to explore the potential of alternative strategies with sufficient latitude and flexibility to allow any positive effects to surface. They require a very formative approach and often involve much trial and error as they go along. Nonexperimental designs that do not impose any restraints on the way in which the demonstration is conducted may be the most suitable designs at this stage.

Model demonstration programs, on the other hand, are aimed at providing much more rigorous tests of the effectiveness of the most promising strategies that emerge from the pilot demonstrations. Here the attempt is to evaluate the causal impact of a strategy, demonstrated in ideal conditions intended to facilitate rather than impede the program's success as much as possible. The question is: Can the strategy produce results in a conducive environment? This stage involves theory testing more than actual program testing and, as such, requires strict controls over any circumstances that might influence the results and confuse the interpretation of the program's direct effects. The internal validity of conclusions about the program's cause and effect relationships is of paramount concern here. Model demonstrations represent the kind of applied program analysis that most closely approximates laboratory conditions; hence true experiments are usually most appropriate at this stage.

When model programs are found to be successful in this constrained type of environment, they must then be tested in settings that resemble the normal operating environment as much as possible. **Prototype demonstration projects** are intended to test the feasibility and utility of mounting the program in circumstances that are as similar as possible to its proposed context. Although experimental designs are often desirable at this stage, it is essential that the design not impose artificial conditions on the evaluation; at this point external validity becomes much more important. Thus, a lower level design from which the results may be more readily generalized may be preferable here.

In the evaluation of ongoing programs, lower level, nonexperimental designs do sometimes prove useful, particularly in providing a preliminary assessment of the program's effectiveness. Most experimental controls are aimed at ruling out rival explanations of apparent positive results; contaminating factors more often make the program look more successful than it really is, not the other way around. Thus, nonexperimental designs may be very appropriate for determining whether a program warrants further, more rigorous evaluation (Rossi, 1972). Often, new program approaches are not found to generate substantial impact, and a nonexperimental or quasi-experimental approach may be sufficient to draw this conclusion without all the time and expense that a more sophisticated evaluation would entail. Or, a nonexperimental approach may suffice in evaluating the worth of a particular program in a particular setting because it indicates that some desirable impacts are occurring for which there are really no viable or plausible rival explanations. In other situations, a nonexperimental evaluation that points to probable program success will suggest that more rigorous evaluations be employed to isolate patterns of cause and effect.

SUMMARY

This chapter has focused on alternate designs in terms of their ability to discern program impacts, structuring the analysis to provide fair comparisons of outcomes among varying programs or treatments; this is the real objective in developing a research design. It should be reemphasized here, however, that providing for fair comparisons of outcomes requires assurance that the alternative programs and treatments are in fact what they are intended or supposed to be. To reiterate an important point made in chapter 2, underlying program theories cannot be adequately tested in evaluations characterized by failure in program.

Thus, in experimental designs it is crucial to make sure that treatments are implemented as designed and that experimental conditions are maintained. With lower level designs it is critical to ascertain how treatments have been applied in order to identify without doubt the program strategies whose outcomes are being measured. This is the primary basis of the need for linking process studies with impact evaluations, as discussed in chapter 1.

In general, research designs must be made appropriate for the purpose at hand and the operating constraints of the program to be evaluated. Where the desire is to measure effects with no ambiguity surrounding the question of underlying cause and effect, there is no substitute for true experimental design, and even these must be replicated in order to determine how widely transferable their results are. However, true experiments often cannot be feasibly interjected into ongoing operating programs, and even when new experiments are mounted, it is often not possible to comprehend the full scope and long term duration of all possible effects (Gramlich and Koshel, 1975). Lower level designs, on the other hand, can often produce useful results when applied selectively and interpreted within their inherent limitations. It is to be hoped that the principles of experimental design can be adhered to more often in the future, but all forms of research design can be used to make contributions to the accumulating body of knowledge about what works and what does not work in public programs.

REFERENCES

Blalock, H. M., Jr. 1972. Social Statistics. 2nd Ed. New York: McGraw-Hill Book Company.

Bernstein, I. (ed.). 1976. Validity Issues in Evaluative Research. Beverly Hills: Sage Publications, Inc.

Borgatta, E. F. 1955. Research: Pure and Applied. Group Psychotherapy 8: 263-267.

Bracht, G. H., and G. V. Glass. 1968. The External Validity of Experiments. Amer. Educ. Res. J. November: 437-474.

California, State of. 1966-72. Department of California Highway Patrol. Operation Planning and Analysis Division. Operational Analysis Section. Operation 101, Final Reports, Phases I-IV.

Campbell, D. T. 1969. Reforms as Experiments. Amer. Psychol. Vol. 24, April.

Campbell, D. T., and J. C. Stanley. 1963. Experimental and Quasi-Experimental Designs for Research. New York: Rand McNally & Co.

Caporaso, J. A. 1973. Quasi-Experimental Approaches to Social Sciences: Perspectives and Problems. In: J. A. Caporaso and L. L. Ross, Jr. (eds.), Quasi-Experimental Approaches: Testing Theory and Evaluating Policy. Evanston, Ill.: Northwestern University Press.

Caporaso, J. A., and L. L. Ross, Jr. (eds.). 1973. Quasi-Experimental Approaches: Testing Theory and Evaluating Policy. Evanston, Ill.: Northwestern University Press.

Doby, J. T. (ed.). 1954. An Introduction to Social Research. Harrisburg, Pa.: Stackpole Books.

Glass, G. V., V. L. Willson, and J. Gottman. 1975. Design and Analysis of Time Series Experiments. Boulder: Colorado Associated University Press.

Gramlich, E. M., and P. P. Koshel. 1975. Educational Performance Contracting. Washington, D.C.: Brookings Institution.

Guba, E. G., and D. L. Stufflebeam. 1968. Evaluation: The Process of Stimulating, Aiding and Abetting Insightful Action. Address delivered at the second National Symposium for Professors of Educational Research. November 21, 1968. Columbus: Evaluation Center, College of Education, Ohio State University.

Huston, T. R. 1972. The Behavioral Sciences Impact-Effectiveness Model. In: P. H. Rossi and W. Williams (eds.), Evaluating Social Programs: Theory Practice and Politics, Chapter 3. New York: Academic Press.

Kelling, G. L., T. Pate, D. Dieckman, and C. E. Brown. 1974. The Kansas City Preventive Patrol Experiment. Washington: Police Foundation.

Meier, P. 1972. The Biggest Public Health Experiment Ever: The 1954 Field Trial of the Salk Polio Myelitis Vaccine. In: J. M. Tanur et al. (eds.), Statistics: A Guide to the Unknown. San Francisco: Holden-Day, Inc.

Michaels, R. M. 1960. The Effects of Enforcement on Traffic Behavior. Public Road, Vol. 31, December.

Pechman, J. A., and P. M. Timpane (eds.). 1975. Work Incentives and Income Guarantees: The New Jersey Income Tax Experiment. Washington: Brookings Institution.

Pennsylvania, Commonwealth of. 1976. An Evaluation of the Traffic Supervision Program. Harrisburg: Office of the Budget.

Poister, T. H., and T. D. Larson. 1976. The Administration of State Mass Transportation Programs. Transportation Research Record, No. 603.

Riecken, H. W., and R. F. Boruch et al. (eds.). 1974. Social Experimentation: A Method for Planning and Evaluating Social Action. New York: Academic Press.

Roethlisberger, F. J., and W. J. Dickson. 1939. Management and the Worker. Cambridge: Harvard University Press.

Ross, H. L., and D. T. Campbell. 1968. The Connecticut Crackdown on Speeding: Time Series Data in Quasi-Experimental Analysis. Law and Society Review, August, pp. 35–53.

Ross, H. L., and G. V. Glass. 1970. Determining the Social Effects of a Legal Reform: The British 'Breathalyser' Crackdown of 1967. American Behavioral Scientist, Vol. 13, (March/April), pp. 493–509.

Rossi, P. H. 1972. Boobytraps and Pitfalls in the Evaluation of Social Action Programs. In: C. H. Weiss (ed.), Evaluating Action Programs: Readings in Social Action and Education. Boston: Allyn & Bacon, Inc.

Rossi, P. H., and W. Williams (eds.), 1972. Evaluating Social Programs: Theory, Practice and Politics. New York: Academic Press.

Stanley, J. C. 1972. Controlled Field Experiments as a Model for Evaluation. In:

P. H. Rossi and W. Williams (eds.), Evaluating Social Programs: Theory, Practice and Politics. New York: Seminar Press Inc.

Suchman, E. A. 1954. The Principles of Research Design. In: J. T. Doby (ed.), Research. Harrisburg, Pa.: Stackpole Books.

Suchman, E. A. 1967. Evaluative Research: Principles and Practice in Public Service and Social Action Programs. New York: Russell Sage Foundation.

Suchman, E. A. 1972. Action for What? A Critique of Evaluative Research. In: C. H. Weiss (ed.), Evaluating Action Programs: Readings in Social Action and Education. Boston: Allyn & Bacon, Inc.

Tanur, J. M., F. Mosteller, W. H. Kruskal, R. F. Link, R. S. Pieters, and G. R. Rising (eds.). 1972. Statistics: A Guide to the Unknown. San Francisco: Holden-Day, Inc.

Vera Institute. 1973. Interim Report: Vera Supportive Programs. New York: Vera Institute.

Weiss, C. H. (ed.). 1972. Evaluating Action Programs: Readings in Social Action and Education. Boston: Allyn & Bacon, Inc.

SURVEY RESEARCH METHODS

10

As has been pointed out in earlier chapters, the development of valid measures and the collection of data are critical factors affecting the quality and usefulness of any study's findings. Furthermore, the fact that data collection and processing are often the most time consuming and costly aspects of program analysis gives added emphasis to the need for adequate planning and development of data collection methods. This chapter builds primarily on chapters 2 and 3 in terms of the kinds of considerations that should go into the design and conduct of one major vehicle of data collection, survey research. Although program analyses use many different types of data, with various data sources often combined in a single study, survey research is discussed in some detail in this book because of its frequent use and its extreme sensitivity in terms of obtaining valid measures.

This chapter focuses on the various types of **interview surveys**, those in which the data are developed by asking people for information. Although all of the measurement issues discussed in chapter 3 apply equally to noninterview surveys, interview surveys require special attention because of their high potential for both good data on one hand *and* misleading or even very damaging results on the other hand. This chapter begins with an introductory discussion of survey research, proceeds with a look at various types of surveys, measurement problems associated with surveys, questionnaire design, and attitude measurement, and concludes with some final comments about the conduct of surveys.

NATURE AND USE OF SURVEY RESEARCH

Survey research is widely used in the analysis of public programs in conjunction with varied research contexts, purposes, and specific analytical approaches. The following section discusses the general nature of survey research and locates it more clearly within the overall framework of program analysis developed in this book.

Types of Studies

First, survey research is *not* a type of study in and of itself. Rather, it is a general approach, and more accurately a method of data development, which may be appropriate for many different kinds of studies. Referring to the typology developed in chapter 1, survey research is frequently employed in needs and demands studies to obtain indications of certain conditions that might warrant a new or expanded program or the perceived need for such a program by members of a particular target group, but it is by no means limited to this purpose. It is often a primary data collection tool in process studies of a program operation or in the actual evaluation of program performance in terms of meeting objectives. Indeed, a given piece of survey research may include elements of all three aspects of program analysis (Webb and Hatry, 1973, chapter 2).

Measures of program effectiveness, and to a lesser extent efficiency, are often developed through surveys of respondents' economic circumstances, activity patterns, or attitudes and perceptions. If an intended impact of a health care program, for example, is to increase the number of physician visits made by members of low income families, a survey might be the most direct way to obtain this measure. Similarly, surveys might be used to assess the adequacy or outreach of a program or to determine whether in the eyes of the community as a whole a certain set of program objectives is appropriate. Recent regional and nationwide surveys, for example, have confirmed that most Americans are in favor of the 55 mph speed limit as a way of improving highway safety and fuel economy.

Another common assumption is that survey research is only useful when it is desired to look at things from the perspective of people on the receiving end of a public program. Surveys are often appropriate vehicles for getting information from program participants, agency clients, and other affected parties, but they have a variety of other applications, too. Some public programs depend for their success on cooperative or facilitating policies on the part of certain actors in the private sector who thus might need to be surveyed. For instance, the planning work in designing a housing rehabilitation program might require a survey of local lending institutions' policies, whereas a formative evaluation of the impact of a job training program might be based in part on a survey of local employers' hiring practices. Surveys are also used to develop information on needs, process, or impacts as seen by service providers. Surveys of social workers, nutritionists, police officers, bus drivers, etc. can be invaluable in obtaining insight as to the causes of the bottlenecks that frustrate efficient service delivery or suggestions for improving the overall effectiveness of a service.

Finally, in some types of program analysis general purpose community surveys or more widespread public opinion surveys can be important inputs in program planning and evaluation. For example, an examination of public receptivity to the federal government's swine flu inoculation program and the reasons why people did not avail themselves of the free inoculations might be best approached through a survey of a representative cross-section of the U.S. population.

Survey Research and Research Design

The "survey research approach" is often erroneously characterized as a low level alternative to more structured experimental and quasi-experimental designs as discussed in the previous chapter, and to some the term connotes a complete methodological approach from start to finish. The tendency to think of survey research as a basic research design, especially salient when a study is based completely on data collected from a single survey, is not particularly dangerous in terms of developing a work plan for completing the study. Yet, it should be recognized that any survey is tied to some overall research design or analytical framework and that the ability to draw causal inferences or generalize conclusions rests *first* on this research design rather than on the quality of the survey instrument.

Survey research has become associated with lower level research design precisely because the bulk of survey research is conducted in conjunction with cross-sectional data analysis with no attempt to use experimental and control groups to make before and after comparisons. This traditional "survey research approach" is to conduct the survey at one point in time with a large enough sample to incorporate wide variation in the behavioral or other characteristics of interest and then to elaborate the apparent system of relationships among these variables as much as possible. Although this is sometimes useful it is often severely limited in terms of the ability to identify cause/effect relationships with any degree of confidence, as discussed in the preceding chapter.

A refinement of this basic approach is the use of **panel studies**, two waves of interviews of the same cross-section of subjects before and after the event or program intervention occurs. Referring to the swine flu inoculation program, a panel study might have been employed to survey a cross-section of the population before the program was initiated and then again after it was completed, on the expectation that some of those in the panel would elect to get the shots and some would not. Such an approach represents an important gain over the one-shot survey in terms of measuring change, and approximates the pretest-posttest nonequivalent comparison group design in some respects, but it is still basically a cross-sectional design and may be subject to glaring threats to internal validity. Primarily, it must be recognized that with this type of panel study there is substantial doubt about who belongs in the experimental versus comparison groups until after the second interviews are completed, as opposed to having a known treatment group and then building a comparison group into the design. Thus, the first wave of interviews might exert a strong influence on whether or not an individual becomes part of the treatment group.

A second approach to expanding on the single-point-in-time cross-sectional survey is the **retrospective pretest**, an attempt to provide an indication of change over time by actually conducting one survey that includes questions relating to both the present and some previous point in time. This may be useful in certain contexts but in general is a very weak research design (Campbell and Stanley, 1963, pp. 66–67).

Survey research is increasingly being employed as a data collection tool in conjunction with more highly structured research designs as these more sophisticated approaches themselves become more prevalent in public program analysis. The Kansas City Preventive Patrol Experiment and the New Jersey Negative Income Tax Experiment both were based on the true experimental designs that relied heavily on the use of survey data (Kelling et al., 1974; Pechman and Timpane, 1975). The New Jersey tax experiment is particularly interesting in this regard as it employed 12 interviews of each family participating in the experiment over a 3-year period. This is indeed a panel study, but one set within the framework of an experimental design as the samples of participating families in each of four cities were randomly assigned to various treatment and control groups before the treatments and data collection were initiated.

Similarly, surveys can readily lend themselves to quasi-experimental designs based on institutional cycles, or employing comparison groups, nonexperimental longitudinal approaches, or regression-discontinuity analysis. In an analysis of a housing rehabilitation program, for example, property owners in both target and comparison neighborhoods may be administered the same survey relating to property improvements they have made or are considering as well as their attitudes toward their neighborhood and property maintenance in general, perhaps at two points in time. Regarding any one of the surveyed neighborhoods by itself, the analysis amounts to cross-sectional data analysis, but the real merit of the surveys is the set of comparisons they facilitate through a quasi-experimental design.

A final misconception regarding surveys and research design, which again relates to the association of surveys with cross-sectional data analysis, is that all surveys are sample surveys. Many surveys used in program analysis are in fact surveys of samples of the population of interest, but quite frequently these studies also employ surveys of the total population. For example, all the participants in a given program might be surveyed, or all the employees engaged in providing a certain service might be surveyed.

Types of Information

The collection of attitudinal data is often the primary objective of surveys, and a later section of this chapter discusses attitude measurement in some detail. A survey conducted in conjunction with a housing rehabilitation program, for example, might include items on the respondents' perceptions of their neighborhoods and general attitudes toward maintaining and improving property along with whether or not respondents would like their homes to be inspected for compliance with codes or are interested in obtaining technical assistance, all for the purpose of gauging receptivity to the program. Furthermore, before and after survey comparisons of residents' satisfaction with their housing conditions and general neighborhood characteristics would provide one kind of assessment of the program's impact.

Surveys are also often aimed at obtaining "factual" data, information regarding actual occurrences, conditions, circumstances, or behavior, with the recognition that such measures taken in a survey may depend on respondents' awareness, memory, interpretation, or familiarity with events and may therefore differ from more objective direct observation. Nevertheless, such "factual" data may be of great use. Many surveys include a number of items on the background and characteristics of the respondent or his family, standard demographic and socioeconomic variables such as sex, age, race, household size, occupation, income, etc., often for purposes of classifying respondents and comparing other measures across these groups.

Other surveys focus on behavioral measures; needs and demands studies, for example, often require extensive descriptions of individual or family activity patterns. Urban transportation planning requires detailed knowledge of household travel patterns, for instance, whereas planning for child day-care services might rely heavily on data relating to work schedules and present arrangements for taking care of young children. Process oriented studies as well as evaluations of program impacts may also depend on this type of factual data. An evaluation of a burglary prevention program, for instance, might use a survey designed to provide information on whether residents in target neighborhoods participated in block meetings or workshops (process), whether they subsequently took additional precautions in securing their homes against burglaries (intermediate effect), and in fact whether or not their homes have been burglarized since the inception of the program (impact).

In addition to attitudinal measures and factual information, surveys may also be used to develop information about respondents' levels of awareness or knowledge about something and indications of their self-perceptions. Returning to the housing rehabilitation illustration, for example, in trying to gain some insight as to relative rates of participation in the program, it might be critical to focus on the awareness of the availability of rehabilitation grants and technical assistance on the part of eligible respondents who did not participate in the program. In general, such measures of knowledge and awareness often help to understand variation in attitudes and opinions picked up in surveys.

Similarly, self-perception items may also increase the explanatory power of a survey instrument. Although the variation in indicators of the degree of satisfaction with the respondent's neighborhood or his attachment to the neighborhood may be partially explained by specific perception and rating type variables, it may also depend on the way in which the respondents see themselves in terms of community involvement, socioeconomic upward mobility, and amount of influence in the neighborhood.

Procedural Overview

The various aspects of designing and conducting a survey can be viewed best within the context of the overall research process, particularly in the case of a piece of program analysis being built primarily around a single survey. Notwithstanding the varied types and purposes of surveys discussed above, the general process of developing and implementing a survey progresses through the steps presented briefly below.

1. **Project Formulation**   Before the survey itself can be designed, the overall substantive and analytical framework must be established,

within which the survey is to function. This includes problem definition, identification of the population to be surveyed and the kinds of variables to be measured, the kinds of relationships to be examined, and the overall research design; in short, the clear identification of the questions to be answered and the research approach to addressing them. This part of the project does not really involve survey research itself—rather it is a question of overall project purpose, systems analysis, and research design as discussed in previous chapters—but it is at this stage that the use and role of survey research in the project are determined.

2. **Survey Mode** Given the overall framework of the survey, an early decision is the determination of the actual mode of collecting the data, i.e., through personal interviews, telephone interviews, mailed questionnaires, or some other means. The survey mode to be used will depend in large part on the amount of data to be included and the degree to which the kinds of questioning lend themselves to the different formats, but there are also other important factors, such as costs, to be taken into consideration, as is discussed in greater detail below.

3. **Sampling Plan** A rough indication of the required or desired number of completed interviews and a general sampling strategy, if it is to be a sample survey, are usually developed in conjunction with the determination of survey mode. Issues relating to overall sample size and the type of sample to best suit the particular analytical purposes are tied to the overall framework developed under project formulation, whereas consideration of alternative sampling strategies is also based on cost and other practical considerations, as discussed in chapter 8.

4. **Questionnaire Design** The heart of the survey design process is the development of the actual survey instrument, which is discussed in depth below. Again, all of these steps are interrelated, and the development of question sequences as well as the working of individual questions will be keyed to the purposes established above and tailored to the survey mode or interview format being planned. Furthermore, the instrument should be developed with the specific population to be interviewed kept in mind.

5. **Interviewer Training** With surveys using interviewers, as opposed to mailed questionnaires or other kinds of self-administered questionnaires, care must be taken in the recruitment and training of the interviewers. Poor interviewing can easily invalidate the data obtained in surveys regardless of the quality of the instrument

being used, and the careful development of good interviewers is an investment that pays off. The skill and sensitivity required of the interviewers varies widely from survey to survey, depending on the instrument and the population being surveyed, but even the simplest surveys require some training and practice. In general, the interviewer must be familiar with the intent of all items on the questionnaire, be able to communicate them clearly and without bias, and be able to record the responses accurately. In addition, he must be motivated to maintain the same high level of interviewing quality throughout the duration of the survey.

6. **Pretesting** Not to be confused with the use of pretest observations in a before-and-after comparative type of research design, pretesting here refers to testing and refining the survey instrument as well as ironing out the bugs in the overall survey procedure before conducting the actual survey. **Pretesting** or **field-testing** the instrument is the process of trying out the questionnaire or parts of it to determine how well it works or how it might be improved; **piloting** sometimes refers to a complete dry run or miniaturized walk-through to test not only the instrument but also the logistics and feasibility of carrying out the full scale survey.

7. **Conduct of the Survey** When all the steps outlined above have been completed satisfactorily, the survey is ready to be fielded. The difficulty of actually conducting the survey depends on the myriad of factors such as length and scope of the instrument, the type of survey format being used, the ability of the people being surveyed to respond, their initial receptivity to the idea of the survey, the relative accessibility of the individuals selected to be interviewed, and the ability and integrity of the interviewers. Some comments relating to the management of the conduct of the field work are made near the end of this chapter.

8. **Data Processing** When the data have been pulled in from the field, there is often a fair amount of work to be done editing and processing the data before they can be analyzed. At this point, suffice it to say that if this involves much coding of the initial responses or a lot of processing of the data in general to get them into machine-readable form, it will be necessary to develop clear procedures for accomplishing this task and control mechanisms to assure that it is completed with an acceptably low rate of error.

9. **Analysis and Interpretation** The final stage of a survey research project, of course, is to analyze the data and develop findings or conclusions. With sample surveys based on probability samples,

inferential statistics are usually appropriate, and the techniques of statistical analysis covered in other sections of this book are generally applicable to survey data.

TYPES OF SURVEYS

The type of survey used will have critical implications regarding the amount and kinds of information to be obtained, possible problems with respect to the quality of data, and the costs of data collection. This section compares the three basic interview formats in these terms, along with the kinds of uses for which they are most appropriate.

Personal Interviews

Personal interview surveys are those in which the survey is conducted by an interviewer in face-to-face contact with the respondent. In general, it is the most informative type of survey because it allows for the kind of in-depth questioning that will not work well with other interview formats. The instrument can contain sequences of questions and follow-up questions that the interviewer can work through, clarifying and interpreting their meaning, if necessary. Furthermore, the interviewer can be trained to probe for explanations of responses where they seem unclear, or to probe for further information when the responses begin to take a direction that might be of interest to the researcher. Thus, personal interviews are advantageous whenever the subject matter is complex and there is a desire to go below the surface in terms of the factors underlying attitudes or behavior or to uncover additional related factors that the survey designer may not be aware of or able to build into set-piece questions.

Whether a survey is being conducted on a total population or sample basis, once the cases to be surveyed have been designated, it is of the utmost importance to actually complete surveys with as many of them as possible. Often obtaining an adequate **response rate**, the proportion of completed surveys, becomes a problem because people are not interested in the nature of the survey or do not want to spend (or waste) their time answering questions or filling out survey forms.

Of course many factors, such as survey content, the type of people to be surveyed, and the extent to which advance work has been done, influence the final response rate, but everything else being equal, the personal interview format produces higher response rates than do other types of surveys. This is first of all because the interviewer has an initial chance to "sell" the survey, to convince the individual that it is a worthwhile survey and that his participation as a respondent is crucial to the success of the project.

Furthermore, once the survey is underway the interviewer can assure a complete return by making sure that questions are not overlooked, that instructions are followed, and in general that adequate responses are given. If the respondent shows signs of fatiguing or losing interest, the interviewer can encourage him to complete it; in fact in some situations the interviewer can develop a rhythm in moving through early question sequences that might serve to counteract the fatigue factor. In general, then, with an interviewer on the spot the probability of obtaining and completing a *usable* interview is greatly increased. Response rates in the neighborhood of 70 to 90 percent are considered acceptable with personal interview surveys.

There are two general types of problems with personal interview surveys to be considered against the kinds of advantages discussed above. First, the interviewer flexibility, which can produce much richer data, can also lead to interviewer bias, which detracts from the quality of the data. With this interview format the interviewer is a communication link between the survey designer and the respondent; he can easily shade the questions either consciously or unconsciously so as to reflect his own biases, and he may color or selectively report responses in the same vein. This problem, always a threat with personal interview surveys, underscores the need for strong interviewer training and motivation.

The second problem relates to costs, which are by far the highest per completed interview with the personal interview format. Personal interviews require many man-hours to complete data collection, particularly with household surveys as opposed to interviewing people who can be scheduled at work places or through agency contacts. With household surveys, much time may be consumed in simply locating the sample households and then making call-backs to contact people who were not found at home initially. Typically, the interviewers are paid wages and also incur travel expenses, and if local interviewers are not used, food and lodging expenditures must also be budgeted. In a general purpose community survey in Harrisburg, Pennsylvania conducted in 1975, for example, with personal interviews covering a wide range of issues and ranging from 30 to 50 minutes in duration, 423 valid interviews were completed for a 76 percent response rate at a total data collection cost of about $15 per completed interview (Poister, McDavid, and Miller, 1976). Costs in some personal interview surveys run much higher.

Mailed Questionnaires

The chief advantage of surveys in which the questionnaire is mailed to the respondent is their low cost. Without a crew of interviewers to pay for, the only costs are those of materials, reproducing the instrument, and postage. A second advantage is that mailed questionnaires preclude the problem of interviewer bias. Offsetting these factors, however, are the very low response rates that characterize many mailed surveys. One implication of this is that surveys must be mailed out to very large samples or populations in order to receive an adequate number of cases for purposes of statistical analysis.

As a follow-up to the Harrisburg community survey mentioned above, for example, the city council conducted a mailed survey, replicating one small portion of the original instrument. The survey was sent to the population of some 19,000 customers of the city water system. Completed returns were received from approximately 2,700 of these, for a 14 percent response rate, and the unit cost of collecting these data was only about $0.22 per completed survey, because no additional mailing costs were incurred (Reemtsen, 1977). If separate postage had been required, the total cost would have amounted to about $1.10 per completed interview.

Although enough surveys were completed to permit data analysis and elaboration, the 14 percent response rate may well mean that the sample represents only a chunk of the city's population, and drawing inferences to the larger population would be very tenuous at best. At worst it could be dangerously misleading. Mailed questionnaires are usually enclosed with a cover letter explaining the purpose and usefulness of the survey and the importance of receiving completed forms, but with no interviewer present the majority of recipients will often discard the questionnaire without a second thought. The greatest problem is that there is a built-in likelihood of a systematic bias in terms of those who actually do complete the survey and return the form; they tend to be those people who are most interested in the issues dealt with by the survey or have strong opinions about them. If the survey findings are generalized beyond the sample of respondents, then, they may well yield gross overstatements about the positions taken on these issues.

Even concerning only those cases for which survey forms are returned, there may be operational problems. In the first place, mailed questionnaires must be kept short, simple, and to the point if there is to be any usable response at all. With no interviewer present, all the items on the questionnaire must be self-explanatory. In addition, for the most part the use of mailed questionnaires precludes the use of open-ended type questioning, and there is little opportunity for the kind of probing that can be done by skilled interviewers.

Other disadvantages stem from the inability to exert control over the interview situation. For example, a survey might be intended for the head of the household, housewives, teenagers, or elderly people in particular, but in actuality it may be completed by any member of the household or by one individual receiving advice from others. Furthermore, although in some surveys the sequencing of questions is of great importance, as is seen below, with mailed surveys the intended order of questions is easily overridden. Also, the use of mailed questionnaires may allow the interested respondent to familiarize himself with the contents and mull over certain questions for a few days before completing the survey; this weighing of responses may or may not be desirable depending on the nature and type of questions being used.

Telephone Surveys

A third alternative that may be appropriate for some kinds of studies is the use of telephone surveys, interviewing people over the telephone instead of face-to-face. In general, telephone surveys present an efficient means of obtaining answers to a few short, direct, nonsensitive questions of fact or fairly straightforward attitude and opinion type questions. They work best with cut-and-dried question sequences that are easily understood and answerable, such as the familiar "Is anyone in your household watching TV at the moment?" and "If so, what program are they watching?" variety.

Telephone surveys tend to fall between personal interviews and mailed questionnaires in terms of both response rates and costs. The interviewer on the telephone has some opportunity to present a sales pitch and convince the intended respondent to answer a few questions, but many people find it easier to refuse interviews over the telephone than in person. In some cases it is more difficult to gain the confidence of the respondent and establish the legitimacy of the survey, as opposed to somebody's idea of a practical joke or a survey actually being undertaken for unstated nefarious purposes. Furthermore, it is always easy for the respondent to terminate the interview at will after it has been started if it becomes too long or tedious.

Telephone surveys must be kept short and to the point if a decent completion rate is to be attained. A good telephone survey, if the type of information being sought lends itself to this format, will probably produce a much higher response rate than would a mailed survey, but it may be less than that obtainable by personal interviewers. On the other hand, it will cost more than mailing out questionnaires, but less than a comparable personal interview survey. The primary disadvantage is the severe limitation on the amounts and depth of questioning permitted by the telephone interview format.

A recently completed telephone survey designed by the author serves as a good case in point. The purpose was to survey residents of a community to determine what kinds of households use the city bus system, attitudes about potential use of an improved system, and in general the degree of support for the provision of this service by a local government unit. The survey contained 16 questions, some of which called for multiple responses, and was fairly ambitious for implementation as a telephone survey. This survey garnered some 980 valid interviews for a 60 percent response rate and an average data collection cost of $0.90 per interview.

This example also provides a good illustration of an inherent problem that may plague telephone surveys, namely that only people with telephones can be respondents. If people living in homes without telephones or people living in group quarters with many individuals sharing only a few phones constitute important elements of the target population, they may be seriously underrepresented in the survey sample. In the present example, it was recognized that because a telephone survey would not adequately represent the lowest income segments of the population and elderly people in senior citizens' homes, two groups that are in fact important targets of transit programming, they would have to be accounted for by other means.

Self-Administered Questionnaires

One variant that combines elements of personal interviews and mailed questionnaires is the use of self-administered questionnaires. This interview format is often used in group situations, such as surveying all the members of a class or participants in some type of program activity at the same time, in which case this interview format is referred to as the use of **group-administered questionnaires**. Whether administered in groups or individually, the self-administered format provides the advantages of having an interviewer present to make sure that the instructions are clear and to clarify certain items, if necessary, and at the same time benefits from the efficiency gained by letting the respondent fill out the form himself. It is especially efficient in group-administered settings, which also facilitate the use of certain stimuli, such as visual aids, and assure that all responses are obtained under the same controlled conditions.

Self-administered questionnaires are often employed in conjunction with direct personal interview techniques, with an interviewer conducting part of the survey that may require careful presentation or probing follow-ups, and the respondent completing the more straightforward portions by himself. This approach was used in a fairly lengthy survey of officers on a city police force designed to obtain some insight as to their perceptions of the performance of the department, relationships between citizens and police officers, and ways of improving police productivity. This survey achieved approximately a 60 percent response rate and incurred an average cost of data collection of $8.00 per case.

SURVEYS AS MEASUREMENT TOOLS

It is important to keep in mind that surveys are measuring instruments—delicate ones at that—and that their sole function is to provide high quality data to address specified issues. The operationalized indicators contained in survey data are essentially responses or reactions to stimuli produced by the questionnaire or interview, and their quality is therefore dependent on the design and conduct of the survey in the first place. Survey data are the most reactive of all types of data; as opposed to unobtrusive measures in which the observations are made in such a way so as not to affect the measure itself, the way in which a survey is conducted and questions are asked can easily influence the responses. In fact, it is fair to say that survey data are *created* rather than collected in their natural state (Babbie, 1973, p. 144).

A concomitant and somewhat more subtle problem is that the use of surveys can easily lead to overstating the importance or significance of the findings. It should be kept in mind that responses are given precisely because they are solicited. The questions may not be biased in any way and the responses may accurately reflect the general direction of an attitude toward some issue; yet the very existence of a positive or negative response, for example, may be interpreted as an indication that the issue is of some concern in the first place, even when it is not. Respondents answer survey questions because they are asked to, whether or not they care about the issues involved, and their responses may not represent strong feelings or well-considered opinions. Thus, a survey limited to cut-and-dried first level questions on some issues, without probing below the surface, may produce a bias not in the direction of the response but in the overstatement of the salience of the issue itself.

The reliability and validity of a survey can be jeopardized by reactive effects stemming from four sources: 1) the interviewer, 2) the respondent, 3) the interview situation, and 4) the survey instrument. Additional errors or distortions can of course occur in the mechanical processing or other preparation of the data for analysis. For example, random errors in the key-punching of the data will weaken their reliability, and selective or biased interpretation of open ended responses can reduce their validity.

Interviewer Effects

In all interview surveys the interviewers themselves may exert great influence over the responses through their appearance, general behavior, and the way in which they conduct the interview. Because the interviewers are the communication links in eliciting responses, the reliability of the data depends on the uniformity with which survey items are presented and responses are recorded. If there are random inconsistencies among interviewers or among the interviews conducted by a single interviewer during the day, reliability is weakened because the operationalized measures are not being taken exactly the same way. Because "sloppy interviewing" can render survey data meaningless even without systematic biases, interviewers must be trained and motivated to be consistent in their conduct of the interviews regardless of mood, fatigue, boredom, or situational factors.

More importantly, interviewers can easily introduce systematic biases in survey responses, weakening the validity of the data. There are two types of problems in this regard. First, the outward characteristics of the interviewer may lead the respondent to systematically temper his responses in a certain direction. Everything else being equal, the response obtained in a given survey may differ systematically by whether the interviewer was male or female, white or black or of a particular ethnic group, younger or older, etc. These differences may relate only to individual items in the survey or to the overall tone of the whole set of responses. For example, in a survey taken in Baltimore, Maryland in which victims of crimes were interviewed regarding their perceptions of police performance in those incidents, some were interviewed by civilians and others by uniformed police officers. The ratings of overall police performance by respondents interviewed by police officers were significantly greater than those reported in the interviews conducted by civilians, especially among black respondents (Furstenberg and Wellford, 1973).

In certain instances the selective assignment of interviewers to cases might be helpful, as with the use of white interviewers in predominantly white neighborhoods and black interviewers in predominantly black neighborhoods in an attempt to obtain more candid responses to race sensitive items that might be withheld from an interviewer of the other race. This is a good idea, however, only if it can be assured that the two sets of interviewers will not differ systematically in the way they conduct the interviews. Beyond this, one strategy that might be used when there is reason to believe that interviewer characteristics might bias responses is the random assignment of interviewers to cases, as mentioned in the previous chapter.

The second type of interviewer bias relates to the way in which he conducts the survey, regardless of his outward characteristics. The psychological balance between interviewer and interviewee will vary considerably from case to case, but often the interviewer will dominate the situation precisely because he is the one conducting the survey. If any of his attitudes, opinions, feelings, or biases are communicated to the respondent through the way in which he presents items, makes side comments, or pursues follow-up questions, the responses that result may reflect his point of view as much as, or more than, that of the person being interviewed. Furthermore, he can inject his own preferences into the data through the way he plays up or plays down the relative importance of certain items, his discretion as to whether or not certain items are applicable to the particular individual responding, and his recording of the responses, particularly in terms of capturing the essence of open-ended responses.

The ability of the interviewer to slant or distort the data obtained in surveys is unquestionable, and this potential problem is a primary factor to be considered in determining whether or not to use the personal interview format. The researcher may begin to counteract this problem somewhat by designing a questionnaire that is unequivocal, but for the most part it is a matter of interviewer recruitment and training. Because much of this interviewer bias can occur unintentionally, good interviewing requires not only the use of responsible, highly motivated individuals but also extensive training (Weiss, 1975). Interviewers must be made aware of the pitfalls of interviewer bias in general and coached through the specific instrument at hand in terms of how to present items and potential biasing factors to guard against.

Respondent Effects

The most varied and perhaps the most intractable set of reactive effects of survey data arise from the person being surveyed, whatever the interview format. How the respondent reacts to the idea of being surveyed and the conscious and unconscious postures he assumes during the survey will have an overriding influence on how he weighs the questions and responds to them. Respondent effects are of particular concern in surveys of social service agency clients, who are likely to be poor, sick, or delinquent, i.e., people who are in stressful circumstances and in need of service (Weiss, 1975, p. 356). These factors may make it difficult for them to respond to survey questions in a meaningful way, and they are apt to govern *how* responses are made. First of all, the kinds of random variation in mood and fatigue and so forth that can result in interviewers performing inconsistently also apply to respondents, decreasing the overall reliability of the data.

Guinea Pig Effects Of much greater concern, however, are a number of potentially biasing factors that can create validity problems with survey data. Foremost in this category are the so-called guinea pig effects, problems arising from the respondent's awareness of being observed or tested, akin to the "Hawthorne effects" discussed in the preceding chapter. Specifically, the idea that his views are being solicited as part of some presumably worthwhile undertaking, or the fact that he has been singled out to be included in a sample survey, may lead the respondent to take greater interest in, or a different attitude toward, the issues under study. In addition, if he thinks that he is being tested somehow and needs to make a good impression, this can easily color all his responses.

Moreover, the respondent may purposefully conceal his true feelings about issues and distort responses about background or behavioral characteristics to create a certain kind of appearance. He may even feel threatened by the interview and knowingly provide responses that are not true in order to avoid what he might perceive as potential unwanted consequences. For example, homeowners may be very reluctant to provide information about improvements they have made on their property if they are worried about public officials finding out about work that has been done without building permits or subsequent increases in their assessed valuation. In introducing the survey it may be wise to emphasize that the findings are to be used for research purposes only and that no individual's responses can be traced back to him, that interest centers on the collective responses of all those interviewed. On the other hand, the very fact that the respondent is told that it is important that he participate in the survey sometimes strengthens the tendency for these guinea pig effects to take hold.

Role Selection More subtle kinds of respondent effects on survey data, particularly with respect to attitudinal data, include role selection and response sets. Even in the absence of overt defensiveness or dishonesty in the responses calculated to create or contradict certain impressions, the respondent may subconsciously select one from the many co-existing perceptions of self and answer the survey questions on that basis. If this **role selection** in the relatively artificial interview situation differs substantially from the more customary roles in natural settings, the responses obtained may not represent true attitudes and feelings very well. Problems of role selection are difficult if not impossible to guard against, but they can sometimes be detected after the fact through inconsistencies among responses.

Response Sets   The term **response set** refers to an underlying psychological perspective from which an individual might approach a survey, a subconscious automatic tendency to respond to survey items in a particular way, almost regardless of the content. If such an underlying tendency governs an individual's responses in part, it can distort his responses so as to become either almost meaningless or systematically biased. One response set, for example, is that of **acquiescence**, the frequently encountered tendency of many respondents to agree rather than disagree with survey items. If all the statements focusing on the quality of a local public service are worded positively, and an individual's responses to all these items are positive, this could reflect either a bona fide favorable attitude or simply the effect of the response set. If the acquiescence response set is indeed the critical factor here, the results can be very misleading. If, however, the set of statements pertaining to the public service is mixed so that some are phrased positively and some negatively, a truly favorable attitude would be expected to produce approximately the corresponding mix of positive and negative responses. If the acquiescence response set were at work with this set-up, the expected response pattern would be basically "agree" type responses to both positive and negative items; these responses could not be substantively interpreted in a meaningful way, but the existence of a response set would be identified.

A second type of response set, which is linked to the guinea pig effect, might be called the **ability to respond** response set. Some individuals may feel a desire to seem knowledgeable and informed about the concerns of the survey, and therefore want to seem able to respond to all or most of the items in a questionnaire, even when they do not have any real basis for responding. With short form multiple choice survey items, it is easy to go through checking off responses or choosing among the alternatives posed by the interviewer with little underlying familiarity, reasoning, or considered opinion. Such responses constitute no more than "random noise," but they may well contribute to the tendency to overstate concern with or positions taken on the issues involved. Therefore, including a few knowledge and awareness "test" questions or asking the respondent a few "why" type follow-up questions may be helpful in identifying when this is the case.

The response set referred to as **prestige bias** is one that prompts people to give responses that they think will put them in a more favorable light, and it applies equally to attitudinal and factual data. People may inflate estimates of income, contributions to charitable organizations, real estate taxes paid, job description, church attendance, and the like to make them seem more prestigious as well as temper their stated opinions for the same reasons. The only way of attempting to counteract this tendency is to present items neutrally, making the low prestige alternatives seemingly as acceptable as the higher prestige responses. For example, instead of asking "Have you read a local newspaper in the past week?" which some respondents might not want to answer negatively because of an implied low prestige factor (not "well informed"), phrasing the question as "Have you had a chance a read a local newspaper in the past week?" might yield more accurate responses by making the low prestige answer more acceptable.

A final response set is that of **social desirability,** the tendency to represent oneself as being in favor of ideas that are generally perceived as being in the public interest or desirable from the larger society's point of view. Upper income respondents in a general community survey, for example, might indicate that they are in favor of improved public recreation facilities in low income areas even when they really do not support the idea. This could occur if these respondents 1) perceive the proposal of improved facilities as something generally considered to be in the public interest, and 2) if they want to give the impression of supporting ideas that reflect the public interest.

Halo Effect Another potentially misleading factor with respect to survey research data is the tendency of some respondents to answer specific questions on the basis of general impressions or their reactions to implied general questions. When ratings of particular characteristics of a particular program, for example, reflect the respondent's overall rating of the program in its entirety rather than a separate evaluation of each specific attribute, the data are clouded by a **halo effect.** Very often a general evaluation of something—a teacher evaluation for instance—will be a net product of more and less favorable evaluations of its specific aspects; this is the assumption on which sets of specific questions arc often based. Yet the respondent may not have a clear idea as to how he would rate the specifics and may simply respond on the basis of his overall general impression. Interpreting them as real indicators of specific ratings can be misleading.

Situational Effects

Beyond the biases introduced by interviewers and interviewees, the situation in which the survey is conducted can also lead to problems with survey data. In household surveys, for example, the responses obtained from an adult in an interview situation characterized by TV and stereo blaring forth, children running around and interrupting frequently, and similar distractions may be far less meaningful than those obtained in a quiet setting in which the respondent is concentrating almost solely on completing the survey.

More importantly, differences in interview situations can produce substantial differences in the nature and direction of the responses. A program participant being asked questions about how well the program is managed or how well it meets his needs, for example, may feel confident to respond freely and perhaps negatively if the interview is being conducted in his home, whereas the same individual may feel more constrained as to how he answers the same questions if the interview is conducted at the agency. Program staffers might respond one way to questions about the program's effectiveness and efficiency in a one-on-one interview situation and respond quite differently if the survey is conducted in a group setting or with his boss present. Similarly, responses given by housewives, in particular, in home interview surveys have been found to vary systematically by whether or not the husband is in the same room. These problems point out the need to anticipate the possible reactive effects of alternative interview situations in a given survey and settle on one type of arrangement that seems likely to enable the person being interviewed to devote adequate attention to the survey and to feel confident in providing honest and forthright responses.

Instrument Effects

The final source of reactive effects on survey data, and the one over which the researcher can exert the most control, is the survey instrument. If items on the survey are vague or ambiguous or if the import of the question is not put across clearly, the result is likely to be a high degree of nonresponse or an unreliable random noise type of response pattern. More importantly, survey instruments are often structured either by design or by accident so as to channel responses in predetermined directions, controlling the outcomes in advance. This can occur through inclusions and omissions of different types of items as well as the use of leading questions and the selective provision of possible responses. The quality of a survey's findings can only be as good as the instrument itself, and if valid information is in fact the objective, care should go into developing a usable and unbiased instrument. The task of questionnaire design is indeed a fine art and is discussed in some detail in the following section.

QUESTIONNAIRE DESIGN

Survey instruments are commonly thought of as consisting solely of questions, but this is not really the case. Most survey questionnaires contain not only questions but also statements to which the respondent is asked to react. The particular types of items that are used and their exact wording are crucial for obtaining valid indicators of the characteristics and attitudes to be measured. In addition, the sequencing of these items and the overall questionnaire format can aid or hinder the effort to obtain valid measures and the conduct of the survey itself.

Question Wording

Survey items must be worded clearly, but in practice the inclusion of items that are vague, incomplete, or ambiguous is a common problem. If the items themselves are open to varying interpretations by the respondents, the individual responses are not really measures on the same scale or against a uniform standard.

Imprecise Questions   Questions that may seem perfectly clear to the researcher may be interpreted differently by respondents if they are not approaching the issue from the same perspective. For example, a survey of teaching faculty at a university might include the question "Do you see a faculty union as having a role here at the university?" on the assumption that a "Yes" response would indicate a positive attitude toward the idea of establishing a union as a collective bargaining agent. However, faculty who are strongly opposed to that idea might still answer "Yes" because they think that a union does have some legitimate role in the university, serving as an information conduit, for example. This would basically be a problem of overinterpretation, reading too much into responses to ambiguous questions.

Imprecise questions can easily ruin the reliability of the data and should be guarded against by carefully specifying the subject or central concern of survey items. If, for example, a sequence of items concerning repairs and improvements that homeowners have made begins with the question "Have you made any major repairs or improvements to this property in the past 2 years?" the responses will depend on how the respondent interprets the word *major*, and this is likely to vary considerably from person to person. If major repairs or improvements are first identified as those that would cost $500 or more, and the instructions specifically indicate that routine repairs such as fixing broken shutters and drainpipes or patching driveways are not to be included, there is much greater certainty that the responses will be made on a common basis.

Some common, everyday words can result in great ambiguity in survey items. If asked whether or not they are in favor of "better counseling policies" in a social service program, for example, some respondents might answer "Yes" on the basis of a desire for closer contact with counselors whereas others may answer "Yes" on the basis of "better" meaning "less" counseling. To be of any use, such a question would have to be made more specific in terms of the type of improvements desired.

The use of more complicated words or specialized terminology can also result in vague or ambiguous survey items. One survey of state budget offices, for example, included a question about the number of appropriation bills that had been submitted to their legislatures in the past fiscal year. The mailed questionnaire included a definition of the term appropriation bill, but somehow (either in spite of, or perhaps because of, this definition) the question was still confusing. The responses ranged from three to several thousand bills—in cases where respondents had apparently counted individual items separately—with the result that the data were meaningless and could not be used. Either the instructions were still imprecise, or this questionnaire required some follow-up contact over the telephone.

Similarly, questions that are indefinite in terms of time can often create problems. The question "Does anyone in your household regularly use city recreational facilities?" begs the question of what constitutes regular usage, for example, with some respondents considering once a month to be regular and others applying a much stricter standard. Such questions are better phrased by specifying a time period such as "Does anyone in your household use city recreational facilities at least once a week?" or further improved by referring to a given point in time. The question "Did anyone in your household use city recreational facilities during the past week?" is a more objective approach because it asks a question of fact related to the immediate past rather than forcing the respondent to make his own estimate of average usage over an unspecified time period.

Double-barreled Questions Double-barreled questions are very ambiguous and should always be avoided, because the respondent may well have different views on the two parts of the question and no way of making the distinction in his response. For example, employees who are asked whether they "think that increased supervision or fairer promotion policies would lead to greater productivity in the agency" will be hard put to respond if they feel that fairer promotion policies would be an improvement but that increased supervision would not. Such a question is likely either to produce a high rate of nonresponse or a set of "yes" and "no" answers that may be quite misleading.

Lengthy Items Short items are preferable to long items and an effort should be made to assure that questions are as concise and to the point as possible. Sometimes the attempt to clarify items leads to complicated statements, with definitions and qualifiers and the like, that are often passed over by many respondents, especially in surveys using mailed questionnaires. This in turn can result in complete misinterpretations of what the question is all about. A safer strategy for constructing items is to assume that respondents will move through them quickly, answering on the basis of first interpretations, and to try to develop items that will be clear and work well under these conditions. An additional precaution along these lines is to refrain from stating items in the negative. The tendency to read through items quickly can easily result in skipping over the word "not" in such statements and basing responses on an interpretation that is 180 degrees off from the intended question.

Irrelevant Questions A second kind of problem encountered in surveys involves asking people questions that they are not really in a position to answer. Not only must survey items be worded clearly; they must also be relevant to the respondent's range of experience or general knowledge so that he is competent to answer them. Although citizens are often asked whether they think that city services are provided efficiently—and if not, how they think this efficiency might be improved—this may have little utility. From casual observation and sometimes more direct contact with city services, citizens are often in a position to evaluate their efficiency, and they may be able to make worthwhile suggestions for improving it. On the other hand, their responses may provide little real contribution if they are unaware of the real world constraints, such as collective bargaining, under which city programs operate. The citizen in this situation may suggest improvements that are obvious to him, given limited familiarity with the operating context, but which unfortunately are not feasible for implementation.

This issue involves posing questions that are relevant for the intended audience. The above example should not be interpreted as indicating that citizen surveys are a waste of time because "They do not know enough to make meaningful responses" as is sometimes contended. To the contrary, citizen surveys can be a valuable tool for obtaining very worthwhile information, but such surveys should not assume an unrealistic level of familiarity or contact with issues. This holds for any group or population being surveyed; it is pointless to interview teachers about the effectiveness of teaching methods they have not used or at least been exposed to, program managers about the receptivity to treatment of types of clientele they are not familiar with, or to ask administrators about the operating characteristics of programs they do not deal with, and so forth.

Loaded Questions A third type of problem in question wording, which is really the crux of the problem of biased survey responses, is the (usually inadvertent) use of **loaded questions**, which channel the responses in a certain direction. As discussed above, to the extent that there is bias in the way survey items are presented, the responses are predetermined and reflect the survey instrument itself rather than true behavior or opinions. Leading questions suggesting a preferred alternative, such as "Don't you think city officials really ought to do something about the rapidly rising crime rate?" for a blatant example, are a primary source of this built-in bias. A somewhat more subtle example would be one in which the respondent is handed a list of local public services and asked "Which of these service areas do you think most urgently requires improvement?" suggesting that at least some of these services are in fact inadequate at present.

Another commonly encountered type of loaded question forces a bias into the responses by providing an unfair set of alternative responses from which one is to be chosen. A program can always be made to look good, for example, by asking participants to rate it on scales that include only positive ratings or scales with many positive positions and relatively few negative ratings, such as the following set of choices: excellent, very good, good, fair, poor. Other question wording techniques that incorporate a built-in bias include the association of certain positions with very popular or unpopular public figures, the use of emotionally charged words that convey a favorable or unfavorable impression of the subject of the question, and damning with faint praise, as in the following example, "Some people say the city's transit system is poor, but others say that it is adequate for the present. How would you rate it?" The point to keep in mind in developing survey items is that in order to provide valid operational indicators, their content must be clear and precise to the respondent without suggesting in any way what his response should be. Thus, when alternative responses are presented, they should be well balanced, and all items should be worded carefully so as not to pronounce judgment or suggest a given attitude or position.

Question Formats

Survey questions are of two general formats, open-ended and closed; nonquestion items are almost always closed-ended. Closed-ended items present a question or statement followed by a set of alternative responses from which the individual is to choose one or more as being most appropriate for him. The validity of the responses then depends on the adequacy of the alternatives provided as well as the working of the question or item in the first place. Closed questions are much quicker and easier to use, and they lend themselves to quantitative data analysis more readily than open-ended questions. Lengthy surveys that cover many areas of concern usually rely on closed questions to a great extent in order to make the conduct of the survey manageable. The chief disadvantage of course is that the "forced" alternatives used in closed questions may introduce further biases in the responses, and in general this type of item precludes any degree of spontaneity or expressiveness in the response.

By contrast, open-ended questions such as asking field representatives of a certain program "How do you think we can make the program more responsive to our clients' needs?" without suggesting any alternatives provides for a free, and potentially most informative, response. Even when used to address more specific issues than the above example, open-ended questions will often generate more complete and less ambiguous information than can be obtained with closed questions. The responses forthcoming with open-ended questions may capture the reasons or whole train of thought behind a particular answer, providing a clear understanding of the intent and basis of the response. In a personal interview with open-ended questioning, the interviewer can probe areas or directions that suggest themselves during the course of the interview either to clarify previous responses or gain further insight into a problem.

Open-ended questioning works best with the personal interview format; the technique is cumbersome in telephone surveys and unlikely to generate complete responses in mailed questionnaire surveys. In terms of content, open-ended questions are most appropriate when 1) the likely responses are not known, in which case the development of a valid closed question is difficult, 2) a great range of responses is anticipated that might not break down neatly into a few categories, 3) it is desired to obtain a response with no prompting whatsoever, 4) indications of in-depth motivations or rationales are desired, or 5) the research is basically exploratory in nature and it is desired to let issues and problems surface.

One problem associated with open-ended questions is that they are unwieldy in terms of writing out lengthy responses and consume much interview time. More importantly, this process, although potentially more informative, is also more vulnerable to interviewer bias. The ideal is for the interviewer to write down the response word-for-word, but this is often impractical, and in effect the interviewer tries to capture the essence of the response with key words and ideas. Consciously or subconsciously, with this process he may be selective, including some elements and screening out others according to his own predilections or previous response patterns he has encountered. Careful treatment of open-ended survey items is probably the most demanding task in the conduct of personal interviews. Furthermore, the responses from open-ended questions often do not lend themselves to quantification very well and prove difficult to incorporate into the data analysis portion of the project.

Fortunately, there are a number of ways of accommodating the advantages of both closed and open-ended questions in a survey instrument. First, where there is a problem of not knowing what the appropriate response alternatives are, open-ended questions might be used in pretesting the instrument as a means of identifying the alternatives for structuring closed form questions in subsequent drafts of the questionnaire. Second, even though it would lengthen the interview, it might be wise to ask crucial questions both ways, first as an open-ended question and then as a more structured closed form question. The closed-ended responses might be relied upon in the data analysis if they seem valid by comparison with the open-ended responses. If, on the other hand, the closed-ended version seems not to have captured the essence of the open-ended responses, the analyst can resort to grappling with the open-ended responses.

Alternatively, in the preparation of the data for analysis, if open-ended responses seem to cluster naturally into a few common types of response, they might be classified accordingly into categories that lend themselves to quantitative analysis. The use of such "coding frames" is discussed below. Another option is to include an open-ended alternative as one possible response in an otherwise closed form question. The list might include a number of anticipated responses plus one labeled "other," to be checked if none of the predetermined responses apply. This "other" alternative can be followed with a "please specify" and a space left vacant for the writing in of open-ended responses, if necessary.

Checklists, Rating Scales and Inventories There is a wide variety of closed question formats ranging from simple "Yes" or "No" questions to fairly complicated forms. Two of the most commonly used types of questions are checklists and rating scales, both of which apply a single question to a whole list of items. **Checklists** present a list of items and ask the respondent to indicate whether each applies in a certain context. Figure 10.1 shows a somewhat elaborate checklist used in a general community survey to obtain an idea of the extent to which various issues are considered to represent problems by local residents. The re-

The first set of questions concerns your feelings about certain aspects of life in _____ Please check only <u>one</u> answer for each item.

	Serious problem	Average problem	Don't know	Minor problem	No problem
1. Drug abuse is:	1	2	3	4	5
2. Unemployment is:	1	2	3	4	5
3. Illness is:	1	2	3	4	5
4. Poor housing is:	1	2	3	4	5
5. Poverty is:	1	2	3	4	5
6. Divorces are:	1	2	3	4	5
7. Crime is:	1	2	3	4	5
8. Idle youth are:	1	2	3	4	5
9. School dropouts are:	1	2	3	4	5
10. Illiteracy is:	1	2	3	4	5
11. Elderly living alone are:	1	2	3	4	5
12. Too much growth is:	1	2	3	4	5
13.	1	2	3	4	5
14.	1	2	3	4	5
15.	1	2	3	4	5
16.	1	2	3	4	5

Figure 10.1.   Checklist question format. Adapted from New England Attitude Data System.

spondent is asked to examine the checklist and indicate in which category each item belongs, in his opinion. The numbers below each possible response are simply codes for processing the data.

Rating scales employ the same kind of checklist but ask the respondent to rate each item according to some specified criterion, using a scale of responses such as "very satisfactory," "satisfactory," "dissatisfactory," and "very dissatisfactory." Rating scales can also be developed to solicit evaluations of a program in a number of different respects, as illustrated in the question shown in Figure 10.2, which asks health teachers to rate drug programs in their schools in terms of a number of different criteria. **Inventories** refer to the same type of checklist format when the items refer to fact or perceived behavior as opposed to attitudinal or opinion type data.

Multiple Choice   Most closed form survey questions are multiple choice questions. The respondent is presented with alternative answers

18. We would like you to evaluate the one drug training program which you considered to be most beneficial in helping you to perform as a health teacher. How effective was this program in the following respects:

	Not at all helpful				Extremely helpful
Recognizing the basic classifications of drugs and the symptoms of their abuse:	1	2	3	4	5
Understanding the reasons for drug use among students:	1	2	3	4	5
Increasing your ability to communicate openly and honestly with students:	1	2	3	4	5
Learning to distinguish between drug experimentation, use, and abuse:	1	2	3	4	5
Learning more about local treatment programs and other community resources:	1	2	3	4	5
Learning to help students to better understand themselves, so that they can make their own decisions regarding the use of drugs:	1	2	3	4	5
Learning to help individual students who may have problems:	1	2	3	4	5
Learning how to involve students in the educational process:	1	2	3	4	5

Figure 10.2.   Rating scale format: program evaluation. From Virginia General Assembly, 1975, p. A-19.

and asked to choose the most appropriate. This is essentially the pro-cedure used in checklists and rating scales as pointed out above. Other formats present just one question at a time and may include many more possible alternatives, which may or may not be ranked in any way. (Whereas closed form questions most frequently yield nominal data, the alternatives to be considered may also represent ordinal or even in-terval scales.)

Figure 10.3 shows one page of a questionnaire used to obtain in-

1. Grade in school: _____   2. Male _____   Female _____

3. Do you consider yourself: Black _____   White _____   Other _____

4. In what city or county do you live?   City _____   County _____

5. How would you describe the level of drug use (not including alcohol) in your
   school: (You may check more than one)

   1. _____   None or very little.
   2. _____   Limited number of experimental users.
   3. _____   Widespread experimental use.
   4. _____   Limited number of occasional users.
   5. _____   Widespread occasional use.
   6. _____   Limited number of habitual users.
   7. _____   Widespread habitual use.

6. Based on your estimate of drug usage, how would you describe the drug problem
   in your school?

   1. _____   No problem.
   2. _____   A problem, but not serious.
   3. _____   A serious problem.

7. What are the most frequently used drugs in your school? For each drug, write
   1, 2, 3, 4 in the space provided, according to whether you believe the drug is
   not used, or is used experimentally, occasionally, or habitually:

   1 – not used   3 – occasional use
   2 – experimental use   4 – habitual use

   _____   Marijuana, hashish.
   _____   LSD, mescaline, hallucinogens.
   _____   Cocaine.
   _____   Heroin.
   _____   Methadrine, methamphetamine ("speed").
   _____   Amphetamines ("uppers, pep pills, bennies, dexies").
   _____   Barbiturates   ("downers, barbs, blues, reds").
   _____   Methaqualone ("sopors, Vitamin Q").
   _____   Tranquilizers   (Darvon, Librium, Valium).
   _____   Alcohol.
   _____   Cough syrup, codeine.
   _____   Glue, inhalants.
   _____   Poly-drug use (more than one drug at one time).

8. How many of your friends turn on with drugs?

   1. _____   None.
   2. _____   Very few.
   3. _____   Several.
   4. _____   Most.

Figure 10.3.   Multiple choice formats. From Virginia General Assembly, 1975, p. A-14.

formation from high school students in the Virginia school system about the use of drugs and alcohol by the student population. Questions 2 and 3 are respondent identification items in multiple choice form, which is typical in most mass surveys. Questions 5 and 6, on the other hand, are aimed at obtaining an indication of the perceived extent of drug and alcohol usage in the respondent's school and the degree to which he considers this to be a problem, if at all. The set of completed responses to these two items would form ordinal scales. Question 7 in the same figure uses the inventory format, designed to take stock of the extent of usage of various kinds of drugs.

Grids Grids are a question format essentially used to record two types of information at once. They employ a checklist of items that may or may not apply to the respondent in the context of the survey and a second variable representing alternative ways in which the items may apply. Figure 10.4 illustrates the use of a grid to identify simultaneously the types of complaints respondents have had with local government and the party with whom each type of complaint was registered. This economical format provides an indication, first, whether the

If you have made any complaints to city officials about city services or problems in the past two years, indicate the nature of each complaint and the official to whom it was made by checking the appropriate boxes below.

To whom was complaint made?

Type of complaint	Mayor	City councilman	Official in city department	Other (specify)
Neighborhood house or yard upkeep				
Trash collection				
Police services				
Recreation facilities				
Parking				
Street lighting				
Street maintenance and cleaning				
Sewer and water				
Other (Specify)				

Figure 10.4.   Grid format illustration.

respondent has had a complaint; second, what type of complaint or complaints they were; and third, with whom these complaints were registered. Notice that with respect to both types of complaint and with whom it was registered, a space is made available for indicating a response that is not already provided for in the listings.

Rankings, Q Sort, and Budget Pies Many surveys present the respondent with a number of items to find out how he would rank them on some criterion or to determine his preferences from among them. Some employ straightforward ranking type questions which ask the respondent to rank the items in order according to whatever the criterion is; this is workable up to about ten items, but the respondent is only asked to indicate the three or four that he would rank highest or lowest, indicating which is first, second, etc.

An alternative approach is to determine the overall rank order among the items with the use of paired comparisons, listing each pair of items separately and asking the respondent which he would prefer or rank higher on the given criterion. One study used this approach in trying to determine the order of importance of various factors influencing motorists' choices of routes (Kannel, 1972). Although paired comparisons may force more careful consideration of rank orders, the technique becomes very cumbersome when more than a few items are involved, and will quickly fatigue respondents. (For computing the number of possible pairs out of a given number of items, refer to the formula for combinations discussed in chapter 6.) Operationally, there is also the problem of possible intransitivities or inconsistencies in the rank orders among pairs (North et al., 1963, pp. 79–89).

Still another approach to determining preferences or distinguishing the important items from the less important items is the **Q sort** technique (Stephenson, 1953; North et al., 1963, pp. 55–77; Gauger and Wyekoff, 1973). The respondent is presented with the pool of items (usually from 35 to 100) and told to sort them into a specified number of groups, e.g., 7 or 9, ranked from lowest to highest or least favorable to most favorable on some criterion. For instance, prisoners in a correctional institution might be presented with a list of grievances or problems regarding regulations and procedures and asked to indicate how serious a problem they consider each item to be.

The distribution of items across the groups is predetermined so that, for example, a respondent must end up with 2, 3, 5, 7, 10, 7, 5, 3, and 2 items, respectively, in the nine groups. The groups are considered to represent equal gradations of change from lowest to highest on the scale so that the data can be coded and analyzed as interval measures, and the use of a unimodal, symmetrical distribution such as that suggested above further facilitates statistical analysis. Although most of the items are clustered around the middle categories, interest centers on those few that are consistently placed at the extreme upper or lower ends of the scale, because they are the items eliciting the strongest reactions. In general, the Q sort technique is a quick and effective way of establishing preference patterns and identifying critical problems or factors in a first round of inquiry, the results of which would then be used to channel attention more closely on these factors.

Frequently in the area of needs assessment and community objectives, interest centers on citizens' priorities concerning relative expenditure amounts among program areas. Although many of the question formats mentioned above have been applied to this issue, one that has been developed with this particular purpose in mind is the **budget pie** approach. As typically presented, the questionnaire shows a circle representing the total budget amount divided into wedges labeled according to program area and the percentage of the total budget currently allocated or being considered for allocation to that area. The respondent is then asked to indicate how he might prefer to have the budget allocated among those, or additional, program areas. Alternatively, the respondent might be presented with an empty circle and asked to divide it into wedges or program allocations "from scratch."

One advantage of this approach is that is sets an overall budget constraint, that is, forces the respondent to play a zero-sum game in which an increased allocation for one type of program or service can be made only by decreasing allocations to other areas. A corresponding limitation is that because it does set an overall budget amount, it does not ask the respondent to weigh his preferences for various total budget amounts along with his consideration of internal allocations. However, several variations have been developed aimed at recording feelings on total budget size. A further alternative is to present respondents with a large number (30 or so) of different budget allocations and ask them to rate each one (Stewart and Gelberd, 1976). In summary, the use of citizen surveys to obtain this type of data on budget priorities, and the use of budget pies in particular, are currently controversial topics; the validity of the measures so generated and the appropriate use of the data are the focal points of the issue (Clark, 1974; Hatry and Blair, 1976; McIver and Ostrom, 1976; Scott, 1976).

Sequencing and Formating

Survey instruments usually consist of series of question or item sequences, and the order in which the items are sequenced and the way in which the various sequences are incorporated into the questionnaire can have a great influence on the workability of the survey and the quality of the resulting data. The objective is to develop an instrument that has good continuity, facilitates moving through the interview smoothly, and does not bias the responses by the order in which items appear.

Funnel Approach Items often come in sequences because it is necessary to include a number of related questions in order to develop a fully rounded set of responses regarding a given issue. In developing a sequence the designer should be concerned with possible biasing effects of some questions on others as well as the need to maintain a sensible continuity among complementary items. One general approach in this regard is called the **funnel approach,** using a sequence of items moving from very broad questions to those more specifically related to the subject of concern.

The idea here is to introduce the subject generally and provide an opportunity for spontaneous response before suggesting specific alternatives. The objective is to finally force the respondent to choose among specific alternatives or address narrowly defined questions, which he might or might not have dealt with if he had been asked the questions in only general terms, but to do this *after* he has been asked the question in broad terms. The funnel approach is designed to counteract the tendency of respondents to answer broad questions in terms of the specifics that have surfaced or been suggested in previous items; it is a way of gaining general impressions uncontaminated by the specifics pointed out by other items.

A funnel sequence aimed at obtaining ratings of neighborhood services, for example, might begin with open-ended questions about the respondent's perceptions of his neighborhood and his general satisfaction with it; then move to open-ended questions about what he thinks should be done, if anything, to improve the quality of the neighborhood; and then move into closed form questions (perhaps using rating scales) aimed at evaluations of specific public services; followed by even more specific questions about those service areas with which the respondent indicates he is least satisfied. One advantage of this approach is that the researcher can check to see whether the responses given to the specific items are reinforced by things that surfaced in response to the open-ended questions. In the neighborhood services example, poor ratings of certain individual services are more meaningful if those same problems were cited spontaneously in response to the preceding general questions.

Quintamensional Plan A somewhat similar approach that also tries to develop a more complete picture of the respondent's views on an issue is the **quintamensional plan** used first by the Gallup Poll. This approach typically begins with a general knowledge or awareness type question to introduce the issue and then moves to general opinion questions about it. These are followed by questions about specific options, which in turn are followed by "why" type questions to probe the thinking behind the response, and finally by questions aimed at assessing the intensity of the opinion stated previously. For example, residents in a community survey might be asked first about the extent of police patrol in their neighborhood and then about their general rating of this service. If interest centers on the perceived need for foot patrol in the area, they would then be asked more specific questions such as "Do you think that police patrolling on foot should be increased in your neighborhood?" Each of these specific questions would be followed up with a "Why do you say that?" type question and an intensity type: "How strongly do you favor (or oppose)...?"

Using this approach, the first knowledge or awareness type question might be employed as a **filter question,** one intended to determine whether the individual respondent should be asked the following sequence of questions or skip on to the next sequence. Filter questions based on behavior or fact are also often used to screen out respondents from answering given sequences. For example, the respondent might first be asked "Do you or any member of your household regularly use the public transit system once a week or more?" with the following sequence of evaluative items used only with those respondents answering "Yes."

Overall Sequence   The overall sequencing of sets of items in a survey instrument can also be important. It is usually best to begin with some "warm-up" questions relating to nonsensitive experimental or general perception type items intended in part to build a rapport between the interviewer and respondent. The interviewer will be trying to establish an atmosphere of natural conversation between the two to gain the respondent's confidence. The instrument might then turn to some of the easier questions of a more substantive nature followed perhaps by more difficult questions in terms of communicating an item clearly and eliciting a valid response. Sensitive issues are better left to the latter portion of the interview, if possible. Questionnaires often conclude with the respondent classification type items, some of which the respondents may be reluctant to answer, particularly items like income and age. If it suits the researcher's purpose, a higher response rate often results from asking income questions in terms of broad interval ranges rather than trying to ask for exact income. Obviously, all these comments on sequencing apply primarily to personal interview surveys; although sequencing on mailed questionnaires can be important in terms of continuity, as has been pointed out, the respondents are likely to scan the whole questionnaire before completing any part of it, thus negating attempts to prevent the stimulus of any one question from influencing the response to any other.

A Note on Format Given good content, structuring of individual questions, and sequencing of items, the instrument can be further improved by making sure that the physical format is adequate. This is perhaps most important with respect to mailed questionnaires that are filled in by respondents themselves. The main objective of course is clarity, leaving no doubt in the respondent's mind (or in the interviewer's mind with other types of surveys) how and where on the page the responses are to be indicated. This is primarily a matter of adequate spacing on the paper to allow space for open-ended responses to be written in and to avoid problems of responses to given items inadvertently being indicated as responses to other items. With some survey forms where numerous items are bunched closely together, one response checked off in the wrong box can result in a whole series of responses being invalidated.

Furthermore, all instructions pertaining to how and where responses are to be indicated must be clear to the respondent using a mailed questionnaire. Precoding the values of responses that will be coded numerically for data processing later on is often a good, time-saving idea, but it should not be done at the expense of confusing the respondent; the precoded numbers should be fairly inconspicuous on the printed page. Finally, if portions of the page are reserved for coding by the research staff later on, these should also be so indicated clearly.

ATTITUDE MEASUREMENT

Because attitudinal data are among the most important types of information obtained in many surveys and because this type of information in particular presents many challenges in terms of developing valid operational indicators, a brief discussion of attitudes and attitude measurement is merited at this point. While there is no firm consensus on exactly what attitudes are in the abstract, many definitions seem to contain the notions of a "mental set" and "readiness to respond" toward the object of the attitude.

Actually, when we talk about attitudes as they relate to public policy and programs, we are usually concerned with what social psychologists increasingly refer to as an entire cognitive structure made of three components or cognitive states: beliefs, attitudes, and intentions (Triandis, 1971; Fishbein and Ajzen, 1975). **Beliefs** constitute the cognitive component, the idea or concept the individual has of the attitude object. In primitive terms these are the categories humans use in thinking, in classifying the object of the attitude in terms of its perceived characteristics. **Attitudes** themselves are the affective or evaluative component of the cognitive structure, the emotional reaction reflecting the perceived value to the individual connoted by the concept. **Intentions**, then, represent the behavioral component, the predisposition to action or "readiness to respond" based on the first two.

Obviously, in gaining an understanding of people's "attitudes" relating to a given public program issue we are really interested in all three components of the cognitive structure. In order to have an attitude toward something a person must first have a concept of what it is, and insight as to that concept of the object will help explain his attitude toward it. Second, that concept must be associated in the individual's mind with pleasant or unpleasant circumstances or outcomes, the affective component, in order for him to formulate an attitude about it. Third, the way and degree to which this concept with its evaluative interpretation relates to the individual's goals and preferences will determine his behavioral intentions relating to the concept.

To a great extent we are interested in attitudes because they are presumed to influence behavior, although the relationship may be circular with behavior and experience contributing to the way in which attitudes develop. Thus, we might be interested in prospective clients' attitudes toward a certain program as a factor influencing their participation in it, or we might be concerned with employees' attitudes toward the same program as a way of explaining their job performance in it. Alternatively, we might specify some attitudinal variable as an impact measure on the assumption that it will trigger subsequent behavioral impacts, for example that improved attitudes toward a respondent's neighborhood will lead to a greater effort to maintain his own property.

Although in some program evaluations attitudes themselves are of primary interest—with respect to some mental health care activities, for instance—usually there is an assumed linkage with behavior. For example, a counseling program for high school students regarded as troublemakers may be designed for improving their attitudes and general outlook on life, but it would be implemented with the objective of improving their performance in the classroom and their deportment in general. In this regard it should be understood that attitudes are by no means the sole determinants of behavior. Although attitudes involve what people think about, how they feel about certain things, and how they would like to behave toward a given attitude object, their behavior might not reflect this. Behavior is influenced by attitudes, what people would like to do, but also by what they think they should do, social norms, by what they have usually done, habits, and by the expected consequences of behavior. Thus, surveys designed to explain why certain patterns of behavior occur or do not occur, or to provide some insight as to what types of behavior are to be expected as the result of some program intervention, may need to explore respondents' perceptions of social norms, their habitual paterns of behavior, and their anticipated consequences of different types of behavior as well as basic attitudes.

Attitude Scales and Indexes

Attitudes and the other components of cognitive structure can be measured or inferred in a number of ways—through the use of physical stimuli, observation of behavior, and physiological measures, for instance, (Fishbein, 1967; Dawes, 1972; Fishbein and Ajzen, 1975)—but in terms of survey research we are interested primarily in verbal specific methods. It should be understood that, in general, attitude measurement is still in its developmental stages and that there are no particularly correct ways of eliciting attitudinal data in surveys. Basically, the researcher can include any straightforward questions or statements relating to attitudes if they have face validity, subject of course to all the problems of clarity and reactive effects of survey research discussed previously.

However, a number of standardized methods that have been developed for obtaining attitudinal data involve the creation of single measures based on responses to multiple survey items. Such attitude scales or indexes are used primarily to improve the quality of measurement but can also be thought of in terms of a gain in efficiency through data reduction when multiple measures are being used.

Scales and indexes are intended to improve reliability and validity by developing well rounded measures, by incorporating multiple measures in a single operational indicator. Any single measure taken from a survey may include extraneous responses or reflect only a single aspect of what a variable is intended to measure. As has been stressed repeatedly in this book, validity is a matter of degree; in this context the inclusion of a set of varied indicators is presumed to increase the probability of cancelling out one-sided extraneous responses and providing a more balanced indicator of the variable of interest.

In developing attitude scales or indexes the primary concern is with **unidimensionality**; the items included should relate to the same general concept. Yet responses to a set of survey items might well constitute several operationalized indicators of the concept, each representing a somewhat different aspect. In selecting items to be included, then, we are looking for indicators that are related to the other items to be included, yet contribute something additional to the scale or index. In general, the **internal validity** of a scale or index refers to its consistency or unidimensionality; techniques for measuring this are discussed below. **External validity**, on the other hand, refers to the ability of the scale or index to predict values on other operationalized indicators considered to represent the variable of interest, begging the question of what the scale or index should measure in the first place.

Scales and indexes are also considered to be advantageous in terms of providing information about the degree and intensity of attitudes. We often think of attitudes almost dichotomously as having a general content or direction, for example a favorable or unfavorable attitude toward a proposed policy, and many survey items will tap only this general attribute. However, attitudes can also be characterized by additional attributes. If we think of an attitude toward an object as running on a unidimensional continuum from extremely positive to extremely negative, we may be interested in the **degree** of positive or negative attitude, the relative position of an individual on that continuum. Furthermore, if we can conceive of, or if empirical evidence indicates, a neutral or zero point on such a continuum, the **intensity** of an attitude is measured by degrees away from this zero point, such that a very negative attitude may be equally as intense as a very positive attitude toward the same object although they differ substantially in location along the continuum (Guttman and Suchman, 1967).

Finally, cognitive states vary in terms of stability, how enduring they are. Social psychologists have classified them in terms of depth ranging from transient opinions, evaluations of a specific subject or issue, to more enduring underlying attitudes, which are based in turn on more deep seated **values**, which are ultimately a reflection of **personality** (Scott, 1968). Scales and indexes can be developed as measures of these attributes of attitudes. The following sections discuss the difference between scales and indexes and introduce the primary standardized techniques for scaling and indexing attitudes (Fishbein, 1967, part II; Fishbein and Ajzen, 1975, pp. 59-89).

Scales Versus Indexes   Although both are single indicators based on multiple responses—and although attitude indexes are often mistakenly referred to as scales—in strict terms scales and indexes differ. A **scale** is a composite measure formed on the basis of the *pattern* of values of the constituent variables, i.e., there is a single value of the scale assigned to each possible combination of responses to the items that make up the scale.

By contrast, an **index** is a measure that is *computed* using some equation that incorporates all the variables that are part of the index. Usually, attitude indexes are computed by summing the values of all the constituent variables, but this need not be the case. As was brought out in chapter 3, the use of indexes is by no means limited to attitudinal data, as witness the consumer price index, air quality index, and the transit level of service index, etc. Nevertheless, the issues in developing them are the same for attitudinal and other types of indexes: 1) the items to be included, 2) the types of relationships among them, i.e., additive, multiplicative, ratio, etc., and 3) how the items are to be weighted.

Attitude Statements   Verbal techniques for measuring the cognitive component or beliefs tend to employ comparisons among attitude objects, asking the respondent to indicate why one of a group of three is different from the other two, or to elicit open-ended or controlled associations in order to gain insight as to the categories people use to classify and differentiate among objects (Triandis, 1971, pp. 29-35). By contrast, most of the scaling and indexing methods to be discussed below are aimed at measuring the evaluative or attitudinal component of cognitive structure. Most of them employ **attitude statements**, statements that identify an attitude object and express an evaluation or rating of it. The items are structured so that the respondent reacts to the attitude expressed in the statement. An example might be the statement "This neighborhood is a good place to bring up children," with five response choices ranging from "strongly agree" to "strongly disagree."

The development of good attitude statements is something of an art in itself. They must be clear, readily understood, and relevant to the attitude object that is the focus of the statement. Some guidelines that might be helpful in developing attitude statements are as follows.

1.   Avoid statements that refer to the past rather than to the present.

2. Avoid statements that are factual or capable of being interpreted as factual.
3. Avoid statements that may be interpreted in more than one way.
4. Avoid statements that are irrelevant to the psychological object under consideration.
5. Avoid statements that are likely to be endorsed by almost everyone or no one.
6. Select statements that are believed to cover the entire range of the affective scale of interest.
7. Keep the language of the statements simple, clear, and direct.
8. Statements should be short, rarely exceeding 20 words.
9. Each statement should contain only one complete thought.
10. Avoid universals such as all, always, none, or never.
11. Words such as only, just, or merely, etc., should be used with care and moderation in writing statements.
12. Whenever possible, statements should be in the form of simple sentences, rather than compound or complex sentences.
13. Avoid the use of words that may not be understood.
14. Avoid the use of double negatives (Edwards, 1957, pp. 13–14).

Semantic Differentials The semantic differential technique is a general method that may be appropriate for measuring the attitude toward any object. As illustrated in Figure 10.5, the attitude object is presented, and the respondent is asked to react to it in terms of a series of scales bound by polar adjectives (Osgood et al., 1957).

The responses are coded numerically and summed for each respondent across the three or four scales, thus forming an **index**, not an attitude scale. If six semantic differentials are used and the responses are coded as shown in Figure 10.5, the scores on each individual scale

The Equal Rights Amendment

	(3)	(2)	(1)	(0)	(−1)	(−2)	(−3)	
good	—	—	—	—	—	—	—	bad
strong	—	—	—	—	—	—	—	weak
passive	—	—	—	—	—	—	—	active
beautiful	—	—	—	—	—	—	—	repugnant
horrible	—	—	—	—	—	—	—	magnificent
merciful	—	—	—	—	—	—	—	cruel

Figure 10.5 Semantic differential illustration.

can range from -3 to $+3$, and the composite index, then, can range from -18 to $+18$. Such indexes can be used for differentiating among survey respondents in terms of both degree and intensity of attitude toward whatever objects the technique is applied to.

Guttman Scales

Guttman scales are developed from responses to a number of items constituting a number of indicators of the same variable. These indicators are ranked from the "easiest" indicators to the "hardest" items with the "hard" indicators representing tougher criteria, stronger endorsements, or higher rating of an attitude object. Taken together, these indicators represent an ordinal scale from weaker to stronger endorsements of the kind of position or attitude being stated.

Presumably, those respondents who endorse the harder indicators will also endorse the weaker indicators, or stated another way, individuals will be expected to endorse a certain number of weaker items up to a point and then not endorse any stronger indicators. The hardest indicator in the series endorsed by a respondent determines his position on the scale. For example, survey respondents who have indicated that in general they favor the idea of consolidation of local governmental jurisdictions in their area might be asked whether they would 1) actually vote for it in an election, 2) encourage other people to vote for it, and 3) contribute money to the campaign on behalf of consolidation. Those who respond that they would contribute money to the campaign would also be expected to say that they would vote for it and encourage others to vote for it. Respondents indicating that they would vote for it but would not encourage others to vote for it or contribute money to the campaign would be scored low on this scale of support for consolidation, whereas those who endorse all three would be scored the highest on this scale.

Guttman scales are scales and not indexes because the single scale score is determined by the pattern of responses to the set of items included in the scale. For example, in this illustration the pattern of responses that endorses the weakest item only (vote for) would be scored with a 1, the pattern that endorses the first two items (vote for and encourage) but not the third (contribute) would be scored with a 2, the pattern endorsing all three would be scored with a 3, whereas the pattern that does not endorse any of the three would be scored with a 0, as shown in Figure 10.6. These four response patterns are all scale types, patterns that are expected given the design and intended rank order of the items. When most of the response patterns turn out to be these scale types, it means that they were consistently perceived by the

Pattern types		(1) Vote for	(2) Encourage	(3) Contribute	Number of respondents	Scale value	Errors	Total scale errors
Scale types	(A)	x	x	x	20	3	0	0
	(B)	x	x	–	30	2	0	0
	(C)	x	–	–	25	1	0	0
	(D)	–	–	–	5	0	0	0
Mixed types	(A)	–	–	x	1	0	1	1
	(B)	–	x	x	4	3	1	4
	(C)	x	–	x	2	3	1	2
	(D)	–	x	–	3	2	1	3
					90			10

Figure 10.6.   Response patterns — Guttman scale.

respondents to represent the intended rank order, and thus the respondents can be compared in terms of degree of attitude by their scale values.

The greater the percentage of individuals surveyed whose responses fit one of these scale types, the more reliable will be the overall scale as an instrument for comparing respondents in terms of their attitude toward the object in question. Conversely, the more **mixed types** of response patterns—those not conforming to the intended rank order of the items, as illustrated in the bottom rank of Figure 10.6—the less reliable will be the scale in indicating relative positions along an attitude continuum. If a researcher is primarily interested in applying a Guttman scale to actually measure attitudes and compare individuals (rather than in the development of a new scale per se) the lesson to be learned here is that to avoid ending up with an unreliable scale, he should 1) use scales that have previously been used successfully with similar populations, or 2) rely on pretesting to validate the items before committing himself to them.

Scalogram Analysis   The development of the **coefficient of reproducibility** (also referred to as scalogram analysis) is useful for assessing the reliability or internal consistency of a Guttman scale. As shown in Figure 10.6, with scale type responses the single score on a Guttman scale (scale value) can be used to accurately reproduce the individual's responses to all the items included in the scale. With mixed response patterns, however, this does not hold. Although there is no universally agreed upon way of assigning scale values to mixed response patterns, in general the objective is to minimize the error in reproducing the responses to individual items. With mixed response type pattern A, for example, the assigned scale value of 0 would lead to only one error in reproducing the responses; this scale value would lead to a reproduced scale type pattern D, which differs from the observed mixed pattern A only in terms of the actual endorsement of the item "contribute" when it would not have been endorsed in the scale type pattern. This is the one error in trying to reproduce the observed mixed response pattern using the assigned scale value. The other possible scale values (1, 2, and 3) would all lead to two or more errors in reproducing the observed mixed pattern. Each of the four possible mixed patterns, then, has been assigned a scale value on this basis as shown in the figure; in each case one error will be made in trying to reproduce the actual (mixed) response pattern on the basis of the assigned scale value.

The coefficient of reproducibility is computed as the percentage of correctly reproduced responses using the scale values. As shown in Figure 10.6, there is a total of 90 respondents, and with responses to three items each there is a total of $(90 \cdot 3)$ or 270 individual responses to be reproduced. Multiplying the number of errors made in reproducing each mixed response type by the number of individuals yielding that response type results in a total of 10 scale errors. The coefficient of reproducibility is then computed as

$$\frac{\text{total predictions} - \text{total scale errors}}{\text{total predictions}}$$

$$= \frac{270 - 10}{270}$$

$$= 96.3\%$$

indicating in this case an extremely reliable ordinal scale. Knowing the scale values of the individual respondents, we could predict their three item responses correctly 96 percent of the time and thus—for the cases at hand—have a high degree of confidence in ranking these individuals in terms of their support for consolidation, using their scale values.

Thurstone Scales

Whereas Guttman scales provide an ordinal level of measurement, **Thurstone scales** involve a great effort to find scale items that represent equal increments along the continuum from weakest to strongest item. The objective is to develop a scale of items, usually 11 or 13, with equal appearing intervals, which can then be validly considered to constitute an interval scale.

The procedure is to begin with perhaps 100 or more items that are considered to represent varying degrees of a given type of attitude, disdain for welfare recipients for instance, and to employ a number of judges to indicate the degree to which each item represents this attitude. These judges are instructed to place each item in one of 11 or 13 piles evenly spaced from the weakest to the strongest indicators of the attitude. This may require 10 or 15 judges drawn from or considered to fairly represent the same general population that is the target of the survey. When the judges' task is completed the next step is to determine which items produced the greatest amount of agreement among them; items that have been placed consistently in a given pile are considered to be reliable indicators of that corresponding degree of the attitude, whereas those whose placement varies widely are discarded immediately. One or possibly two items in each pile or category that are placed there most consistently are selected to be included in the survey instrument.

Given a set of items that are consistently percieved as representing these incrementally stronger degrees of a given attitude, the resulting pattern of responses should achieve the efficiency of Guttman scales—respondents who endorse item number 6, for example, should also endorse items 1 through 5—and a single scale value can be assigned based on the strongest item endorsed, with the added advantage of equal appearing intervals and the subsequent treatment of the data as an interval scale. In practice, however, Thurstone scales are not widely used because of the tremendous effort involved in developing the set of items in the first place.

Likert Indexes

An attitude measurement technique frequently used in program evaluation is the **Likert index** or **summated rating method**. The researcher develops attitude statements relating to the object of concern, each of which he considers to indicate either a definite positive or definite negative attitude toward that object; neutral items should not be included. The survey respondents are presented with these statements and asked to respond to them, usually on a five-point scale ranging from "strongly agree" to "strongly disagree," as illustrated in Figure 10.7.

The responses to these statements are coded numerically, usually on a scale of 1 through 5 with 1 representing the least favorable attitude and 5 indicating the most favorable attitude toward the object. For the positively worded statements, then, "strongly agree" would be

	Strongly agree	Agree	Neutral	Disagree	Strongly disagree
The police provide good service to this neighborhood.	5	4	3	2	1
Residents of this neighborhood are often mistreated by policemen.	1	2	3	4	5
The police do a good job in solving crimes that are committed in this neighborhood.	5	4	3	2	1
People in this neighborhood are frequently the victims of crimes.	1	2	3	4	5

(Numbers show numerical coding of responses.)

Figure 10.7.   Sample Likert items.

coded with a 5, "agree" with a 4 and so on, while with the negatively worded items "strongly agree" would be coded with a 1, "agree" with a 2, and so forth. Mixing the order of positive and negative items as shown in Figure 10.7 is also a good idea in terms of providing a check on the acquiescence response set (always tending to agree) mentioned earlier.

A Likert index is formed by summing the individual's coded responses across the set of items to be included in the index. If the four items shown in Figure 10.7, for example, are to constitute the index, it would range from 4 to 20, with a 4 representing the least favorable attitude toward neighborhood police services and 20 representing the most favorable attitude. It should be pointed out that there is no provision for equal intervals in these indexes, but that by convention Likert indexes are often treated as interval data in statistical analysis, for example using two-sample t tests to determine whether one subpopulation has a significantly more favorable attitude than another subpopulation. However, this assumption of the interval level of measurement is not as fully justified with Likert indexes as with Thurstone scales.

Item Analysis   The items to be included in the Likert index may be selected solely on the basis of **face validity**, items that make sense to the researcher himself, but usually the criterion of internal consistency is applied to screen out items that do not seem to be measuring the same general attitude. **Item analysis** is a method of determining whether a given item belongs in the index based on the criterion of being strongly associated with the other items in the index. Usually the data are considered to be interval measures, and the appropriate measure of the strength of association among variables is Pearson's correlation coefficient, discussed in chapter 14.

The item analysis proceeds as follows: the set of items that are candidates for inclusion in the index are determined by face validity, and tentative index scores for each individual are computed on the basis of including all these items. Then, each of these items is tested separately by measuring its association with this tentative index (or better yet, its association with an index including all the items but the one being analyzed). If this association is sufficiently strong, the item is included on the basis that it serves as an operationalized indicator of the same dimension or type of attitude of interest, whereas a lesser degree of association leads to excluding the item from the index on the basis that it is an indicator of something else.

How strong the association should be in order for the item to be included is problematic. A strong correlation is desired as an indication of unidimensionality; yet a perfect association would mean that the new item does not add anything new to the index. On the other hand, a moderately strong association would indicate that some different aspect of attitude is being reflected, whereas at some point a lesser degree of association is taken as an indication that the assumption of unidimensionality is being violated. The researcher is thus left to his discretion as to the strength of association required for the item to be included in the index.

Factor Analysis   Although Likert indexes and item analysis have been in use for decades, in more recent years a statistical technique called factor analysis has been employed for both selecting and weighting the items to be included in an index. Factor analysis itself is not covered in any depth in this book, but briefly it can be thought of as a technique that analyzes the set of intercorrelations among all the variables under consideration and identifies the fundamental dimensions (factors) underlying that multivariant domain (Rummel, 1967; Nie et al., 1975, chapter 25). Its principal output is an identification of the factors that have been encountered along with an indication of the **loadings** of each variable on each factor; these loadings indicate the extent to which that variable is bound up in that underlying dimension. A high factor loading indicates that the variable represents an important aspect of the core of that factor.

Variables that load highly on a given factor are selected to create an index representing that underlying factor. When the initial variables are responses to Likert type statements, the result is an attitude index representing varying degrees of that type of attitude. This approach might be useful in validating a set of preconceived items for inclusion in an index (essentially a form of hypothesis testing) or in identifying a number of dominating types of attitudes reflected in a data set developed with a large pool of Likert items that might relate to a number of different types of attitudes. A second optional output from a factor analysis is a set of **factor score coefficients**, which for our purposes can be thought of as mathematical expressions of the functional relationships between the individual items as components of the factors and the overall factor itself. These factor score coefficients can be used to weight the items being included in a Likert index as follows. The raw scores on each item to be included in the index are transformed into normal deviate scales (Z scores), and the factor score or index score for each respondent is computed by summing his scores on the respective constituent items, each weighted by the corresponding factor score coefficient, or:

$$\text{Index score} = \Sigma(\text{item } Z \text{ score} \cdot \text{factor score coefficient})$$

The index scores thus computed for each respondent are taken as representing relative degrees of the type of attitude being analyzed.

Factor analysis is a statistical technique that is primarily useful as a means of data reduction and for identifying sets of variables that are linked together on the basic dimensions underlying a given set of data. It is by no means limited to applications involving attitude measurement, and it may be used with any type of measures to identify the major subsets of variables in a data set or perhaps identify a few key variables that lack redundancy and seem to represent different kinds of factors for use in further analysis. With respect to attitude measurement, in addition to use in developing Likert indexes, factor analysis is also employed in identifying the different types of categories or concepts underlying the patterns of belief represented by different types of survey responses (Triandis, 1971, pp. 29–32).

Factor analysis permits a more comprehensive approach to the selection of variables to be incorporated in Likert indexes than individual item analysis does, and it has the added advantage of providing a means for weighting the constituent variables in the creation of the index. Yet it should be understood that neither method of variable selection can assure the external validity of the resulting index. Rather, they are aimed at the internal consistency of the index given the limitation of the set of variables they are applied to and the set of cases on which those measures were taken; this is no guarantee that the resulting index really represents degrees of the type of attitude it purports to measure.

Social Distance Scales

The Bogardus social distance scale is aimed at assessing the respondent's behavioral intentions toward certain types of people, usually as classified according to race, religion, or nationality. Essentially it works like a Guttman scale, but the items are clearly rank ordered beforehand. The attitude object (here a type of person) is identified, and the respondent is asked about a series of possible behaviors representing differing degrees of interaction, such as whether he would:

—Marry into this group?
—Have members of this group as close friends?
—Have them as next door neighbors?
—Work in the same office with them?
—Have a speaking acquaintance with them?
—Have as citizens of his country?
—Have as visitors to his country?

These items are clearly rank ordered with some representing very close contact and some only minimal contact. As with Guttman scales, endorsement of the harder items would almost require endorsing easier items and responses would be expected to "scale" well. Thus, the items can be coded numerically from easiest to hardest, with a respondent's scale value assigned on the basis of the hardest items endorsed.

Program analyses often use assessments of attitudes both in terms of gauging inputs and measuring the effects of programs. In general, indicators of attitudes are most commonly obtained through surveys, and this often involves the use of scales and indexes rather than single measures. Frequently this entails the development of original scales using one of the methods discussed above, but the reader should also note that for many types of attitudes, standardized scales have already been developed and are available for use if they suit the purpose of a particular project (Bonjean et al., 1965; Shaw and Wright, 1967).

CONDUCT OF A SURVEY

This final section briefly discusses some points concerning the overall conduct of a piece of survey research. First, given a general plan for proceeding with a survey and a tentative design of the instrument, pretesting is a critical stage in which problems can be anticipated and resolved before it is too late. Second, once these problems have been resolved and the researcher is ready to proceed with the actual field work, the quality of the data obtained will depend on how well and how carefully this work is actually carried out. Third, when the field work is completed, the process of coding the data and preparing them for analysis can well enhance or detract from their ultimate usefulness. The following comments apply primarily to personal interview surveys but also pertain to other survey formats on a selective basis.

The Importance of Pretesting

Pretesting is important in a number of ways, most of all in developing and improving the survey instrument. Depending on the scope of the topics to be covered, the population to be surveyed, the complexity of the questions to be included and the researcher's previous experience or familiarity with similar types of surveys, the questionnaire might be pretested in total or in parts, once or repeatedly. Usually, if time and resources permit, it is a good idea to **pilot** the complete questionnaire as discussed below, once the researcher is quite confident that the current version of the instrument is the one he will use in the actual field work, possibly with a few minor changes. During the earlier stages of instrument design, however, concern may center on a few key sections or individual questions that may have to be pretested separately and revised more than once before the questionnaire as a whole is ready for pretesting or piloting.

In developing a questionnaire, especially those portions for which previous experience in other surveys is not available, pretesting is the only way of obtaining worthwhile feedback as to how well different questions work. In developing new question sequences, researchers will often consider alternative question formats or alternative versions of the wording of particular items; pretesting these alternatives and comparing the results can be a great help in either selecting one to field or in determining that none is sufficient. After pretesting, the researcher may well go back to the drawing board to develop a certain set of questions, but even here the experience gained in the pretest may be of help in suggesting new alternative approaches.

It is a good idea to pretest the complete questionnaire once, because even with respect to those portions with which no particular problems are anticipated, difficulties or possible improvements may surface in a pretest. In terms of conducting the survey, the researcher can use the pretest to determine whether there are any items with which the interviewers themselves have trouble, and if so, exactly what these problems are and how they might be avoided. During the pretest the interviewers should also take note of items that seem to present difficulties to the respondents, questions that they do not seem to understand or be able to answer very well. In this respect it is important to pretest a refined version of the questionnaire with respondents fairly representative of the target population, as some instruments will work well with some groups of respondents and not others. Finally, as has been mentioned earlier, pretesting can identify the kinds of responses that will be prompted by open-ended questions, determine whether or not they seem to cluster into a set of meaningful categories, and possibly suggest a set of likely alternative responses and determine whether the item should be converted into a closed type question.

Statistical Analysis   Surveys produce responses as operationalized indicators that are usually analyzed statistically in terms of the distributions of responses to individual items as well as patterns of associations among them, often with both descriptive and inferential techniques. Needless to say, it is a good idea to think through this statistical analysis while the instrument is being developed, in terms of sets of dependent and independent variables, the levels of measurement involved, appropriate statistical techniques, and so on. Often it is useful to develop "dummy" statistical tables as the questionnaire is being developed to block out the way in which the data analysis will be operationalized and make sure that the types of statistical analysis that are being planned will be appropriate for the kinds of measures generated by the survey. Pretesting can be a valuable aid along these lines as the limited data generated can be used to walk through the statistical analysis.

Piloting the Survey   A pilot survey amounts to a dress rehearsal, a miniaturized run through the field work intended to test the actual conduct of the survey as well as provide a final assessment of the complete survey instrument. Obviously, to be of much use the pilot should approximate the actual survey conditions as much as possible. Although prior pretesting might be done by the researcher himself with a few associates, the pilot survey should be conducted by those who will actually be doing the field work, if possible. This gives them final training in the field and provides an opportunity for the researcher to assure that the interviewers are indeed capable of conducting the survey under actual working conditions.

Furthermore, the pilot serves to test the sampling plan and the logistics of carrying out the field work. It provides an idea of the response rate to be expected in terms of the difficulty in finding people at home for personal interviews or reaching them by telephone, as the case may be. In addition, in the case of personal interview surveys, piloting may be helpful in resolving problems in logistics, for example in terms of the interviewers gaining familiarity with the territory, transportation arrangements, etc. In general, piloting is advantageous in testing the feasibility of actually conducting the field work as planned, making sure that the field work gets off to a good start, and helping to keep the cost per completed interview to a minimum.

Management of the Field Work

Given a sound instrument, well trained interviewers, and a feasible logistics plan, how well or poorly the field work is managed can still make or break a survey. There are basically two concerns along these lines: 1) obtaining a favorable response rate and 2) assuring the completeness and legitimacy of those interviews that are conducted. Particularly with respect to personal interview surveys, a number of steps can be taken to increase the likelihood of obtaining an adequate number of responses. First, it may help to send out advance letters to individuals or households included in the sample introducing the survey in general terms and explaining why it is important that they be interviewed. With sample surveys this letter should point out that the person or household was selected at random and emphasize that interest centers on the aggregate distributions of responses and not with any individual's response per se.

When an interviewer first contacts the designated respondent, either in person or over the telephone, he should be prepared with a low key sales pitch to convince reluctant individuals that the survey is legitimate and worth their time. Again, this introductory spiel should stress the relevance of the survey, its practical utility, and the random sampling and anonymity factors. With respect to legitimacy, with surveys sponsored by a governmental unit or a particular agency, the interviewers frequently carry letters of introduction, signed by the appropriate government official or agency head, pointing out the importance of the survey and asking for cooperation. With local community surveys, it might also be a good idea to indicate the phone number of the sponsoring agency that the respondent can call to confirm the identity of the interviewer and the legitimacy of the survey. (It should also be noted that in some jurisdictions, conducting door-to-door surveys requires advance permission from local authorities.)

One issue that requires a decision somewhere along the line, once the researcher has a good feel for the likely response rate and the degree of difficulty in contacting respondents and completing interviews, is the number of call-back attempts to be made in an effort to conduct interviews with designated respondents who prove difficult to find at home or reach by telephone. An across-the-board call-back policy might be set, such as make five call-back attempts before discarding the particular case, or if in monitoring the completed returns the researcher sees that differential response rates are developing for different subsamples, he might set a greater priority making call-backs for those subsamples that seem to be underrepresented.

In any event, when an attempt to contact a respondent fails, this information should be noted along with the date and time of day, and in general call-backs should be attempted at different times of the day. Furthermore, early evenings and weekends often prove fruitful for obtaining interviews from people who were not able to be contacted during normal daytime working hours. With home interview surveys conducted by personal interviewers, it is often useful to develop a call-back form that can be left at the door when an interviewer fails to find anyone at home. It can inform the intended respondent that an interviewer has been there and either indicate the next time the interviewer will come by or ask the respondent to indicate a convenient time for the interview. The interviewer can pick up the call-back form later to see if an appointment has been set; needless to say, following through when a convenient time has been indicated is essential. With mailed surveys where it is not considered essential to guarantee complete anonymity, survey forms or envelopes are sometimes precoded numerically to permit a second mailing to those recipients who have not responded within some designated time period.

Field Checks   With most types of surveys, some individual has to be in charge of coordinating the field work. Telephone surveys are managed most successfully when the interviewers for the most part are working in the same location under the supervision of this coordinator or field captain. Personal interview surveys that are conducted out in the field, e.g., at the respondent's home, should also be coordinated from some central control point. In large scale surveys over a geographically dispersed area there may need to be a number of localized control points from which assignments and materials are handed out and to which completed questionnaires are returned.

Completed questionnaires should be edited at that control point very soon after they have been turned in, at least on a sample basis. This is to determine whether the returned forms are indeed complete, and whether the pattern of responses seems to be legitimate as opposed to having been invented by the interviewer himself, an occurrence not unknown in the practice of survey research. If certain omissions are found in these forms, the interviewer might be able to clear them up himself if they are pointed out to him soon after the interview is conducted. If not, and if the effort seems warranted in terms of importance of those particular items of information, he may be instructed to try to contact the respondent again to obtain the missing information. In part, the purpose of this editing process at the outset is to make the interviewers fully aware of the kinds of items that are easily overlooked —things they should watch out for—as well as to let them know that their work is being carefully monitored.

Given the possibility of interviewers faking the responses instead of actually conducting the interviews, it is often a good idea to make validity checks for a random sample of the completed questionnaires that are turned in. The most direct procedure here is for the field captain to try to contact the respondent listed on the form by telephone and establish that the interview did in fact take place. Because interviewers working in surveys involving long or complicated questionnaires have also been known to actually conduct partial interviews and then fake the rest of the responses, it may also be a good idea in these validity checks to mention one or two of the items again to see whether the responses indicated on the returned form are correct. The kinds of problems with interviewers alluded to above fortunately do not occur in the majority of surveys undertaken, and depending on his familiarity with and confidence in the interviewers, the researcher may not feel the need to institute such procedures; yet, it should be remembered that their primary value is as a deterrent aimed at keeping the interviewers honest. Because these problems are more likely to set in after the survey has been on the ground for awhile and the interviewers may be fatiguing, such validity checks should be made intermittently throughout the duration of the field work.

Data Processing

The last activity, which needs to be mentioned briefly at this point, involves the processing and preparation of the data for analysis once the field work is completed. More often than not, this step involves getting the data into machine readable form so that they can be entered into a computer for analytical purposes. The responses to closed form items are often coded numerically to facilitate this conversion process, even with data representing the nominal and ordinal levels of measurement. This should not present any particular problem, but the researcher must always be cognizant of the level of measurement of individual variables and not fall into the trap of treating certain category type variables as interval data simply because the values happen to be coded 1, 2, 3, etc.

Coding Frames A greater challenge is usually presented by the desire to sort the responses to open-ended items into a set of stand-ardized categories in order to facilitate the use of quantitative data analysis with the items. Such **coding frames** consist of a list of categories with working definitions as to the types of responses they include. For a given item or variable, the open-ended response is read and assigned to one of these categories, which is usually represented by a number in the computerized data set. Although the use of coding frames does facilitate statistical analysis, it invariably involves a concurrent loss of information, but the researcher can still interpret the free-flow open-ended responses to complement the statistical analysis if this is helpful.

This process also incurs a reliability problem, namely the lack of assurance that different answers that were intended to indicate the same general type of response will be coded the same with the use of the coding frame. This is particularly a problem when a number of individuals share the coding tasks, which is common in large scale surveys; the problem here relates to the possibility that two or more coders would assign the same open-ended response to different categories. Although a procedure has been developed for measuring the extent of this kind of reliability—namely, the **coefficient of inter-coder reliability** (Scott, 1955, pp. 321–325)—it really tests the adequacy of the given coding frame as used by the particular individuals whose assignments of responses to categories the computation is based on; with additional coders the lack of reliability may well increase.

Open-ended coding frames are developed by selecting a random or systematic sample of the completed questionnaires, reading each individual response, and listing apparently similar responses together while keeping unlike responses separate. If, after a sufficient number of responses have been read and treated in this manner, there seem to be a limited number of types of responses cropping up repeatedly, these types will comprise the core of the coding frame. In addition, there may well be a number of very different individualistic responses that do not cluster at all, and these may have to be lumped together in an "other" category. One never knows how useful such an open-ended coding procedure will be until the codes have been developed and applied to the responses; with a very diverse set of responses, the codes may be next to meaningless, too vague, general, or ambiguous to indicate any real patterns of variation. On the other hand, if the responses happen to fall into a few neat clusters, developing a coding frame may be well worth the effort.

REFERENCES

Abramson, J. H. 1974. Survey Methods in Community Medicine. London: Churchill Livingstone.

Babbie, E. R. 1973. Survey Research Methods. Belmont, Cal.: Wadsworth Publishing Co. Inc.

Backstrom, C. H., and G. D. Hursh. 1963. Survey Research. Evanston, Ill.: Northwestern University Press.

Bonjean, C. M., R. J. Hill, and S. D. McLemore. 1965. Sociological Measurement: An Inventory of Scales and Indices. San Francisco: Chandler Publishing Company.

Campbell, D. T., and J. C. Stanley. 1963. Experimental and Quasi-Experimental Designs for Research. New York: Rand McNally & Co.

Clark, T. N. 1974. Can You Cut a Budget Pie? Policy and Politics 3:3–31.

Dawes, R. M. 1971. Fundamentals of Attitude Measurement. New York: John Wiley & Sons, Inc.

Edwards, A. L. 1957. Techniques of Attitude Scale Construction. New York: Appleton-Century-Crofts.

Fishbein, M. (ed.). 1967. Readings in Attitude Theory and Measurement. New York: John Wiley & Sons, Inc.

Fishbein, M., and I. Ajzen. 1975. Belief, Attitude, Intention and Behavior: An Introduction to Theory and Research, 2nd Ed. Reading, Mass.: Addison-Wesley Publishing Co.

Furstenberg, F. F., Jr., and C. F. Wellford. 1973. Calling the Police: The Evaluation of Police Service. Law and Society Review (Spring) pp. 393–406.

Gauger, S. E., and J. B. Wyekoff. 1973. Aesthetic Preferences for Water Resources Projects: An Application of Q Methodology. Water Resources Bulletin, Vol. 9 (June), pp. 522–528.

Glock, C. Y. (ed.). 1967. Survey Research in the Social Sciences. New York: Russell Sage Foundation.

Guttman, L., and E. A. Suchman. 1967. Intensity and a Zero Point for Attitude Analysis. In: M. Fishbein (ed.), Readings in Attitude Theory and Measurement, pp. 96–107. New York: John Wiley & Sons, Inc.

Hatry, H. P., and L. H. Blair. 1976. Citizen Surveys for Local Governments: A Copout, Manipulative Tool, or a Policy Guidance and Analysis Aid? Policy and Politics, Vol. 4, pp. 129–140.

Kannel, E. J. 1972. A Disaggregate Analysis of Urban Travel Behavior, Joint Highway Research Project. Lafayette, Ind.: Purdue University.

Kelling, G. L., T. Pate, D. Dieckman, and C. E. Brown. 1974. The Kansas City Preventive Patrol Experiment. Washington: Police Foundation.

Linzey, G., and E. Aronson (eds.). 1968. The Handbook of Social Psychology, Vol. 2, 2nd Ed. Reading, Mass.: Addison-Wesley Publishing Co.

McIver, J. P., and E. Ostrom. 1976. Using Budget Pies to Reveal Preferences: Validation of a Survey Instrument. Policy and Politics, Vol. 4, pp. 87–110.

Nie, N. H., C. H. Hull, J. G. Jenkins, K. Steinbrenner, and D. H. Bent. 1975. SPSS: Statistical Package for the Social Sciences, 2nd Ed. New York: McGraw-Hill Book Company.

North, R. C., O. R. Holsti, M. G. Zaninovich, and D. A. Zinnes. 1963. Content Analysis. Evanston, Ill.: Northwestern University Press.

Oppenheim, A. N. 1966. Questionnaire Design and Attitude Measurement. New York: Basic Books.

Osgood, C., G. J. Suci, and P. H. Tannenbaum. 1957. The Measurement of Meaning. Urbana: University of Illinois Press.

Pechman, J. A., and P. M. Timpane (eds.). 1975. Work Incentives and Income Guarantees: The New Jersey Negative Income Tax Experiment. Washington: Brookings Institution.

Poister, T. H., J. C. McDavid, and S. K. Miller. 1976. A Report of Harrisburg Residents' Evaluation and Preferences for Local Governmental Programs and Services. University Park: Institute of Public Administration, The Pennsylvania State University.

Reemtsen, W. 1977. A Report of Citizens' Priorities Determined by the Harrisburg Water Billing Survey. University Park: Institute of Public Administration, The Pennsylvania State University.

Rummel, R. J. 1967. Understanding Factor Analysis. Journal of Conflict Resolution, Vol. 11, pp. 444–480.

Scott, D. 1976. Measures of Citizen Evaluation of Local Government Services. Policy and Politics, Vol. 4, pp. 111–128.

Scott, W. A. 1955. Reliability of Content Analysis: A Case of Nominal Scale Coding. Public Opinion Quarterly, Vol. 19, pp. 321–325.

Scott, W. A. 1968. Attitude Measurement. In: G. Linzey and E. Aronson (eds.), The Handbook of Social Psychology, Vol. 2, 2nd Ed., pp. 204–273. Reading, Mass.: Addison-Wesley Publsihing Co.

Shaw, M. E., and J. M. Wright. 1967. Scales for the Measurement of Attitudes. New York: McGraw-Hill Book Company.

Stephenson, W. 1953. The Study of Behavior: Q-Technique and Its Methodology. Chicago: University of Chicago Press.

Stewart, T., and L. Gelberd. 1976. Analysis of Judgment Policy: A New Approach for Citizen Participation in Planning. Journal of the American Institute of Planners, Vol. 42 (January), pp. 33–41.

Struening, E. L., and M. Guttentag (eds.). 1975. Handbook of Evaluation Research, Vol. 1. Beverly Hills, Cal.: Sage Publications, Inc.

Triandis, H. C. 1971. Attitudes and Attitude Change. New York: John Wiley & Sons, Inc.

Webb, K., and H. P. Hatry. 1973. Obtaining Citizen Feedback: The Application of Citizen Surveys to Local Governments. Washington, D.C.: Urban Institute.

Weiss, C. H. 1975. Interviewing in Evaluation Research. In: E. L. Struening and M. Guttentag (eds.). 1975. Handbook of Evaluation Research, Vol. 1, pp. 355–395. Beverly Hills, Cal.: Sage Publications, Inc.

11

METHODS OF ECONOMIC ANALYSIS

The primary emphasis of this text is the evaluation of the performance of public programs in terms of effectiveness, the extent to which they achieve specified objectives. Although other evaluative criteria, such as efficiency, have been discussed at various points, the major thrust has been at the attainment of objectives, without giving much consideration to the costs involved. The more structured research designs discussed in chapter 9, for example, are intended primarily to assure the validity of conclusions to be drawn about causal relationships between program means and ends. The primary objective is to establish whether certain program strategies produce desired outcomes, although consideration of costs can also be built into these designs. For example, in an experimental design employing more than one treatment group, the alternative treatments can be compared in terms of cost measures as well as effects.

TYPES OF ECONOMIC ANALYSIS

For our purposes the term **economic analysis** is used to refer to any analysis designed to examine the relationships between the resources consumed by a program and the outputs and impacts it produces. Benefit-cost analysis and cost-effectiveness analysis are two prominent approaches that use the techniques of economic analysis, but the term itself refers to any attempt to measure productivity through an investigation of inputs, conversion processes, outputs, and products at any level. This ranges from a macro level analysis of the desirability of a federal income maintenance program, or the overall value of a state's special education program to a comparison of the costs and performance of three alternative boiler plants in a Veterans Administration hospital. (For some case studies illustrating the range of application of economic analysis, see Hinrichs and Taylor, 1969.)

Operating efficiencies are pointless if not oriented to achieving a program's objectives; it is also not very useful to study a program's effectiveness in a vacuum, unrelated to the costs incurred. This is particularly true in that most program analysis is ultimately aimed at providing input into the budgetary process, a process concerned with the allocation of scarce resources and which therefore cannot assess the worth of a proposed program or strategy without consideration of the resource requirements and opportunity costs attached to it.

This chapter introduces benefit-cost analysis and cost-effectiveness analysis in terms of the types of issues they address and their general methodological approach and then moves into a more detailed discussion of the steps involved in carrying out a benefit-cost analysis. The bulk of the chapter focuses on the many problems in operationalizing benefit-cost models, which may or may not also create problems in doing cost-effectiveness analysis. The chapter then looks at cost-effectiveness as an alternate type of economic analysis and concludes with a discussion of the general applicability of all forms of economic analysis.

Benefit-Cost Analysis

Beyond the question of a program's effectiveness is the larger issue of whether its positive impacts outweigh the costs, both direct and indirect, of producing them. **Benefit-cost** analysis is intended to address this issue. It is an economist's tool for assessing the net worth of public programs or projects or comparing the net benefits produced by alternative programs or projects. It is an analytical approach founded on the theory of welfare economics and developed to address the issue of whether resources should be withdrawn from the private sector of the economy and invested in public programs. The approach involves the systematic comparison of alternatives in order to maximize benefits derived by the society as a whole (McKean, 1958; Burkhead and Miner, 1971, chapter 7; Layard, 1972; Mishan, 1973, 1975; Prest and Turvey, 1975).

Benefit-cost analysis is directed toward resource allocation decisions on a global scale. It is used to address the question of whether a public program or project should be undertaken and at what level such programs and projects should be supported; it is a tool designed to evaluate the feasibility of specific projects, to select preferred projects from a range of possible projects, and to justify projects in the budgetary process. Formal benefit-cost models are most typically used in preinvestment analysis based on before-the-fact estimates of costs and benefits. Benefit-cost analysis differs from the other forms of evaluation research discussed in this text in that it is designed to provide an appraisal of proposed programs and projects, not an ex post facto evaluation of impacts. Nevertheless, benefit-cost analysis should not be viewed as an alternative to program impact evaluation. Rather, it is best used as a complement to ex post facto evaluation, a planning tool designed to project the total outcome of undertaking a program in terms of both costs and impacts.

Furthermore, there is a strong interdependency between benefit-cost analysis and ex post facto evaluation in that building the structural relationships in a benefit-cost model is based largely on knowledge accumulated through evaluation research of similar kinds of programs or projects. Estimates of future costs and benefits can only be based on evidence obtained from previous experience. On the other hand, while formal benefit-cost models are usually established with a prospective framework, the principles of benefit-cost analysis are increasingly employed in evaluation research. This is particularly true of cost-effectiveness analysis, a technique that incorporates some of the same principles as benefit-cost analysis but is aimed at addressing more limited issues and is especially useful in formative program analysis.

Benefit-cost analysis is also used most frequently in evaluating the worthiness of proposed infrastructure improvements or research and development projects; it has been applied much more to capital investment problems than to operating program decisions. It was initially developed—and probably has reached its most sophisticated state—in water resources management, applied to projects designed to improve navigation, irrigation, and flood control, and to provide hydro-electric power, water supply, and recreational facilities (Eckstein, 1958; Krutilla and Eckstein, 1958; Hirschleifer, DeHaven, and Milliman, 1960). It has also been used widely in the field of transportation (Kuhn, 1962; Mohring and Harwitz, 1962; Adler, 1971) and more recently has been extended to urban renewal and human resource program areas, including education and health (Schultz, 1964; Dorfman, 1965; Ribich, 1968; Barsby, 1972; Perry, 1975).

The overriding criterion employed in benefit-cost analysis is **economic efficiency** in a global sense, as defined in chapter 1. Resources are allocated efficiently when they lead to the maximization of total benefits to society, when they are used most productively to maximize the satisfaction derived by society from their use. A benefit-cost analysis will indicate that funds should be invested in a public program or project if this will produce greater benefits than would result from leaving the funds in the private sector or investing them in alternative public enterprises. This global definition of economic efficiency clearly encompasses the concept of effectiveness as used in this text in that the benefits to be measured represent the attainment of objectives set by the society.

In terms of the evaluation criteria discussed in chapter 1, benefit-cost analysis can also be thought of as an indicator of appropriateness, addressing the question "Is this activity or project something that a governmental unit should be engaged in?" Appropriateness is an indicator of the public interest, of whether a program's goals and objectives are in line with the public's concerns and value systems, and benefits are program outcomes valued by society. If the benefits to be derived from a public program or project are insufficient, therefore, that activity is an inappropriate public undertaking.

A major criticism mounted against the principles underlying benefit-cost analysis is that it ranks projects only in terms of the economic efficiency criterion, whereas many programs and policies have other, nonefficiency objectives relating to income redistribution and the concept of equity (Maass, 1966). Transfers from one party to another can and should be incorporated in benefit-cost models and, as is seen below, can be weighted to reflect desirable distributional consequences. However, traditional benefit-cost analysis assumes that public policy has already dealt with the stabilization and distribution functions of fiscal policy and that what remains is to allocate resources efficiently within this context (Musgrave and Musgrave, 1976, chapter 1). Traditional benefit-cost analysis, then, is based on the assumption that a dollar has the same value to one individual or group as any other.

Cost-Effectiveness Analysis

Cost-effectiveness analysis is the application of benefit-cost principles to compare alternative programs or projects in terms of effectiveness or efficiency, usually within a more limited framework. Its purpose is to analyze the productivity of the alternatives, but not to address the larger question of net addition to society's welfare. Cost-effectiveness analysis relates more to *how* resources should be used in a project or program area, rather than *whether* they should be allocated to that area. In fact, it is interesting to note that in the parlance of systems analysis we tend to inventory resources and assume that they are to be used. The operational question for which cost-effectiveness analysis is appropriate is frequently posed in terms of how best to employ these resources so as to maximize the attainment of system objectives. Alternatively, we might first determine the need for a given level of effort in a certain program area and then use cost-effectiveness analysis to compare the efficiency of various program designs that could provide that level of effort. Cost-effectiveness analyses are often geared more to the criterion of *technological efficiency* than macro level economic efficiency, as discussed in chapter 1.

For example, currently there is great interest in exploring ways of providing transportation service to elderly and handicapped persons in urban areas, using conventional bus service, taxis, social service agency vehicles, and other alternatives. Once these alternatives are defined for a given area, they can be compared by specifying a required level of service—for example, the capacity to provide for an average of five round trips per person per week to and from common destinations— and pricing out the cost of providing this service level for each alternative; the cost-effective strategy is that which provides the specified service at the lowest cost. Notice that although this approach does identify the most efficient alternative, it makes no attempt to determine whether it is worthwhile or appropriate to provide the service in the first place, whether the benefits gained exceed the costs of even the least cost strategy.

Although in some respects it is a more modest tool than benefit-cost analysis, cost-effectiveness analysis is receiving increasingly widespread use, in part because it is a more manageable technique but also because it is more applicable to many of the operating questions at hand. This chapter dwells on benefit-cost analysis because it is the more comprehensive method. Cost-effectiveness entails the same kind of comparisons between a program's costs and its products and involves many of the same kinds of analytical approaches to model development, but by its more limited frame of reference some of the more elusive measurement problems may be avoided. Benefit-cost applications treating major categories of intangibles in solely descriptive terms, for example, actually constitute cost-effectiveness in the strict sense.

Although benefit-cost analysis was first developed in the area of water resource projects involving tangible benefits to economic development, cost-effectiveness was pioneered by the Department of Defense in evaluating alternative weapons systems and strategies (Goldman, 1967), activities whose products are far from the economic marketplace. As the use of the two approaches has expanded into many other fields, the lines between them have become fuzzy, principally because of the application of benefit-cost analysis in contexts which force the compromising of its basic tenets or limit the **choice set** (set of alternatives) in a suboptimizing manner.

Nevertheless, certain useful distinctions can be made between cost-effectiveness and formal benefit-cost analysis. In operational terms, benefit-cost analysis attempts to measure all the relevant factors in dollars, while cost-effectiveness mixes measurement units. Costs (but not necessarily all costs) are usually measured in dollar outlays, or budget costs, whereas effectiveness factors and unintended impacts are often measured in substantive units relating to objectives or other desirable conditions. This mixing of measurement units, then, precludes the summarization of the analysis in a single ratio, which characterizes benefit-cost analysis. In addition, with benefit-cost analysis the levels of both benefits and costs are variable in order to observe the productivity over a wide range of alternatives. However, cost-effectiveness often is used to provide closer, though more limited, comparisons of alternatives by holding either costs or effectiveness levels constant.

With respect to purpose, whereas the formal benefit-cost model addresses the issue of whether a program or project's rate of return justifies its undertaking, cost-effectiveness looks at the question of which among a number of alternatives is the most productive, without regard to the issue of whether the program in general is justified in benefit-cost terms. While benefit-cost analysis is a more comprehensive method, cost-effectiveness often provides a more detailed partial analysis. Furthermore, the two differ in terms of applications. As has been seen, benefit-cost is used most frequently in conjunction with the assessment of set-piece capital projects. Cost-effectiveness, on the other hand, is being applied increasingly to the analysis of ongoing operating programs, particularly in relation to program budgeting systems. It may also be geared to shorter time frames, which in turn means that cost-effectiveness tends to be based more on adequate data and dominated less by future uncertainties than benefit-cost analysis.

BENEFIT-COST MODELS

The general principle underlying benefit-cost analysis is deceptively simple: Add up the dollar values of all the benefits to be derived from a project and all the costs to be incurred by the project, and compare them. In general, if the total amount of benefits exceeds total costs, the project is justified and should be undertaken or included in the pool of alternatives from which one project will be selected. This justification is based on the assumption that the present value of the benefits that will accrue from the investment of resources in the private sector equals the present value of those resources. Thus, if a public investment will produce benefits in excess of the dollar value of the resources consumed, it is advantageous.

Benefit-cost analysis has been described as consisting of five elements: 1) objectives, 2) alternatives, 3) costs, 4) a model, and 5) a criterion (McKean, 1968). Program objectives have been discussed elsewhere in this text; they are the desired changes or improvements the program is intended to produce in the environment. In benefit-cost applications there must be no ambiguity about objectives because the identification and measurement of benefits are derived from program objectives.

Benefits are outcomes that move toward specified objectives, the achievement of intended impacts. They may represent change from present conditions or the maintenance of conditions that would be expected to deteriorate if the program or project were not implemented. The **alternatives** represent competing possible uses of resources. They may consist of one individual program or project versus no public project (where the alternative is to leave the resources in the private sector and not undertake such a project) or a number of specified projects differing in terms of purpose, scope, location, size, or design characteristics. Regardless, the alternatives must be described in sufficient detail to differentiate among their anticipated costs and benefits.

Costs represent forgone benefits of some kind. These include resources that are directly consumed by the project (budget costs) and thus not available for alternative uses, and secondary costs that are imposed by the project's undertaking. These secondary costs usually represent existing benefits of some sort that are reduced or eliminated by virtue of undertaking the project. Benefits can be thought of as moving toward the achievement of objectives; costs are best conceived of as representing a retrogression away from desired conditions. Benefits and costs are really two sides of the same coin, in that costs can be evaluated only in terms of forgone benefits. The cost of resources is given by the value of the benefits that could be produced by alternative use of the resources; thus, the cost of undertaking a given project is measured by foregone opportunities of employing the resources elsewhere.

The purpose of a benefit-cost **model** is to develop the structural relationships between characteristics of the alternatives and their impacts in order to trace through the anticipated costs and benefits of each of the alternatives. This model building is the real core of the analysis and is the stage that exerts the heavy demands on evaluation research, as mentioned above. The validity of the cost and benefit estimates generated by the model is only as sound as the existing knowledge of the relevant causal relationships on which the model is based. Finally, the **criterion** is the basis upon which the preferred alternative will be determined; for example it might be to select that project that has the highest ratio of total benefits to total costs.

Procedural Overview

The guiding principle in benefit-cost analysis is to list all the parties affected by a project and then to value its effects on each party as they would value them in money terms (Layard, 1972, p. 14). **Externalities**, or **spillover** costs and benefits are those that accrue to parties other than the producers or intended users of a good or service. One purpose of macro level economic analysis is to **internalize** all externalities by taking all benefits and costs into account. The output of the model should be the present dollar value of all costs and all benefits summed across all the affected parties. Where possible, the dollar values of costs and benefits are taken from market prices that reveal people's willingness to pay for something, but these prices sometimes must be adjusted to compensate for market imperfections. More difficult problems arise concerning the dollar valuation of impacts for which no market prices are available, as well as the discounting of future benefits and costs to their present value.

The application of a benefit-cost analysis, then, can be considered to proceed in five steps as follows.

1. Establish the alternatives. Although the analyst often takes the alternatives as already given, setting the scope of the choice set in the first place is a critical element in benefit-cost analysis. Because public projects are characterized by a high degree of interdependencies, incompatibilities, and trade-offs necessitated by budget constraints, care must be taken to develop a choice set of alternatives with common constraints or to take interproject consequences into account. An important criticism of practical applications of the technique is that sophisticated models are commonly applied to alternatives that are chosen haphazardly in the first place (Steiner, 1974, pp. 313–319).
2. Identify all affected parties and the types of benefits and costs expected to result from the alternatives.
3. Given the types of benefits and costs, develop separately for each alternative measure or estimate the extent to which each type of impact will occur. While step 2 is conceptual in nature, step 3 is highly analytical.
4. Evaluate these varying amounts of different types of costs and

benefits in dollar terms. The dollar values of costs and benefits expected to occur at different points in time must then be discounted to their present value.

5. Finally, compare the alternatives in terms of the present value of their benefits and costs, selecting the most desirable alternative based on some previously determined criterion.

The most difficult steps for the analyst are 2 through 4, particularly steps 3 and 4, which are highly sensitive to the particular design characteristics of the alternatives and the context into which the program or project is to be introduced, as well as heavily dependent on the general state of knowledge in the substantive area. Steps 3 and 4 often constitute great challenges for valid measurement, really the crux of the problem facing the analyst, and are often based on general assumptions and approximations. Given these problems and the attendant lack of precision or accuracy in the resulting estimates, benefit-cost analysis is often considered to be most applicable to long range planning decisions rather than more detailed program management. Clearly, the outcome of a benefit-cost analysis cannot be substituted for a decision, but rather is used to sharpen the judgment used to make the decision (Fisher, 1972).

Classes of Benefits and Costs

A major strength of benefit-cost analysis in theory is that it provides a comprehensive framework for incorporating all costs and benefits in the analysis, including externalities. However, this same strength presents corresponding dangers to the practical application of the method; a major difficulty is ascertaining "when to stop counting and what not to count" (Burkhead and Miner, 1971, p. 225). Although the general principle is to include all costs and benefits, some kinds of impacts must be interpreted differently in differing contexts, and care must be taken to avoid double counting. A second problem, how to count, is discussed later, but it should be recognized that in practice the measurability of costs and benefits and the availability of data often have a strong bearing on which factors are actually included in the analysis.

Real Versus Pecuniary   There are many classes of benefits and costs, the foremost distinction being that between real, sometimes called technological, benefits and costs as opposed to pecuniary impacts. **Real** benefits and costs represent changes in society's satisfaction derived from production and consumption. Real benefits reflect an addition to the welfare of the community or society as a whole, while real costs represent an actual decrease in this overall welfare or the loss of an opportunity to increase society's welfare in some manner.

Pecuniary costs and benefits do not reflect gains or losses to the society as a whole, but rather gains to some individuals or groups that are offset by losses incurred by others. Pecuniary effects are attributable to changes in relative prices brought about by the introduction of new facilities or services. They do not affect the overall benefit-cost ratio of a proposal, but they are relevant in assessing distributional consequences. If all costs and benefits to all affected parties are listed, pecuniary items will appear twice and cancel out one another.

Direct Versus Indirect   Real costs and benefits can be further classified in a number of ways, in particular according to the distinction between direct (sometimes referred to as primary) versus indirect (or secondary) benefits and costs. It has been pointed out that it is incorrect to talk about secondary benefits that should be excluded from the analysis because there are no such things. Rather, **indirect** or **secondary** impacts are benefits and costs in relation to secondary, perhaps nonefficiency oriented, objectives (Maass, 1966, p. 211). For example, with respect to a proposed dam whose primary objective relates to the provision of hydroelectric power, recreational benefits would be considered as secondary benefits. Whether such secondary benefits should be included in the benefit-cost computations is partly a matter of legislative intent; if the sole purpose is energy oriented, perhaps it is inappropriate to use recreational benefits as a partial justification for building the project. (Recent federal standards for water resources planning include recreation as a benefit subject to dollar valuation. See Water Resources Council, 1973.) In practice, secondary benefits are usually included, but the by-product nature of some of them raises the issue of whether some impacts should be weighted more heavily than others when multiple objectives are taken into account. On the other hand, there has often been a failure in practice to take important indirect costs into consideration, thereby biasing the analysis in favor of undertaking the project.

Direct costs are those incurred to establish and operate a program or to build a facility including one-time fixed costs, investment costs, and recurring costs. They have been itemized as follows.

1.   **One-time fixed costs:**
     Research
     Planning
     Test and evaluation

2. **Investment costs:**
    Land
    Building and facilities
    Equipment and vehicles
    Initial training
3. **Recurring costs (operating and maintenance costs):**
    Personnel salaries, wages, and fringe benefits for direct operations
    Maintenance of equipment, vehicles, and buildings
    Replacement and recurring training costs
    Direct contributions and payments to citizens, e.g., welfare payments to the needy
    Payments to extra-governmental institutions for services for citizens, e.g., payments to agencies for foster home services
    Miscellaneous materials and supplies
    Miscellaneous support (overhead) costs. (Hatry, Winnie, and Fisk, 1973, p. 89)

These types of direct costs are the central concern of much budget and financial analysis, and some types of economic analysis are limited to consideration of direct costs in relation to output levels, intermediate effects and anticipated impacts. However, a comprehensive benefit-cost analysis incorporates all direct costs *plus* indirect costs, all third party costs and negative impacts of the program.

Tangible Versus Intangible   It has also been pointed out that it is incorrect to classify costs and benefits as "economic" and "noneconomic" because all impacts, including nonmonetary benefits and costs, have economic value. If a potential impact will have no worth to anyone, it is not appropriately labeled a cost or benefit (McKean, 1968, pp.140–141). Rather, the distinction that the economic/noneconomic dichotomy is intended to make is between tangible and intangible impacts. **Tangible** benefits and costs are those that may seem to be more economic in nature because they can be valued in the marketplace. **Intangible** benefits and costs may be no less important than tangible impacts, but they often are much more difficult to evaluate in dollar terms because they are not priced in the marketplace.

Inside Versus Outside   **Inside** costs and benefits occur within the jurisdiction for which the benefit-cost analysis is being performed, whereas **outside** costs and benefits relate to jurisdictions other than that which is undertaking the project. For example, a dam and reservoir built upstream might reduce the threat of flooding in another jurisdiction downstream; this would be a real outside benefit. Given such spillover effects, along with the nature of intergovernmental financing, the outcome of a benefit-cost analysis can be altered dramatically depending on the perspective from which it is conducted.

For example, any large scale construction project will create a sizeable number of local jobs that may be important to the state or local economy, but from a national perspective these should not be computed as benefits because if the project is not undertaken the funds will presumably be invested elsewhere and provide a similar number of jobs. From the national perspective, then, this would be a pecuniary benefit, generating jobs in one area at the expense of jobs that might otherwise be created in another area. However, from the local and state perspective, if not undertaking the project means that the federal funds will be invested in a similar type project in another state, the increased employment that would be generated constitutes a very real benefit and should be included in the analysis.

A brief example may help to clarify differences among types of costs and benefits. The real, direct benefits of a highway project accrue to the users in the form of reduced accidents, travel time, and operating costs, while the real, direct costs include right-of-way, construction, and maintenance costs borne by the taxpayers. There are likely to be important secondary impacts relating to nontransportation objectives, such as degradation of or improvements to the physical environment in the vicinity of the new highway and the loss of low income housing stock displaced by the facility. The cost of relocating displaced families to comparable housing is a real, direct cost that formerly was borne by the families themselves and is now borne by the taxpayers. If, as is provided for by the Uniform Relocation Assistance Act, such families are relocated in housing that is superior to their previous housing, the improvement of their housing conditions is a pecuniary and indirect benefit that represents a transfer payment from the taxpayers to these families.

The indirect cost of relocation is a tangible cost that can be evaluated readily in the marketplace. Other secondary impacts, such as air and noise pollution, are intangible costs for which no market data are available. However, indirect methods may be used to place dollar values on these items. Another intangible, secondary cost might be a loss of the sense of community shared by residents of neighborhoods that have been fragmented by the highway construction. This is more difficult to measure in any quantitative terms, much less to evaluate in dollars. A different kind of secondary impact that might be taken into account is change in land values because of the new facility. In suburban areas, at least, the value of land adjacent to the highway may increase as a result of improved accessibility, but for the most part this is a pecuniary benefit that represents a change in the locus of value rather than a real benefit. The land adjacent to the new highway will be more attractive to industry and other users who otherwise might have located elsewhere. The increase in property value then, is a transfer of value from one site to another. To include this item in the analysis would produce double counting because the improved accessibility is already taken into account by the benefits of reduced travel time and operating costs.

However, the increased land values in the suburban jurisdiction are real benefits to the jurisdiction and would be incorporated into its calculus of costs and benefits. Similarly, the loss of tax base in the central city through which the highway is built is a real cost to the municipal government, although from a metropolitan perspective there will be only pecuniary costs and benefits as activities, forced to move by the highway, are relocated elsewhere. While these are examples of inside benefits and costs that are real to the local jurisdiction but not relevant from the larger perspective, the opposite situation can pertain. For example, if this highway is being built with 70 percent federal funding, from the state perspective only 30 percent of the direct costs are relevant, whereas the other 70 percent constitute an outside cost.

Measuring Costs and Benefits

Given the identification of the various kinds of costs and benefits to be considered, the more challenging aspect of model development involves estimating how much of each class of impact should be anticipated and affixing dollar values to them. The final output of the formal model is the **present dollar value** of all benefits and all costs, or the net worth of the project at present. This entails making two sets of dollar valuations, pertaining to 1) the value of costs and benefits at the time they occur, and 2) their value discounted to the present, as discussed in a later section.

A whole host of measurement problems arises in moving to this point. Many of these problems stem from uncertainty surrounding future impacts. The benefit-cost analyst is plagued by uncertainties about what all the costs and benefits will be and the extent to which they will materialize in future years, as well as uncertainties about the dollar value of these impacts and the appropriate rate for discounting them to their present value. Dealing with these uncertainties begs the very question that benefit-cost analysis is intended to address: What are the advantages and disadvantages of a given proposal?

A second type of problem is that some classes of costs and benefits do not lend themselves very well to dollar valuation or quantitative measurement in any units. For example, it is very difficult to incorporate esthetics or psychological values in cost-benefit accounts. Benefit-cost analysis attempts to quantify all the relevant factors in a common denominator, dollars, but often this must be supplemented with qualitative analysis. When qualitative aspects are ignored, secondary impacts and intangibles are most likely to be excluded, and this can bias the conclusions tremendously. The more costs and benefits that must be excluded from the formal model, the more important it is to complement the model with qualitative analysis. If these qualitative factors are judged not to vary much among the alternatives, however, this task is greatly simplified.

Often, benefit-cost analysis breaks down in the model building stage because we are unable to make sound estimates of the amounts of impacts and their dollar values. The technique frequently serves as a good framework for structuring a problem, but we are unable to piece it together. The substantive understanding needed to develop the model comes from basic research and repeated applied program analysis efforts. Although problems of uncertainties and difficulties of quantitative measurement are bound to persist, as knowledge in a given substantive area continues to accumulate, benefit-cost applications should become more precise and defensible. Most of the research in the area is concentrating on resolving these measurement problems; yet, as one critic concludes, "Much work remains to be done" (Steiner, 1974, p. 326).

Although direct costs are usually considered to be the easiest effects to measure, often even these factors prove elusive and open to widely differing interpretations. A good case in point involves the controversial lock and dam project on the Mississippi River at Alton, Illinois. The U.S. Corps of Engineers' cost estimate for an on-site rehabilitation of the existing facilities is $401 million, whereas an estimate prepared by critics of the project is about $46 million, a magnitude of difference that casts doubt on the soundness of any such estimate (Congressional Budget Office, 1976).

As an example of the difficulties in operationalizing a complete benefit-cost analysis in a "soft" program area, consider the comparison of four alternative employment and training activities of the federal government shown in Table 11.1. The cost estimates are based on di-

Table 11.1. Costs and benefits of employment and training programs

Activities	Fiscal year 1975 cost per participant (dollars)	Potential future increases in annual earnings (dollars)
I. Skill development	1,600-1,900	400-800
II. Job development (direct employment creation)	4,700-5,800	300-700
III. Employability development	2,600-3,500	200-400
IV. Work experience (direct part-time employment creation)	500-2,300	0-200

From Congressional Budget Office, 1976.

rect expenditure amounts only, shown for one fiscal year, whereas the projected benefits are limited to an estimate of the annual increases in earnings by program participants. On this basis, the skill development strategies would seem to be the most successful, but it must be noted that a "number of relevant benefits and costs are not included because they are difficult to quantify," including reductions in the administrative costs of income maintenance programs and the foregone earnings during training of participants in those programs (Perry, 1975, p. 76). For the work experience (job creation) programs, immediate income assistance would be an important benefit as well. Even in terms of future increase in earnings, a lack of information on the persistence in annual earnings gains precludes an estimate of the total value of this direct benefit; the figures in the table pertain to the year or years immediately after participation in these programs. Furthermore, a complete analysis would have to include many more types of benefits and costs to the participants, taxpayers, and the society at large (Barsby, 1972, pp. 9-10).

Discount Rates

A crucial step in calculating benefits and costs is the **discounting** of all dollar values to their present worth. This is necessary because the value of a particular benefit or cost depends on when it will occur. Future benefits are less valuable than present benefits; a dollar now is worth more than a dollar a year from now because presumably it can be invested and generate a total worth of, say, $1.10 a year from now. The further into the future a given cost or benefit is expected to occur, the lower its present value. Because most kinds of projects to which benefit-cost analysis is applied generate differential flows in the levels of costs and benefits across time, the only fair basis for evaluating the relationship of benefits to costs is to discount both cost and benefit streams to their present value. For example, many investments in human resource program areas such as health and education are characterized by heavy concentrations of costs early in the life of the project, while the benefits accrue slowly at first, then rise rapidly to a peak and level off (Johnson and Pierce, 1975). Comparing undiscounted benefits and costs would overstate the desirability of the project.

In general, there is great controversy over the way in which future benefits and costs should be discounted, and with respect to any given project there may be much uncertainty about the proper discount rate to be applied. The continuing debate among economists over appropriate discount rates is heavily value laden, with those favoring an expansion of the public sector rationalizing arguments for a low discount rate and those who would restrict public sector investment attempting to justify a high discount rate (Burkhead and Miner, 1971, p. 228). The issue is critical because theoretically at the macro level what is at stake is the allocation of resources between the public and private sectors (Baumol, 1969).

Discount rates used by the federal government range from 3 to 15 percent, and the time span may easily extend to 50 years or more. The rate actually employed in a given analysis is critical because the benefit-cost ratio may turn out to be greater or less than 1, depending solely on the discount rate. For example, a study by the General Accounting Office on the cost-effectiveness of the purchase versus leasing of a fleet of tankers indicated that with a discount rate of 6 percent the Navy should purchase the tankers, but that at a 10 percent discount rate leasing would be the preferred alternative (Comptroller General of the United States, 1975, pp. 73-74).

The problem of which discount rate is appropriate involves many complex macroeconomic considerations, revolving in part around private households' propensity to save, government policy regarding economic growth, and benefit trade-offs between present and future generations. In terms of economic principles there is no clearly correct discount rate, and the selection of a rate to be applied in a given piece of analysis may be highly judgmental.

Private Rates   Either private rates or social rates may be employed. Private discount rates represent interest rates, the cost of borrowing money, in the private sector. It is often held that these are appropriate because in a perfectly competitive market the prevailing private rate represents the time preference of individuals and households making marginal valuations between savings and consumption (Mishan, 1967). Moreover, it is argued that because the private sector is the source of funds for public investment, the private rate is appropriate for discounting the benefits of public projects because it measures the benefits that will accrue if the funds are left in the private sector.

One problem with using the private rate is that in actuality with imperfect markets there are many private rates, and the choice of a discount rate ceases to be obvious. Other problems with the use of private rates are that they do not reflect the full range of external costs incurred by private investment (Burkhead and Miner, 1971, p. 233), and there is a discrepancy, occasioned by taxes on income, between the gross rate of return and the after-tax rate of return (Baumol, 1969, pp. 493–496). In addition, it has been argued that private interest rates are inappropriate for discounting public sector investment because they are based in part on the risk of loss involved in making private loans. Because loans to governments have been largely risk free, moral obligation bonds and New York City's recent problems notwithstanding, private rates have been considered too high for discounting the costs and benefits of public projects (Lee and Johnson, 1977, p. 167). The point here is that in acknowledging risk, investors will require a higher interest rate than the return they actually expect to receive from all their investments in the long run, thereby overstating the discounting of future yields to present values.

Social Rates   Many critics of the use of private rates advocate that the discount rate be set lower than private rates as an instrument of public policy to correct for the "myopia" of private households that fail to see the importance of saving, investment, and future consumption. The theory underlying such a social time preference rate is based on the notion of delayed rewards and a concern for the welfare of future generations; reduced consumption and increased investment will produce greater future benefits. Furthermore, using a lower, social discount rate may be more appropriate in terms of undertaking public projects aimed at guaranteeing a clean, healthy physical environment for future generations. In addition, advocates of a social rate point out that social time preference is not simply an aggregation of individual time preferences, because individuals may be better off undertaking more investment collectively than by undertaking the sum of the investments they would find it desirable to make privately (Marglin, 1963).

Clearly there are problems in applying social rates of discount,

too. Operationally there is no obvious social time preference rate to select, and theoretically there is a problem relating to whether the resources to be withdrawn from the private sector would be diverted from
consumption or investment (Musgrave and Musgrave, 1976, pp. 175,
179–180). On a different plane, the whole notion of setting a social rate
to correct for deficiencies of the private rate is in direct contrast to the
principle of citizen/consumer sovereignty on which the philosophy of
benefit-cost analysis is based.

Furthermore, it is not really clear that the social rate would be
lower than the prevailing private rate. An opposing trend of thought
would reason that because individuals do not foresee the rise in income
attributable to technological progress, they overestimate the value of
consumption derived from present savings. Therefore, to correct for this
the proper social rate should be greater than the private rate. Also in
support of this position is the fact that in many underdeveloped nations, policies of deficit financing of economic development and consequent "forced savings" already overstate the value of future benefits as
compared with consumer preferences at present.

Practical Approaches In the face of abovementioned kinds of
difficulties in conceptualizing what the appropriate discount rate should
be, rather crude rules of thumb are applied in practice. The most common
approach is to base the discounting of the benefit stream not on the
prevailing rate of return in the private sector nor on an estimate of the
social time preference, but rather on the government's cost of borrowing
funds. Usually the long term borrowing rate is considered appropriate.
A variation used by some federal agencies is to adjust this rate upward
to allow for the loss of tax revenue that results from the decrease in
private sector activity. The present value of benefits so derived is compared to actual project costs (Musgrave and Musgrave, 1976, pp.
175–176).

Similarly, it has been advocated that state and local governments
use the rates at which they can borrow money even though there is
wide variation in these rates among regions and units of government,
because the problem facing them is the efficient allocation of resources
within their regions. In part, this convention is based on a financial,
rather than economic, justification. In the face of difficulties in determining discount rates based on real opportunity costs, government
should undertake projects up to the point beyond which its money out-
lay is not expected to be recovered.

Given a lack of assurance that a comparison of benefits and costs
based on one assumed discount rate is valid, the analysts may prefer to

treat the appropriate discount rate as an uncertainty and evaluate costs and benefits using a range of reasonable rates. This can be used to indicate how sensitive the results are to the assumption of a discount rate and the ranges within which different alternatives are preferred. Finally, an alternative to the assumption of a discount rate is the internal rate of return method, which is discussed later.

Computing Present Value   The present value of a future benefit or cost is computed by applying a discount factor to the future dollar value in question. The discount factor can be computed, given a discount rate and the number of years over which the future dollar value is to be discounted.

When cost and benefit streams are uneven, that is when the dollar values vary from year to year over the time span involved, each future year benefit and cost must be discounted separately to present value. The formula for the discount factor for a single future dollar value is

$$\frac{1}{(1 + r)^N}$$

where r denotes the discount rate and N stands for the number of years by which the dollar value is to be discounted. Figure 11.1 shows the computation of the discount factor for computing the present value of a $230,000 future benefit to be discounted by a 10 percent discount rate over 5 years. The discount factor is shown to be 0.621; this can be interpreted as the present value of $1.00 discounted at 10 percent over 5 years. (Table A-10 in the appendix shows the discount factors computed for a wide range of time horizons and discount rates.) As shown in Figure 11.1 then, the discount factor is applied to the dollar value of the future benefit resulting in a present value of $142,830. This can be read as follows: "At a 10 percent discount rate, a benefit of $230,000 occurring 5 years from now has a present value of $142,830."

In some analyses benefit or cost streams may be uniform over the duration of the project, with an *annual* cost or benefit of a certain amount. When this is the case, the discounting procedure can be simplified by summarizing the discounts for the various years in a single computation. Essentially an annuity factor, the present value of $1.00 received annually for N years can be computed with the formula

$$\frac{1 - \left(\dfrac{1}{1 + r}\right)^N}{r}$$

where r again denotes the discount rate. (Table A-11 in the appendix

Problem: Compute the present value of a $230,000 benefit expected to occur
5 years in the future, discounted by 10% per year.

Present value   =   discount factor · dollar benefit

Discount factor   = $\dfrac{1}{(1 + r)^N}$

                      = $\dfrac{1}{(1 + 0.10)^5}$

                      = $\dfrac{1}{1.6105}$

                      =   0.621

Present value   =   0.621 · $230,000

                      = $142,830

Figure 11.1.   Discount computation — single benefit or cost.

shows the annuities of $1.00 received annually for a range of time spans and discount rates.)

Figure 11.2 illustrates the calculation of the present value of a $90,000 annual cost over the next 20 years, using a 10 percent discount rate. First the annuity factor is computed using the formula above, then this is applied to the dollar value of the annual cost. The result is

Problem: Compute the present value of an annual cost of $90,000 over the
next 20 years, discounted by 10% per year.

Present value   =   annuity discount factor · annual dollar value

Annuity factor   = $\dfrac{1 - \left(\dfrac{1}{1 + r}\right)^N}{r}$

                  = $\dfrac{1 - \left(\dfrac{1}{1 + 0.10}\right)^{20}}{0.10}$

                  =   8.514

Present value   =   8.514 · $90,000

                  = $766,260

Figure 11.2.   Discount computation — uniform annual benefit or cost.

read as: "The present value of an annual cost of $90,000 over the next 20 years, discounted at 10 percent, is $766,260."

Comparing Benefits and Costs

There are as many variations of benefit-cost models as there are different ways of expressing the choice set and various procedures for selecting the preferred alternative. This section presents summaries of two applications of benefit-cost analysis to illustrate how the various classes of costs and benefits can be pulled together in order to compare alternatives.

Highway Project Illustration   The first case pertains to a hypothetical highway project in which two alternative expansion levels are considered in comparison with the no-build alternative, retaining the existing facility at the pre-expansion level (Musgrave and Musgrave, 1976, pp. 184–188). In this application the alternatives are compared incrementally, so that the benefits and costs of the first expansion level, F_1, are derived by comparing it with the pre-expansion level, F_0, and those corresponding to the second expansion level, F_2, are based on its incremental costs and benefits beyond F_1. Sequentially, then, the analysis addresses the issue of whether it is justified to move to the first expansion level, which might be a four-lane highway, and if so, whether it is further justified to move to the second expansion level, which might be a six-lane facility.

The illustration is instructive by its deficiencies as well as its stronger points. Only the most direct costs and benefits are taken into account: the benefits of time savings and other variable (operating) costs and the costs of construction and maintenance. No attempt is made to incorporate any of the kinds of externalities discussed in a previous section in relation to highway projects. If there is a bias in these computations, it is likely to be in favor of justifying one of the expansion levels, because of the exclusion of real secondary costs.

As shown in Table 11.2, the value of time savings is set at $2.00 per hour, and as the average time spent per trip declines dramatically with the first expansion level and then modestly as we move to the second expansion level, the average time cost per trip (line 2) decreases accordingly. Other trip costs increase slightly at the first expansion level, because of higher and less efficient operating speeds, and then decrease slightly at the second expansion level because of improved maneuverability in dispersed traffic. Total variable cost per trip (line 4) also follows the pattern of a dramatic decrease at the first expansion level and a much lesser decrease at the second expansion level.

Table 11.2.   Benefit-cost computations for hypothetical highway project[a]

	Pre-expansion level F_0	After expansion to F_1	After expansion to F_2
Estimation of benefits to users			
1. Time per trip (min)	30	18	16
2. Time cost of trip ($2/hr)	$1.00	$0.57	$0.53
3. Other cost per trip	$1.75	$1.90	$1.85
4. Total variable cost per trip			
(2 + 3)	$2.75	$2.47	$2.38
5. Number of trips per year	1,000,000	1,500,000	1,750,000
5a. Increase in trips		500,000	250,000
6. Total variable costs per year			
(4 · 5)	$2,750,000	$3,705,000	$4,165,000
7. Cost savings per trip		$0.28	$0.09
8. Cost savings on previous no.			
of trips		$280,000	$135,000
9. Cost savings on additional			
trips ($1/2(7 · 5a)$)		$70,000	$11,250
10. Total benefits per year			
(8 + 9)		$350,000	$146,250
11. Present value of benefits			
(8%, 25 years)		$3,736,172	$1,561,186[b]
Estimation of project cost			
12. Capital cost		$2,000,000	$2,000,000
13. Annual maintenance cost	$20,000	$30,000	$50,000
14. Increase in maintenance cost		$10,000	$20,000
15. Present value of mainte-nance cost (8%, 25 years)		$106,748	$213,496
16. Total project cost, present value (12 + 15)		$2,106,748	$2,213,496
Evaluation			
17. Benefit-cost ratio (line 11 ÷ line 16)		1.77	0.71

Adapted from *Public Finance in Theory and Practice* by Musgrave, R. A. and P. B. Musgrave. Copyright 1973 by McGraw-Hill, Inc. Used with permission of McGraw-Hill Book Company.

[a] Computation of direct benefits and cost only, moving incrementally from existing highway facility, F_0, to expansion level F_1, and then from F_1 to expansion level F_2.

[b] Computed as follows:

$$\frac{1 - \left(\frac{1}{1 + 0.08}\right)^{25}}{0.08} \, (\$146,250) = \$1,561,186$$

Next, the total number of trips per year using the facility is taken into account, showing the additional volumes of travel induced by the advantage of quicker travel. (Obviously, the structural relationships between the facility's capacity and travel characteristics that underlie these computations are critical; this illustration shows only the summarization of costs and benefits.) An additional 500,000 annual trips are forecast to be generated by the first expansion level and an additional 250,000 annual trips beyond that are forecast for the second expansion level.

In economists' terms, this additional travel is induced by the reduction of the average cost per trip, as shown in Figure 11.3. Given a demand curve for travel in this particular transportation corridor, as the unit cost decreases from $2.75 per trip to $2.47 per trip, the volume of trips rises from 1 million to 1.5 million. Similarly, with the further reduction in cost to $2.38 per trip, the volume of trips rises to 1.75 million annually. The reduction in costs yields a primary class of benefit in many economic analyses: **consumer surplus**, measured by the difference between what users or consumers would be willing to pay for use of a facility or service and what they actually do pay. In Figure 11.3 this consumer surplus generated by the first expansion level for the previous number of trips is represented by the area shaded with diagonal stripes. This is the difference between what these trips cost at the pre-expansion level and what they would cost at the first expansion level. For the additional travel generated by the first expansion level, the consumer surplus is shown in the area shaded with vertical stripes. In Table 11.2 the consumer surplus for previous trips and for additional

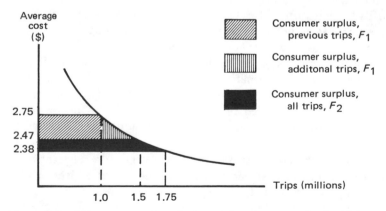

Figure 11.3.   Trip costs, number of trips, and consumer surplus for highway alternatives.

trips is computed in lines 8 and 9, respectively; for additional trips the computation is one-half the number of new trips times the average cost savings as the best straight line approximation of that portion of the demand curve which lies between the costs of $2.75 and $2.47 per trip.

As consumer surplus is the sole source of benefits included in the analysis, total benefits are computed by adding these cost savings for both the previous and additional trips. Finally, the present value of the benefit stream is computed by assuming that the same amount of benefits will accrue for each of 25 years into the future and discounting them by 8 percent. In this example, no attempt is made to determine how the level of benefits might be expected to vary across time due to, for instance, the gradual buildup of additional travel over the project's life.

The cost computations are less complex. The cost of constructing the facility to first expansion level specifications is estimated at $2 million, and that for moving to the second expansion level is $2 million more. Maintenance costs will increase from $20,000 to $30,000 per year for the first expansion level and up to $50,000 for the second expansion level; again, no effort is made to represent the greater maintenance needs that will be incurred later in the project's life as more than routine preventive maintenance measures are required. Total project costs are arrived at by discounting the cost of maintenance by 8 percent over the 25 years and adding this to the present value of construction costs. Finally, the ratio of benefits to costs is calculated for each expansion level, with the results showing that moving to the first expansion level will yield benefits in excess of costs but that moving beyond that to the second expansion level will incur costs that outweigh the additional benefits to be obtained. Regarding the second expansion level, the question is sometimes posed as to whether the investment would be more attractive if a toll were to be charged for use of the roadway, thereby reducing the net costs of the facility. The answer is "no" as this would constitute a pecuniary benefit, a transfer of money from the users to the authority operating the highway. Furthermore, imposing a toll would actually be expected to lead to a reduction in net benefits because it would increase average trip costs, resulting in decreased usage of the facility.

Bridge Construction Illustration   The second case concerns the construction of a bridge designed to carry traffic across a river, replacing the existing ferry service. It has a somewhat different format from the previous illustration in that it assumes that failing to build the bridge and retaining the ferry service instead as the only means of transport across the river would entail capital expenditures for new ferries and terminal expansions at various points in time as well as increased operating costs. The illustration is drawn from a series of applications of benefit-cost analyses to development projects in Pakistan; the benefits and costs are valued in millions of rupees (Adler, 1971, pp. 92–103).

This case also includes only direct costs and benefits, but the computations shown in Table 11.3 are based on more detailed analysis than in the previous example. The project life is set at 45 years, and costs and benefits are shown to vary over that period as inputs and usage rates are altered. The capital costs are borne during the 4 years the project will be under construction, with maintenance costs beginning the first year the facility is open and increasing in one step function near the midlife of the project. Total costs for each year are the sum of the two categories.

The first class of benefits is made up of costs of the ferry service, which will not be continued if the bridge is built; thus they become savings if the bridge is built. There is wide variation in this class of benefits because it includes the purchase of new ferries in 1971, 1976, 1980, 1983, and 1986, as well as the construction of two new terminals in 1980. These new ferries would be needed to expand the fleet to accommodate increasing traffic, and in addition, other replacement ferries would have to be purchased. The second class of benefits includes the elimination of delay and time savings valued in terms of vehicle costs, drivers' wages, and passenger time. These calculations are also based on a forecast of a much greater buildup over time of traffic across the river than would materialize if the bridge is not built.

Both costs and benefits, then, vary from year to year based on projections of occurrences in response to the bridge being built or not being built. The two columns to the right in Table 11.3 show the cost and benefit streams discounted to their present value. The present value, or net present worth, is determined to be 2.42 million rupees. In short, this would indicate that the project should be undertaken. However, as an interesting footnote, the author notes that when the contingency of a 25 percent cost overrun is incorporated into the analysis, it would result in a negative net present value. As 25 percent cost overruns are not all that uncommon, the project's justification might well be reviewed after firm bids are received.

Selection Criteria

The newcomer to benefit-cost analysis might assume that once problems involved in model development have been overcome, there is no

Table 11.3. Benefit-cost discounting: construction of a bridge (in Rs. million)

| Year | Costs | | | Benefits | | | Present worth | |
	Capital costs (1)	Maintenance costs (2)	Total costs (3)	Ferry costs (4)	Cost of delay (vehicles and drivers) (5)	Total benefits (6)	Discounted at 12 percent Costs (7)	Benefits (8)
1967	3.00		3.00				3.00	
1968	5.00		5.00				4.47	
1969	5.00		5.00				3.99	
1970	5.00		5.00				3.55	
1971		0.04	0.04	4.85	0.34	5.19	0.03	3.32
1972		0.04	0.04	0.75	0.40	1.15	0.02	0.65
1973		0.04	0.04	0.75	0.45	1.25	0.02	0.63
1974		0.04	0.04	0.75	0.50	1.25	0.02	0.56
1975		0.04	0.04	0.75	0.55	1.30	0.02	0.52
1976		0.04	0.04	2.90	0.60	3.50	0.01	1.26
1977		0.04	0.04	1.10	0.70	1.80	0.01	0.58
1978		0.04	0.04	1.10	0.75	1.85	0.01	0.54
1979		0.04	0.04	1.10	0.85	1.95	0.01	0.50
1980		0.04	0.04	3.80	0.95	4.75	0.01	1.09
1981		0.04	0.04	1.50	1.05	2.55	0.06	0.51
1982		0.04	0.04	1.50	1.15	2.65	0.06	0.48
1983		0.04	0.04	3.65	1.25	4.90	0.06	0.78
1984		0.04	0.04	1.85	1.35	3.20	0.06	0.48
1985		0.04	0.04	1.85	1.50	3.35	0.06	0.44
1986		0.04	0.04	4.00	1.65	5.65	0.06	0.67
1987		0.04	0.04	2.20	1.80	4.00	0.06	0.40
1988		0.04	0.04	2.20	2.00	4.20	0.06	0.39
1989		0.04	0.04	2.20	2.20	4.40	0.06	0.36
1990		0.05	0.05	2.20	2.40	4.60	0.06	0.34
1991		0.05	0.05	6.30	2.40	8.70	0.02	0.57

Year							
1992	0.05	0.05	2.20	2.40	4.60	0.02	0.27
1993	0.05	0.05	2.20	2.40	4.60	0.02	0.24
1994	0.05	0.05	2.20	2.40	4.60	0.02	0.22
1995	0.05	0.05	2.20	2.40	4.60	0.02	0.19
1996	0.05	0.05	4.00	2.40	6.40	0.02	0.24
1997	0.05	0.05	2.20	2.40	4.60	0.02	0.15
1998	0.05	0.05	2.20	2.40	4.60	0.02	0.14
1999	0.05	0.05	2.20	2.40	4.60	0.02	0.12
2000	0.05	0.05	4.50	2.40	6.90	0.02	0.16
2001	0.05	0.05	2.20	2.40	4.60	0.02	0.10
2002	0.05	0.05	2.20	2.40	4.60	0.02	0.09
2003	0.05	0.05	4.00	2.40	6.40	0.02	0.11
2004	0.05	0.05	2.20	2.40	4.60	0.02	0.07
2005	0.05	0.05	2.20	2.40	4.60	0.02	0.06
2006	0.05	0.05	4.00	2.40	6.40	0.02	0.08
2007	0.05	0.05	2.20	2.40	4.60	0.02	0.05
2008	0.05	0.05	2.20	2.40	4.60	0.02	0.04
2009	0.05	0.05	2.20	2.40	4.60	0.02	0.04
2010	0.05	0.05	2.20	2.40	4.60	0.02	0.03
2011	0.05	0.05	5.30	2.40	7.70	0.02	0.05
2012	0.05	0.05	2.20	2.40	4.60	0.02	0.03
2013	0.05	0.05	2.20	2.40	4.60	0.02	0.02
2014	0.05	0.05	2.20	2.40	4.60	0.02	0.02
2015	0.05	0.05	2.20	2.40	4.60	0.02	0.02
2016	0.05	0.05	4.00	2.40	6.40	0.02	0.02
2017	0.05	0.05	2.20	2.40	4.60	0.02	0.02
2018	0.05	0.05	2.20	2.40	4.60	0.02	0.02
2019	0.05	0.05	2.20	2.40	4.60	0.02	0.01
2020	0.05	0.05	2.20	2.40	4.60	0.02	0.01
2021			-5.00	2.40	-5.00	0.02	-0.01
						15.25	17.67

Net present worth = 2.42 million Rs.

From H. Adler, 1971. *Economic Appraisal of Transport Projects*. Bloomington: Indiana University Press, pp. 100-101.

difficulty in selecting the preferred alternative. This, however, is not the case. There are a few different procedures for determining which alternative is the most advantageous, and certain dangers are associated with the application of each. On a theoretical plane, there is also a normative question of what the objective of public investment should be.

The most conservative position would require that any public investment produce a **Pareto improvement,** a change in which none of the affected parties suffers losses while at least one party gains something. For the most part, this is a hypothetical situation, and application of this criterion would mean that hardly any projects would be undertaken. In practice, the objective applied is a net welfare improvement, a stipulation that projects should be undertaken only if the gainers could compensate the losers and still have some leftover benefits. Given this norm, public policy is increasingly providing for compensation to groups or affected parties incurring losses, to be charged off as project costs. This policy is aimed at an equity objective and does not alter the economic worth of a project because compensation payments are pecuniary rather than real impacts.

The **net welfare improvement** requirement, then, states that projects should be undertaken if total benefits exceed total costs. When the analysis focuses on a single project, and the decision is to undertake that project or no project, it should be undertaken if the *ratio* of benefits to costs exceeds 1 or, stated alternatively, if the **net present value** (benefit minus costs) is greater than 0. This is based on the assumption that the present value of the benefits that will result from resources left in the private sector equals the present value of the investment. The benefit-cost ratio of the investment of resources in the private sector equals 1 by definition, as the opportunity cost of using a resource in the public sector equals its face value in dollars.

Internal Rate of Return   An alternative to the discounting of costs and benefits and comparing their present values is the use of the **internal rate of return**. With this method the benefit stream is discounted at whatever rate sets the present value of benefits equal to the original investment or sets present net value equal to 0. The project is justified if this internal rate of return is greater than the cost of borrowing funds to finance the project (the applicable interest rate), or the appropriate discount rate for costs. This method has been applied more frequently to analyses of ongoing programs than to capital projects, but it has been recommended as being especially appropriate in circumstances requiring the allocation of a given capital budget among a number of potential investment projects (Mishan, 1973, chapter 4).

Operationally, use of the internal rate of return would seem to be most appealing in situations in which there is little uncertainty about how to discount costs but no clear guide to the appropriate rate for discounting benefits. Indeed, the operational problem most often cited is determining the appropriate discount rate for costs to serve as the basis of comparison for the internal rate of return. What is the cutoff point of minimum acceptable rate of return? (Burkhead and Miner, 1971, pp. 218–219). This problem is largely avoided, however, if the following two conditions are imposed for use of the internal rate of return: 1) no investment after the initial period, and 2) a constant opportunity cost of capital over the life of the project (Besen, Fechter, and Fisher, 1967, footnote 4).

Determination of the internal rate of return is quite straightforward if the project is characterized by uniform annual benefits. The annuity factor is computed by dividing the annual dollar benefit into the present value of total costs. This annuity factor is then used to enter Table A-11 for the appropriate number of years to determine what the implied discount rate would be; this is the internal rate of return.

Referring to the hypothetical highway project shown in Table 11.2, the annuity factor is the ratio of present value of costs (line 16) to annual benefit (line 10), or

$$\frac{\$2,106,748}{\$350,000} = 6.019$$

for the first expansion level. Taking this annuity factor into Table A-11 in the line corresponding to 25 years, we find that the internal rate of return is just slightly greater than 16 percent. Given 8 percent as the appropriate rate for discounting costs or the jurisdiction's cost of borrowing money, the internal rate of return clearly justifies this first expansion level. Applying the same procedure to the second expansion level yields an annuity factor (\$2,213,496/\$146,250) of 15.135 and an internal rate of return equal to slightly more than 4 percent; thus the second expansion level would not be justified. With uneven benefit streams, the simplest way to determine the internal rate of return is a trial and error approach, computing the present value of benefits with a guessed internal rate of return and adjusting it upward or downward as needed to arrive at a figure that is equal to the present value of total costs.

Project Rankings   When the choice set consists of alternative versions of a project or alternative kinds of projects, it is conventional to rank them for purposes of selecting the preferred alternative. The choice of selection criteria is particularly salient here as the benefit-cost ratio, net present value, and internal rate of return criteria do not result in the same rankings. Interest usually centers on the difference between using benefit-cost ratios and the net present value, illustrated in Table 11.4. Given the choice between the two projects, characterized by two different levels of investment, use of the highest benefit-cost ratio criterion would lead to the selection of project 1 as the preferred alternative, whereas the highest net present value criterion would result in the selection of project 2.

There is no systematic relationship between these two criteria other than the fact that when present net value equals 0, the benefit-cost ratio equals 1. A common mistake in comparing projects of different magnitudes is using benefit-cost ratios. They are intuitively appealing because they represent the rate at which benefits are yielded by investments, and obviously it is desirable to maximize these benefits. However, use of the highest benefit-cost ratio does not necessarily lead to maximum welfare improvement; in and of themselves the ratios are irrelevant.

Given a valid choice set, the proper criterion is to maximize the present value of net benefits. As in the case shown in Table 11.4, this may well result in choosing an alternative with a lower benefit-cost ratio, but it must be remembered that the primary issue is the extent to which resources should be withdrawn from the private sector to be invested in a type of public project. Investing more resources in a public program will clearly produce benefits at a diminishing rate, but as long as benefits continue to exceed costs the net effect is superior to leaving the resources in the private sector. Theoretically, this means that the amount of activity in a given public program area should be pushed to that point where the incremental benefit-cost ratio is 1, the point where marginal productivity in the public sector activity is equated with that in the private sector.

Table 11.4.   Selection between two hypothetical projects (values in million of dollars)

Present value	Project 1	Project 2
Costs	$100	$200
Benefits	$150	$260
Net present value	$ 50	$ 60
Benefit/cost ratio	1.5	1.3

When many alternative versions of a project are being compared, and when they differ primarily in terms of magnitude or level of effort, a least total cost variant may be the most appropriate model for identifying the preferred alternative. For example, a number of composite transportation plans for a metropolitan area might range from a very low to a very high level of new construction. If capital construction costs (amortized on a daily basis) vary directly with the additional mileage called for while the benefits, reductions in travel costs, increase at a diminishing rate with additional mileage, then total transportation costs would follow the relationship shown in Figure 11.4, decreasing rapidly at first, leveling off, and then increasing as the savings in travel costs made possible by still more new facilities are outweighed by the cost of constructing those additional facilities.

Net benefits are maximized in the "saddle" of the total costs curve, where total cost is minimized; according to the figure, plan *C* is the preferred alternative. Plan *A* has the greatest benefit-cost ratio, and moving incrementally from left to right, each successively larger plan shows fewer benefits per unit of increased cost. In the saddle of the total cost curve the incremental benefits equal incremental costs (beyond those of the previous plan), whereas the plans to the right of the saddle would have negative incremental benefit-cost ratios.

In theory, investment in public projects should be pushed to the point resulting in least total costs. In practice, however, this rule is rarely applied completely because: 1) Most programs and particularly

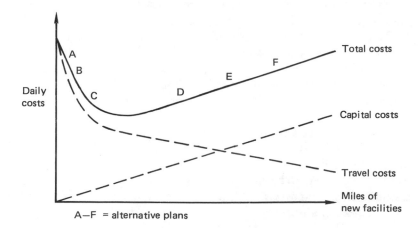

Figure 11.4.   Least cost criterion.

capital projects are "lumpy," i.e., not finely divisible into very small increments, 2) given the uncertainties surrounding most such analyses, there is usually a perceived need to maintain a healthy margin of safety, requiring benefit-cost ratios much greater than 1, for a project to be undertaken, and 3) everything is usually *not* equal, particularly in terms of the alternative use of resources if the low cost alternatives are selected.

Alternatives Specification   This leads directly to the critical issue of defining the choice set in the first place. If the choice set is the relevant one for the decision to be made, i.e., if it really represents the alternative uses to which resources might be committed, then the maximization of net present value is the correct criterion to be applied. However, when projects of different magnitudes are being compared, interest centers on the alternative use of the resources that would not be used if the smaller project were selected. The assumption underlying benefit-cost analysis is, of course, that they would be used in the private sector, but if this is not the case the alternatives should be built into the choice set.

In practice, most public agencies have budget ceilings and undertake to finance projects up to those ceilings. Referring to Table 11.4, the choice set depicted arouses the suspicion that if project 1 were to be undertaken, requiring an investment of $100 million while $200 million is apparently available, some additional project, project 3, might also be undertaken that could not be financed in the event of undertaking project 2. If such is the case, the choice set should be specified as a decision between project 2 and the package of project 1 and project 3. If project 3 generated similar benefits to those of project 1, the same size and scale project in a different location for example, the package of projects 1 and 3 would yield net benefits of $100 million for the $200 million investment and thus be preferable to project 2. Application of benefit-cost analysis, then, is only as useful as the degree to which the formalized choice set represents the real options at hand.

If benefit-cost analysis is to be employed to identify the optimal use of resources, an obvious requirement is that all the realistic alternatives be included. Given the circumstance in which a total sum is likely to be invested by an agency or governmental unit one way or another, the alternatives should be specified where relevant as combinations or packages of projects so as to permit a true assessment of total benefits and costs. A comprehensive benefit-cost analysis requires specification of the choice set to reflect **incompatibilities**—projects that would not be feasible if other projects are undertaken—and **complementarities**—sets of projects that logically should be undertaken together—in order to fully assess the consequences of undertaking any project.

For example, a major conceptual criticism of the Corps of Engineers benefit-cost analysis of the Alton Locks and Dam project mentioned earlier is that the project is really just the first step in a package of improvements in the Upper Mississippi Navigation System, that the Corps is considering other projects logically related to the Alton project, and that full benefits would materialize only if the whole set of projects were undertaken (Congressional Budget Office, 1976). Thus, economic analysis would be more meaningful in the long run if it were applied to whole systems of improvements rather than to individual projects.

Distributional Consequences

The net present value criterion ranks alternatives in terms of economic efficiency alone, without regard to distributional consequences. A project is justified if the gainers could compensate the losers and still have some benefits left over, but there is no concern built into the model for who those gainers and losers are. In problems without substantial negative externalities, or third party losses, there is still no consideration of the incidence of the benefits among various groups. However, although benefit-cost analysis is an efficiency oriented method that has been criticized for ignoring equity considerations, distributional effects can be observed and even adjusted for in the interpretation of benefit-cost results. This can be accomplished by either 1) building desired distributional effects into the benefit-cost model with a weighting scheme, or 2) applying nonefficiency criteria in conjunction with, or even in place of, the net present value criterion.

Weighting Schemes   Use of a weighting scheme may be appropriate when interest centers directly on the costs and benefits affecting different income groups. Traditional benefit-cost analysis is based on the assumption that one dollar has the same worth for one individual or party as for any other, although we can be fairly certain that in reality this is not the case. Furthermore, if public policy does not assure that the losers will be compensated somehow, projects can be justified on efficiency grounds, which flagrantly violates the notion of equity. For example, a project involving large, secondary costs imposed on low income groups with benefits accruing primarily to higher income groups may be considered undesirable from an equity standpoint although it may be found to contribute net benefits to the society as a whole.

One response to this kind of concern is the idea of attaching utility weights to the costs and benefits pertaining to different income groups. In operational terms there is a difficulty in determining exactly what those weights should be, but the idea is to apply a set of weights that reflect the varying degrees of utility that a dollar has for differing income groups. If a dollar benefit were thought to have three times as much utility to a low income family as to a high income family, it would be weighted accordingly (Mishan, 1973, chapter 4). Essentially, the use of such a weighting scheme would alter the dollar values placed in the benefit and cost accounts, and the net present value criterion could then be employed to select that alternative with the greatest net benefit in terms of units of utility instead of absolute dollars.

Alternative Criteria Although the inclusion of all pecuniary benefits and costs in the model will have no effect on the computation of net benefits, it does serve to indicate the distribution of positive and negative impacts among all affected parties. This can be used to interpret the relative merits of the alternatives as separate from their contributions to economic efficiency. For example, the analyst might consider all those alternatives with positive benefit-cost ratios and then rank them in terms of their effects on a particular party, perhaps in terms of their income benefits to families below the poverty level. Alternatively, he might screen out some of the alternatives by use of a specified equity constraint, eliminating all projects that would reduce the housing stock in the predominantly black areas of a city for example, and then proceed to select the preferred alternative from the remaining ones on the basis of net present value.

Such distributional considerations are often taken into account in planning developmental strategy in developing nations. For example, the desire to promote industrial development in a particular region in which the general standard of living is substantially below that of the country as a whole might lead to locating infrastructure facilities there even when their installation elsewhere would clearly provide greater net benefits. This kind of issue also becomes bound up in the question of perspective regarding inside versus outside benefits (Prest and Turvey, 1975).

An example of the kind of trade-off to be made between efficiency and equity considerations concerns the alternative strategies considered in the general debate leading up to the 1965 Housing Act (Maass, 1966, pp. 221–225). The Administration's proposal apparently would have resulted in greater total direct benefits produced by the planned investment (i.e., more housing units) than did the action ultimately undertaken by Congress. However, in the congressional plan the benefits were aimed directly at low income households rather than the moderate income households that would have been the direct beneficiaries of the administration's program. In this case, the policy preference exerted by the Congress had an equity orientation first and an efficiency orientation second.

A methodological extension of benefit-cost analysis that is aimed in part at analyzing the distributional effects of proposals is the matrix approach, cross-classifying the affected parties by multiple categories of objectives or impacts. The prototype among these is Lichfield's comprehensive **balance sheet of development** designed to assess the overall worth of a city plan (Lichfield, 1960). The method is characterized by the classification of various categories of producers and consumers, the estimation of costs and benefits in nonmonetary units where dollar values cannot readily be assigned, and the summarization (in both quantitative and qualitative terms) of the impacts affecting each group separately. The format of the balance sheet, which lacks a single overall benefit-cost ratio, has been cited as an advantage in terms of communicating the complexities of projects and in avoiding the misleading impressions that are often conveyed by single numerical indicators (Burkhead and Miner, 1971, p. 244). The method has, however, been criticized as being abstract in that it mixes together many classes of costs and benefits relating to different objectives, when relationships among those objectives are unclear (Hill, 1968). This has led to attempts to further refine the general methodology by determining the relative importance of these objectives through referendums or citizen surveys, thus making it possible to weight costs and benefits on a scale that would measure their relative contribution to, or detraction from, the public welfare (Hill, 1968; Weiner and Deak, 1972).

SPECIALIZED MEASUREMENT PROBLEMS

In previous sections, the problems of measuring and selecting pertinent costs and benefits have been raised. This section describes several ways of addressing these problems and achieving workable results in the face of inherent imperfections or uncertainties.

Treatment of Uncertainty

The problem of uncertainty is one of the major hurdles in an applied benefit-cost analysis, and the way in which uncertainties are resolved can be the primary determinant of the results. Often uncertainties are dealt with in an arbitrary fashion, but in some cases more systematic treatments are possible. To understand the problem of dealing with uncertainties it is necessary to distinguish among various sources of uncertainty. Dollar values of impacts and appropriate discount rates are two classes of uncertainties. The first stems largely from a lack of understanding about individual and group preferences, and the latter is in part a normative issue, as has been discussed. Other uncertainties relate in substantive terms to the impacts themselves; with respect to the highway example these might concern such issues as:

—How much additional travel will be induced by the new facility?
—By how much will accident rates and travel times be reduced?
—Will vehicle operating costs actually increase or decrease?
—What maintenance efforts will be required?
—What will happen to fuel prices in the future and how will that affect travel volumes?
—Will the speed limit change?
—Will noise levels actually be increased or reduced? Will there be any other positive or adverse environmental effects?
—Will there be any spinoffs on local economies?
—In the long run will land use patterns change so as to affect travel volumes on the facility?

Difficulties in estimating costs and benefits in substantive terms stem from three sources of uncertainty (Fisher, 1972, p. 190). The first involves uncertainty about cause/effect relationships between programs or projects and benefits and costs. It depends on the state of knowledge about observed effects of similar programs or projects in the past and is thus the primary focus of most ex post facto program or project evaluation. In the above example, for instance, projections of future benefits will be based in part on past findings regarding the amount of additional travel that is generated by the opening of new highways. The more complete and situation-specific the past research findings, the better able we are to estimate future impacts of a given proposal.

The second source of uncertainty involves the question of whether observed or apparent relationships will hold for the future as well as uncertainty about future outcome states of controlling environmental factors. Can additional travel be expected to develop on new highways in the future at the same rate at which this phenomenon has been observed in the past? Furthermore, will fuel prices or speed limits (environmental factors beyond the control of the transportation planners) be altered dramatically, exerting in turn an influence on travel volume? Addressing these issues requires attempts at forecasting trends and making judgments about probable changes in the future.

The third type of uncertainty is statistical uncertainty relating to chance effect, the random component of experimental error, sometimes referred to as **risk** as opposed to uncertainty. This last category can be disposed of most easily as many quantitative techniques are available to deal with risk—inferential statistics as well as operations research probability models as discussed in other chapters—and where relevant these should be employed. However, it should be noted that if the problem is swamped with uncertainty about cause/effect patterns and the nature of future outcome states, elaborate statistical treatments of chance effect may be of little use. Although uncertainties by definition will reduce the precision of a benefit-cost model, their implications for the overall worthiness of a proposal can be taken into account with the following approaches.

Contingency Analysis One strategy is to investigate how the ranking of the alternatives is affected by the assumption of contingency plans for changes in environmental constraints. For example, a construction project might be costed at a specified amount, given an assumption of normal working conditions. In the event of unanticipated difficulties in excavation or a sudden increase in the cost of materials, the estimated cost might be overrun considerably. What would this do to the benefit-cost ratio? Similarly, a local unit of government might be evaluating the benefits and costs of a new program for which state grants are available and basing its costs on the local share only; if the state assistance is eliminated, what is the effect on the program's net benefits?

Sensitivity Analysis Often estimates of benefits and costs are based on point projections of the level of some important environmental variable that is known to fluctuate considerably. Rather than working with expected values only, a more conservative approach is to develop projections based on both high and low levels to produce interval estimates of costs and benefits. For example, projections of anticipated highway user revenues to be available for future construction and maintenance activities are based in part on annual vehicle miles traveled (VMT). As VMT cannot be forecast with a high degree of certainty, it may be informative to develop multiple projections of VMT and a range of estimated revenue. Separate benefit-cost comparisons can then be made based on the varying revenue estimates.

Table 11.5 illustrates the use of sensitivity analysis to develop a

Table 11.5.   Incremental cost of Indianapolis police fleet plan

ANNUAL OPERATING OR RECURRING COST	Mileage increase		
	40%	60%	70%
Direct (Expense Budget))			
Case A—7.3¢ per mile			
Incremental miles driven	1,970,242	2,955,362	3,447,923
Cost per mile	0.073	0.073	0.073
Total mileage cost	$ 143,828	$ 215,741	$ 251,698
Radio and insurance	$ 84,668	$ 84,668	$ 84,668
Direct recurring cost	$ 228,496	$ 300,409	$ 336,366
Case B—5.5¢ per mile			
Incremental miles driven	1,970,242	2,955,362	3,447,923
Cost per mile	0.055	0.055	0.055
Total mileage cost	$ 108,363	$ 162,545	$ 189,636
Radio and insurance	$ 84,668	$ 84,668	$ 84,668
Direct recurring cost	$ 193,031	$ 247,213	$ 274,304
Case C—4¢ per mile			
Incremental miles driven	1,970,242	2,955,362	3,447,923
Cost per mile	0.04	0.04	0.04
Total mileage cost	$ 78,810	$ 118,215	$ 137,917
Radio and insurance	$ 84,668	$ 84,668	$ 84,668
Direct recurring cost	$ 163,478	$ 202,883	$ 222,585

Indirect—Car Replacement (Capital Budget) Based on Pre-Fleet Plan	Yearly replacement cycle		
	2	2½	3
Number of patrol cars	455	455	455
Annual car replacement	228	190	152
Pre-fleet plan replacement	85	85	85
Net annual replacement	143	105	67
Cost per car (accessories transferred)	$ 2,000	$ 2,000	$ 2,000
Indirect recurring cost	$ 286,000	$ 210,000	$ 134,000

TOTAL ANNUAL RECURRING COST—MOST LIKELY CASE

Direct (Expense Budget) 5.5¢ per mile—60% mileage increase	$ 247,213
Indirect—Car Replacement (Capital Budget) 2½ year replacement	$ 210,000
Total annual recurring cost	$ 457,213

From Fisk, 1970, p. 49.

range of estimates of the recurring costs of the Indianapolis Police Fleet Plan, on which marked cars were assigned to individual patrolmen who used them during off duty hours for personal and family use and responded to emergency calls in their areas even while off duty. Uncertainties in terms of operating and maintenance costs related to both the unit cost per mile and the extent of the overall increase in vehicle mileage; thus projections were developed on ranges of estimates for both of these factors. The uncertainty regarding the necessary schedule for phasing cars out of the fleet and replacing them with new vehicles was dealt with in a similar fashion. In this example the "middle" estimates based on the two sets of computations were then selected to provide a "most likely" single point estimate of the total annual recurring costs of the program.

A Fortiori Analysis This strategy is appropriate in situations in which intuitive judgment favors one alternative, X, while the objective analysis seems to point toward a second alternative, Y. With a fortiori analysis, the analyst arbitrarily resolves all uncertainties of any consequence in favor of X; if Y still emerges as the most advantageous alternative in benefit-cost terms, there is a much stronger case for this alternative. An example would be a choice between a new expressway and a rapid rail line in a transportation corridor in which there is strong sentiment for building the rapid rail line even though the expressway seems to be preferable from a benefit-cost standpoint. The two major uncertainties, fuel prices and parking availability could be set at levels that would discourage commuting by automobile; if the expressway continues to seem advantageous, it is a stronger indication that rapid rail cannot compete in that situation.

Assigning Probabilities A fourth procedure is to assign probabilities to various outcome states, based on subjective judgment, probability sampling, or forecasting models (Vedder, 1970). For instance, the benefits to be derived from a job training program will be partially dependent on the state of the local labor markets when the program is completed. If the analyst can derive some reasonable probabilities that the demand for the skills being developed will be high, moderate, or low, either judgmentally or based on previous experience, he can gain further insight as to the probable worth of the program.

It has also been pointed out that analysis of uncertainties using the above techniques may be of use in developing new alternatives. Through such examination of the impact of uncertainties, the analyst may gain a further understanding of the really critical, least controllable uncertainties. This could lead to the design of a new alternative that would "provide a reasonably good hedge against a range of the more significant uncertainties" (Fisher, 1972, p. 191).

Shadow Pricing

Tangible benefits and costs in general are measured by their market prices, as these usually provide the best indication of what people are willing to pay for the use of resources. However, if observed prices are distorted by market imperfections, they will not represent true social values and costs and thus may have to be adjusted. Such adjustments are often termed **shadow prices**, corrections made to represent more accurately substitution ratios among resources or products or the real consequences of an investment decision in terms of alternative uses and opportunity costs.

There are many sources of market price distortion that might have to be adjusted for in a given benefit-cost analysis. In general, any restrictions on competition, such as monopoly or oligopoly conditions, restrictions on imports, or limited entry into an industry or occupation, may limit the supply of an input and inflate prices to levels above actual costs plus a normal rate of return. The real opportunity cost of the use of such inputs would be measured by the value of the product resulting from the alternative employment of the same factors of production in a competitive situation without excess profits. Indirect taxes and price support programs also inflate market prices above the opportunity costs of the factors of production.

The notion of unemployed or underemployed resources can create measurement difficulties in depression periods. The usual assumption in benefit-cost analysis is that all resources used in a program or project, particularly labor, will be used elsewhere if the project is not undertaken. If, however, this is not the case—when there is widespread unemployment in the construction industry, for example—there is no opportunity cost incurred by using them to undertake the project.

The prospect of unemployed labor can also affect benefit computations. Employment opportunities afforded by a project are usually not counted as benefits because it is assumed that if the project is not undertaken, the funds will be invested in other projects, whether in the public or private sector, and comparable employment opportunities will still be provided. If this is not the case, however, perhaps the income derived from employment in the project should be reckoned as a benefit. In assessing the consequences of halting a state's highway construction program, for example, the loss of construction jobs would probably be taken into account because most of the funds are federal monies earmarked for highways. If the construction program is phased out, these funds would be forfeited by the state altogether, resulting in a real decrease in income in the state (Poister, Larson, and Rao, 1978).

Use of Shadow Prices The kinds of price distortions mentioned above can introduce serious biases in benefit-cost calculations and in certain applications should be adjusted for in order to reflect true opportunity costs. This cataloging should not suggest, however, that shadow prices are always preferable to observed market prices. With respect to observed prices that are distorted by market restrictions, for example, it has been argued that if such restrictions are anticipated to remain binding in the future, observed prices provide the more accurate indication of opportunity cost or sacrifice (McKean, 1972, p. 126). Similarly, in terms of changing supply and demand conditions, if price changes attributable to independent factors or even the project itself can be forecast, they should be taken into account. The appropriate prices to use depend on the anticipated real world situation at the time the inputs are to be used.

Market distortions create discrepancies between purely economic valuations and **financial appraisals**, the former representing opportunity costs in terms of technological relationships and the latter representing money outlays based on market prices. Money outlays certainly represent opportunity costs too, in the sense of how much of other kinds of inputs cannot be purchased if a given project is undertaken. In general, projects should be undertaken only if justified in both economic and financial terms, but situations can still arise in which one alternative is superior economically whereas another is the preferred alternative in financial terms (Adler, 1971, pp. 47–48).

Intangible Costs and Benefits

Intangibles are much more difficult to measure in dollar values because there is no direct market experience to serve as the basis for the valuation. Benefit-cost analysis seeks to measure all impacts in dollar terms as they would be valued by the affected parties; the problem is that the preferences of the affected parties for intangibles are not revealed in the market. Some intangibles are readily quantifiable, such as travel time, whereas others are difficult to quantify, such as psychological stress engendered by driving in heavy traffic. Rather than affixing dollar values to them, the former type may be summarized quantitatively in substantive measures and the latter type summarized descriptively as a complement to the benefit-cost computations. This is certainly preferable to ignoring them altogether, which can severely bias the conclusions to be drawn, but the use of different measuring units necessarily precludes the possibility of arriving at a single measure of net benefit.

The alternative is to attempt to impute dollar values to intangible costs and benefits through indirect approaches. This has the advantage of expressing the value of all costs and benefits in a common unit of measurement, but often the methods for imputing dollar values to intangibles are based on tenuous assumptions, hinging the analysis on questionable measures. This can be crucial, especially when the more prominent impacts are intangibles. For example, one of the major benefits attributed to most transportation improvements is savings in travel time, but there is a notable lack of consensus on how such time should be valued. The effect of using an average value of $2.75 per hour as opposed to $2.50 per hour can easily be the difference between a justified and unjustified project.

Comparable Prices One way of imputing dollar values to intangiables is to observe price relationships for similar items in the market. A frequent application of this approach is the use of area wage rates as the value of time saved in travel because of the construction of a new transportation facility, equating travel time with work time. This is questionable even for working time (travel on the job) because travel time saved does not always represent a real gain in opportunity; often the time saved is not converted into economic value (Harrison and Quarmby, 1972). For nonworking time it is an even more doubtful measure. What are the opportunity costs of spending time in travel? Clearly there is a wide range of answers to this question depending on what people could or would do instead of traveling and how much satisfaction they derive from these other activities. If the time saved from travel could be used to earn additional income, it has a certain value, but if the time is spent in leisure activity, its value may be quite different.

Consumer Choice Situations A second approach to measuring the dollar value of intangibles is to observe consumer behavior in certain choice situations or experiments that provide clues as to how people value trade-offs between a given intangible and money. For example, an estimate of how commuters value their time can be derived by observing the choices they make between a less expensive, time consuming travel mode and a more expensive but quicker means of making the same trip (Foster and Beesely, 1963). However, such a measure is valid only if the consumers are known to have complete information about the alternatives and if all other possible influences on the decision can be assumed to be neutral or accounted for in some way. In the example the commuters would have to know the time consequences of the alternatives, and the two travel modes would have to be alike in all other respects. If there is a difference in comfort between the two, the choices observed cannot necessarily be attributed solely to time and cost considerations. Furthermore, there may be difficulty in inferring that the same trade-offs apply to a larger group of consumers. For example, if the experiment involved the choice between express and local subway trains, there would be no assurance that the dollar value established would pertain to commuters in general, other than subway users.

Derived Demand   In some situations the demand curve for a service or facility provided for free can be derived by computing indirect costs. For example, consider a large state park for which there is no entry fee. Users come from different locations and thus incur different costs in reaching the park; fewer visitors come from farther away because of the higher costs to them. If it can be assumed that the trip has no other purpose and no inherent utility, the travel demand is derived from the desire to visit the park, and the travel costs incurred can be considered to represent the actual prices paid to use the park.

This information can be used to develop a measure of the satisfaction received by visitors to the park, a final benefit for which no direct dollar valuation is available. Zones around the park can be delineated according to average travel costs and the number of annual visitors per 1,000 residents can be computed for each zone. Aggregating the zones with different average travel costs will produce a demand curve for the park, and the usage rate will decline as the price rises. If the zones can be considered similar in terms of the preferences of their residents for use of the park, the demand curve can be applied to each zone separately and compared with actual usage. The difference between this demand curve and the flat price (the average travel cost from the zone to the park) for those people who do visit the park will represent the consumer surplus, the difference between the costs actually incurred in getting to the park and what the visitors would be willing to pay to use the park if they had to (Clawson, 1959; Clawson and Knetsch, 1966; Mansfield, 1972).

Social Surveys   A different approach to imputing dollar values to intangibles is to ask people how they value a certain service. This can be used to replicate an experiment in consumer choice, but it involves additional threats to validity. For instance, to evaluate the benefits of a proposed new bus route, a survey might be used to ask potential riders how many trips per week they would make on the route at varying fare levels. The demand curve so generated can be compared with the proposed flat fare, with the recognition, however, that people tend to inflate their responses in such surveys. In general the validity of the dollar value estimates is subject to all the measurement problems associated with survey research discussed in the preceding chapter.

Cost of Compensation   Sometimes costs, particularly negative externalities, can be valued by pricing out what it would actually cost to physically overcome them. For example, the costs of detrimental physical environmental impacts of a project might be valued in dollar terms by the direct costs of mounting the necessary abatement programs to effect a return to the noise levels and air quality that prevailed before construction of the project (Weiner and Deak, 1972, p. 97).

Using similar logic in reverse, the dollar value of benefits produced by a public health program that provides free inoculations against an anticipated epidemic might be imputed from **cost avoided.** Theoretically, the benefits are worth whatever people would be willing to pay for them, but in practice they might be evaluated by estimates of potential medical costs and lost earnings that were avoided by virtue of being protected against the disease in question.

Value of Human Life   The difficulties involved in trying to place a dollar value on the saving of a human life, or the loss of human life, illustrate well the frustration of coming to grips with intangibles in economic analysis. A number of alternative approaches have been developed—based on projected earnings, the dollar value implied by governmental policies, insurance premiums paid, etc. (Mishan, 1973, pp. 101–104)—but they all raise as many questions as they answer. Yet, many programs, such as police protection, highway safety, health care, and ambulance services, are aimed in part at saving human lives, and their evaluation in large part hinges on this question.

It should be pointed out that although there is much interest in devising methodologies for placing dollar values on intangible costs and benefits, one school of thought cautions that this may not be desirable. This position holds that if there is no clear indication of the values people place on impacts based on market experience, they can be evaluated only through budget determination by the political process (Musgrave and Musgrave, 1976, p. 162). The principles of economic analysis can then be applied to a more limited problem constrained by the specification of intangible benefits to be pursued or ignored and intangible costs to be tolerated or avoided. This approach, referred to as cost-effectiveness, is discussed in the following section.

COST—EFFECTIVENESS ANALYSIS

Not surprisingly, the difficulties associated with the practical application of benefit-cost analysis increase with the complexity of the problem being addressed. On the other hand, benefit-cost principles are being applied increasingly to issues that are less comprehensive than the question of whether resources should be used by the public sector. Under the general rubric of cost-effectiveness, methods of economic analysis are being employed to address the kinds of questions most often facing program analysts: Can existing resources be used differently so as to increase effectiveness, or can productivity be improved so as to maintain or increase effectiveness while holding the line on costs?

The use of cost-effectiveness analysis is occasioned by the need to address questions that are not feasible for benefit-cost analysis applications in an operational sense or are too constrained for the scope of benefit-cost analysis. This is the case with social goods, activities whose product is of a collective nature shared in equal amounts by all citizens; such as national defense, for example.

People do not reveal their preferences for more or less national defense in the economic marketplace, and the benefits of defense programs are not measured in dollars. In analyzing the deployment of strategic forces, for example, effectiveness might be measured in terms of "the numbers of particular types of forces which can be deployed to specific areas by a specific time" (Niskanen, 1967, p. 29). Alternative sites for basing such forces could then be compared both in terms of this measure of effectiveness and the costs of transporting the forces.

Second, cost-effectiveness has been found to be an attractive approach to problems characterized by major externalities or intangibles. Where these factors cannot readily be measured in dollar terms as required by benefit-cost analysis, they can be dealt with substantively in cost-effectiveness analysis, either by setting them equivalent across the alternatives or holding the alternatives to constraints set in terms of the intangibles. In developing an industrial park or airport, for example, rather than attempting to put dollar values on negative impacts on the physical environment, these impacts can be dealt with by excluding from consideration all those alternatives generating negative impacts above certain specified levels. Those alternatives meeting these constraints expressed in physical terms can then be analyzed and compared in the traditional benefit-cost format. Selection of the preferred alternative plan will be based on differences in the tangible factors only, and there may be no precise indication of true net worth.

Fixed Utility

In the absence of the ability to determine real net benefit, alternative program strategies are often compared by holding the level of effectiveness constant and analyzing differences in their costs, or by holding costs constant and comparing levels of effectiveness. The former, referred to as the **fixed utility** approach, is commonly used in national defense analysis; a prescribed level of deterrent capability may be established and alternative systems configurations analyzed in terms of both deterrent capability and costs; the cost-effective alternative is the one that meets the prescribed level of effectiveness at least cost.

Examples of the usefulness of the fixed utility approach abound. A city planning department may set the objective of reducing the number of families housed in substandard dwelling units by 50 percent and compare the costs of attaining this objective through the construction of new housing and the rehabilitation of existing, substandard housing. Differences in social or psychological effects should also be noted and adjusted for if possible to ensure the validity of the comparison.

It should be understood that fixed utility will not always refer to final impacts in the sense in which the term effectiveness is used in this text, but rather the fixed utility may also be set in terms of intermediate effects and outputs. In essence then, the cost-effective alternative would be that which produces the specified type and level of outputs at least cost. One notable application of this approach was a study comparing the costs of five integrated transportation modes in providing service levels along a given route as specified in terms of carrying capacity, travel time, and convenience in terms of such factors as seat availability and waiting time (Meyer, Kain, and Wohl, 1966).

Fixed Budget

Cost-effectiveness analysis is perhaps used more frequently in the allocation of fixed budget amounts. It should be noted that resource allocation decisions made within the framework of budget constraints beg the central question addressed by traditional benefit-cost analysis: What level of resources, if any, should be invested in a given public program or project? In such a context, however, benefit-cost principles can be used to suboptimize within the budget constraint (Prest and Turvey, 1975, p. 95).

Given a fixed budget to be allocated between two program categories, they should be funded where their marginal benefits are equal. This will maximize the effectiveness of the program as a whole, but does not examine the more important question of whether the budget should be augmented or cut, with funds diverted to other programs. The use of the internal rate of return method has also been advocated for this kind of context, for example, in allocating job training program funds between programs teaching general skills and those teaching specialized skills. If one program's rate of return is higher than that of another, funds should be shifted from the first to the second until the point where the returns at the margin are equalized (Besen, Fechter, and Fisher, 1967, pp. 144–145).

With respect to ongoing, operating programs the fixed budget approach may be used more often than the fixed utility approach because the actual constraint is frequently a budget ceiling and because the available data often lend themselves to this method. For example, if a city police department has experimented with a fleet utilization plan and found that it was associated with a 10 percent decrease in the commission of certain types of crimes, it can measure the cost-effectiveness of that strategy by relating this observed effect to the cost of mounting the plan. If the department then wishes to compare this performance with those of other strategies, a foot patrol effort or a burglary prevention program, for example, it can do so more readily by holding costs constant than by trying to obtain exactly the same degree of effectiveness with each strategy. It can invest the same amount of funds spent on the fleet plan in each of the other two strategies, separately, and then compare the percent decrease in crimes associated with each of the three alternatives.

Human Resources Illustration

A good illustration of the applicability of cost-effectiveness analysis to ongoing programs in the general area of human resources is a comparison of vocational-technical curricula and nonvocational curricula in senior high schools for training and educating students who do not go to college (Kaufman, Hu, Lee, and Stromsdorfer, 1969). The objective is to compare both the costs and benefits of two alternative types of programs in terms of their relative contributions to society's welfare. Obviously, they are not mutually exclusive alternatives, but rather the question relates to the optimal balance between the two in the educational system.

Because these are operating programs for which much data are available, in some respects the model development is more precise than in many capital project benefit-cost applications. A cross-section of school districts was analyzed to determine the costs of operating these programs, and a sample of their graduates was studied in a follow-up survey to obtain a measure of the benefits derived from their education. In the study, actual costs were measured by current operating costs plus the replacement costs of capital facilities and then approximated by a statistical procedure known as regression analysis in order to estimate costs for varying levels of output. It was found that on the average the marginal costs of vocational-technical curricula were roughly $100 to $200 greater than those for nonvocational curricula.

The benefits were computed by using time employed and earnings as proximate measures, as these were thought to reflect the major differences in benefits received by graduates of the two curricula. Statistical analysis was used to control for other factors that might influence the levels of these benefits such as sex, race, marital status, city, IQ, and father's income, this last a general indicator of socio-economic status and background. On the average, it was found that vocational-technical graduates were employed 4.3 months more than nonvocational graduates during the first 6 years after graduation and that they earned $3,456 more than the nonvocational graduates during the same period. By comparing these figures it was found that these differences in benefits outweighed the cost differentials between the types of curricula, and on this basis it was recommended that funds be shifted to vocational-technical programs from nonvocational programs.

This study uses all the principles and techniques of benefit-cost analysis—benefits and costs were discounted to present value for example—but it addresses a more limited question. The purpose was to compare the productivity of the two types of programs, but no attempt was made to assess the overall net benefits of either, a much more challenging issue. Therefore, factors that were found not to differentiate between the two curricula were excluded, even though they would constitute critical variables in a full blown benefit-cost analysis. For example, earnings foregone by the students while they were in school were not incorporated in the analysis because they would be roughly equivalent for the two groups. Similarly, actual earnings after the sixth year upon graduation were not included because they too were found to be roughly equivalent; the earning advantage of the vocational-technical programs occurs in the first few years after graduation. Furthermore, the study looked separately at a set of nonmonetary benefits such as voting behavior (a citizenship benefit to the society), job congruence with real interests, and psychological and motivational characteristics. In this case these factors were not found to have notable differences, but if they had, the interpretation of net effects in terms of these benefits and the monetary benefits would have been made judgmentally. Although the focus of such a study is certainly more circumscribed than a comprehensive benefit-cost framework, the information provided by this more limited approach may be as useful or more useful to administrators and decision makers.

Recidivism Illustration

Brief consideration of a second example of cost-effectiveness analysis, this one a hypothetical comparison of alternative strategies for reducing recidivism among released prisoners, is useful because it illustrates the use of economic analysis in conjunction with an experimental design as well as a comparison of the use of cost criteria versus purely effectiveness considerations (Levin, 1975, chapter 5). It is based on a hypothetical experiment in which, upon release, male prisoners are randomly assigned to one of four strategies including 1) job placement, 2) psychological services, 3) a combination of these two, and 4) normal existing arrangements for reporting periodically to parole officers. During a 6-month period, 10,000 released prisoners are assigned to each strategy. The programs are kept in operation for 5½ years; the primary impact measure is the number of participants in each group who have remained nonrecidivous at the end of that period.

Table 11.6 shows the comparison of the strategies in terms of cost-effectiveness. The normal existing arrangements strategy incurs the least direct cost, whereas the combined treatment has the highest costs. In general, the four treatments rank in the same order in terms of nonrecidivous participants as they do in terms of cost, but the computation of average cost per nonrecidivist shows this unit to vary substantially among the four treatments. On this basis the normal arrangement is also seen to be the least costly.

However, use of the number of nonrecidivists overstates the effectiveness of all these programs because it can be presumed that many of these former prisoners would not become recidivists in the absence of any program. This overstatement would presumably be greatest for the normal arrangements. Furthermore, the normal arrangement cannot be eliminated because of legal constraints, and it is incorporated in each of the other treatments; the real question is whether or not one of the three new treatments should be implemented in addition. Thus, both the number of nonrecidivists and costs are converted to incremental amounts representing change from the prevailing program. These can be considered more validly to represent the additional direct costs and real impact produced by implementing these treatments on top of the normal reporting requirements.

The summary indicator, then, is the additional or marginal cost

Table 11.6. Cost-effectiveness comparison of antirecidivism programs for released prisoners

Comparison criteria	Treatment			
	Job placement	Psychological services	Combination of these	Normal program
Experimental population	10,000	10,000	10,000	10,000
Five-year rate of recidivism	0.15 (2)[a]	0.26 (3)	0.12 (1)	0.37 (4)
Number of persons not recidivous	8,500 (2)	7,400 (3)	8,800 (1)	6,300 (4)
Total cost	$10,000,000	$9,000,000	$16,000,000	$5,000,000
Average cost per subject	$1,000 (3)	$ 900 (2)	$ 1,600 (4)	$ 500 (1)
Average cost per nonrecidivous subject	$1,176 (2)	$1,216 (3)	$1,818 (4)	$ 794 (1)
Number of persons not recidivous in comparison with normal program	2,200 (2)	1,100 (3)	2,500 (1)	
Additional cost beyond normal program	$ 5,000,000 (2)	$4,000,000 (1)	$11,000,000 (3)	
Marginal cost per additional non-recidivous subject	$2,273 (1)	$3,636 (2)	$4,400 (3)	

From Levin, 1975, p. 96.
[a] Numbers in parentheses show program rankings on various criteria.

per additional nonrecidivous participant for each of the three strategies. Based on this criterion, the job placement treatment is the most productive although the combined treatment produced slightly greater impact overall (2,500 additional nonrecidivists compared with 2,200 for job placement only). This is as far as the cost-effectiveness approach can take us. There is no attempt here to compare total benefits and costs. The value judgment as to whether one additional nonrecidivist is worth \$2,273 (job placement) or whether it might even be worth \$4,400 per nonrecidivist for a further gain of 300 additional nonrecidivists (combined program) would have to be determined on other grounds.

APPLICABILITY OF ECONOMIC ANALYSIS

Economic analysis of alternative public programs and strategies is essential for rational decision making in governmental agencies. Given real constraints on resources, administrators must know not only which programs and strategies produce the desired results, but also the relative costs and productivities of each. Although many of the requirements of the formal benefit-cost model cannot be met in many instances, the method nevertheless is valuable because it serves to identify the most important quantitative relationships as well as focus attention on the major contingencies. Benefit-cost is basically a tool of systems analysis, the application of economic measurement and criteria to comprehensively defined problems. Use of economic analysis methods to lower level problems, or partial analyses, often yields more precise and operational kinds of information, and although the questions addressed are more modest, this is frequently more responsive to the needs of the managers of ongoing programs.

There is little doubt that in general the theory of benefit-cost analysis is far ahead of practice, as might be expected. In part this is because the theory as yet has not been able to provide clear indications of appropriate procedures, in relation to discount rates for instance, but it may also be a function of the difficulty of operationalizing elaborate and costly procedures in actual field applications. Ways of dealing with uncertainties and measurement problems are being explored and refined, but often in practice the applications are grossly simplified and sometimes ignore critical problems. Many applications arbitrarily exclude important secondary or intangible factors from consideration and compute the values of costs and benefits based on rule of thumb type approximations and expected values that are potentially misleading. Still, even these applications often serve to size and structure the problem; the important point is not to rely too heavily on their findings or confide too much in their validity.

It has been observed that benefit-cost applications have a tendency to overestimate the benefit-cost ratios and net present values of programs or projects, sometimes drastically (Maass, 1966, pp. 211–212). This can result from any number of procedural errors such as the double counting of benefits through inclusion of pecuniary benefits without the corresponding costs, omission of important negative externalities, and the overvaluation of direct benefits. This last category is crucial, because the objective is to place dollar values on benefits as the beneficiaries would do. When a state highway department's benefit-cost calculations show, for example, that a multitude of new construction projects around the state are economically justified, primarily on the grounds of the value of savings to motorists, and at the same time the electorate (which is quite similar to the group of motorists) overwhelmingly rejects a proposal to increase user taxes in order to finance these projects, it is an indication that the valuation of these benefits is way out of line with user preferences. Motorists may desire that new roads be built but yet value these roads lightly relative to alternative uses of resources. A more disturbing explanation of the chronic overestimation of net benefits is the observation that benefit-cost analysis has often been used as a means of predetermined project justification instead of an objective evaluation of alternatives (Marglin, 1967, p. 18).

Benefit-cost analysis is most applicable to relatively narrow problems of choice in which the alternatives are similar and 'the objective function clear. (McKean, 1968, p. 144). Thus its greatest contributions have been evaluating alternative projects in such fields as water resources and transportation. Clearly, benefit-cost applications are more precise in the comparison of alternatives that are expected to generate the same kinds and magnitudes of externalities, particularly when those externalities are not great in relation to other project impacts. In addition, problems of dealing with uncertainties and sensitivity to discount rate approaches are less severe in conjunction with projects of shorter duration.

Benefit-cost analysis is usually applied at a level far below its global context; it is applied to intraprogram choices rather than interprogram choices (Steiner, 1974, pp. 300–319). It is not used to compare investment in food stamps as opposed to school construction, for example, but it might be used to determine where schools should be built. At any level public investment is characterized by interdependencies and incompatibilities among alternatives, so that structuring the choice set is critical. Especially in the allocation of fixed budget amounts, where the opportunity costs are the benefits that would be derived from investing in competing projects rather than in the private sector, failure to delineate the alternatives in a complete manner will negate the value of the analysis. In such situations, where essentially a decision has been made to undertake a program or series of projects and benefit-cost analysis is used to compare alternative versions or packages of projects, benefit-cost is merged with cost-effectiveness, leading to suboptimization within the specified program and budget constraints.

At this level, economic analysis, whether in the guise of benefit-cost or cost-effectiveness, is of great operational relevance to program administrators and decision makers. Often their decisions are characterized by sufficiently narrow ranges of options, shorter time spans, fewer uncertainties, and more adequate information bases, so that the analysis provides more specific and usable information than that yielded by macro level benefit-cost applications. Although program analysis in general comprehends many different criteria and techniques to address program performance, economic analysis is an essential part of it because public agencies are at least as sensitive to cost considerations in their decision making as to perceived effectiveness.

REFERENCES

Adler, H. 1971. Economic Appraisal of Transport Projects. Bloomington: Indiana University Press.

Barsby, S. L. 1972. Cost-Benefit Analysis and Manpower Programs. Lexington, Mass.: D.C. Heath.

Baumol, W. J. 1969. On the Discount Rate for Public Project. Joint Economic Committee, The Analysis and Evaluation of Public Expenditures. 91st Congress, 1st Session, Vol. 1, pp. 489–503.

Besen, S. M., A. E. Fechter, and A. C. Fisher. 1967. Cost-Effectiveness for the 'War on Poverty.' In: T. A. Goldman (ed.), Cost Effectiveness Analysis, pp. 140–154. New York: Frederick A. Praeger, Inc.

Burkhead, J., and J. Miner. 1971. Public Expenditures. Chicago: Aldine-Atherton, Inc.

Clawson, M. 1959. Methods of Measuring the Demand and Values of Outdoor Recreation. Reprint No. 10. Washington, D.C.: Resources for the Future.

Clawson, M., and J. L. Knetsch. 1966. Economics of Outdoor Recreation. Baltimore: Johns Hopkins Press.

Comptroller General of the United States. 1975. Annual Report, 1974. Washington, D.C.: U.S. Government Printing Office.

Congressional Budget Office. 1976. Alton Locks and Dam: A Review of the Evidence. Staff working paper. Washington, D.C.: U.S. Government Printing Office.

Dorfman, R. (ed.). 1965. Measuring Benefits of Government Investments. Washington, D.C.: Brookings Institution.

Eckstein, O. 1958. Water Resource Development. Cambridge: Harvard University Press.

Fisher, G. H. 1972. The Role of Cost Utility Analysis in Program Budgeting. In: F. J. Lyden and E. G. Miller (eds.), Planning—Programming—Budgeting: A Systems Approach to Management, pp. 265–281. Chicago: Markham Publishing Company.

Foster, C. D., and M. E. Beesely. 1963. Estimating the Social Benefit of Constructing an Underground Railway in London. Journal of the Royal Statistical Society Vol. 126, part 1, pp. 46–78.

Goldman, T. A. (ed.). 1967. Cost-Effectiveness Analysis. New York: Frederick A. Praeger, Inc.

Harrison, A. J., and D. A. Quarmby. 1972. The Value of Time. In: R. Layard (ed.), Cost-Benefit Analysis, pp. 173–208. Harmondsworth, England: Penguin Education.

Hatry, H. P., R. E. Winnie, and D. M. Fisk. 1973. Practical Program Evaluation for State and Local Governments. Washington, D.C.: Urban Institute.

Hill, M. 1968. A Goals-Achievement Matrix for Evaluating Alternative Plans. Journal of the American Institute of Planners, Vol. 34 (January), pp. 19–29.

Hinrichs, H. H., and G. M. Taylor (eds.). 1969. Program Budgeting and Benefit-Cost Analysis: Cases, Texts and Readings. Pacific Palisades, Cal.: Goodyear Publishing Co., Inc.

Hirschleifer, J., J. C. DeHaven, and J. W. Milliman. 1960. Water Supply: Economics, Technology, and Policy. Chicago: University of Chicago Press.

Johnson, R. W., and J. M. Pierce. 1975. The Economic Evaluation of Policy Impacts: Cost Benefit and Cost Effectiveness Analysis. In: F. P. Scioli and T. J. Cook (eds.), Methdologies for Analyzing Public Policies, Chapter 13. Lexington, Mass.: D.C. Heath & Company.

Kaufman, J. J., T. W. Hu, M. L. Lee, and E. W. Stromsdorfer. 1969. A Cost-Effectiveness Study of Vocational Education: A Comparison of Vocational and Nonvocational Education in Secondary Schools. A report for the Institute for Research on Human Resources. University Park: The Pennsylvania State University.

Krutilla, J. V., and O. Eckstein. 1958. Multiple Purpose River Development. Baltimore: Johns Hopkins Press.

Kuhn, T. E. 1962. Public Enterprise Economics and Transport Problems. Berkeley: University of California Press.

Layard, R. (ed.). 1972. Cost-Benefit Analysis. Harmondsworth, England: Penguin Education.

Lee, R. D., Jr., and R. W. Johnson. 1977. Public Budgeting Systems. 2nd Ed. Baltimore: University Park Press.

Levin, H. M. 1975. Handbook of Evaluation Research. Beverly Hills: Sage Publications, Inc.

Lichfield, N. 1960. Cost-Benefit Analysis in City Planning. Journal of The American Institute of Planners, Vol. 26 (November), pp. 273–279.

Lyden, F. J., and E. G. Miller (eds.). 1972. Planning-Programming-Budgeting: A Systems Approach to Management. Chicago: Markham Publishing Company.

Maass, A. 1966. Benefit-Cost Analysis: Its Relevance to Public Investment Decisions. Quarterly Journal of Economics, Vol. 80 (May), pp. 208–226.

McKean, R. N. 1958. Efficiency in Government Through Systems Analysis. New York: John Wiley & Sons, Inc.

McKean, R. N. 1968. Public Spending. New York: McGraw-Hill Book Company.

McKean, R. N. 1972. The Use of Shadow Prices. In: R. Layard (ed.), Cost-Benefit Analysis, pp. 119–139. Harmondsworth, England: Penguin Education.

Mansfield, N. W. 1972. The Value of Recreational Facilities. In: R. Layard (ed.), Cost Benefit Analysis, pp. 209–218. Harmondsworth, England: Penguin Education.

Marglin, S. A. 1963. The Social Rate of Discount and the Optimal Rate of Investment. Quarterly Journal of Economics, Vol. 77 (February), pp. 95–111.

Marglin, S. A. 1967. Public Investment Criteria: Benefit-Cost Analysis for Planned Economic Growth. Cambridge: M.I.T. Press.

Meyer, J. R., J. F. Kain, and M. Wohl. 1966. The Urban Transportation Problem. Cambridge: Harvard University Press.

Mishan, E. J. 1967. Criteria for Public Investment: Some Simplifying Suggestions. Journal of Political Economy (April), pp. 139–146.

Mishan, E. J. 1973. Economics for Social Decisions: Elements of Cost-Benefit Analysis. New York: Frederick A. Praeger, Inc.

Mishan, E. J. 1975. Cost-Benefit Analysis: An Informal Introduction, 2nd Ed. London: Allen & Unwin, Ltd.

Mishan, E. J. 1976. Cost-Benefit Analysis. New York: Frederick A. Praeger, Inc.

Mohring, H., and M. Harwitz. 1962. Highway Benefits: An Analytical Framework. Evanston, Ill.: Northwestern University Press.

Musgrave, R. A., and P. B. Musgrave. 1976. Public Finance in Theory and Practice, 2nd Ed. New York: McGraw-Hill Book Company.

Niskanen, W. A. 1967. Measures of Effectiveness. In: T. A. Goldman (ed.), Cost-Effectiveness Analysis, pp. 17–32. New York: Frederick A. Praeger, Inc.

Perry, C. R., B. E. Anderson, R. L. Rowan, H. R. Northrup, P. P. Amons, S. A. Schneider, M. E. Sparrough, H. Goldberg, L. Matlock, and C. A. McGuinness. 1975. The Impact of Government Manpower Programs. Philadelphia: The Wharton School Industrial Research Unit.

Poister, T. H., T. D. Larson, and S. Rao. 1978. Fiscal Planning and Highway Programming: The Pennsylvania Response to a Changing Environment. Transportation Research Record.

Prest, A. R., and R. Turvey. 1975. Cost-Benefit Analysis: A Survey. Economic Journal (December), pp. 683–735.

Ribich, T. 1968. Education and Poverty. Washington, D.C.: Brookings Institution.

Schultz, T. W. 1964. The Economic Value of Education. New York: Columbia University Press.

Scioli, F. P., and T. J. Cook (eds.). 1975. Methodologies for Analyzing Public Policies. Lexington, Mass.: D.C. Heath & Company.

Steiner, P. O. 1974. Public Expenditure Budgeting. In: Economics of Public Finance, pp. 241–357. Washington, D.C.: Brookings Institution.

Vedder, J. 1970. Planning Problems with Multidimensional Consequences. Journal of the American Institute of Planners, Vol. 36 (March), pp. 112–119.

Water Resources Council. 1973. Water and Related Land Resources: Establishment of Principles and Standards for Planning. Federal Register, Vol. 38, no. 174, part 3 (September 10).

Weiner, P., and E. J. Deak. 1972. Environmental Factors in Transportation Planning. Lexington, Mass.: D.C. Heath & Company.

BIVARIATE
AND MULTIVARIATE
STATISTICS

12

CONTINGENCY ANALYSIS AND RANK-ORDER CORRELATION

Much of chapter 5 was concerned with the display and descriptive interpretation of statistical associations between two or more category type variables using crosstabulations. The present chapter builds on that discussion in terms of analyzing the strength and statistical significance of such associations. **Contingency analysis** is the term used to refer to the analysis of crosstabulations of nominal scales or ordinal scales. There are also techniques for analyzing associations among strictly ordinal measures, generally referred to as methods of **rank-order correlation.** This chapter first looks at significance tests for nominal level associations, proceeds to various measures of the strength of such associations, and then moves to a discussion of rank-order correlation techniques.

CHI SQUARE SIGNIFICANCE TESTS

Chi square is a bivariate inferential statistical technique used to test hypotheses concerning associations between two nominal variables. Ordinal measures and even collapsed interval measures are often incorporated in crosstabulations to which chi square is applied, but the conclusions drawn from such tests relate only to the nominal properties of the variables being examined.

Chi square, or χ^2, is actually a statistic whose sampling distribution is known, depending on the number of categories the variables have, based on the assumption that the null hypothesis of no association is true. The procedure for applying the χ^2 test follows the underlying logic of inferential statistics developed in chapter 7; we compute the value of χ^2 for our (random) sample and compare it with the known sampling distribution to determine the probability of drawing the sample if the null hypothesis is true.

Observed and Expected Frequencies

The value of χ^2 is based on the extent to which the observed frequencies in a crosstabulation between two nominal variables deviate from the joint frequencies that would be expected if there were no association between the two variables. These **expected frequencies** would be such that the relative frequency distribution (or proportional breakdown) of the dependent variable would be the same for every category of the independent variable.

It will be recalled from chapter 5 that the best way to examine associations between two nominal variables is to crosstabulate them with the dependent variable in the rows and convert the frequencies into vertical proportions. If the proportions differ from column to column, conditional frequencies are different from marginal frequencies, and the two variables are statistically associated; the distribution of the dependent variable is **contingent** to some degree on the category of the independent variable. The greater the deviation of conditional frequencies from marginal frequencies, the stronger the association. On the other hand, if the relative frequencies are identical from column to column, conditional frequencies equal marginal frequencies and there is a complete lack of association between the two variables. This is the kind

Table 12.1.   Housing inspection preference by whether respondents felt repairs were needed

Housing inspection preference	Repair service		Totals
	Repairs needed	Repairs not needed	
A. Observed frequencies			
Would like it inspected	63 (47.0%)	32 (29.9%)	95 (39.4%)
Neutral	36 (26.9%)	44 (41.1%)	80 (33.2%)
Would not like it inspected	35 (26.1%)	31 (29.0%)	66 (27.4%)
Totals	134 (100.0%)	107 (100.0%)	241 (100.0%)
B. Expected frequencies			
Would like it inspected	52.8 (39.4%)	42.2 (39.4%)	95 (39.4%)
Neutral	44.5 (33.2%)	35.5 (33.2%)	80 (33.2%)
Would not like it inspected	36.7 (27.4%)	29.3 (27.4%)	66 (27.4%)
Totals	134 (100.0%)	107 (100.0%)	241 (100.0%)

of joint distribution that the null hypothesis postulates for the population as a whole.

Table 12.1*A* shows the crosstabulation of responses to two items in a community sample survey, preference for housing inspection by whether or not repairs on the property are needed. The proportions show a modest association between the two in which respondents who indicate that their property is in need of repair have a greater tendency to say that they would like the property inspected, while respondents indicating that their property is not in need of repair are more likely to be neutral about housing inspection and have a slightly greater tendency to say that they would not like the property to be inspected.

Table 12.1*B* shows the expected frequencies for the same cross-tabulation based on the assumption of no association. They are developed by applying the marginal proportions (0.394, 0.332, and 0.274) to the total number of cases in each category of the independent variable (134 cases for "repairs needed" and 107 for "repairs not needed"). As a check, expected frequencies should sum to observed marginal totals. Note that the crosstabulation shown in *B* is not the only joint distribution that would satisfy the null hypothesis, because any distribution of the two variables in which conditional probabilities equal marginal probabilities would do so. In fact, *B* is not even a realistic expectation of an expected sample distribution, inasmuch as any sample would have whole numbers of cases, and no fractions, in each category jointly classified by the two variables. Nevertheless, the relative frequencies in the margins of both variables provide unbiased point estimates of their corresponding parameters, and the expected frequencies in *B*, based on these marginal frequencies, provide the best estimate in a hypothetical sense of what the sample would look like if it were totally representative of the population as hypothesized by the null hypothesis.

Applying the Test

The formula for computing chi square is:

$$\chi^2 = \Sigma \frac{(f_o - f_e)^2}{f_e}$$

or the sum of the squared differences between the observed and expected frequency of each cell divided by their corresponding expected frequencies. An alternative formula for computing chi square, which some find more convenient, is:

$$\chi^2 = \Sigma \frac{f_o^2}{f_e} - N$$

As the deviations between observed and expected frequencies increase, the value of χ^2 will also increase.

With random sampling from a population in which two variables are completely unassociated, the sampling distribution of χ^2 will be generally skewed to the right, indicating that higher values of χ^2 will result by chance with decreasing probabilities, with extremely high values occurring very rarely by chance. Like the t distribution discussed in chapter 7, χ^2 really refers to a family of curves that correspond to different numbers of degrees of freedom. In this case, however, rather than relating to sample size, degrees of freedom are given by the numbers of categories in the two variables by the formula

$$df = (r - 1)(c - 1)$$

in which r represents the number of rows and c the number of columns in the crosstabulation. Table A-7 in the appendix shows the χ^2 distributions corresponding to 1 through 30 degrees of freedom.

Figure 12.1 shows the application of the χ^2 test to the problem presented above. The test is based on the assumptions of 1) random sampling, and 2) the null hypothesis that in the population expected frequencies equal observed frequencies. Testing at the 0.05 level with 2 degrees of freedom, the critical value of χ^2 is 5.991; a computed χ^2 of that size or greater would occur by chance with a probability of 0.05 or less, given the assumptions stated above. The computed χ^2 of 8.28 does fall in the critical region, and thus we reject the null hypothesis and conclude that the association is significant for the population as a whole.

Interpretation and Comments

Although the critical region lies only in the right-hand tail of the sampling distribution, the χ^2 test is actually a two-tailed test in terms of being insensitive to the direction of association between the two variables. Formally, the alternate hypothesis states only that observed frequencies are not equal to expected frequencies. In the example above we concluded that the two variables are significantly associated, with the implication that the nature of the association in the population would reflect that observed in the sample. Yet this is not necessarily the case; in the population there might well be a reversal in the "would not like it inspected" response such that respondents indicating that repairs were necessary were more likely to give this response than were those who said repairs were not needed.

H_0: $F_o = F_e$

H_1: $F_o \neq F_e$

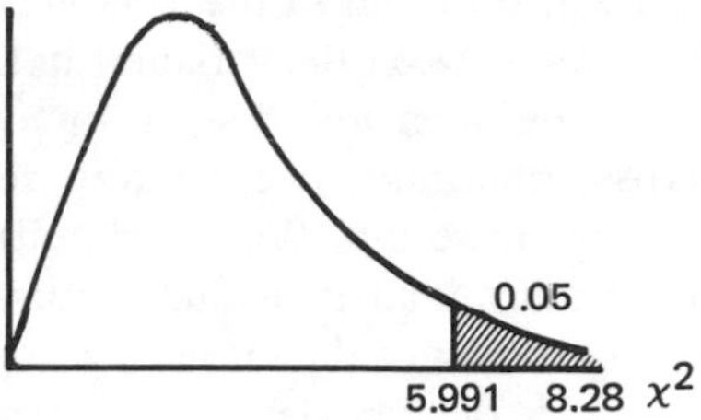

$$\chi^2 = (f_o - f_e)^2/f_e$$

0.05

5.991   8.28 χ^2

f_o	f_e	$(f_o - f_e)$	$(f_o - f_e)^2$	$(f_o - f_e)^2/f_e$
63	52.8	10.2	104.04	1.97
36	44.5	−8.5	72.25	1.62
35	36.7	−1.7	2.89	0.08
32	42.2	−10.2	104.04	2.47
44	35.5	8.5	72.25	2.04
31	29.3	1.7	2.89	0.10
241	241.0	0.0		$\Sigma = 8.28$

$$df \quad = (r - 1)\,(c - 1)$$

$$= (3 - 1)\,(2 - 1)$$

$$= (2)\,(1)$$

$$df \quad = 2$$

at 0.05 level with 2 degrees of freedom critical $\chi^2 = 5.991$

Conclusion: Reject H_0

Figure 12.1. Computation for chi square test of significance.

With respect to the association between the independent variable and whether respondents would like their property inspected as opposed to being neutral (the obvious part of the overall association), we are safe in concluding that this represents the direction of the association in the general population. If, in the population, this association were reversed—with those indicating that repairs were *not* needed being *more* likely to want their property inspected—the observed sample would have an even lower probability of occurring by chance than it would given the null hypothesis. With crosstabs involving variables with many categories, a significant χ^2 should not be taken to mean that all categories are involved in the association. In general, the only fair interpretation is that there is some significant association in the population and that the joint distribution in the sample provides the best estimate of the contingencies between the variables in the population.

The interpretation is the most straightforward with two-by-two crosstabulations, because any degree of association must be in one of two opposite directions, e.g., either the female employees of an agency tend more than their male counterparts to fall into a given civil service classification or the males have a greater tendency to fit that classification than do the females. Thus, if a significant association is observed in a sample it is safe to conclude that the association in the population is in the same direction.

However, it should also be noted that with a two-by-two crosstabulation, a significant χ^2 can be produced by equally strong associations in the opposite direction. If, in fact, the alternate hypothesis is simply that there is some association, without specifying a direction, the null should be rejected if a strong association in either direction emerges in the sample by chance. On the other hand, if the alternative hypothesis would specify a direction of association, and the sample data reflect this direction, only one-half of those samples that could produce a χ^2 of a certain magnitude are relevant; the other half logically could not lead to rejecting the null and accepting the alternate. Thus, when the alternate hypothesis specifies a direction of association, the real probability of a type I error is *one-half* the significance level obtained using the table. Rejecting the null hypothesis with a χ^2 significant at the 0.10 level according to the table, for example, only incurs a 0.05 probability of a type I error.

Chi Square and Sample Size   It should also be pointed out that the χ^2 test requires fairly large samples in order for sample chi squares to follow the sampling distribution given in Table A-7. The required sample size depends on the marginal frequencies of the two variables, but a conventional rule of thumb states that all *expected* frequencies should be 5 or greater in order to use χ^2 as illustrated above. With expected frequencies of less than 5, χ^2 should be employed only as adjusted with **corrections for continuity**, but in practice this is rarely done for greater than two-by-two crosstabs and is not presented in this text. Also for two-by-two crosstabs with small N's, a more precise method is available, termed **Fisher's Exact Test**, which also will not be discussed in this book (Blalock, 1972, pp. 285–291).

One common strategy when expected cell frequencies of less than 5 are encountered with greater than two-by-two crosstabs is to consider collapsing one or both of the nominal scales into fewer categories with more cases in each. Obviously, this reduces the refinement of the scales and should be done only when the combined categories make intuitive sense, i.e., when the collapsed categories still provide meaningful differentiation among cases. Second, collapsing the categories increases the likelihood of distortion in the measure of association due to grouping error (Loether and McTavish, 1976, pp. 202–204).

A second point regarding chi square and sample size is that the test does not take sample size into account directly, either in computing χ^2 or determining the critical region. Thus, chi square tests are not scaled to sample size as are t tests and other inferential statistics, and as a result very weak associations can produce "significant" chi squares with large samples. In the example above, for instance, χ^2 was significant at the 0.05 level, but it would not have been significant at the 0.01 level. However, if all the frequencies are doubled, as shown in Table 12.2, the strength of association is unchanged, but χ^2 increases from 8.28 to 16.56 and is now significant at the *0.001 level.*

The result is that conclusions about associations often are most meaningful when χ^2 proves to be significant with relatively small samples. On the other hand, in research contexts in which sensitivity to weak, but real, differential effects is of concern—in determining whether apparently modest results are due to a program as opposed to chance effect for example—this feature of χ^2 may be appropriate.

STRENGTH OF NOMINAL ASSOCIATIONS

There are a number of statistics available for measuring the strength of association between nominal measures, some based on chi square and others completely apart from chi square. In general, these measures are useful, especially for comparing the relative strength of different associations, although their interpretation is not as clear as might be desired.

Table 12.2.   Chi square with double sample size[a]

Housing inspection preference	Repairs needed	Repairs not needed	Totals
Would like it inspected	126 (47.0%)	64 (29.9%)	190 (39.4%)
Neutral	72 (26.9%)	88 (41.1%)	160 (33.2%)
Would not like it inspected	70 (26.1%)	62 (29.0%)	132 (27.4%)
Totals	268 (100.0%)	214 (100.0%)	482 (100.0%)

[a] Crosstab from Figure 12.1 with cell frequencies doubled.

Chi Square Based Measures

Although chi square does vary with the strength of association, as seen above it does not provide a consistent measure of association because it also varies directly with sample size. Because χ^2 increases proportionally to sample size, it makes sense to scale it down by dividing by N, producing the measure known as phi squared. Actually, the measure that is usually reported is **phi**, computed as

$$\phi = \sqrt{\chi^2/N}$$

Phi is a **normed** measure of association, one that takes on a given value to represent a given strength of association regardless of sample size, which is appropriate for two-by-two or two-by-K crosstabs. Continuing our sample problem shown in Table 12.1:

$$\phi^2 = \chi^2/N$$
$$= 8.28/241$$
$$= 0.0343$$
$$\phi = \sqrt{0.0343}$$
$$= 0.1854$$

As a confirmation of the consistency of this measure, consider the crosstab shown in Table 12.2, in which the sample size has doubled while the strength of association remains the same:

$$\phi = \sqrt{\chi^2/N}$$
$$= \sqrt{16.56/482}$$
$$= 0.1854$$

For any two-by-K crosstabulation, ϕ ranges from 0 to 1, with 1 indicating a perfect association and 0 indicating a complete lack of association. Obviously, ϕ's close to 0 indicate very weak relationships and ϕ's near 1 represent very strong ones, but in between there are no standard guidelines for interpreting the magnitude of ϕ.

For crosstabulations with more than two columns and two rows, the upper limit of ϕ is greater than unity; thus its use is usually limited to two-by-K crosstabs.

Cramer's V   A more generally applicable measure of association is Cramer's V, given by the formula

$$V = \sqrt{\frac{\chi^2}{N \cdot \min\,(r - 1)\,(c - 1)}}$$

in which the denominator is sample size times whichever is smaller (minimum), the number of rows minus 1 or the number of columns minus 1. For our sample problem

$$V = \sqrt{\frac{8.28}{241 \, (2 - 1)}}$$
$$= 0.1854$$

In this case Cramer's V equals ϕ, as it will for any two-by-K crosstabulation. The advantage of Cramer's V is that it ranges from 0 to 1 for any size crosstabulation, whether or not the numbers of columns and rows are equal.

As mentioned above, the interpretation of these measures is vague and highly judgmental and a review of several studies using them is likely to reveal a Cramer's V of 0.27, for example, described as indicating a modest association in one study and a strong association in another. Phi and Cramer's V rarely turn out to be 0.80 or greater, and although there is no general consensus as to what constitutes a strong or weak association, the following is offered as a guideline for interpreting values of these two statistics:

0–0.0999	negligible association
0.10–0.1999	weak association
0.20–0.3999	moderate association
0.40–0.5999	fairly strong association
0.60–0.9999	very strong association

Proportional Reduction in Error

As pointed out in chapter 5, one interpretation of a statistical relationship is in terms of the ability to predict values of the dependent variable taken on by cases on the basis of knowing their values on the independent variable. Some measures of the strength of association for normal crosstabulations are based on this interpretation and are known as indicators of proportional reduction in error. These **PRE measures** involve computing the difference in error of prediction based on knowing the aggregate distribution of the dependent variable only (original error) and that based on knowing, in addition, the dependent variable distribution for each category of the independent variable (new error) and then computing this difference (reduction in error) as a proportion of original error. Thus, the general formula is

$$PRE = \frac{\text{original error} - \text{new error}}{\text{original error}}$$

Lambda The critical factor in operationalizing the PRE concept relates to how the predictions are to be made with or without knowledge of the independent variable. The objective should be to minimize errors made in predicting the value of the dependent variable taken on by each case. With one such measure, **lambda** (λ), the prediction is based on assigning all cases to the modal category; the number of errors will be the number of cases that do not belong in that category.

Referring back to Table 12.1A, knowing the marginal frequency distribution only, we would predict the modal category "would like it inspected" and be correct for 95 cases. The number of errors—original error—would be $(80 + 66)$ or 146 errors. Now suppose that we know the frequency distribution for the "repairs needed" column and are given those 134 cases and told to predict the value of the dependent variable for each case. Again, we would predict the modal category for all cases, and here it would also be "would like it inspected." Here the number of new errors would be $(36 + 35)$ or 71. For the other part of the sample in the "repairs not needed" column, however, the modal category of the dependent variable is "neutral." Using this as the basis of prediction will produce $(32 + 31)$ or 63 new errors. Thus, the total new error

$$\lambda = \frac{\text{original error} - \text{new error}}{\text{original error}}$$

$$= \frac{146 - 134}{146}$$

$$= 0.0822$$

is $(71 + 63)$ or 134, indicating an 8.2 percent reduction in error of predicting values of the dependent variable with this method.

Although λ is an easy measure to compute, it is really only suitable for crosstabulations in which there are "reversals" in the joint distribution, when the modal category of the dependent variable is not the same for all categories of the independent variable. Without such reversals there will be no reduction in error using this particular method of prediction, even though the association is quite strong. For example, given a joint distribution as follows:

	A	B	Total
C	45	55	100
D	55	45	100
Total	100	100	200

λ will be 0.10, indicating some degree of association. However, with the joint distribution,

	A	B	Total
C	90	55	145
D	10	45	55
Total	100	100	200

a much stronger association, λ will be 0. In general, with greater than two-by-two crosstabs, λ is a somewhat crude measure in that it is keyed solely to modal category reversals and is insensitive to differences in distributions across other categories.

Goodman and Kruskal's Tau$_y$ Tau$_y$ (τ_y) is another PRE measure, based on a different procedure for predicting values of the dependent variable. According to this prediction rule, cases are *randomly* assigned to all categories of the dependent variable such that the overall distribution equals the known distribution, and then probabilities are used to compute the number of *expected errors*. Referring back to our sample problem in Table 12.1, to compute original error we would *randomly* assign the 241 cases to the three categories of the dependent variable with the distribution 95, 80, and 66, respectively. Given a random assignment, the expected number of errors out of the total number of cases assigned to each category would be given by the probability that a case does *not* belong in that category.

For example, the probability that any individual case belongs in the "would like it inspected" category is 0.394 while the probability that any given case does *not* fit in that category is $1 - 0.394$, or $0.332 + 0.274$ (the sum of the probabilities that the case belongs in other categories). Computing the probabilities of error for each assigned category, applying them to their respective assigned frequencies, and summing these expected errors over the categories, we obtain

Original error $= 95 (0.606) + 80 (0.668) + 66 (0.726)$

$57.57 + 53.44 + 47.92$

$= 158.93$

as our estimate of expected errors in predicting values of the dependent variable for each case not knowing the values of the independent variable.

Similarly, we can apply the same procedure to each category of the independent variable and sum these expected errors across the categories to obtain the expected *new* error. Thus,

$$\text{new error} = 63\,(0.53) + 36\,(0.731) + 35\,(0.739)$$
$$+ 32\,(0.701) + 44\,(0.589) + 31\,(0.71)$$
$$= 155.94$$

Goodman and Kruskal's τ_y, then, can be computed as

$$\tau_y = \frac{\text{original error} - \text{new error}}{\text{original error}}$$
$$= \frac{158.93 - 155.94}{158.93}$$
$$= 0.0188$$

As suggested in this example, τ_y will usually be less than λ, if there are reversals in the joint distribution, but τ_y has the advantage of being sensitive to associations in which there are no reversals. Although τ_y can range from 0 to 1, an extremely strong association is required to obtain a value greater than 0.50. A given association will almost always produce a higher value of Cramer's V than τ_y; thus, values of τ_y should be interpreted more "generously" than indicated by the guidelines for Cramer's V presented earlier.

The two PRE measures discussed differ from the chi square based measures presented earlier in another respect. Phi and Cramer's V (as well as χ^2 itself) are both **symmetrical** measures, meaning that they are insensitive to the presumed direction of influence from an independent to a dependent variable. That is, if the two variables in Table 12.1 were interchanged so that the "repairs needed" variable were in the rows with the "inspection preference" variable in the columns, χ^2, ϕ and Cramer's V would turn out the same. With λ and τ_y, however, this will usually *not* be the case, as they are **asymmetrical** measures that relate to the error in predicting a designated dependent variable on the basis of the other, independent variable.

In general, the measures presented above should provide adequate alternatives for assessing the strength of nominal level associations. Others are available such as Tschuprow's T, Pearson's Contingency Coefficient and Yule's Q, but for the most part they share the same problems of interpretation (Blalock, 1972, chapter 15).

ELABORATING NOMINAL LEVEL ASSOCIATIONS

As discussed in chapter 5, the analysis of statistical relationships often moves into the elaboration of bivariate associations in order to see how an initial bivariate association holds up when statistical controls are taken into account and to examine the pattern of associations among larger systems of variables. With crosstabulated data the elaboration process essentially boils down to breaking the sample down by categories of the control variable(s) and comparing the bivariate associations among these subsamples or conditional tables. While chapter 5 discusses the elaboration process in some detail on a purely descriptive basis, chi square and the measures of association presented above can be applied throughout the elaboration of nominal level associations, as outlined below.

Subsample Comparisons

Table 12.3 shows the same survey responses on needed repairs and housing inspection, broken down by whether the respondent is classified as a homeowner or renter. It is apparent that the association between housing inspection preference and repairs needed observed in the aggregate is *not* replicated for homeowners and renters. Rather, the association is fairly strong for the renter subsample and almost nonexistent for the homeowner subsample. As it turns out, χ^2 is highly significant for the renters and insignificant for the homeowners, as shown in Table 12.4. With these three variables the analysis might well be terminated at this point, concluding that housing inspection preference and property repairs needed are significantly associated among renters but not at all among homeowners.

Tests for Interaction

Whenever a bivariate association between two nominal level variables is not replicated in all categories of a control variable, there is some pattern of interaction, as discussed in chapter 5. Thus, another way of stating the interpretation of the example above is that there is an interaction "effect" of property repairs needed and home ownership on housing inspection preference such that the association between repairs needed and housing inspection preference is strong for renters and nonexistent for homeowners.

Table 12.3. Housing inspection preference by housing tenure and by whether respondents felt repairs were needed

Housing inspection preference	Tenure type																	
	Homeowner						Renter						Totals					
	Repairs needed		Repairs not needed		Total		Repairs needed		Repairs not needed		Total		Repairs needed		Repairs not needed		Total	
	No.	%	No.	%	No.	%	No.	%	No.	%	No.	%	No.	%	No.	%	No.	%
Would like it inspected	20	24.7	19	25.7	39	25.2	43	81.1	13	39.4	56	65.1	63	47.0	32	29.9	95	39.4
Neutral	28	34.6	27	36.5	55	35.5	8	15.1	17	51.5	25	29.1	36	26.9	44	41.1	80	33.2
Would not like it inspected	33	40.7	28	37.8	61	39.4	2	3.8	3	9.1	5	5.8	35	26.1	31	29.0	66	27.4
Totals	81	100.0	74	100.0	155	100.1	53	100.0	33	100.0	86	100.0	134	100.0	107	100.0	241	100.0

Table 12.4. Associations between housing inspection preference and property repairs needed, controlling for home ownership

Cases	Cramer's V	χ^2	Significance level
Total sample	0.1854	8.28	0.05
Homeowners	0.0298	0.138	NS[a]
Renters	0.4278	15.74	0.001

[a]NS = not significant.

This is a fairly safe conclusion given the very pronounced differential effect in the direction expected between homeowners and renters in the example, but in analyses based on sample data there is always some possibility that an observed pattern of interaction in the sample is a result of chance effect in the sampling process. Inevitably there will be some differences among subsamples, and the question is whether they are statistically significant. If the analyst wishes to pursue this issue, a technique that is appropriate when the variables involved are all dichotomies is the difference of differences of proportions test mentioned in chapter 7.

The example shown in Table 12.5, based on data drawn from a random sample victimization survey, is a good case in point. In the aggregate, there is a strong association between victims who expressed satisfaction with police response time and their perception of how long the response time was, and the association is highly insignificant for the population (at the 0.01 level with 1 degree of freedom, the critical $\chi^2 = 6.635$). In general, the association holds for both white and nonwhite respondents, but it is much stronger for nonwhites.

The test of whether this difference in degree of association is statistically significant is shown in Figure 12.2. The null hypothesis is that the difference between those respondents with perceived response times of less than 10 minutes and greater than 10 minutes in terms of the proportion who were satisfied with response time is the same among nonwhites as it is among whites. In this example, the four sample proportions are used as estimates of their respective parameters, as opposed to the more conservative approach in which each population proportion, p_u, is set at 0.5. In this case the results indicate that if the null hypothesis is true, the observed difference in differences of proportions would occur by chance with random sampling with a probability of only 0.0038. Testing at the 0.01 level, we conclude that in the larger population the association between perceived response time and satisfaction with response time is stronger for nonwhites than for whites.

Table 12.5. Satisfaction with response time by estimated response time and race

Satisfaction with response time	Nonwhites minutes						Whites minutes						Total minutes					
	Less than 10	%	More than 10	%	Total	%	Less than 10	%	More than 10	%	Total	%	Less than 10	%	More than 10	%	Total	%
Satisfied	34	94.4	4	22.2	38	70.4	66	84.6	24	48	90	70.3	100	87.7	28	41.2	128	70.3
Dissatisfied	2	5.6	14	77.8	16	29.6	12	15.4	26	52	38	29.7	14	12.3	40	58.8	54	29.7
Total	36	100%	18	100%	54	100%	78	100%	50	100%	128	100%	114	100%	68	100%	182	100%

Nonwhites: $\chi^2 = 30.05$, $V = 0.7460$

Whites: $\chi^2 = 19.58$, $V = 0.3912$

Total: $\chi^2 = 44.20$, $V = 0.4928$

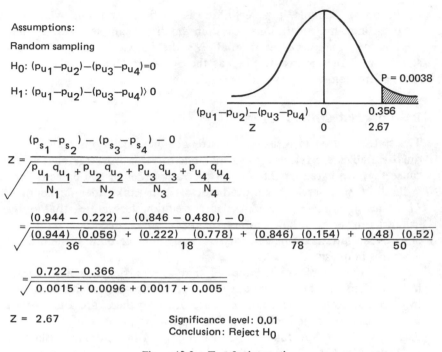

Assumptions:

Random sampling

H_0: $(p_{u_1}-p_{u_2})-(p_{u_3}-p_{u_4})=0$

H_1: $(p_{u_1}-p_{u_2})-(p_{u_3}-p_{u_4})\rangle\ 0$

$P = 0.0038$

$(p_{u_1}-p_{u_2})-(p_{u_3}-p_{u_4})$ 0   0.356

Z   0   2.67

$$Z = \frac{(p_{s_1}-p_{s_2}) - (p_{s_3}-p_{s_4}) - 0}{\sqrt{\dfrac{p_{u_1}q_{u_1}}{N_1} + \dfrac{p_{u_2}q_{u_2}}{N_2} + \dfrac{p_{u_3}q_{u_3}}{N_3} + \dfrac{p_{u_4}q_{u_4}}{N_4}}}$$

$$= \frac{(0.944 - 0.222) - (0.846 - 0.480) - 0}{\sqrt{\dfrac{(0.944)\ (0.056)}{36} + \dfrac{(0.222)\ (0.778)}{18} + \dfrac{(0.846)\ (0.154)}{78} + \dfrac{(0.48)\ (0.52)}{50}}}$$

$$= \frac{0.722 - 0.366}{\sqrt{0.0015 + 0.0096 + 0.0017 + 0.005}}$$

$Z = 2.67$ Significance level: 0.01
Conclusion: Reject H_0

Figure 12.2. Test for interaction.

Third Variable Controls

Apart from the issue of interaction, it may be desirable to ask whether two variables are significantly associated, controlling for a third variable. This can be addressed by conducting separate χ^2 tests within each category of the control variable, as with the above example, which indicated that estimated response time and satisfaction are significantly associated for both whites and nonwhites.

An alternative procedure is to compute separate chi squares for each subsample and then to sum both the chi squares and their corresponding degrees of freedom, applying a single test with these sums. In the above example, χ^2 would equal (30.05 + 19.58) or 49.63 and the total degrees of freedom would be 2. At the 0.01 level with 2 degrees of freedom the critical χ^2 equals 9.210, and therefore we conclude that the original bivariate association is significant, controlling for race.

This technique can be used with more than one control variable simultaneously and with variables having more than two categories; the degrees of freedom take this into account. Although not really necessary in the above example, this technique is particularly useful when statistical controlling operations result in small subsample sizes. It may well happen that because of small N's the individual subsample chi squares are not significant, whereas the overall test based on more degrees of freedom does prove to be significant.

RANK-ORDER CORRELATION

The statistics used to measure the strength of associations between ordinal variables are referred to as methods of **rank-order correlation** because they are based on the idea of the rank order of two cases on one ordinal measure serving as a predictor of their rank order on another. There are a number of rank-order correlation techniques that differ primarily in terms of how ties are treated; a **tie** occurs whenever a pair of cases fall into the same category or rank of one or both of the ordinal measures in question.

Although there are techniques that are particularly appropriate for situations in which there are few ties, if any—essentially when the two ordinal scales have as many categories as there are cases—they would seem to be of limited use in applied program analyses. These measures include Spearman's r_s and Kendall's Tau_a and Tau_b (Blalock, 1972, pp. 416–421). By contrast, the techniques presented here are more applicable when ties are the rule rather than the exception, when the data are conveniently displayed in crosstabulations because the variables have relatively few categories with numerous cases "grouped" in each category.

Two points should be kept in mind in considering the use of these measures. First, they are measures of the strength of *linear* association, the degree to which one variable tends either to increase or decrease as the other one increases from the lowest rank to the highest rank. Two ordinal measures could have a strong nonlinear association that would not be reflected by these measures. Second, these measures are often accorded a PRE interpretation, indicating the extent to which prediction of the rank order of cases with respect to values of one variable is improved by virtue of knowing the rank order of cases for values of the other variable (Loether and McTavish, 1976, p. 22).

Concordant and Discordant Pairs

In setting up a crosstabulation between two ordinal measures, two conventions that will facilitate computations of rank-order correlation measures are 1) placing the dependent variable in the rows, and 2) arranging the values of the variables in *descending order* from top row to bottom row and from right-hand column to left-hand column. This is illustrated in Table 12.6, showing the joint distribution of survey respondents' reported level of use of a particular public service and their general rating of that service. The crosstab exhibits some degree of negative association with service rating tending to increase as usage level decreases.

With 140 cases in the sample, there are a total of 9,730 pairs, i.e., $(140 \cdot 139)/2$. Each pair can be classified as one of the following types:

—Concordant pairs (C) with the same rank order on both variables. For example, a case in the "Good-Frequent" cell is ranked higher than one in the "Poor-No use" cell on both variables.
—Discordant pairs (D) with opposite rank orders on the two variables. For example, cases in the "Fair-Frequent" cell are ranked higher than those in the "Good-Infrequent" cell on the usage scale but lower on the service rating scale.
—Pairs tied on the *dependent* variable (T_y) but not on the independent variable. Cases in the "Fair-Infrequent" cell, for example, are tied with those in the "Fair-Frequent" cell on the service rating scale but not on the usage scale.
—Pairs tied on the *independent* variable (T_x) but not on the dependent variable. Cases in the "Fair-Infrequent" cell are tied with cases in the "Poor-Infrequent" cell on usage level but not on service rating.
—Pairs tied on both variables (T_{xy}), any two cases in the same cell of the crosstabulation.

For our purposes it is necessary only to compute the number of pairs of the first three types, but it is a good idea to do so for all five types and sum them as a check on arithmetic, because the five account for all possible pairs. The numbers of pairs of each type are shown in Table 12.7.

With the variables arranged as illustrated in Table 12.6, the num-

Table 12.6.   Service rating by usage level

| Service rating | Usage level | | | |
	No use	Infrequent	Frequent	Total
Good	28	19	8	55
Fair	21	22	10	53
Poor	11	9	12	32
Total	60	50	30	140

Table 12.7. Concordant, discordant, and tied pairs

Type	Number
Concordant (C)	1,554
Discordant (D)	2,607
Tied on Y (T_y)	2,139
Tied on X (T_x)	2,210
Tied on both (T_{xy})	1,220
Total	9,730

ber of concordant pairs is computed by summing the products of the frequency of each cell times the frequencies of any cells to the left and below. It is convenient to begin with the cell in the upper right-hand corner and move diagonally across the table. Thus,

$$C = 8 (22 + 21 + 9 + 11) +$$
$$10 (9 + 11) +$$
$$19 (21 + 11) +$$
$$22 (11)$$
$$= 504 + 200 + 608 + 242$$
$$= 1,554$$

The computation of discordant pairs moves in the other direction. Given the arrangement of Table 12.6, it is the sum of the products of the frequency of each cell times the frequencies of the cells to the right and below:

$$D = 19 (10 + 12) +$$
$$22 (12) +$$
$$28 (10 + 12 + 22 + 9) +$$
$$21 (9 + 12)$$
$$= 418 + 264 + 1484 + 441$$
$$= 2607$$

To compute the number of pairs that are tied on the dependent variable only, sum the products of each cell frequency times the other cells frequencies in the same row:

$$T_y = 8 (19 + 28) + 19 (28) +$$
$$10 (22 + 21) + 22 (21) +$$
$$12 (9 + 11) +$$
$$9 (11)$$
$$= 376 + 532 + 430 + 462 + 240 + 99$$
$$= 2139$$

Computations for the numbers of cases tied on the independent variable only and tied on both variables are not shown because they are not needed to compute the following measures of rank-order correlation.

Kendall's Tau$_c$

All the measures presented in this section are ratios of the difference between concordant and discordant pairs to some total number of predictions. The first of these measures, Tau$_c$ is computed as:

$$\text{Tau}_c = \frac{C - D}{1/2 \, N^2 \, [(m - 1)/m]}$$

where m denotes the minimum of rows or columns. In our sample problem, then,

$$\text{Tau}_c = \frac{1554 - 2607}{1/2 \, (140)^2 \, [(3 - 1)/3]}$$

$$= \frac{- 1053}{1/2 \, (19,600) \, (0.667)}$$

$$= \frac{- 1053}{6,536.6}$$

$$= -0.161$$

for any size crosstab, Tau$_c$ will range from -1 to $+1$ with 0 representing no association; a Tau$_c$ of -0.161 would represent a modest negative association.

Gamma

Tau$_c$ is sometimes criticized on the grounds of underrepresenting the strength of association between ordinal variables because it fails to discount the role of ties in the data. Excluding the ties from the denominator—not counting tied pairs as predictions to be made because they show no rank order—will result in a reduced base of the ratio and a corresponding increase in PRE. This is the logic underlying a second measure called **gamma**, computed as follows:

$$\gamma = \frac{C - D}{C + D}$$

In our sample problem,

$$\gamma = \frac{1554 - 2607}{1554 + 2607}$$

$$= \frac{-1053}{4161}$$

$$= -0.253$$

Gamma also ranges from -1 to $+1$ and can be thought of as providing a much more generous indication of the strength of association between ordinal variables. One set of guidelines for interpreting values of γ is as follows:

0.00	no association
±0.01–0.09	negligible association
±0.10–0.29	low association
±0.30–0.49	moderate association
±0.50–0.69	substantial association
±0.70–0.99	very strong association
±1	perfect association (Davis, 1971, p. 49)

Thus, the variables in our sample problem would be interpreted according to these guidelines as having a low negative association.

Somers' d_{yx}

The two measures discussed above are symmetrical because all ties are treated uniformly; with Tau_c predictions are made on all pairs of cases whereas with γ no predictions are made on pairs that are tied on either variable. A third ordinal measure of association, however, includes predictions on pairs that are tied on the dependent variable (Y) but not tied on the independent variable (X). With **Somers' d_{yx}** predictions are not made for pairs that are tied on the independent variable only or on both variables. Thus, Somers' d_{yx} is an asymmetrical measure that requires identifying the dependent variable. It is computed as:

$$d_{yx} = \frac{C - D}{C + D + T_y}$$

For our sample problem, then:

$$d_{yx} = \frac{1554 - 2607}{1554 + 2607 + 2139}$$

$$= \frac{-1053}{6,300}$$

$$= -0.167$$

As in this example, Somers' d_{yx} is usually less than γ but greater than Tau$_c$. There is no clear-cut preference among these measures, and the analyst may want to use all three. Obviously, their greatest utility is in comparing the strength of association between different pairs of variables. Tests of significance for these measures are also available based on the sampling distribution of $C - D$ (Loether and McTavish, 1976, pp. 550–567).

Although chi square and the nominal measures of association can be used with ordinal measures, the rank order statistics are more informative because they are sensitive to any tendency of one variable to increase or to decrease as the other variable increases. Furthermore, the analysis of ordinal associations can be elaborated with additional variables in the same way discussed above with reference to nominal measures. One additional feature of this process with ordinal measures is that Tau$_c$, γ, and Somers' d_{yx} are signed measures that show whether an association is positive or negative; examination of whether the signs change or hold constant is an obvious part of this elaboration.

REFERENCES

Blalock, H. M., Jr. 1972. Social Statistics. 2nd Ed. New York: McGraw–Hill Book Company.

Davis, J. A. 1971. Elementary Survey Analysis. Englewood Cliffs, N.J.: Prentice-Hall, Inc.

Loether, H. J., and D. G. McTavish. 1976. Descriptive and Inferential Statistics: An Introduction. Boston: Allyn & Bacon, Inc.

PRACTICE PROBLEMS FOR CHAPTER 12

1. Refer to Table 5.12 and perform the following operations.
   a. For the aggregate association between social class and opinion on affirmative action compute χ^2 and apply the test of significance at the 0.05 level. What do you conclude?
   b. Perform the same analysis using data from the white subsample in the table. What do you conclude?
   c. Compute phi (ϕ) as a measure of strength of association for the same proportions of the table. How would you characterize the strength of each association?
   d. Compute Goodman and Kruskal's τ_y for both the black and white subsamples. Based on the results, how would you characterize the strength of these associations?
2. Refer to the table on the following page, "Sales experience by timber development organization by predominant wood type." Perform the following analyses.
   a. Compute χ^2 and apply the test of significance at the 0.01 level for the aggregate association between sales experience and timber development organization (TDO). What do you conclude about the significance of this association?
   b. Compute χ^2 and apply the test of significance at the 0.01 level for each subsample association (Hardwoods and Softwoods) in the table. Is the association between sales experience and timber development significant within each subsample?
   c. Compute lambda (λ) for the association between sales experience and type of wood. What do you conclude about the strength of the association based on your computations?
   d. Compute Cramer's V as a measure of strength of association for the aggregate association between sales experience and TDO. What does this computation indicate about the strength of this association? Perform the same analysis for the associations in the Hardwood and Softwood subsample. What does Cramer's V indicate about the strength of association between sales experience and TDO in these subsamples?
3. Refer to Table 5.16. The presumed pattern of association is that age influences the type of program, which in turn is related to job status and that age also influences job status directly, apart from its effect through program type.
   a. Compute χ^2 and ϕ for the association between job status and type of program in the aggregate and for each age subsample.

Sales experience by timber development organization by predominant wood type

Sales experience	Softwoods				Hardwoods				Total			
	TDO	No TDO	Total		TDO	No TDO	Total		TDO	No TDO	Total	
No increase	0	20	20	(10%)	10	50	60	(50%)	10	70	80	(25%)
Mild increase	40	80	120	(60%)	6	34	40	(33.3%)	46	114	160	(50%)
High increase	40	20	60	(30%)	4	16	20	(16.7%)	44	36	80	(25%)
Total	80	120	200		20	100	120		100	220	320	

    b. Is the association between program type and age statistically significant at the 0.05 level?

    c. Compute χ^2 and Cramer's V for the association between job status and age in the aggregate and then separately for each type of program. Overall, are these data consistent with the presumed relationships stated above?

4. The table below shows the distribution of responses to a survey item stating that "housing conditions in this neighborhood have improved over the past 3 years." The respondents are categorized by race and whether they reside in program target areas or comparison areas.

    a. Is there an association between the response variable and area in the aggregate? Compute χ^2 and ϕ and discuss your interpretation. Test at the 0.05 level.

    b. Do your interpretations change when you control for race? Compute χ^2 and ϕ for both subsamples and discuss your findings. Overall, is the association between response and area significant at the 0.05 level when you control for race?

Aggregate

		Total		
			Area	
	Response	Program	Comparison	Total
	Agree	44	24	68
	Disagree	58	53	111
		102	77	179

By Race

	Whites			Nonwhites		
	Area			Area		
Response	Program	Comparison	Total	Program	Comparison	Total
Agree	37	5	42	7	19	26
Disagree	53	16	69	5	37	42
Total	90	21	111	12	56	68

5. An analyst in an MHMR agency, which funds both schools and sheltered workshops for mentally retarded people, wants to know the extent to which clients' progress is contingent upon the length of time they have been enrolled in their program. The following

table shows these data separately for school and workshop participants. What is the nature of the association between progress and
enrollment for each group? Use γ to compare the strength of this
association for those in schools as opposed to those in workshops.
State your conclusions.

Client progress by length of enrollment and type of program

	Schools			
	Enrollment			
Progress indicator	1–2 years	3–4 years	5+ years	Total
No progress	24	50	71	145
Minimal progress	31	53	52	136
Substantial progress	43	46	60	149
Total	98	149	183	430
	Workshops			
	Enrollment			
Progress indicator	1–2 years	3–4 years	5+ years	Total
No progress	9	16	50	75
Minimal progress	15	35	46	96
Substantial progress	40	39	32	111
Total	64	90	128	282

ANALYSIS OF VARIANCE 13

As has been seen in the chapter 5 discussion of statistical associations and relationships, interest often centers on comparing mean averages of an interval level measure across two or more groups of cases as represented in comparison of means tables. The primary method for analyzing such data beyond a visual inspection and descriptive interpretation is **analysis of variance**, often referred to as ANOVA. Although the technique primarily entails a test or series of tests of statistical significance, ANOVA can also be used to develop measures of the strength of associations between nominal or category type independent variables and interval level dependent variables.

The simplest application of analysis of variance is a significance test between the means of two samples or subsamples, in which case it is equivalent to a two-tailed two-sample t test. As a matter of fact, researchers are often in the position of choosing between ANOVA and t test procedures in approaching certain problems, and as is seen below the two are often used as complementary statistical tools. In terms of usage, analysis of variance can be thought of as an extension of the two-sample t test in two important respects. First, when the independent variable of interest has more than two *categories*, ANOVA provides a single test of significance among the mean averages of all the categories, a task that would require a whole series of t tests. Second, and more important, ANOVA can be used to take into consideration two or more *independent variables* simultaneously, testing for significant differences in means across the categories of one independent variable while fixing for the effects of others. Thus, it is a **multivariate statistical technique** that can be used as a way of operationalizing the process of elaboration beyond bivariate associations.

The classic application of ANOVA is in analyzing data generated by highly structured experiments; it was initially developed in the 1920's by the British statistician R. A. Fisher for use with agricultural experiments replicated over many field plots. With true experiments the dependent variables are the responses of impacts observed across all groups, whereas the independent variables represent the factors (treatments, blocks, replications) built into the experimental design. The primary purpose of ANOVA in this context is to provide statistical controls over the random component of experimental error, rather than drawing inferences for larger populations, as discussed in chapter 9. The technique does, however, have widespread applications apart from experimental designs, including the analysis of cross-sectional sample data, and basically may be considered a candidate for use whenever the dependent variable of interest is an interval level measure and the independent variables are nominal measures or otherwise categorized variables.

ONE-WAY ANALYSIS OF VARIANCE

The concept that forms the basis of analysis of variance is sometimes difficult to grasp at first because it uses estimates of population variance, a measure of dispersion, to examine hypotheses about population means, measures of central tendency. As is seen below, the test statistic is the F **statistic**, which is the ratio of two separate estimates of population variance based on sample data. If the null hypothesis about population means is true, the sampling distribution of the F ratio is known and the probabilities associated with it indicate the likelihood of observed differences among sample means occurring as a function of chance effect in a random sampling process.

F Ratio and Estimates of Variance

One-way ANOVA involves the comparison of means across the two or more categories of a single independent variable, and the cases falling within each category are thought of as subsamples or groups. For example, Table 13.1 shows the number of subsequent job offers received and a sample of participants in two alternative skills training programs and a sample of persons not participating in either program. The means of the three groups differ markedly, and the question is whether these differences might easily have occurred by chance if the means of the respective populations are identical.

Given an interval level measure and a random sample broken down into two or more groups, three different ways of estimating the population variance are possible: 1) a **total** estimate of the variance of cases around the overall means, 2) a **between group estimate** of population variance based on the variation of the group means around the grand mean, and 3) a **within group estimate** based on the variation of individual cases around their respective group means. The F statistic is computed as the ratio of the between group estimate of population variance to the within group estimate:

$$F = \frac{\text{between } s^2}{\text{within } s^2}$$

Given random sampling, the between and within group estimates are independent of each other even though they are based on the same set of observations. The total estimate of variance is not used in F ratios because it is not independent of the between and within group estimates.

The within group estimate always provides an unbiased estimate of total population variance. Stated in another way, no matter how a random sample is subdivided into groups, the estimate based on the variation of cases around their group means will be an unbiased estimate of the overall population variance. The null hypothesis in ANOVA problems states that the means of the population subgroups are equal, in effect that the subsamples on which the analysis is based are independent random samples drawn from the same population. If H_0 is true, any observed differences in sample means will be a random effect of sampling error, and the between group estimate of population variance will also be unbiased.

Therefore, if H_0 is true, the expected value of the F ratio is unity; the expected value of each of these unbiased estimates of variance is the same, and the ratio of the two will be greater or less than unity only by chance effect. Actual computed F ratios might be greater or less than 1 because of sample error, but extremely low or high values would occur only with a very slight probability.

On the other hand, if H_0 is false and the population means are not equal, the between group estimate will provide a biased estimate, tending to overestimate the population variance because of the systematic deviation of group means from the overall population means. If H_0 is false, then, with an upward-biased between group estimate and a still unbiased within group estimate of variance, the expected value of F will be greater than unity. The question is, what is the probability of getting a high F ratio by chance if H_0 is true? If this probability is sufficiently low, we reject H_0 with a known chance of a type I error, and conclude H_1, that the population means are in fact different and that this is what produced the high F ratio.

Estimates of population variance depend in part on degrees of freedom, and there is a different F distribution for every combination of degrees of freedom associated with the numerator and denominator. Each sampling distribution of F represents the relative frequencies of the ratios based on all sample estimates of the population variance with a given number of degrees of freedom to all sample estimates of population variance based on some other specified number of degrees of freedom using random samples from the same population. The F distribution for 2 and 15 degrees of freedom is shown in Figure 13.1.

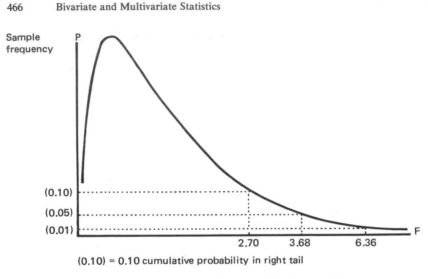

(0.10) = 0.10 cumulative probability in right tail

Figure 13.1. *F* distribution. Degrees of freedom = 2,15.

If the between and within group estimates are in fact both unbiased estimates of the common population variance, based on separate sub-samples drawn from the same population, the sampling distribution of *F* has a mean of unity and a mode of less than unity, and is highly skewed to the right. By chance, in some pairs of estimates the within group estimate will exceed the between group estimate, resulting in an *F* ratio between 0 and 1. Also by chance a number of pairs of such unbiased estimates will yield *F* ratios of greater than unity because the between group estimate exceeds the within group estimate. The *F* values in the extreme right tail of the distribution represent pairs of estimates in which the between group estimate exceeds the within group estimate by very substantial margins, and these would occur with a very low probability by chance. It is therefore in this tail that we test hypotheses that population means are equal and that sample differences in means occur by chance.

Variation and Estimates of Variance   Estimates of population variance are sums of squared deviations of cases around mean averages, divided by the corresponding number of degrees of freedom. The sum of squared deviations of cases around mean averages are referred to as measures of **variation**, indicating the magnitude of dispersion around the mean. It will be remembered that one property of the mean average is that the sum of the squared deviations around the mean is minimized, less than the **sum of squares (SS)** around any other value in a distribution. Because analysis of variance, and the techniques of regression and correlation analysis, are based on this special property of minimized SS, they are often referred to as **least squares** techniques.

If we take all the cases in each subgroup of a sample, compute their deviations from the single, overall mean, square these deviations and sum the squared deviations across all the subgroups, the result is the **total variation** of all the cases around the grand mean, sometimes called **total variation corrected for the mean**. Using the notation, X_{jk} for the kth individual case of the jth subgroup (or column as shown in Table 13.1), and $\overline{X}$ for the grand mean, the formula for total variation is:

$$\text{Total SS} = \underset{jk}{\Sigma\Sigma}\, (X_{jk} - \overline{X})^2$$

The double summation sign, $\Sigma\Sigma$, represents summing the squared deviations first within each subgroup or column and then across all the columns.

Total variation can be partitioned into two components, the first representing the variation of the group means around the grand means, and the second being the variation of the individual cases around their respective group means. One thing we are interested in is the extent to which the deviation of an individual case from the grand mean is due to the deviation of its group mean. In computing the **between group variation**, each group mean, $\overline{X}_j$, is taken as representing the value of each individual case in that group; in effect the variation within each group is ignored to see how much variation there would be if all the

Table 13.1.   Number of job offers by program type

	Program 1	Program 2	Control
$X_{jk} =$	5	4	2
	6	1	3
	4	2	4
	7	5	2
	5	3	2
	3	3	2
	$\Sigma = 30$	$\Sigma = 18$	$\Sigma = 15$
	$\overline{X}_j = 5$	$\overline{X}_j = 3$	$\overline{X}_j = 2.5$

$$\Sigma X_{jk} = 63$$
$$\overline{X} = 3.5$$

cases within a group took on the same value. Between group variation, then, is computed as:

$$\text{Between SS} = \underset{jk}{\Sigma\Sigma}\,(\overline{X}_j - \overline{X})^2$$

Again, the double summation indicates the summing of the SS for every case within each group (which will now be the same for each case in the group and can therefore be accomplished by multiplying by the number of cases in the group) and then across the groups.

The **within group variation** represents the sum of the variation of all the individual cases around their respective group means, again summed across all groups:

$$\text{Within SS} = \underset{jk}{\Sigma\Sigma}\,(X_{jk} - \overline{X}_j)^2$$

As indicated above, the total variation corrected for the mean is equal to the between group variation plus the within group variation:

$$\underset{jk}{\Sigma\Sigma}\,(X_{jk} - \overline{X})^2 = \underset{jk}{\Sigma\Sigma}\,(\overline{X}_j - \overline{X})^2 + \underset{jk}{\Sigma\Sigma}\,(X_{jk} - \overline{X}_j)^2$$

In practice we can compute any two of these measures of variation and obtain the third by a residual method.

Estimates of variance are computed by dividing measures of variation by the corresponding number of degrees of freedom. For example, the variance estimate based on total variation (which is not used in the F ratio) would be:

$$s^2 = \frac{\underset{jk}{\Sigma\Sigma}\,(X_{jk} - \overline{X})^2}{N - 1}$$

This is the measure of sample variance corrected so as to provide an unbiased estimate of population variance.

Application of the F test Referring to the problem presented in Table 13.1 involving the number of job offers for sample cases drawn from two skills training programs and a control group, the null hypothesis states that the means of the respective populations are identical, while the alternate hypothesis states that the population means are themselves different. The assumptions on which the F test is based include 1) that number of job offers is an interval measure and that program type is a nominal measure, 2) that the sets of cases in each of the three program types constitute independent random samples, 3) that the variances of the three respective populations are equal, and 4) that the number of job offers variable follows a normal distribution in each of the three populations. Given the assumed H_0 that the population means are equal and the assumption that their variances are also equal, the test is based on the general assumption that the three subsamples are in effect three independent samples drawn from the same population. Analysis of variance is a **parametric technique**, requiring the interval level of measurement and normal distributions in the dependent variable; yet with larger samples the normality assumptions are relaxed. It should also be noted that the ANOVA F test does *not* test hypotheses concerning equal variances, although a different F test application can be used in this way. For ANOVA purposes, however, the F test requires the prior assumption of equal variances.

Specification of the critical region depends on the numbers of degrees of freedom involved and the desired significance level. The degrees of freedom associated with the between group variation equal the number of categories minus one ($c - 1$), while for the within group variation the degrees of freedom are given by the sample size minus the number of categories, $N - c$. Thus, the between group degrees of freedom plus the within group degrees of freedom equal the degrees of freedom associated with total variation, the sample size minus one, $N - 1$. For our problem, then, there are 2 degrees of freedom with the between group variation ($3 - 1$) and 15 degrees of freedom associated with the within group variation ($18 - 3$). Table A-8 in the appendix shows cutoff points of the F distributions for various combinations of degrees of freedom at the 0.05 and 0.01 significance levels. Testing at the 0.05 level with 2 df in the numerator and 15 df in the denominator, the critical F value is 3.68. Thus, assuming that H_0 is true, and with three random samples of six cases each drawn from the same population, the probability of obtaining a calculated F ratio of greater than 3.68 by chance is 0.05, and we will reject H_0 if our computed F exceeds 3.68. (To see this, refer to Figure 13.1.)

Table 13.2 shows the computation of total variation and within group variation by summing up squared deviations within and across categories, as discussed above. The between group or between column SS is then obtained by subtracting the within group SS from total SS. Alternatively, the between column SS might be computed directly, as follows:

Between column SS $= \sum_j N_j (\bar{X}_j - \bar{X})^2$

$$= 6\,(5 - 3.5)^2 + 6\,(3 - 3.5)^2 + 6\,(2.5 - 3.5)^2$$
$$= 6\,(1.5)^2 + 6\,(-.5)^2 + 6\,(-1)^2$$
$$= 6\,(2.25) + 6\,(.25) + 6\,(1)$$
$$= 13.5 + 1.5 + 6$$
$$= 21$$

Multiplying each squared deviation by subsample size accounts for summing SS across the six cases within each category, as noted earlier.

Table 13.2   Computation of sum of squares: one-way ANOVA

Total SS		Within columns SS	
$X_{jk} - \bar{X}$	$(X_{jk} - \bar{X})^2$	$X_{jk} - \bar{X}_j$	$(X_{jk} - \bar{X}_j)^2$
$5 - 3.5 =$ 1.5	2.25	$5 - 5$ $=$ 0	0
$6 - 3.5 =$ 2.5	6.25	$6 - 5$ $=$ 1	1
$4 - 3.5 =$ 0.5	0.25	$4 - 5$ $= -1$	1
$7 - 3.5 =$ 3.5	12.25	$7 - 5$ $=$ 2	4
$5 - 3.5 =$ 1.5	2.25	$5 - 5$ $=$ 0	0
$3 - 3.5 = -0.5$	0.25	$3 - 5$ $= -2$	4
$4 - 3.5 =$ 0.5	0.25	$4 - 3$ $=$ 1	1
$1 - 3.5 = -2.5$	6.25	$1 - 3$ $= -2$	4
$2 - 3.5 = -1.5$	2.25	$2 - 3$ $= -1$	1
$5 - 3.5 =$ 1.5	2.25	$5 - 3$ $=$ 2	4
$3 - 3.5 = -0.5$	0.25	$3 - 3$ $=$ 0	0
$3 - 3.5 = -0.5$	0.25	$3 - 3$ $=$ 0	0
$2 - 3.5 = -1.5$	2.25	$2 - 2.5 = -0.5$	0.25
$3 - 3.5 - -0.5$	0.25	$3 - 2.5 =$ 0.5	0.25
$4 - 3.5 =$ 0.5	0.25	$4 - 2.5 =$ 1.5	2.25
$2 - 3.5 = -1.5$	2.25	$2 - 2.5 = -0.5$	0.25
$2 - 3.5 = -1.5$	2.25	$2 - 2.5 = -0.5$	0.25
$2 - 3.5 = -1.5$	2.25	$2 - 2.5 = -0.5$	0.25

$$\sum_{jk}\sum (X_{jk} - \bar{X})^2 = 44.50 \qquad\qquad \sum_{jk}\sum (X_{jk} - \bar{X}_j)^2 = 23.50$$

Between columns SS $=$ Total SS $-$ Within columns SS
$$= 44.50 - 23.50$$
$$= 21.00$$

The measures of variation, degrees of freedom, variance estimates, and F ratio are usually presented in the ANOVA table format, as shown in Table 13.3.

Mean square is the term used for variance estimate; it represents an average amount of variation per degree of freedom. In this example, the F ratio of the between estimate of variance to the within estimate of variance exceeds the critical F, and thus we reject the null hypothesis (with a probability of a type I error of less than 0.05) and conclude that the observed differences in sample mean number of job offers do represent differences in means in the corresponding populations.

Percent Variation Explained

The measure of strength of association derived from analysis of variance is based on the concept of explained variation. Total SS as computed above is an indication of the total amount of variation around the mean average of the dependent variable. As discussed above, total SS is the sum of the variation represented by the spread of the group means around the grand mean and the variation of the individual cases around their respective group means, or the sum of between group and within group variation. The between group variation is considered to represent **explained variation**, that proportion of total variation that can be explained by the breakdown of the cases into the categories of the independent variable. By contrast, the within group variation is **unexplained variation**, remaining variation among the cases within groups that is not explained away by the categorization of cases according to the particular independent variable being examined.

The most straightforward way of measuring the strength of association between a nominal level independent variable and an interval level dependent variable is to look at the reduction in unexplained variation in the dependent variable due to the independent variable, or the proportion that the explained variation attributable to the inde-

Table 13.3.   ANOVA table—one-way ANOVA

Source	SS	df	Mean square	F ratio
Total	44.50	$(N-1)$ 17	2.62	
Between	21.00	$(c-1)$ 2	10.50	$\dfrac{10.50}{1.57} = 6.69*$
Within	23.50	$(N-c)$ 15	1.57	

*Computed F exceeds 3.68. Program type significant at 0.05 level.

pendent variable constitutes of the total variation in the dependent variable. The most common indicator of the strength of this kind of association is sometimes referred to as R^2, and more properly as Eta^2 (E^2), the percent variation explained. It is computed as the proportion that between group variation constitutes of total variation, or:

$$R^2 = E^2 = \frac{\text{between SS}}{\text{total SS}}$$

In the sample problem above:

$$E^2 = \frac{21.0}{44.5}$$

$$= 0.472$$

$$= 47.2\% \text{ variation explained}$$

Eta^2 or the **correlation ratio**, is a descriptive statistic measuring the degree of association between the two variables in the sample, but it also provides an estimate of the strength of their association in the larger population. With small samples, however, it tends to be a biased estimate in the direction of overestimating the strength of association, because of the tendency of the sample standard deviation to underestimate the variability in the population. With small samples, then, the bias in the correlation ratio can be corrected for with a computation involving the variance estimates directly:

$$\epsilon^2 = 1 - \frac{\text{within mean sq}}{\text{total mean sq}}$$

In our sample problem, the estimate of variance based on total deviation would be 44.5 SS divided by 17 degrees of freedom, or 2.62. Thus, the *unbiased* correlation ratio, denoted by E^2, is:

$$E^2 = 1 - \frac{1.56}{2.62}$$

$$= 1 - 0.595$$

$$= 0.405$$

Notice that this corrected estimate of variation explained in the larger population is more conservative than the uncorrected version. With samples of more than a few cases per category, or when the interpretation pertains solely to the cases at hand, the uncorrected correlation ratio is customarily used.

Alternative Computing Formulas

Alternative, short-cut formulas for computing total variation and between group variation are available, as shown in Table 13.4.

Notes on Interpretation

The results of the ANOVA conducted above indicate that there are significant differences at the 0.05 level among the mean number of job offers received by individuals in the two different programs and the control group. There are a number of points that should be made as to the interpretation of these results and how the analysis might be further pursued. First, these findings do not necessarily indicate that

Table 13.4. Alternative computing formulas

	X_{jk}	X_{jk}^2	Formula
	5	25	Total SS $= \sum_{jk}\sum X_{jk}^2 - \dfrac{\left(\sum_{jk}\sum X_{jk}\right)^2}{N}$
	6	36	
	4	16	
$\Sigma X_{jk} = 30$	7	49	$= 265 - \dfrac{63^2}{18}$
	5	25	
	3	9	$= 265 - 220.5$
			$= 44.5$
	4	16	Between SS $= \sum_j \dfrac{\left(\sum_k X_{jk}\right)^2}{N_j} - \dfrac{\left(\sum_{jk}\sum X_{jk}\right)^2}{N}$
	1	1	
$\Sigma X_{jk} = 18$	2	4	
	5	25	$= \dfrac{30^2}{6} + \dfrac{18^2}{6} + \dfrac{15^2}{6} - \dfrac{63^2}{18}$
	3	9	
	3	9	$= 150 + 54 + 37.5 -$ 220.5
			$= 21.0$
	2	4	Within SS $=$ total SS $-$ between SS
	3	9	
$\Sigma X_{jk} = 15$	4	16	$= 44.5 - 21.0$
	2	4	$= 23.5$
	2	4	
	2	4	
	$\Sigma = 63$	$\Sigma = 265$	

there are significant differences between each possible pair of means, but only that it is unlikely that all three population means are equal. Referring to Table 13.1 we see that the mean number of job offers for the individuals in program 1 is much greater than the means of the other two groups and that the difference in means between the other two groups, program 2 and the control group, is much less. Perhaps there is a highly significant difference between program 1 versus the other groups, and the observed difference of three job offers between program 2 and the control group is a result of chance effect. A one-way ANOVA applied simultaneously across all three groups has no way of discerning these possible differences.

Often ANOVA is used to take a first cut in analyzing such data and then followed up with more specific comparisons of means. Particularly interesting pairs of means might be compared using either ANOVA or two-sample t tests, or all pairs of means might be compared to determine which, if any, are statistically significant. This latter procedure has often been criticized on the grounds that if many pairs of means are involved, a few differences would be expected to be statistically significant by pure chance, even if H_0 is actually true. The integrity of the test remains, however, and such erroneous conclusions would simply be a product of the known probability of a type I error. In practice, with only a few categories and pairs of means, this does not usually present a problem.

In addition to comparing the means of two specific categories, methods have also been developed to test for the "average effects" of two or more categories as opposed to still other categories. For example, in our sample problem we might wish to test the significance of the average effects of program 1 and program 2 as opposed to the control group. This would involve comparing the average mean of the first two groups ($\overline{X} = 24$) with that of the control group ($\overline{X} = 15$) using modified estimates of standard error. (For a discussion of this averaged effects method, as well as an alternative approach based on least significant differences, see Snedecor and Cochran, 1967, pp. 268–275.)

Another observation that should be noted in this regard is that the F test is essentially a two-tailed test and therefore insensitive to which of two means is greater. Although the critical region is always located in the right tail only, a computed F ratio will fall in the critical region if either of two means exceeds the other by a sufficiently wide margin. As mentioned above, the F test of significant difference between two means is equivalent to a two-tailed two-sample t test, and the square root of a computed F will equal the t statistic computed for the same data. To verify this, consider a comparison of the means of the first two groups of six cases each in our sample problem, five job offers per case in program 1 and three job offers per case for program 2. The computed F for this problem equals 6.00 and the computed t statistic equals $\sqrt{F}$ or 2.449. Testing at the 0.05 level, with 1 and 10 degrees of freedom, the critical F is 4.96 and thus the observed difference in means between the two groups is significant. Similarly, applying a two-tailed t test at the 0.05 level with $(N_1 + N_2 - 2)$ 10 degrees of freedom, the critical value of t is 2.228, or the square root of F, $\sqrt{4.96}$.

The point is that in making comparisons of specific pairs of means, ANOVA and the two-tailed version of the t test will produce the same results. However, very often we are in a position to specify the direction of expected differences between means, in this case for example that program 1 is expected to be more effective than program 2 in terms of attracting job offers. In these situations one-tailed tests are always preferable, and therefore one-tailed two-sample t tests are often used rather than ANOVA in comparing specific pairs of means.

TWO-WAY ANALYSIS OF VARIANCE

Suppose that the data in our sample problem were generated from a demonstration project in which the skills training experiment was replicated across two blocks of participants, the first categorized as having limited previous experience in related occupations and the second as having extensive experience. The results might be displayed in a comparison of means format as shown in Table 13.5, and on a descriptive level we can examine the main effects of both the program variable and the previous experience variable as well as their interaction, as defined in chapter 5. We have already noted the differences among the program and control groups, and Table 13.5 indicates that, in general, individuals with extensive previous experience tended to receive more subsequent job offers than those with limited previous experience. Furthermore, some degree of interaction is indicated by the fact that although the program 2 mean exceeds the control group mean for the extensive previous experience block, the sample means for program 2 and the control group in the limited previous experience block are equal.

Analysis of variance extended to two or more independent variables provides a way of testing for the statistical significance of main effects and interactions, testing each effect while fixing for the effects of the

Table 13.5.   Average number of job offers by program treatment and previous experience

Previous experience	Program 1	Program 2	Control	Total
Extensive	5 6 $\overline{X}_{21} = 6$ 7	4 5 $\overline{X}_{22} = 4$ 3	2 3 $\overline{X}_{23} = 3$ 4	$\overline{X}_i = 4.33$
Limited	4 5 $\overline{X}_{11} = 4$ 3	1 2 $\overline{X}_{12} = 2$ 3	2 2 $\overline{X}_{13} = 2$ 2	$\overline{X}_i = 2.67$
Total	$\overline{X}_j = 5$	$\overline{X}_j = 3$	$\overline{X}_j = 2.5$	$\overline{X} = 3.5$

other factors. The general ANOVA procedure presented below is based on the requirement of equal frequencies of cases in each cell of the breakdown or comparison of means table, as is the case of our example with three individuals per cell. When this condition pertains, the independent variables, here program type and previous experience, are statistically independent of each other and this facilitates sorting out their statistical effects on the dependent variable. (The reader should recognize that the question of association between these two nominal level measures would be examined in a crosstabulation; equal cell frequencies would indicate a complete lack of association.)

As mentioned above, the classic use of ANOVA is in analyzing data drawn from true experiments, which are purposefully designed with the objective of maintaining uncorrelated factors or independent variables. Such **orthogonal designs**, those in which the independent variables are statistically independent of each other, provide the "cleanest" kind of data for multivariate analysis.

Two-way ANOVA is used to test for significant differences in means across the categories of one independent variable, controlling for the effects of the other independent variable, and vice versa, and to test for the significance of differences in means due to interaction beyond the main effects of the two independent variables. With orthogonal designs, the controls are inherent in the structure of the data itself, i.e., the main effects of the two independent variables and their interaction effects are statistically independent of each other, and conducting the ANOVA is a relatively straightforward process. With **nonorthogonal designs**, there is overlap among the various effects on the dependent variables, and the procedure must be modified to develop statistical controls for fixing for the effects of one variable while testing the significance of the other variable's effects.

Components of Variation

As with one-way ANOVA, the total variation in a two-way ANOVA problem represents the amount of spread of individual cases around the grand mean and can be broken down into explained and unexplained variation. The explained portion of total variation is that which can be attributed to the breakdown of cases into subcells according to the two independent variables, in our example the breakdown of the cases into the six cells of Table 13.5 by program type and previous experience. The unexplained variation is the remaining variation of the individual cases around their respective subcell means. Thus,

$$\text{Total SS} = \text{between subcell SS} + \text{within SS}$$

With orthogonal designs the main effects and interaction effects are additive such that the variation attributable to the column variable is one component of explained variation, that attributable to the row variable is a separate component of explained variation, and the variation attributable to their joint interaction is a third component. Thus,

$$\text{Subcell SS} = \text{between column SS} + \text{between row SS} + \text{interaction SS}$$

Computing Test Statistics

The two-way ANOVA is based on the same set of assumptions discussed with the one-way ANOVA example with the addition of the assumed statistical independence between the two independent variables. Furthermore, there are now three null hypotheses to be tested: 1) that the population means of the different program types are equal, 2) that the population means of the two levels of previous experience are equal, and 3) that in the larger population there is no interaction effect of program type and previous experience on the number of job offers.

Table 13.6 shows the computation of the various sums of squared deviations. Total variation and the between column variation have already been computed in the one-way ANOVA exercise and do not change by virtue of introducing a second independent variable into an orthogonal design. Subcell SS and between row SS are computed directly and then measures of interaction and within subcell variation are obtained through residual methods; interaction SS equals subcell SS minus the combined column and row SS. The conventional notation used is as follows:

Table 13.6.   Computations of sum of squares: two-way ANOVA

$$\text{Between row SS} = \sum_{ik}\sum (\overline{X}_i - \overline{X})^2$$
$$= 9(4.33 - 3.5)^2 + 9(2.67 - 3.5)^2$$
$$= 12.40$$

$$\text{Subcell SS} = \sum_{ijk}\sum\sum (\overline{X}_{ij} - \overline{X})^2$$
$$= 3(6 - 3.5)^2 + 3(4 - 3.5)^2 + 3(3 - 3.5)^2$$
$$\quad + 3(4 - 3.5)^2 + 3(2 - 3.5)^2 + 3(2 - 3.5)^2$$
$$= 34.50$$

$$\text{Total SS} = \sum_{ijk}\sum\sum (X_{ijk} - \overline{X})^2$$
$$= 44.50 \text{ (computed in Table 13.2)}$$

$$\text{Between column SS} = \sum_{jk}\sum(\overline{X}_j - \overline{X})^2$$
$$= 21.00 \text{ (computed in Table 13.2)}$$

$$\text{Interaction SS} = \text{subcell SS} - (\text{column SS} + \text{row SS})$$
$$= 34.50 - (21.00 + 12.40)$$
$$= 1.10$$

$$\text{Within SS} = \text{total SS} - \text{subcell SS}$$
$$= 44.50 - 34.50$$
$$= 10.00$$

X_{ijk} = kth unit or case in the ith row and jth column

$\overline{X}_{ij}$ = mean of the subcell in the ith row and jth column

$\overline{X}_i$ = mean of the cases in the ith row

$\overline{X}_j$ = mean of the cases in the jth column

$\overline{X}$ = grand mean

The degrees of freedom associated with the different measures of variation are the number of cases minus one ($N - 1$) for total variation, the number of subcells minus one ($rc - 1$) for subcell variation, the number of columns minus one ($c - 1$) for the between column variation, the number of rows minus one ($r - 1$) for the between row variation, the number of columns minus one times the number of rows minus one ($r - 1$) ($c - 1$) for interaction, and the number of cases minus the number of subcells ($N - rc$) for the within subcell variation.

The output from this analysis is presented in the ANOVA format in Table 13.7.

Three separate F tests are being applied in this two-way ANOVA problem, one for each of the main effects and one for the interaction effect. Each computed F statistic is the ratio of the variance estimate based on the corresponding main or interaction effect to the variance estimate based on within subcell variation. If the null hypothesis concerning a column, row, or interaction effect is true, then its corresponding variance estimate will be unbiased, regardless of whether or not the other variance estimates are biased or unbiased. The variance estimate based on the within subcell variation is always unbiased, and therefore if a particular H_0 is true the expected value of its F ratio is unity.

It should be noted that the computed F ratio for the column variable, program type, is substantially different from that computed in the one-way ANOVA, increasing from 6.69 to 12.65. This change occurs because a second independent variable, previous experience, is now being taken into account. Although the variation attributed to program type (SS = 21.00) is unchanged in the two-way ANOVA, it is now being related to a reduced amount of unexplained variation within subcells, 10.00 SS as compared to 23.5 SS in the one-way ANOVA. This is the statistical control for testing the significance of the column variable beyond the effects of the row variable. The question is, after subtracting the portion of total variation that can be attributed to the row variable, previous experience, how much of the remaining variation can be explained by the column variable, program type, and how likely is

Table 13.7.   ANOVA table—two-way ANOVA

Source	SS	df		Mean square	F
Total	44.50	$(N-1)$	17		
Between subcell	34.50	$(rc-1)$	5		
Columns—program	21.00	$(c-1)$	2	10.50	12.65*
Rows—experience	12.40	$(r-1)$	1	12.40	14.94**
Interaction	1.10	$(r-1)(c-1)$	2	0.55	0.66
Within subcell	10.00	$(N-rc)$	12	0.83	

*F exceeds 3.89. Program type significant at 0.05 level.
**F exceeds 4.75. Previous experience significant at 0.05 level.

this to have occurred by chance effect if in the larger population none of the dependent variation can be attributed to program type?

In the two-way ANOVA the variance estimate based on the between column variation is set in ratio to the variance estimate based on a reduced amount of within subcell variation *and* fewer degrees of freedom than in the one-way ANOVA. In this example the changes resulted in a much higher computed F ratio. As is seen below, the critical F for testing the significance of the column variable has also changed slightly, because of the decrease of degrees of freedom associated with the within subcell estimate of variance.

Interpreting the Results

With two-way ANOVA we are making three F tests of three different null hypotheses. The critical values of F to be used as benchmarks depend on the degrees of freedom associated with the variance estimates used in computing the F ratios; the degrees of freedom in the denominator will not change from test to test because they are all based on the same within subcell variance estimate, but the degrees of freedom in the numerator may well change, depending on the number of categories in the independent variables. In our sample problem, the tests concerning the column effects and interaction effects are based on the sampling distribution of F with 2 and 12 degrees of freedom, while that for the row effect is based on the F distribution with 1 and 12 degrees of freedom.

Referring to Table 13.7 we see that the computed F values for both of the main effects do exceed their corresponding critical F's at the 0.5 level, and thus we conclude that there are significant differences in the mean number of job offers by program type beyond any effects of previous experience, and that there are also significant differences in mean number of job offers between the two previous experience categories beyond the effects of program type. Whereas the visual inspection of means in Table 13.5 does indicate some interaction effects of program type and previous experience on number of job offers for the sample data, the F test applied in Table 13.7 does not show this interaction effect to be statistically significant.

If the interaction effect in an orthogonal design turns out to be significant, at least one of the main effects will also be significant, but one or more of the main effects can easily be significant without any significant interaction. Usual practice in social science research is to look at interaction effects first and, if they are not significant, to pool them with the unexplained subcell estimate of variance before testing the main effects. In our sample problem the interaction effect is not significant, and thus we would throw it back into the "error term" or variance estimate based on unexplained variation, as shown in Table 13.8.

Although this procedure augments the within subcell or error term variation, it also increases the degrees of freedom associated with it. As in our sample probelm, this often results in a decreased within subcell variance estimate and increases the likelihood of finding the main effects to be statistically significant. The reader should also note that the critical values of F change again due to this change in degrees of freedom. In this case, then, our final conclusion is that both program type and previous experience have significant effects on the number of job offers received, each beyond the effects of the other, and that there is no significant interaction effect of the two beyond their combined additive effects.

Interaction represents dissimilarity in the differential effects of one independent variable across categories of the other. These differences in differential effects may be spread across many of the cells in the table or concentrated in one part of it. When interaction proves to be significant, it may merit close attention to identify the pattern of interaction suggested by the data. In program evaluations, the greatest practical significance may lie in identifying important interactions, for example in terms of which combinations of program strategies produce the greatest results, or combinations of program treatments and environmental conditions that maximize results.

When significant interactions are identified, this may warrant further research and analysis being concentrated on particular categories of the independent variables. Even when the overall pattern of interaction is not statistically significant, visual inspection may indicate certain differences that should be investigated more closely. In our ex-

Table 13.8. ANOVA table—pooled interaction

Source	SS	df	Mean square	F
Between columns—program	21.00	2	10.50	13.24*
Between rows—experience	12.40	1	12.40	15.64**
Error	11.10	14	0.79	

*F exceeds 3.74. Program type significant at 0.05 level.
**F exceeds 4.60. Previous experience significant at 0.05 level.

ample one important implication of the findings is that differences in number of job offers by program type are more pronounced for those with extensive previous experience than for those with limited previous experience.

Strength of Association

The strength of each bivariate association in a two-way ANOVA, as well as that between the combination of independent variables and the dependent variable, can be measured with the Eta^2 statistic. Referring to Table 13.7 we can relate the amount of variation attributed to each variable to the total amount of variation. The column variable, program type, still accounts for 47.2 percent of total variation, while the row variable, previous experience, accounts for 27.9 percent of total variation, computed as follows:

$$E^2 = \frac{\text{row SS}}{\text{total SS}}$$

$$= \frac{12.40}{44.50}$$

$$= 0.279$$

By the same token, the interaction of the two variables apart from their main effects is seen to "explain" 2.4 percent of total variation, and because these effects are additive (given the orthogonal design) the two variables taken together can account for a total (47.2 + 27.9 + 2.4) of 77.5 percent of the total variation in the number of job offers. This can be verified by the direct computation:

$$E^2 = \frac{\text{subcell SS}}{\text{total SS}}$$

$$= \frac{34.50}{44.50}$$

$$= 0.775$$

COMPARISONS OF SPECIFIC MEANS

As a second example of two-way analysis of variance, consider the hypothetical teaching strategy experiment outlined in Table 13.9. It involves the testing of a newly devised teaching strategy in a particular curriculum as compared with the current method, the control. A stan-

Table 13.9. Teaching strategy experiment

A	Four Group Design			
R	0	X	0	
R	0		0	
R		X	0	
R			0	

B	Individual scores on posttest	
	Pretested and posttested	Posttested only
Test group	93	85
	90	87
	90	83
	87	81
Control group	72	70
	70	71
	74	73
	72	74

C	Mean average posttest scores		
	Pretested and posttested	Posttested only	Total
Test group	90	84	87
Control group	72	72	72
Total	81	78	79.5

dard pretest-posttest experimental design was desired to compare the amount of improvement on a uniform test achieved by groups of students randomly assigned to the two teaching methods. However, because the researchers are interested in measuring the amount of improvement in these test scores due to the use of the two teaching methods and are concerned about the possible effects of pretesting on the posttest scores, a Solomon four-group design is employed as shown in Table

13.9*A*. A total of 16 students were randomly assigned to the four groups of four individuals each; the scores of these individuals on the posttest are shown in Table 13.9*B*; *C* shows the means of the posttest scores broken down by treatment and testing situation. (This example employs a very limited sample size and widely divergent test scores to provide a clear illustration; in practice, a much larger *N* would be desired.)

In this example we proceed first with an analysis of variance applied to these posttest scores and then continue with the use of *t* tests to make some more specific comparisons. Taking all four sets of posttest scores into account simultaneously we can use ANOVA to test for the significance of 1) the main effects of the treatment variable on posttest scores, 2) the main effects of the pretest versus posttest-only variable on posttest scores, and 3) the interaction of these two on posttest scores. Making a descriptive interpretation of the comparison of means table shown in Table 13.9*C*, we see that for the 16 cases at hand there is a difference of 15 points between the mean average scores of the test group and control group in the direction expected. There is also a difference of 3 points between the means of those who were pretested and those who were not and some degree of interaction between the two inasmuch as the pretest can account for a 6-point difference in the scores of the test groups but cannot account for any difference between the scores of the two control groups.

Table 13.10 shows the computation of the amounts of variation (sum of squares) associated with the different factors in the experiment. Because this is an orthogonal design the column SS (due to pretest versus posttest only) and the row SS (due to the difference in teaching method) are independent, and thus the interaction SS is the difference between overall subcell SS and the sum of the column and row SS. In this example, total SS is not computed directly as in the previous example, but rather is derived from summing the overall subcell SS and the within group SS.

Table 13.11 shows the ANOVA table developed for this experiment. With only two categories of treatment and two categories of testing situation there is 1 degree of freedom associated with each main effect and with interaction. Thus, testing at the 0.01 level of significance, the critical *F* for each of the three tests is 9.33, and only the row effect (treatment effect) is found to be significant. Because the interaction does not prove significant, we throw it back into the error term and use the revised ANOVA table shown in Table 13.11*B* to test for the column and row effects. With this test the row variable is seen to be

Table 13.10.   Computations for teaching strategy: ANOVA example

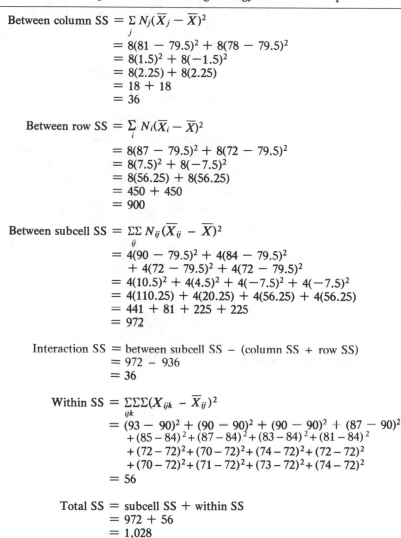

Between column SS $= \sum_{j} N_j(\overline{X}_j - \overline{X})^2$

$\qquad = 8(81 - 79.5)^2 + 8(78 - 79.5)^2$
$\qquad = 8(1.5)^2 + 8(-1.5)^2$
$\qquad = 8(2.25) + 8(2.25)$
$\qquad = 18 + 18$
$\qquad = 36$

Between row SS $= \sum_{i} N_i(\overline{X}_i - \overline{X})^2$

$\qquad = 8(87 - 79.5)^2 + 8(72 - 79.5)^2$
$\qquad = 8(7.5)^2 + 8(-7.5)^2$
$\qquad = 8(56.25) + 8(56.25)$
$\qquad = 450 + 450$
$\qquad = 900$

Between subcell SS $= \sum\sum_{ij} N_{ij}(\overline{X}_{ij} - \overline{X})^2$

$\qquad = 4(90 - 79.5)^2 + 4(84 - 79.5)^2$
$\qquad\quad + 4(72 - 79.5)^2 + 4(72 - 79.5)^2$
$\qquad = 4(10.5)^2 + 4(4.5)^2 + 4(-7.5)^2 + 4(-7.5)^2$
$\qquad = 4(110.25) + 4(20.25) + 4(56.25) + 4(56.25)$
$\qquad = 441 + 81 + 225 + 225$
$\qquad = 972$

Interaction SS $=$ between subcell SS $-$ (column SS $+$ row SS)
$\qquad = 972 - 936$
$\qquad = 36$

Within SS $= \sum\sum\sum_{ijk}(X_{ijk} - \overline{X}_{ij})^2$

$\qquad = (93 - 90)^2 + (90 - 90)^2 + (90 - 90)^2 + (87 - 90)^2$
$\qquad\quad + (85 - 84)^2 + (87 - 84)^2 + (83 - 84)^2 + (81 - 84)^2$
$\qquad\quad + (72 - 72)^2 + (70 - 72)^2 + (74 - 72)^2 + (72 - 72)^2$
$\qquad\quad + (70 - 72)^2 + (71 - 72)^2 + (73 - 72)^2 + (74 - 72)^2$
$\qquad = 56$

Total SS $=$ subcell SS $+$ within SS
$\qquad = 972 + 56$
$\qquad = 1,028$

significant and the column variable is not, and we therefore conclude that the teaching method had a significant effect on posttest scores beyond any effect of pretesting, but that the use of a pretest versus no pretest did not significantly affect posttest scores.

Table 13.11.   ANOVA for teaching strategy experiment

A		ANOVA table			
Source	SS	df		Mean square	F
Total	1,028	$(N - 1)$	15		
Subcell	972	$(rc - 1)$	3		
Col.—testing	36	$(c - 1)$	1	36	7.71
Row—treatment	900	$(r - 1)$	1	900	192.72*
Interaction	36	$(r - 1)(c - 1)$	1	36	7.71
	56	$(N - rc)$	12	4.67	

*Significant; $F (0.01, df = 1,12) = 9.33$
Interaction not significant at 0.01 level. Throw it back into error term.

B	ANOVA table with interaction thrown into error term			
Source	SS	df	Mean square	F
Column—testing	36	1	36	5.08
Row—treatment	900	1	900	127.12*
Error	92	13	7.08	

*Significant; $F (0.01, df = 1,13) = 9.07$
Treatment effect significant at 0.01, pretest not significant.

Comparing Experimental Groups

In the analysis of variance discussed above, the pretest versus posttest only variable was not found to have a significant effect on posttest scores in the aggregate, that is in comparing the scores of the eight individuals who were pretested with those of the eight who were not. Because in the descriptive interpretation of the data we noticed that the pretest variable seemed to account for a difference in the scores of the two experimental groups but not between the two control groups, we might wish to examine the difference in the mean posttest scores of the two experimental groups more closely. The concern here would focus on the issue of whether or not pretesting should be expected to inflate posttest scores, when used in conjunction with the new teaching strategy. This could be viewed as a subexperiment in which the pretest is the experimental variable; we have eight cases randomly divided between two groups that both have received the new teaching strategy and presumably have been treated the same in other respects except that one was pretested and one was not.

The individual posttest scores of these two groups, along with means and standard deviations, are shown in Table 13.12A. The mean average score of those who were pretested is 6 points greater than that of those who were not, suggesting that perhaps the pretest experience has the effect of increasing posttest scores, at least among those who are exposed to the new teaching strategy. The question of whether this difference is statistically significant as opposed to having a high probability of occurring by chance in the random assignment process can be addressed by a two-sample t test, as shown in Table 13.12B.

Because, according to the alternate hypothesis, the mean score of those who were pretested would be expected to exceed that of the group that was not pretested, a one-tailed test is applicable. As the computed t value is greater than the critical t at the 0.01 level, we conclude that for the experimental groups the difference in scores between the pretested and nonpretested groups is significant, and given the controlled nature of the experiment we would be fairly confident, then, that the pretest did in fact produce added increments in posttest scores among the participants in the experimental group.

This result implies fairly strongly that there is indeed an interaction between teaching method and pretest versus no pretest in affecting posttest scores, because there is a significant difference between mean posttest scores of the experimental pretested and nonpretested groups, while there is no observed difference in mean scores between the pretested and nonpretested control groups. Yet, the lack of observed difference between the mean scores of the two control groups could be a result of chance effect in the random assignment process, and we have no indication of the probability of a type II error in concluding that in the long run the means of these two groups would be the same.

Comparing Gain Scores

In comparing the degree of improvement registered by the two groups who were exposed to both a pretest and a posttest, we cannot use two-sample t tests to compare mean pretest and posttest scores for each group because both sets of scores pertain to the same samples. Rather,

Table 13.12. Comparison of experimental groups pretested and nonpretested

A	Posttest scores		
	Pretested	Posttested only	
	93 $\overline{X}_1 = 90$ 90 90 $s_1 = \sqrt{4.5}$ 87	85 $\overline{X}_2 = 84$ 87 83 $s_2 = \sqrt{5}$ 81	

B	Two-sample t test

H_0: $\mu_1 = \mu_2$

H_1: $\mu_1 > \mu_2$

$$t = \frac{(\overline{X}_1 - \overline{X}_2) - (\mu_1 - \mu_2)}{\sqrt{\dfrac{s_1^2}{N_1 - 1} + \dfrac{s_2^2}{N_2 - 1}}}$$

$$t = \frac{(90 - 84) - 0}{\sqrt{\dfrac{4.5}{3} + \dfrac{5}{3}}}$$

$$= \frac{90 - 84}{\sqrt{3.17}}$$

$$= 6/1.78$$

$t = 3.37$

t (one-tailed, df $= 6$, 0.01) $= 3.143$

Conclusion: reject H_0

the appropriate measure is the **gain score**, the difference between an individual's posttest and pretest scores. We can, however, use a two-sample t test to compare mean average gain scores between the experimental and control group, as these are independent samples.

These gain scores are computed in Table 13.13, which shows a dramatic difference between the two groups, an average of 20 points improvement for those in the test group and only 3 points improvement for

Table 13.13.   Comparison of gain scores

Group	Pretest scores		Posttest scores	Gain scores	
Test	68		93	25	
	67	$\bar{X} = 70$	90	23	$\bar{X}_1 = 20$
	73		90	17	$s_1 = \sqrt{17}$
	72		87	15	
Control	67		72	6	
	70	$\bar{X} = 69$	70	0	$\bar{X}_2 = 3$
	68		74	6	$s_2 = \sqrt{6.5}$
	71		72	1	

H_0: $\mu_1 = \mu_2$

H_1: $\mu_1 > \mu_2$

$$t = \frac{(20 - 3) - 0}{\sqrt{\dfrac{17}{3} + \dfrac{6.5}{3}}}$$

$$= 17/2.8$$

$$= 6.07$$

t (one-tailed, df = 6, 0.01) = 3.143
Conclusion: reject H_0

those in the control. The t statistic computed in the table lands deep in the critical region, testing at the 0.01 level, and we therefore conclude that the degree of test score improvement on the part of the test group was significantly greater than that of the control group. Again, a one-tailed test was used because the alternate hypothesis specifies a direction of difference, namely that the experimental group performance would be superior to the control group performance.

An additional test that might be made would involve a comparison of the mean average pretest scores of the two groups to determine whether there was an initial selection bias between them. In this case the test is not conducted because the observed means differ by only 1 point. If, however, the mean pretest score of the control group were substantially lower than that of the test group, it would bring into question a rival explanation, namely that a difference in the ability of the students in the two groups rather than the difference in teaching methods is the factor that resulted in difference in gain scores. Thus, the use of specific t tests within the overall ANOVA framework can provide additional insight regarding the variation of test scores.

One additional comment relating to the example concerns the ultimate question of how much improvement in test scores we can attribute to the new teaching strategy. Looking at Table 13.13 we see an average 20-point gain score for the test group and a 3-point score for the control; our single best point estimate of the difference due to the new strategy *and* pretesting is 17 points, and we could develop a confidence interval estimate around this figure. However, referring back to Table 13.9, showing posttest scores for all four groups, we see that the point differential between test and control groups is an average of 18 points for those who were pretested and 12 points for those who were posttested only. In addition, a comparison of the two test groups shows an average posttest score for the pretested group that is 6 points higher than that for the group that was not pretested. Thus, in Table 13.9, it would appear that the treatment itself accounts for an increase of 12 points while the interaction of pretesting and treatment accounts for an additional 6 points. To summarize, then, referring to both Table 13.9 and Table 13.13, we would conclude that the treatment itself produced a gain of from 12 to 17 points in posttest scores.

THREE OR MORE INDEPENDENT VARIABLES

Analysis of variance is often used with three or more independent variables, particularly with data generated by experiments involving more than two treatment or blocking variables. With both experimental and nonexperimental data the key constraint on how many independent variables can be introduced into the analysis is the number of cases. Even with a large sample size in the aggregate, breaking the observations down by categories of multiple independent variables can soon result in having only a few cases per cell, almost automatically reducing within group variation. With nonorthogonal designs, using cross-sectional data for example, where the frequency of cases in certain categories might be low, breaking down by an additional independent variable might result in empty cells in the comparison of means table and the **confounding** of two or more variables. This refers to the lack of distribution of one independent variable across categories of another, making it impossible to sort out their effects on the dependent variable.

Table 13.14.   Number of physician visits per year—raw data

Age group	Metropolitan areas		
	5% Co-insurance	20% Co-insurance	Control
<20	4, 5, 8, 2, 5	4, 5, 3, 4, 5	4, 6, 4, 2, 6
	6, 3, 1, 9, 7	2, 6, 4, 5, 7	4, 5, 5, 2, 4
21-64	6, 7, 5, 7, 9	5, 6, 4, 7, 5	5, 3, 6, 5, 4
	6, 7, 2, 7, 6	4, 6, 3, 8, 6	5, 6, 5, 7, 4
65 and over	8, 8, 7, 8, 9	10, 7, 6, 8, 11	7, 8, 7, 8, 7
	8, 10, 11, 6, 9	9, 7, 5, 9, 8	6, 7, 7, 8, 7

Age group	Nonmetropolitan areas		
	5% Co-insurance	20% Co-insurance	Control
<20	4, 4, 5, 4, 4	3, 4, 5, 6, 4	4, 6, 3, 3, 2
	9, 3, 4, 2, 1	3, 4, 4, 3, 2	3, 3, 1, 4, 3
21-64	5, 5, 4, 4, 6	4, 6, 5, 9, 5	1, 4, 3, 4, 4
	4, 4, 6, 3, 7	4, 6, 4, 5, 2	7, 5, 3, 4, 5
65 and over	7, 6, 4, 8, 6	6, 3, 5, 6, 9	9, 6, 5, 7, 6
	6, 7, 6, 6, 6	4, 6, 8, 6, 5	5, 2, 6, 3, 4

Table 13.14 introduces data from a hypothetical experiment on public health insurance in which two treatments are compared with a control. The two treatments provide individuals with health insurance benefits at different rates of co-insurance, the proportion of costs to be paid by the individual, while the control group individuals are receiving no health insurance benefits, public or private. The experiment is in force for 1 year with the dependent variable, number of physician visits during that year, measured at the end of that period. As age is known to be highly associated with physician visits, three age groups are set up as blocks with the full experiment run for each block. Furthermore, the experiment is replicated intact on a group of residents of metropolitan areas and residents of nonmetropolitan areas. Essentially the experiment is being run on six blocks of participants as grouped by age and place of residence.

Table 13.14 shows the number of physician visits for the 10 individuals in each block, while Table 13.15 is a complete comparison of means breakdown of the 180 observations by treatment, age, and place of residence. Given the statistical independence among the three independent variables, computing the sums of squares is a straightforward extension of the two-way ANOVA presented above. For example, the treatment SS would be based on the variation of the three overall treatment means shown in columns IX through XI (5.77, 5.42, and 4.82, respectively) around the grand mean of 5.34. The main effect of place of residence SS would be computed on the basis of the variation of the overall means of columns IV and VIII around the grand mean, while the SS due to age would be based on the variation of the overall means of rows A, B, and C around the grand mean.

In addition to these main effects, the sum of squares can be computed for the interaction effect of each pair of independent variables and for the three-way interaction effect of all three independent variables. To develop the SS due to interaction between treatment and age, for example, we would use the bottom portion of the table, columns IX through XII and rows A through D, and treat it as a two-way ANOVA. For the interaction SS attributable to age and place of residence we would extract all of the columns IV, VIII and XII from Table 13.15 and treat them in similar fashion. For the SS due to the interaction effect of treatment and place of residence, we could set up a comparison of means table involving all the means in row D, ignoring the age breakdown, and proceed in the same way. Finally, the three variable interaction SS equals the overall subcell SS minus the sum of the SS attributable to the three main effects and the three two-way interaction SS already computed. The overall subcell SS is based on the variation of the means of the 18 subcells in the top rank of Table 13.15 around the grand mean.

Table 13.16 shows the ANOVA table for this exercise. The degrees of freedom, mean square variance estimates, and F ratios are all arrived at in the same manner as with the two-way ANOVA, each F being the ratio of the corresponding mean square to the within group mean square. The critical value of F at a given significance level depends on the degrees of freedom associated with the particular factor being tested and with the within group estimate of variance. Thus, to test the effect of the treatment variable at the 0.01 level, with 2 and 162 degrees of freedom the critical F is roughly 4.7. It is preferred procedure to test the three-way interaction first, throwing it back into the error term if it is not significant, then testing the two-way interactions and throwing them back into the error term if they are not significant, before testing the main effects; however, this is often not done in practice. In Table 13.16

Table 13.15. Number of physician visits per year by type of program, age, and place of residence

Age group		Metropolitan				Nonmetropolitan			
		I 5% Co-insurance	II 20% Co-insurance	III Control	IV Total	V 5% Co-insurance	VI 20% Co-insurance	VII Control	VIII Total
A	<20	5.00	4.50	4.20	4.57	4.00	3.80	3.20	3.67
B	21–64	6.20	5.40	5.00	5.53	4.80	5.00	4.00	4.60
C	65 and over	8.40	8.00	7.20	7.87	6.20	5.80	5.30	5.77
D	Total	6.53	5.97	5.47	5.99	5.00	4.87	4.17	4.68

Age group		Total			
		IX 5% Co-insurance	X 20% Co-insurance	XI Control	XII Total
A	<20	4.50	4.15	3.70	4.12
B	21–64	5.50	5.20	4.50	5.07
C	65 and over	7.30	6.90	6.25	6.82
D	Total	5.77	5.42	4.82	5.34

Table 13.16.   ANOVA table: three-way ANOVA

Source	SS	df	Mean square	F
Total	763.99	179	4.268	
Subcell	347.80	17	20.459	7.964
Treatment	27.70	2	13.850	5.391*
Age	225.10	2	112.550	43.810*
Residence	77.356	1	77.356	30.111*
Treatment and age	0.500	4	0.125	0.049
Treatment and residence	1.411	2	0.706	0.275
Age and residence	14.011	2	7.006	2.727
Treatment, age, and residence	1.722	4	0.431	0.168
Within	416.186	162	2.569	

*Significant at the 0.01 level

these interactions are not thrown back into the error term although they are not significant, yielding the final conclusion that each of the main effects is significant at the 0.01 level and that none of the interactions is significant beyond the main effects. Thus, we conclude that the effect of the treatment variable on physician visits is significant beyond the effects of age and place of residence.

It should be reiterated that with experimental designs such as those discussed in the preceding examples, inferential statistics very often are not applied directly in the context of drawing conclusions about larger populations based on sample data. The experimental units observed very often do not constitute any kind of probability sample from the population of interest, and, therefore, there is no basis for making probabilistic inferences to the larger populations. Analysis of variance is a primary statistical technique for use with experimental data, but the interpretation of the F tests is often based on the *random assignment* of cases to treatments rather than *random sampling*. In this situation, a statistically significant difference in means is interpreted as one that would have a low probability of occurring by chance if the cases were observed and then randomly assigned to blocks or treatment groups. This represents the use of inferential statistics to take the random component of experimental error into account and strengthen internal validity, as opposed to the usual external validity-oriented function of inferential statistics. When experimental data are based on random samples from larger populations, of course, both kinds of interpretations can be drawn from inferential tests of significance.

NONORTHOGONAL DESIGNS

With unequal frequencies of cases in the cells of comparison of means tables, two and three-way ANOVA problems are compounded by the lack of statistical independence among the independent variables. The unequal cell frequencies indicate statistical associations among the independent variables such that there may be some overlap in their effects on the dependent variable that cannot be sorted out. When this is the case, the additivity properties of the main and interaction effects no longer pertain, and if the variation associated with each effect is computed separately, there is no reason to expect that their sum will equal total subcell, or explained, variation.

As we saw in the chapter 5 discussion of elaboration, the statistical relationship between two variables in the aggregate can be affected in any number of ways by interrelationships with additional variables. The apparent association between a nominal level independent variable and an interval level dependent variable may be exaggerated, diminished, or altered altogether by the disproportionate representation of cases in different categories of the independent variable across categories of some third variable which is also statistically related to the dependent variable. In the example shown in Table 5.15 in chapter 5, for instance, there is absolutely no association between employee sex and absenteeism within given income groups. Yet because of the strong relationship between income and absenteeism and that fact that more women tend to be in the low income group while more men tend to be in the upper income group, in the aggregate women are shown to be absent twice as much as men. It is this aggregate association which is encompassed by the term, main effects, in analysis of variance, and the problem in ANOVA with unequal cells is to assess these effects "fairly" in a way that is not distorted by the differential effects of other variables.

Adjusted Means

By convention this problem is usually dealt with by attributing to each main effect the portion of total variation that the variable can account for apart from the effects of the other independent variables included in the analysis. Another way of saying this is that all the variation that might be attributed to the other variables is subtracted out or neutralized before computing the amount of variation explained by the independent variable of interest. This is done in turn for each independent variable under consideration. (It should be noted that with unequal cell frequencies, interaction effects can also bias apparent main effects and that packaged computer programs often provide options for attributing explained variation to independent variables in different ways, depending on the researcher's purpose.)

Up to this point our discussion of statistical controls has centered around the examination of bivariate associations within separate categories of control variables to see whether they are replicated, further specified, distorted, or washed out, etc. A different way of operationalizing this concept when mean averages are involved, however, entails adjusting means in a table so as to "erase" the variation in the dependent variable that might be attributable to the control variable, and then comparing these adjusted means across the categories of the other independent variable.

Table 13.17 shows hypothetical data on highway patrol levels and accident rates discussed in chapter 5. The association between patrol

Table 13.17.   Accidents per 100 million vehicle miles by patrol level and traffic flow

A	Unadjusted		
	Patrol level		
Traffic flow	Low (N)	High (N)	Total (N)
Light	2.70 (60)	2.40 (8)	2.66 (68)
Intermediate	3.40 (30)	3.00 (25)	3.22 (55)
Heavy	4.20 (5)	3.90 (50)	3.93 (55)
Total	3.00 (95)	3.48 (83)	3.22 (178)

B	Adjusted for traffic flow		
	Patrol level		
Traffic flow	Low (N)	High (N)	Total (N)
Light	3.26 (60)	2.96 (8)	3.22 (68)
Intermediate	3.40 (30)	3.00 (25)	3.22 (55)
Heavy	3.49 (5)	3.19 (50)	3.22 (55)
Total	3.32 (95)	3.11 (83)	3.22 (178)

level and accident rates is distorted by a third variable, traffic flow, which is associated with both the independent and dependent variables. Thus, although for each level of traffic flow a lower accident rate is associated with a high level of patrol, in the aggregate the mean accident rate for roadways with a high patrol level is greater than that for the roads with low patrol levels.

In Table 13.17B the means have been adjusted for the traffic flow variable. This is akin to asking what the accident rates would be if traffic flow had no effect on them, and involves adding 0.56 to each observation in the light traffic flow category and subtracting 0.71 from each heavy traffic flow observation so as to represent this hypothetical situation. Note that if this procedure were used with an orthogonal design it would have no effect on the aggregate mean averages for the categories of the independent variables, because the association between one independent variable and the dependent variable is inherently separate from the effects of other independent variables.

However, because the aggregate category means are in effect weighted averages across the subcells within the category, with nonorthogonal designs adjusting the means for one variable often results in changes in the category means of the other variables, as is the case in Table 13.17B. The adjusted means in that table can be interpreted as the mean accident rates that would be expected if traffic flow had no effect on accident rates. Notice that in this example the direction of the association between patrol level and accident rates has been reversed and that the variation of the adjusted column means around the grand mean has also been decreased; the column sum of squares computed on the basis of the adjusted means and interpreted as variation explained by patrol level would be less than that based on the unadjusted means.

The differences in these adjusted means represent the association between patrol level and accident level rates beyond any association between either of these variables and traffic flow, which has now been controlled for. In fact, this adjusting procedure is really what is meant by the term "fixing for the effects of" a given variable. With ANOVA problems involving unequal cell frequencies and more than two independent variables, means can be adjusted for all but one, and the resulting variation among categories of that variable can be fairly attributed to it. Computing sums of squares on the basis of these adjusted means is basically the way in which two or three-way ANOVA proceeds, although the computational procedures may not involve this step directly. It is also the case that the computation of sums of squares incorporates a weighting procedure to compensate for unequal subsamples and satisfy the assumptions underlying the F test. The details of these computations will not be presented in this text (they are rarely performed manually in any case), but the use of the technique is illustrated in the following two examples.

Fire Loss Example   Table 13.18 shows the average fire loss in hundreds of dollars for 219 reported fires in a city as broken down by the type of alarm, the property type, and the form of ignition. This example begins with two adjusted means exercises and then shows how these effects are reflected in the ANOVA procedure. Comparing the unadjusted aggregate means shows a substantial differential between types of alarm ($5.15 for telephoned alarms versus $31.76 for those reported by other methods), a lesser differential effect of form of ignition ($12.07 for fuel sources, $14.76 for electrical or smoke ignited fires, versus $13.26 for other forms of heat ignition), a very slight difference in average fire loss by property type ($13.45 for buildings versus $13.39 for open spaces). In table 13.18B these data have all been adjusted for the effect of the form of ignition. This results in only slight changes in the aggregate means of type of alarm and property type, primarily because of the weak differential effect of form of ignition in the first place and its fairly weak associations with the other two variables. Thus, form of ignition is not acting as a suppressor variable, as might have been expected.

Table 13.19 shows average fire loss broken down by type of alarm and property type only, similar to the lower portion of Table 13.18A, but now adjusted for type of alarm. Thus, in Table 13.19 the variation in fire loss associated with type of alarm has been subtracted, and in this case the result has been to heighten the apparent effect of property type. While with the unadjusted means the differential effect of property type was only a few cents, by adjusting the means for type of alarm it has been increased to almost $4. This indicates that the statistical relationship between property type and fire loss is largely suppressed by the overall effect of the type of alarm variable in the unadjusted comparison of means table. This heightened effect of property type, when type of alarm is controlled for, is borne out in the following analysis of variance.

Table 13.20 shows ANOVA tables for one, two, and three-way analyses of these data. In A the effect of property type is tested without consideration of either of the other two independent variables; the sum of squares attributable to property type is inconsequential and its computed F is just about 0. In B a two-way ANOVA is shown involving type of alarm and property type as independent variables. The sum of squares for each has been computed on the basis of means having been adjusted for the other. Thus, the sum of squares attributed to property type is based on the adjusted means shown in Table 13.9. This sum of squares attributed to property type, 845.364, is greatly increased above the amount shown in A, because fixing for the effects of alarm type reveals a much greater differential effect of property type, as seen in Table 13.19.

In Table 13.20 B the sum of squares attributed to type of alarm, property type, and their interaction effect on fire loss add up to greater than the total subcell or explained variation, due to the increased differential effect of property type when the means are adjusted for type of alarm. Thus, each variable is being tested independently of the other; we have no way of beginning with total subcell variation and breaking it down into portions fairly attributable to the two independent variables. With respect to the F tests, although the sum of squares due to property type has increased substantially, only type of alarm is found to have a significant effect on fire loss.

Table 13.20 C shows the three-way ANOVA table. Note here that further adjusting the means for form of ignition in applying the F tests to the previous two variables has resulted in a minimal decrease in the sum of squares attributed to type of alarm and a very slight increase in the variation attributed to property type. In other words, incorporating form of ignition as an additional variable in the ANOVA has a negligible impact on the apparent effect of type of alarm and property type, as seen in Table 13.18B. In addition, the variation attributed to the interaction effect of type of alarm and property type has declined by virtue of taking form of ignition into account. Still, of all the possible main and interaction effects, only the main effect of type of alarm is found to be statistically significant. It might also be noted that although subcell SS increases substantially from the two-way to the three-way ANOVA, on the whole it represents a fairly small proportion of total variation with E^2, the proportion of explained variation, moving from 4.8 to 7.2 percent.

Analysis of Variance with Proportions

With dichotomous or binomial variables, which can be represented as taking on the values 1 and 0, the most common descriptive statistic is the proportion and the most common way of examining statistical associations is through the use of contingency analysis. Yet, as discussed in chapter 7 on introductory inferential statistics, it was pointed out that the proportion can be considered to represent a special case of mean average and that statistical inferences regarding population proportions and differences in proportions can be made on that basis using the Z score methodology. With large samples this approach can be extended to analysis of variance, even though the assumption of interval level measurement is clearly violated. Experiments have shown that the con-

Table 13.18. Average fire loss by type of alarm, property type, and form of ignition (hundreds of dollars)

A   Unadjusted

Type of alarm	Fuel			Electric or smoke			Other		
	Building	Open	Total	Building	Open	Total	Building	Open	Total
Telephone	1.40 (20)	2.20 (20)	1.80 (40)	15.45 (22)	1.64 (25)	8.11 (47)	2.75 (32)	7.41 (32)	5.08 (64)
Other	27.00 (8)	44.44 (9)	36.24 (17)	61.25 (8)	10.73 (13)	29.67 (21)	21.50 (6)	33.00 (24)	30.70 (30)
Total	8.71 (28)	15.31 (29)	12.07 (57)	27.67 (30)	4.58 (38)	14.76 (68)	5.71 (38)	18.38 (56)	13.26 (94)

Total

Type of alarm	Building	Open	Total
Telephone	6.16 (74)	4.18 (77)	5.15 (151)
Other	37.95 (22)	28.80 (46)	31.76 (68)
Total	13.45 (96)	13.39 (123)	13.42 (219)

B

Adjusted for form of ignition

Type of alarm	Fuel			Electric or smoke			Other		
	Building	Open	Total	Building	Open	Total	Building	Open	Total
Telephone	2.75	3.55	3.15	14.11	0.30	6.77	2.91	7.57	5.24
Other	28.35	45.79	37.59	59.91	8.89	28.33	21.66	33.16	30.86
Total	10.06	16.66	13.42	26.33	3.24	13.42	5.87	18.53	13.42

Total

Type of alarm	Building	Open	Total
Telephone	6.20	4.16	5.16
Other	38.00	28.77	31.76
Total	13.49	13.37	13.42

Table 13.19.   Average fire loss by type of alarm and property type (adjusted for type of alarm)

| Type of alarm | Property type | | |
	Building	Open	Total
Telephone	$14.43 (74)	$12.45 (77)	$13.42 (151)
Other	19.61 (22)	10.46 (46)	13.42 (68)
Total	15.62 (96)	11.71 (123)	13.42 (219)

clusions drawn from F tests and χ^2 tests will usually be the same and that where the results differ there is no basis for favoring one or the other (Li, 1964, pp. 471–475). In situations in which the effects of multiple independent variables on a binomial dependent variable are of interest, therefore, analysis of variance may well be preferable to elaborate χ^2 analysis because ANOVA is a multivariate technique that can incorporate many independent variables simultaneously. To replicate a three or four-way ANOVA with a series of χ^2 tests may be impossible because of the resulting few numbers of cases in the cells of the differentiated crosstabulations.

Table 13.21 shows the responses to a survey question about increasing expenditures on the police in a given city. The responses have been coded with a 1 representing "yes" and a 0 representing "no" so that the mean average of this variable for any given set of cases indicates the proportion who responded "yes." In Table 13.21A the proportion favoring increased police expenditures is shown for the sample of respondents broken down by their general rating of police services in their neighborhood and by whether or not someone in their household had been a victim of any crime over the past 15-month period. In general, it can be seen that a greater proportion favoring an increased expenditure is associated with the lower ratings of police performance and that respondents from victimized households tend less to favor an increased expenditure. Furthermore, there is also an association between the two independent variables (as indicated by the percentages shown in parentheses) such that respondents from victimized households tend to give the police a low general rating while those from nonvictimized households tend to give the police a high rating.

Table 13.20.   Analysis of variance with nonorthogonal design

A	One-way ANOVA			
Source	SS	df	Mean square	F
Total	725966.562	218		
Property type	0.179	1	0.179	0.000
Within	725966.383	217	3345.467	

B	Two-way ANOVA			
Source	SS	df	Mean square	F
Total	725966.562	218	3330.122	
Subcell	34599.500	3	11533.167	
Type of alarm	34050.641	1	34050.641	10.589*
Property type	845.364	1	845.364	0.263
Interaction	548.661	1	548.661	0.171
Within	691367.062	215	3215.661	

C	Three-way ANOVA			
Source	SS	df	Mean square	F
Total	725966.562	218	3330.122	
Subcell	51932.750	11	4721.159	
Alarm	34042.582	1	34042.582	10.455*
Property type	861.607	1	861.607	0.265
Form of ignition	221.884	2	110.942	0.034
Alarm and property	294.572	1	294.572	0.090
Alarm and ignition	818.961	2	409.481	0.126
Property and ignition	10623.703	2	5311.852	1.631
Alarm, property and ignition	5519.258	2	2759.629	0.847
Within	674033.812	207	3256.202	

*Significant at the 0.01 level.

Table 13.21B shows the same set of responses with the means (or proportions) adjusted to cancel out the effect of general police rating. The result is a slight increase in the differential effect of the victimization variable, again an indication that the association between victimization and the expenditure preference is somewhat suppressed in the aggregate by the general police rating variable.

Table 13.21. Proportion favoring increase in police expenditures by general police rating and victimization

A	Unadjusted means		
General police rating	Victimized	Not victimized	Total
Low	0.59 (27) (28%)	0.68 (29) (14%)	0.64 (56) (19%)
Medium	0.50 (36) (38%)	0.61 (67) (33%)	0.57 (103) (34%)
High	0.43 (33) (34%)	0.50 (108) (53%)	0.48 (141) (47%)
Total	0.50 (96) (100%)	0.56 (204) (100%)	0.54 (300) (100%)

B	Adjusted for general police rating		
Rating	Victimized	Not victimized	Total
Low	0.49 (27)	0.58 (29)	0.54 (56)
Medium	0.47 (36)	0.58 (67)	0.54 (103)
High	0.49 (33)	0.56 (108)	0.54 (141)
Total	0.48 (96)	0.57 (204)	0.54 (300)

Table 13.22 shows the results of a one-way and two-way ANOVA of this problem. In *A*, the victimization variable is the sole independent variable and is seen not to be significantly associated with the survey response variable. In *B*, both victimization and general police rating are taken into account. The sum of squares attributed to the victimization variable is increased somewhat by virtue of fixing for the effects of police rating, but in general both of the mean effects and the interaction effect are weak, and none turns out to be statistically significant. The great bulk of the variation in the expenditure preference variable goes unexplained by either of the two independent variables or their joint effect.

SUMMARY

Analysis of variance is a multivariate technique that is very useful in assessing the statistical relationships between interval level dependent variables and nominal, or category type, independent variables. In the

Table 13.22.   Analysis of variance with proportions

A	One-way ANOVA table			
Source	SS	df	Mean square	F
Total	74.435	299		
Victimization	0.265	1	0.2650	1.065
Within	74.170	298	0.2489	

No significant association

B	Two-way ANOVA table (Police rating and victimization controlled)			
Source	SS	df	Mean square	F
Total	74.435	299		
Subcell	1.740	5		
Victimization	0.554	1	0.554	2.243
Police rating	1.459	2	0.730	2.955
Interaction	0.016	2	0.008	0.032
Within	72.695	294	0.247	

No significant association

analysis of public programs it has many applications, with effectiveness and efficiency indicators often measured in dollars or other interval scales and independent variables often consisting of alternative program strategies, levels of input, modes of implementation, or environmental conditions specified as category type variables.

In some developmental stages of programming in which treatment effects are being evaluated with true experimental designs, the data may lend themselves to the classic use of ANOVA with orthogonal designs. More often, however, this is not the case. The data are collected from the field without the controlled structure of an experimental design, with unequal numbers of cases in the cells, and adjusted means are used to fix for the effects of control variables while testing for significant differences in means across categories of the independent variables of interest. Although the actual computations of sums of squared deviations are much more complicated in ANOVA with nonorthogonal data, and rarely performed manually in any sizeable problem, the availability of packaged computer programs incorporating these computational modifications has extended the practical use of analysis of variance to a much wider range of program analysis applications.

REFERENCES

Krishnan Nambroodiri, N., L. F. Carter, and H. M. Blalock. 1975. Applied Multivariate Analysis and Experimental Designs. New York: McGraw-Hill Book Company.

Li, J. C. R. 1964. Statistical Inference I. Ann Arbor: Edwards Brothers.

Neter, J., and W. Wasserman. 1974. Applied Linear Statistical Models. Homewood, Ill.: Richard D. Irwin, Inc.

Ostle, B., and R. W. Mensing. 1967. Statistics in Research, 6th Ed. Ames, Iowa: Iowa State University Press.

Snedecor, G. W., and W. G. Cochran. 1967. Statistical Methods, 6th Ed. Ames, Iowa: Iowa State University Press.

Winer, B. J. 1962. Statistical Principles in Experimental Design. New York: McGraw-Hill Book Company.

PRACTICE PROBLEMS FOR CHAPTER 13

1. Ten years ago a program was begun in four rural provinces in Peru to reduce the rate of population increase by educating peasants about birth control devices and making these devices available. In two of these provinces the program also included continued counseling on family planning.

   The evaluation of the effect of this program was based on a random selection of a few families from each pair of provinces as well as two other provinces where the program had never been implemented. The primary measure used is the number of children 10 years old or less per family:

Provinces

I & II No program	III & IV Program—no counseling	V & VI Program and counseling
4	2	2
2	4	1
6	3	2
3	4	3
4	1	1
5	3	0
6	2	0
3	5	2

Using inferential statistics determine whether the program had a significant impact on the birth rate for the population as a whole.

2. Below is the output of an analysis of variance:

	SS	df	Mean square	F
Total	5218	219		
Between columns	2218	4	554	69.2
Between rows	837	3	279	34.9
Interaction	511	12	43	5.4
Within	1652	200	8	

a. What is the number of observations in the sample?
b. How many categories does the column variable have?
c. Is the interaction effect significant at the 0.01 level?
d. How much of the total variation is left unexplained by the analysis?

3. In an attempt to determine the influence of the residential density and type of pickup on the cost of household refuse collection, the relevant data were collected from 12 collection agencies, selected in a stratified random sample. The table below shows the individual observations as well as the mean average annual costs per household for each group of three agencies.

Average annual cost per household

Type of pickup	Density		Total
	Low	High	
Curb	37 38 $\bar{X} = 38$ 39	32 32 $\bar{X} = 32$ 32	$35
Alley	44 46 $\bar{X} = 46$ 48	41 44 $\bar{X} = 44$ 47	$45
Total	$42	$38	$40

With reference to the sample both density and type of pickup seem to be associated with cost of collection. Use the ANOVA technique to test for the significance of these assocations for the population at large.
a. Compute the variation (SS) attributed to the density variable.

    b.   Compute the variation (SS) attributed to the type of pickup.
    c.   Compute total subcell SS.
    d.   Compute the interaction SS.
    e.   Compute within group variation.
    f.   Complete an ANOVA table for this problem.
    g.   Which effects, if any, are significant at the 0.05 level?

4.   A city Personnel Department conducted a training program to increase tolerance for ambiguity in decision-making situations. Personnel of three position classifications were involved in the training
program. The position classifications were Maintenance, Managerial,
and Clerical. Assume that those receiving the training (treatment
"X") were randomly chosen. The measuring instrument employed
to show the effects of the training program on the various personnel categories was an examination. This measuring instrument
was scaled from 0 to 10; with 0 = low tolerance and 10 = very
high tolerance for ambiguity.

Present position classification

Treatment	Maintenance	Managerial	Clerical	Total
No training	1 3 2 $\bar{X}_{11} = 2$	2 1 0 $\bar{X}_{12} = 1$	1 2 0 $\bar{X}_{13} = 1$	$\bar{X}_1 = 1.33$
	0 5 1	0 0 3	1 1 1	
Total	12	6	6	24
Training	9 6 7 $\bar{X}_{21} = 8.33$ 10 10 8	3 1 2 $\bar{X}_{22} = 4.16$ 6 8 5	3 8 6 $\bar{X}_{23} = 6.16$ 4 9 7	$\bar{X}_2 = 6.22$
Total	50	25	37	112
Total	$\bar{X}_1 = 5.16$	$\bar{X}_2 = 2.58$	$\bar{X}_3 = 3.5$	$\bar{X} = 3.77$

Using the data, test for statistically significant interaction effect between the treatment and Present Position classification on tolerance
scores. Are both main effects significant at the 0.05 level?

14

REGRESSION AND CORRELATION ANALYSIS

Regression analysis and correlation analysis are complementary techniques, developed for the examination of associations among interval level measures. The techniques consist of a whole set of summary measures and statistical tests which, taken together, yield more complete and more precise findings than do the other techniques discussed in this book, mostly because of the greater amount of information contained in interval measures. These techniques, like analysis of variance, are often termed least squares methods because the computations are based on minimizing unexplained variation. In fact, in some ways regression can be thought of as an extension of ANOVA in which each level of an interval measure, independent variable, is a separate and discrete category. Conversely, ANOVA can be thought of as an extension of regression analysis where the independent variable only has a small number of possible values; in the next chapter the use of categorical variables in a regression model is discussed, and this point should become more clear.

Regression and correlation are highly useful techniques because they enable the researcher to examine the precise nature of an association as well as obtain good approximations of the strength of association and make tests of statistical significance. The two are often merged in that while a regression equation represents the trend of an association and correlations indicate its strength, measures of strength of association are closely related to the nature of association, and significance tests for both regression and correlation really amount to the same thing.

Regression models can be developed for purely descriptive purposes, predictive or forecasting purposes, and explanatory uses. That is, regression can be used to simply describe a statistical association, predict values of the dependent variable in additional observations based on known or projected values of the independent variables, and examine hypotheses about causal relationships. These least squares techniques have many applications ranging from needs and demands studies to program impact evaluations. They are most often used in cross-sectional data analysis, but they are also frequently applicable to more structured research designs, particularly time series.

The conventional notation used with regression analysis is to represent the dependent variable with Y and the independent variables with X's. All the variables are operated on as interval measures. The **regression of Y on X** is the path through the mean average values of Y for each level of X represented in the data. This curve shows the direction and to what extent Y changes as X changes. The true regression of Y on X in the population may be of any form, from a horizontal line to a very irregular curve. We often work with straight line, or linear, regressions, one type of curve, but the true regression might not be linear.

Visual inspection of scatterplots showing the joint distribution of Y and X will often provide an idea of what type of regression model is appropriate. The true regression could be a horizontal straight line at the mean value of Y, indicating a complete lack of association as the level of Y does not change at all with changing levels of X. A regression of any other form means that prediction of Y improves with knowledge of X, but some represent more systematic associations and lead to more reasonable interpretations. Figure 14.1 illustrates a horizontal linear regression and a curvilinear regression.

Typically, regression analysis is performed on sample data, although it can be used to approximate the true regression for data that are available for a whole population. The usual procedure is to postulate a model, specifying the form of regression that we hypothesize for the population, and then estimate the parameters of that model with sample data. The resulting regression is evaluated using a number of statistics, and if it seems to be an appropriate model (i.e., if it provides a good fit to the joint distribution), interpretations are drawn. If not, the information gained from inspection of that first model may lead the ana-

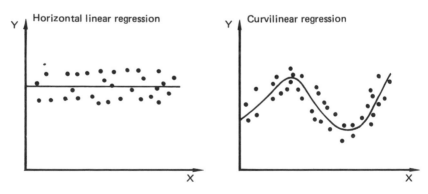

Figure 14.1.   Regression lines.

lyst to postulate a different form of regression and move through the process again.

As a final preliminary comment, it should be reemphasized that regression analysis, like all other statistical techniques, is concerned with describing and testing the statistical significance of associations among variables; the findings do not necessarily lead to conclusions about causal relationships. The technique is totally insensitive to the specification of dependent and independent variables, so that one can easily obtain highly significant regressions that clearly do not reflect a direction of causality, showing age as a function of education, for example.

The particular model that is developed depends on one's purposes. For example, if the intent is to look for differential effects of some program treatment variable, then the direction of cause and effect is clear and should be specified in the model. The finding of a highly significant regression in such a situation, however, still does not confirm the causal relationship, but rather indicates that the hypothesized effects *may* be being produced by the program treatments. Guarding against rival explanations such as self-selection, etc., is incumbent on the research design within which the regression analysis is conducted, not on the statistical analysis itself. If the purpose is to explain the variation in some dependent variable with independent variables that are thought to exert some causal influence, the model should be based on some underlying theory. If the purpose is simply to explore associations or develop a predictive model, the direction (or directness) of causality is less important. If for some reason it were desired to predict the ages of children in a school system using some readily available information, for example, a model that regressed age on grade would be helpful, although grade level certainly does not cause age.

SIMPLE LINEAR REGRESSION

The great bulk of applications of regression analysis in social science research have employed linear models, representing linear associations in which Y changes at a constant rate with unit changes in X. This is both because linear regressions are the easiest to work with and because frequently the state of existing knowledge about a subject is not developed enough to facilitate the use of more exacting models. Although the true regression might not be linear, a linear model may still approximate the true regression and provide useful information, as illustrated in Figure 14.2.

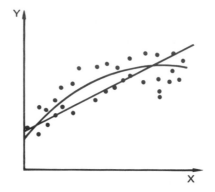

Figure 14.2.   Linear regression as approximation of curvilinear association.

This chapter concentrates on linear regressions, while curvilinear regressions are introduced briefly in the next chapter. A **simple linear regression** is one with a single independent variable. The regression model is stated as

$$Y = \beta_0 + \beta_1 X_1 + \epsilon$$

in which the parameters β_0 and β_1 represent a constant and the regression coefficient of X_1, respectively. The symbol ϵ represents the error term, the extent to which the regression fails to account for the variation in Y at a given level of X. In the case of a perfect linear association, for example, the functional relationship between fuel tax proceeds and gallons of fuel sold, there is no error and all observations would fall directly on the regression line. Most of the associations that are analyzed, however, are statistical associations in which the dependent variable is not completely determined by the independent variable; for such imperfect associations the error term represents the variation of cases around the regression line. Figure 14.3 illustrates true regressions for both perfect and imperfect associations.

Assumptions Underlying Regression Analysis

Regression analysis is based on the assumption of the interval level of measurement in all variables; the specification of the precise nature of the association as well as conducting tests of significance requires scales with equal intervals, but not necessarily ratio scales. Second, the interpretation of results should never be extended beyond the range of observed X's. As shown in Figure 14.4, the regression fit to a sample of

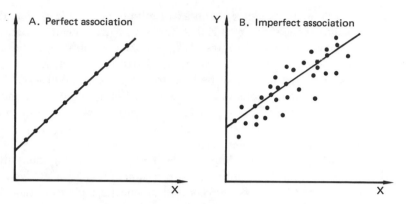

Figure 14.3.   Regression lines and associations.

cases within a particular range of X may be quite different from that which would pertain to a different or enlarged range of X values.

Error Term Assumptions   In using a regression model one usually has a statistical relationship instead of a functional relationship due to the error term, ϵ, in the equation. Certain assumptions about the error term must be made to conduct statistical inferences or tests for the regression analysis. The error referred to here is caused by measurement error (in the Y variable) and other factors acting on the Y variable. These other causal factors, therefore, may be numerous, singly unimportant, not highly interrelated, and of course unrelated and independent of X. (If these factors have a major impact, they should be included in the analysis with the use of multiple regression, which is

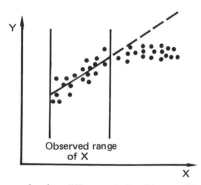

Figure 14.4.   Scattergram showing different relationships outside of observed range of X.

discussed later in the chapter.) The assumption then made is that the expected value of the error term is 0, $E\,(\epsilon) = 0$, with a mean of 0 and a constant variance across all values of X. Another assumption necessary for the analysis is that the error is normally distributed about X.

If these assumptions cannot be met, for example, if we observe that the error terms tend to increase or decrease or change signs as we move across levels of X, this linear regression is probably not the appropriate model. The appropriate model may not be linear, or the truly important independent variables have not been taken into account.

Assumptions for Making Significance Tests   In applying inferential statistical tests, random sampling is also assumed. As with analysis of variance, there are both fixed effects and stochastic regression models. **Fixed effects models** are those in which the values of X are established at certain levels. In the area of program analysis, the X's may represent treatment variables whose values are set or controlled for in experimental designs. Interpretations, then, are limited to these set values.

In stochastic models, also referred to as organismic or **random effects models,** the X's are random variables, and a random sample of cases to be observed will be random in terms of both X and Y. Interpretations are valid for all values of X within the range of observed values. With random effects models, the inference is to the population of all cases within the range of the observed values of X and Y, while with fixed effects models the inference extends only to populations characterized by those same levels of X.

In addition, it is assumed that Y is normally distributed at each value of X. Another assumed property is called **homoscedasticity,** which means there are equal variances of Y around the population mean of Y for each value of X as shown in Figure 14.5.

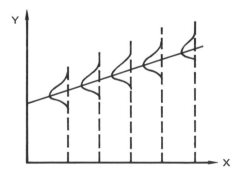

Figure 14.5.   Homoscedasticity around the regression line.

Developing the Estimating Equation

Given the assumption of a linear model for the true regression, we can use sample data to develop the estimating equation seen below:

$$\hat{Y} = b_0 + b_1 X_1$$

The parameters β_0 and β_1 have now been replaced by their best estimators, b_0 and b_1. The computations shown below provide unbiased estimates of these parameters, but they are still only estimates of the true relationship. By removing the error term the equation will no longer yield the observed value of Y. Therefore, we use the notation $\hat{Y}$ (called Y-**hat**) to denote the **predicted value of** Y, that is, the value of Y predicted by the estimating equation for a given level of X. Solving for b_0 and b_1 provides us with the least squares linear regression of Y on X for the sample and our best estimate of the model hypothesized for the population.

Computing b_1 and b_0   The formula for b_1, the **regression coefficient,** is:

$$b_1 = \frac{\Sigma(X_i - \overline{X})(Y_i - \overline{Y})}{\Sigma(X_i - \overline{X})^2}$$

or the ratio of the co-variation of X and Y to the variation (sum of squares) in X. The nature of the co-variation can be seen to determine the direction of the slope. If the association is positive, then deviations from means will tend to be either positive or negative for both X and Y for individual cases and the overall co-variation will be positive. For a negative association, the deviation from the mean of Y will tend to be negative when the deviation from X is positive and vice versa; thus, summing the products of deviations, primarily for cases with one positive and one negative deviation, will result in a negative co-variation.

After computing the regression coefficient we can use the formula below for computing Y **intercept, b_0**:

$$b_0 = \overline{Y} - b_1 \overline{X}$$

This term, b_0, is a constant in the estimating equation. We can think of the linear regression as beginning at that value of Y and then getting larger or smaller at a constant rate as we move up the scale of X. Another property of the estimating equation is that it passes through the point, $\overline{X}$, $\overline{Y}$, the center of the joint distribution.

Figure 14.6 gives an illustration of the computation of b_1 and b_0 using a sample problem of the effects of housing rehabilitation funds,

Property value increase	Rehabilitation funds			Co-variation	Variation in X
Y	X_1	$(Y - \bar{Y})$	$(X_1 - \bar{X}_1)$	$(X_1 - \bar{X}_1)(Y - \bar{Y})$	$(X_1 - \bar{X}_1)^2$
$30	$10	5	0	0	0
25	8	0	−2	0	4
10	9	−15	−1	15	1
45	12	20	2	40	4
20	11	− 5	1	− 5	1
15	8	−10	−2	20	4
40	13	15	3	45	9
5	6	−20	−4	80	16
35	12	10	2	20	4
25	11	0	1	0	1
$\Sigma Y = 250$	$\Sigma X_1 = 100$	$\Sigma = 0$	$\Sigma = 0$	$\Sigma = 215$	$\Sigma = 44$
$\bar{Y} = 25$	$\bar{X}_1 = 10$				

$$b_1 = \frac{\Sigma (X_1 - \bar{X}_1)(Y - \bar{Y})}{\Sigma (X_1 - \bar{X}_1)^2}$$

$$= \frac{215}{44}$$

$$b_1 = 4.8864$$

$$b_0 = \bar{Y} - b_1 \bar{X}_1$$

$$= 25 - 4.8864(10)$$

$$= 25 - 48.864$$

$$b_0 = -23.864$$

$$\hat{Y} = -23.864 + 4.8864 X_1$$

Figure 14.6. Computation of b_1 and b_0: housing rehabilitation example.

the independent variable (X_1), on the dependent variable, change in property values. In this example, the unit of analysis is the target neighborhood, 10 of which are displayed in Figure 14.6. Both variables represent mean averages for all the dwelling units in the neighborhood, expressed in units of $100.

Deviations of the observed values of Y from the least squares regression line $(Y - \hat{Y})$ sum to 0, i.e., the positive and negative deviations balance out. Furthermore, the sum of these squared deviations is at a minimum; this is really the *criterion* of the "best" regression line and the basis of significance tests and interpretations that follow. The **least squares regression line** is that one straight line passing through the joint distribution about which the variation of observed values of Y is minimized.

From this it follows that the regression of Y on X is not the same as that of X on Y unless the linear association between the two is perfect. Each would be minimizing the variation of a different variable around it. This illustrates why it is necessary to postulate the direction of the hypothesized relationship and specify the model accordingly. Figure 14.7 gives a graphic example of the regressions of Y on X and X on Y.

Characteristics of Regression Equations   The regression coefficient, b_1, equals the slope, indicating the direction and average amount of change in Y per unit increase in X. In our example it seems that for every dollar increase in rehabilitation funds there is an average \$4.88 increase in property values. The other estimating statistic, b_0, is the Y- intercept, indicating the point at which the regression line crosses the Y axis.

The dependent and independent variables are often measured in different scales; b_1 represents the functional relationship between them. The value of b_1, then, reflects the relative orders of magnitude of the two variables as well as the extent to which Y changes per unit change in X. If one changes the scale of X, b_1 changes accordingly but not b_0. For instance, in Figure 14.6 if we leave Y in hundreds of dollars and

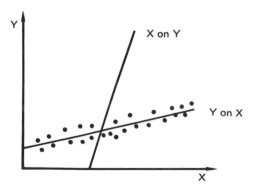

Figure 14.7.   Simple regressions—Y on X and X on Y.

change X_1 to simply dollars, b_1 will be reduced from 4.8864 to 0.048864. A change in the scale of Y would produce changes in both b_0 and b_1.

From this example we can see that the scales involved can be altered to facilitate computations; this may be desired in terms of both accuracy in computations as well as ease of interpretation. It should be noted that regressions are highly sensitive to rounding error and, therefore, computations should be carried out to more decimal places than is common with the less exacting statistical methods discussed in previous chapters.

For example, a measure of a very high order of magnitude might be divided by some constant in order to scale it down, or, conversely, one of a very low order of magnitude might be multiplied by a constant to eliminate decimal places. Similarly, because some of the computations that might be used require all positive numbers, some constant number might be added to each observation of Y to eliminate negative numbers. In such a case, b_0 will change, but not b_1.

Examining the Regression Equation

Having developed a simple regression equation, we can examine it to address three kinds of questions: 1) Statistical significance—is the linear regression found in a sample likely to have occurred by chance with a population in which there is no linear association? 2) Appropriateness of the *linear* model—is it apparent that the true association between the two variables is really nonlinear? 3) Strength of association—how much of the variation in the dependent variable is explained *by the linear regression*? All of the information needed to address these questions is contained in the **residuals**, the variation of the observed values of the dependent variable around the regression line. If there are no residuals, i.e., all the observations fall on the line, there is a perfect linear association that is highly significant for the population as a whole, such as the functional relationship of fuel tax to gallons of gas.

Significance of Regression   The statistical significance of a linear regression is tested with the analysis of variance F test. The null hypothesis is that there is no linear association in the population, that the regression of Y on X would be a horizontal line at the mean of Y. When this is true, our best prediction of Y for a given case is $\overline{Y}$ and is not improved by knowledge of X. Formally, ANOVA is used to test the assumption that the degree of linear association is 0. As will be seen later in this chapter, the parameter measuring the degree of linear association between two interval variables is **rho**; thus the null hypothesis being tested is that rho equals 0. This is synonymous with a test of the null hypothesis that the slope of the regression, β_1, is 0.

The total variation corrected for the mean is the sum of the squared deviations of the observed values from the mean; in our example $\Sigma(Y - \overline{Y})^2$ = 1,500 (see Figure 14.9). This total variation can be partitioned into two components: 1) remaining variation around the regression line, $(Y - \hat{Y})^2$ and 2) variation explained by the regression line, $(\hat{Y} - \overline{Y})^2$ both of which are computed in Figure 14.9. It should be noted that the unsquared deviations of observed values from predicted values, $\Sigma(Y - \hat{Y})$, sum to -0.04 rather than 0.00 because of rounding error. These two components sum to total variation as illustrated in Figure 14.8:

$$Y - \overline{Y} = (Y - \hat{Y}) + (\hat{Y} - \overline{Y})$$

Squaring both sides of this identity and summing across all cases ultimately results in the equation:

$$\Sigma(Y - \overline{Y})^2 = \Sigma(Y - \hat{Y})^2 + \Sigma(\hat{Y} - \overline{Y})^2$$

showing that total variation is indeed the sum of the variation due to regression (predicted values deviating from the mean) and the residual variation of individual cases around the regression (Blalock, 1972, pp. 321, 390–391).

The value of F is the ratio of the estimate of population variance based on the variation explained by the regression line to that based on the variation remaining around the regression. The variance estimates are comparable to the between group and within group estimates, respectively, used in analysis of variance. Given the assumption of homoscedasticity, the variance estimate based on the remaining, unexplained variation around the regression, or the residual mean square, will always

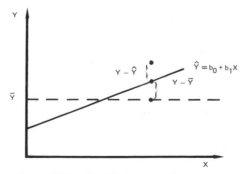

Figure 14.8.   Partitioning sum of squares.

Y	X_1	b_0	$b_1 X_1$	$\hat{Y}$	$(Y - \hat{Y})$
$30	$10	−23.86	48.86	25.00	5.00
25	8	−23.86	39.09	15.23	9.77
10	9	−23.86	43.98	20.12	−10.12
45	12	−23.86	58.64	34.78	10.22
20	11	−23.86	53.75	29.89	− 9.89
15	8	−23.86	39.09	15.23	− 0.23
40	13	−23.86	63.52	39.66	0.34
5	6	−23.86	29.32	5.46	− 0.46
35	12	−23.86	58.64	34.78	0.22
25	11	−23.86	53.75	29.89	− 4.89

$\Sigma = 250$

$\overline{Y} = 25$

$\Sigma | = -0.04$

rounding error

Residual variation $(Y - \hat{Y})^2$	Total variation $(Y - \overline{Y})^2$
25.00	25
95.45	0
102.41	225
104.45	400
97.81	25
0.05	100
0.12	225
0.21	400
0.05	100
23.91	0
$\Sigma = 449.46$	$\Sigma = 1,500$

ANOVA table

Source	SS	df	Mean square	F
Total (corrected)	1,500.00	9		
Regression	1,050.54	1	1,050.54	18.700 *
Residual	449.46	8	56.18	

*Significant at the 0.01 level

Figure 14.9. ANOVA for simple regression. Calculations of residual and total variation using least squares technique.

be *unbiased.* If the null hypothesis (H_0:rho $= 0$) is true, and in the population the values of Y are distributed evenly around $\overline{Y}$ without regard to values of X, the direction and slope of the linear regression in the sample will be results of sample error, dependent solely on the amount of variability in Y. The estimate of population variation based on the variation of points on the regression line around the mean, or regression mean square, then, will also be an unbiased estimate. Thus the expected value of the F ratio will be unity, and the distribution of F values resulting from all possible samples will follow the known F distribution for the corresponding number of degrees of freedom. If H_0 is false, however, the regression mean square will tend to overestimate the population variance, and the expected value of the F ratio will be greater than unity.

The ANOVA table for our sample problem is shown in Figure 14.9.

The residual sum of squares is computed with the formula, residual SS $= \Sigma(Y - \hat{Y})^2$, and equals 449.46. The regression sum of squares was obtained in this instance by subtracting the residual SS from total SS. With an N of 10, there are 9 degrees of freedom associated with the total variation corrected for the mean, while the regression SS has 1 degree of freedom because the variance estimate based on regression assumes that all the observations fall on the line. This is analogous to the assumption used in computing the between group variance estimate in analysis of variance that all observations fall on their respective category means. Thus with 1 degree of freedom associated with b_0 and one with b_1, there are 8 degrees of freedom ($N - 2$) associated with the residual variation.

The regression and residual mean squares, or variance estimates, are computed by dividing their respective SS by the corresponding df. The resulting F ratio of 18.700 exceeds the critical F at the 0.01 level for 1 and 8 df, and therefore the regression is found to be statistically significant. Our interpretation is that if H_0 is true and there is no linear association in the population, the probability of selecting a random sample where $N = 10$ yielding this particular regression is less than 0.01. Therefore, in this example we can reject the null hypothesis with the probability of a type I error of less than 0.01.

Test for Lack of Fit   Underlying a linear regression model is the assumption that the expected value of the error term in predicting Y for any level of X is 0, that the error is due to random variation, measurement error, and numerous, singly unimportant variables that might influence Y but are outside the model. If, however, the model is incorrect, we can think of the error term as having systematic components or bias error as well as random variation. A **bias component** represents a systematic connection between the sign or magnitude of the residual and the level of X. This might be apparent in an examination of residual plots, as discussed below.

The random variation component is sometimes referred to as **pure error** and the biased component is called "lack of fit." In addition to a visual inspection of residual plots, we can compute pure error and test for lack of (linear) fit if we have repeated observations for values of X. An estimate of the population variance based on the dispersion of Y for repeated values of X is said to represent pure error because X is fixed, therefore only random variation can account for differences in the values of Y. To be conservative in testing for linearity we assume that all the remaining variation in the error term is due to the lack of fit of the linear model, that all the observed values of Y fall on the true, curvilinear regression, however implausible that might seem. The formula for computing pure error (P.E.) at each level of $X_K (K = 1 \ldots n)$ having repeated observations is:

$$\text{P. E. SS} = \Sigma (Y_{X_K} - \overline{Y}_{X_K})^2$$

In our sample problem, then, we have repeated observations where X equals 8, 11, and 12:

At $X = 8$: $\text{P.E.} = (25 - 20)^2 + (15 - 20)^2$

$$= (5)^2 + (-5)^2$$

$$= 50$$

As summarized below, pure error SS for the whole problem equals 112.5 with 3 degrees of freedom; at any level of X, the degrees of freedom associated with pure error are 1 less than the number of observations at that level

X	$\Sigma(Y_{X_K} - \overline{Y}_{X_K})^2$	df
8	50.0	1
11	12.5	1
12	50.0	1
	112.5	3

After calculating pure error we can subtract it from the residual SS to obtain a measure of lack of fit, and expanding the ANOVA table we have the following result for our sample problem as seen in Table 14.1.

At the 0.01 level the critical F for 5 and 3 degrees of freedom is 28.24. Thus the lack of fit in the residual is not significant, and we have no reason to doubt the adequacy of the linear model. When lack of fit proves to be significant, we reject the linear model and explore some curvilinear models, as discussed in the next chapter.

Table 14.1 Test for lack of fit

Source	SS	df	Mean square	F
Total	1,500.00	9		
Regression	1,050.54	1	1,050.54	18.700
Residual	449.46	8	56.18	
Lack of fit	336.96	5	67.39	1.797
Pure error	112.5	3	37.50	

$F (0.01, \text{df} = 5,3) = 28.24$

This test does not prove that the linear regression is the correct model, but rather that it is plausible and not disputed by the data. We are always in the position of entertaining the model at hand rather than confirming that it is the only correct model. Nevertheless, the ability to test for lack of fit is an important advantage made possible by multiple observations for given levels of X. Therefore, in designing research in which one has some control over the independent variables, it is desirable to build such replications into the design.

Residual Plots The residuals of a regression can be plotted in scattergrams against values of X, $\hat{Y}$, or a time dimension to obtain an idea of how well the regression fits the data. Those for the simple regression computed above are plotted on X_1 in Figure 14.10. One purpose of examining residual plots is to determine the appropriateness of a linear model, as a complement to an F test for lack of fit discussed above or an alternative approach in situations in which the researcher lacks repeated observations of X. The fit of a linear regression to the data points can also be seen in a scattergram of the original values of Y on X, as shown in Figure 14.2. Sometimes because of differences in scale the pattern of cases around the regression can be better examined in residual plots, and furthermore, such graphical analysis of residuals also serves to examine the validity of certain assumptions on which the regression analysis is based. From this plot we can see that there is no systematic pattern to the residuals and therefore we can assume that the linear regression model is appropriate in this regard.

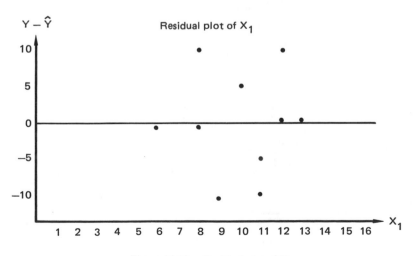

Figure 14.10.   Residual plot of X_1.

Figure 14.11 illustrates four prototype residual plots. If a linear model is appropriate, we would expect no connection between the residuals with either X or $\hat{Y}$ as shown in panel A (as in Figure 14.10). The residuals tend to fall in a horizontal band centering on 0, with no systematic variation in sign or values across the range of X or $\hat{Y}$. Figure 14.11B illustrates a situation in which the linear model is clearly inappropriate, and would lead us to develop some type of curvilinear regression. The pattern of fluctuation in the residuals of this prototype would indicate what type of curvilinear model would be appropriate.

In C the values of the residuals are shown to increase as X or $\hat{Y}$ increases, an indication that the error term in the regression model is greater at higher levels of X. As X increases, the variance around $\overline{Y}$ also increases, and thus the initial assumption of homoscedasticity (constant variance in Y around $\overline{Y}$ for all levels of X) is not met. Whenever a

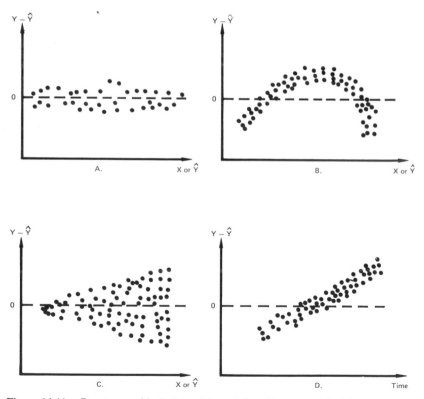

Figure 14.11.   Prototype residual plots. Adapted from Draper and Smith, 1966, Figures 3.3 and 3.4, p. 89.

residual plot indicates that the distribution of Y around X is hetero-scedastic, with a magnitude of variance in Y varying systematically with levels of X, the researcher should reconsider the appropriate model to use. With a residual plot as shown in Figure 14.11C, a linear model is still appropriate, but the simple regression of Y on X will not be the least squares solution and the F test for significance will not necessarily be valid. This situation can be accommodated by using a weighted least squares procedure (Neter and Wasserman, 1974, pp. 131–136).

If the cases vary across time and a time variable is included in the data base, it may also be useful to plot the residuals against the time measure (Draper and Smith, 1966, pp. 88–90). A residual plot against time such as that shown in D is particularly salient because it shows that error terms are correlated across time, with the regression over-estimating the earlier cases and underestimating the latter cases. When this situation arises, the time variable should be entered into a multiple regression model. By putting such a variable into the model, the systematic deviations will be absorbed by the time variable, and we will be left with residuals that are a function of other (hopefully nonsystematic) causes.

Standard Error of b_1 The estimated standard error of b_1 is the square root of the residual mean square ($\sqrt{s^2}$) divided by the variation in X. For our sample problem on property value increases this would be:

$$\text{s.e. } b_1 = \sqrt{\frac{s^2}{\Sigma_i(X - \overline{X})^2}}$$

$$= \sqrt{\frac{56.18}{44}}$$

$$= \sqrt{1.2768}$$

$$\text{s.e. } b_1 = 1.1300$$

The standard error can be used in t tests of hypotheses regarding the population parameter β_1; most commonly the null hypothesis is $H_0{:}\beta_1 = 0$ as opposed to the alternative hypothesis that β_1, the slope of the linear regression in the population, is not 0. This test is synonymous with the F test of the H_0 that the population parameter, rho = 0, discussed above. If rho is 0, there is a complete lack of linear association between X and Y, and β_1 is also equal to 0. To test $H_0{:}\beta_1 = 0$, we compute:

$$t = \frac{b_1 - \beta_1}{\text{s.e. } b_1}$$

$$= \frac{4.8864 - 0}{1.13}$$

$$t = 4.3242$$

Because in this case the alternate hypothesis is that $\beta_1 > 0$, a one-tailed test is appropriate; testing at the 0.01 level with 8 degrees of freedom, the critical value of t equals 2.896. Therefore, we conclude that there is a positive slope in the linear regression of Y on X in the population with a probability of a type I error of less than 0.01. Testing at the same significance level, an F test of rho $= 0$ will always produce the same results as a t test that $\beta_1 = 0$. It is interesting in this regard to note the relationship between the t and F distributions: t for $N - 2$ degrees of freedom is the square root of F with 1 and $N - 2$ degrees of freedom. In our example $t^2 = 18.70 = F$. It should be pointed out that indiscriminate use of this t test procedure—for instance with 20 separate simple regressions using the same dependent variable—will result in an inflated probability of type I error, as pointed out in the preceding chapter. In practice, with only a few independent variables and selective use of these t tests, this will usually not present a problem.

Standard error can also be used to construct confidence intervals for β_1, as follows:

$$b_1 \pm t \cdot \text{s.e. } b_1$$

In the example, at the 95 percent confidence level (for 8 df with a two-tailed test at the .05 level, $t = 2.306$) the confidence interval estimate is given by:

$$4.8864 \pm 2.306 \cdot 1.13$$

$$\pm 2.6058$$

$$P(2.2806 < \beta_1 < 7.4922) = 0.95$$

Standard Error of b_0   The estimating equation also provides a point estimate for β_0. Similar to b_1, we can calculate the standard error of b_0 using the formula shown below:

$$\text{s.e. } b_0 = \frac{\Sigma X^2}{\sqrt{N \Sigma (X - \overline{X})^2}} \cdot \sqrt{s^2}$$

This can be included in the equation shown below to calculate the confidence interval around the point estimate of β_0. In this example we are calculating a 99 percent confidence interval for the point estimate of β_0:

$$b_0 \pm t\,(N - 2, 0.01)\ \text{s.e.}\ b_0$$

(The t value is for a two-tailed test with $(N - 2)$ degrees of freedom at the 99 percent confidence level.)

Confidence Intervals for $\overline{Y}$ The least squares estimating equation developed for the sample provides us with our best point estimate of the mean of Y in the population for any specified level of X. Accuracy of the prediction depends in part on strength of association—a more compact distribution of Y about the regression yields greater accuracy in prediction. Another indicator is residual mean square—the smaller this estimate of population variance, the less the error of predicting $\overline{Y}$.

To get an idea of precision and accuracy in predicting $\overline{Y}$, we can develop interval estimates at specified levels of confidence. The confidence interval for $\overline{Y}$ at a given level of X is computed with the formula:

$$\hat{Y}_{X_K} \pm t \cdot \text{s.e.}\ Y_{X_K}$$

Where $\hat{Y}$ is the point estimate of $\overline{Y}$ at $X = K$ and s.e. $\hat{Y}_{X_K}$ is the standard error of $\hat{Y}$ at $X = K$, and t corresponds to the desired confidence level. The t value is that t for a two-tailed test with the number of degrees of freedom in the residual. The standard error for $\hat{Y}$ at X_K is given by:

$$\text{s.e.}\ Y_{X_K} = \sqrt{s^2}\ \sqrt{\frac{1}{N} + \frac{(X_K - \overline{X})^2}{\Sigma\,(X - \overline{X})^2}}$$

where s^2 is the residual mean square. The standard error of $\hat{Y}$ will vary with levels of X; it is minimized at the mean of X and increases with X's below and above $\overline{X}$. This can be understood intuitively by remembering that the true regression will pass through the point $\mu_x\mu_y$. To the extent that the slope of the estimating equation deviates from that of the true regression, the range of error in predicting Y will increase as the level of X moves away from its mean. Figure 14.12A shows the development of a 95 percent confidence interval estimate of $\overline{Y}$ where $X = 10$, while Figure 14.12B lists the computed 95 percent confidence intervals for various levels of X. Figure 14.12C, then, illustrates this confidence band of interval estimates across the range of X's, showing that the

$$\text{s.e. } \hat{Y}_{X_K} = \sqrt{s^2} \sqrt{\frac{1}{N} + \frac{(X_K - \bar{X})^2}{\Sigma(X - \bar{X})^2}}$$

A. 95% confidence interval calculation for $X_1 = 10$

If $X_1 = 10$, $\hat{Y} = 25$

From Figure 14.6

$$\text{s.e. } \hat{Y}_{|10} = \sqrt{56.18} \sqrt{\frac{1}{10} + \frac{(10 - 10)^2}{44}} \qquad \Sigma(X - \bar{X})^2 = 44$$

From Figure 14.9

$$= \sqrt{56.18} \sqrt{0.10} \qquad s^2 = 56.18$$

$$= \sqrt{5.618}$$

$$= 2.37$$

$t\ (0.05, 8\ df) = 2.306$

$25 \pm 2.306 \cdot 2.37$

± 5.4652

$P\ (19.53 \langle \bar{Y} \langle 30.47)\ 0.95$, when $X_1 = 10$

B. 95% confidence intervals for selected values of X

Y values

X	Lower limit	Upper limit	Range
6	−6.32	17.22	23.54
8	7.67	22.77	15.10
9	17.06	26.16	12.10
10	19.64	30.48	10.84
11	23.84	35.94	12.10
12	27.22	42.32	15.10
14	32.76	56.30	23.54

Figure 14.12.   Confidence intervals for $\bar{Y}$.

precision of interval estimates at a given confidence level decreases as we move away from $\bar{X}$.

In the above example confidence intervals are developed for estimating the population mean of Y for a specified level of X. If one is interested in making an interval estimate of the value of Y for an individual case at a given level of X, he will obviously have much less preci-

C. Confidence Interval Band for $\bar{Y}$

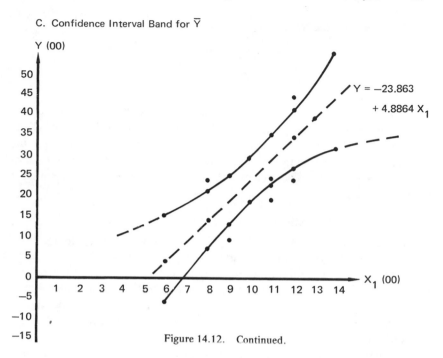

Figure 14.12.   Continued.

sion. For this kind of problem, the computing formula for the standard error is:

$$\text{s.e. } \hat{Y}_{X_K} = \sqrt{s^2} \sqrt{1 + \frac{1}{N} + \frac{(X_K - \bar{X})^2}{\Sigma(X - \bar{X})^2}}$$

Strength of Association   As indicated above, the SS due to regression can be considered to represent the amount of total variation in Y that is *explained* by the linear association of Y on X because it measures the amount by which variation in Y is reduced by virtue of using the regression line rather than the mean as a predictor of Y. The balance of the total variation is measured by the residual SS, unexplained variation in Y around the regression line. Our most direct measure of the strength of the linear association is the proportion of total variation explained by the regression. This measure is commonly referred to as R^2, **the coefficient of determination:**

$$R^2 = \frac{\text{regression SS}}{\text{total SS}}$$

In the example the R^2 for the regression line would be:

$$R^2 = \frac{1050.54}{1500.00}$$

$$= 0.70$$

R^2 is a measure of the compactness or dispersion of the observations around the regression line relative to the general degree of variability in Y. It varies between 0 and 1, with 0 indicating a complete lack of association (the regression line would be $\overline{Y}$) and 1 indicating a perfect linear association. The visual interpretation for R^2 is illustrated in Figure 14.13.

Alternative Computations

The computations illustrated to this point become very tedious with greater sample sizes and much more complex when additional variables are taken into consideration. Although such computations increasingly are being performed by computers, it is worthwhile to note that an alternative approach for computing these statistics is matrix algebra, which some individuals find is more manageable (Draper and Smith, 1966, pp. 88–90).

There are also alternative algebraic formulas for computing many of these statistics, which some are inclined to feel are more operationally convenient. Alternative formulas for computing b_1, total SS, and SS attributable to regression are illustrated below using the same data as before:

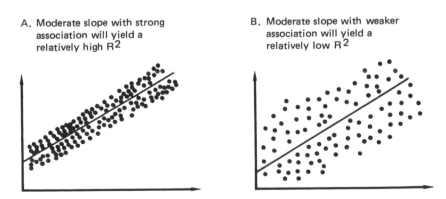

A. Moderate slope with strong association will yield a relatively high R^2

B. Moderate slope with weaker association will yield a relatively low R^2

Figure 14.13.   Visual interpretation of R^2.

$$b_1 = \frac{N\Sigma XY - (\Sigma X)(\Sigma Y)}{N\Sigma X^2 - (\Sigma X)^2}$$

$$= \frac{10 \cdot 2715 - 100 \cdot 250}{10 \cdot 1044 - (100)^2}$$

$$= \frac{27,150 - 25,000}{10,440 - 10,000}$$

$$b_1 = 4.8864$$

$$\text{Total SS} = \Sigma Y^2 - \frac{(\Sigma Y_i)^2}{N}$$

$$= 7,750 - \frac{(250)^2}{10}$$

$$= 7,750 - 6,250$$

$$\text{Total SS} = 1,500$$

$$\text{Regression SS} = b_1 \left[\Sigma X_1 Y - \frac{(\Sigma X_1)(\Sigma Y)}{N} \right]$$

$$= 4.8864 \left[2,715 - \frac{(100)(250)}{10} \right]$$

$$= 4.8864 \, [2,715 - 2,500]$$

$$= 4.8864 \, (215)$$

$$\text{Regression SS} = 1,050.58$$

CORRELATION

The word correlation is often used to refer to the strength of associations among variables. Pearson's **correlation coefficient**, r, sometimes termed a product moment correlation, is a measure of the degree of linear association among interval level variables. The formula for computing Pearson's r is

$$r = \frac{\Sigma(X - \bar{X})(Y - \bar{Y})}{\sqrt{\Sigma(X - \bar{X})^2 \Sigma(Y - \bar{Y})^2}}$$

or the covariation in X and Y divided by the square root of the product of the variation in X times the variation in Y.

A **zero order correlation** is one involving the original values of the variables as opposed to residuals; the zero order correlation between two variables is called a **simple correlation**. For our sample problem (refer to

Figures 14.6 and 14.9), the sample correlation between X_1 and Y would be:

$$r_{yx_1} = \frac{215}{\sqrt{(44)\,(1500)}}$$
$$= 215/\sqrt{66{,}000}$$
$$= 215/256.90$$
$$r_{yx_1} = 0.8369$$

Interpretation of Correlations

Although correlations are often examined before, or separate from, regressions in research projects, correlation is logically subsequent to regression in that a correlation is a measure of linear association, the extent of concentration of the observations around the regression line relative to their dispersion around the mean. Pearson's r varies from -1, indicating a perfect negative association to $+1$, indicating a perfect positive association. An r of 0 indicates a complete lack of **linear** association.

A Pearson's r computed for sample data provides a point estimate of the population parameter, rho. As mentioned earlier, the F test is really a test of the null hypothesis that rho $= 0$. A simple correlation coefficient, r, can be tested for significance without having computed the regression statistics illustrated above by use of the alternate formula (for simple correlations only):

$$F = \frac{r^2\,(N - 2)}{(1 - r^2)}$$

The value of this computed F is compared with the critical F for 1 and $N - 2$ degrees of freedom at the desired significance level. The standard error of r can also be computed and used to construct confidence intervals or compare correlations between samples or pairs of variables (Blalock, 1972, pp. 401–402).

The correlation coefficient does not have a direct, intuitive interpretation as does R^2, the proportion of variation in one variable that is explained by another. Notice that R^2 is usually used when we are talking about the total variation of the dependent variable explained by the independent variable(s). In fact, one must take care not to attach such an interpretation to correlation coefficients. This would produce an inflated impression of the strength of association, especially at midrange and lower values of r, as shown in Table 14.2. Furthermore, it can only be used to interpret the strength of a linear relationship; for example, an r of 0 may exist for a perfect curvilinear relationship. Simple correlations tend to be most useful in exploratory work or the early stages of analysis, when one wants to identify those variables that should be examined more closely. As is seen later in this chapter, an important use of correlation is to select variables to be used in developing regression models.

Relationship of Correlation and Slope

Relationships among correlation and slope and statistical significance are shown schematically in Figure 14.14. The correlation or strength of association depends upon the slope of the regression and the general degree of variability in X and Y. The correlation can be conceived as a function of these two as illustrated below:

$$r_{yx} = b_{yx}(s_x/s_y)$$

where b_{yx} is the slope and s_x/s_y is the ratio of the sample standard deviations. Given a degree of variability in Y relative to that in X, a steeper slope will indicate a stronger linear association. Conversely, a moderate slope will signify a strong association if the variability in Y is low relative to that in X and a weaker association if the variability in Y is high relative to that in X, as illustrated in Figure 14.13.

Similarly, given the strength of association, the probability of a type I error in rejecting the null hypothesis of no linear association will decrease as N increases, because the F distribution is more compact with larger sample sizes. Conversely, given a sample size N, statistical significance of an association increases with the strength of association. P in Figure 14.14, therefore, represents both the probability of a type I

Table 14.2.   Relationship of correlation coefficient to coefficient of determination

r	R^2
0.90	0.81
0.80	0.64
0.70	0.49
0.60	0.36
0.50	0.25
0.40	0.16

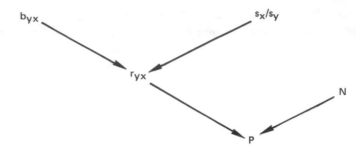

Figure 14.14.   Linkages among the nature, strength, and statistical significance of linear associations.

error and statistical significance of an association. In looking at associations between interval measures, our goal is to move upwards in the diagram, to go beyond the questions of statistical significance and look at the strength and precise nature of linear associations.

Partial Correlation

A partial correlation is the product moment correlation between two variables, fixing for the effects of one or more control variables. It is an indication of the degree of linear association between two variables which goes beyond any association that might be explained by the effects of a control variable. In our sample problem, for instance, we might be interested in examining the association between Y, the average increase in property values, and X_2, the percentage of dwellings that have been inspected for codes violations, beyond the association of Y with X_1 rehabilitation funds expended per dwelling unit—$r_{yx_2|x_1}$—which means the partial correlation of Y and X_2 controlling for X_1. In systems analysis terms, does the inspection component of a housing program have an observable impact on property values beyond the effects of rehabilitation funds? This would be a **first order partial correlation**, the correlation between two variables controlling for one other variable. If two variables were being treated as control variables, we would be computing a second order partial correlation, and so on.

    Computation of Partial Correlations   In computing partial correlations, we are looking at the association not between the original variables, nor total variation of the two variables, but between the remaining variation in each after the variation that is attributable to the control variable has been subtracted out. This remaining variation is represented by the residuals around the regressions of each of the variables on the control variable or variables. Thus, the partial correlation between Y and X_2, given X_1, $(r_{yx_2|x_1})$ is the product moment correlation between the residuals of Y regressed on X_1 and those of X_2 regressed on X_1.

In Figure 14.15, the computations for partial correlation are presented. To begin with, we must ascertain the least squares equation for the regression of X_2 on X_1. This is done simply by using the previously presented calculations for simple regression. The result of these calculations is the regression line $X_2 = -2.5 + 6.25\, X_1$. The next step is to subtract to find the residuals of both equations $(Y - \hat{Y}$ and $X_2 - \hat{X}_2)$. To avoid confusion between the sets of residuals we use the notation $Y_{|x_1}$ and $X_{2|x_1}$ to denote the residuals of the regressions of Y on X_1 and X_2 on X_1, respectively. We then square the deviations from the mean for each set of residuals. This process is facilitated by the fact that the mean of any set of residuals is 0, and therefore we need only sum the squares of each residual. Finally, these calculations are used in the formula for zero order correlations presented above. Thus, the final result is the zero order correlation between the residuals of two simple regressions.

While the above procedure is presented because it illustrates more clearly the logic of partial correlation as representing the association between two variables beyond their associations with a control variable, partial correlations are usually computed directly by a formula involving simple correlation coefficients and coefficients of determination. The same partial correlation, that between Y and X_2 given X_1, is computed using this formula in Figure 14.16. It should be kept in mind that this partial correlation, 0.535, is *not* a measure of percentage of variation explained. Rather, its square, $r^2_{yx_2|x_1}$, measures the percentage of *residual* variation of Y regressed on X_1 that can be explained by X_2.

MULTIPLE REGRESSION

Frequently in developing explanatory or predictive models we desire to examine the association or simultaneous "effects" of two or more independent variables on a dependent variable. When all the variables in consideration are interval measures, this is facilitated by the use of multiple regression analysis. A multiple linear regression model postulates the dependent variable as a linear combination of a number of independent variables, such that:

$$Y = \beta_0 + \beta_1 X_1 + \beta_2 X_2 + \cdots + \beta_K X_K + \epsilon$$

X_2	X_1	$(X_2 - \bar{X}_2)$	$(X_1 - \bar{X}_1)$	$(X_1 - \bar{X}_1)(X_2 - \bar{X}_2)$	$(X_1 - \bar{X}_1)^2$
70	10	10	0	0	0
55	8	-5	-2	10	4
30	9	-30	-1	30	1
70	12	10	2	20	4
60	11	0	1	0	1
35	8	-25	-2	50	4
90	13	30	3	90	9
50	6	-10	-4	40	16
75	12	15	2	30	4
65	11	5	1	5	1
$\Sigma = 600$	$\Sigma = 100$	$\Sigma = 0$	$\Sigma = 0$	$\Sigma = 275$	$\Sigma = 44$

$$\bar{X}_2 = 60 \qquad \bar{X}_1 = 10$$

$$b_1 = \frac{\Sigma (X_1 - \bar{X}_1)(X_2 - \bar{X}_2)}{\Sigma (X_1 - \bar{X}_1)^2} = \frac{275}{44} = 6.25$$

$$b_0 = \bar{X}_2 - b_1 \bar{X}_1$$

$$= 60 - 6.25(10)$$

$$= 60 - 62.5$$

$$b_0 = -2.5$$

Estimating equation:

$$\hat{X}_2 = -2.5 + 6.25\, X_1$$

Figure 14.15. Partial correlation of Y and X_2, given X_1.

This model can be estimated using empirical data with a least squares equation of the form:

$$Y = b_0 + b_1 X_1 + b_2 X_2 + \cdots + b_K X_K$$

such that remaining variation around the regression is minimized. With two independent variables this least squares solution can be visualized as a plane, as shown in Figure 14.17, with the height of the dependent variable, Y, varying with values of both X_1 and X_2. The beta coefficients in a multiple regression are partial regression coefficients and will generally differ from those obtained in simple regressions. A **partial regression coefficient** represents the net effect of the corresponding variable on the dependent variable apart from the effects of the other independent variables in the equation. b_2, for example, represents the slope of Y on X_2 at given levels of X_1, or the effect of X_2 on Y fixing for the effects of X_1.

X_2	X_1	$\hat{X}_2 / X_1$	$(X_2 - \hat{X}_2)$	$(Y - \hat{Y})$
70	10	60.00	10.00	5.00
55	8	47.50	7.50	9.77
30	9	53.75	−23.75	−10.12
70	12	72.50	− 2.50	10.22
60	11	66.25	− 6.25	− 9.89
35	8	47.50	−12.50	− 0.23
90	13	78.75	11.25	0.34
50	6	35.00	15.00	− 0.46
75	12	72.50	2.50	0.22
65	11	66.25	− 1.25	−4.89

$$\Sigma = 0 \qquad \Sigma = -0.04 \text{ (rounding)}$$

$$(X_2 - \hat{X}_2) = X_{2|x_1} \qquad (X_{2|x_1} - \overline{X}_{2|x_1})^2 = (X_{2|x_1} - 0)^2 = (X_{2|x_1})^2$$

$$(Y - \hat{Y}) = Y_{|x_1} \qquad (Y_{|x_1} - \overline{Y}_{|x_1})^2 = (Y_{|x_1} - 0)^2 = (Y_{|x_1})^2$$

$(X_{2|x_1})(Y_{|x_1})$	$(X_{2|x_1})^2$	$(Y_{|x_1})^2$
50.00	100.00	25.00
73.28	56.25	95.45
240.35	564.06	102.41
−25.55	6.25	104.45
61.81	39.06	97.81
2.88	156.25	0.05
3.83	126.56	0.12
− 6.90	225.00	0.21
0.55	6.25	0.05
6.11	1.56	23.91
$\Sigma = 406.36$	$\Sigma = 1,281.24$	$\Sigma = 499.46$

$$r_{y x_2 | x_1} = \frac{(X_{2|x_1})(Y_{|x_1})}{\sqrt{(X_{2|x_1})^2 (Y_{|x_1})^2}}$$

$$= \frac{406.36}{\sqrt{(1,281.24)(449.46)}}$$

$$= 406.36/758.86$$

$$r_{y x_2 | x_1} = 0.535 = \text{partial correlation between}$$

Y and X_2, given X_1

Figure 14.15.   Continued.

$$r_{yx_2 \mid x_1} = \frac{r_{yx_2} - (r_{yx_1})(r_{x_2x_1})}{\sqrt{1 - r_{yx_1}^2}\sqrt{1 - r_{x_2x_1}^2}}$$

$$= \frac{0.8249 - (0.8369)(0.7569)}{\sqrt{1 - 0.7004}\sqrt{1 - 0.5728}}$$

$$= \frac{0.8249 - 0.6334}{\sqrt{0.2996}\sqrt{0.4272}}$$

$$= \frac{0.1915}{\sqrt{0.127989}}$$

$$= 0.1915/0.357755$$

$$r_{yx_2 \mid x_1} = 0.535$$

Figure 14.16.   Alternative formula for calculating partial correlation.

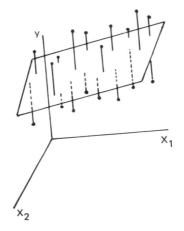

Figure 14.17.   Least squares plane. From *Social Statistics* by Hubert M. Blalock. Copyright 1960 by McGraw-Hill Book Company. Used with permission of McGraw-Hill Book Company.

The calculations necessary for multiple regression are very complicated and are normally carried out using the computer; the computations are not shown in this book. The example presented here concerns the effects of rehabilitation funds and codes inspection on property value increase. This will be a continuation of the simple regression problem where the analyst was looking at rehabilitation funds as the only independent variable. The data for the example are given in Figure 14.18. After putting the data through a computer program we find that the least squares regression line is:

$$Y = -23.06 + 2.91X_1 + 0.316X_2$$

Examination of Multiple Regressions

Multiple regressions can be examined in many ways to determine the statistical significance and strength of association for both the overall regression and the individual independent variables.

Analysis of Variance The ANOVA table shown in Figure 14.18 tests the overall statistical significance of Y regressed on X_2 beyond the effects of X_1. The total variation explained by the regression, regression $SS|b_0$, is shown as the sum of that explained by X_1 alone (SS due to $b_1|b_0$) plus the additional variation explained by X_2, (SS due to $b_2|b_0$, b_1). Total variation and that due to the simple regression of Y on X_1 are drawn from Figure 14.9, while residual SS is computed anew for the multiple regression as shown in the lower part of Figure 14.18. The SS due to $b_2|b_0$, b_1 is the difference between the overall regression SS and that explained by X_1 alone. This represents the additional contribution of X_2 beyond that of X_1 in explaining the variation of Y. There are now 7 degrees of freedom left in the residual because there are 2 degrees, one for each independent variable, associated with the variation explained by the regression.

Two F ratios are computed in the ANOVA table. The first is the overall F computed as the ratio of the regression mean square to the residual mean square. As compared with the critical F for 2 and 7 degrees of freedom, this F of 12.87 is significant at the 0.05 level. Thus, the multiple regression as a whole is found to be statistically significant.

The F of 2.81 is the ratio of the mean square variance estimate based on the additional variation explained by X_2 to the residual mean square. This is used to make a partial F test of the effect of X_2 on Y; a test of the statistical significance of X_2 when entered into the regression model last. This F ratio is less than the critical F for 1 and 7 degrees of freedom at the 0.05 level, and indicates that X_2 does not have a significant effect on Y beyond the effects of X_1.

$$Y = -23.06 + 2.91X_1 + 0.316X_2$$

Y	X_1	X_2	b_0	$2.91X_1 + 0.316X_2$
30	10	70	−23.06	29.10 + 22.12
25	8	55	−23.06	23.28 + 17.38
10	9	30	−23.06	26.19 + 9.48
45	12	70	−23.06	34.92 + 22.12
20	11	60	−23.06	32.01 + 18.96
15	8	35	−23.06	23.28 + 11.06
40	13	90	−23.06	37.83 + 28.44
5	6	50	−23.06	17.46 + 15.80
35	12	75	−23.06	34.92 + 23.70
25	11	65	−23.06	32.01 + 20.54

Y	$\hat{Y}$	$(Y - \hat{Y})$	$(Y - \hat{Y})^2$
$30	28.16	1.84	3.38
25	17.60	7.40	54.76
10	12.61	−2.61	6.81
45	33.98	11.02	121.44
20	27.91	−7.91	62.56
15	11.28	3.72	13.83
40	43.21	−3.21	10.30
5	10.20	−5.20	27.04
35	35.56	−0.56	0.31
25	29.49	−4.49	20.16
		$\Sigma = 0.00$	$\Sigma = 320.59$

ANOVA table

Source	SS	df	Mean square	F
Total (corrected)	1,500.00	9		
Regression$\|b_0$	1,179.41	2	589.70	12.87 *
due to $b_1\|b_0$	1,050.54	1	1,050.54	22.94 **
due to $b_2\|b_1, b_0$	128.87	1	128.87	2.81
Residual	320.59	7	45.79	

* F (0.05, df = 1, 7) = 5.59
** F (0.05, df = 2, 7) = 4.74

Figure 14.18.   ANOVA table for multiple regression.

A **partial F test** is a test of the statistical significance of a single independent variable or block of independent variables in a multiple regression when entered into the regression last. It is based on the variation picked up by that variable that cannot be attributed to other variables in the model, or the extra sum of squares principle. Thus the partial F test is a significance test of the additional contribution in explaining the variation of the dependent variable that is gained by adding the particular variable to the model. A partial F test of the effect of X_1, for example, would require a different ANOVA table to be constructed that would show the additive effect of X_1 on Y beyond the sum of squares due to the regression of Y on X_2. As illustrated in Table 14.3, this test does not prove to be significant either. Both rehabilitation funds and dwelling inspection are highly associated wth increase in property values, but these two independent variables are also intercorrelated. Therefore, neither has a significant effect on property values beyond the effects of the other.

Strength of Association The R^2 for this example, using the formula presented above, is:

$$R^2 = \frac{\text{regression SS}}{\text{total SS}}$$

$$= \frac{1,179.41}{1,500.00}$$

$$= 0.7862$$

This 78.62 percent represents a gain in R^2 percentage points beyond that for the simple regression of Y on X_1. As a check to understand more clearly why this is so, we could compute the ratio of additional regression SS when X_2 is included to the residual SS when X_2 is not the model

$$\frac{SSb_2 | b_0, b_1}{\text{residual SS} | b_0, b_1} = \frac{128.75}{449.46} = 0.2865$$

to obtain the percentage of the residual variation around the regression of Y on X_1 that is explained by adding X_2 into the model. (As a computational check, we can see that the residual variation explained, 0.2865, is indeed the square of the partial correlation of Y and X_2, given X_1, computed earlier in Figure 14.16 to equal 0.535.) In simple regression of Y on X_1, the residual SS amounted to 30 percent of total variation

Table 14.3. ANOVA table (showing partial F test for X_1)

Source	SS	df	Mean square	F
Total (corrected)	1,500.00	9		
Regression $\mid b_0$	1,179.41	2	589.70	12.87
due to $b_2 \mid b_0$	1,020.60	1		
due to $b_1 \mid b_0, b_2$	158.81	1	158.81	3.46
Residual	320.59	7	45.79	

$F(0.05,\ df = 1,7) = 5.59$

$(1 - R^2)$. If we multiply this 30 percent by the partial R^2 of 0.2865, we obtain an improvement in the overall R^2 of 8.59 percentage points (this differs from 8.62 solely because of rounding error).

The **multiple correlation coefficient**, r, of Y with X_1 and X_2 in this example is $\sqrt{0.7862}$ or 0.8867. It is defined as the product moment correlation between the observed values of the dependent variable and the values that would be predicted for each case by the multiple regression equation. As independent variables are added one by one into multiple regression models, R^2 and the multiple r increase if these variables are associated with previously unexplained variation in the dependent variable. An increase in multiple r or R^2, however, does not necessarily indicate an improved ability to predict values of the dependent variable. If the square root of the residual mean square, $\sqrt{\text{residual SS/df}}$, or standard error of estimate, is not reduced, then we can say that the addition of a new independent variable to the model does not produce a gain in accuracy or precision in predicting values of Y. This may be the case even though there is some increase in R^2 due to the addition of another independent variable, because the decrease in residual SS is offset by the loss of 1 degree of freedom associated with the residual.

Developing Multiple Regression Models

As has been seen in the discussion of simple regression, the uses of regression analysis include 1) making statistical inferences about the regression parameters β_0 and β_1, 2) making point and interval estimates about the mean value of the dependent variable given a value of the independent variable, and 3) making such estimates for the value of the dependent variable for a single case or the next observation. Inferential tests for the parameters in multiple regression models have been illustrated above; although we have not explored methods for calculating estimates of $\overline{Y}$ and of the next observation of Y, given values of X_1, X_2, X_3, etc., suffice it to say there are such methods available (Neter and Wasserman, 1974, pp. 244–246).

Given the ability to examine simultaneous and additive statistical effects of multiple independent variables on a dependent variable, the question still remains as to which variables to include in the multiple regression model. In other words, given a dependent variable whose sources of variation are of interest, what are the relevant independent variables and multiple regressions to examine? In general, multiple regression models are developed either on an a priori basis, usually founded on substantive theory or expectations, or with a more mechanical selection procedure based on statistical criteria.

"Hand-built" Models Clearly, the inclusion of variables in regression models and the sequence of tests made should be geared to one's purposes in doing the analysis. In general, all of the independent variables included in the data set for possible consideration will have been adjudged to have some degree of face validity. "Hand-built" models are those developed in situations in which the researcher exerts complete control over variable selection in order to examine the effects of certain combinations of variables he is interested in, usually from a theoretical perspective.

Such models can range all the way from the all inclusive type models, often characteristic of exploratory work, to very carefully selected regressions designed to test the additive effects of specific variables. The former type is often used in the development of basically predictive models where the researcher is mainly interested in the combined strength of association. For example, in the area of policy analysis, states' expenditure on some function might be regressed on whole sets of demographic variables and economic development variables in an attempt to develop a typology of states relative to that function. In applied program analysis, such an approach might have its greatest applicability in exploratory needs and demands studies.

At the other end of the spectrum are efforts to test very specific hypotheses. For example, one might wish to determine whether the clearance rate of crimes reported in individual patrol sectors is dependent upon the number of follow-up investigations conducted, beyond the effects of number of calls for service and average response time. One would build the model in such a way as to examine the incremental increase in R^2 and partial F value of the follow-up variable with the other two variables, number of calls and response time, already in the model.

Interest should be given to the sequence in which variables are entered in a model when the researcher has a hypothesis about the relative "predictive power" of independent variables that may well have inter-associations among themselves. This is because the simple association of each with the dependent variable is likely to represent, to some degree, the associations among the dependent variables. Thus the hypothesis that the relative "predictive power" of three independent variables is in the order $X_1 > X_2 > X_3$ is most likely to be confirmed by the model, $y = b_0 + b_1X_1 + b_2X_2 + b_3X_3$. In this case, however, use of the conservative model, $y = b_0 + b_3X_3 + b_2X_2 + b_1X_1$, would provide the most stringent test.

Selection Procedures In between the all inclusive model development and models developed to test very specific hypotheses are procedures used to select variables according to specified statistical criteria. Such procedures are most useful in situations characterized by the absence of a very definitive theory and a desire to identify the more relevant variables and examine their relative influence. In some instances they are used as mechanisms to develop strong predictive models, and in others they can be thought of as variable reduction devices aimed at separating from the larger pool of variables those that would bear close scrutiny.

There are basically five types of selection procedures that have come into increasing use with the widespread availability of computers (see Draper and Smith, 1966, chapter 6). These are: 1) all possible regressions, 2) maximization of R^2, 3) backward elimination, 4) forward selection, and 5) stepwise selection.

The first selection procedure, all possible regressions, is inherently the most precise of the five procedures. This procedure merely results in all combinations of variables being incorporated into regression models. Each of these models can then be compared to discover the best model for the particular problem. The drawback to this approach is the number of possible models with even a few independent variables (for example, because there are 2^K possible combinations of variables, six independent variables will yield 64 models). However, with only a small number of independent variables this method is advisable because it yields the greatest amount of information of the five methods.

The second selection procedure, **Max R^2**, is intended to build the model that explains the greatest amount of variation in the dependent, or response, variable in the most efficient manner. The first independent variable is selected on the basis of the highest simple correlation with the response variable; the corresponding simple regression is computed and the value of R^2 noted. From among the remaining variables outside the model, the next variable is chosen that will add the greatest increment to explained variation, that which has the highest partial correlation with the response variable fixing for the effects of the independent variable already in the model. Additional variables are then added one by one on the same basis with the resulting R^2 being noted each time. The increments in R^2 will diminish and total R^2 will usually begin to level off after a few variables have been entered. The procedure terminates when 1) all the variables in the pool have been exhausted, 2) no further improvement in R^2 is achieved, or 3) some previously specified cutoff point in R^2 improvement has been reached. This procedure is used when the researcher is interested in determining the greatest amount of explained variation that is possible by a pool of independent variables. Its chief deficiency is that it does not take the significance of association into account.

By contrast, the other three selection procedures presented here incorporate partial F tests of the statistical significance of individual variables beyond the effects of other variables in the model. The third procedure, **backward elimination**, begins with a model including all the independent variables and computes a partial F value for each as though it were the last variable to be entered in the equation. The lowest partial F value is compared with a predetermined significance level, and if it exceeds that significance level, the all-inclusive regression is retained. If, however, the partial F test indicates that the corresponding variable is not significant at the predetermined level, that variable is selected out of the equation and the whole process repeated with the regression including all the other independent variables save that one. Variables are discarded one by one in this procedure until the first equation is obtained in which each independent variable has a significant partial F value. The backward elimination procedure has the advantage of producing a final regression in which each variable makes a significant contribution to explaining the dependent variation while beginning with the all-inclusive model that allows the researcher "not to miss anything."

The fourth procedure, **forward selection**, moves in the opposite direction to the backward selection in developing multiple regression. It is similar to the Max R^2 procedure in that it begins with the "best" simple regression (based on R^2) and builds the model incrementally with one variable at a time so as to maximize R^2 improvement with each new variable. However, in contrast with the Max R^2 approach, the forward selection process also employs significance tests (partial F tests) at each step and terminates when no new variable can be entered and make an additional contribution to R^2 that is significant at the previously established level. The advantage of this procedure is that it applies significance tests to each new variable while permitting the analyst to watch the model develop from the bottom up beginning with the "most important" variables. A deficiency of the forward selection process is that it does not register the effects of a new variable on the importance of variables that have been entered at earlier stages. A variable that may have been highly associated with the dependent variable at the initial stage and entered first, therefore, may become superfluous a few steps later because of relationships between it and variables entered subsequently.

The fifth procedure, **stepwise selection**, accounts for such effects by applying the partial F test to each independent variable in the model at each step. If a variable that was entered previously proves to be insignificant at a later stage due to the effect of additional variables brought into the model, it is discarded. The procedure then goes on to try other new variables that will add to the total R^2 and terminates when *no* single additional variable can be added to the most recent model or substituted for one or more of the variables already in that model, while producing a significant F value and an increase in R^2. This procedure, then, builds a model "up from scratch" while controlling stringently for statistical significance. Many authorities believe the stepwise method to be the best of the variable selection procedures when the all possible regressions procedure is unfeasible. Like the other procedures discussed, however, it can easily be abused by the "amateur" statistician (Draper and Smith, 1966, p. 17).

SUMMARY

Regression and correlation analysis are useful and powerful statistical tools when interval level variables are available. Through the use of regression and correlation, the analyst cannot only determine the direction and degree of association as well as test its statistical significance, but also can examine the specific nature of the association in terms of the amount of change in the dependent variable per unit increase in an independent variable.

Regression and correlation are also multivariate techniques that permit the examination of the simultaneous effects of multiple independent variables. By using partial correlation analysis it is possible to discover the association between one independent variable and the dependent variable while fixing for the effects of one or more other independent variables. By examining partial regression coefficients we can determine the amount of change in the dependent variable per unit increase in an independent variable while holding constant the other independent variables in the equation; significance tests for certain independent variables while fixing for the effects of other are also possible with the partial F test.

With these capabilities it is clear that regression and correlation analysis can be extremely useful for analyses that deal with prediction and forecasting, describing statistical associations, or examining causal hypotheses. In this chapter the fundamentals of regression and correlation analysis, including the assumptions behind the model and the computations involved, have been presented. In the next chapter this discussion is extended by examining certain problems in using the regression model and by looking at applications of regression and correlation to topics in public program analysis.

REFERENCES

Blalock, H. M., Jr. 1972. Social Statistics, 2nd Ed. New York: McGraw-Hill Book Company.

Draper, N. R, and H. Smith. 1966. Applied Regression Analysis. New York: John Wiley & Sons, Inc.

Mood, A. M., and F. A. Graybill. 1963. Introduction to the Theory of Statistics. New York: McGraw-Hill Book Company.

Neter, J., and W. Wasserman. 1974. Applied Linear Statistical Models. Homewood, Illinois: Richard D. Irwin, Inc.

PRACTICE PROBLEMS FOR CHAPTER 14

1. In an attempt to develop a model to forecast the need for transportation facilities, data on household size and number of trips were collected for the 10 sample households below:

X No. of persons	Y Trips
1	5
2	6
4	12
2	3
3	8
4	9
2	4
3	6
5	16
4	11
$\Sigma X = 30$	$\Sigma Y = 80$
$\overline{X} = 3$	$\overline{Y} = 8$

a. Locate these households on a scattergram.

b. From the graph, would household size and number of trips seem to be unassociated, positively associated, or negatively associated?

c. Derive the regression equation estimating the number of trips as a function of household size.

d. Compute total variation, regression SS, and residual SS, and complete an ANOVA table for this problem.

e. Is the association between household size and number of trips per household significant at the 0.01 level?

f. What percentage of the variation in number of trips is explained by number of persons?

2. The following data have been collected in an attempt to develop a model to explain or predict the demand for national parks. Each observation corresponds to a geographic zone located at a known distance from a park. The dependent variable is the number of visitors per 1,000 population going to the park, and the independent variable is the average expense incurred per visit. As the expense increases the rate of visitors is expected to decrease.

Zone	Expense per visit		Visitors/1,000 population	
A	$20		50	
B	$25		40	
C	$40		20	
D	$30		10	
E	$20	$\overline{X} = \$25$	30	$\overline{Y} = 30$
F	$10		25	
G	$ 5		35	
H	$10		50	
I	$55		10	
J	$35		30	

$(X - \overline{X})$	$(Y - \overline{Y})$	$(X - \overline{X})^2$	$(Y - \overline{Y})^2$	XY	Y^2	X	Y
− 5	20	25	400	1,000	2,500	20	50
0	10	0	100	1,000	1,600	25	40
15	−10	225	100	800	400	40	20
5	−20	25	400	300	100	30	10
− 5	0	25	0	600	900	20	30
−15	− 5	225	25	250	625	10	25
−20	5	400	25	175	1,225	5	35
−15	20	225	400	500	2,500	10	50
30	−20	900	400	550	100	55	10
10	0	100	0	1,050	900	35	30
		2,150	1,850	6,225	10,850	250	300

a. Compute Pearson's correlation coefficient between the two variables.
b. Complete an analysis of variance for the problem. Is the regression significant at the 0.01 level?
c. What percentage of variation in park visitors/1,000 population is explained by the expense variable?
d. Derive the regression equation estimating the number of visits as a function of expense.

3. A state budget office analyst is interested in the extent to which highway accidents are associated with the level of police patrol. Using a sample of 215 segments of highways across the state, he begins by regressing TOTAL ACCIDENTS PER MILE on (an environmental variable) TRAFFIC VOLUME, and obtains the following output:

ANOVA

Source	SS	df	Mean square	F
Total	157.16	214		
Regression	101.28	1	101.28	386.56
Residual	55.88	213	.262	

a. Is this simple regression significant at the 0.01 level?
b. What percent of the total variation in accidents per mile is explained by TRAFFIC VOLUME?
    The simple regression is:

    ACCIDENTS = 0.22239 + 0.00006 TRAFFIC VOLUME

c. How would you describe the precise nature of the association between accidents and traffic volume?

Further computer output from this first run included first order partial correlation coefficients for three additional independent (program operation) variables:

Variable	Partial correlation
PATROL HOURS PER MILE	−.23861
RADAR HOURS PER MILE	−.03934
TOTAL ARRESTS PER MILE	−.25520

    d. How do you interpret the association between ACCIDENTS and PATROL HOURS beyond the effects of TRAFFIC VOLUME?

    e. The analyst wants to build a stepwise multiple regression model; which of the above variables should he enter as the second independent variable?

The table below shows the ANOVA output for the regression of ACCIDENTS on all four independent variables.

ANOVA

Source	SS	df	Mean square	F
Total	157.15	14		
Regression	107.76	4	26.94	114.64
Traffic	101.28	1	101.28	430.98
Arrests	4.59	1	4.59	19.53
Patrol hours	.72	1	.72	3.06
Radar hours	1.17	1	1.17	4.98
Residual	49.39	210	.235	

    f. Is the overall multiple regression significant at the 0.01 level?

    g. The last variable to be entered into the model was RADAR HOURS. Is the partial F for this variable significant at the 0.01 level?

    h. How much of total variation is now explained by virtue of including the three additional variables?

15

SPECIAL TOPICS AND APPLICATIONS IN REGRESSION ANALYSIS

The preceding chapter on regression was concerned with presenting the basic computations and procedures for developing correlations and multiple regression models. As has been seen, regression and correlation are useful tools for addressing various types of questions, and many different kinds of models are possible. These techniques are appropriate for a wide range of applications. This final chapter briefly discusses some common problems in using regression analysis and surveys some further variations and extensions of the technique. The discussion of such topics as path analysis and causal interpretations is intended solely to point out their availability and potential usefulness for certain kinds of problems. Before actually employing them, the reader should refer to the sources listed at the end of the chapter. The chapter also illustrates applications of regression analysis in various kinds of program analyses.

PROBLEMS WITH IMPLEMENTING THE REGRESSION MODEL

As with any statistical technique, problems can easily occur when using regression analysis. These problems basically fall into two categories: variable selection and violations of underlying assumptions. This section discusses variable selection problems and the problem of exceptional pieces of data.

Outliers

Outliers are cases that deviate a great distance from the regression line, relative to the general range of variability of the joint distribution. They are perplexing because when using the least squares method, outliers exert more influence on the estimating equation than do other cases. Because it is the sum of squared deviations that is to be minimized, the regression is pulled disproportionately toward outliers, producing a regression that differs from that which would best summarize the variation of Y on X for the more compact set of cases excluding outliers. Since the outliers can exert such a strong influence, often a good first step is to check the reliability of the data to determine whether these values represent a real case or an error in coding.

Figure 15.1 shows a joint distribution of two variables with the presence of an outlier. It is apparent that this one case falls a great distance from the otherwise compact distribution around the regression line. In this figure, the solid line represents the least squares line with the outlier included in the data. As one can easily see, this line deviates considerably from the least squares line with the outlier excluded, represented by the dashed line.

Outliers should not be routinely rejected from the data set, however, because they may contain important information. If a case lies out of the main portion of the joint distribution in terms of X or both X and Y, it may represent a change in the trend of the association between X and Y. In this situation it would be preferable to enlarge the set of observations to include more cases in the midrange of X so as to obtain a more complete indication of the co-variation of X and Y. Of course, if the researcher is interested only in the lower levels of X he may exclude the outlier arbitrarily. Alternatively, and particularly if the outlier is unique in the larger population, he may compute the regression both with

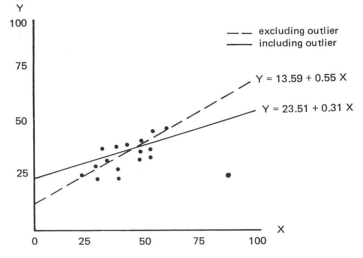

Figure 15.1.   Estimating equations, with and without outlier.

and without the outlying case (as in Figure 15.1), as always being careful to report the range of observations with his findings.

Cases that are outliers only in terms of Y, the dependent variable, may be more difficult. They may be a result of an error in measurement or coding, and if so should be corrected or discarded. If this is not the case, it is safer to include them in the analysis, because they may convey significant information about interactions between X and Y with some additional variable outside the model. In the proper context, the existence of such an outlier may lead the researcher to examine that case closely in search of a clue as to why it differs from the bulk of the cases.

Multicollinearity

The problem of multicollinearity in regression analysis has been referred to, if not by name, throughout the preceding chapter. **Multicollinearity** refers to high intercorrelations among the independent variables being considered for inclusion in multiple regressions. The problem is that if two or more independent variables are correlated among themselves, it is difficult or impossible to sort out their effects on the dependent variable; the greater these intercorrelations, the more of a problem multicollinearity presents.

The problem of multicollinearity gives rise to the need for partial correlations and partial F tests in developing multiple regressions, as discussed in the previous chapter. Although these statistics do permit an examination of the association between one dependent and one independent variable "beyond the effects of" another independent variable on that dependent variable, this is a controlling operation in a statistical sense only. Using the extra sum of squares principle, the overlapping effect of two intercorrelated independent variables on a dependent variable is not double counted, but as was seen in chapter 14, the relative importance of the independent variables as stated in an ANOVA table is partly a function of the order in which they were entered into the model.

Multicollinearity can be a very perplexing problem, depending on its severity and the ultimate purpose of the regression analysis. In general, intercorrelation among independent variables in a model does not prevent obtaining a good fit to the data nor does it prevent making inferences about mean values of the dependent variable or making predictions for new observations. However, it does create problems in measuring the relative importance of independent variables as determinants of dependent values and makes causal interpretations much more difficult. When independent variables are highly intercorrelated, the estimated regression coefficients tend to vary widely from sample to sample leading to less precise estimates. Thus, each estimated coefficient may be found not to be statistically significant even when a definite relationship exists between the dependent variable and a set of independent variables.

When independent variables are highly intercorrelated, it is difficult to isolate the effects of one variable from another. In the example on property values in the preceding chapter, for instance, the code inspection variable was not found to have a significant effect on property values beyond the effects of rehabilitation funds expended. However, the two treatment variables were highly correlated ($r = 0.7569$), and when they were entered into the model in reverse order the results were the opposite. The effect of the two variables together is quite clear, but it would not be wise to conclude that code inspections had no effect. Rather, it might have been that apart from the rehabilitation program the codes inspections resulted in property values being increased, an effect that is obscured in the regression analysis by the fact that the two strategies seem to have been targeted together.

Predictive Models The importance of the purpose of analysis in terms of the problem of multicollinearity can be illustrated in the case of needs and demands studies. Regression models are often used to forecast the demand for a service, such as a transit trip generation model that postulates the number of transit trips as a function of population density, number of employed persons, and automobile availability. Here we are less concerned about the exact pattern of causal relationships. The density variable in particular might be a surrogate for a number of other factors that directly influence transit demand, but if it has been observed to have a consistent association with transit usage, we can use it as a predictor of transit demand.

Predictive models are less sensitive to multicollinearity because they depend only on the constancy of the associations involved. If we are talking about actually forecasting the demand for transit for a future time period as opposed to predicting the number of trips generated by a given zone at present, two additional points should be noted. A forecast assumes that the same underlying causal laws will continue to hold for the future, but this may not be the case; the association between density and transit usage may be changing over time because of increased automobile ownership. In addition, because forecasts are necessarily based on values of independent variables that have been projected or forecasted—in this case, density—there may also be slippage at multiple points in the model.

Causal Interpretation   Some needs and demands studies are aimed at examining the causes of a problem as well as its magnitude. An example might be an analysis of the problem of abandoned housing to identify a likely point of intervention for devising a program strategy to combat the problem. Analysis of data for a large sample of census tracts might indicate that many of the variables thought to be relevant are highly intercorrelated, but development of these associations by itself would not be sufficient. Abandonment might well influence, as well as be influenced by, other variables in the analysis, and the importance of key variables might be obscured by multicollinearity. To design a program strategy, however, the analyst must have a clearer idea of the causal sequence.

Essentially, multicollinearity represents a problem inherent in cross-sectional data analysis. Part of the problem is that the "natural" data may not be characterized by sufficient variation. If many independent variables are highly intercorrelated, this may suggest a number of rival explanations, and the data do not permit the analyst to examine bivariate associations while controlling for the effects of third variables. Clearly, what is desirable would be to obtain additional cases in the sample that would break up the pattern of intercorrelations, but this is often not feasible. Failing this, some might advocate excluding some variables, supposedly redundant, from the analysis, but this obviously can result in ignoring what are really the critical variables. At least by retaining them the analysis remains open to alternative explanations.

Problems in causal interpretation in regression analysis are not solely a function of multicollinearity, but also can result from incorrect postulation of the model in the first place. Although the dependent variable in a model is usually specified on some a priori, theoretical basis, the flow of causality in the model may be in the opposite direction. For example, transit trip models often include service accessibility as an independent variable thought to influence usage, but in the absence of experimentation the validity of this assumption cannot be tested. A strong association between accessibility and usage may well be the result of the service being targeted primarily to those areas generating transit trips. Any conclusions drawn about the effect on usage with changes in service accessibility may be quite misleading. One technique that has been developed for approaching the question of causal sequence among many interval level variables with cross-sectional data is **path analysis**, a procedure that cannot demonstrate causal relationships but can serve to illuminate the possibilities and indicate some of the more likely interpretations (Blalock, 1964, 1971; Duncan, 1966; Heise, 1970).

Incorrect Specification

Related to the problems of causal interpretation is the problem of incorrect specification of variables. This problem occurs in two forms. The first of these occurs when the relevant variables are not included in the model. A regression may yield a fairly strong R^2 and not have the important variables in the model. It is very possible that the variables in the model are only incidental to the dependent variation and are not the major explanatory variables. This becomes a problem when the analyst tries to posit a causal link or when he tries to predict or forecast. For example, if we are trying to predict an occurrence using the wrong variables, we may find the forecast to be far off if the spurious relationship does not continue in the future. The solution to this problem is to try to find all the relevant variables and to make sure that the causal linkages make intuitive sense.

The second problem occurs when the right variables are included but the wrong model is used. An analyst may have a fine R^2 but could achieve a much higher one by using an interaction term or nonlinear model. At this point it should be emphasized that merely obtaining a statistically significant model should not necessarily end the search for the best model.

MORE COMPLEX MODELS

Up to this point we have only discussed regression with interval level variables that have not been changed from their original units. In this section we begin by showing regression models that incorporate variables computed through the use of two other variables (cross-products) and variables that are straightforward extensions of original variables (transformations). The next two sections discuss models that incorporate categorical variables as independent variables. Finally, we introduce analysis of co-variance, which incorporates both regression and analysis of variance when the analyst wishes to control for some variable while studying the effects of others.

Cross-products

Some regression models include a variable based on the interaction of two variables. This is appropriate when it is not either of the main effects of two variables that is important, but rather their interaction. A **cross-product** is the multiplication of the values of two variables for each case in the data. We normally use cross-products when we have two variables that are not significant but can be intuitively perceived to be important when both are present in large or small amounts at the same time.

For example, consider an attempt to develop a predictive model in a study of urban transit usage. In this instance the unit of analysis would be geographic zone and the dependent variable would be the number of daily transit trips generated by each zone. Because the analyst is interested in the best predictive model, an attempt is made to accumulate all the relevant variables. The analyst employs a stepwise regression procedure to limit the number of variables to those with the greatest predictive power. This results in a model with four independent variables—population, number of blue collar workers, a service level index, and the average number of automobiles per household—and a fairly low R^2. Two of the variables—blue collar workers and service level—were almost insignificant. However, the analyst further hypothesizes that if there were many blue collar workers (blue collar workers ride the transit system in a disproportionately large number) but not much service provided in a zone, or a high level of service but few blue collar workers, the zone would not generate many transit trips. Conversely, if both levels were large then there should be a large number of transit riders. In other words, neither variable by itself is a sufficient condition for strong ridership, but the interaction of the two might have a great effect on ridership.

Working with this hypothesis the analyst used a cross-product of the two variables instead of the two separate variables in his model. The new model with the three variables included does indeed show a much higher R^2 and therefore much better predictive capability. Simply by theorizing about the relationships between the variables, the analyst was able to greatly increase the usefulness of the model. The use of interaction terms is very flexible because there is no limit to the number of interaction terms.

Transformations and Curvilinear Regressions

Transformations of variables are changes in original variables brought about by applying some mathematical operations to them, in effect the creation of new variables from existing ones. Variable transformations are performed to alter the scale or type distribution of variables or to capture additional empirical content. One commonly used transformation, for example, is the conversion of variables from their original measurement units into Z scores. When applied to variables expressed in such normal deviate units, regression is referred to as **regression in standard form**. This is often done as an aid to interpretation, especially when multiple independent variables are measured in widely differing scales. Because all transformed variables are expressed in a common unit, the betas, now called **standardized regression coefficients,** can be compared directly in terms of magnitude. The values of the betas will range from -1 to $+1$, indicating the slopes representing the amount of change in standard deviation units of Y associated with standard deviation unit changes in each of the X's. Regression in standard form is also referred to as regression through the origin; the β_0 is eliminated (Y intercept $= 0$) and the regression will lie in two quadrants of the coordinate system.

Although much of the regression analysis that is used in practice employs simple and multiple linear regression models, often the data indicate that the association under study is not linear in nature. In such cases it may be preferable to use nonlinear, or curvilinear, models. Even when a linear model provides a satisfactory fit to the data, a curvilinear model may more closely summarize the joint distribution of two variables.

There are a great many possible curvilinear regression models, but in practice only the simplest of these are used. These would include two general classes, 1) those that can be "rectified" into linear models and 2) lower degree polynomials. Many curvilinear regressions of Y on X are intrinsically linear in that with variable transformations using reciprocals or logarithms, they become linear. Polynomial regressions are those that include an independent variable X taken to some higher power in addition to X to the first power; these polynomials cannot be rectified, but the least squares estimates are derived using the same computations as for linear models. Other, more complex curvilinear models are not dealt with in this text.

Figure 15.2 illustrates two models using reciprocal transformation. In both examples the plot of Y on X_1 is not linear. Such models can be easily rectified by substituting the reciprocal of X_1 for X_1. In the upper portion of Figure 15.2, Y decreases as X_1 increases; therefore, Y increases as the reciprocal of X_1 increases. The lower portion shows the regression of employees' hourly earnings as a function of their years of experience. Earnings increase at a decreasing rate with years of experience, and decrease at a constant rate with the reciprocal of years of experience.

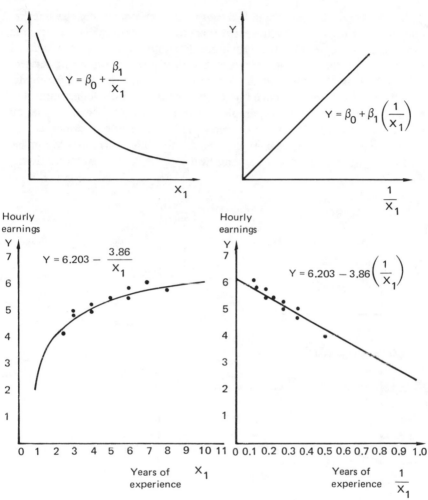

Figure 15.2.   Reciprocal transformations.

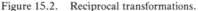

A second type of transformation frequently used to rectify intrinsi-cally linear regressions employs logarithmic functions. The **logarithm** of a number represents the power that a given base must be taken to equal that number. The base of the logarithm is conventionally noted as a subscript and the number is written in parentheses. Thus, $\log_2 (8) = 3$; 2 taken to the third power equals 8. Common logarithms are logs with the base of 10, so if a variable is transformed to common logs, all values are expressed as powers of 10. This will usually produce decimal numbers; for example, $\log_{10}(40) = 1.6021$, $\log_{10}(81) = 1.9085$, $\log_{10}(150) = 2.1761$, and $\log_{10}(2.812) = 0.449$. (Students not familiar

with the computations should consult any standard college mathe-
matics text.) Figure 15.3 illustrates three models employing logarithmic
functions. In Figure 15.3A, the joint distribution follows the type of
curve that is often used to represent the demand for a good or service,
in which Y is the quantity demanded and X_1 the price. This model
can be rectified by transforming both Y and X_1 into logarithms and
estimating the least squares simple linear regression; β_0 will be the log
of the A shown in the untransformed model. The linear model can be
converted to the curvilinear expression by finding A, the antilog of β_0,
and plugging A and β_1 into the equation $Y = A(X_1) + \beta_1$ with original

A Demand curve

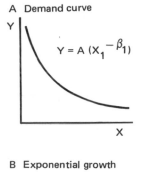

$$Y = A\,(X_1^{-\beta_1})$$

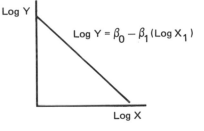

$$\text{Log } Y = \beta_0 - \beta_1\,(\text{Log } X_1)$$

B Exponential growth

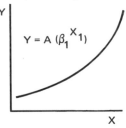

$$Y = A\,(\beta_1^{X_1})$$

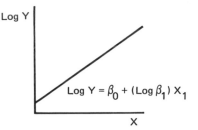

$$\text{Log } Y = \beta_0 + (\text{Log } \beta_1)\,X_1$$

C Exponential decay

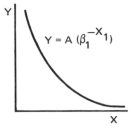

$$Y = A\,(\beta_1^{-X_1})$$

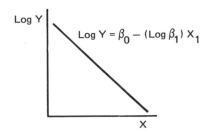

$$\text{Log } Y = \beta_0 - (\text{Log } \beta_1)\,X_1$$

Figure 15.3.   Logarithmic transformations.

values of X_1. (Again, see a college text for log and antilog tables and their use.)

Figure 15.3B illustrates a regression following the exponential growth curve, in which the increase in Y for any level of X_1 is proportional to the value of Y for the next lower value of X_1. With this kind of curve, the plot of log Y will be linear on X_1. The model log $Y = \beta_0 + \beta_1X_1$ can be estimated with linear least squares and then converted to the model $Y = A(\beta_1)^{X_1}$, where log $A = \beta_0$. Figure 15.3C illustrates an exponential decay curve in which Y decreases at a diminishing rate as X_1 increases. This can also be rectified by transforming Y to log Y, as with the exponential growth curve.

Figure 15.4 shows a plot of hypothetical data obtained in a study of the productivity of agency personnel in the coding and filing of incoming data on new clients. The independent variable is the number of cases processed by an employee in a week, and the dependent variable is the number processed correctly. As can be seen from the scatterplot, the number of correct cases seems to decrease with the volume processed until $X_1 = 150$ and then levels off or increases after that point. The linear regression of Y on X_1 yielded the estimating equation $Y = 96.5333 - 0.0428X_1$, with an R^2 of 0.736.

In an attempt to obtain a closer fit to the data, a polynomial model was developed to include, as a new variable, the square of X: $Y = \beta_0 + \beta_1X_1 + \beta_{12}X_1^2$. This is a polynomial of the second degree, with X_1 taken to the second power, and was used because the joint distribution seemed to have one reversal in the direction of the association between Y and X. For a joint distribution with two such reversals (Y increasing, then decreasing, and then increasing again as X increases, for example) a third degree polynomial, $Y = \beta_0 + \beta_1X_1 + \beta_{12}X_1^2 + \qquad$ would have been appropriate. In the example, the regression obtained was $Y = 100.6529 - 0.1455X_1 + 0.00047X_1^2$, with an R^2 equal to 0.951. The increase in R^2 represents the better fit obtained by the polynomial, as can be seen by a visual comparison of Figure 15.4, A and B.

Curvilinear regressions are usually evaluated in terms of an additional explanation of the dependent variation beyond that obtained by the best linear equation. In addition to the improvement in R^2, this can be measured by a partial F test, as shown in Table 15.1, a test of the null hypothesis that the additional explained variation attributed to the polynomial would be likely to occur by chance. The residual variation around the curvilinear model is subtracted from that around the best linear model to obtain the reduction in residual sum of squares. This reduction is the amount of variation attributed to the curvilinear

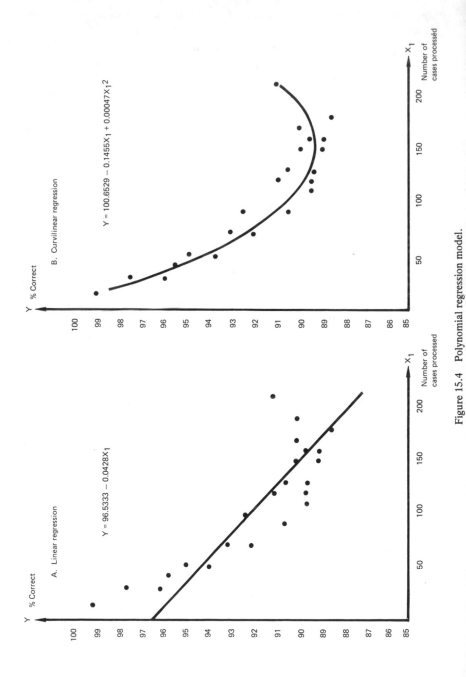

Figure 15.4   Polynomial regression model.

Table 15.1.   Significance test for departure from linear regression

Source	SS	df	Mean square	F
Deviations from linear regression	53.404	23		
Deviations from curvilinear regression	9.856	22	0.448	
Reduction (attributable to curvilinear regression)	43.548	1	43.548	97.205

models. The corresponding mean square is divided by the residual mean square (variance around the curvilinear regression) to obtain an F statistic, in this case 97.205. As this F is highly significant (critical F for 1 and 22 degrees of freedom = 14.38 at the 0.001 significance level) we conclude that the curvilinear model is an improvement over the linear model. This same procedure can be used with multiple curvilinear regressions and higher degree polynomials.

"Dummy" Variables

An important limitation on the applicability of regression analysis to program evaluation is that much of the data consists of noninterval measures. Analysis involving nominal and ordinal measures commonly employ other, less informative, statistical techniques as has been shown earlier. However, when regression is used because the bulk of the variables are interval measures, or because the dependent variable is interval, nonquantitative measures can be brought into the analysis through the use of dummy variables. Essentially, **dummy variables** are variables that are fabricated in order to represent as interval measures factors that are not naturally quantitative.

One commonly used type of dummy variable is an indicator variable, one that has two values, 1 and 0, indicating the presence or absence of some characteristic. For example, in the example on codes inspection and housing rehabilitation in the previous chapter, it might be of interest to know whether previous urban renewal status has an effect on property values. A dummy variable, X_3, could be developed as follows:

$X_3 = 1$, if census tract contained urban renewal project
$X_3 = 0$, if not

If the estimating equation $Y = b_0 + b_1X_1 + b_2X_2 + b_3X_3$ is solved, the slope b_3 is an estimate of the differential effect of urban renewal status.

In general, b_3 would represent how much more (or less) increase in property value was experienced by those neighborhoods having contained an urban renewal project than neighborhoods without such projects at comparable levels of both code inspection and rehabilitation funds.

In general, nominal variables with more than two categories can be incorporated in regression analysis with the use of more than one dummy variable; the number of dummy variables required to represent a nominal variable is one less than the number of categories that variable has $(c - 1)$. A trichotomy, then, would require two dummy variables, coded as follows:

$$X_1 = 1, X_2 = 0, \text{ if tract had urban renewal project}$$

$$X_1 = 0, X_2 = 1, \text{ if tract had flood control project}$$

$$X_1 = 0, X_2 = 0, \text{ if tract had neither}$$

If the percentage of substandard dwellings is regressed on this trichotomized, prior project status variable, the model would be:

$$Y = \beta_0 + \beta_1 X_1 + \beta_2 X_2$$

in which β_1 would represent the effect of urban renewal projects and β_2 would represent the effect of flood control projects.

Ordinal level variables are frequently introduced into regression models by the use of allocated codes. For example, if clients of a service have been categorized as occasional users, regular users, and heavy users, this variation might be represented by a variable coded as follows:

$$X_1 = 1, \text{ if occasional user}$$

$$X_1 = 2, \text{ if regular user}$$

$$X_1 = 3, \text{ if heavy user}$$

However, this practice is questionable in that it imputes an interval metric to a noninterval scale; the assumption that the difference between occasional and regular users equals that between regular and heavy users is untested.

Piecewise Regression

Piecewise regression models are appropriate for use in any situation in which the existence of different regressions over different ranges of an independent variable is to be assumed or tested. Piecewise regression is particularly appropriate for analyzing data generated by the use of the regression-discontinuity design in which treatment and comparison groups are selected on the basis of some eligibility criterion, which is also expected to influence the results. Basically, there are two kinds of piecewise regression, continuous and discontinuous; the basic difference between the two is that for continuous piecewise regression the lines have a point in common, but for discontinuous piecewise regression there is no such point.

For example, as illustrated in Figure 15.5, a treatment group may be selected from a larger class on the basis of pretest scores of 80 or higher, to be treated as an advanced class and taught with different methods. The purpose of the evaluation is to determine whether these special methods work to improve the scores of the treatment group, on a common posttest administered at the end of the course, beyond what they would have scored if they had been taught with the same conventional methods which were continued in use with the other part of the class. Formally, the question is whether there is one common regression of posttest scores on pretest scores for all the students, or whether there is discontinuity in the regression between the students who were exposed to the treatment and those who were not.

If Y is the posttest score and X_1 the pretest score, we can code two indicator variables as follows:

$$X_2 = 1, \quad \text{if } X_1 \geq 80 \qquad X_3 = 1, \quad \text{if } X_1 \geq 80$$
$$X_2 = 0, \quad \text{if } X_1 < 80 \qquad X_3 = 0, \quad \text{if } X_1 < 80$$

The estimating equation, then, would be:

$$Y = b_0 + b_1 X_1 + b_2(X_1 - 80)X_2 + b_3 X_3$$

The hypothesis that the regression is discontinuous, that there is a step

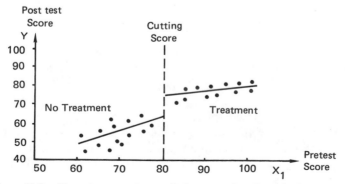

Figure 15.5.   Piecewise regression applied to regression discontinuity design.

function in the regression at $X_1 = 80$, can be tested with a t test of the null hypothesis that $b_3 = 0$.

Piecewise regression models can either be used when they seem appropriate for a specific theory or when a residual analysis of some other form of regression shows that there is a significant change in the pattern of the residuals at some point of an independent variable. In the discussion of time-series analysis an example of continuous piecewise regression is shown.

Analysis of Co-variance

Very often in program analysis, the analyst is presented with the problem of controlling for variables while looking at the effects of one or more other variables. We have already seen that we can use partial correlation when we have interval level dependent and independent variables. **Analysis of co-variance** is used when the dependent variable is interval but the independent variables are a mix of interval and categorical variables. In true experimental designs the analyst can fix for the effects of independent variables by using blocking designs. If we cannot do this experimentally, then we must take out this possible experimental bias statistically. The method is flexible because it does not matter whether the categorical variable is the control variable or the variable under study, and because any number of independent variables may be used.

The primary application of analysis of co-variance can best be pictured as a regression model with all the control variables entered and then an ANOVA performed on the residuals. The assumptions behind the model are the same as those for ANOVA, with the inclusion of the assumption of no interaction. The test for interaction between the variable under study and the control variable(s) is simply an F test for interaction with the interaction term entered last in a regression model with all the other variables in the model (see the section on interaction above).

For example, suppose the analyst would like to find out if a new set of training modules in a particular graduate professional degree program has an effect on graduate grade point averages (GPA). Although he has randomly assigned students to the new and old programs, the analyst would like to control for any possible pretreatment differences between the two groups, that is, take into account any relevant concomitant variables. In order to do this he selects scores on the Graduate Record Examination (GRE) as the control variable. In dealing with a problem, an analyst might have assumed that random sampling itself is a sufficient control and simply do a one-way ANOVA with program type and GPA. In Table 15.2 the data are presented along with a one-way ANOVA on program type. The F of 0.01 is far below the critical F and therefore the analyst would conclude that program type has no effect on GPA. A two-tailed t test on this data will, of course, produce the same result.

However, a more alert analyst would want to make sure that there are no confounding effects from other variables. Instead of a simple ANOVA, the analyst would use analysis of co-variance. Because the first step in analysis of co-variance is to make sure that there are no inter-actions, he uses a regression model with GRE scores, program type, and an interaction term. In Table 15.3 we can easily see that the interaction term is not significant. If the interaction had been significant, then the analyst would have to use a regression approach with the interaction term included. This is undesirable because it becomes very difficult to

Table 15.2.   Data for analysis of co-variance example

New program		Old program	
GRE score	GPA	GRE score	GPA
749	3.900	684	3.660
589	3.400	614	3.300
693	3.730	745	4.000
585	3.200	733	3.850
699	3.850	633	3.370
743	3.900	636	3.420
551	3.250	737	3.870
722	4.000	610	3.300
579	2.900	741	4.000
712	3.820	635	3.380
608	3.450	665	3.540
686	3.700	724	3.760
730	4.000	612	3.000
547	3.000	636	3.420
655	3.500	745	3.900

One-way ANOVA

Source	SS	df	Mean square	F
Total	3.114	29		
Program	0.001	1	0.001	0.01
Error	3.113	28	0.111	

F (0.05, df = 1, 28) = 4.20

Table 15.3.   Test for interaction

Source	SS	df	Mean square	F
Total	3.114	29		
Regression	2.810	3	0.937	78.08
Main effects	2.800	2	1.400	
Interaction	0.010	1	0.010	0.83
Error	0.304	26	0.012	

$F\,(0.05,\,df = 1,26) = 4.23$

sort out the effects of program type as opposed to the control variable, GRE scores. As stated before, analysis of co-variance can be thought of as an ANOVA on the residuals of a regression model with the control variable(s). In Figure 15.6 the results of a regression of GRE on GPA are given. By using different symbols for the two different program types we can see that the new program participants tend to be above the

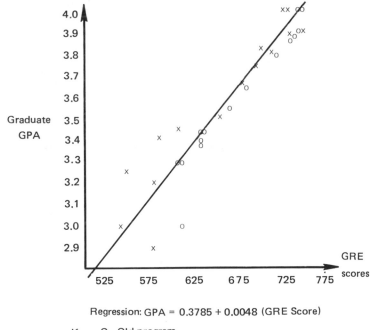

Regression: GPA = 0.3785 + 0.0048 (GRE Score)

Key: O Old program
     X New program

Figure 15.6.   Regression of GRE scores on graduate GPA.

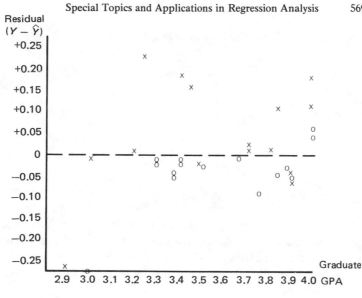

Key: O   Old program
      X   New program

Figure 15.7.   Residual plot of regression of GPA on GRE—residuals plotted on GPA.

least squares regression line and the old program participants tend to have GPA's below the line.

In Figure 15.7, a residual plot of the regression in Figure 15.6, we can see this effect more clearly. In this figure, the residuals between observed and predicted values of GPA are plotted against the observed values.

Because the actual calculations for analysis of co-variance are basically the same as those for regression and ANOVA, only the results of the test are shown. In Table 15.4, the ANOVA table shows the variation in GPA scores attributable to the program variable after the SS due to the regression of GPA on GRE, called a **covariate,** has been accounted for. In this instance the computed F ratio for the program factor with 27 degrees of freedom is 4.821. Thus, fixing for the effects of GRE's, the association between GPA and the program variable is indeed significant at the 0.05 level.

Analysis of co-variance can also be used when controlling for a categorical variable. For example, we might have a job training program that has two different types of programs, specialized skills and general skills. The program length for both types varies in weeks of duration.

Table 15.4   ANOVA table—analysis of covariance

Source	SS	df	Mean square	F
Total	3.114	29	0.107	
Explained	2.801	2	1.400	
Covariate-GRE	2.745	1	2.745	
Groups-Program	0.056	1	0.056	4.821*
Residual	0.313	27	0.012	

*$F(0.05, \mathrm{df} = 1,27) = 4.20$

The problem for the analyst is to discover whether time spent in the program influences future earnings of the participants. Because the analyst knows that those in the specialized skills program will earn more regardless of weeks in the program, he wishes to control for this categorical variable.

In Figure 15.8 we can clearly see that duration has an influence when the program types are controlled for. The calculations are .not shown; however, one can see that in this case the regression is done with the assumption of two different lines with equal slopes. The absolute difference in earnings is therefore the distance between the two lines.

Analysis of co-variance is a statistical tool used to control for variables when experimental controls are impossible. Any number of variables can be controlled for and they may be either categorical or interval. The independent variable must be interval but it does not matter which type of variable we are actually studying or controlling for. We use analysis of co-variance primarily to make sure that there are no confounding effects from other variables when testing for the variable under study.

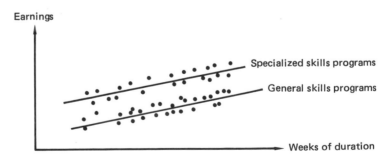

Figure 15.8.   Analysis of co-variance model controlling for a categorical variable.

REGRESSION WITH HIGHER LEVEL DESIGNS

Various applications of regression analysis are often used in conjunction with data generated by some of the more sophisticated research designs, as indicated above in the discussion of the use of piecewise regression in conjunction with regression-discontinuity designs. The use of ANOVA and regression with data developed in true experiments and highly structured quasi-experiments represents a particularly potent combination of research design and statistical technique. As discussed in the preceding section, analysis of co-variance is often used with experimental data to take into account the effect of concomitant variables in addition to category type treatment variables. With other experimental designs, straightforward multiple regression analysis is most appropriate for data analysis, as discussed below. Finally, regression analysis is frequently applied to time series data.

Experimental Designs

As has been stressed throughout this text, the validity of conclusions about the effects of program strategies on target conditions is much more dependent on research design than statistics. Multicollinearity and the problem of identifying directions of causality in regression analysis arise from the use of less structured, lower level designs. Where regression analysis is used in examining experimental data, it can produce results that are precise and highly informative. For instance, when levels of program treatment variables are set by the experimenter and assigned randomly to individual cases, the regression model should be orthogonal, with very little association between the treatments and other relevant independent variables. In this situation there is much less difficulty in interpreting the results, because of the properties of true experiments.

An example would be a factorial design in an experiment with job training programs intended to measure the effects of class size and length of program on the earnings of participants after completing the program. Three class sizes and four program durations could be specified and the participants assigned randomly to each of the 12 sections. Any observed effects of the two treatment variables would be manifested independently in a multiple regression model because they would be orthogonal variables. Furthermore, if other independent variables, such as client characteristics, have an effect on income subsequent to the program, these effects should not have strong systematic associations with the treatment variables because of the random assignment of cases to treatments, and multicollinearity should still be less of a problem than with lower level designs. If clients were instead allowed to select their preferred sections, the problem of self-selection could confound analysis of the effects of the treatments. For example, the most highly motivated clients might be those with the greatest amount of work experience, and they might tend to choose the sections with longer durations.

In designing such an experiment, the analyst has control over how many levels of X are built into the model. While in many program evaluations more variation is generally preferred over less variation, that is not necessarily the case here. Because the standard error of b_1, the slope, is minimized when the variation in X is maximized, and because this occurs when cases fall only at the extremes of the relevant range of X, the precision of the estimates is enhanced by limiting the number of levels of X that are used. If only linear models are to be considered, 2 or 3 levels of X should suffice, and fortunately this is often more feasible than numerous treatment levels. If curvilinear models are to be considered, a few additional levels of X might be needed.

Time Series Applications

Regression analysis is often applied to time series designs to summarize trends in the data before and after the intervention point. Random variation in the dependent variable and that associated with factors other than time frequently make it difficult to interpret patterns in the data before or after the intervention. Regression models can be used to "smooth out" this variation as an aid to visual interpretation and to permit inferential tests to be made concerning the consistency of the data before and after the intervention.

A continuous piecewise regression model is appropriate when the

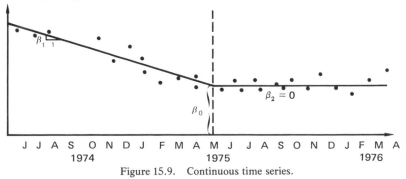

Figure 15.9.   Continuous time series.

slope of the raw scores across time seems to change at the intervention point, with postintervention series beginning at approximately the same point where the preintervention series terminates. Such a situation is illustrated in Figure 15.9 showing monthly totals of revenue passengers on a bus system before and after the initiation of a senior citizen free fare program in May, 1975.

Such a "two-piece" regression equation can be estimated by the model:

$$Y = b_0 + b_1X_1 + b_2X_2$$

where X_1 and X_2 are dummy variables designed to represent the time trend and intervention point as follows:

Month	Year	X_1	X_2	Month	Year	X_1	X_2
June	1974	−11	0	June	1975	0	1
July	1974	−10	0	July	1975	0	2
August	1974	− 9	0	August	1975	0	3
September	1974	− 8	0	September	1975	0	4
October	1974	− 7	0	October	1975	0	5
November	1974	− 6	0	November	1975	0	6
December	1974	− 5	0	December	1975	0	7
January	1975	− 4	0	January	1976	0	8
February	1975	− 3	0	February	1976	0	9
March	1975	− 2	0	March	1976	0	10
April	1975	− 1	0	April	1976	0	11
May	1975	0	0				

In this model, b_0 is the estimate of Y_1 revenue passengers at the intervention point, b_1 is the estimate of slope between the intervention, and b_2 the slope estimate after the intervention.

A discontinuous time series model is appropriate when the criterion variable seems to have a jump-point at the intervention as well as a change in slope. Such a case, involving changes in monthly scores on a productivity index of municipal employees before and after implementation of a new incentives plan, is illustrated in Figure 15.10. The productivity level is seen to fluctuate around a stationary mean before the incentives plan, take a dramatic jump upward upon implementation, and then decrease gradually over time toward the former level.

This discontinuous regression can be estimated by the equation:

$$Y = b_0 + b_1X_1 + b_2X_2 + b_3X_3$$

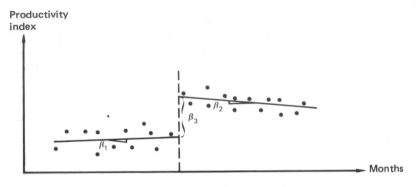

Figure 15.10.   Discontinuous time series.

where X_1 and X_2 are defined the same way as in the previous example and X_3 is set equal to 1 for those months after and including the intervention and equal to 0 for those months before the intervention. In this model, b_0 estimates the Y intercept, b_1 the slope before the intervention, b_2 the slope after the intervention, and b_3 the difference in the predicted values at the intervention point by the two different slopes.

Significance Tests   If the usual assumptions underlying regression analysis are thought to hold for a given time series design, standard errors of regression coefficients can be used to test hypotheses about these parameters, as discussed in a previous section. Statistical tests of significance are employed to determine the probability that observed values occur by chance, assuming that the null hypotheses are true. In the case of time-series analysis the null hypotheses hold that postintervention observations are continuations of preintervention series, that the only deviations from this are caused by chance effects. As discussed in chapter 9, two-sample t tests of difference in means between one preintervention observation and one postintervention observation are inadequate because they do not take into account any long range trends in the data across time, which is really the advantage of time series designs over simple pretest/posttest designs. Rather, with time series designs, regressions can be developed to represent such trends and significance tests can be applied to test hypotheses about differences in pre- and postintervention series.

One test that is suitable for continuous time series applications, particularly when interest centers on an immediate change or when multiple postintervention observations are not available, is the **single Mood test.** A regression is fitted to the preintervention series, and used to predict the value of the first observation after the intervention. This predicted value is then compared with the observed value using a t test to determine the probability of the observed value occurring by chance if the trend represented by the regression still prevails. For discontinuous time series such as illustrated in Figure 15.10, the hypothesis that the difference in point estimates by the pre- and postintervention regressions is due to chance effect can be tested by applying a t test to the null hypothesis that $\beta_3 = 0$.

With respect to slopes in the case of either continuous or discontinuous time series, a two-sample t test can be employed to test the null hypothesis that $\beta_1 = \beta_2$, using the notation shown in Figures 15.9 and 15.10. This is equivalent to the **Walker-Lev test three**, testing the null hypothesis that a common regression fits both the preintervention and postintervention series. In this test separate regression estimates are computed for both series and then the beta coefficients are compared by the use of an F test to determine the probability that they were drawn from the same population.

Autocorrelation   It should be understood that although the above-mentioned tests are frequently employed with time series data, such applications are often not valid in strict terms, in that time series often do not meet the assumptions on which regression analysis is founded. For example, most time series are not made up of a set of randomly selected observations, but rather observations of interest at periodic intervals in time.

One of the most troublesome problems in analyzing time series data is **autocorrelation**, the tendency of time ordered observations not to have independent error terms. This occurs most often because of the continuing effects of certain variables outside the model creating the same kind of disturbance in consecutive observations, i.e., the error term is not solely a function of numerous, singly unimportant varibles that are unrelated to the time dimension.

For example, the observations in the bus passenger example presented above are almost certain to be autocorrelated because the number of passengers riding the bus each month in a city is a function of gradually changing parameters such as population size and automobile ownership. Autocorrelation can also occur as a result of the level of the criterion variable in one time period having a direct effect on its level in the subsequent time period. A time series designed to analyze the effect of the introduction of an early detection program on the incidence of venereal disease, for example, would be subject to autocorrelation due to the nature of the pattern of exposure to such diseases.

With an autocorrelated series, least squares regression coefficients will still be unbiased, but many of the associated statistics will not be valid. The standard error of the regression coefficients as well as the estimated variance around the regression may be underestimated, and the use of the confidence intervals and tests using the t and F distributions may not be applicable. The presence of autocorrelation can often be detected in residual plots on time, but it can also be tested for using the **Durbin-Watson test** statistic:

$$D = \frac{\Sigma(e_t - e_{t-1})^2}{\Sigma e_t^2}$$

where e_t is the residual of a given observation and e_{t-1} the residual of the preceding observation. This statistic is compared with upper and lower bounds shown in appendix Table A-9 for various significance levels, sample sizes, and independent variables. If D is below the lower bound, this indicates that the series is autocorrelated. If D exceeds the upper bound, this leads to the conclusion that the series is not autocorrelated, whereas a D falling in the range between the two bounds is inconclusive. Autocorrelation can be taken into account by elaborating the model:

$$Y = \beta_0 + \beta_1 X + e$$
$$Y = \beta_0 + \beta_1 X_1 + \rho e_{t-1} + u_t$$

where ρ is the autocorrelation parameter relating the error term of one observation to that of the next and u_t is the random disturbance in each observation. Iterative approaches have been designed for estimating ρ. However, a simpler approach is to assume that the autocorrelation parameter equals 1 and use **first differencing**, in which each observation is transformed into the difference between its original value and that of the preceding observation:

$$Y_t' = Y_t - Y_{t-1}$$
$$X_t' = X_t - X_{t-1}$$

Thus, the transformed model:

$$Y_t' = \beta_1' X_t' + u_t$$

can be estimated to reduce error due to autocorrelation. The first differences approach is thought to be appropriate for many times series applications. (For discussion of time series analysis and autocorrelation, see Box and Tiao, 1965; Neter and Wasserman, 1974, pp. 352–366; Glass et al., 1975.)

Seasonal Adjustments   As the general approach to the analysis of time series data is to statistically explain the variation in the preintervention series in order to determine whether the postintervention series represents a significant deviation from the pattern of observations that might be expected if trends continued unchanged after the intervention point, it is often helpful to incorporate additional independent variables in the model. If the standard error of estimate is reduced with the use of additional variables, comparisons between preintervention and postintervention series will be more discriminating. A frequent use of additional variables involves **seasonal adjustments**, to account for that part of the dependent variation that is tied systematically to changes in months or seasons across the year.

Figure 15.11 shows the data obtained for a time series analysis of the effects of a substantial fare reduction (from 40¢ to 15¢ per ride) on the transit system in Atlanta, Georgia (Kemp, 1974). Ridership as measured by revenue passengers per month seems to have increased after the fare cut, which was implemented in March 1972, but in general there is substantial instability in the data from month to month. The preintervention series does evidence a gradual downward trend, which in part is overshadowed by a systematic pattern of peaks and valleys: low in the summer months and high in the spring and fall months.

In order to determine whether the postintervention series represents a significant departure from the preintervention trend, a regression was developed for the preintervention data and then extrapolated into the postintervention period. In developing this model, the objective was to explain the preintervention variation in revenue passengers as a function of the secular time trend and season. Time trend in this case was represented by a single variable in which the observations were numbered consecutively from 1 = January, 1970; 2 = February, 1970; and so on. The seasonal variation from month to month was captured with a set of 12 dummy variables, one for each month coded as follows: $D_1 = 1$ for January, 0 for any other month; $D_2 = 1$ for February, 0 for any other month, and so forth. The regression of revenue passengers on the time varible (actually a log function was used with time) and the 12-month variables over the 26 preintervention series provided a good fit to the data, with an R^2 of 0.882.

Figure 15.12 shows the actual passenger volumes along with the volume for each month predicted by this regression. Note that with other variables in addition to the time variable, the prediction values no longer fit on a straight line across the series. The dashed line represents the predicted values, which were then projected into the postintervention

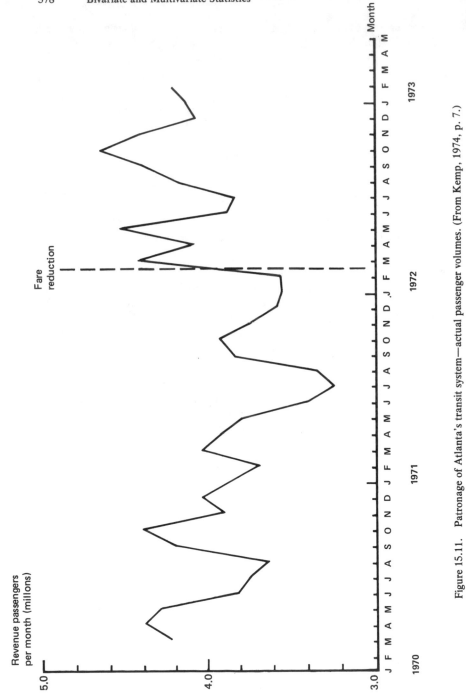

Figure 15.11.   Patronage of Atlanta's transit system—actual passenger volumes. (From Kemp, 1974, p. 7.)

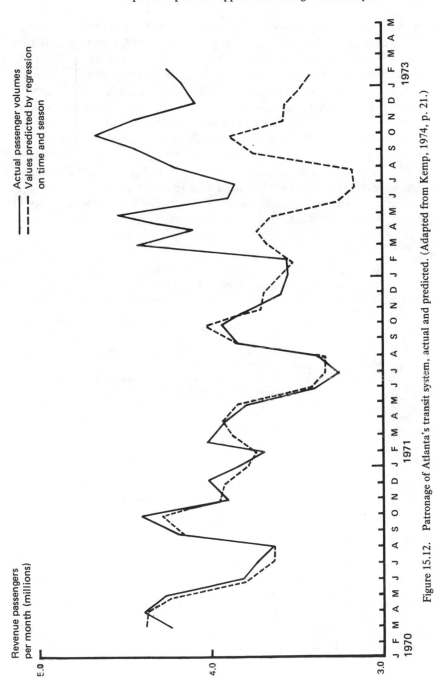

Figure 15.12.   Patronage of Atlanta's transit system, actual and predicted. (Adapted from Kemp, 1974, p. 21.)

series on the basis of the time and season variables in the same regression. This projection follows the same general downward trend, punctuated by the Spring-Summer-Fall-Winter pattern of variation observed in the preintervention series. In this case it is clear that the actual postintervention ridership was much greater than what would have happened if the preintervention trend had continued unchanged. Significance tests could be made by using the standard error of estimate to test the hypothesis that $Y = \hat{Y}$ for each postintervention observation. If the regression had been a less accurate predictor on the preintervention series, this testing might have been a good idea, but in this particular example, a visual comparison will suffice to conclude that after a fare cut, ridership on the system did in fact increase substantially above what it would have been if previous ridership trends had continued.

REFERENCES

Blalock, H. M., Jr. 1964. Causal Inferences in Nonexperimental Research. Chapel Hill: University of North Carolina Press.

Blalock, H. M., Jr. (ed.). 1971. Causal Models in the Social Sciences. Chicago: Aldine-Atherton.

Blalock, H. M., Jr. 1972. Social Statistics, 2nd Ed. New York: McGraw-Hill Book Company.

Bock, D. R. 1975. Multivariate Statistical Methods in Behavioral Research. New York: McGraw-Hill Book Company.

Borgatta, E. F., and G. W. Bohrnstedt (eds.). 1970. Sociological Methodology 1970. San Francisco: Jossey Bass Inc., Publishers.

Box, G. E. P., and G. C. Tiao. 1965. A Change in Level of a Non-stationary Time Series. Biometrika, Vol. 52, #1 and 2, pp. 181-192.

Draper, N. R., and H. Smith. 1966. Applied Regression Analysis. New York: John Wiley & Sons, Inc.

Duncan, O. D. 1966. Path Analysis: Sociological Examples. Am. J. Sociol. 72:1-16.

Glass, G. V., V. L. Willson, and J. Gottman. 1975. Design and Analysis of Time Series Experiments. Boulder: Colorado Associated University Press.

Heise, D. R. 1970. Causal Inference from Panel Data. In: E. F. Borgatta and G. W. Bohrnstedt (eds.), Sociological Methodology 1970. San Francisco: Jossey Bass Inc., Publishers.

Jorgenson, D. W. 1964. Minimum Variance, Linear, Unbiased Seasonal Adjustment of Economic Time Series. Am. Statistical Assoc. J. 59:681-724.

Kemp, M. A. 1974. Transit Improvements in Atlanta: The Effects of Fare and Service Changes. Washington: Urban Institute.

Mood, A. M., and F. A. Graybill. 1963. Introduction to the Theory of Statistics. New York: McGraw-Hill Book Company.

Neter, J., and W. Wasserman. 1974. Applied Linear Statistical Models. Homewood, Illinois: Richard D. Irwin, Inc.

Snedecor, G. W., and W. C. Cochran. 1967. Statistical Methods, 6th Ed. Ames, Iowa: Iowa State University Press.

Appendix

Table A-1. Squares and square roots

k	$\sqrt{k}$	$\sqrt{10k}$	k^2	k	$\sqrt{k}$	$\sqrt{10k}$	k^2
1	1	3.16228	1	51	7.14143	22.5832	2601
2	1.41421	4.47214	4	52	7.2111	22.8035	2704
3	1.73205	5.47723	9	53	7.28011	23.0217	2809
4	2	6.32456	16	54	7.34847	23.2379	2916
5	2.23607	7.07107	25	55	7.4162	23.4521	3025
6	2.44949	7.74597	36	56	7.48331	23.6643	3136
7	2.64575	8.3666	49	57	7.54983	23.8747	3249
8	2.82843	8.94427	64	58	7.61577	24.0832	3364
9	3	9.48683	81	59	7.68115	24.2899	3481
10	3.16228	10	100	60	7.74597	24.4949	3600
11	3.31662	10.4881	121	61	7.81025	24.6982	3721
12	3.4641	10.9545	144	62	7.87401	24.8998	3844
13	3.60555	11.4018	169	63	7.93725	25.0998	3969
14	3.74166	11.8322	196	64	8	25.2982	4096
15	3.87298	12.2474	225	65	8.06226	25.4951	4225
16	4	12.6491	256	66	8.12404	25.6905	4356
17	4.12311	13.0384	289	67	8.18535	25.8844	4489
18	4.24264	13.4164	324	68	8.24621	26.0768	4624
19	4.3589	13.784	361	69	8.30662	26.2679	4761
20	4.47214	14.1421	400	70	8.3666	26.4575	4900
21	4.58258	14.4914	441	71	8.42615	26.6458	5041
22	4.69042	14.8324	484	72	8.48528	26.8328	5184
23	4.79583	15.1658	529	73	8.544	27.0185	5329
24	4.89898	15.4919	576	74	8.60233	27.2029	5476
25	5	15.8114	625	75	8.66025	27.3861	5625
26	5.09902	16.1245	676	76	8.7178	27.5681	5776
27	5.19615	16.4317	729	77	8.77496	27.7489	5929
28	5.2915	16.7332	784	78	8.83176	27.9285	6084
29	5.38516	17.0294	841	79	8.88819	28.1069	6241
30	5.47723	17.3205	900	80	8.94427	28.2843	6400
31	5.56776	17.6068	961	81	9	28.4605	6561
32	5.65685	17.8885	1024	82	9.05539	28.6356	6724
33	5.74456	18.1659	1089	83	9.11043	28.8097	6889
34	5.83095	18.4391	1156	84	9.16515	28.9828	7056
35	5.91608	18.7083	1225	85	9.21954	29.1548	7225
36	6	18.9737	1296	86	9.27362	29.3258	7396
37	6.08276	19.2354	1369	87	9.32738	29.4958	7569
38	6.16441	19.4936	1444	88	9.38083	29.6648	7744
39	6.245	19.7484	1521	89	9.43398	29.8329	7921
40	6.32456	20	1600	90	9.48683	30	8100
41	6.40312	20.2485	1681	91	9.53939	30.1662	8281
42	6.48074	20.4939	1764	92	9.59166	30.3315	8464
43	6.55744	20.7364	1849	93	9.64365	30.4959	8649
44	6.63325	20.9762	1936	94	9.69536	30.6594	8836
45	6.7082	21.2132	2025	95	9.74679	30.8221	9025
46	6.78233	21.4476	2116	96	9.79796	30.9839	9216
47	6.85565	21.6795	2209	97	9.84886	31.1448	9409
48	6.9282	21.9089	2304	98	9.89949	31.305	9604
49	7	22.1359	2401	99	9.94987	31.4643	9801
50	7.07107	22.3607	2500	100	10	31.6228	10000

From Loether and McTavish, 1976, pp. 605–607.

Table A-1. *Continued.*

k	$\sqrt{k}$	$\sqrt{10k}$	k^2	k	$\sqrt{k}$	$\sqrt{10k}$	k^2
101	10.0499	31.7805	10201	151	12.2882	38.8587	22801
102	10.0995	31.9374	10404	152	12.3288	38.9872	23104
103	10.1489	32.0936	10609	153	12.3693	39.1152	23409
104	10.198	32.249	10816	154	12.4097	39.2428	23716
105	10.247	32.4037	11025	155	12.4499	39.37	24025
106	10.2956	32.5576	11236	156	12.49	39.4968	24336
107	10.3441	32.7109	11449	157	12.53	39.6232	24649
108	10.3923	32.8634	11664	158	12.5698	39.7492	24964
109	10.4403	33.0151	11881	159	12.6095	39.8748	25281
110	10.4881	33.1662	12100	160	12.6491	40	25600
111	10.5357	33.3167	12321	161	12.6886	40.1248	25921
112	10.583	33.4664	12544	162	12.7279	40.2492	26244
113	10.6301	33.6155	12769	163	12.7671	40.3733	26569
114	10.6771	33.7639	12996	164	12.8062	40.4969	26896
115	10.7238	33.9116	13225	165	12.8452	40.6202	27225
116	10.7703	34.0588	13456	166	12.8841	40.7431	27556
117	10.8167	34.2053	13689	167	12.9228	40.8656	27889
118	10.8628	34.3511	13924	168	12.9615	40.9878	28224
119	10.9087	34.4964	14161	169	13	41.1096	28561
120	10.9545	34.641	14400	170	13.0384	41.2311	28900
121	11	34.7851	14641	171	13.0767	41.3521	29241
122	11.0454	34.9285	14884	172	13.1149	41.4729	29584
123	11.0905	35.0714	15129	173	13.1529	41.5933	29929
124	11.1355	35.2136	15376	174	13.1909	41.7133	30276
125	11.1803	35.3553	15625	175	13.2288	41.833	30625
126	11.225	35.4965	15876	176	13.2665	41.9524	30976
127	11.2694	35.6371	16129	177	13.3041	42.0714	31329
128	11.3137	35.7771	16384	178	13.3417	42.19	31684
129	11.3578	35.9166	16641	179	13.3791	42.3084	32041
130	11.4018	36.0555	16900	180	13.4164	42.4264	32400
131	11.4455	36.1939	17161	181	13.4536	42.5441	32761
132	11.4891	36.3318	17424	182	13.4907	42.6615	33124
133	11.5326	36.4692	17689	183	13.5277	42.7785	33489
134	11.5758	36.606	17956	184	13.5647	42.8952	33856
135	11.619	36.7423	18225	185	13.6015	43.0116	34225
136	11.6619	36.8782	18496	186	13.6382	43.1277	34596
137	11.7047	37.0135	18769	187	13.6748	43.2435	34969
138	11.7473	37.1484	19044	188	13.7113	43.359	35344
139	11.7898	37.2827	19321	189	13.7477	43.4741	35721
140	11.8322	37.4166	19600	190	13.784	43.589	36100
141	11.8743	37.55	19881	191	13.8203	43.7035	36481
142	11.9164	37.6829	20164	192	13.8564	43.8178	36864
143	11.9583	37.8153	20449	193	13.8924	43.9318	37249
144	12	37.9473	20736	194	13.9284	44.0454	37636
145	12.0416	38.0789	21025	195	13.9642	44.1588	38025
146	12.083	38.2099	21316	196	14	44.2719	38416
147	12.1244	38.3406	21609	197	14.0357	44.3847	38809
148	12.1655	38.4708	21904	198	14.0712	44.4972	39204
149	12.2066	38.6005	22201	199	14.1067	44.6094	39601
150	12.2474	38.7298	22500	200	14.1421	44.7214	40000

Table A-1. *Continued.*

k	$\sqrt{k}$	$\sqrt{10k}$	k^2	k	$\sqrt{k}$	$\sqrt{10k}$	k^2
201	14.1774	44.833	40401	251	15.843	50.0999	63001
202	14.2127	44.9444	40804	252	15.8745	50.1996	63504
203	14.2478	45.0555	41209	253	15.906	50.2991	64009
204	14.2829	45.1664	41616	254	15.9374	50.3984	64516
205	14.3178	45.2769	42025	255	15.9687	50.4975	65025
206	14.3527	45.3872	42436	256	16	50.5964	65536
207	14.3875	45.4973	42849	257	16.0312	50.6952	66049
208	14.4222	45.607	43264	258	16.0624	50.7937	66564
209	14.4568	45.7165	43681	259	16.0935	50.892	67081
210	14.4914	45.8258	44100	260	16.1245	50.9902	67600
211	14.5258	45.9347	44521	261	16.1555	51.0882	68121
212	14.5602	46.0435	44944	262	16.1864	51.1859	68644
213	14.5945	46.1519	45369	263	16.2173	51.2835	69169
214	14.6287	46.2601	45796	264	16.2481	51.3809	69696
215	14.6629	46.3681	46225	265	16.2788	51.4782	70225
216	14.6969	46.4758	46656	266	16.3095	51.5752	70756
217	14.7309	46.5833	47089	267	16.3401	51.672	71289
218	14.7648	46.6905	47524	268	16.3707	51.7687	71824
219	14.7986	46.7974	47961	269	16.4012	51.8652	72361
220	14.8324	46.9042	48400	270	16.4317	51.9615	72900
221	14.8661	47.0106	48841	271	16.4621	52.0577	73441
222	14.8997	47.1169	49284	272	16.4924	52.1536	73984
223	14.9332	47.2229	49729	273	16.5227	52.2494	74529
224	14.9666	47.3286	50176	274	16.5529	52.345	75076
225	15	47.4342	50625	275	16.5831	52.4404	75625
226	15.0333	47.5395	51076	276	16.6132	52.5357	76176
227	15.0665	47.6445	51529	277	16.6433	52.6308	76729
228	15.0997	47.7493	51984	278	16.6733	52.7257	77284
229	15.1327	47.8539	52441	279	16.7033	52.8205	77841
230	15.1658	47.9583	52900	280	16.7332	52.915	78400
231	15.1987	48.0625	53361	281	16.7631	53.0094	78961
232	15.2315	48.1664	53824	282	16.7929	53.1037	79524
233	15.2643	48.2701	54289	283	16.8226	53.1977	80089
234	15.2971	48.3735	54756	284	16.8523	53.2917	80656
235	15.3297	48.4768	55225	285	16.8819	53.3854	81225
236	15.3623	48.5798	55696	286	16.9115	53.479	81796
237	15.3948	48.6826	56169	287	16.9411	53.5724	82369
238	15.4272	48.7852	56644	288	16.9706	53.6656	82944
239	15.4596	48.8876	57121	289	17	53.7587	83521
240	15.4919	48.9898	57600	290	17.0294	53.8516	84100
241	15.5242	49.0918	58081	291	17.0587	53.9444	84681
242	15.5563	49.1935	58564	292	17.088	54.037	85264
243	15.5885	49.295	59049	293	17.1172	54.1295	85849
244	15.6205	49.3964	59536	294	17.1464	54.2218	86436
245	15.6525	49.4975	60025	295	17.1756	54.3139	87025
246	15.6844	49.5984	60516	296	17.2047	54.4059	87616
247	15.7162	49.6991	61009	297	17.2337	54.4977	88209
248	15.748	49.7996	61504	298	17.2627	54.5894	88804
249	15.7797	49.8999	62001	299	17.2916	54.6809	89401
250	15.8114	50	62500	300	17.3205	54.7723	90000

Table A-2.   Random numbers

I.	1-4	5-8	9-12	13-16	17-20	21-24	25-28	29-32
1	74 44	80 91	21 41	40 25	98 81	57 12	30 13	24 93
2	72 59	62 28	26 74	90 62	91 20	70 31	19 10	23 06
3	33 76	63 60	48 79	23 76	28 61	87 65	79 30	38 27
4	78 02	65 54	17 61	60 15	00 81	18 07	66 38	88 33
5	32 46	64 91	77 63	26 35	94 81	54 90	10 70	10 66
6	19 68	47 39	30 75	39 71	13 14	55 59	25 38	79 00
7	06 34	06 19	72 70	53 47	57 70	04 07	54 81	04 98
8	62 23	31 49	29 34	39 38	99 54	66 13	94 08	17 03
9	97 69	04 44	89 07	31 84	66 59	86 21	61 78	60 26
10	71 00	49 40	32 08	38 57	58 59	69 72	31 52	94 75
11	32 40	60 49	51 52	47 01	29 40	59 31	14 60	26 91
12	63 42	42 91	61 34	02 22	44 76	88 32	06 36	71 39
13	09 20	12 10	05 86	08 66	45 84	84 80	69 45	65 08
14	62 50	89 39	48 02	24 64	45 60	20 27	83 65	33 82
15	73 95	05 00	52 98	08 57	74 19	05 58	27 46	23 26
16	62 43	84 11	42 38	74 13	04 57	80 26	28 04	20 52
17	07 00	14 03	55 80	14 27	69 56	24 43	30 82	55 08
18	83 26	53 43	70 61	67 23	07 36	49 78	40 25	09 66
19	14 67	02 60	21 02	64 47	54 86	62 88	81 12	28 29
20	33 60	94 02	89 25	44 73	03 85	01 95	17 85	70 51
21	02 73	10 59	69 74	76 11	57 27	04 63	94 15	74 96
22	75 46	82 03	13 43	64 34	96 68	23 86	38 49	83 98
23	79 06	02 26	58 82	81 17	91 27	44 27	71 89	17 90
24	85 16	88 13	08 97	13 08	73 28	25 34	79 27	16 34
25	37 30	30 55	08 17	55 15	93 34	10 60	00 95	60 26
II.								
1	24 25	56 63	72 28	28 39	91 61	34 21	52 63	73 21
2	50 63	56 77	89 77	80 28	03 14	79 27	86 26	35 33
3	03 65	03 42	90 08	30 90	14 39	85 94	74 39	97 71
4	63 60	97 32	86 61	10 39	07 30	89 99	09 11	21 55
5	54 69	75 00	63 95	78 98	01 93	93 77	57 30	50 82
6	88 05	23 40	46 42	52 55	27 85	28 12	00 51	23 76
7	97 38	25 33	16 78	32 87	47 58	19 34	31 76	44 97
8	03 12	82 62	94 17	66 36	56 10	23 73	50 93	15 55
9	19 66	44 73	79 92	31 66	72 70	27 72	90 95	46 77
10	46 32	77 62	36 51	73 93	57 25	09 15	50 30	50 95
11	40 78	23 70	51 26	87 86	69 22	21 85	62 27	39 01
12	20 66	67 60	26 95	80 64	02 42	97 88	48 34	27 23
13	97 77	58 66	34 10	91 71	94 82	79 59	14 11	53 84
14	91 93	21 80	20 91	19 52	71 42	20 08	35 28	35 91
15	14 88	89 71	48 84	32 22	13 63	78 02	72 97	61 13
16	90 97	01 01	01 59	01 39	96 96	74 40	66 88	44 01
17	85 29	86 31	19 55	37 86	04 56	98 35	78 82	29 06
18	22 06	90 91	84 64	81 65	63 51	54 35	94 73	79 48
19	53 69	65 88	46 28	13 02	00 17	27 22	69 94	45 92
20	66 42	58 45	92 71	40 83	59 73	64 04	42 92	38 84
21	91 09	52 38	46 27	17 09	95 13	43 45	80 94	98 07
22	88 72	65 18	16 79	80 82	75 47	29 46	95 09	91 01
23	86 63	79 92	70 95	28 32	95 25	95 25	81 18	30 16
24	46 70	03 50	46 40	34 78	59 35	93 12	24 69	37 37
25	25 50	24 15	01 82	38 36	21 15	71 91	31 52	52 51

From Loether and McTavish, 1976, pp. 589-592.

Table A-2. *Continued*

III.	1–4	5–8	9–12	13–16	17–20	21–24	25–28	29–32
1	81 18	43 25	80 75	71 96	48 88	91 61	85 37	12 99
2	30 49	80 30	38 91	62 72	55 48	26 82	31 66	09 47
3	47 11	18 80	57 00	16 38	30 49	09 74	15 77	52 68
4	00 31	08 24	87 17	23 04	98 29	30 98	14 95	03 98
5	24 25	33 96	83 92	12 02	80 63	80 41	49 40	62 49
6	93 06	35 71	31 25	38 38	01 14	75 19	72 11	92 52
7	45 33	21 67	02 64	92 85	74 74	82 52	68 19	23 78
8	44 45	81 92	53 10	78 28	17 76	84 74	60 37	34 08
9	95 75	30 09	08 93	87 81	68 63	71 84	96 91	86 02
10	13 99	84 18	43 72	24 15	33 59	11 97	95 69	24 43
11	46 15	99 32	14 87	23 20	44 45	84 19	35 65	20 97
12	74 00	80 33	52 32	96 66	57 94	25 86	63 40	57 70
13	59 47	85 05	51 89	52 12	75 48	61 99	99 11	48 07
14	84 22	38 10	92 68	34 81	15 10	03 01	30 59	79 03
15	58 57	59 12	18 06	15 63	10 13	58 18	49 60	64 86
16	13 95	54 28	92 78	95 64	71 57	33 08	46 27	18 31
17	77 32	46 87	82 56	39 99	81 79	87 57	12 82	24 62
18	52 58	01 90	82 77	99 53	71 20	22 50	41 28	99 16
19	73 26	35 54	15 57	67 00	28 84	47 57	10 46	36 12
20	86 83	39 22	37 11	93 21	01 40	14 71	20 98	40 01
21	12 70	37 38	82 24	18 01	45 58	72 29	70 45	18 50
22	41 31	79 58	62 06	58 38	72 38	13 63	51 70	38 27
23	24 40	09 84	72 10	84 64	50 20	85 02	37 12	46 34
24	99 76	09 25	14 33	44 93	20 35	18 69	50 99	24 73
25	29 74	34 46	74 62	58 08	68 78	60 16	83 98	86 80
IV.								
1	81 66	77 08	85 13	41 90	28 77	60 13	59 55	15 06
2	32 42	50 81	08 01	90 10	43 28	89 50	05 42	05 95
3	11 50	29 08	16 39	76 94	70 66	53 71	23 03	41 38
4	93 65	51 22	55 70	86 61	59 58	64 86	29 00	65 26
5	33 43	08 85	65 24	55 58	73 81	50 89	58 50	57 14
6	59 87	34 45	41 02	32 95	98 53	54 21	95 66	01 13
7	15 52	12 97	14 84	23 98	01 13	04 26	20 79	37 97
8	75 02	13 24	27 60	50 77	97 95	06 07	52 64	86 71
9	14 52	99 22	31 39	70 43	58 93	43 52	61 47	51 75
10	59 22	81 73	42 89	96 56	46 75	39 39	37 10	70 70
11	12 07	71 71	64 45	62 43	10 27	48 73	88 72	28 81
12	51 12	39 78	31 47	77 80	94 00	57 79	54 64	08 44
13	25 52	91 93	90 49	05 47	33 28	40 98	13 58	92 30
14	30 63	79 24	45 48	15 83	74 00	62 15	54 44	71 02
15	84 21	76 60	10 79	48 36	76 51	74 52	04 72	96 63
16	02 22	20 00	82 36	33 25	60 45	80 70	93 29	33 61
17	77 24	43 56	80 48	10 29	45 33	44 14	19 76	26 11
18	62 79	14 00	69 80	81 05	33 52	93 34	10 31	55 89
19	76 87	06 38	98 93	50 50	06 33	95 12	52 93	92 72
20	18 90	97 14	95 07	88 30	69 06	75 51	75 45	32 65
21	17 27	41 02	29 40	58 56	16 66	35 38	58 29	04 01
22	94 73	05 06	86 43	55 58	55 70	43 35	53 80	43 49
23	68 94	03 23	79 95	89 33	64 51	68 19	87 45	29 13
24	96 34	44 78	24 04	72 98	17 07	13 28	49 56	68 69
25	53 55	99 99	13 59	25 54	41 52	27 17	05 74	28 03

Table A-2. *Continued*

V.	1–4	5–8	9–12	13–16	17–20	21–24	25–28	29–32
1	61 81	17 50	68 00	35 10	30 90	59 71	09 95	01 14
2	78 95	64 65	24 82	14 05	27 63	33 96	10 41	88 70
3	84 28	44 68	07 47	21 46	56 81	32 87	28 40	40 50
4	92 33	63 98	99 22	09 21	97 81	10 03	79 46	17 13
5	15 79	75 50	29 36	12 37	63 39	02 47	57 02	97 17
6	80 16	09 75	22 28	35 25	53 57	72 64	09 98	63 50
7	68 20	33 03	43 73	80 96	21 13	97 61	90 37	35 77
8	55 26	85 04	30 60	68 10	73 53	89 35	58 45	83 23
9	60 00	37 51	42 89	52 32	46 00	57 02	71 97	44 16
10	59 69	31 20	16 37	66 34	99 76	07 23	40 85	64 91
11	84 42	33 66	58 54	17 16	45 73	67 20	09 27	90 96
12	57 46	65 19	78 34	57 12	77 45	54 65	17 17	30 90
13	78 17	51 47	69 22	41 48	01 99	66 46	00 28	21 74
14	27 66	33 21	49 11	24 15	33 70	06 95	04 67	98 56
15	82 54	98 27	81 86	77 35	87 56	32 72	60 90	26 75
16	33 06	79 71	73 57	96 74	85 94	36 97	87 79	82 00
17	77 94	61 11	69 61	78 78	36 51	45 21	82 94	39 22
18	87 15	49 66	56 55	34 99	05 26	45 35	59 83	55 47
19	24 98	52 45	79 85	15 67	32 21	29 94	98 90	02 27
20	05 66	15 23	83 66	24 98	06 75	60 69	64 26	58 24
21	84 90	70 29	01 36	90 78	56 40	61 00	58 40	75 37
22	49 50	30 71	87 38	70 10	80 71	12 54	60 76	62 13
23	27 53	95 47	04 78	61 85	56 15	71 76	25 31	96 39
24	56 17	07 83	96 29	88 39	67 86	98 23	95 03	82 62
25	41 67	05 42	29 18	54 76	71 82	04 81	82 63	00 23
VI.								
1	59 63	29 38	35 59	02 05	68 55	03 47	95 17	41 48
2	11 94	21 16	54 90	92 80	80 91	71 76	54 03	81 00
3	97 62	76 15	96 67	40 92	96 85	18 84	70 89	87 05
4	07 02	78 73	21 58	12 95	04 96	66 91	42 11	11 86
5	13 40	90 19	67 10	34 15	62 59	21 10	30 33	62 02
6	45 48	25 79	20 34	96 33	32 28	66 64	75 37	10 31
7	41 01	61 47	38 60	24 86	08 42	37 27	16 65	20 86
8	49 89	46 70	52 25	93 67	00 76	10 78	72 86	63 18
9	83 90	36 74	50 40	54 90	71 78	80 65	48 29	01 80
10	94 53	17 86	40 96	47 83	02 53	42 68	21 55	96 13
11	73 09	63 85	30 66	78 74	91 82	64 54	81 95	50 35
12	42 47	76 36	12 49	28 49	39 61	49 16	69 42	98 75
13	36 77	54 32	75 18	69 35	54 26	99 87	86 21	94 49
14	65 15	36 03	51 29	64 85	08 56	58 27	32 20	94 21
15	25 25	78 24	08 31	20 26	82 28	54 65	30 00	70 33
16	61 33	06 70	01 51	70 43	38 01	21 94	08 89	77 54
17	59 55	83 53	92 99	57 59	52 24	07 21	82 57	97 42
18	54 63	59 93	45 39	87 90	49 18	71 36	19 88	79 46
19	42 26	36 54	15 06	45 23	61 47	59 31	30 37	08 64
20	84 41	06 96	39 93	14 09	66 32	58 24	55 92	10 76
21	77 00	01 88	33 81	04 10	26 96	38 07	08 44	34 62
22	92 12	15 04	18 73	45 98	64 20	60 93	35 60	29 32
23	59 19	35 73	78 60	18 44	27 97	71 69	44 70	30 76
24	83 17	41 05	62 05	10 84	51 42	68 31	85 75	87 63
25	74 41	13 36	38 79	52 23	86 67	34 06	15 75	62 86

Table A-2.   *Continued*

VII.	1–4	5–8	9–12	13–16	17–20	21–24	25–28	29–32
1	38 72	32 95	74 46	76 67	68 09	89 22	60 57	82 64
2	11 82	49 29	40 38	95 27	81 69	93 47	66 37	58 35
3	95 03	45 03	70 47	62 85	98 97	30 77	42 07	56 81
4	27 08	80 32	56 82	94 55	08 77	65 06	96 89	25 01
5	85 28	95 84	92 94	24 58	44 70	29 77	51 65	30 77
6	24 20	59 89	51 58	35 01	11 42	28 86	74 92	98 59
7	43 99	91 57	41 65	31 50	92 26	73 23	69 01	73 61
8	60 40	15 37	73 20	69 70	55 57	15 29	04 80	55 84
9	46 21	83 42	72 91	77 61	43 03	99 51	61 55	95 52
10	65 16	18 75	61 81	63 65	90 58	08 61	91 93	12 82
11	94 09	28 63	60 84	61 72	33 05	21 22	62 33	08 64
12	73 29	16 49	23 94	04 08	56 16	50 82	71 54	41 85
13	40 89	53 52	52 24	71 12	67 11	81 57	14 17	41 61
14	17 26	53 28	16 02	11 05	00 16	90 00	92 59	31 17
15	97 21	81 57	15 12	72 51	77 72	39 16	37 90	14 82
16	95 97	68 82	11 37	52 15	14 17	56 10	38 80	19 31
17	13 74	46 34	72 76	97 12	89 94	79 35	53 65	57 47
18	96 84	74 54	51 90	61 57	86 10	63 29	91 78	63 30
19	07 23	87 56	36 47	49 13	08 05	60 03	41 28	97 32
20	07 30	14 39	08 34	67 36	77 48	42 73	38 26	76 46
21	79 92	18 02	31 87	99 28	29 12	86 94	42 93	92 15
22	67 55	96 52	20 18	23 86	06 70	04 88	18 43	14 06
23	79 27	82 62	05 89	98 67	55 36	11 38	00 68	15 01
24	09 79	13 97	33 12	37 47	52 10	37 21	15 39	17 63
25	54 08	82 23	41 24	83 94	36 43	69 56	55 29	06 16

VIII.	1–4	5–8	9–12	13–16	17–20	21–24	25–28	29–32
1	55 75	40 42	28 16	15 56	85 90	22 52	87 75	06 06
2	53 93	89 69	57 62	00 50	26 55	37 24	65 06	64 78
3	84 57	05 82	38 34	07 71	97 01	91 60	45 25	33 38
4	03 05	40 70	93 45	19 14	58 44	31 03	79 85	07 37
5	65 05	52 06	67 02	47 09	67 69	07 49	67 57	91 35
6	50 47	01 71	99 25	67 79	31 22	22 06	54 11	75 95
7	60 33	68 59	90 87	16 12	28 04	74 19	58 23	70 65
8	72 59	23 82	08 63	50 57	22 08	93 19	04 14	97 89
9	90 76	09 09	51 31	94 39	66 42	80 81	52 57	75 01
10	55 08	70 65	08 89	97 03	10 80	17 66	02 34	05 62
11	75 34	83 06	54 74	25 75	21 66	70 25	56 88	94 85
12	35 12	26 18	99 18	94 62	15 62	67 31	20 64	11 94
13	31 34	34 41	42 27	82 69	18 17	43 38	34 60	27 82
14	11 06	90 62	46 36	29 49	16 61	59 17	06 05	30 10
15	45 39	91 03	75 07	44 92	10 88	83 66	36 38	60 00
16	25 39	41 17	27 38	47 37	53 47	24 61	14 26	63 71
17	09 89	05 38	91 35	66 23	35 07	24 25	70 97	04 84
18	05 08	88 91	65 32	98 80	67 94	01 96	67 42	37 23
19	25 77	61 05	66 95	67 51	95 05	31 65	11 81	80 88
20	80 27	99 51	62 04	97 57	64 38	74 62	66 96	88 31
21	77 63	69 24	66 53	10 06	53 68	30 75	58 69	66 09
22	60 36	08 06	17 43	89 37	19 21	29 61	41 54	17 80
23	72 25	43 32	87 36	99 15	39 77	47 45	28 97	90 13
24	82 42	03 82	40 22	17 69	64 42	39 68	44 19	83 56
25	41 38	49 33	89 76	67 76	87 32	94 70	01 81	90 14

Table A-3. Areas under the normal curve

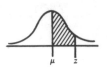

z	.00	.01	.02	.03	.04	.05	.06	.07	.08	.09
0.0	.0000	.0040	.0080	.0120	.0160	.0199	.0239	.0279	.0319	.0359
0.1	.0398	.0438	.0478	.0517	.0557	.0596	.0636	.0675	.0714	.0753
0.2	.0793	.0832	.0871	.0910	.0948	.0987	.1026	.1064	.1103	.1141
0.3	.1179	.1217	.1255	.1293	.1331	.1368	.1406	.1443	.1480	.1517
0.4	.1554	.1591	.1628	.1664	.1700	.1736	.1772	.1808	.1844	.1879
0.5	.1915	.1950	.1985	.2019	.2054	.2088	.2123	.2157	.2190	.2224
0.6	.2257	.2291	.2324	.2357	.2389	.2422	.2454	.2486	.2518	.2549
0.7	.2580	.2612	.2642	.2673	.2704	.2734	.2764	.2794	.2823	.2852
0.8	.2881	.2910	.2939	.2967	.2995	.3023	.3051	.3078	.3106	.3133
0.9	.3159	.3186	.3212	.3238	.3264	.3289	.3315	.3340	.3365	.3389
1.0	.3413	.3438	.3461	.3485	.3508	.3531	.3554	.3577	.3599	.3621
1.1	.3643	.3665	.3686	.3708	.3729	.3749	.3770	.3790	.3810	.3830
1.2	.3849	.3869	.3888	.3907	.3925	.3944	.3962	.3980	.3997	.4015
1.3	.4032	.4049	.4066	.4082	.4099	.4115	.4131	.4147	.4162	.4177
1.4	.4192	.4207	.4222	.4236	.4251	.4265	.4279	.4292	.4306	.4319
1.5	.4332	.4345	.4357	.4370	.4382	.4394	.4406	.4418	.4429	.4441
1.6	.4452	.4463	.4474	.4484	.4495	.4505	.4515	.4525	.4535	.4545
1.7	.4554	.4564	.4573	.4582	.4591	.4599	.4608	.4616	.4625	.4633
1.8	.4641	.4649	.4656	.4664	.4671	.4678	.4686	.4693	.4699	.4706
1.9	.4713	.4719	.4726	.4732	.4738	.4744	.4750	.4756	.4761	.4767
2.0	.4772	.4778	.4783	.4788	.4793	.4798	.4803	.4808	.4812	.4817
2.1	.4821	.4826	.4830	.4834	.4838	.4842	.4846	.4850	.4854	.4857
2.2	.4861	.4864	.4868	.4871	.4875	.4878	.4881	.4884	.4887	.4890
2.3	.4893	.4896	.4898	.4901	.4904	.4906	.4909	.4911	.4913	.4916
2.4	.4918	.4920	.4922	.4925	.4927	.4929	.4931	.4932	.4934	.4936
2.5	.4938	.4940	.4941	.4943	.4945	.4946	.4948	.4949	.4951	.4952
2.6	.4953	.4955	.4956	.4957	.4959	.4960	.4961	.4962	.4963	.4964
2.7	.4965	.4966	.4967	.4968	.4969	.4970	.4971	.4972	.4973	.4974
2.8	.4974	.4975	.4976	.4977	.4977	.4978	.4979	.4979	.4980	.4981
2.9	.4981	.4982	.4982	.4983	.4984	.4984	.4985	.4985	.4986	.4986
3.0	.49865	.4987	.4987	.4988	.4988	.4989	.4989	.4989	.4990	.4990
4.0	.4999683									

Illustration: For $z = 1.93$, shaded area is 0.4732 out of total area of 1.

From Neter and Wasserman, 1966, p. 708.

Table A-4. Poisson probabilities

X	0.1	0.2	0.3	0.4	μx 0.5	0.6	0.7	0.8	0.9	1.0
0	.9048	.8187	.7408	.6703	.6065	.5488	.4966	.4493	.4066	.3679
1	.0905	.1637	.2222	.2681	.3033	.3293	.3476	.3595	.3659	.3679
2	.0045	.0164	.0333	.0536	.0758	.0988	.1217	.1438	.1647	.1839
3	.0002	.0011	.0033	.0072	.0126	.0198	.0284	.0383	.0494	.0613
4		.0001	.0002	.0007	.0016	.0030	.0050	.0077	.0111	.0153
5				.0001	.0002	.0004	.0007	.0012	.0020	.0031
6							.0001	.0002	.0003	.0005
7										.0001

X	1.5	2.0	2.5	3.0	μx 3.5	4.0	4.5	5.0	6.0	7.0
0	.2231	.1353	.0821	.0498	.0302	.0183	.0111	.0067	.0025	.0009
1	.3347	.2707	.2052	.1494	.1057	.0733	.0500	.0337	.0149	.0064
2	.2510	.2707	.2565	.2240	.1850	.1465	.1125	.0842	.0446	.0223
3	.1255	.1804	.2138	.2240	.2158	.1954	.1687	.1404	.0892	.0521
4	.0471	.0902	.1336	.1680	.1888	.1954	.1898	.1755	.1339	.0912
5	.0141	.0361	.0668	.1008	.1322	.1563	.1708	.1755	.1606	.1277
6	.0035	.0120	.0278	.0504	.0771	.1042	.1281	.1462	.1606	.1490
7	.0008	.0034	.0099	.0216	.0385	.0595	.0824	.1044	.1377	.1490
8	.0001	.0009	.0031	.0081	.0169	.0298	.0463	.0653	.1033	.1304
9		.0002	.0009	.0027	.0066	.0132	.0232	.0363	.0688	.1014
10			.0002	.0008	.0023	.0053	.0104	.0181	.0413	.0710
11				.0002	.0007	.0019	.0043	.0082	.0225	.0452
12				.0001	.0002	.0006	.0016	.0034	.0113	.0264
13					.0001	.0002	.0006	.0013	.0052	.0142
14						.0001	.0002	.0005	.0022	.0071
15							.0001	.0002	.0009	.0033
16									.0003	.0014
17									.0001	.0006
18										.0002
19										.0001

Illustration: If $\mu X = 1$, $P(X = 2) = 0.1839$

Abridged from Molina, 1949, p. 709. © Litton Educational Publishing Inc.

Table A-5. Probabilities in right tail of exponential probability distribution

X

$\dfrac{X}{\mu x}$	Prob.	$\dfrac{X}{\mu x}$	Prob.	$\dfrac{X}{\mu x}$	Prob.	$\dfrac{X}{\mu x}$	Prob.
0.0	1.000	2.5	0.082	5.0	0.0067	7.5	0.00055
0.1	0.905	2.6	0.074	5.1	0.0061	7.6	0.00050
0.2	0.819	2.7	0.067	5.2	0.0055	7.7	0.00045
0.3	0.741	2.8	0.061	5.3	0.0050	7.8	0.00041
0.4	0.670	2.9	0.055	5.4	0.0045	7.9	0.00037
0.5	0.607	3.0	0.050	5.5	0.0041	8.0	0.00034
0.6	0.549	3.1	0.045	5.6	0.0037	8.1	0.00030
0.7	0.497	3.2	0.041	5.7	0.0033	8.2	0.00028
0.8	0.449	3.3	0.037	5.8	0.0030	8.3	0.00025
0.9	0.407	3.4	0.033	5.9	0.0027	8.4	0.00022
1.0	0.368	3.5	0.030	6.0	0.0025	8.5	0.00020
1.1	0.333	3.6	0.027	6.1	0.0022	8.6	0.00018
1.2	0.301	3.7	0.025	6.2	0.0020	8.7	0.00017
1.3	0.273	3.8	0.022	6.3	0.0018	8.8	0.00015
1.4	0.247	3.9	0.020	6.4	0.0017	8.9	0.00014
1.5	0.223	4.0	0.018	6.5	0.0015	9.0	0.00012
1.6	0.202	4.1	0.017	6.6	0.0014	9.1	0.00011
1.7	0.183	4.2	0.015	6.7	0.0012	9.2	0.00010
1.8	0.165	4.3	0.014	6.8	0.0011	9.3	0.00009
1.9	0.150	4.4	0.012	6.9	0.0010	9.4	0.00008
2.0	0.135	4.5	0.011	7.0	0.0009	9.5	0.00008
2.1	0.122	4.6	0.010	7.1	0.0008	9.6	0.00007
2.2	0.111	4.7	0.009	7.2	0.0007	9.7	0.00006
2.3	0.100	4.8	0.008	7.3	0.0007	9.8	0.00006
2.4	0.091	4.9	0.0007	7.4	0.0006	9.9	0.00005

Illustration: If $\mu x = 600$, the probability of exceeding $X = 900$ is .223.

From Neter and Wasserman, 1966, p. 710.

Table A-6. Student's t distribution

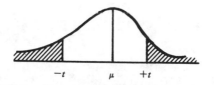

	Level of Significance for one-tailed test					
	0.10	0.05	0.025	0.01	0.005	0.0005
	Level of Significance for two-tailed test					
df	0.20	0.10	0.05	0.02	0.01	0.001
1	3.078	6.314	12.706	31.821	63.657	636.619
2	1.886	2.920	4.303	6.965	9.925	31.598
3	1.638	2.353	3.182	4.541	5.841	12.941
4	1.533	2.132	2.776	3.747	4.604	8.610
5	1.476	2.015	2.571	3.365	4.032	6.859
6	1.440	1.943	2.447	3.143	3.707	5.959
7	1.415	1.895	2.365	2.998	3.499	5.405
8	1.397	1.860	2.306	2.896	3.355	5.041
9	1.383	1.833	2.262	2.821	3.250	4.781
10	1.372	1.812	2.228	2.764	3.169	4.587
11	1.363	1.796	2.201	2.718	3.106	4.437
12	1.356	1.782	2.179	2.681	3.055	4.318
13	1.350	1.771	2.160	2.650	3.012	4.221
14	1.345	1.761	2.145	2.624	2.977	4.140
15	1.341	1.753	2.131	2.602	2.947	4.073
16	1.337	1.746	2.120	2.583	2.921	4.015
17	1.333	1.740	2.110	2.567	2.898	3.965
18	1.330	1.734	2.101	2.552	2.878	3.922
19	1.328	1.729	2.093	2.539	2.861	3.883
20	1.325	1.725	2.086	2.528	2.845	3.850
21	1.323	1.721	2.080	2.518	2.831	3.819
22	1.321	1.717	2.074	2.508	2.819	3.792
23	1.319	1.714	2.069	2.500	2.807	3.767
24	1.318	1.711	2.064	2.492	2.797	3.745
25	1.316	1.708	2.060	2.485	2.787	3.725
26	1.315	1.706	2.056	2.479	2.779	3.707
27	1.314	1.703	2.052	2.473	2.771	3.690
28	1.313	1.701	2.048	2.467	2.763	3.674
29	1.311	1.699	2.045	2.462	2.756	3.659
30	1.310	1.697	2.042	2.457	2.750	3.646
40	1.303	1.684	2.021	2.423	2.704	3.551
60	1.296	1.671	2.000	2.390	2.660	3.460
120	1.289	1.658	1.980	2.358	2.617	3.373
∞	1.282	1.645	1.960	2.326	2.576	3.291

Illustration: The t value for 9 degrees of freedom corresponding to an area of 0.05 in both tails is 2.262; the t value for 9 degrees of freedom corresponding to an area of 0.05 in one tail is 1.833.

Adapted from Table III of Fisher and Yates, 1974, p. 46.

Table A-7. Distribution of Chi Square

x^2

df	Probability													
	0.99	0.98	0.95	0.90	0.80	0.70	0.50	0.30	0.20	0.10	0.05	0.02	0.01	0.001
1	0^3157	0^3628	0^3393	0^2158	0^2642	.148	.455	1.074	1.642	2.706	3.841	5.412	6.635	10.827
2	.0201	.0404	.103	.211	.446	.713	1.386	2.408	3.219	4.605	5.991	7.824	9.210	13.815
3	.115	.185	.352	.584	1.005	1.424	2.366	3.665	4.642	6.251	7.815	9.837	11.341	16.268
4	.297	.429	.711	1.064	1.649	2.195	3.357	4.878	5.989	7.779	9.488	11.668	13.277	18.465
5	.554	.752	1.145	1.610	2.343	3.000	4.351	6.064	7.289	9.236	11.070	13.388	15.086	20.517
6	.872	1.134	1.635	2.204	3.070	3.828	5.348	7.231	8.558	10.645	12.592	15.033	16.812	22.457
7	1.239	1.564	2.167	2.833	3.822	4.671	6.346	8.383	9.803	12.017	14.067	16.622	18.475	24.322
8	1.646	2.032	2.733	3.490	4.594	5.527	7.344	9.524	11.030	13.362	15.507	18.168	20.090	26.125
9	2.088	2.532	3.325	4.168	5.380	6.393	8.343	10.656	12.242	14.684	16.919	19.679	21.666	27.877
10	2.558	3.059	3.940	4.865	6.179	7.267	9.342	11.781	13.442	15.987	18.307	21.161	23.209	29.588
11	3.053	3.609	4.575	5.578	6.989	8.148	10.341	12.899	14.631	17.275	19.675	22.618	24.725	31.264
12	3.571	4.178	5.226	6.304	7.807	9.034	11.340	14.011	15.812	18.549	21.026	24.054	26.217	32.909
13	4.107	4.765	5.892	7.042	8.634	9.926	12.340	15.119	16.985	19.812	22.362	25.472	27.688	34.528
14	4.660	5.368	6.571	7.790	9.467	10.821	13.339	16.222	18.151	21.064	23.685	26.873	29.141	36.123
15	5.229	5.985	7.261	8.547	10.307	11.721	14.339	17.322	19.311	22.307	24.996	28.259	30.578	37.697
16	5.812	6.614	7.962	9.312	11.152	12.624	15.338	18.418	20.465	23.542	26.296	29.633	32.000	39.252
17	6.408	7.255	8.672	10.085	12.002	13.531	16.338	19.511	21.615	24.769	27.587	30.995	33.409	40.790
18	7.015	7.906	9.390	10.865	12.857	14.440	17.338	20.601	22.760	25.989	28.869	32.346	34.805	42.312
19	7.633	8.567	10.117	11.651	13.716	15.352	18.338	21.689	23.900	27.204	30.144	33.687	36.191	43.820
20	8.260	9.237	10.851	12.443	14.578	16.266	19.337	22.775	25.038	28.412	31.410	35.020	37.566	45.315
21	8.897	9.915	11.591	13.240	15.445	17.182	20.337	23.858	26.171	29.615	32.671	36.343	38.932	46.797
22	9.542	10.600	12.338	14.041	16.314	18.101	21.337	24.939	27.301	30.813	33.924	37.659	40.289	48.268
23	10.196	11.293	13.091	14.848	17.187	19.021	22.337	26.018	28.429	32.007	35.172	38.968	41.638	49.728
24	10.856	11.992	13.848	15.659	18.062	19.943	23.337	27.096	29.553	33.196	36.415	40.270	42.980	51.179
25	11.524	12.697	14.611	16.473	18.940	20.867	24.337	28.172	30.675	34.382	37.652	41.566	44.314	52.620
26	12.198	13.409	15.379	17.292	19.820	21.792	25.336	29.246	31.795	35.563	38.885	42.856	45.642	54.052
27	12.879	14.125	16.151	18.114	20.703	22.719	26.336	30.319	32.912	36.741	40.113	44.140	46.963	55.476
28	13.565	14.847	16.928	18.939	21.588	23.647	27.336	31.391	34.027	37.916	41.337	45.419	48.278	56.893
29	14.256	15.574	17.708	19.768	22.475	24.577	28.336	32.461	35.139	39.087	42.557	46.693	49.588	58.302
30	14.953	16.306	18.493	20.599	23.364	25.508	29.336	33.530	36.250	40.256	43.773	47.962	50.892	59.703

Illustration: The value on the x^2 scale associated with 4 degrees of freedom with an area of 0.05 in the right tail is 9.488.

Adapted from Table IV of Fisher and Yates, 1974, p. 47.

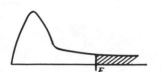

Table A-8. Distribution of F

df_2 \ df_1	Probability = 0.05							
	1	*2*	*3*	*4*	*5*	*6*	*8*	*10*
1	161.4	199.5	215.7	224.6	230.2	234.0	238.9	241.9
2	18.51	19.00	19.16	19.25	19.30	19.33	19.37	19.40
3	10.13	9.55	9.28	9.12	9.01	8.94	8.85	8.79
4	7.71	6.94	6.59	6.39	6.26	6.16	6.04	5.96
5	6.61	5.79	5.41	5.19	5.05	4.95	4.82	4.74
6	5.99	5.14	4.76	4.53	4.39	4.28	4.15	4.06
7	5.59	4.74	4.35	4.12	3.97	3.87	3.73	3.64
8	5.32	4.46	4.07	3.84	3.69	3.58	3.44	3.35
9	5.12	4.26	3.86	3.63	3.48	3.37	3.23	3.14
10	4.96	4.10	3.71	3.48	3.33	3.22	3.07	2.98
11	4.84	3.98	3.59	3.36	3.20	3.09	2.95	2.85
12	4.75	3.89	3.49	3.26	3.11	3.00	2.85	2.75
13	4.67	3.81	3.41	3.18	3.03	2.92	2.77	2.67
14	4.60	3.74	3.34	3.11	2.96	2.85	2.70	2.60
15	4.54	3.68	3.29	3.06	2.90	2.79	2.64	2.54
16	4.49	3.63	3.24	3.01	2.85	2.74	2.59	2.49
17	4.45	3.59	3.20	2.96	2.81	2.70	2.55	2.45
18	4.41	3.55	3.16	2.93	2.77	2.66	2.51	2.41
19	4.38	3.52	3.13	2.90	2.74	2.63	2.48	2.38
20	4.35	3.49	3.10	2.87	2.71	2.60	2.45	2.35
21	4.32	3.47	3.07	2.84	2.68	2.57	2.42	2.32
22	4.30	3.44	3.05	2.82	2.66	2.55	2.40	2.30
23	4.28	3.42	3.03	2.80	2.64	2.53	2.37	2.27
24	4.26	3.40	3.01	2.78	2.62	2.51	2.36	2.25
25	4.24	3.39	2.99	2.76	2.60	2.49	2.34	2.24
26	4.23	3.37	2.98	2.74	2.59	2.47	2.32	2.22
27	4.21	3.35	2.96	2.73	2.57	2.46	2.31	2.20
28	4.20	3.34	2.95	2.71	2.56	2.45	2.29	2.19
29	4.18	3.33	2.93	2.70	2.55	2.43	2.28	2.18
30	4.17	3.32	2.92	2.69	2.53	2.42	2.27	2.16
40	4.08	3.23	2.84	2.61	2.45	2.34	2.18	2.08
60	4.00	3.15	2.76	2.53	2.37	2.25	2.10	1.99
80	3.96	3.11	2.72	2.48	2.33	2.21	2.05	1.95
120	3.92	3.07	2.68	2.45	2.29	2.17	2.02	1.91
∞	3.84	3.00	2.60	2.37	2.21	2.10	1.94	1.83

Illustration: The value on the F scale associated with 3 degrees of freedom in the numerator and 10 degrees of freedom in the denominator corresponding to an area 0.05 in the right tail is 3.71.

Adapted from Table V of Fisher and Yates, 1974, p. 48.

Table A-8. *Continued*

Probability = 0.05

df_2 \ df_1	12	15	20	30	40	60	120	∞
1	243.9	245.9	248.0	250.1	251.1	252.2	253.3	254.3
2	19.41	19.43	19.45	19.46	19.47	19.48	19.49	19.50
3	8.74	8.70	8.66	8.62	8.59	8.57	8.55	8.53
4	5.91	5.86	5.80	5.75	5.72	5.69	5.66	5.63
5	4.68	4.62	4.56	4.50	4.46	4.43	4.40	4.36
6	4.00	3.94	3.87	3.81	3.77	3.74	3.70	3.67
7	3.57	3.51	3.44	3.38	3.34	3.30	3.27	3.23
8	3.28	3.22	3.15	3.08	3.04	3.01	2.97	2.93
9	3.07	3.01	2.94	2.86	2.83	2.79	2.75	2.71
10	2.91	2.85	2.77	2.70	2.66	2.62	2.58	2.54
11	2.79	2.72	2.65	2.57	2.53	2.49	2.45	2.40
12	2.69	2.62	2.54	2.47	2.43	2.38	2.34	2.30
13	2.60	2.53	2.46	2.38	2.34	2.30	2.25	2.21
14	2.53	2.46	2.39	2.31	2.27	2.22	2.18	2.13
15	2.48	2.40	2.33	2.25	2.20	2.16	2.11	2.07
16	2.42	2.35	2.28	2.19	2.15	2.11	2.06	2.01
17	2.38	2.31	2.23	2.15	2.10	2.06	2.01	1.96
18	2.34	2.27	2.19	2.11	2.06	2.02	1.97	1.92
19	2.31	2.23	2.16	2.07	2.03	1.98	1.93	1.88
20	2.28	2.20	2.12	2.04	1.99	1.95	1.90	1.84
21	2.25	2.18	2.10	2.01	1.96	1.92	1.87	1.81
22	2.23	2.15	2.07	1.98	1.94	1.89	1.84	1.78
23	2.20	2.13	2.05	1.96	1.91	1.86	1.81	1.76
24	2.18	2.11	2.03	1.94	1.89	1.84	1.79	1.73
25	2.16	2.09	2.01	1.92	1.87	1.82	1.77	1.71
26	2.15	2.07	1.99	1.90	1.85	1.80	1.75	1.69
27	2.13	2.06	1.97	1.88	1.84	1.79	1.73	1.67
28	2.12	2.04	1.96	1.87	1.82	1.77	1.71	1.65
29	2.10	2.03	1.94	1.85	1.81	1.75	1.70	1.64
30	2.09	2.01	1.93	1.84	1.79	1.74	1.68	1.62
40	2.00	1.92	1.84	1.74	1.69	1.64	1.58	1.51
60	1.92	1.84	1.75	1.65	1.59	1.53	1.47	1.39
80	1.88	1.80	1.70	1.60	1.54	1.49	1.41	1.32
120	1.83	1.75	1.66	1.55	1.50	1.43	1.35	1.25
∞	1.75	1.67	1.57	1.46	1.39	1.32	1.22	1.00

Table A-8. *Continued*

Probability $= 0.01$

df_2 \\ df_1	1	2	3	4	5	6	8	10
1	4052	4999.5	5403	5625	5764	5859	5982	6056
2	98.50	99.00	99.17	99.25	99.30	99.33	99.37	99.40
3	34.12	30.82	29.46	28.71	28.24	27.91	27.49	27.23
4	21.20	18.00	16.69	15.98	15.52	15.21	14.80	14.55
5	16.26	13.27	12.06	11.39	10.97	10.67	10.29	10.05
6	13.75	10.92	9.78	9.15	8.75	8.47	8.10	7.87
7	12.25	9.55	8.45	7.85	7.46	7.19	6.84	6.62
8	11.26	8.65	7.59	7.01	6.63	6.37	6.03	5.81
9	10.56	8.02	6.99	6.42	6.06	5.80	5.47	5.26
10	10.04	7.56	6.55	5.99	5.64	5.39	5.06	4.85
11	9.65	7.21	6.22	5.67	5.32	5.07	4.74	4.54
12	9.33	6.93	5.95	5.41	5.06	4.82	4.50	4.30
13	9.07	6.70	5.74	5.21	4.86	4.62	4.30	4.10
14	8.86	6.51	5.56	5.04	4.69	4.46	4.14	3.94
15	8.68	6.36	5.42	4.89	4.56	4.32	4.00	3.80
16	8.53	6.23	5.29	4.77	4.44	4.20	3.89	3.69
17	8.40	6.11	5.18	4.67	4.34	4.10	3.79	3.59
18	8.29	6.01	5.09	4.58	4.25	4.01	3.71	3.51
19	8.18	5.93	5.01	4.50	4.17	3.94	3.63	3.43
20	8.10	5.85	4.94	4.43	4.10	3.87	3.56	3.37
21	8.02	5.78	4.87	4.37	4.04	3.81	3.51	3.31
22	7.95	5.72	4.82	4.31	3.99	3.76	3.45	3.26
23	7.88	5.66	4.76	4.26	3.94	3.71	3.41	3.21
24	7.82	5.61	4.72	4.22	3.90	3.67	3.36	3.17
25	7.77	5.57	4.68	4.18	3.85	3.63	3.32	3.13
26	7.72	5.53	4.64	4.14	3.82	3.59	3.29	3.09
27	7.68	5.49	4.60	4.11	3.78	3.56	3.26	3.06
28	7.64	5.45	4.57	4.07	3.75	3.53	3.23	3.03
29	7.60	5.42	4.54	4.04	3.73	3.50	3.20	3.00
30	7.56	5.39	4.51	4.02	3.70	3.47	3.17	2.98
40	7.31	5.18	4.31	3.83	3.51	3.29	2.99	2.80
60	7.08	4.98	4.13	3.65	3.34	3.12	2.82	2.63
80	6.96	4.88	4.04	3.56	3.25	3.04	2.74	2.55
120	6.85	4.79	3.95	3.48	3.17	2.96	2.66	2.47
∞	6.63	4.61	3.78	3.32	3.02	2.80	2.51	2.32

Table A-8.—*Continued*

Probability = 0.01

df_2 \ df_1	12	15	20	30	40	60	120	∞
1	6106	6157	6209	6261	6287	6313	6339	6366
2	99.42	99.43	99.45	99.47	99.47	99.48	99.49	99.50
3	27.05	26.87	26.69	26.50	26.41	26.32	26.22	26.13
4	14.37	14.20	14.02	13.84	13.75	13.65	13.56	13.46
5	9.89	9.72	9.55	9.38	9.29	9.20	9.11	9.02
6	7.72	7.56	7.40	7.23	7.14	7.06	6.97	6.88
7	6.47	6.31	6.16	5.99	5.91	5.82	5.74	5.65
8	5.67	5.52	5.36	5.20	5.12	5.03	4.95	4.86
9	5.11	4.96	4.81	4.65	4.57	4.48	4.40	4.31
10	4.71	4.56	4.41	4.25	4.17	4.08	4.00	3.91
11	4.40	4.25	4.10	3.94	3.86	3.78	3.69	3.60
12	4.16	4.01	3.86	3.70	3.62	3.54	3.45	3.36
13	3.96	3.82	3.66	3.51	3.43	3.34	3.25	3.17
14	3.80	3.66	3.51	3.35	3.27	3.18	3.09	3.00
15	3.67	3.52	3.37	3.21	3.13	3.05	2.96	2.87
16	3.55	3.41	3.26	3.10	3.02	2.93	2.84	2.75
17	3.46	3.31	3.16	3.00	2.92	2.83	2.75	2.65
18	3.37	3.23	3.08	2.92	2.84	2.75	2.66	2.57
19	3.03	3.15	3.00	2.84	2.76	2.67	2.58	2.49
20	3.23	3.09	2.94	2.78	2.69	2.61	2.52	2.42
21	3.17	3.03	2.88	2.72	2.64	2.55	2.46	2.36
22	3.12	2.98	2.83	2.67	2.58	2.50	2.40	2.31
23	3.07	2.93	2.78	2.62	2.54	2.45	2.35	2.26
24	3.03	2.89	2.74	2.58	2.49	2.40	2.31	2.21
25	2.99	2.85	2.70	2.54	2.45	2.36	2.27	2.17
26	2.96	2.81	2.66	2.50	2.42	2.33	2.23	2.13
27	2.93	2.78	2.63	2.47	2.38	2.29	2.20	2.10
28	2.90	2.75	2.60	2.44	2.35	2.26	2.17	2.06
29	2.87	2.73	2.57	2.41	2.33	2.23	2.14	2.03
30	2.84	2.70	2.55	2.39	2.30	2.21	2.11	2.01
40	2.66	2.52	2.37	2.20	2.11	2.02	1.92	1.80
60	2.50	2.35	2.20	2.03	1.94	1.84	1.73	1.60
80	2.41	2.28	2.11	1.94	1.84	1.75	1.63	1.49
120	2.34	2.19	2.03	1.86	1.76	1.66	1.53	1.38
∞	2.18	2.04	1.88	1.70	1.59	1.47	1.32	1.00

Table A-9. Durbin-Watson test bounds

Probability = 0.05

	$p - 1 = 1$		$p - 1 = 2$		$p - 1 = 3$		$p - 1 = 4$		$p - 1 = 5$	
n	d_L	d_U	d_L	d_U	d_L	d_U	d_L	d_U	d_L	d_U
15	1.08	1.36	0.95	1.54	0.82	1.75	0.69	1.97	0.56	2.21
16	1.10	1.37	0.98	1.54	0.86	1.73	0.74	1.93	0.62	2.15
17	1.13	1.38	1.02	1.54	0.90	1.71	0.78	1.90	0.67	2.10
18	1.16	1.39	1.05	1.53	0.93	1.69	0.82	1.87	0.71	2.06
19	1.18	1.40	1.08	1.53	0.97	1.68	0.86	1.85	0.75	2.02
20	1.20	1.41	1.10	1.54	1.00	1.68	0.90	1.83	0.79	1.99
21	1.22	1.42	1.13	1.54	1.03	1.67	0.93	1.81	0.83	1.96
22	1.24	1.43	1.15	1.54	1.05	1.66	0.96	1.80	0.86	1.94
23	1.26	1.44	1.17	1.54	1.08	1.66	0.99	1.79	0.90	1.92
24	1.27	1.45	1.19	1.55	1.10	1.66	1.01	1.78	0.93	1.90
25	1.29	1.45	1.21	1.55	1.12	1.66	1.04	1.77	0.95	1.89
26	1.30	1.46	1.22	1.55	1.14	1.65	1.06	1.76	0.98	1.88
27	1.32	1.47	1.24	1.56	1.16	1.65	1.08	1.76	1.01	1.86
28	1.33	1.48	1.26	1.56	1.18	1.65	1.10	1.75	1.03	1.85
29	1.34	1.48	1.27	1.56	1.20	1.65	1.12	1.74	1.05	1.84
30	1.35	1.49	1.28	1.57	1.21	1.65	1.14	1.74	1.07	1.83
31	1.36	1.50	1.30	1.57	1.23	1.65	1.16	1.74	1.09	1.83
32	1.37	1.50	1.31	1.57	1.24	1.65	1.18	1.73	1.11	1.82
33	1.38	1.51	1.32	1.58	1.26	1.65	1.19	1.73	1.13	1.81
34	1.39	1.51	1.33	1.58	1.27	1.65	1.21	1.73	1.15	1.81
35	1.40	1.52	1.34	1.58	1.28	1.65	1.22	1.73	1.16	1.80
36	1.41	1.52	1.35	1.59	1.29	1.65	1.24	1.73	1.18	1.80
37	1.42	1.53	1.36	1.59	1.31	1.66	1.25	1.72	1.19	1.80
38	1.43	1.54	1.37	1.59	1.32	1.66	1.26	1.72	1.21	1.79
39	1.43	1.54	1.38	1.60	1.33	1.66	1.27	1.72	1.22	1.79
40	1.44	1.54	1.39	1.60	1.34	1.66	1.29	1.72	1.23	1.79
45	1.48	1.57	1.43	1.62	1.38	1.67	1.34	1.72	1.29	1.78
50	1.50	1.59	1.46	1.63	1.42	1.67	1.38	1.72	1.34	1.77
55	1.53	1.60	1.49	1.64	1.45	1.68	1.41	1.72	1.38	1.77
60	1.55	1.62	1.51	1.65	1.48	1.69	1.44	1.73	1.41	1.77
65	1.57	1.63	1.54	1.66	1.50	1.70	1.47	1.73	1.44	1.77
70	1.58	1.64	1.55	1.67	1.52	1.70	1.49	1.74	1.46	1.77
75	1.60	1.65	1.57	1.68	1.54	1.71	1.51	1.74	1.49	1.77
80	1.61	1.66	1.59	1.69	1.56	1.72	1.53	1.74	1.51	1.77
85	1.62	1.67	1.60	1.70	1.57	1.72	1.55	1.75	1.52	1.77
90	1.63	1.68	1.61	1.70	1.59	1.73	1.57	1.75	1.54	1.78
95	1.64	1.69	1.62	1.71	1.60	1.73	1.58	1.75	1.56	1.78
100	1.65	1.69	1.63	1.72	1.61	1.74	1.59	1.76	1.57	1.78

$p - 1 =$ number of independent variables.

From Durbin and Watson, 1951, p. 175.

Table A-9.—*Continued*

Probability = 0.01

n	$p - 1 = 1$		$p - 1 = 2$		$p - 1 = 3$		$p - 1 = 4$		$p - 1 = 5$	
	d_L	d_U	d_L	d_U	d_L	d_U	d_L	d_U	d_L	d_U
15	0.81	1.07	0.70	1.25	0.59	1.46	0.49	1.70	0.39	1.96
16	0.84	1.09	0.74	1.25	0.63	1.44	0.53	1.66	0.44	1.90
17	0.87	1.10	0.77	1.25	0.67	1.43	0.57	1.63	0.48	1.85
18	0.90	1.12	0.80	1.26	0.71	1.42	0.61	1.60	0.52	1.80
19	0.93	1.13	0.83	1.26	0.74	1.41	0.65	1.58	0.56	1.77
20	0.95	1.15	0.86	1.27	0.77	1.41	0.68	1.57	0.60	1.74
21	0.97	1.16	0.89	1.27	0.80	1.41	0.72	1.55	0.63	1.71
22	1.00	1.17	0.91	1.28	0.83	1.40	0.75	1.54	0.66	1.69
23	1.02	1.19	0.94	1.29	0.86	1.40	0.77	1.53	0.70	1.67
24	1.04	1.20	0.96	1.30	0.88	1.41	0.80	1.53	0.72	1.66
25	1.05	1.21	0.98	1.30	0.90	1.41	0.83	1.52	0.75	1.65
26	1.07	1.22	1.00	1.31	0.93	1.41	0.85	1.52	0.78	1.64
27	1.09	1.23	1.02	1.32	0.95	1.41	0.88	1.51	0.81	1.63
28	1.10	1.24	1.04	1.32	0.97	1.41	0.90	1.51	0.83	1.62
29	1.12	1.25	1.05	1.33	0.99	1.42	0.92	1.51	0.85	1.61
30	1.13	1.26	1.07	1.34	1.01	1.42	0.94	1.51	0.88	1.61
31	1.15	1.27	1.08	1.34	1.02	1.42	0.96	1.51	0.90	1.60
32	1.16	1.28	1.10	1.35	1.04	1.43	0.98	1.51	0.92	1.60
33	1.17	1.29	1.11	1.36	1.05	1.43	1.00	1.51	0.94	1.59
34	1.18	1.30	1.13	1.36	1.07	1.43	1.01	1.51	0.95	1.59
35	1.19	1.31	1.14	1.37	1.08	1.44	1.03	1.51	0.97	1.59
36	1.21	1.32	1.15	1.38	1.10	1.44	1.04	1.51	0.99	1.59
37	1.22	1.32	1.16	1.38	1.11	1.45	1.06	1.51	1.00	1.59
38	1.23	1.33	1.18	1.39	1.12	1.45	1.07	1.52	1.02	1.58
39	1.24	1.34	1.19	1.39	1.14	1.45	1.09	1.52	1.03	1.58
40	1.25	1.34	1.20	1.40	1.15	1.46	1.10	1.52	1.05	1.58
45	1.29	1.38	1.24	1.42	1.20	1.48	1.16	1.53	1.11	1.58
50	1.32	1.40	1.28	1.45	1.24	1.49	1.20	1.54	1.16	1.59
55	1.36	1.43	1.32	1.47	1.28	1.51	1.25	1.55	1.21	1.59
60	1.38	1.45	1.35	1.48	1.32	1.52	1.28	1.56	1.25	1.60
65	1.41	1.47	1.38	1.50	1.35	1.53	1.31	1.57	1.28	1.61
70	1.43	1.49	1.40	1.52	1.37	1.55	1.34	1.58	1.31	1.61
75	1.45	1.50	1.42	1.53	1.39	1.56	1.37	1.59	1.34	1.62
80	1.47	1.52	1.44	1.54	1.42	1.57	1.39	1.60	1.36	1.62
85	1.48	1.53	1.46	1.55	1.43	1.58	1.41	1.60	1.39	1.63
90	1.50	1.54	1.47	1.56	1.45	1.59	1.43	1.61	1.41	1.64
95	1.51	1.55	1.49	1.57	1.47	1.60	1.45	1.62	1.42	1.64
100	1.52	1.56	1.50	1.58	1.48	1.60	1.46	1.63	1.44	1.65

Table A-10. Present value of $1

Discount rate

Years Hence	1%	2%	4%	6%	8%	10%	12%	14%	15%	16%	18%	20%	22%	24%	25%	26%	28%	30%	35%	40%	45%	50%
1	0.990	0.980	0.962	0.943	0.926	0.909	0.893	0.877	0.870	0.862	0.847	0.833	0.820	0.806	0.800	0.794	0.781	0.769	0.741	0.714	0.690	0.667
2	0.980	0.961	0.925	0.890	0.857	0.826	0.797	0.769	0.755	0.743	0.718	0.694	0.672	0.650	0.640	0.630	0.610	0.592	0.549	0.510	0.476	0.444
3	0.971	0.942	0.889	0.840	0.794	0.751	0.712	0.675	0.658	0.641	0.609	0.579	0.551	0.524	0.512	0.500	0.477	0.455	0.406	0.364	0.328	0.296
4	0.961	0.924	0.855	0.792	0.735	0.683	0.636	0.592	0.572	0.552	0.516	0.482	0.451	0.423	0.410	0.397	0.373	0.350	0.301	0.260	0.226	0.198
5	0.951	0.906	0.822	0.747	0.681	0.621	0.567	0.519	0.497	0.476	0.437	0.402	0.370	0.341	0.328	0.315	0.291	0.269	0.223	0.186	0.156	0.132
6	0.942	0.888	0.790	0.705	0.630	0.564	0.507	0.456	0.432	0.410	0.370	0.335	0.303	0.275	0.262	0.250	0.227	0.207	0.165	0.133	0.108	0.088
7	0.933	0.871	0.760	0.665	0.583	0.513	0.452	0.400	0.376	0.354	0.314	0.279	0.249	0.222	0.210	0.198	0.178	0.159	0.122	0.095	0.074	0.059
8	0.923	0.853	0.731	0.627	0.540	0.467	0.404	0.351	0.327	0.305	0.266	0.233	0.204	0.179	0.168	0.157	0.139	0.123	0.091	0.068	0.051	0.039
9	0.914	0.837	0.703	0.592	0.500	0.424	0.361	0.308	0.284	0.263	0.225	0.194	0.167	0.144	0.134	0.125	0.108	0.094	0.067	0.048	0.035	0.026
10	0.905	0.820	0.676	0.558	0.463	0.386	0.322	0.270	0.247	0.227	0.191	0.162	0.137	0.116	0.107	0.099	0.085	0.073	0.050	0.035	0.024	0.017
11	0.896	0.804	0.650	0.527	0.429	0.350	0.287	0.237	0.215	0.195	0.162	0.135	0.112	0.094	0.086	0.079	0.066	0.056	0.037	0.025	0.017	0.012
12	0.887	0.788	0.625	0.497	0.397	0.319	0.257	0.208	0.187	0.168	0.137	0.112	0.092	0.076	0.069	0.062	0.052	0.043	0.027	0.018	0.012	0.008
13	0.879	0.773	0.601	0.469	0.368	0.290	0.229	0.182	0.163	0.145	0.116	0.093	0.075	0.061	0.055	0.050	0.040	0.033	0.020	0.013	0.008	0.005
14	0.870	0.758	0.577	0.442	0.340	0.263	0.205	0.160	0.141	0.125	0.099	0.078	0.062	0.049	0.044	0.039	0.032	0.025	0.015	0.009	0.006	0.003
15	0.861	0.743	0.555	0.417	0.315	0.239	0.183	0.140	0.123	0.108	0.084	0.065	0.051	0.040	0.035	0.031	0.025	0.020	0.011	0.006	0.004	0.002
16	0.853	0.728	0.534	0.394	0.292	0.218	0.163	0.123	0.107	0.093	0.071	0.054	0.042	0.032	0.028	0.025	0.019	0.015	0.008	0.005	0.003	0.002
17	0.844	0.714	0.513	0.371	0.270	0.198	0.146	0.108	0.093	0.080	0.060	0.045	0.034	0.026	0.023	0.020	0.015	0.012	0.006	0.003	0.002	0.001
18	0.836	0.700	0.494	0.350	0.250	0.180	0.130	0.095	0.081	0.069	0.051	0.038	0.028	0.021	0.018	0.016	0.012	0.009	0.005	0.002	0.001	0.001
19	0.828	0.686	0.475	0.331	0.232	0.164	0.116	0.083	0.070	0.060	0.043	0.031	0.023	0.017	0.014	0.012	0.009	0.007	0.003	0.002	0.001	
20	0.820	0.673	0.456	0.312	0.215	0.149	0.104	0.073	0.061	0.051	0.037	0.026	0.019	0.014	0.012	0.010	0.007	0.005	0.002	0.001	0.001	
21	0.811	0.660	0.439	0.294	0.199	0.135	0.093	0.064	0.053	0.044	0.031	0.022	0.015	0.011	0.009	0.008	0.006	0.004	0.002	0.001		
22	0.803	0.647	0.422	0.278	0.184	0.123	0.083	0.056	0.046	0.038	0.026	0.018	0.013	0.009	0.007	0.006	0.004	0.003	0.001	0.001		
23	0.795	0.634	0.406	0.262	0.170	0.112	0.074	0.049	0.040	0.033	0.022	0.015	0.010	0.007	0.006	0.005	0.003	0.002	0.001			
24	0.788	0.622	0.390	0.247	0.158	0.102	0.066	0.043	0.035	0.028	0.019	0.013	0.008	0.006	0.005	0.004	0.003	0.002	0.001			
25	0.780	0.610	0.375	0.233	0.146	0.092	0.059	0.038	0.030	0.024	0.016	0.010	0.007	0.005	0.004	0.003	0.002	0.001				
26	0.772	0.598	0.361	0.220	0.135	0.084	0.053	0.033	0.026	0.021	0.014	0.009	0.006	0.004	0.003	0.002	0.002	0.001				
27	0.764	0.586	0.347	0.207	0.125	0.076	0.047	0.029	0.023	0.018	0.011	0.007	0.005	0.003	0.002	0.002	0.001	0.001				
28	0.757	0.574	0.333	0.196	0.116	0.069	0.042	0.026	0.020	0.016	0.010	0.006	0.004	0.002	0.002	0.002	0.001	0.001				
29	0.749	0.563	0.321	0.185	0.107	0.063	0.037	0.022	0.017	0.014	0.008	0.005	0.003	0.002	0.002	0.001	0.001					
30	0.742	0.552	0.308	0.174	0.099	0.057	0.033	0.020	0.015	0.012	0.007	0.004	0.003	0.002	0.001	0.001	0.001	0.001				
40	0.672	0.453	0.208	0.097	0.046	0.022	0.011	0.005	0.004	0.003	0.001	0.001										
50	0.608	0.372	0.141	0.054	0.021	0.009	0.003	0.001	0.001	0.001												

Illustration: The present value of $1.00 discounted at 10% over 20 years is $0.149.

Table A-11. Present Value of $1 Received Annually for N Years

Discount Rate

Years (N)	1%	2%	4%	6%	8%	10%	12%	14%	15%	16%	18%	20%	22%	24%	25%	26%	28%	30%	35%	40%	45%	50%
1	0.990	0.980	0.962	0.943	0.926	0.909	0.893	0.877	0.870	0.862	0.847	0.833	0.820	0.806	0.800	0.794	0.781	0.769	0.741	0.714	0.690	0.667
2	1.970	1.942	1.886	1.853	1.783	1.736	1.690	1.647	1.626	1.605	1.566	1.528	1.492	1.457	1.440	1.424	1.392	1.361	1.289	1.224	1.165	1.111
3	2.941	2.884	2.775	2.673	2.577	2.487	2.402	2.322	2.283	2.246	2.174	2.106	2.042	1.981	1.952	1.923	1.868	1.816	1.696	1.589	1.493	1.407
4	3.902	3.808	3.630	3.465	3.312	3.170	3.037	2.914	2.855	2.798	2.690	2.589	2.494	2.404	2.362	2.320	2.241	2.166	1.997	1.849	1.720	1.605
5	4.853	4.713	4.452	4.212	3.993	3.791	3.605	3.433	3.352	3.274	3.127	2.991	2.864	2.745	2.689	2.635	2.532	2.436	2.220	2.035	1.876	1.737
6	5.795	5.601	5.242	4.917	4.623	4.355	4.111	3.889	3.784	3.685	3.458	3.326	3.167	3.020	2.951	2.885	2.759	2.643	2.385	2.168	1.983	1.824
7	6.728	6.472	6.002	5.582	5.206	4.868	4.564	4.288	4.160	4.039	3.812	3.605	3.416	3.242	3.161	3.083	2.937	2.802	2.508	2.263	2.057	1.883
8	7.652	7.325	6.733	6.210	5.747	5.335	4.968	4.639	4.487	4.344	4.078	3.837	3.619	3.421	3.329	3.241	3.076	2.925	2.598	2.331	2.108	1.922
9	8.566	8.162	7.435	6.802	6.247	5.759	5.328	4.946	4.772	4.607	4.303	4.031	3.786	3.566	3.463	3.366	3.184	3.019	2.665	2.379	2.144	1.948
10	9.471	8.983	8.111	7.360	6.710	6.145	5.650	5.216	5.019	4.833	4.494	4.192	3.923	3.682	3.571	3.465	3.269	3.092	2.715	2.414	2.168	1.965
11	10.368	9.787	8.760	7.887	7.139	6.495	5.937	5.453	5.234	5.029	4.656	4.327	4.035	3.776	3.656	3.544	3.335	3.147	2.752	2.438	2.185	1.977
12	11.255	10.575	9.385	8.384	7.536	6.814	6.194	5.660	5.421	5.197	4.793	4.439	4.127	3.851	3.725	3.606	3.387	3.190	2.779	2.456	2.196	1.985
13	12.134	11.343	9.986	8.853	7.904	7.103	6.424	5.842	5.583	5.342	4.910	4.533	4.203	3.912	3.780	3.656	3.427	3.223	2.799	2.468	2.204	1.990
14	13.004	12.106	10.563	9.295	8.244	7.367	6.628	6.002	5.724	5.468	5.008	4.611	4.265	3.962	3.824	3.695	3.459	3.249	2.814	2.477	2.210	1.993
15	13.865	12.849	11.118	9.712	8.559	7.606	6.811	6.142	5.847	5.575	5.092	4.675	4.315	4.001	3.859	3.726	3.483	3.268	2.825	2.484	2.214	1.995
16	14.718	13.578	11.652	10.106	8.851	7.824	6.974	6.265	5.954	5.669	5.162	4.730	4.357	4.033	3.887	3.751	3.503	3.283	2.834	2.489	2.216	1.997
17	15.562	14.292	12.166	10.477	9.122	8.022	7.120	6.373	6.047	5.749	5.222	4.775	4.391	4.059	3.910	3.771	3.518	3.295	2.840	2.492	2.218	1.998
18	16.398	14.992	12.659	10.828	9.372	8.201	7.250	6.467	6.128	5.818	5.273	4.812	4.419	4.080	3.928	3.786	3.529	3.304	2.844	2.494	2.219	1.999
19	17.226	15.678	13.134	11.158	9.604	8.365	7.366	6.550	6.198	5.877	5.316	4.844	4.442	4.097	3.942	3.799	3.539	3.311	2.848	2.496	2.220	1.999
20	18.046	16.351	13.590	11.470	9.818	8.514	7.469	6.623	6.259	5.929	5.353	4.870	4.460	4.110	3.954	3.808	3.546	3.316	2.850	2.497	2.221	1.999
21	18.857	17.011	14.029	11.764	10.017	8.649	7.562	6.687	6.312	5.973	5.384	4.891	4.476	4.121	3.963	3.816	3.551	3.320	2.852	2.498	2.221	2.000
22	19.660	17.658	14.451	12.042	10.201	8.772	7.645	6.743	6.359	6.011	5.410	4.909	4.488	4.130	3.970	3.822	3.556	3.323	2.853	2.498	2.222	2.000
23	20.456	18.292	14.857	12.303	10.371	8.883	7.718	6.792	6.399	6.044	5.432	4.925	4.499	4.137	3.976	3.827	3.559	3.325	2.854	2.499	2.222	2.000
24	21.243	18.914	15.247	12.550	10.529	8.985	7.784	6.835	6.434	6.073	5.451	4.937	4.507	4.143	3.981	3.831	3.562	3.327	2.855	2.499	2.222	2.000
25	22.023	19.523	15.622	12.783	10.675	9.077	7.843	6.873	6.464	6.097	5.467	4.948	4.514	4.147	3.985	3.834	3.564	3.329	2.856	2.499	2.222	2.000
26	22.795	20.121	15.983	13.003	10.810	9.161	7.896	6.906	6.491	6.118	5.480	4.956	4.520	4.151	3.988	3.837	3.566	3.330	2.856	2.500	2.222	2.000
27	23.560	20.707	16.330	13.211	10.935	9.237	7.943	6.935	6.514	6.136	5.492	4.964	4.524	4.154	3.990	3.839	3.567	3.331	2.856	2.500	2.222	2.000
28	24.316	21.281	16.663	13.406	11.051	9.307	7.984	6.961	6.534	6.152	5.502	4.970	4.528	4.157	3.992	3.840	3.568	3.331	2.857	2.500	2.222	2.000
29	25.066	21.844	16.984	13.591	11.158	9.370	8.022	6.983	6.551	6.166	5.510	4.975	4.531	4.159	3.994	3.841	3.569	3.332	2.857	2.500	2.222	2.000
30	25.808	22.396	17.292	13.765	11.258	9.427	8.055	7.003	6.566	6.177	5.517	4.979	4.534	4.160	3.995	3.842	3.569	3.332	2.857	2.500	2.222	2.000
40	32.835	27.355	19.793	15.046	11.925	9.779	8.244	7.105	6.642	6.234	5.548	4.997	4.544	4.166	3.999	3.846	3.571	3.333	2.857	2.500	2.222	2.000
50	39.196	31.424	21.482	15.762	12.234	9.915	8.304	7.133	6.661	6.246	5.554	4.999	4.545	4.167	4.000	3.846	3.571	3.333	2.857	2.500	2.222	2.000

Illustration: At a 10% discount rate, the present value of an annuity of $1.00 for the next 20 years is $8.514.

From PROGRAM BUDGETING AND BENEFIT COST ANALYSIS by Harley H. Hinrichs and Graeme M. Taylor (p. 378). Copyright © 1969 by Goodyear Publishing Company. Reprinted by permission.

REFERENCES

Durbin, J., and G. S. Watson. 1951. Testing for serial correlation in least squares regression II. Biometrika 38:175.

Fisher, R. A., and F. Yates. 1974. Statistical Tables for Biological, Agricultural and Medical Research. 6th Ed. Harlow, Essex: Longman Group Limited.

Loether, H. J., and D. G. McTavish. 1976. Descriptive and Inferential Statistics: An Introduction. Boston: Allyn & Bacon, Inc.

Molina, E. C. 1949. Poisson's Exponential Binomial Limit, p. 709. Huntington, N.Y.: R. E. Krieger Pub. Co., Inc.

Neter, J., and W. Wasserman. 1966. Fundamental Statistics for Business and Economics. Boston: Allyn & Bacon, Inc.

LIST OF SYMBOLS

X_i	value for individual case	Q_1	first quartile
$\overline{X}$	sample mean average	Q_2	second quartile
μ	(mu) population mean average	Q_3	third quartile
		X	independent variable, in regression analysis
s	sample standard deviation		
σ	(sigma) population standard deviation	Y	dependent variable, in regression analysis
s^2	sample variance	$\hat{Y}$	(Y-hat) predicted value of Y
σ^2	(sigma squared) population variance	r	correlation coefficient
		R^2	coefficient of determination
CV	coefficient of variation	χ^2	chi square
m_1	first moment	ϕ	phi
m_2	second moment	V	Cramer's V
z	normal deviate or standard score	λ	lambda
		γ	gamma
N	sample size	τ_y	Goodman and Kruskal's Tau$_y$
n	population size		
P	probability	d_{yx}	Somers' d
p	proportion	Tau$_c$	Kendall's Tau$_c$
q	$1 -$ proportion	F	F ratio (ratio of variance estimates)
Σ	summation		
E(x)	expected value of x	PRE	proportional reduction in error
H_0	null hypothesis		
H_1	alternate hypothesis	SS	sum of squares
t	Student's t distribution	β	regression parameters
df	degrees of freedom	ρ	(rho) autocorrelation parameter
s.e.	standard error		
f	frequency	E^2	(Eta^2) correlation ratio
f_e	expected frequency	ϵ^2	unbiased correlation ratio
f_o	observed frequency	b_1	regression coefficient (slope)
%	percent	b_0	Y- intercept
U	upper limit of a range	ϵ	error term in regression
L	lower limit of a range	D	Durbin-Watson test statistic
Q	semi-interquartile range		

INDEX

methodological overview of, 27-28
performance evaluation criteria for,
    9-15
program objectives in, levels of,
    17-18
research principles in, 24-27
responsive, 23-24
scale of programming in, 18-19
systems approach to, 40-57
utilization of, 20-23
Program operation variables, 47
Program-related administrative
    studies, 14
Program-related policy analysis, 8-9
Program strategy evaluations, defini-
    tion and function of, 19
Programming
    and evaluation, 15-19
    scale of, 18-19
Projects
    alternative
        ranking of, in benefit-cost
            analysis, 405-408
        specification of, in benefit-cost
            analysis, 408-409
    evaluations of, definition and
        function of, 19
    formulation of, in survey research,
        326-327
    rating of, definition and function
        of, 19
Proportional reduction in error as
    measures of strength of
    nominal associations,
    443-447
Proportional stratified random
    sample, 240-241
Proportions
    analysis of variance with, 499,
        502-504, 505
    confidence intervals for, 224-225
    difference in, 229-232
    difference of differences in pro-
        portions, 449, 451
    extensions of tests with, 232
    and probabilities, relationship
        between 177
    as relational measures, 107-108,
        109

tests involving, 218-226
Prototype demonstration projects,
    purpose of, 314
Proximate measures, definition and
    application of, 69-70
Public policies, definition of, 5
Pure error, in linear regression
    model, 521-522

Q sort, applications of, for surveys,
    351-352
Quartile deviation, as measure of
    dispersion, 112
Quartiles as positional measures, 105
Quasi-experimental research designs,
    290-306
Questionnaires, in survey research,
    327
    design of, 341-355
    mailed, advantages and disad-
        vantages of, 331-332
    pretesting of, 369-370
    self-administered, advantages and
        disadvantages of 333-334
Questions, in survey research
    closed-ended, applications of,
        345, 346, 347-348
    double-barreled, disadvantages of,
        343
    filter, in sequencing survey items,
        354
    formats for, effects of, 345-346
    imprecise, effects of, 341-342
    irrelevant, effects of, 343-344
    loaded, effects of, 344-345
    multiple choice, applications of,
        348-350
    open-ended
        applications of, 345-347
        responses to, coding frames in
            analysis of, 373-374
        wording of, effect of, 341-345
Quintamensional plan, in sequencing
    survey items, 353-354
Quota sample, 249

Random assignment of cases in ex-
    perimental design, 276-278